BUSINESS LAWS

[As per New Syllabus (CBCS) for First Semester, B.Com. (Hons.), Delhi University *w.e.f.* 2015-16]

AF731668

DR. S.N. MAHESHWARI

PROFESSOR EMERITUS AND ACADEMIC ADVISOR
DELHI INSTITUTE OF ADVANCED STUDIES
DELHI – 110085
[Formerly, Principal, Hindu College, Delhi University,
Professor & Dean, Faculty of Commerce and
Business Management, Goa University]

DR. SUNEEL K. MAHESHWARI

PROFESSOR OF ACCOUNTING
EBERLY COLLEGE OF BUSINESS AND INFORMATION TECHNOLOGY
INDIANA UNIVERSITY OF PENNSYLVANIA, U.S.A
[Formerly, Professor of Accounting
in the Division of Accountancy and
Legal Environment, Marshall University, U.S.A.]

Himalaya Publishing House

ISO 9001:2008 CERTIFIED

© Authors

No part of this publication may be reproduced, stored in a retrieval system, or transmitted in any form or by any means, electronic, mechanical, photocopying, recording and/or otherwise without the prior written permission of the publishers.

First Edition : 2016

Published by : Mrs. Meena Pandey for **Himalaya Publishing House Pvt. Ltd.,**
"Ramdoot", Dr. Bhalerao Marg, Girgaon, **Mumbai - 400 004.**
Phone: 022-23860170/23863863, Fax: 022-23877178
E-mail: himpub@vsnl.com; Website: www.himpub.com

Branch Offices :

New Delhi : "Pooja Apartments", 4-B, Murari Lal Street, Ansari Road, Darya Ganj, New Delhi - 110 002. Phone: 011-23270392, 23278631; Fax: 011-23256286

Nagpur : Kundanlal Chandak Industrial Estate, Ghat Road, Nagpur - 440 018. Phone: 0712-2738731, 3296733; Telefax: 0712-2721216

Bengaluru : Plot No. 91-33, 2nd Main Road Seshadripuram, Behind Nataraja Theatre, Bengaluru-560020. Phone: 08041138821, 9379847017, 9379847005

Hyderabad : No. 3-4-184, Lingampally, Besides Raghavendra Swamy Matham, Kachiguda, Hyderabad - 500 027. Phone: 040-27560041, 27550139; Mobile: 09390905282

Chennai : New-20, Old-59, Thirumalai Pillai Road, T. Nagar, Chennai - 600 017. Mobile: 9380460419

Pune : First Floor, "Laksha" Apartment, No. 527, Mehunpura, Shaniwarpeth (Near Prabhat Theatre), Pune - 411 030. Phone: 020-24496323/24496333; Mobile: 09370579333

Lucknow : House No 731, Shekhupura Colony, Near B.D. Convent School, Aliganj, Lucknow - 226 022. Phone: 0522-4012353; Mobile: 09307501549

Ahmedabad : 114, "SHAIL", 1st Floor, Opp. Madhu Sudan House, C.G. Road, Navrang Pura, Ahmedabad - 380 009. Phone: 079-26560126; Mobile: 09377088847

Ernakulam : 39/176 (New No: 60/251) 1st Floor, Karikkamuri Road, Ernakulam, Kochi - 682011, Phone: 0484-2378012, 2378016; Mobile: 09344199799

Bhubaneswar : 5 Station Square, Bhubaneswar - 751 001 (Odisha). Phone: 0674-2532129, Mobile: 09338746007

Kolkata : 108/4, Beliaghata Main Road, Near ID Hospital, Opp. SBI Bank, Kolkata - 700 010, Phone: 033-32449649, Mobile: 09883055590, 07439040301

DTP by : Sunanda

Printed at : Infinity Imaging System, New Delhi. On behalf of HPH.

PREFACE

We are pleased to place before the esteemed readers a book on ***Business Laws*** for B.Com. (Hons.) students of Delhi University as per Choice Based Credit System.

The book has several distinctive features. These include the following:

- Comprehensively covers the course content requirements of the students appearing in the paper "Business" Laws at B.Com. (Hons.) I Semester Examination of Delhi University and those having similar course contents.
- Written in simple and straight style.
- Gives a lucid explanation of the basic provisions of law with plenty of illustrations supported by case laws.
- Incorporates at the end of each chapter:
  - Objective type questions with short answers to enable the students to test their understanding.
  - Essay type questions for review, discussion and practice.
  - Practical problems with short answers for sharpening the knowledge of students.
- Broadly classified into Three Sections, each covering a separate enactment(s) and conveniently divided into several concise but complete chapters covering specific topics.
- Provides Learning Objectives at the beginning of each chapter to tell the students what he will learn after studying the chapter.
- Defines Key Terms introduced, at the end of each chapter, for recapitulation and better grasp over the subject.
- Incorporates in the preliminary pages topic wise coverage of the relevant syllabus in the book.
- Bound to prove a refreshing guide for business executives.

We are confident that, with all these *PLUS* features, the readers will find the book extremely useful and rewarding for them. Constructive and helpful suggestions for improvement in the book will be gratefully acknowledged.

A-2/156, Paschim Vihar
New Delhi - 110 063

DR. S.N. MAHESHWARI
DR. S.K. MAHESHWARI

SYLLABUS

B.Com (Hons.): Semester I

Paper BCH1.3: Business Laws

Duration: 3 Hrs

Objective: To impart basic knowledge of the important business laws along with relevant case laws.

Contents

Contents	Coverage in the Book: Section	Coverage in the Book: Chapter(s)
Unit I: The Indian Contract Act, 1872 (a) Contract – meaning, characteristics and kinds (b) Essentials of valid contract – Offer and acceptance, consideration, contractual capacity, free consent, legality of objects (c) Void agreements (d) Discharge of contract – modes of discharge including breach and its remedies (e) Contingent contracts (f) Quasi – contracts (d) Contract of Indemnity and Guarantee (e) Contract of Bailment (f) Contract of Agency	1	1 to 15
Unit II: The Sale of Goods Act, 1930 (a) Contract of sale, meaning and difference between sale and agreement to sell (b) Conditions and warranties (c) Transfer of ownership in goods including sale by non-owners (d) Performance of contract of sale (e) Unpaid seller – meaning and rights of an unpaid seller against the goods and the buyer.	2	1 to 6

Unit III: The Limited Liability Partnership Act, 2008		
(a) Salient Features of LLP (b) Difference between LLP and Partnership, LLP and Company (c) LLP Agreement (d) Nature of LLP (e) Partners and Designated Partners (f) Incorporation Document (g) Incorporation by Registration, Registered office of LLP and change therein (h) Change of name (i) Partners and their Relations (j) Extent and Limitation of liability of LLP and partners (k) Whistle blowing (l) Taxation of LLP (m) Conversion of LLP (n) Winding up and dissolution	3	1
Unit IV: The Information Technology Act, 2000		
(a) Definitions under the Act (b) Digital signature (c) Electronic governance (d) Attribution, acknowledgement and dispatch of electronic records (e) Regulation of certifying authorities (f) Digital signatures certificates (g) Duties of subscribers (h) Penalties and adjudication (i) Appellate Tribunal (j) Offences	3	2

CONTENTS

Section 2

THE SALE OF GOODS ACT, 1930

Section 3

MISCELLANEOUS

INTRODUCTORY

LEARNING OBJECTIVES

A careful study of this chapter will enable you to :

- understand the concept of law;
- differentiate between Law and Mercantile Law;
- identify the different sources of Indian Mercantile Law; and
- explain the meaning of certain key terms.

MEANING OF LAW

The term law refers to rules of conduct enforced by the State to maintain peace and order in the society. Their objective is to provide security and uniformity by regulating human actions. In the absence of law, life and business will become a matter of survival not only of the fittest but also of the most ruthless. Since laws are backed by the authority and the power of the State, they are enforceable against all individuals irrespective of their social status.

It will be appropriate here to give definitions of the term law by some eminent scholars :

"Law is the body of principles recognised and applied by the State in administration of justice."

—*Salmond*

"A law is a rule of conduct imposed and enforced by the sovereign." —*Austin*

"Law in its most general and comprehensive sense signifies a rule of action and is applied indiscriminately to all kinds of actions whether animate or inanimate, rational or irrational."

—*Blackstone*

Thus, law may be defined as the system of rights and obligations which the State enforces.

MEANING OF MERCANTILE OR BUSINESS LAW

The term 'Mercantile or Business Law' or 'Law Merchant' refers to those legal rules which govern and regulate mercantile or business transactions. These rules, regulations, etc. bring a sense of seriousness and definiteness in business dealings. They provide for rules regarding the validity of making contracts and their performance. They deal with various types of contracts such as those relating to partnership, sale of goods, agency, bailment, indemnity and guarantee. Mercantile Law also includes in its fold the laws relating to the joint stock companies, carriage of goods, insurance, insolvency, etc.

SOURCES OF INDIAN MERCANTILE OR BUSINESS LAW

The main sources of Indian Mercantile or Business Law are as follows :

(1) **English Mercantile Law :** Indian Mercantile Law is largely based on English Mercantile Law. As a matter of fact, even after independence, in the absence of provisions regarding

any matter of the Indian law, the provisions of the English law are generally accepted in the Indian Courts.

(2) **Statutes of Indian Legislatures :** Most of the Indian laws are in the form of Acts passed by the Legislatures. Both the Central Legislatures (*i.e.,* the Parliament) and the State Legislatures are empowered to enact laws relating to matters which come within their jurisdiction. For example, the Companies Act, 1956 has been enacted by the Parliament while the different State Legislatures have enacted the Sales Tax Acts applicable to their respective States.

(3) **Judicial Decisions :** Past judicial decisions acquire the force of precedents and are generally followed by law courts in deciding similar cases. In our country, the courts have been divided into three groups : (*i*) the Supreme Court, (*ii*) the High Courts and (*iii*) the Sub-ordinate Courts. The Supreme Court is the final court of appeal. For the court of same stature, earlier decisions have only a guiding and persuasive value. However, for a court of a lower stature, the decision given by the court of a higher stature regarding the same subject matter is usually taken as having binding effects.

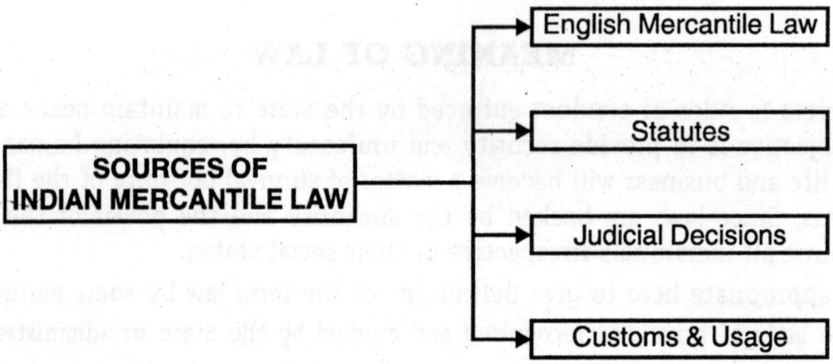

(4) **Customs and Usage :** Customs and Usage also play a significant role in regulating business transactions. This fact has been accepted by many Indian statutes. For example, section 1 of the Indian Contract Act states that 'nothing therein contained shall affect any usage or customs of trade'. Similarly Section 1 of the Negotiable Instruments Act also provides that 'nothing therein contain shall affect any legal usage relating to Instruments in an oriental language[1].

KEY TERMS

❑ **Law :** Rules of conduct enforced by State to maintain peace and order in the society.

❑ **Mercantile Law :** Legal rules which govern and regulate mercantile transactions.

TEST QUESTIONS

Objective Type : ***Test Your Knowledge***

1. State whether each of the following statements is *True* or *False*

(*i*) Laws are framed by the State to maintain peace and order in the society.

(*ii*) Mercantile Law and Law Merchant are synonymous terms.

1. These Instruments are popularly termed as 'Hundis'.

(*iii*) Customs and usages have no role to play in regulating business transactions.
(*iv*) Past judicial decisions have to be accepted by the law courts while giving decisions in future.
(*v*) Both the Parliament and State Legislatures have the power to make laws.

[*Ans.* (i) True; (ii) True; (iii) False; (iv) False; (v) True]

2. Fill in the blanks:

(*i*) The decisions of a High Court are binding on all the ___________ Courts.
(*CS Foundation, June 2008*)

(*ii*) Law means a ___________ of rules. (*CS Foundation, June 2008*)

[*Ans.* (i) Subordinate (ii) Set]

Essay Type : *For Review, Discussion and Practice*

1. Explain the meaning of the term 'law'. Differentiate it from Mercantile Law.
2. State the main sources of Indian Mercantile Law. (*CS Foundation, Dec. 2004, June 2011*)

SECTION 1

THE INDIAN CONTRACT ACT, 1872

Chapter 1

GENERAL PRINCIPLES

LEARNING OBJECTIVES

A careful study of this chapter will enable you to :

- understand the meaning of the term contract;
- identify the essentials of a valid contract;
- classify the contracts into different categories; and
- explain the meaning of certain key terms.

SCOPE AND APPLICATION

The Indian Contract Act is the most important constituents of Indian Mercantile Law. It affects every person since every one of us enters into a contract virtually every day. When a person takes a seat in a bus or lends a book to his friend or deposits money in a bank account or purchases goods on credit, he enters into a contract though he may not be conscious of this fact. The law of contracts is of immense importance to a businessman since all his transactions are based on contracts.

The Indian Contract Act came into force from 1st September, 1872. It has been amended several times. The notable amendments have been in 1886, 1891, 1899, 1930, 1932 and 1997. The Act has been mainly enacted to ensure that the obligations prescribed by agreements and the reasonable expectations created by them are fulfilled by the concerned parties to the agreements. The Act applies to the whole of India except the state of Jammu and Kashmir.

The Act largely deals with :

(*i*) the general principles applicable to contracts;

(*ii*) the conditions necessary for making a valid contract;

(*iii*) the principles applicable to quasi contracts; and

(*iv*) the principles applicable to some special contracts like those of Indemnity, Guarantee, Bailment and Agency.

It may be noted that the Contract Act is not applicable to all types of contracts. There are certain contracts which are governed by special laws. *For example,* the Transfer of Property Act is applicable to all contracts, relating to immovable property. Similarly, the Negotiable Instruments Act regulates all contracts regarding cheques, bills of exchange and promissory notes. The Sale of Goods Act deals with contracts of sale of goods, etc. The provisions of the Contracts Act are mostly general in nature and they are applicable to special contracts mentioned above only to the extent that they are not contrary to the provisions of the special Acts governing them. Similarly, the Contract Act does not affect particular custom and usage of trade unless otherwise specifically agreed by the parties.

TYPES OF RIGHTS

Rights available to a person may be divided as rights *in rem* and rights *in personam.* Right *in rem* implies a right available against the whole world. Right *in personam* is available only against a particular individual. The Contract Act deals with rights *in personam* and not with rights *in rem.*

Examples : (*i*) *A* is the owner of a house. As owner of the house he has the right of its quiet possession and enjoyment against the whole world. This is, therefore, his right *in rem.*

(*ii*) *A* is indebted of *B* to the extent of ₹ 1000. *B's* right to recover money from *A* will be termed as right *in personam* as it is available only against *A* and none else.

Thus, rights to property are right *in rem* and rights arising out of contracts are rights *in personam.*

MEANING OF CONTRACT

It will be appropriate to go through definitions given by some eminent jurists to understand the meaning of the term contract.

"An agreement creating and defining obligations between the parties". —*Salmond*

"A contract is an agreement enforceable at law made between two or more persons, by which rights are acquired by one or more to acts or forbearances on the part of the other or others".

—*Sir William Anson*

"Every agreement and promise enforceable at law is a contract". —*Sir Federick Pollock*

Sec. 2 (*h*) of The Indian Contract Act defines a contract as, 'an agreement enforceable at law'. Every contract, thus, combines two essential elements (*i*) agreement and (*ii*) obligation. It creates rights and obligations between the parties to the contract, which are correlative. In case a party refuses to honour a contracted obligation it will give right of action to the other party.

The essential requirements of a contract, based on the above definitions can be put as follows:

(1) **Two Parties :** Two parties are necessary to make a contract. The person who makes the promise is known as the 'promisor' and the person to whom the promise is made is known as the 'promisee'. As a matter of fact, in a contract, each party is a promisor as well as a promisee. *For example*, when *A* promises to sell his car for a sum of ₹ 10,000 to *B*, *A* is a promisor because he has promised to sell his car while he is also a promisee because there is a promise from *B* to pay a sum of ₹ 10,000 to him. The same is also applicable to *B*.

(2) **An Agreement :** There has to be an agreement between two parties. An offer when accepted becomes an agreement. Thus, an agreement implies an 'offer' and acceptance. The term offer implies the willingness of a person to do or not to do something and its communication to the other, while acceptance means assent by the party to whom the offer has been made. *For example*, if *A* says to *B* that he is willing to sell him his car for a sum of ₹ 10,000, it is an offer from *A*. If *B* gives his assent to this offer, it will be said that he has accepted the offer and an agreement will come into existence.

(3) **Legal Obligation :** The agreement should give rise to a legal obligation, *i.e.*, obligation which is enforceable at law. Agreements which give rise only to social or domestic obligations

cannot be termed as contracts. An agreement to go to a picture or attend a marriage ceremony is not a contract as it does not give rise to any legal obligation. They are often not intended to be binding in law. The most usual form of agreements, which do not constitute a contract, are the agreements made between husband and wife. They are not contracts because the parties do not intend that they should be attended by legal consequences.[1] But where *A* agrees *B* to supply him 1,000 bales of cotton at ₹ 100 per bale, there is a contact, because if any party is not prepared to fulfil his part, the other party can have recourse to legal remedies.

From the above following conclusions can be drawn:

(*a*) *All agreements are not contracts :* Agreement is a much wider term than a contract. As stated above, an agreement may or may not give rise to legal obligations. An agreement which does not create legal obligation, is not a contract. Agreements which the parties declare not to be binding also do not constitute contract. They may be just 'honourable pledges' and expressly stated to be 'outside the jurisdiction of any court.'[2]

Examples : (*i*) If *A* agrees to come to the house of *B* for a dinner at *B*'s request, there is an agreement, but it cannot be termed as a contract because it does not carry any legal obligation.

(*ii*) *A* of Ceylon came to England with his wife for a holiday. While returning to Ceylon on the expiry of his leave, he promised his wife, who on medical grounds had to remain in England, a household allowance of £ 30 a month until she joined him in Ceylon. After some time when the two parties separated from each other, the wife claimed the allowance. The Court did not allow the claim on the ground that domestic arrangements are outside the realm of contract altogether.[3]

(*b*) *All obligations also do not constitute contracts* : Any obligation which arises independently of an agreement, cannot be the basis of a valid contract. According to *Anson,* only that obligation is a contract, which directly contemplates and creates an obligation and is intended to have any legal consequences. Obligation to maintain wife and children does not arise out of contract. Obligation to observe the provisions of the various Acts also does not arise out of a contract.

Therefore, to sum up, a contract results from a combination of agreement and obligation. But, it is not necessary that all agreements should create an obligation between the parties to the agreement. An agreement may exist without any legal obligation, but a contract cannot. In order that an agreement should be a contract, it must create legal obligation on both the parties. It must impose compulsion upon a person or persons to do or not to do a certain act. Obligations may also relate to either social or legal matters. But the Law of Contracts is confined only to such legal obligations as are traceable only to agreements. Agreements giving rise to social obligations will also not constitute binding contracts. Obligations arising from a trust, a decree or from statutes do not fall within the scope of the Contract Act. Hence 'the law of contracts is not the whole law of agreements nor is it the whole law of obligations. It is the law of those agreements which create obligations, and those obligations which have their sources in agreements.' — *Sir John William Salmond**

1. Balfour *v.* Balfour (1919) 2 K.B. 571.
2. Rose & Frank Co. *v.* Crompton & Bros. (1925) A.C. 445.
* (3rd Dec. 1862 - 19th Sept. 1924) Legal Scholar, Judge, New Zealand.

ESSENTIAL ELEMENTS OF A VALID CONTRACT

The following are the essential elements of a valid contract :

(1) **Agreement :** Agreement means communication by the parties to one another their intention to create relationship. This requires a proposal from the side of one party and its acceptance by the other party. Thus, a contract requires two parties—one making the proposal and the other accepting it.

(2) **Competent Parties :** Both the parties entering into an agreement should be competent to make contract. Every person who has attained the age of majority, possesses sound mind and is not subject to any other legal disqualifications, is considered competent to enter into a contract.

(3) **Free Consent :** The term consent means understanding the same thing in the same sense by the parties entering into an agreement. Consent is said to be free if it has been given by the parties independently without any fear or favour. In order to make a contract valid, it is necessary that parties to the contract not only give their consent, but should also be free.

(4) **Consideration :** A contract enforceable by law must also be supported by consideration. Consideration means 'something' in return. This implies that the parties entering into an agreement should get something in return for the promises they are making to make such promises a valid contract.

(5) **Legal Object :** The object of the agreement should be legal. In other words the agreement should not violate the provisions of some law or it should not relate to matters which are forbidden by law.

(6) **Not Expressly Declared Void :** The agreement must have not been expressly declared void by any law in force in the country.

(7) **Compliance with the Legal Formalities :** The prescribed legal formalities of writing, registration etc., if necessary, for the agreement to make it enforceable by law, must have been observed. Certain other Acts also prescribe some legal formalities, which if not observed, will make the agreements void.

A list of such agreements is given below :

Contracts which must be in writing : Following are some of the contracts or documents which must be in writing, otherwise they will not be valid :

(1) A promise to pay a time-barred debt.

(2) An arbitration agreement.

(3) Lease agreements for a period of more than three years.

(4) Contracts of insurance.

(5) Negotiable Instruments *e.g.,* bills of exchange, cheques or promissory notes.

(6) Memorandum and Articles of Association of a company.

(7) Contracts relating to transfer of immovable properties.

Contracts which must be registered : Following are some of the contracts (or documents containing contracts) which must be registered:

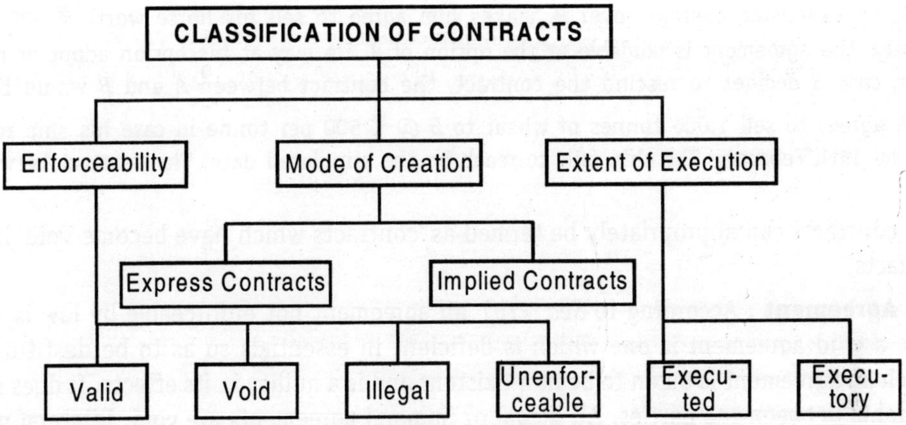

(1) A promise made without consideration on account of natural love and affection between parties standing in near relation.

(2) Documents of which registration is compulsory under *Sec. 17* of The Registration Act, 1908.

(3) Contracts relating to the transfer of immovable properties under The Transfer of Property Act, 1882.

(4) Memorandum and Articles of Association, debentures, mortgages and charges under The Companies Act, 1956.

CLASSIFICATION OF CONTRACTS

Contracts may be classified into different categories depending upon their (*i*) enforceability, (*ii*) mode of creation and (*iii*) extent of execution. This has been given in the chart as follows:

1. Classification of Contracts on the Basis of Enforceability

(*a*) **Valid Contracts :** Contracts which satisfy all the essential elements of a valid contract as laid down by Section 10, are enforceable in a court of law. Such contracts are termed as valid contracts.

(*b*) **Void Contracts :** An agreement may be enforceable at the time when it was made but later on, due to certain reasons, it may become void and unenforceable. Such agreements are known as void contracts.

Following are some of such contracts :

(*i*) A contract becomes void by supervening impossibility or illegality (*Sec. 56*).

(*ii*) A voidable contract becomes void, when the party, who had the option to avoid it, decides to repudiate the contract.

(*iii*) A contingent contract to do or not to do something on the happening of an event becomes void when the event becomes impossible (*Sec. 32*).

Examples : (*i*) On 15th January. *A* agrees with *B* to sell him horse for a sum of ₹ 500 on 20th

February. The horse dies on 21st January. The performance of the agreement was possible at the time when it was made, but now its performance becomes impossible on account of supervening impossibility. It is, therefore, a void contract.

(*ii*) *A*, by exercising coercion over *B*, makes him agree to sell his horse worth ₹ 500 for a sum of ₹ 100 only. The agreement is voidable at the option of *B*. He may at his option adopt or rescind the contract. In case *B* decides to rescind the contract, the contract between *A* and *B* would be void.

(*iii*) A agrees to sell 1,000 tonnes of wheat to *B* @ ₹ 500 per tonne in case his ship reaches the port safely by 15th February. The ship fails to reach by the stipulated date. The contract between *A* and *B* is void.

Such contracts can appropriately be termed as 'contracts which have become void' in place of 'void contracts'.

Void Agreement : According to *Sec. 2(g)* 'an agreement not enforceable by law is said to be void.' Thus, a void agreement is one which is deficient in essentials so as to be destitute of legal effects. Such an agreement is taken to be non-existent and is a nullity in its effects. It does not create any legal rights between the parties. All illegal or immoral agreements are void. Bilateral mistake of a material fact also makes an agreement void.

Example : *A* agrees with *B*, in consideration of ₹ 100, to draw two parallel lines in such a way as to cross each other. The agreement is impossible to perform and, therefore void.

Void Agreement and Void Contract

Thus, a void agreement is void from the very beginning, *i.e.*, void *ab initio*, while a void contract was valid at the time when it was made but becomes void later. An agreement, which is found to be void *ab initio* or which becomes void subsequently, as stated earlier, will have the following effects :

(*a*) The agreement shall be unenforceable.

(*b*) Money paid or property transferred by one party to another is recoverable. This principle will not apply where both the parties knew or were expected to know about the illegal or void nature of the agreement at the time when it was made. This has been discussed in detail at the end of Chapter 12 in this Section.

(*c*) Collateral transactions shall not become void unless the agreement has also been illegal.

Example : *A* test match is going on between India and Pakistan. *A* agrees to pay a sum of ` 100 to *B* if India wins the match. India wins and in order to pay off *B*, *A* borrows a sum of ` 100 from *C*. *C* knows the purpose. The agreement between *A* and *C* is a collateral transaction. Since a wagering agreement is void and not illegal (except in the old State of Bombay), notwithstanding the original agreement between *A* and *B* being void, the collateral agreement between *A* and *C* is perfectly valid.

(*d*) All lawful promises which are severable shall remain valid and can be enforced.

(*c*) **Voidable Contracts :** 'An agreement which is enforceable by law at the option of one or more of the parties thereto, but not at the option of other or others, is voidable contract.' [*Sec. 2(i)*]. Thus, a voidable contract is a contract with a flaw of which the aggrieved party may, at his option, take benefit. He has the option either to affirm it and elect to carry out the contract in spite of the defect or to reject it. The other party will have no right to avoid it. The contract shall remain valid so long as it is not repudiated or avoided by the party entitled to do so. Agreements induced by coercion, undue influence, fraud or misrepresentation are voidable at the option of the party whose consent has been so obtained.

Example : *A* by giving false description persuades *B* to purchase certain goods. *B* on discovering the misrepresentation can repudiate the contract or elect to carry out the contract in spite of the defect.

The party rescinding the contract is entitled to get damages for any loss that he might have suffered from the other party on account of making that contract. But in case he (the aggrieved party) has received some benefit under the contract, he must restore such benefit to the person from whom it was received.

Difference between Void Agreements and Voidable Contracts

1. *Enforceability :* Void agreements are unenforceable from the very beginning. They are *void ab initio*. A voidable contract becomes unenforceable only when the party at whose option contract is voidable chooses to rescind it. It continues to be valid till it is repudiated by the person entitled to do so. A void agreement cannot be enforced at all. A voidable contract can be enforced if the option is exercise to enforce it.

No one can acquire any title on goods contained under a void agreement. But a *bona fide* holder for value will acquire better title on goods obtained from a person who had title to the same under a voidable contract.

2. *Restitution and Compensation :* (*a*) In the case of void agreements, restitution is always allowed except where illegality or void nature of the agreement was known or expected to be known to both the parties from very beginning, *e.g.*, where a minor who had not misrepresented his age was a party to the contract.

But in voidable contract, when they are rescinded, benefit will be restored as far as may be possible.

(*b*) As a void agreement cannot be enforced at law, there arises no question of the compensation on account of the non-performance of the agreement. But, in case of voidable contract, if a person rightfully rescinds a contract, he is entitled to compensation for loss or damages suffered by him on account of the rescission of the contract.

3. *Effect on Collateral Agreements :* A voidable contract also does not affect the collateral contract just as a void agreement. But where the agreement is void on account of the illegality of the object and consideration, the collateral agreements will also become void.

Following examples will explain the difference between void agreements and voidable contracts:

Examples : (*i*) *A*, a doctor by exercising undue influence over his patient *B*, makes him agree to sell his car worth ₹ 10,000 for a sum of ₹ 5,000. The contract is voidable at the option of *B*; but if he does not exercise his option the contract will remain valid.

(*ii*) *B* has two cars, one blue and other red. He wishes to sell his blue car. He makes an offer to sell his car to *A* for a sum of ₹ 5,000. *A* accepts the offer thinking that it is about the red car. There is no *consensus ad idem* (identity of mind) and, therefore, the agreement is void.

(*d*) **Illegal Contracts :** It will be appropriate to use the term illegal agreement in place of illegal contract. The term 'illegal agreement' has a wider conception than void agreement. *All illegal agreement are void but all void agreements are not necessarily illegal, e.g.*, a wagering agreement is void but not illegal or an agreement with a minor is void but not illegal. An illegal agreement is destitute of legal effect *ab initio* (*i.e.*, from the very beginning) but a contract may become void subsequently on the happening of an event which makes it illegal. Money paid or property transferred by one party to the other, in the case of an illegal agreement, shall in general be not recoverable. But incase of agreements which were valid in the beginning but had become illegal on account of the happening of some event or where the parties did not know of illegality, the money paid or property transferred might be recovered. A void agreement does not affect the performance of collateral transactions, but illegality of the original contract will make even the collateral transactions tainted with illegality. Illegal agreements need not necessarily be criminal in nature. When the contract is illegal, the court will, of its own motion, refuse to enforce it even though the illegality has not been pleaded by the defendant.

Examples : (*i*) *A* promises to pay a sum of ₹ 100 to *B* if he *B* gives a good beating to *C*. *B* gives a good beating to *C* and *A*, in order to pay *B*, borrows from *D* a sum of ₹ 100, *D* knows the purpose for which money has been borrowed from him. The agreement between *A* and *B* being illegal, the collateral transaction between *A* and *D* will also be illegal.

(*ii*) *A* agrees to pay *B* a sum of ₹ 100 if it rains tomorrow. It rains tomorrow and in order to pay *B*, *A* borrows a sum of ₹ 100 from *D*. *D* knows the purpose for which money has been borrowed from him. The agreement between *A* and *B*, being of wagering nature, shall be void (except in Maharashtra and Gujarat where wagering agreements are illegal on account of Bombay Act) but the collateral transaction between *A* and *D* will be perfectly valid.

Difference between Void and Illegal Agreements

1. All illegal agreements are void, but all void agreements are not illegal.
2. Unlike illegal agreements, there is no punishment to the parties to a void agreement.
3. Agreements collateral to void agreements are valid but agreements collateral to illegal agreements are void *ab-initio*.
4. Illegal agreements are void from the very beginning, but sometimes valid contracts may subsequently become void.

(*e*) **Unenforceable Contracts :** Certain contracts become void because the law courts will not enforce them. These contracts have all the essential characteristics of a contract and are perfectly valid in their substances yet they cannot be enforced because of certain technical defects. They include contracts which are incapable of being enforced on account of non-observance of certain formalities required by special provisions of law such as those of writing, attestation, registration, etc. Some of them can be enforced if the technical defect is removed. *For example*, if a document embodying a contract is understamped, the contract is unenforceable, but if the requisite stamp is affixed (if allowed), the contract becomes enforceable.

2. Classification of Contracts on the Basis of Mode of Creation

(*a*) **Express Contracts :** Contracts entered into between the parties by words spoken or written, are termed as express contracts. In such contracts, parties make oral or written declaration of their intentions and of the terms of the transaction.

Example : *A* writes to *B*, 'I am prepared to sell my horse for a sum of rupees five hundred. *B* accepts *A*'s offer by a telegram. The contract will be termed as express contract.

(*b*) **Implied Contracts :** Contracts which come into being on account of the act or conduct of the parties and not by their express words, written or spoken, are known as implied contracts. Blackstone defines implied contracts as those 'which reason and justice dictate and which the law, therefore, presumes that every man undertakes to perform.'

Example : *A* takes a seat in a bus. There is an implied contract that he will pay the prescribed fare for taking him to his destination.

In some cases, in spite of no agreement between the parties, the law takes it for granted on account of the circumstances that the contractual relationship exists between two parties. Actually such obligations do not arise out of agreements, and therefore, properly speaking they cannot be termed as contracts. The Contracts Act calls such obligations as *'relations resembling to those of controls'.* These relations have been discussed in detail in Chapter 11 of this section.

Example : A sends a parcel of fruits to his friend *B*. The parcel is misdelivered to *C*, who takes it as a birthday present from his friend. *C* must pay for the price of the fruits.

3. Classification of Contracts on the Basis of the Extent of Execution

(*a*) **Executed Contracts :** Where both the parties to the contract have fulfilled their respective obligations, contract is said to be executed. In other words, an executed contract is one where nothing remains to be done by either party.

Example : *A* sells a radio set to *B* for ₹ 300. *B* pays the price. Both the parties have performed their respective obligations, and therefore, it is an executed contract.

(*b*) **Executory Contract :** Where one or both the parties to the contract have still to perform certain things in future or under the terms of the contract something remains to be done, the contract is termed as an executory one, *e.g.*, delivery of goods has been given but price has not been paid or both the delivery of goods and payment of price have to be made at a future date.

Example : *A* agrees to paint a picture for *B* and *B* in consideration promises to pay *A* a sum of rupees one hundred. The contract is executory.

In a contract where one party has performed his promise but the other has still to perform his part, the contract will be taken as *partly executed* and *partly executory*.

Example : *A* agrees to paint a picture for *B* and *B* in consideration pays a sum of ₹ 100 to *A*. The contract is executed as regards *B*, but executory as regards *A*.

On the basis of execution, the contracts may also be divided as :

(1) Unilateral contracts.

(2) Bilateral contracts.

(1) ***Unilateral Contracts :*** A contract is said to be unilateral where one party has performed his obligation either before or at the time when the contract comes into existence. It is only the obligation of the other party which remains outstanding at the time of formation of the contract. Such contracts are also termed as contracts with executed consideration.

Example : *A*, a coolie, puts *B*'s luggage in the carriage. The contract comes into existence as soon as the luggage is put. It is now for *B* to perform his obligation by paying the charges to the coolie.

(2) ***Bilateral Contracts :*** A contract is bilateral if the obligations of both the parties are outstanding at the time of the formation of the contract. They are, therefore, executory contracts with executory consideration.

Example : *A* promises to sell his car to *B* after 15 days. *B* promises to pay the price on the delivery of the car. The contract is bilateral as obligations of both the parties are outstanding at the time of the formation of the contract.

It is to be noted that the contract comes into existence on the date on which it is entered into between the parties. The date of its execution is immaterial for determining the validity of the contract. The mere fact that the performance of the contract has been postponed does not mean that the contract was never entered into.

Example : *A* agrees to supply 500 bags of rice to *B* three months after 15th January the date on which he will enter into a contract with *B*. Though performance of the contract has been deferred for three months but the contract will be taken to have come into existence right on 15th January.

From the above, it follows that a contract is a contract from the time it is made and not from the time its performance is due.

KEY TERMS

- ❑ **Agreement :** An offer when accepted becomes an agreement.
- ❑ **Contract :** An agreement enforceable by law.
- ❑ **Illegal Agreement :** An agreement against the provisions of law.
- ❑ **Void Agreement :** An agreement enforceable at the time when it was made; but later on becomes unenforceable.
- ❑ **Voidable Contract :** An agreement enforceable at the option of one or more parties thereto; but not at the option of the other or others.

TEST QUESTIONS

Objective Type : *Test Your Knowledge*

1. Fill in the blanks

(*i*) A contract is an agreement ....

(*ii*) A void agreement is void from the ....

(*iii*) A voidable contract is void at the option of one of the contracting parties but not at the option of the ....

(*iv*) All illegal agreements are .... but not all void agreements are ....

(*v*) Collateral agreements are also void in case of .... agreements.

(*vi*) A contract to contract is .... a contract.

(*vii*) An agreement not enforceable by law is......................... (*CCS Foundation Dec. 2012*)

[***Ans.*** (*i*) enforceable by law; (*ii*) very beginning; (*iii*) other or others; (*iv*) void, illegal; (*v*) illegal; (*vi*) not; (*vii*) void-ab-initio.]

2. Select the most appropriate answer

(*i*) *A* contract is made where :

(*a*) *X* agrees with *Y* to discover a treasure by magic.

(*b*) *X* bids at a public auction.

(*c*) *A* takes a sit in a public omni bus.

(*d*) *X* promises in writing to give ₹ 500 to *Y*.

(*ii*) Right *in rem* implies :

(*a*) a right available against the whole world.

(*b*) a right available against a particular individual.

(*c*) a right available against the Government.

(*iii*) A void contract

(*a*) is void from the very beginning.

(*b*) becomes void later on due to certain contingencies.

(*c*) is enforceable at the option of one of the contracting parties only.

(*iv*) A void agreement is one which is
(*a*) Valid but not enforceable.
(*b*) Enforceable at the option of both the parties.
(*c*) Enforceable at the option of one party.
(*d*) Not enforceable in a court of law. *(CS Foundation, June 2007)*

(*v*) In case of void agreements, collateral transactions are
(*a*) Also void
(*b*) Unenforceable
(*c*) Not affected
(*d*) Illegal *(PCE, ICAI, Nov. 2007)*

[**Ans.** (*i*) (*c*); (*ii*) (*a*); (*iii*) (*b*); (*iv*) (*d*); (*v*) (*c*)]

Essay Type : *For Review, Discussion and Practice*

1. Explain the essentials which must be fulfilled before an agreement becomes enforceable at law.
2. "The law of contracts is not the whole law of agreements nor is it the whole law of obligations." —(*Salmond*). Comment.
3. How do you distinguish between Void, Voidable, Unenforceable and Illegal Contracts?
4. Differentiate between (*i*) Executed and Executory Contracts, (*ii*) Formal and Simple Contract.
5. Differentiate between :
   (*a*) Unilateral and Bilateral Contracts *(CA Inter, Nov. 1987, 1990)*
   (*b*) Void and Illegal Agreements *(CA Foundation, Nov. 2000; CA Inter, Nov. 1991, CS Foundation, Dec. 2003, B.Com. (Hons.), Delhi 1987, B.Com. (Pass) 2000)*
6. 'A contract is a contract from the time it is made and not from the time performance is due.' Comment.
7. Explain the following :
   (*i*) A voidable contract is valid till the aggrieved party opts to avoid it. *(ICWA Foundation, June 1998)*
   (*ii*) Is there any difference between agreement and contract? *(ICWA Foundation, June 2000)*
   (*iii*) Illegal agreements and void agreements are the same. *(ICWA Foundation, Dec. 1999; Dec. 2000)*
   (*iv*) An agreement to agree is a valid contract. *(ICWA Foundation, June 2000)*
   (*v*) Distinguish between void agreement and voidable contract. *(ICWA Foundation, Dec. 2000)*
   (*vi*) "All illegal agreements are void"—Comment. *(ICWA Foundation, Dec. 2000)*
   (*vii*) What are essentials for validity of a contract? *(ICWA Foundation, June 2001)*
8. Distinguish between 'Void' and 'Voidable' contracts with relevant examples. *(GGSIPU, BBA (H), May 2002, B.Com. (Pass), Delhi 2005)*
9. Define 'Contract'. Explain essential elements of a valid contract. *(GGSIPU, BBA (H), May 2002, 2004)*
10. "All contracts are agreements, but all agreements are not contracts." Discuss this statement in the light of section 10 of the act. *(B.Com. (Hons.) Delhi 1999 & 2003; GGSIPU, BBA (H), May 2003)*
11. "In commercial and business agreements, the presumption is that the parties intend to create legal obligations." Comment. *(B.Com. (Hons.), Delhi, 1988)*
12. "The law of contract is not the whole law of obligations." Comment. *(B.Com. (Hons.), Delhi, 1991)*

13. "An agreement enforceable at law is a contract." Explain. (*B.Com. (Pass), Delhi 2005*)
14. Distinguish between 'void contract' and 'voidable contract'. (*CS Foundation, June 2008*)
15. State the essential elements of a valid contract. (*CS Foundation, Dec., 2011*)
16. Comment on the following statements:
    (*i*) All contracts are agreements but all agreements are not contracts (*B.Com (Hons.) Delhi 2010*)
    (*ii*) In social agreements, the usual presumptions is that the parties intend to create legal obligations. (*B.Com (Hons.) Delhi 2011*)
    (*iii*) A void contract is one which is void ab-initio (*B.Com (Hons.) Delhi 2012*)
    (*iv*) All void agreements are not illegal but all illegal agreements are void. (*B.Com (Hons.) Delhi 2010*)
    (*v*) Collateral transactions to an illegal agreement do not become void. (*B.Com (Hons.) Delhi 2011*)

PRACTICAL PROBLEMS

1. Do the following constitute valid contracts :
   (*a*) when you board a bus;
   (*b*) when you enrol for a correspondence course;
   (*c*) when you call a taxi;
   (*d*) when you buy an evening paper;
   (*e*) when you put a penny in the slot of a weighing machine;
   (*f*) when you eat a meal at a restaurant.

   [***Ans.*** Yes, in all cases.]
2. Father promised to pay his son a sum of ₹ 1 lakh if the son passed CA examination in the first attempt. The son passed the examination in the first attempt, but father failed to pay the amount as promised. Son files a suit for recovery of the amount. State along with reasons whether son can recover the amount under the Indian Contract Act, 1872. (*PEE II, May 2005*)

   [***Ans.*** The son cannot recover the amount of ₹ 1 lakh from father since there was no intention to create legal relationship.]
3. W, the wife of H, who is lunatic, purchased a diamond set of ₹ 10 lakhs from Beauty Jeweller on credit. Referring to the provisions of the Indian Contract Act, 1872, decide whether the Beauty Jeweller is entitled to claim the above amount from the property of H.(PEE-II, ICAI, June 2009)

   [***Ans.*** Beauty Jeweller is not entitled to claim the price of diamond set from the property of H because diamond set of worth ₹ 10 lakhs is not a necessity for W.]

Chapter 2
OFFER AND ACCEPTANCE

LEARNING OBJECTIVES

A careful study of this chapter will enable you to :

- understand the meaning of the term agreement;
- identify the essential requisites of a valid offer and a valid acceptance;
- describe when communication of offer and acceptance and their revocation is complete; and
- explain the meaning of certain key terms.

According to section 2(*e*) 'every promise and every set of promises forming consideration for each other is called an agreement.' A proposal when accepted by another party becomes a promise.

PROPOSAL OR OFFER

Sec. 2(*a*) defines proposal as 'when one person signifies to another his willingness to do or to abstain from doing anything with a view to obtaining the assent of that other to such an act or abstinence, he is said to make a proposal.' Thus, an offer consists of two parts :

(*i*) a promise by the offerer to do or abstain from doing something and

(*ii*) a request to the offeree for giving his acceptance.

Offerer is not bound by his promise until the offeree accepts it unconditionally.

Essentials of a Valid Offer

The essentials of a valid offer can be put as follows :

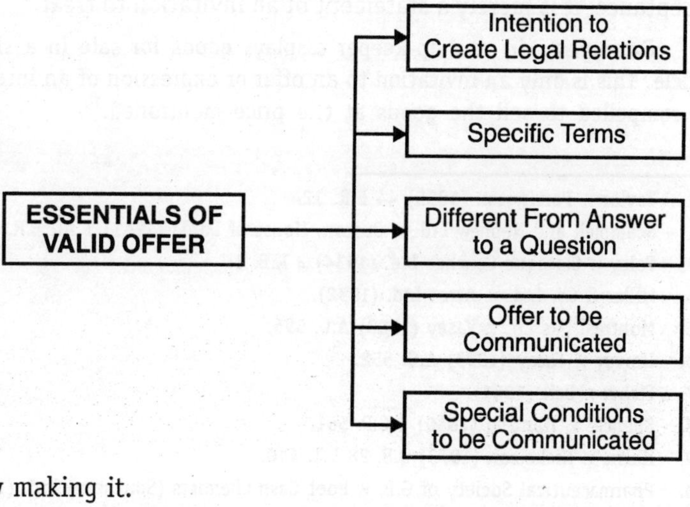

1. **The offer must disclose an intention to create legal relations:** A proposal will not become a promise even after it has been accepted unless it was made with a view to create legal obligations *e.g.,* invitation to a dinner which has no intention to create legal relationship. An offer to perform social or moral acts, without any intention of creating legal relations, will not be a valid offer. Thus, an offer must impose some duty on the party making it.

2. **The terms of an offer must be clear and specific and not loose or vague :** An offer must not be based on a condition which is uncertain or incapable of performance.[1] It must contain certain terms on which the proposer is willing to act. Though the proposer is free to lay down any terms and conditions in his offer, hard or ridiculous, but they should be certain and legal, otherwise its acceptance will conclude a vague agreement which the courts will not enforce.[2] But where an agreement contains its own definitions for clarifying a vague term, the agreement will not be vague in law.[3] The previous course of dealings between the parties to an agreement may also be referred to in order to clarify a vague term.[4] In some circumstances, the courts might imply a term based upon the presumed intention of the parties.

Examples : (*i*) *A* offers to purchase one more horse from *B* if the horse purchased earlier from *B* proves lucky. The offer is vague and hence not valid.

(*ii*) *A* made a contract with *B* and promised that if he was satisfied with him as a customer, he would favourably consider his application for the renewal of the contract. The promise is too vague to create any legal relationship.

3. **An offer is different from an answer to a question, an invitation to an offer and a statement of intention.**

Mere answer to a question : An answer to a question cannot be taken as an offer nor a mere statement of the lowest price at which a person may agree to sell goods amounts to a proposal.

Example : *H* telegraphed to *F*, 'Will you sell us white car? Telegraph lowest cash price.' *F* telegraphed in answer, 'Lowest cash price for white car is £ 900.' *H* telegraphed: 'We agree to buy white car for £ 900 asked by you. Please send us your title deeds.' To this *H* received no reply. It was held that there was no contract because *F* communicated only the lowest price. He did not state that he was prepared to sell and the mere statement about the lowest price could not be taken as an offer from *F*.[6]

Mere invitation to an offer : Offer is also to be distinguished from a mere invitation to an offer or treat. Catalogue of goods, and advertisement for tenders or inviting applications for job, a prospectus of a company, an auctioneer's request for bids or display of goods in the show-case with prices marked upon them[7] etc., are mere invitations to offers and not actual offers.[8] They disclose an intention of making an offer but in reality an offer is not made. The person, who responds to an invitation to an offer, makes the actual offer. The party issuing an invitation for the offers has a right to accept or not to accept them. Similarly, an advertisement regarding an auction sale is not an offer capable of acceptance; it is merely a statement of an invitation to treat.[9]

Examples : (*i*) *A* shop-keeper displays goods for sale in a shop with price tags attached to each article. This is only an invitation to an offer or expression of an intention to sell. The shop-keeper cannot be compelled to sell the goods at the price mentioned.[10]

1. Taylor *v.* Portington (1855) 44 E.R. 124.
2. Scammell and Nephew Ltd. *v.* Ouston, House of Lords (1941) 1 All E.R. 14.
3. Foley *v.* Classque Coaches Ltd. (1934) 2 K.B. 1.
4. Hillas & Co. Ltd. *v.* Acros Ltd. (1932).
5. Montreal Gas Co. *v.* Vasey (1900) A.C. 595.
6. Hervey *v.* Facey (1893) A.C. 552.
7. Fisher *v.* Bell (1961).
8. Spencer *v.* Harding (1870) 5 C.P. 561.
9. Harris *v.* Nickelson (1873) Q.B. 28 L.T. 410.
10. Pharmaceutical Society of G.B. *v.* Boot Cash Chemists (Southern) Ltd. (1921) 2 Q.B.

(*ii*) *A* person makes an announcement to sell goods by tender. He does not declare that the goods will be sold to the highest bidder. This amounts only to an invitation to offer and not an offer.

In case of an invitation for an offer, there is no intention on the part of the person sending out the invitation to obtain the assent of the other person to such an invitation. His object is merely to circulate information of his willingness to deal with anybody, who on such information is willing to open negotiations with him.

The above principles have also been followed by the Supreme Court in the Case of *McPherson v. Appana.*[11] The facts of the case are being given in the following example.

Example : *M* offered to purchase a lodge by *A* for ₹ 1,000. He wrote to *A*'s agent asking whether his offer was accepted. He also added that he was ready to accept any higher price if found reasonable. The agent replied, 'Won't accept less than rupees ten thousand.' *M* gave a telegram to the agent accepting the price. *M* brought a suit for specific performance on the refusal of *A* to sell the lodge. It was held that *A* was merely inviting offers. There was no binding contract because he had not given assent to *M*'s offer to buy for ₹ 10,000.

Mere statement of intention : A declaration by a person that he has the intention to do something does not amount to an offer. The person making the declaration will not be liable to the person who has suffered some loss because of reliance on the declared intention.[12]

An advertisement in the newspaper by a person to effect sale of goods on a particular date or a price tag fixed with the goods in the show case is merely a statement of intention and not an offer. It has also been held recently by the Supreme Court that the announcements made on loudspeakers do not result into any binding contracts.[13]

Examples : (*i*) A father, on his daughter's marriage, wrote to the intended son-in-law, 'You are aware that with my large family Eliza Mill has a little fortune, she will have a share of what I leave after the death of her mother.' The letter was held to contain a mere statement of intention.[14]

(*ii*) *T* paid in conversation to *W* that he would give ₹ 1,000 to him who married his daughter with his consent. *W* married *T*'s daughter with his consent. He, therefore, filed a case against *T* for the alleged promise. It was held that the words used by *T* were a mere statement of intention and were general words to excite suitors.[15]

(*iii*) *A* gives an advertisement in a newspaper to effect sale of his goods on a particular day. This amounts only to a mere statement of intention and not an offer.

4. **The offer must be made with a view to obtain the consent of the other party to the act or abstinence which the proposer is willing to do :** The communication of accep-tance cannot be dispensed with by any of the terms of the offer. A proposer cannot also dictate terms under which the offer can be refused. At best he can lay down the mode of acceptance.

5. **Every offer must be communicated :** Merely, by acting according to the terms of the offer without their knowledge, a party cannot accept an offer and, therefore, no valid contract can rise.

As Lord Lindlay puts it, 'A state of mind not communicated cannot be regarded as dealings between man and man.' This is applicable both to specific as well as general offers.

11. A.I.R. 1951 S.C. 184.
12. Harris *v.* Nickelson (1873).
13. Banwarilal *v.* Sukdarshan Dayal (1973) Sec. 294, 295.
14. Farina *v.* Fickus (1900) 1 Ch. 331.
15. Weeks *v.* Tybald (1605) Nov. 11.

Example : G's nephew had absconded. He sent his munim *L* in search of the missing nephew. In the meantime *G* issued handbills offering ₹ 501 to any person who would find out the missing boy. *L* found out the missing nephew before seeing the handbills. Later on, he came to know of the reward and sued *G* for the reward. It was held that he could not claim the reward as he did not know of the offer.[16]

6. **Special conditions attached to an offer must also be communicated :** A proposer is free to lay down any terms and conditions in his offer. The other party, if accepts the offer, will have to abide by all the terms and conditions of the offer. It will be immaterial whether the terms were harsh or ridiculous. The only responsibility of the proposer is to bring all the terms of the offer to the notice of the other party. Notice of conditions must be contemporaneous with the making of the contract. The acceptor can be held liable for the fulfilment of the conditions only when they have expressly been communicated to him or they are so clearly written that he ought to have known them or reasonable notice of the existence of the conditions is given to him. He will also be bound by the conditions if he knew of their existence though they are in a language not known to him. It is his duty to get them explained.

Examples : (*i*) *T*, an illiterate, purchased a railway ticket on the front of which was printed 'for conditions see back'. One of the conditions was that the railway company would not be liable for personal injuries to passengers. An accident caused some injuries to *T*. Suit for damages brought by *T* was dismissed as he was bound by the conditions printed on the reverse of the ticket.[17]

(*ii*) *R* booked her luggage on the ship. She was given a ticket folded in such a way that no writing was visible. The ticket contained a condition in small type stating that the ship-owner's liability was limited to £ 100. *R* knew that there was printing on the ticket but did not know that it was about some condition. It was held that *R* was not bound by the conditions as she having regard to the smallness of the type, it could not be taken that ship-owners had made sufficient arrangement for the communication of the condition.[18]

Thus, it is to be noted that a person, who accepts without objection a document containing terms of the offer, which he know or ought to have known, will be bound by those terms even if he had not read them. However, this rule will not be applicable if the conditions are so irrelevant or unreasonable that an assent to them cannot reasonably be presumed.[19] Similarly, where a condition attached to an offer is against public policy, it will not be enforced merely because it has been impliedly accepted by the acceptor.

Example : *R* delivered some clothes to a laundry. On the reverse of the laundry receipt handed over to him, it was mentioned that the customer would be entitled to recover only 15% of the market price or value of the article in the event of its being lost. A garment of *R* was lost due to the negligence of laundry owner. In a suit by *R*, it was held that the term being *prima facie* opposed to public policy and to the fundamental principles of contracts, could not be enforced merely because it was printed on the back side of the bill and there was tacit acceptance of the term when the bill was received.[20]

---

16. Lalman Shukla *v.* Gauri Dutt (1913) 11 All. L.J. 489.
17. Thompson *v.* L.M. & S. Rly. (1930) IK.B.41.
18. Richardson *v.* Rowntree (1894) A.C. 217.
19. Geband *v.* Great Eastern Rly. Co. (1920) 3 K.B. 689. This case is to be differentiated from the two cases given above. In case of a railway company or a shipping company the conditions have some sort of statutory backing. These conditions may be incorporated in the Act or the charter of creation of these companies besides being widely circulated. Public interest is, therefore, duly cared for. But a dry cleaner or a tailor may get certain conditions printed on the receipts which he gives to his customers and these conditions may have been framed by him only for his convenience without caring for the public interest. Hence, such conditions cannot be enforced.
20. Lily White *v.* R. Munnuswami, A.I.R. 1966 (Mad.) 13.

It will be very appropriate to state here the judgement given by the House of Lords in the case of *Richardson v. Rowntree.*[21] It was observed that mere delivery and acceptance of the ticket with the conditions upon it was not sufficient to make those conditions part of the contract. But the acceptor would be bound by the conditions if all of the following conditions are satisfied :

(*i*) The acceptor knew about the writing or printing on the ticket.

(*ii*) He also knew that the writing or printing on the ticket contained conditions regarding the terms of the contract.

(*iii*) The offerer had done all that what was reasonably sufficient to give to the acceptor notice of the conditions.

(*iv*) The notice of the conditions should be given before or at the time of the contract. A subsequent notice will amount to alteration of the original contract which will not bind the other party unless he has assented thereto.

Example : *A* and his wife hired a room at a hotel for seven days. After paying the rent in advance when they entered the room there was a notice on its walls. It read, 'the proprietors will not hold themselves responsible for articles lost, or stolen unless handed to the manager for safe custody.' On account of the negligence of the hotel staff, their property was stolen. On a suit being filed by *A*, the court held that the notice was not a part of the contract and, therefore, the proprietors of the hotel were liable to compensate *A* for the loss suffered by him. *A* had completed the contract when he had paid the rent and signed the visitors book.[22]

TYPES OF OFFER

Offers may be of the following types :

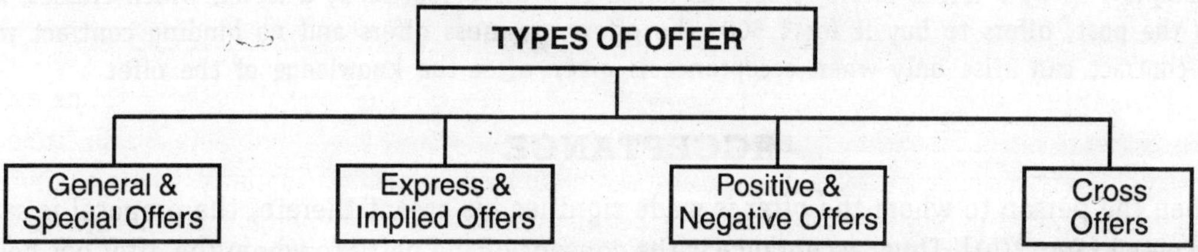

1. **General and Special Offers :** General offer means an offer made to the world at large, while a specific offer means offer made to some specific individual or individuals. General offer can be accepted by any person having notice of the offer by doing what is required under the offer. However, specific offer can be accepted only by the person or persons to whom it has been made and by no one else.[23] Thus, it follows that an offer need not be made to an ascertained person, but it must be accepted by a definite person.

Example : Carbolic Smoke Ball Company advertised in the newspapers that whosoever would take smoke balls, manufactured by it, according to the printed instructions would not contract influenza. The company offered a reward of £ 100 to anyone who contracted influenza after taking its smoke balls according to the printed instructions. It was added that £ 1000 was deposited with Alliance Bank to show the sincerity of the Company. One Mrs. Carlill used the smoke balls according to the directions given, but contracted influenza. It was held that the offer was general one, and Mrs. Carlill had accepted

21. (1894) A.C. 217.
22. Olley *v.* Marlbrough Court Ltd. (1949) 1 K.B. 532.
23. Boulton *v.* Jones (1878).

it by acting according to the advertisement and, therefore, the company could not get away from responsibility by saying that it was a mere puff. She was entitled to get the reward.[24]

In India the principle of the Carbolic Smoke Ball Company case was followed in the case of Harbhajan Lal *v.* Harcharan Lal.[25] In this case a young boy had run away from his father's house. The father issued a pamphlet stating, 'Anybody who finds trace of the boy and brings him home will get ₹ 500.' Harbhajan Lal who knew of the reward, found out the boy at a Railway Station Dharamshala, and took to the police station. It was held that the handbill was a general offer and, therefore, he was entitled to the reward.

2. **Express and Implied Offers :** When an offer is expressed by words spoken or written, it is termed as an express offer. Implied offer means an offer made by conduct. When one person allows the other to perform certain acts under such circumstances that nobody would accept them without consideration it will amount to an offer by conduct and the permission of the party, who is benefited by such performance, will amount to his acceptance. Such an acceptor will be asked to pay for it.

Example : A bus company runs buses between Maurice Nagar and Kashmere Gate. There is an implied offer from the bus company to take any person on the route who is prepared to pay the prescribed fare. The offer will be said to be accepted by a passenger as soon as he takes seat in the bus.

3. **Positive and Negative Offers :** A person may express his willingness to do something or to abstain from doing something *e.g.*, it may be an offer to construct a wall to provide privacy or not to construct a wall so that free passage of light and air may not be obstructed.

4. **Cross Offers :** Two offers similar in all respects, made by one party to the other, in ignorance of each other's offer, are termed as cross offers. They shall not constitute acceptance of one's offer by the other.

Example : *A,* by a letter, offers to sell his house to *B* for ₹ 500. *B,* by a letter, which crosses, *A*'s letter in the post, offers to buy it for ₹ 500. The offers are cross offers and no binding contract will arise. A contract can arise only when acceptance is given after the knowledge of the offer.

ACCEPTANCE

When the person to whom the offer is made signifies his assent thereto, the proposal is said to be accepted [*Sec.* 2(*b*)]. Thus, acceptance is the consent of the party to whom the offer has been made to the establishment of legal relations between himself and the offerer. It is an assent to the terms of the offer.

Who can give Acceptance : Acceptance can be given only by the person to whom offer has been made. But, where the offer has been made to the world at large, any person or persons who have the notice of the offer, can come forward and accept the offer.

Example : *B* sold his business to his manager without disclosing the fact to his customers. On the afternoon of the day on which the sale was carried through, customer *J* who has a running account sent an order for some goods addressed to the vendor of the business by name. The new owner without disclosing the fact of himself having purchased the business and become owner thereof, executed the order. *J* came to know of the change in ownership only when he received an invoice and by that time he had already consumed the goods. He had a set off against the old proprietor of the business and, therefore, refused to pay the price. It was held that the new owner could not recover the price. 'The

24. Carlill *v.* Carbolic Smoke Ball Co. 1 Q.B. 256, 1893.
25. A.I.R. (1925) All. 539.

rule of law is clear that if you propose to make a contract with *A*, then *B* cannot substitute himself for *A* without your consent and to your disadvantage, securing to himself all the benefits of the contract.'[26]

ESSENTIALS OF VALID ACCEPTANCE

1. **Acceptance may be express or implied :** Acceptance given by words spoken or written is express acceptance, while that given by conduct is termed as implied acceptance. Implied acceptance may be given :

(*a*) by doing some particular act, the doing of which by the terms of the offer is made in evidence of assent;

(*b*) by accepting a service or benefit offered by the person making the offer.

Examples : (*i*) In the case of *Carlill v. Carbolic Smoke Ball Co.*, the latter company offered by an advertisement a reward of £ 100 to anyone who contracted influenza after using their smoke balls for a fortnight according to the instructions and the mode prescribed by the company. Mrs. Carlill, on the faith of the advertisement purchased and used the smoke balls for a fortnight as directed. But she was attacked by influenza and hence used for the advertised reward. Her suit was decreed by the court on the ground that the advertisement was not a mere statement of an intention to give reward but a definite proposal which became an agreement on having been accepted by Mrs. Carlill by acting in the manner prescribed by the offerer. Though the offer was made open to the whole world but it had been accepted by a specified person and the offerer had by the terms of the offer waived communication of acceptance to him. Acceptance of the offer by conduct does not require any formal acceptance.

(*ii*) A lady invited her niece to stay with her in the same house and promised to settle on her an immovable property. The niece stayed with her in her residence till the time of her death. Niece was held to be entitled to property because she had accepted the offer of the aunt by going to her house and staying with her as desired.[27]

(*iii*) A bus offers to carry passengers from Red Fort to the University of Delhi bus stop for 50 paise. *A* takes a seat in the bus and is taken to the University stop. *A* shall be considered to have accepted the offer of the bus driver by receiving the benefit of service thereof and shall be bound to pay 50 paise, the price of the ticket.

2. **Acceptance must be absolute and unqualified :** It must correspond with all the terms of the offer. Offer must be accepted *in toto*. Conditional acceptance is no acceptance.[28] It will not give rise to any contract. It will be a counter offer, which the proposer may or may not accept.[29]

Examples : (*i*) An offer of land by *M* for £ 280 was accepted by *N*, who enclosed £ 80 with his letter of acceptance and promised to pay the balance by monthly instalments of £ 50. *N* cannot bind *M* by his acceptance for it has not been unqualified. It does not being any contract into existence.

(*ii*) *A* offers to sell his car to *B* for a sum of ₹ 10,000. *B* sends his acceptance stating that he is prepared to purchase it for a sum of ₹ 8,000. This is no acceptance. Later on, *B* changes his mind and writes to *A* that he is prepared to purchase his car for ₹ 10,000. This be taken as a new offer from *B*, which may or may not be accepted by *A*.

(*iii*) *A* offers to buy *B*'s mare on *B*'s giving a warranty that the mare was quiet in harness. *B* gave a warranty that the mare was 'sound and quiet in double harness'. It was held that this was not an acceptance of the offer.[30]

26. Boulton *v.* Jones (1857) H. & N. 564.
27. V. Rao *v.* A. Rao (1919) 39 Mad. 509.
28. Haji Mohd. *v.* Spinner (1900) 24 Bom. 510, 524.
29. Hyde *v.* Wrench (1940) 49 E.R. 132.
30. Jordon *v.* Norton (1838) 4 M. and W. 155.

3. **Acceptance must be in the mode prescribed :** The proposer may lay down the manner of acceptance in his offer. In case the acceptance is not given in the prescribed mode, the proposer may reject the acceptance and inform the offeree within a reasonable time. But if he fails to do so, he shall be taken to have accepted the acceptance.

If the proposer has not prescribed any mode of acceptance, the acceptance must be given in some usual and reasonable manner.

Examples : (*i*) An offer is made to take shares indicating that the answer is to come by a telegram. It is accepted but the acceptance is sent by an ordinary letter. The offerer can reject the acceptance as not being in the prescribed mode.

(*ii*) *A*, a merchant, sent his son, *B* to Agra with a letter for *C*, an Agra merchant. In the letter *A* offered to sell to *C* a quantity of cloth and required *C* to give his reply to *B*. *C* sent away *B* without a reply but decided later to accept *A*'s offer by a telegram. The telegram reached *A* before *B*'s return.

A can refuse *C*'s acceptance on the ground that the acceptance was not given by him in the prescribed mode. But *A* should inform *C* of his objection within a reasonable time. In case he fails to do so it will be presumed that he has accepted the acceptance and a valid contract will arise between *A* and *C*.

(*iii*) *K* wrote to *S*, 'I intend to sell my house for ₹ 7,000. If you are willing to have it, write to *F* at his address.' Instead of writing to *F*, *S* sent his agent in person to *F* and agreed to purchase the property for ₹ 7,000. On being contended that the acceptance was not in the mode prescribed, it was held that the letter ought to be read in a reasonable manner and it did not preclude *S* from putting into direct communication with *F*. Hence, it was a valid acceptance.[31]

This decision may perhaps be doubted, and a safer ground would have been that on the oral acceptance being communicated to the vendor he did not insist upon the proposal being accepted in writing.[32]

4. **Silence cannot be prescribed as mode of acceptance :** Proposer has the right to prescribe the manner in which the proposal may be accepted, but not the manner in which it may be refused. The offerer cannot impose this burden on the person to whom the offer is made that he will have to reply to the offer under all circumstances.

Example : *F* offered by a letter to purchase his nephew's horse for £ 30, adding, 'If I hear no more about it I shall consider the horse as mine for £ 30.' Nephew did not give any reply to his letter but he instructed the auctioneer, with whom his horse was for sale, not to sell it as it was sold to *F*. By mistake *B* sold that horse. *F* filed a suit against the auctioneer for conversion of his property. He failed in his suit. The court held that there was no concluded contract between *F* and his nephew and the horse did not belong to *F* at the time *B* sold it as the nephew had never signed his acceptance to the offer made by *F*. Silence cannot be prescribed as a mode of acceptance because if that was so, the offerer will be put to a great deal of inconvenience because he shall have to write in clear terms that he is not accepting the offer.[33]

5. **Acceptance can be given only for that offer which has been communicated :** There can be no acceptance of an uncommunicated offer. Acts done in ignorance of proposal will not amount to acceptance of the offer. Acceptance cannot precede an offer. A person who has no knowledge of an offer cannot be said to have accepted it merely because he happened to act just by chance in the manner prescribed by the offer.[34] Counter offer made in ignorance of each offer's offer will not

31. Surendra Nath *v.* Kedar Nath, A.I.R. (1936) Cal. 87.
32. Pollock and Mulla 'Indian Contract and Specific Relief Acts', p. 91 cd. 1972.
33. Felthouse *v.* Bindley (1862) C.B.N.S. 869.
34. Lalman Shukla *v.* Gauri Dutt (1913) 11 All L.J. 489.

amount to acceptance. Counter offers put an end to the original offer. Subsequent acceptance of the original offer also cannot give rise to a contract.[35]

Example : *X,* the captain of a ship, after resigning from his post during the course of a voyage changed his mind and continued to be incharge of the ship. His resignation, however, was accepted. It was held that the captain could not recover remuneration for the period subsequent to his resignation, as the offer to serve had not been communicated by the captain.[36]

6. **Acceptance must be communicated :** Acceptance must be communicated to the offerer to create a binding contract. 'Mere mental acceptance not evidenced by words or conduct is in the eyes of law no acceptance. But where the offer is to be accepted by being acted upon, no communication to the offerer will be necessary unless the communication is stipulated for in the offer itself.

Examples : (*i*) The manager of a railway company received a draft agreement relating to the supply of coal, wrote the word 'approved' on it and kept it in his drawer. It was held that there was no contract as the acceptance had not been communicated.[37]

(*ii*) The plaintiff was a candidate for a post. The appointing authority selected him for the post. But the plaintiff was not intimated of his selection. Subsequently, the appointing authority cancelled his selection. The suit of the plaintiff was dismissed on the basis that in the absence of any communication to him, the contract was not complete. A mere mental assent to an offer not evidenced by words or by conduct, therefore, will not constitute an acceptance.[38]

7. Acceptance of the proposal will mean acceptance of all the terms of the offer.

8. **Acceptance must be given within the time stipulated or within a reasonable time :** In any case it must proceed before the lapse of the offer or its revocation.

9. **If the proposal is made through an agent, it is enough if the acceptance is communicated to him :** If *A* sends the offer to *B* by agency of *C*, and *B* in turn gives his acceptance to *C*, the acceptance is complete even if *C* fails to communicate it to his principal *A*.

10. Acceptance, in order to be valid, must be made under circumstances which would show that the acceptor is able and willing, then and there, to fulfil the promise. An acceptance to do something which a person has no intention to perform shall not be a valid acceptance.

11. If Acceptance has been given by a person 'subject to a formal contract' or 'subject to approval by certain persons—such as solicitors etc.,' no contract will arise till a formal contract is entered into or consent of such persons is obtained.

Example : *C* and *E* signed an agreement for the purchase of *E*'s house by *C*. The agreement was made 'subject to a proper contract' to be prepared by *E*'s solicitors. The solicitors prepared the contract and *E* signed it, but in the meantime *C* changed his mind and refused to sign the contract. It was held that agreement being conditional, there was no contract between the parties.[39]

COMMUNICATION OF OFFER AND ACCEPTANCE

Where contracting parties are facing each other, it can be conveniently said that a valid contract arises as soon as the acceptor says 'yes' to the proposal put forward by the offerer. But, where contracting

35. Hyde *v.* Wrench (1940) 49 E.R. 132.
36. Taylor *v.* Laird (1856) 25 L.J. Ex. 329.
37. Brogden *v.* Metropolitan Railway Co. (1877) A.C. 66.
38. Powel *v.* Lee (1908) 99 L.T. 284.
39. Chillingworth *v.* Esche (1924) 1 Ch. 97.

parties are living at a distance and the services of the post office are utilised, the following rules as laid down in sections 4, 5 and 6 will be applicable.

Communication of offer (*Sec.* 4) : The communication of an offer is complete when it comes to the knowledge of the person to whom it is made.

When a proposal is made by post, its communication will be complete when the proposal in the letter comes to the knowledge of the person to whom the offer has been made. Mere delivery of the letter will not make the communication of offer by post complete.

Example : *A* proposes to sell a cow at a certain price and makes this offer by a letter sent to *B*. The communication of the offer will be complete when the proposal in the letter comes to the knowledge of *B*.

Communication of acceptance (*Sec.* 4) : Communication of an acceptance is complete :

(*a*) as against the *proposer* when it is put in course of transmission to him as to be out of the power of the acceptor to withdraw the same;

(*b*) as against the *acceptor* when it comes to the knowledge of the proposer.

When a proposal is accepted by a letter sent by post, the communication of the acceptance will be complete as against the proposer when the letter of acceptance is posted and as against the acceptor when the letter reaches the proposer.

Example : *B* accepts *A's* proposal by a letter sent by post. The communication of the acceptance is complete :

as against *A*, when the letter is posted;

as against *B*, when the letter is received by *A*.

'Receiving the letter' here means 'Receiving the message given in the letter'. Mere delivery of letter will not make the communication of acceptance complete.

An acceptance may be held to be communicated in spite of the fact that it has not come to the knowledge of the offerer. The proposer becomes bound by the contract from the moment the letter of acceptance is posted by the offeree. Loss of letter in the post, late delivery or miscarriage etc. will not affect the validity of the contract.[40] Thus, it is correct to say that an acceptance is complete when communicated, but in order to draw the line as to what is communication, it has been held that where the offeree has done all in his power to convey his intention to the offerer and agency used being within the spirit of the offer fails, such failure will not affect the case, communication will be taken to be complete. But the acceptor will be bound by his acceptance only when the letter of acceptance has reached the proposer.

Examples : (*i*) *D*, in answer to an inquiry as to the price of pig iron, wrote to *H*: 'We shall be glad to supply you with 2,000 tonnes of pig iron at the price you have offered us.' On account of bad state of roads the post was delayed, acceptance was received six hours later than the hour at which the post ought to have arrived. On *D's* refusal to sell iron, it was held that the posting of the letter was accepting the offer. The offeree by putting his letter into the post on the correct day, has done everything that he was bound to do. Hence he cannot be held responsible for that over which he has no control?[41]

---

40. Household Fire Insurance Co. *v.* Grant (1879) 4 Ex. D. 216.
The current feeling is that even in postal communications the principle of *concensus ad idem* should be applied and there should be no contract till the acceptance is received (Holwell Securities *v.* Hughes (1973) 1 W.L.R. 757.

41. Dunlop *v.* Higgins (1866) 1 H.L. Cas. 381.

(ii) On receipt of a notice for payment of premium for revival of a life insurance policy, the premium was sent by money order. But before the premium could reach the insurance company, the assured died. On a claim being made by *H* the widow of the deceased, it was held that she could recover the money, since the policy had received from the date of the money order and not from the date of its receipt by the insurance company.[42]

In all cases of contracts by post, it is now the accepted view that the contract is deemed to have been made at the place where the letter of acceptance is posted.[43]

In those cases where acceptance is to be given by doing the act, no formal communication of acceptance is necessary. Similarly, no notice of acceptance is necessary when the offerer dispenses with notice to himself, *e.g.*, the offerer has also sent the consideration with the proposal and the same has been accepted by the offeree.

The difference between the communication of proposal and communication of acceptance is that an offer is not held to be communicated until it is brought to the knowledge of acceptor, while the acceptance may be held to be communicated though it has not come to the knowledge of the offerer.

REVOCATION OF OFFER AND ACCEPTANCE

The word 'revocation' means taking back'. Both an offer as well as an acceptance may be revoked. The communication of revocation is complete :

(a) *As against the person who makes it*, when it is put into the course of transmission to the person to whom it is made so as to be out of the power of the person who makes it to withdraw, and

(b) *As against the person to whom it is made*, when it comes to his knowledge.

Example : *A* revokes his proposal to *B* by telegram. *B*'s revocation is complete as against *A* when the telegram is despatched. It is complete as against *B* when *B* receives it.

B revokes his acceptance to *A* by telegram. *B*'s revocation is complete as against him when the telegram is despatched and as against *A* when it reaches him.

Revocation of an Offer or a Proposal

According to Section 5, a proposal may be revoked any time before its acceptance is complete as against the proposer but not afterwards. Revocation of a proposal after its acceptance is ineffective.

Example : *A* proposes, by a letter sent by post, to sell his house to *B*.

B accepts the proposal by a letter sent by post.

A may revoke his proposal at any time before *B* posts his letter of acceptance but not afterwards.

A proposal may be revoked in any of the following ways (*Sec. 6*) :

(a) **By communication of the notice of revocation :** Revocation by the proposer may give notice to the offeree before the offer is accepted by the offeree either expressly or by conduct. Notice of revocation will take effect only when it comes to the knowledge of the offeree. It is to be noted that notice of revocation must come from the proposer or his agent duly appointed. If the offeree comes to know offerer's intention to revoke the offer from any other source, it will not be taken as good notice of revocation.

42. Hairoon Bibi *v.* United India Life Insurance Company A.I.R. 1947 Mad 122.
43. Manilal *v.* Vakatachalapthy, 1944, I.L.R.M., Baroda Oil Cake Traders *v.* Parshottam, A.I.R. 1954, Bom. 49.

(*b*) **By lapse of the specified time :** The offer stands revoked after the lapse of the speci-fied time. However, if no time is mentioned, the offer will stand revoked by expiry of a reasonable time within which the acceptance of the offer has not been communicated to the offerer.

Example : *M* applied for shares in company in June. No allotment letter was received till November. His offer was held to have lapsed on account of the expiry of a reasonable time.

(*c*) **By the failure of the acceptor to fulfil a condition precedent to the acceptance :**

Example : *A* offers to sell his house to *B* for a sum of ₹ 500 provided *B* sends an advance of ₹ 100 with his acceptance. *B* accepts the offer but does not send the advance. The offer may be taken as revoked.

(*d*) **By the death or insanity of the proposer :** The death or insanity of the proposer results in revocation of the offer if the fact of his death or insanity comes to the knowledge of the acceptor before acceptance. If the proposer dies after the acceptance of the offer, the legal representatives of the proposer shall be bound by the contract. The proposal will not be taken to be revoked. (According to English Contract Law, supervening insanity of the proposer does not operate as a ground for the revocation of the proposal. But death, however, shall by itself put an end to the offer irrespective of the fact whether it has come to the knowledge of the offeree or not).

No provision has been made in the Act for a case where the person to whom the proposal is made dies before the acceptance. Obviously, the proposal comes to an end by operation of law because death automatically beings about termination of the proposal. The proposal can never be meant to be made to a dead person or his executors.

(*e*) **By a counter offer :** A counter offer will also amount to a revocation of the original offer.

Fixing a Time for Acceptance

In case the proposer fixes some time for giving acceptance, he is not bound to keep the proposal open during the whole time fixed unless he gets some consideration for it. The effect of fixing a time for acceptance is merely to fix a time beyond which the proposal shall not be accepted. The proposer may, notwithstanding the fixing of such a time, revoke his proposal by properly communicating notice of revocation to the other party.

Examples : On 1st November, 1998, *A* offered to sell a bicycle to *B* for ₹ 100 and said that the offer would remain open for three days. State what would be the position in each of the following cases :

(*i*) On November 2, 1998, *B* tells *A* that he will buy the bicycle for ₹ 80. But on *A*'s refusal, *B* agrees to pay ₹ 100.

(*ii*) On November 3, 1998, *B* tells *A* that he accepts the offer, but in fact on the previous day *A* had sold the bicycle to *C*

(*iii*) On November 5, 1998, *B* tells *A* that he accepts the offer.

The following decisions will be valid in the above cases :

(*i*) The original offer to *A* lapses when *B* puts a counter offer to buy the bicycle for a sum of ₹ 80. The subsequent offer of *B* to buy the bicycle for a sum of ₹ 100 is a new offer from *B* which may or may not be accepted by *A*.

(*ii*) *A* is not bound to keep the offer open without any consideration. He can revoke the offer before the expiry of fixed time provided, he gives a proper notice of revocation to *B*. In the absence of such a notice *A* can be held liable to pay damages to *B* for the any loss suffered by him.

(*iii*) The acceptance is late as the offer lapsed on 4th November 1998. *A* is, therefore, not bound by *B*'s acceptance.

Revocation of Acceptance

According to Section 5, an acceptance may be revoked at any time before the communication of acceptance is complete as against the acceptor but not afterwards.

Examples : (*i*) *A*, a resident of Delhi, posted an offer on 1st November to *B* of Kanpur to sell some specific property for ₹ 50,000. The offer was to remain open for a week. *B* posted his letter of acceptance on 6th November, which reached *A* on 8th November.

How would the contract be affected if (*i*) *A* from Delhi posted a letter of revocation on 5th November which reached *B* at Kanpur on 7th November, (*ii*) *B* despatched a telegram from Kanpur, cancelling his acceptance which reached *A* in Delhi on 7th November.

The effect on the contract will be as follows :

(*a*) Acceptance is complete as against the offerer as soon as the letter of acceptance is posted, while revocation of an offer is complete as against the offeree only when it comes to his knowledge. In the present case the letter of acceptance was posted on 6th November while the letter of revocation was received by the acceptor only on 7th November. Thus, the contract between *A* and *B* exists.

(*b*) Acceptance can be revoked at any time before it is complete as against the acceptor. The letter of acceptance was received by *A* on 8th November while he gets telegram for revocation on 7th November. The revocation is therefore valid, and there is no contract between *A* and *B*.

(*ii*) *A* applied for shares in a bank. On October 26th he withdrew his application. His letter of withdrawal was received by the company at 8.30 a.m. on October 27th. At 7.30 a.m. the company had handed a letter of allotment (acceptance) to a postman to post, but the letter was not actually posted till after 8.30 a.m. Held, the acceptance was too late, as the letter was not actually posted till after the offer had been revoked. Of course, if the letter of acceptance had been actually posted before 8.30 a.m. the acceptance would have been binding as against the proposer.[44]

CONTRACTS BY POST

An offer by post may be accepted by post, unless the offer indicates anything to the contrary. An offer by post is complete only when the letter containing the offer actually reaches the offeree and not before. An acceptance by post is complete as soon as the letter of acceptance is posted, prepaid and properly addressed, whether it reaches the offerer or not. But if the acceptance, instead of being properly posted, is handed over to a peon to post, the contract will not be complete until the acceptance is actually received by the offerer. A revocation of offer by post will not be complete until it actually reaches the offeree before the acceptance of the offer.

In case, the letter of acceptance and the letter of revocation of acceptance reach simul-taneously, which of the two is opened first, decides the issue. But where acceptance is revoked by a telegram, a person is more likely to open the telegram first. Acceptance will, therefore, be treated as revoked. In case the two messages, *i.e.*, one accepting the offer and the other revoking the acceptance are received simultaneously, the acceptance is deemed to be revoked.

CONTRACTS OVER TELEPHONE

Contracts over telephone or telex are treated on the same principles as those when the parties are facing each other. No binding contract can arise unless the offeree's acceptance is audible, heard

44. Re. London and Norther Bank (1900) 1 Ch. 220.

and understood by the offerer, *i.e.*, acceptance should be in such words which have the effect of communicating it.[45] In such cases, the contract will be complete only when the acceptance is received by the offerer and not merely when transmitted.

In case a person makes an offer to another person and in the course of his reply the line goes dead abruptly on account of which the offerer does not hear the acceptor's words, the contract will not come into existence at that time. It will come into existence when the parties again talk and acceptance is heard by the offerer.[46]

The Supreme Court, in the case of *Bhagwandas Goverdhandas Kedia v. Girdharilal Purshottamdas & Co.*,[47] ruled by a majority judgement that post office rules of communication are not applicable to contracts over telephone or telex. In case of such contracts, the contract will be complete only when the acceptance has been communicated to the offerer (and not when it is put in the course of transmission, whether received or not by the offerer). The contract will come into existence at the place where the acceptance has been received.

Example : *B* made an offer from Ahmedabad to *G* of Khamgaon by telephone to purchase certain goods. The offer was accepted by *G* over telephone. On a dispute being arisen about the place of coming of contract into existence, it was held that the contract was made at Ahmedabad where acceptance was received.

When the parties negotiate a contract face to face or over telephone, the question of revocation does not arise because in such instantaneous communications a definite offer is made and accepted at the same time.

Anson has beautifully put the effect of accepting an offer and their revocation in the following words : 'Acceptance is to an offer what a lighted match is to a train of gunpowder. It produces something which cannot be recalled or undone. But the powder may have laid until it has become damp, or the man who laid the train may remove it before the match is applied. So an offer may lapse for want of acceptance or be revoked before acceptance. Acceptance converts the offer into a promise and then it is too late to remove it.'[48]

Aanson compares an offer with a train of gunpowder and acceptance with a lighted match. As soon as a lighted match is brought near the gunpowder, it explodes. Similarly, an offer when accepted becomes a contract and will give rise to legal obligations. However, explosion can be prevented if the gunpowder becomes damp or is removed before the lighted match is brought near it. Similarly, no contract arises if the offer has already lapsed on account of acceptance not being given within a reasonable or fixed time or it has been withdrawn by offerer before its acceptance.

AGREEMENT TO MAKE CONTRACT

An agreement to enter into a contract in the future cannot create contractual obligations. Unless the terms of the contract have been finalised, the matter shall remain in the stage of negotiations.

Lord Wensleydale in Ringway v. Wharton[49] observed : 'An agreement to be finally settled must comprise all the terms which the parties intend to introduce into the agreement. An agreement to

45. Entores Ltd. *v.* Miles Far East Corporation (1955) 2 All E.R. 493.
46. *Law of Contract,* Anson 21 Ed., p. 54.
47. A.I.R. 1966 Sc. 543.
48. (1856-57) 6 H.L.C. 283 at p. 24.
49. (1856-57) 6 H.L.C. 238.

enter into an agreement upon terms to be afterwards settled between the parties is a contradiction in terms. It is absurd to say that a man enters into an agreement till the terms of the agreement are settled; until those terms are settled, he is perfectly at liberty to retire from the bargain.'

Lord Maugham also observed in *Foley v. Classque Coaches*[50] that 'unless all material terms of the contract are agreed, there is no binding obligation. An agreement to agree in future is not a contract nor is there a contract if a material terms is neither settled nor implied by law and the document contains no machinery for ascertaining it.'

KEY TERMS

- **Agreement :** Every promise and every set of promises forming consideration for each other.
- **Acceptance :** The consent of the parties to whom the offer has been made.
- **Cross Offers :** Two offers similar in all respects made by one party to the other in ignorance of each other's offers.
- **Proposal :** A communication by one person to other of his willingness to do or abstain from doing with the objective of getting the acceptance of the other.
- **Revocation :** Taking back of an offer or acceptance.

TEST QUESTIONS

Objective Type : *Test Your Knowledge*

1. Fill in the blanks
   (*i*) General offers means an offer made to the ....
   (*ii*) Acceptance can be given only by the person to whom .... has been made.
   (*iii*) An offer is different from mere invitation to ....
   (*iv*) Mere mental assent is no ....
   (*v*) A proposal may be revoked any time before the communication of its acceptance is complete against the ....
   (*vi*) An acceptance may be revoked at a.m. time before the communication of the acceptance is complete against ....
   (*vii*) An agreement not enforceable by law is .... *(CS Foundation, Dec. 2012)*
   [***Ans.*** (*i*) world at large; (*ii*) the offer; (*iii*) an offer; (*iv*) acceptance; (*v*) proposer; (*vi*) acceptor; (*vii*) void-ab-initio.]
2. State whether each of the following statement is *True* or *False*
   (*i*) Acceptor may revoke his acceptance even if the letter of acceptance sent by him to the offeree is lost in the transit. *(CS Foundation, Dec. 1998)*
   (*ii*) A standing offer cannot be revoked. *(CS Foundation, Dec. 1998)*
   (*iii*) The offer lapses by the death of offeree before acceptance.
   (*iv*) Silence cannot be prescribed as mode of acceptance.
   (*v*) An agreement to settle terms of agreement in future makes a valid contract.
   (*vi*) 'Revocation of offer does not take effect until it is actually communicated to the offeree'. *(CS Foundation, Dec. 2006)*

50. (1934) 2 K.B. 1.

(*vii*) 'Specific offer can be accepted by any member of the general public'.
(*CS Foundation, June 2008*)

(*viii*) 'The law of contracts is not the whole law of agreements'. (*CS Foundation, Dec. 2008*)

(*ix*) An invitation to offer is not an offer. (*B.Com. (Hons.) Delhi 2010*)

(*x*) Communication of offer is complete when the letter of offer is posted
(*B.Com. (Hons.) Delhi 2011*)

(*xi*) Acceptance can be made ever without knowledge of the offer. (*B.Com. (Hons.) Delhi 2011*)

(*xii*) Cross-offers constitute a valid contract between the parties. (*CS Foundation, Dec. 2012*)

(*xiii*) A voidable contract is one which cannto be enforced in a court of law.
(*B.Com. (Hons.) Dehi, Nov., 2012*)

(*xiv*) Collateral transactions to an illegal agreement do not become void.
(*B.Com. (Hons.) Delhi, Nov., 2012*)

(*xv*) A proposal may be revoked by the proposer before the posting of the letter of acceptance.
(*CA IPC, Nov., 2012*)

(*xvi*) Acceptance of a General Offer is not required to be communicated.
(*B.Com. (Hons.) Delhi, Nov., 2012*)

[***Ans.*** (*i*) True; (*ii*) False; (*iii*) True; (*iv*) True; (*v*) False; (*vi*) True; (*vii*) False; (*viii*) True; (*ix*) True; (*x*) False; (*xi*) False; (*xii*) False; (*xiii*) False; (*xiv*) False; (*xv*) True; (*xvi*) True]

3. Select the most appropriate answer

(*i*) General offer can be accepted by

(*a*) any person (*b*) specific person

(*c*) any person having notice of it.

(*ii*) Silence

(*a*) cannot be provided as a mode of acceptance.

(*b*) can be provided as a mode of acceptance.

(*c*) can be rejected as a mode of acceptance.

(*iii*) Communication of acceptance is complete against the acceptor when

(*a*) it is put in the course of transmission by him.

(*b*) it comes to the knowledge of the proposer.

(*c*) a reasonable time expires.

(*iv*) Which of the following does not constitute valid acceptance :

(*a*) It has been communicated.

(*b*) It is absolute and unqualified.

(*c*) It has been presumed from silence of offeree.

(*d*) The offer has been accepted by the proper person. (*CS Foundation, June 2007*)

[***Ans.*** (*i*) (*c*); (*ii*) (*a*); (*iii*) (*b*); (*iv*) (*c*)]

Essay Type : *For Review, Discussion and Practice*

1. Define a proposal and distinguish between an offer and invitation to offer.
2. Explain clearly the meaning of 'acceptance' of an offer. When is communication of acceptance not necessary? How does an offer lapse? Explain.
3. When is the communication of an offer and acceptance complete? How and when can an offer and acceptance be revoked?

4. (*a*) 'A mere mental acceptance not evidenced by words or conduct is, in the eyes of law, no acceptance.' Comment giving examples. (*B.Com. (Hons.), Delhi 1991, 1995*)
   (*b*) 'There cannot be a contract to make a contract.' Comment.
5. 'A contract is formed when the acceptor has done something to signify his intention to accept, not when he has made up his mind to do so.' Explain.
6. Briefly discuss the law relating to offer and acceptance by post.
7. How and on what grounds do proposals stand revoked? Is there any limit in time after which revocation of proposal and acceptance cannot be made?
8. 'Acceptance is to an offer what a lighted match is to a train of gunpower.' —*Anson*. Comment. (*B.Com. (Hons.), Delhi 1996*)
9. State the rules relating to 'acceptance' of a consumer. (*C.A. Foundation, Nov. 2000*)
10. Explain the following :
    (*i*) Acceptance must be absolute and unqualified. (*ICWA, Foundation, June 1998; Dec. 1999*)
    (*ii*) A proposal may be revoked at any time before acceptance but not afterwards. (*ICWA, Foundation, June 1998*)
    (*iii*) An acceptance must be absolute and unqualified. (*ICWA, Foundation, June 1998*)
    (*vi*) The offer lapses by death or insanity of the offerer. (*ICWA, Foundation, June 1998*)
    (*v*) A proposal cannot be revoked at any time. (*ICWA, Foundation, Dec. 1999*)
    (*vi*) Can an acceptance be revoked? (*ICWA, Foundation, June 2000*)
    (*vii*) Offer must be capable of being accepted and giving rise to legal relationship. (*ICWA, Foundation, Dec. 1998*)
    (*viii*) Counter offer constitutes an acceptance of offer. (*ICWA, Foundation, June 1999; Dec. 2000*)
11. What is acceptance to an offer? Discuss the legal rules for a valid acceptance.
12. Discuss the circumstances under which an offer stands revoked. (*GGSIPU, BBA (H), June 2001*)
13. Explain the legal rules relating to the 'Offer' and 'Acceptance'. (*GGSIPU, BBA (H), May 2002*)
14. Distinguish between 'offer' and 'an invitation to offer'. (*B.Com. (Hons.), Delhi 1989, 1992, 2001, B.Com. (Pass), Delhi 2001*)
15. Define acceptance. Who can give acceptance? What conditions must be fulfilled to convert an offer into an acceptance? (*B.Com. (Pass), Delhi 2004*)
16. How and on what grounds can an offer be revoked. (*B.Com. (Hons.), Delhi 2002*)
17. Define an offer. Explain the rules regarding a valid offer. When does an offer lapse? (*B.Com. (Pass), Delhi 2002*)
18. Distinguish between specific offer and general offer. When does an offer come to an end? (*B.Com. (Pass), Delhi 2003*)
19. How can the offer and acceptance be revoked? Explain with the help of an example. (*B.Com. (Hons.), Delhi 2012*)

PRACTICAL PROBLEMS

1. *M* owned a house at Calcutta. *A* offered to buy that house for ₹ 26,000 and *M*'s agent, to whom the offer was given cabled to *M* : 'Have had offer for the house at Calcutta for ₹ 26,000.' Then the agent got reply from *M* : 'Will not accept less than ₹ 30,000.' Then *A* accepted *M*'s price of ₹ 30,000, and confirmed the acceptance by a letter to the agent. But *M* sold the house for a higher price to *K*. *A* then sues *M* for damages for breach of contract. Is the suit maintainable? Decide stating reasons.

   [***Ans.*** No, there was no offer but only an invitation to an offer.]

2. *X* at Delhi on 1st August, 1998 sends a letter to *Y* in Bombay offering to sell his car for ₹ 16,000. *Y* on 2nd August, 1998 sends a letter to *X* accepting the offer. This acceptance letter reaches *X* on 4th August, 1998. But on 3rd August 1998 *X* has sold the car to *Z* and wired *Y* revoking the offer. This wire reaches *Y* on 3rd August 1998 itself. Is there a breach of contract committed by *X*? Give reasons.

[***Ans.*** Yes. Acceptance against *X* was complete on 2nd August, 1998 and binding contract came into existence on that date.]

3. The defendants writing from Bombay on 1st July, 1997, made an offer to the plaintiff at Calcutta asking for a reply by post. The plaintiff received the letter of offer on 8th and at once accepted in the manner requested. In the meantime, however, the defendants had on the 4th July 1997, posted a letter revoking the offer. This letter of revocation did not reach the plaintiff until the 12th July, 1997. Is there a contract? State reasons for your answer.

[***Ans.*** There is a contract. Revocation is ineffective.]

4. *A* owes ₹ 5,000 to his friend *B*. *B* assures *A* that he will not file a suit against him. Does this assurance constitute a proposal in the legal sense of the term?

[***Ans.*** Yes. Abstaining from doing something]

5. *A* offers to *B* 'I shall sell my house for ₹ 500 to you if you give me my mule.' *B* agrees in writing to buy the horse but refused to deliver the mule to *A*. Is there any binding contract?

[***Ans.*** No. All terms of offer not accepted.]

6. *A* offers to sell 100 bales of cotton to *B* @ ₹ 250 per bale. The offer is open for acceptance till 5 p.m. of that day. At 3 p.m. *A* sells the cotton bales to *C* @ ₹ 300 per bale. *B* accepts the offer at 4 p.m. Is *A*, bound by *B*'s acceptance?

[***Ans.*** No. But he will have to pay damages.]

7. *X* offers to sell his radio to *Y* for ₹ 300. *Y* replies, 'I will pay ₹ 250 for it.' *X* refuses to sell at this price. *Y* then offers ₹ 300 to *X*. In reply *X* said. 'I do not want to sell radio.' Discuss the rights of *X* and *Y*.

[***Ans.*** No contract at all. No rights against each other.]

8. *M* agreed on Monday to sell his property to *N* by a written agreement which stated that 'this offer be left open until Saturday 10 a.m.' In the meantime, on Wednesday *M* enters into a contract to sell his property to *O*. *N* who was, sitting in the next room, hears about the deal between *M* & *O*. On Friday *N* accepts the offer and delivers to *M*, the letter of acceptance. Is *N*'s acceptance valid. Give reasons.

[***Ans.*** *N*'s acceptance is not valid since the offer had already been revoked to the knowledge of *N*.]

9. Ram's son absconded from home. He sent his servant in search of the boy. When the servant had left, Ram, by handbills, offered to pay ₹ 500 to anybody discovering the boy. The servant came to know of this offer only when he had already traced the missing child. He, however, brought an action to recover the reward. Will he succeed in his attempt? Give reasons.

[***Ans.*** The servant will not succeed since there can be no acceptance without the knowledge of the offer.]

10. Land Development Authority advertised for sale of a prime plot by auction on Sunday, the 7th July, 2001. Large number of people had come from far and distant places to participate in the auction after spending lot of money. On the fixed date, an official of the authority appeared at the venue of the auction and announced that the auction had been postponed by a month and expressed regrets for the inconvenience caused to the prospective bidders. Can the bidders claim any compensation from the authority for the inconvenience and damage caused to them by postponement of the auction without any valid reasons?

[***Ans.*** No compensation can be claimed by the prospective bidders for postponement of auction.]

11. *A* offers to sell his car to *B* for ₹ 80,000 and *B* agrees to buy it for ₹ 75,000. On rethinking, *B* is ready to pay ₹ 80,000 for the car. Is *A* bound to sell the car?

(*ICWA, Foundation, June 1998*)

[**Ans.** It is a counter offer and not an acceptance. Hence *A* is not bound to sell his car to *B*.]

12. The Managing Committee of a school in response to *P*'s application for the post of Headmaster passed a resolution appointing *P* to the post. But this decision was not communicated to *P*. However, *P* came to know about this decision from some source. *P* files a suit for breach of contract.

(*ICWA, Foundation, June 1998*)

[**Ans.** *P* will not succeed since there was no communication of acceptance to him.]

13. *M* offers to buy shares of a company on June 8, 1997. The company informed him about allotment on November 23, 1997. *M* refused to accept the shares. Can the company compel *M* to accept the allotment of shares?

(*ICWA, Foundation, June 1998*)

[**Ans.** The company shall fail since *M*'s offer to buy shares had lapsed because it was not accepted within a reasonable time by the company.]

14. *A* duly posts a letter to *B*. But the letter is lost transit by the negligence of the post office. What effect, if any, does this have on the formation of the contract? (*ICWA, Foundation, June 1999*)

[**Ans.** There is a valid contract if the letter has been properly addressed.]

15. *A* agrees to *B* to sell his house for ₹ 10 lakhs. *B* offers ₹ 8 lakhs but *A* rejects it. After a month *B* agrees to pay ₹ 10 lakhs but *A* refuses to sell at that price. Advise *B* about his right against *A*.

(*ICWA, Foundation, Dec. 1999*)

[**Ans.** There is a counter offer by *B* and hence there is no contract.]

16. *A* duly posts a letter of acceptance to *B*. But the letter is lost in transit by the negligence of the Post Office. What effect, if any, does this have on the formation of the Contract?

(*ICWA, Foundation, Dec. 2000*)

[**Ans.** The acceptance is complete as against proposer. Hence the contract has been formed as per Section 4.]

17. *G* sent his servant *L* to trace his lost nephew. When the servant had left, *G* announced a reward of ₹ 500 to any one who traces the boy. *L* found the boy and brought him home. Will be get this reward?

(*ICWA, Foundation, June 2000, 2001*)

[**Ans.** The servant cannot claim the reward since he had no knowledge of the offer at the time of tracing the boy.]

18. Agreement to spend a holiday together is only a social obligation. This cannot lead to legal consequences. *B* cannot sue and the will fail if he does so. (*ICWA, Foundation, Dec. 1999*)

[**Ans.** There is no legal obligation and hence there is no contract.]

19. *A* proposes by a letter sent by post to sell his house to *B*. *B* accepts the proposal by a letter sent by post. State the legal position regarding revocation of offer and acceptance by *A* and *B* respectively.

(*B.Com. (Hons.), Delhi, 1986*)

[**Ans.** *A* may revoke his offer or proposal to sell his house to *B* at any time before *B* posts his letter of acceptance but not afterwards. B may revoke his acceptance at any time before the communication of *B*'s acceptance is complete against *B* himself, *i.e.*, when *B*'s letter of acceptance is received by *A*).

20. Shambhu Dayal started "self service" system in his shop. Smt. Prakash entered the shop, took a basket and after taking articles of her choice into the basket reached the cashier for payments. The cashier refuses to accept the price. Can Shambhu Dayal be compelled to sell the said articles to Smt. Prakash? Decide.

(*PEE II, May 2004*)

[**Ans.** Shambhu Dayal cannot be compelled to sell the said articles since the display of articles with a price in it in a self-service shop is merely an invitation to offer. It is in no sense an offer for sale, the acceptance of which constitutes a contract.]

21. *A* sent an offer to B. B sent a letter of acceptance. Then, changing his mind, he sent a telegram to revoke his acceptance. Both the communications reach A at the same time. Can there be a contract between them? *(GGSIPU, BBA (H), May 2004)*

[***Ans.*** Acceptance will be taken as revoked since he is expected to open it first.]

22. *P* was appointed Principal of a school. One of the members of the governing body privately informed *P* that he had been appointed Principal. But no official communication was sent to *P* by the governing body. Later the governing body did not appoint *P* as the Principal. *P* filed a suit against the governing body to claim damages. Advise him, giving full reasons as to whether he would succeed. *(B.Com. (Hons.), Delhi 2000)*

[***Ans.*** No, *P* cannot succeed since no contract had yet been reached between *P* and the appointing authority, *i.e.*, Governing Body.]

23. *A* offered to sell his estate to *B* for ₹ 1,000 lakhs. *B* offered ₹ 950 lakhs which *A* refused. After some time *B* wrote to *A* accepting the original offer of ₹ 1,000 lakhs. A having refused to sell the property, *B* sued for specific performance. Decide, giving reasons. *(B.Com. (Hons.), Delhi 2002)*

[***Ans.*** *B* will not succeed because the original offer has lapsed.]

24. *X* duly posts a letter of acceptance to *Y*. But the letter is lost in the transit by the negligence of the post office. What effect does it have on the formation of legal contract? Give reasons for your answer. *(B.Com., (Hons.), Delhi 2005)*

[***Ans.*** Section 4 of the Indian Contract Act states that acceptance is complete as against the proposer, as soon as the duly addressed letter of acceptance is put into the course of transmission. Thus, in the present case, the contract is valid.]

25. Ramaswami proposed to sell his house to Ramanathan. Ramanathan sent his acceptance by post. Next day, Ramanathan sends a telegram withdrawing his acceptance. Examine the validity of the acceptance in the light of the following :

(*i*) The telegram of revocation of revocation of acceptance was received by Ramaswami before the letter of acceptance.

(*ii*) The telegram of revocation and letter of acceptance both reached together. *(PEE-II, ICAI, May 2006)*

[***Ans.*** Section (*i*) Yes the revocation of acceptance by Ramanathan (the acceptor) is valid.

(*ii*) If Ramaswami opens the telegram first (and this would be normally so in case of a rational person) and reads it, the acceptance stands revoked. If he opens the letter first and reads it, revocation of acceptance is not possible, as the contract has already been concluded.]

26. Ram wrote to Shyam to sell him apples at the rate of 150 per kg. On the same day, Shyam wrote to Ram to buy apples at the rate of 150 per kg. Their letters cross in the post. Shyam now requires Ram to sell him applies as there was an enforceable contract between them. Will Shyam succeed? Give reasons. *(CS Foundation, Dec., 2011)*

[***Ans.*** No, Shyam will not succeed, 'Cross-offers' do not constitute acceptance of one's offer by the other and as such there is no completed agreement.]

27. Mr. *D* started "Self-Service" system in his shop. Mr. *A* entered the shop, took a basket and after taking article of his choice into the basket reached the cashier for payments. The cashier refused to accept the price. Can Mr. *D* be compelled by Mr. *A* to sell the said article? Decide. *(CAIPC, May, 2013)*

[***Ans.*** The display of articles with a price on it in a self service shop is merely an invitation to offer. It is in no sense an offer for sale, the acceptance of which may constitute a contract. Hence, if the cashier does not accept the price. the interested buyer cannot compel him to sell.]

28. *A* posts an offer to *B* on July 1, 2013. *B* posts his acceptance on July 5, 2013. In the meantime, *A* posts his letter of revocation of offer to *B* on July 4, 2013 which is received by *B* on July 6, 2013. Is there an enforceable contract in this case? Explain with reasons.

[*B.Com., (Hons.), Delhi, Nov. 2013*]

[***Ans.*** Yes, there is an enforceable contract between *A* and *B*, as *A* has put his acceptance into transmission on July 5, 2013 and revocation of offer is communicated to him on July, 6, 2013.]

29. *X* advertises in a newspaper that he would pay ₹ 1,00,000 to anyone who trace his missing son. *Y* traced that boy claimed the amount of reward. State whether *Y* is entitled to receive the amount of reward (a) if he did not know about the reward, (b) if he knew about the reward. Defend your choice with reasons. [*B.Com., (Hons.), Delhi, Nov. 2013*]

[***Ans.*** (a) *Y* is not entitlted to receive the amount of reward if he did not know about the reward. (b) *Y* is entitled to receive the amount of reward, i.e., ₹ 1,00,000 if he knew about the reward.]

Chapter 3

COMPETENCE OF CONTRACTING PARTIES

LEARNING OBJECTIVES

A careful study of this chapter will enable you to :

- identify the persons who are not competent to enter into contracts;
- describe the privileged position of a minor;
- enumerate persons disqualified by specific laws to enter into contracts; and
- explain the meaning of certain key terms.

Capacity to contract implies competence of the parties to contract. Section 11 of the Contract Act specifies that "Every person is competent to contract, who is of the age of majority according to the law to which he is subject and who is of sound mind and is not disqualified from contracting by any law to which he is subject." Thus, following persons are incapable of contracting :

(1) A minor.

(2) A person of unsound mind.

(3) Persons disqualified from contracting by any other law.

MINOR

Who is a minor? According to Indian Majority Act, 1875, a person who has not completed his 18th year of age is considered to be a minor.

In case a guardian to the person or property of the minor is appointed by the court or the property of the minor is put under the charge of a Court of Wards, during the period of his minority, the person shall become major on the completion of the age of 21 years. In England, a person becomes major on the completion of 18 years of age for all purposes.

Law relating to minor's agreements : Indian Contract Act has given a specially privileged position to a minor. He is allowed to take advantage of his acts but does not incur any kind of obligations. He can not be held personally liable for any of his wrongs. No legal action can be taken against him for his misbehaviour or false promises. The parents of a minor are not legally responsible for his contracts unless he acts as their agent. Following important provisions govern agreements made with a minor.

1. **Absolutely Void :** An agreement with a minor has been held to be void *ab initio*. It is not only void, but is absolutely void.[1] It is considered to be a nullity and non-existent from the very

1. Mohori Bibi *v*. Dharmodas Ghose (1903) 30 Cal. 539.

beginning and is, therefore, devoid of any consequences. In case a minor is carrying on a business, he cannot be held liable for the agreements made by him in the course of trade.

Example : A minor executed a mortgage for ₹ 20,000 and received ₹ 8,000 from the mortgage. He sued for setting aside the mortgage. The mortgagee wanted the refund of sum which he had actually paid, *i.e.,* ₹ 8,000. The Privy Council held that as the minor's contract was absolutely void, no question of refunding money could arise in these circumstances (*Mohori Bibi v. Dharmodas Ghose*).

However, if the minor has carried on his obligations, he can bring a suit against the other party for the enforcement of the other party's obligation.

Examples : (*i*) *R*, a minor girl, was allotted by *P*, a film producer, the role of an actress in a film. The agreement was made with *R*'s father. Later on of *P* allotted this role to some other artist. On a suit being filed by *R* for breach of contract, it was held that neither *R* not her father could sue *P*. This was because the girl was not bound by the agreement, and therefore, mutuality of the obligation was completely absent. The father could not sue because there was no consideration from him because promise of the minor girl being unenforceable it could not be a valid consideration for *P*'s promise to pay her a salary.[2]

(*ii*) *M* entered into a contract on behalf of a minor with *S* to purchase some immovable property for him. On a suit being filed by the minor for specific performance of the contract, it was held that the agreement was void and, therefore, his plea could not be accepted.[3]

(*iii*) *A, a minor advanced money to* B against a mortages executed in his favour. It was held that the mortgage was enforceable by him or by any other person on his behalf.[4]

(*iv*) A minor under a contract of sale delivered goods to the purchaser. It was held that he was entitled to maintain a suit for the recovery of the price.[5]

Please not the difference between illustrations (*i*), (*ii*), & (*iii*), (*iv*). In case of illustrations (*i*) & (*ii*), the contract is still executory, the minor has not performed his part, and therefore, the agreements are unenforceable. In case of illustrations (*iii*) & (*iv*) the minor has performed his part. He can, therefore, sue for the enforcement of the contract.

But a contract entered into by a minor though void is not unlawful. If a person after attaining majority pays a debt incurred during his minority, he cannot subsequently bring a suit for the refund of that amount.

2. **No Ratification :** Since a contract by a minor is altogether void, he cannot ratify contracts entered into by him during his minority, even after becoming major. There can be no ratification of a contract void *ab initio*.[6] A promise by a person on attaining majority to repay money lent and advanced to him during minority cannot be enforced, as consideration given during minority is held to be no consideration at all.

Example : *A*, a minor, borrows ₹ 5,000 from *B* and executes a promissory note in *B*'s favour. After attaining majority *A* executes a fresh promissory note in favour of *B* for this amount. *B* cannot sue on this promissory note as the agreement is void for lack of consideration.[7]

However, a minor who, on attaining majority, takes up and carries on a transaction commenced while he remained under disability will bind himself for the whole transaction.

2. Raj Rani *v.* Prem Adib, A.I.R. (1949) Bom. 215.
3. Mir Sarwarjan *v.* Fakhrudin Md. Chowdhury (1912) 39 Cal. 432 (P.C.).
4. Satyadev *v.* Tribeni, A.I.R. (1936) Pat. 153. S.C. 519.
5. Abdul Gafar *v.* Piare Lal (1935) 16, Lah. 1.
6. Mohendra *v.* Kailash (1927) 555 Cal. 842.
7. Indran Ramaswami *v.* Anthappa Chettiar (1906) 16 M.L.J. 422.

Examples : (*i*) *P* renders certain services to *D* during *D*'s minority on *D*'s request. On attaining majority *D* requests *P* to continue his services and later on promises to compensate *P* for such services as a whole. The agreement is valid and enforceable.[8]

(*ii*) *A*, a minor, takes a loan of ₹ 1,000 from *B* during his minority. On attaining majority he applies to *B* for a further loan of ₹ 1,000. *B* gives this loan and obtains from *A* a combined promissory note of ₹ 2,000 for the two loans. This will be taken as a new contract and *A* will be liable on the pronote.

3. **No Restitution :** A minor is not liable to repay any money or compensate for any benefit that he might have received under a void contract. Court may, however, in certain cases, while ordering for the cancellation of an instrument at the instance of the minor, require him to pay compensation to the other party to the instrument under Sec. 33 of the Specific Relief Act.

Examples : (*i*) *A*, a minor, sold a shop to *B*. The consideration was paid to *A* but the sale deed could not be registered as *A* was a minor. On a suit by *B* for recovery of the consideration, it was held that the agreement being void, the amount of consideration was not recoverable.

(*ii*) *V*, minor, agreed with *C*, to be a tenant in his house and to pay £ 100 for the furniture therein. *V* paid £ 68 in cash and gave a promissory note for the balance. After occupying and using the furniture for some time, *V* brought a suit for (*i*) cancellation of the promissory note and (*ii*) refund of £ 68 to him. The court ordered the cancellation of the promissory note but on grounds of natural justice refused the refund of £ 68 as *V* had used the premises and the furniture for some time.

However, the court will not grant 'restitution' in the following cases :

(*i*) where the other party was aware of infancy.[9]

(*ii*) where the other party was unscrupulous in his dealings with the minor.[10]

(*iii*) where the other party entered into a contract with the minor on account of reasons other than misrepresentation of his age.[11]

(*iv*) where the other party fails to satisfy the court that justice requires the application of the principle of restitution in his favour.[12]

There can be no specific performance of a contract entered into by a minor since such contracts are void *ab initio*.

4. **No Estoppel :** A minor is not bound by his misrepresentations. If a minor enters into a contract by fraudulently representing himself to be a minor, he cannot be prevented from pleading his minority in defence. He will not be held liable under the contract. The contract will be void. Therefore, a minor is not estopped from pleading minority even though he may be guilty of misrepresentation as to his age. The rule of estoppel cannot be applied against a minor.[13]

However, this does not mean that the minor shall be allowed to retain and enjoy the fruits of his own fraud. Court will order, on equitable considerations, for restitution if the minor is still in possession of the money or the things purchased out of it.[14] The minor shall have no liability if the money or things cannot be traced out in his hands.

---

8. Sindha *v*. Abraham (1895) 20 Bom. 755.
9. Bhim Mandal *v*. Magaram Corain, A.I.R. 1961 Pat. 61.
10. Muhammad Said *v*. Bishambher Nath, A.I.R. (1924) All. 156.
11. K. Maugle *v*. Mahda On. (1939) Rang. 545.
12. Kamta Prasad Singh *v*. Sheo Gopal Lal (1904) 26 All. 342.
13. Sadiq Ali Khan *v*. Jai Kishore, A.I.R. (1928) P.C. 152.
14. Section 33 of the Specific Relief Act. 1963.

Examples : (*i*) A minor borrowed ₹ 1,000 on a fraudulent representation that he was a major. Can the creditor sue for the realisation of the amount so advanced?

Creditor, in this case, cannot sue for the realisation of the money so advanced by him. Minor, in spite of his earlier fraudulent representation to the effect that he was a minor, cannot be estopped from pleading his minority in defence of the suit filed against him by the creditor. Since all contracts by a minor are void, he shall escape the liability for the return of the debt. An order of restitution can be issued if the amount can be found with the minor or if he has purchased certain articles out of that money, those articles can be taken but if he has spent the whole of the money, nothing can be recovered from him.

(*ii*) *L*, a minor, induced *J* to purchase property from him. *J* did not know about *L*'s minority and rather he was misled by him. On a suit being filed by *L* to recover back the property sold, it was held that on principles of equity *L* must return to *J*, the consideration received by him for the sale of property.[15]

5. **Minor Beneficiary :** All such contracts under which the minor is to receive some benefit or which are beneficial to him are valid. But in no case, he is personally liable. Only his property is liable for liability arising out of such contracts. These contracts include agreements which provide for the teaching, instruction or employment of a minor, if reasonable and for the benefit of the minor.[16] A minor is bound by a contract under which he obtains education, training for a trade or profession or beneficial experience in a trade or profession. Restraints imposed upon a minor by an agreement granting him articles of apprenticeship shall be valid and binding upon the minor if they are reasonable and substantially for the benefit of the minor. Such a contract is also protected by the Indian Apprentices Act, 1985 which states as its object to train children especially the orphans and the poor, in trades, crafts and employment so that they may gain a livelihood when they come of age. Similarly, contracts involving recurring rights and duties by which a minor acquires an interest in some property shall be binding on him unless he repudiates them within a reasonable time of becoming major or earlier.

Examples : (*i*) The father of a minor girl on her behalf entered into a contract with *M*, whereby *M* promised to marry the minor girl. On *M*'s refusal to marry, it was held that the contract was for the benefit of and on behalf of the minor and, therefore she could maintain a suit for damages for breach of the contract.[17]

(*ii*) *D*, an infant professional boxer, held a licence from British Boxing Board under the terms of which his money was to be stopped if he was disqualified. In a Boxing match *D* was disqualified and the Board withheld the money. *D* sued to recover the money on the ground that the clause in the agreement was burdensome. The court held that the clause was burdensome but was binding since contract as a whole was beneficial for the infant.[18]

It may be noted that all contracts in India by a minor are void. However, majority of the contracts for the benefit of the minor have been held to be enforceable by courts perhaps on the ground that it will be unjust in the circumstances to deprive a minor of a benefit which he may be entitled to get under a contract.

6. **Minor's Liability for Necessities :** All contracts relating to the necessities of the life supplied to a minor are valid. A person can claim reimbursement out of the property of the minor, the amount

15. Jagan Nath Singh *v.* Lalta Prasad (1908) 21 All. 21.
16. Roberts *v.* Gray (1913) 1. K.B. 520.
17. Rose Fernandez *v.* Joseph Gonsalves (1924) 48 Bom. 673. Of course minor can get a contract of marriage enforced against the other party but such contract is not enforceable against him.
18. Doyle *v.* White City Stadium Ltd. (1935).

of necessities suitable for the position in life supplied to him or to the members of his family whom he was bound to support. A minor shall have no personal liability for such debts.

The term 'necessities' is limited to such things as are absolutely necessary to keep the minor or persons dependent on him alive, but extends to all such things which a reasonable man would supply to the minor in that class of society to which the minor belongs and which are required by him to keep that position. Articles should be necessities for the minor both at the time of sale and delivery. Loan given to a minor to purchase necessities will also come within the definition of the term 'necessities'. (For detailed explanation refer to chapter on *'Quasi Contracts'* later in this section)

Examples : (*i*) *A*, the wife of a minor, purchases goods on credit from *B*. Does it constitute a valid contract?

It will be a valid contract only if the goods supplied are necessities (*Sec. 68*). The property of a minor is liable for all the necessities supplied to him or to any of his dependents according to their status in life.

(*ii*) *A* sold some articles from his shop to *B* on credit, not knowing that *B* a minor. The time fixed for payment expired and no payment was made. Sometime later, when *B* attained majority, *A* sued him for the price. What remedies should the court give to *A* under the law.

An agreement with a minor is void. Therefore, *A* will have no rights and cannot recover payment for the goods supplied except when they were of the nature of necessities to the minor and then also, the price can be recovered from his property and not from his personal self. *B*, the minor, cannot ratify, after becoming major, contracts entered into by him during his minority.

At best, court can allow *A* to recover the articles supplied, if they can still be traced in the hands of the minor.

Contracts relating to trade in which the minor is engaged shall not be necessities and shall, therefore, be void.

7. **Minor Promisee :** A minor can be a promisee. A promissory note executed in favour of the minor can be enforced. He can draw, negotiate or endorse a negotiable instruments so as not to incur any liability upon himself.

8. **Minor Agent :** A minor can be appointed as an agent. He can represent his principal in dealing with other parties. The principal will be responsible to third parties for the acts of his minor agent but he cannot hold the minor agent personally responsible for any wrongful acts. In the absence of any personal liability of the minor agent, the principal runs a great risk. He cannot recover any compensation from his minor agent for loss caused to him by any fault of the minor agent.

9. **Minor Partner :** A minor cannot be a partner. He can, however, be admitted to the benefits of the partnership. His liability is limited to the extent of his interest in the partnership. He has no right to take part in the management of the firm or copy or inspect any of the books of accounts of the firm.

10. **Surety for a Minor :** A person who stands as a surety for a loan taken by the minor will be liable to the creditor for payment of the loan, though the minor is not liable.[19] Similarly, an adult who along with a minor sings a bond in favour of a third party is bound by the promise though the minor is not liable on the same.[20]

19. Kashiba *v.* Shripat (1894) 19 Bom. 69.
20. Jamna Bai *v.* Vasanta Rao (1916) 39 Mad. 409.

11. **Minor as Member of a Company :** A minor cannot become a member of a company since he is incompetent to enter into a contract.[21] In case a minor inherits certain shares, the name of his lawful guardian will be entered as a member in the Register of Members. However, if a minor has been allotted shares through ignorance and his name has been entered in the Register of Members, both the company and the minor can repudiate the allotment of shares during his minority. But if none of them repudiate the contract, the minor may continue to enjoy the benefits of his shareholding without being liable for the payment of calls.

12. **A minor cannot be declared as an insolvent** because even for necessities of life he is not personally liable.

13. **Minor's Liability for Tort :** In case a minor is found guilty of a tort. (*i.e.*, civil wrong) he can be held liable. However, if a minor in the course of doing, what he is entitled to do under the contract, is found guilty of negligence, he cannot be made liable for a tort if he is not liable on the contract.

Examples : (*i*) A minor hired a horse for riding under express instructions not to jump it. He lent the horse to one of his friends who jumped it over a long distance whereby it became sick and ultimately died. The court held the minor liable for tort since ... it was bare trespass, not within the object and purpose of hiring for which the defendant was liable.[22]

(*ii*) A minor hired a horse for riding. The horse was injured on account of over-riding. It was held that minor was not liable since the injury was due to his negligence in the course of what he was entitled to do under the contract. He was not liable on the contract himself and, therefore, he was not liable for this tort too.[23]

Thus, the contracts made with the minors can be put under three heads :

1. *Valid contracts :* They include (*i*) contract for necessities which include goods as well as services; and (*ii*) contracts for loan taken for purchasing articles of necessities.
2. *Voidable contracts :* No such category of voidable contracts made by the minors has been recognised in our country. Contracts made with the minor are either void or valid. But contracts in which minor is a promisee or payee (in the case of negotiable instruments) or is beneficiary, are enforceable by him but not by the other party and, therefore, they can reasonably be called as contracts voidable at the option of the minor.
3. *Void contracts :* All contracts by a minor other than those referred above shall be void.

Position of Minor's Parents : The parents of a minor are not liable for agreements made by a minor, though the articles purchased may amount to necessities. The parents may feel a moral obligation for money borrowed by their minor children and may, therefore, pay the money, but there is no legal obligation for such payment. The parents can be held liable for contracts of their minor children only when they are acting as their agents.

Minority—A Boon : Looking to the privileges available to a minor it may be said that minority is not a disqualification but a shield which gives necessary protection to the minors. This protection has been given to minors because the law takes them a immature persons who can be easily misled by interested persons. Sir John William Salmond has defined their privileged position in the following words :

21. Palaniappa *v.* Pasupati Bank (1942) 1 M.L.I. 425.
22. Burnard *v.* Haggis (1863) 14 C.B. 45.
23. Jennings *v.* Rundell (1799) 8. T.R. 335.

'The law protects their persons; preserves their rights and estates, excuseth their laches and assists them in their pleadings, the Judges are their counsellors, the Jury are their servants and Law is their guardian.'

PERSONS OF UNSOUND MIND

According to *Section 12*, 'A person is said to be of sound mind for the purpose of making a contract if at the time when he makes it, he is capable of understanding it and of forming a rational judgement as to its effect upon his interests.'

Thus idiots, lunatics and drunkards are not considered to be persons of sound mind.

Idiot : A person who is devoid of any faculties of thinking or rational judgement is called an idiot. All agreements, other than those for necessities of life, with idiots are absolutely void.

Lunatic : A person, whose mental powers are deranged, is called a lunatic. Agreements made with lunatics, except those made during lucid intervals, (period in which he is in his senses) are void. Agreements for necessities of life are, however, valid.

For necessaries supplied to an idiot or lunatic, the property of such person is liable. He does not have any personal liability.

Necessities of life to an idiot or to a lunatic also include necessities of life to his wife and children. However, an agreement entered into by a person of unsound mind for his benefit can be enforced.[24]

Drunkards : A person under the influence of drink or drug stands on the same footing as a lunatic. An agreement made during drunkenness is void. But it should be shown that, at the time of contracting, the person, pleading drunkenness, was so drunk that temporarily he was deprived of reason, and therefore, could not give valid consent to the contract.

Examples : (*i*) A patient in a lunatic asylum, who, at intervals is of sound mind, may contract during those lucid intervals.

(*ii*) A sane man, who is delirious from fever or who is so drunk that he cannot understand terms of a contract or form a rational judgement as to its effect on his interest, cannot contract whilst such delirium or drunkenness lasts.

A contract made during mental disability can be ratified during a lucid interval.

PERSONS DISQUALIFIED BY OTHER LAWS

1. **Alien Enemy :** A person who is not a citizen of India is called an alien. In case the Sovereign or State of the alien is at peace with India, he is an alien friend, otherwise he is an alien enemy. An alien friend living in India has full contractual capacity subject to certain restrictions put up by the Government of India, *e.g.*, an alien cannot acquire any ownership interest in any Indian ship. In case of outbreak of war between India and alien's country, the following rules will apply :

(*a*) No contract can be made with an alien enemy during the subsistence of war except with the prior approval from the Central Government.

(*b*) Performance of the contracts made before the outbreak of war will be suspended during the course of war. They will be performed after the war is over. The Government, of course,

24. Jugal Kishore *v.* Cheddu (1903) All. L.J. 43.

can put restrictions on the performance of these contracts if it considers them necessary for national interest.

2. **Foreign Sovereigns :** Foreign Sovereigns and their accredited representatives can be sued in Indian courts only with the previous permission of the Central Government. They can, if they choose, enter into contracts and enforce them in our courts. Of course, an ex-king is not entitled to this privilege. He can be sued as an ordinary citizen in any of the Indian courts.

3. **Convicts :** While undergoing sentence, a convict is incapable of entering into a contract. This inability comes to an end on the expiration of the sentence or if he has been pardoned.

4. **Corporations :** A corporation or a company is only an artificial person created by law. It is a legal entity. It can only contract through its Board of Directors. It can hold property, can sell or purchase goods and can sue or be sued in relation to any of the contracts entered into by it. Being a mere creature of law, it cannot go beyond those objectives which have been laid down in the charter of its creation, *i.e.,* Memorandum of Association. In a case where a company had powers under its memorandum of association to purchase and work tramways, it was held that it could not work omnibuses.[25] Contracts which are *ultra vires* the objects of the company shall not be binding upon the company. Such *ultra vires* contracts cannot be ratified even by the unanimous vote of all its members.[26]

Besides that a company cannot make certain contracts at all, *e.g.,* a contracts to marry.

5. **Married Women :** Law does not make any distinction between the contractual capacities of males and females. In India, a woman (married or single) enjoys the same contractual capacity as man. Whatever property a female possesses, she enjoys right of absolute ownership over it. She can deal with her personal property in any way she likes and for these contracts her husband will not be responsible. Of course, for necessities of life, she can make her husband liable under certain conditions.

KEY TERMS

- **Minor :** A person who has not completed eighteenth year of age.
- **Idiot :** A person who is devoid of any faculties of thinking or rational judgement.
- **Lunatic :** A person whose mental powers are deranged.

TEST QUESTIONS

Objective Type : *Test Your Knowledge*

1. State whether each of the following statements is *True* or *False*

(*i*) A contract to supply articles of necessities to a minor can be enforced against him.

(*ii*) Contracts with a lunatic during lucid intervals are valid.

(*iii*) A woman does not have the same contractual capacity as a man.

(*iv*) A minor can be declared as an insolvent.

(*v*) A minor can be a promisee.

(*vi*) A minor cannot be appointed as an agent. (*PCE, ICAI, Nov. 2007*)

25. London Country Council *v.* Attorney General, 1902 (A.C. 165).
26. Ashbury Railway Carriage Co. *v.* Richie (1875), 7 H.L. Cas 653.

(vii) 'Besides minors and persons of unsound mind, there are others too who are disqualified from contracting by law.' *(CS Foundation, June 2007)*

(viii) 'A minor, who is of sound mind, is competent to contract.' *(CS Foundation, June 2008)*

(ix) A minor can always plead minority. *[B.Com., (Hons.) Delhi, 2011]*

(x) Law does not debar a minor from becoming a promisee in a contract. *[B.Com., (Hons.) Delhi, 2012]*

(xi) The Minor's Liability for necessaries supplied to him can be enforced only against Minor's Property. *[B.Com., (Hons.) Delhi, Nov. 2012]*

[***Ans.*** (*i*) False; (*ii*) True; (*iii*) False; (*iv*) False; (*v*) True; (*vi*) False; (*vii*) True; (*viii*) False; (*ix*) True; (*x*) True; (*xi*) True]

2. Select the most appropriate answer

(*i*) A minor

(*a*) cannot be an agent

(*b*) cannot be a principal

(*c*) can be a promisee

(*d*) can ratify a contract on attaining majority.

(*ii*) *X*, a minor misrepresenting that he is a major induces *Y* to enter into a contract. *X* is :

(*a*) liable on the contract

(*b*) not liable on the contract

(*c*) liable to pay compensation

(*d*) liable on the contract on attaining majority.

(*iii*) A minor can be

(*a*) an agent (*b*) a partner in a firm

(*c*) a member of a company.

[***Ans.*** (*i*) (*c*); (*ii*) (*b*); (*iii*) (*a*)]

Essay Type : *For Review, Discussion and Practice*

1. Explain the law regarding contracts made by minors.
2. What do you know about contracts entered into with a minor from the legal point of view in India? Do you know of any contracts with a minor to be valid? What are they?
3. A contract made by an infant may be (1) valid, (2) void and (3) voidable. What contracts come under each of these heads?
4. Can a married woman enter into a valid contract? To what extent has a wife authority to pledge her husband's credit?
5. What do you understand by capacity to contract. Examine the position of agreements made by a minor. *(CS Foundation, Dec. 1999, B.Com. (Pass), Delhi 2000, 2003 & 2004)*
6. Examine the legal position of :
   (*i*) Minor Promisor; (*ii*) Minor Promisee; (*iii*) Minor Agent *(CS Foundation, June 2000)*
7. Explain the concept of 'misrepresentation' in matters of contract. *(PEE II, November 2003)*
8. Explain the legal position of a minor under the Indian Contract Act, 1872 for necessaries supplied to him. *(CS Foundation, June 2005)*
9. Explain, with suitable examples, the circumstances under which a minor's estate is liable to reimburse for necessaries supplied to him.
   (CS Foundation, December 2005; B.Com. (Hons.), Delhi, 1990, 1992)
10. Can a minor be liable for payment of supplies of necessaries to him?
   (ICWAI, Inter Grade I, December 2005; CS Foundation, June 2007)

11. Explain the position of minor in relation to the Indian Contract Act.
(*GGSIPU, BBA (H), May 2004*)
12. Discuss the validity of contracts by minors. (*B.Com. (Hons.), Delhi, 1993, 2000 & 2004*)
13. What do you understand by 'competence to contract'? Examine the position of contracts made by minors. (*B.Com. (Hons.), Delhi, 1989, 2000*)
14. What is the legal effect of a minor's misrepresentation of his age while entering into an agreement? (*B.Com. (Hons.), Delhi, 1995*)
15. Explain the protection given to a minor by the Indian Contract Act, 1872. In what circumstances, a minor is bound by his contracts for necessaries? (*B.Com. (Hons.), Delhi, 2005*)
16. "Every person is competent to contract." Comment. (*ICWA Inter, June 2009*)
17. "A minor can be appointed as an Agent." Comment. (*ICWA Inter, June 2009*)
18. State with suitable examples the circumstances under which a minor is bound by his contracts for necessaries as per Indian Contract Act. Whether a contract of person service by a minor is valid? Explain. (*B.Com. (Hons.), Delhi, 2011*)

PRACTICAL PROBLEMS

1. *X*, a minor, lent ₹ 1,000 to *Y* at the market rate of interest on the basis of a promissory note? *A* year thereafter, when *X* attained majority, he filed a suit against *Y* for recovery of the amount thereon. *Y* contended that since X was minor at the time when loan was advanced, the contract was void. Will *Y* succeed?
[***Ans.*** No. A contract for the benefit of minor can be enforced by him.]
2. *A* grocer supplies monthly rations for 6 months to *B* who is aged 17 years. On *B*'s failure to pay, he sues him for realisation of his dues. Will he succeed?
[***Ans.*** Yes. For necessaries *B*'s property is liable.]
3. *X*, a minor, lends ₹ 10,000 and gets a mortgage executed in his favour. Is the borrower liable to repay the money?
[***Ans.*** Yes]
4. *A*, minor, borrows ₹ 5,000 from *B* and executes a pronote in favour of *B*. After attaining majority. *A* executes another pronote in settlement to the first pronote. Will *B* succeed in recovering the money from *A*? Give reasons in support of your answer.
[***Ans.*** *B* will not succeed since the pronote does not have any validity because of *A* being a minor. Even the ratification after majority will not help.]
5. Teji, a minor broke his right leg in a football match. He engaged Curewell, a doctor to set it. Does the doctor have a valid claim for his services? Give reasons. (*CS Foundation, June 2000*)
[***Ans.*** Doctor can claim for his services out of the property of the minor.]
6. Sohan induced Suraj to buy his motorcycle saying that it was in a very good condition. After taking the motorcycle, Suraj complained that there were many defects in the motorcycle. Sohan proposed to get it repaired and promised to pay 40% cost of repairs. After a few days, the motorcycle did not work at all. Now Suraj wants to rescind the contract. Decide giving reasons.
(*PEE II, November 2003*)
[***Ans.*** Suraj cannot rescind the contract, as his acceptance to the offer of Sohan to bear 40% of the cost of repairs impliedly amount to final acceptance of the sale.]
7. Amit, who is sixteen years of age, fractures his leg while playing cricket. He goes to a doctor and gets his leg plastered. The doctor demands a fee of ₹ 1,000, but Amit refuses to pay on the ground that he is a minor. The doctor files a suit against Amit. Will the doctor succeed? Give reasons.
(*CS Foundation, June 2004*)
[***Ans.*** The Doctor will succeed.]

8. Rajesh, a director of Volatile Ltd., died in an air crash. It has been decided to appoint Kamal in his place. Will the company be required to call an extraordinary general meeting to approve of the latter's appointment as a director? When appointed, how long would Kamal remain in office? *(CS Foundation, June 2005)*

   [***Ans.*** There is no need to call an EGM for the purpose. The vacancy being a casual vacancy can be filled by the Board of Directors.]

9. Sandeep, a minor lends ₹ 1,000 against a Promissory Note executed in his favour by the borrower. Is the borrower liable to repay the money to Sandeep? *(GGSIPU, BBA (H), June 2001)*

   [***Ans.*** The borrower is liable since a minor can be a promisee.]

10. Ramesh, a minor, by misrepresenting himself to be of 19 years, obtains a loan of ₹ 10,000 from Suresh stating that the amount was badly needed by him to complete his education. Suresh without making any further inquiry, lent the amount to Ramesh. Can Suresh recover the amount from Ramesh? *(B.Com. (Hons.), Delhi 1988)*

    [***Ans.*** Suresh cannot recover the amount from Ramesh.]

11. *A* executed a pronote in favour of *B* while he was a minor. The pronote was renewed by *A* in favour of *B* when he attained the age of majority. *B* brings a suit against *A* on the basis of the second pronote. Will he succeed? Give reasons. *(B.Com. (Hons.), Delhi 2001)*

    [***Ans.*** Since minor's agreement is void *ab initio*, it cannot be validated by any subsequent action. Thus, *B* will not succeed in recovering money from *A*.]

12. A minor borrowed ₹ 10,000 and signed a pronote. On becoming major he signed another pronote replacing the earlier one. Later, he refused to make the payment. Discuss the rights of the creditor with reasons. *(B.Com. (Pass), Delhi 2001)*

    [***Ans.*** A minor cannot ratify the agreement on attaining the age of majority as the original agreement is void *ab initio*. Hence, in the present case, creditor cannot claim for ₹ 10,000 from minor as per rule.]

13. *X*, a minor was studying in M.Com. in a college. On 1st July, 2005 he took a loan of ₹ 10,000 from *B* for payment of his college fees and to purchase books and agreed to repay by 31st December, 2005. *X* possesses assets worth ₹ 2 lakhs. On due date *X* fails to payback the loan to *B*. *B* now wants to recover the loan from *X* out of his (*X*'s) assets. Referring to the provisions of Indian Contract Act, 1872 decide whether *B* would succeed. *(PEE, ICAI, Nov. 2006)*

    [***Ans.*** Yes, *B* can proceed against the assets of *X*.]

14. *R*, is the wife of *P*. She purchased some sarees on credit from *Q*. *Q* demanded the amount from *P*. *P* refused. *Q* filed a suit against *P* for the said amount. Decide in the light of provisions of the Indian Contract Act, 1872, whether *Q* would succeed. *(PEE, ICAI, Nov. 2006)*

    [***Ans.*** *Q* will succeed. He can recover the said amount from *'P'* if sarees purchased by *R* are necessaries for her.]

15. *P*, a minor borrowed ₹ 50,000 from *Q*, a money-lender, by misinterpretating his age to be above 18 years. On discovering the truth *Q* waited for *P* to become a major and got a promissory note signed from *P* for ₹ 60,000. Is *P* liable to pay? *(B.Com. (Hons), Delhi 2010)*

    [***Ans.*** No, *P* is not liable to pay *Q* on the new promissory note executed by him after attaining majority. An agreement with a minor is void ab initio, there is no possibility of its ratification by the minor after attaining majority.

16. Ramesh, aged 16 years, was studying in an engineering college. On 1 March, 2011 he took a loan of ₹ 1 lakh from Suresh for the payment of his college fee and agreed to pay by 30th May, 2012. Ramesh possesess assets worth ₹ 10 lakhs. On due date, Ramesh fails to pay back the loan to Suresh. Suresh now wants to recover the loan from Ramesh out of his assets. Whether Suresh would succeed? Decide, referring to the provisions of the Indian Contract Act, 1872.

    (CA IPC, Nov. 2012)

    [***Ans.*** Suresh will be entitled to recover the amount of loan given to Ramesh for payment of the college fees from the property of the minor]

17. *M* lends a type-writer to *N*, a minor, for typing practice for a period of two months. It was agreed that *N* would pay montly hire charges of ₹ 500. At the end of two months, *N* refuses to pay the hire charges. Can *M* recover hire charges from *N* (A) if the typewriter was lent for necessaries? (B) if the typewriter was not lent for necessaries? Discuss. (*B.Com. (Hons), Delhi, Nov. 2010*)

[***Ans.*** (A) Yes, *M* can recover hire charges of the typewriter from the property of *N*, if it was lent for necessaries. (B) No, *M* cannot recover any charges from *N*, if the typewriter was not lent for necessaries, because an agreement by a minor is absolutely void and inoperative against him.]

Chapter 4

CONSENT : NATURE AND REQUISITES

LEARNING OBJECTIVES

A careful study of this chapter will enable you to :

- understand the meaning of consent;
- identify the cases where the consent is not said to be free;
- differentiate between coercion and undue influence and misrepresentation and fraud;
- study the effect of mistake on the validity of a contract; and
- explain the meaning of certain key terms.

CONSENT

According to *Sec. 13* 'two or more persons are said to consent when they agree upon the same thing in the same sense.' This means that there should be perfect identity of mind (*consensus ad idem*) regarding the subject-matter of the contract. When each party has a different thing in mind or understands the thing in a different way, there is no real consent, *e.g.*, if two persons enter into a contract concerning a particular person or thing and it turns out later that they were misguided by a similarity of name and actually had a different person or thing in mind, no contract would exist between them. This happens in case of mistake, where consent is altogether absent. Salmond has described it as *'Error in Consensus'*.

FREE CONSENT

To make a contract valid, not only consent is necessary but the consent should also be free. According to *Sec. 14* consent is said to be free when it is not caused by any of the following :

1. Coercion
2. Undue influence
3. Fraud
4. Misrepresentation
5. Mistake

A clear distinction must be made between 'no consent' and 'no free consent'. In the first-four cases, consent is there but the consent is not free. *Salmond* calls it *'error in causa.'* In the last case, there is no identify of mind and, therefore, consent is altogether absent. A person cannot acquire any title, whatsoever, in the goods without the consent of the real owner and in the absence of any title to himself, he cannot convey any title, good or bad, even to a person who acquires those goods in good faith and for valuable consideration. A man cannot transfer what he himself does not possess.

On the other hand a person acquiring title without free consent, can convey a better title to a transferee in good faith and for consideration before his title is challenged by the real owner. In the first case of no consent, the agreement is void *ab initio*. In the latter case of 'no free consent', the agreement is voidable at the option of the party whose consent has not been free and until he exercises his right to avoid the contract, the possessor of the goods can convey a better title and the *bonafide* transferee for value will acquire them free from all defects.

Examples : (*i*) *A* has two cars, one blue and the other red. He wants to sell his blue car. *B* who knows of only *A*'s red car, offers to purchase *A*'s car for ₹ 20,000. *A* accepts the offer thinking that it is for his blue car. This is no consent because both the parties are not understanding the same thing in the same sense.

(*ii*) In the above example, if *B* goes to *A* and on the point of pistol asks *A* to sell his red car for a sum of ₹ 20,000 to him, there is consent because both are understanding that red car is the subject-matter of the conduct, but the consent is not free because it has been obtained by coercion.

COERCION

According to *Section 15*, 'coercion is the committing or threatening to commit any act forbidden by the Indian Penal Code, or the unlawful detaining or treatening to detain any property, to the prejudice of any person, whatsoever, with the intention of causing any person to enter into an agreement.'

It is immaterial whether the Indian Penal Code is or is not in force in the place where coercion is employed.

On analysing this definition, we arrive at the following essential characteristics of coercion :

(1) Committing or threatening to commit any act forbidden by the Indian Penal Code amounts to coercion.

Examples : (*i*) After giving a good beating to *A*, *B* makes him to agree to sign a promissory note for ₹ 1,000. The beating amounts to coercion.

(*ii*) The relatives of a widow threatened her that they would not carry the dead body of her husband for cremation, unless she signed a document stating adoption of *B* as her son. It was held that the threat amounted to coercion.[1]

Threat to commit suicide : An attempt to commit suicide is an offence under the Indian Penal Code, but a threat to commit suicide is no offence, and therefore, consent obtained by giving a threat to commit suicide cannot strictly be termed as caused by coercion. However, Madras High Court has held by a majority judgement that even a threat to commit suicide is coercion even though it is not punishable under the Indian Penal Code. The following observation made by the Court is worth noting:

'The term 'any act forbidden by the Indian Penal Code' is wider than the term 'punishable' by the Indian Penal Code, simply because a man escapes punishment, it does not follow that the act is not forbidden by the Indian Penal Code. For example, a lunatic or a minor may not be punished. This does not show that their criminal acts are not forbidden by the Indian Penal Code.'

Example : A person by giving a threat to commit suicide, induces his wife and son to execute a release deed in favour of his brother in respect of certain properties which they claimed to be their own. Held that the consent of the wife and son has been taken by coercion.[2]

---

1. Ramganayakamma *v*. Alwar Chetty (1889) 13. Mad. 214.
2. Amiraju *V*. Seshamma (1918) 41 Mad. 33.

Threat to file a suit : A threat to file a civil or criminal suit does not amount to coercion since the act is not forbidden by the Indian Penal Code. However, a threat to file a suit on a false charge amounts to coercion since such an act is forbidden by the Indian Penal Code.[3]

(2) Detaining or threatening to detain unlawfully property of another person also amounts to coercion.

Example : An agent refuses to hand over the books of account relating to the agency business to his principal unless the principal releases him from all past transactions. Held, the release has been obtained by coercion and, therefore, is not binding.[4]

(3) The act must have been done with the intention of causing any person to enter into an agreement.

(4) Coercion can be applied either by a party to the contract or even by a stranger. It may be applied against a party to the contract or any other person.

Example : *P* threatens *A* that he will shoot *P's* son *Q* unless *P* signs a contract with *B* agreeing to sell his house to him. *A* signs the contract. It is not binding on him because his consent has been obtained by coercion.

(5) It is not necessary that the Indian Penal Code should be applicable at the place where coercion is exercised.

Example : *A* on board an English ship on the high seas, causes *B* to enter into an agreement by an act amounting to criminal intimidation under the Indian Penal Code.

A afterwards sues *B* for breach of contract at Calcutta.

A has employed coercion, although his act is not an offence by the law of England, and although Section 566 of the Indian Penal Code was not in force at the time when or place where the act was done.

Effect of Coercion

When the consent of a party to an agreement is obtained by coercion, the contract becomes voidable at the option of the party, whose consent is so obtained (*Sec. 19*). The burden of proving that the consent was obtained by coercion shall be upon the party who wants to set aside the contract on the plea of coercion.

Example : *A* executes a transfer bond for the house under fear of assault. It will be a contract voidable at the option of *A* since his consent was obtained by coercion.

According to Section 72 of the Act, which is based on the principle of equitable restitution, a person to whom anything has been delivered or money paid under coercion must return or repay it.

Example : A railway company refuses to deliver certain goods to the consignee, except upon the payment of an illegal charge for carriage. The consignee pays the sum charged in order to obtain the goods. He is entitled to recover so much of the charge as was illegal and excessive.

UNDUE INFLUENCE

Undue influence is the improper use of any power possessed over the mind of the contracting party. According to *Section 16* a contract is said to be affected by undue influence when :

3. Askari Mirya *v.* Bibi Jai Kishori (1912) 16, I.C. 344.
4. Muthian Chettiya *v.* Karuppanchetti, 50 Mad. 786.

(a) the relations subsisting between the parties are such that one of the parties is in a position to dominate the will of the other, and

(b) uses that position to obtain an unfair advantage over the other.

The three ingredients in the definition of undue influence are :

(i) that the relations subsisting between the parties are such that one of the parties is in a position to dominate the will of the other;

(ii) that the dominant party obtains and unfair advantage over the other;

(iii) that the dominant party uses his dominant position to obtain that unfair advantage.

A contract made under statutory compulsion cannot be regarded as one made under undue influence.

Example : *A*, a cane grower, had the freedom to offer cane to the factory of his area or not. But, if he made an offer, the factory was bound an Act to accept. The Supreme Court held that though factory was required to give its consent under law, it could not be taken as coercion undue influence.[5]

Persons deemed to be in a position to dominate the will of the other : In the following three cases law presumes a person to be in a position to dominate the will of the other :

(i) Where he holds a real or apparent authority over the other (master or servant, parent and child). Real or apparent authority may arise due to inequality of the parties.

(ii) Where he stands in a fiduciary relationship (religious guru and disciple, trustee and beneficiary, doctor and patient, lawyer and client).

(iii) Where he makes a contract with a person whose mental capacity is temporarily or permanently affected by reason of age, illness or mental or bodily distress [*Sec. 16 (2)*].

The above presumptions can be rebutted if it is proved that :

(a) All material facts were disclosed to the party who is alleging exercise of undue influence.

(b) The consideration was adequate.

(c) The party alleging exercise of the undue influence was in receipt of independent advice and was free to exercise it.

Examples : (i) *A*, having advanced money to his son *B* during minority, upon *B*'s coming of age obtains by misuse of parental influence, a bond from *B* for a greater amount than the actual sum advanced by him. The agreement shall be voidable at the option of *B* for the reason of his consent having obtained by employing undue influence.

(iii) *A*, being in debt to *B*, the moneylender of his village, contracts for a fresh loan on terms which appear to be unconscionable. It lies on *B* to prove that the contract was not induced by undue influence.

(iv) *A* applied to a banker for a loan at a time when there is stringency in the money market. The banker declines to make the loan except at an unusually high rate of interest. *A* accepts the loan on these terms. This is a transaction in the ordinary course of business, and the contract is not influenced by undue influence.

(v) A person was suffering from a number of ailments. He was confined to a nursing home and from there he gifted all his properties to one of his sons excluding all others. It was held by the Supreme Court that they could presume exercise of undue influence.[6]

5. Andhra Sugar Ltd. *v.* State of Andhra Pradesh (1968) 1 S.C.R. 705.

6. Lakshmi Amma *v.* T. Narayan, A.I.R. (1970) S.C. 1367.

Undue influence, is a type of moral coercion. Importunity or threats such as the promisor has not the courage to resist, moral command asserted and yielded for the sake of peace and quiet or of escaping from distress of mind or social discomfort, these if carried to a degree in which the free play of the promisor's judgement, discretion or wish is overborne, will constitute undue influence, though no force is either used or threatened. However, where the parties are on equal footing merely that the contract puts a party to some hardships or that the contract was unconscionable or the consideration is inadequate will not allow to the contract to avoid it on the ground of undue influence.

Burden of Proof : To prove that the contract has been effected by undue influence, all the three ingredients discussed before must be proved in the order in which they are written. When the first two ingredients are proved in a contract, the burden of proving the absence of the use of the dominant position to obtain the unfair advantage will lie on the party in a position to dominate the will of the other.

Pardanashin Woman : A pardanashin woman is one who, by the custom of the country or the usage of the particular community to which she belongs is obliged to observe complete seclusion.[7] Such ladies are more exposed to undue influence and require special protection from the courts. A contract with a pardanashin woman is presumed to have been induced by undue influence. In order to prove that the constent of the pardanashin lady has not been effected by undue influence, following additional things must be proved :

(*a*) the terms of the contract are fair and equitable,

(*b*) the transaction is real and *bona fide,*

(*c*) the lady had an independent advice in the matter.

(*d*) she acted at an arm's length from the other party to the contract,

(*e*) the deed was explained to her, and

(*f*) she understood it and its effect on her interests in full.

The protection given to a pardanashin woman by the above rules is also extended to an illiterate and ignorant woman who is equally exposed to the danger and risk of an unfair deal.[8]

Effect of Undue Influence : An agreement caused by undue influence shall be voidable at the option of the party whose consent has been so obtained. Such an agreement may be set aside absolutely or if the party, who was entitled to set aside, has received any benefit the court may set it aside upon such terms and conditions as may appear to be just (*Sec. 19A*).

Examples : (*i*) *A*'s son has forged *B*'s name to a promissory note. *B*, under the threat of prosecuting *A*'s son, obtains a bond from *A* for the amount of the forged note. If *B* sues on the bond, the court may set the bond aside.

(*ii*) *A*, a money-lender, advances ₹ 100 to *B*, an agriculturist, and by undue influence induces *B* to execute a bond for ₹ 200 with interest at 6% per month. The court may set the bond aside ordering *B* to repay ₹ 100 with such interest as may seem just.

Difference between Coercion and Undue Influence

1. **Mode of Obtaining Consent :** In both coercion and undue influence, the consent of the aggrieved party is not free. But in coercion, the consent of the aggrieved party is taken

7. Fayyaz-ud-din *v.* Kutub-ud-din (1929) 10, Lah. 761, 766. It is to be noted that a woman who observes some degree of seclusion (quasi-pardanshin) will not get this benefit.

8. Sonia Parashini *v.* S.M. Baksha (1950), A.I.R. Cal. 17.

by committing or threatening to commit an act forbidden by the Indian Penal Code or detaining or threatening to detain some property unlawfully. While in undue influence, the consent of the aggrieved party is obtained by dominating the party by taking an unfair advantage of his position.

2. **Type of Force :** In case of coercion physical force is exercised while in undue influences, moral force is used.
3. **Existence of Relationship :** In case of coercion, relationship between the promisor and the promise is not necessary. While in case of undue influence, some sort of relationship *must* (whether parental or fiduciary) exist between the two parties to the contract.

FRAUD

Misrepresentation of facts may be intentional or innocent. Intentional misrepresentation has been termed as 'Fraud' and innocent misrepresentation has been termed simply as 'Misrepresentation' in the Contract Act.

Definition : According to *Section 17* Fraud means and includes any of the following acts committed by a party to a contract, or by any one with his connivance or by his agent with intent to deceive another party thereto or his agent or to induce him to enter into the contract :

(*a*) A suggestion as to a fact of that which is not true by one who does not believe it to be true.

(*b*) An active concealment of a fact by one having knowledge or belief of the fact.

(*c*) A promise made without any intention of performing it.

(*d*) Any other act fitted to deceive.

(*e*) Any such act or omission as the law specially declares to be fraudulent.

Elements of Fraud : The main elements of fraud are :

1. The act must have been committed by a party to the contract or with his connivance or by agent. It should not have been committed by a stranger.

Examples : (*i*) The directors of a company issued a prospectus containing some false particulars on the basis of which *S* applied for allotment of shares in the company. The shares were allotted to *S*, but subsequently he wanted to avoid the contract on the ground of fraud. It was held that the directors of the company were agents of the company as regards publication of the prospectus, and therefore, *S* could set aside the contract on the ground of fraud played by the company with him.[9]

(*ii*) A person was induced to buy shares in a company on account of a false statement made by a stranger. It was held that he could not get out of the bargain because false statement was not made by the company or its agent.[10]

2. Acts committed may be of the following nature :

(*a*) *Suggestion of an untrue fact :* If a person knowingly states an untrue fact or fact which he does not believe to be true, it will be taken as a fraud on his part.

Example : *A* says to *B* his coat is made of pure wool, though he knows that is untrue. *B* purchases the coat believing *A*'s statement to be true. It is a fraud by *A*, and therefore, contract is voidable at *B*'s option.

---

9. Reese River Silver Mining Co. *v.* Smith, L.R. 4H.L. 64.
10. Nicols' case, 28 L.J. Ch. 257.

It is important to note that the fraudulent representation must always relate to the assertion of a fact and not of an opinion, statement of expression or intention. A declaration of an opinion, or a mere expression of opinion will not amount to fraud.

Examples : *(i) A*, who is about to sell a horse to *B* says. 'The horse is a beauty and worth ₹ 1,000.' *B* buys the horse for ₹ 800. Afterwards *B* learns that *A* had bought it for ₹ 400, and *B* cannot get more than ₹ 300 for it. What is *B*'s remedy?

B does not have any remedy against *A*, as the statement made by *A* is a mere expression of an opinion and cannot be taken as fraud.

(ii) In the above case if *A* says to *B* 'The horse is a beauty and only yesterday I had purchased it for ₹ 1,000.' Actually he had purchased it only for ₹ 400. *B* buys the horse believing *A*'s statement. *A* has knowingly misrepresented a fact and, therefore, it will be taken as a fraud on his part.

There will be no fraud if a false statement is made by a person who honestly believes it to be true. It will simply amount to misrepresentation.

(b) Active concealment of a fact : If a person conceals a fact which is his duty to disclose, it will be taken as a fraud on his part. It is to be noted that mere concealment of facts does not amount to fraud because as a rule the seller is not bound to disclose faults in the goods he is going to sell. It is the duty of the buyer to satisfy himself regarding the quality or price of the goods before purchasing them. However, in contracts of *uberrimae fidei* or absolute faith (as discussed later), silence of the seller about material facts will be taken as fraud.

Examples : *(i) A* contracts to sell to *B* a piece of silk, *B* thinks that it is English silk. *A* knows that *B* thinks so, but knows that it is Japanese silk. *A* does not correct *B*'s impression. Subsequently, *B* discovers that it is not English silk. Can he repudiate the contract?

B cannot repudiate the contract. There is no fraud on the part of *A* because he is under no duty to disclose that piece of silk is a Japanese one. *A*'s silence cannot be taken as fraud.

(ii) A has house. Its foundation had been badly shaken on account of an earthquake. He sells this house to *B* without disclosing this fact to him. *B* later on comes to know about the dangerous nature of the foundation of the house. He can repudiate the contract on the ground of fraud because a contract for sale of an immovable property is a contract of *uberrimae fidei*. Concealment of a material fact about the house by *A* will be taken as a fraud on his part.

Concealment of a latent defect (defect not visible through ordinary inspection) will amount to fraud.

Example : *A*, a horse dealer, sold a mare to *B*, *A* knew that the mare had a cracked hoof which he filled in such a way that it was not visible through ordinary inspection. The defect was subsequently discovered by *B*. It was held that concealment of a latent defect amounted to a fraud on the part of *A* and, therefore, *B* could set aside the contract.

(c) A promise made without any intention of performance it : If a party while entering into a contract has no intention to perform his promise, it will be taken as a fraud on his part.

Examples : *(i) A* purchases certain goods from *B*. He does not have any intention to pay the price of the goods. It is a fraud on the part of *A*.

(ii) A man and a woman went through a ceremony of marriage. The husband had no intention to regard it as a real marriage. It was held that the consent of wife was obtained by fraud.[11]

---

11. Shireen Mall *v.* Johan James Taylor, A.I.R. (1952) Punj, 227.

(*d*) *Any other act fitted to deceive :* This sub-section is meant for covering all such cases which cannot appropriately be covered by other sub-sections. Thus, this sub-section covers all tricks, dissembling and other unfair ways, which are used by cunning people to cheat others.

(*e*) *Any such act or omission which the law specially declares to be fraudulent, e.g.,* under the Transfer of Property Act, any transfer of immovable property with the intention of defrauding the creditors, is taken as a fraud.

(3) ***The act must have been committed with the intention of inducing the deceived party to act upon it :*** It implies that the assertion should be such that it would necessarily influence and induce the other party to act.

Example : *A* company's prospectus contained a statement that one Mr. *P* was a director of the company. *A* person, *B*, who never heard of *P* applied for allotment of shares to him on the basis of company's prospectus. As a matter of fact *P* was not actually on the Board of Directors of the company. *B* wanted to set aside the contract on the ground of mis-statement in the prospectus. It was held that *B* could not do so because the untrue statement was immaterial to him, and it had in no way induced him to purchase shares in the company.[12]

(4) ***The act must have in fact deceived the other party :*** If a person has committed a fraudulent act to deceive the other party, but the other party has not been actually been deceived by his act, it will not be taken as a fraud on his part. It has been observed, "A deceit which does not deceive is no fraud."

Examples : (*i*) *A* had a cannon. It had a defect. In order to conceal it, he puts a metal plug on it. He sold it to *B*, who accepted the cannon without examining it. The cannon burst before it was paid for. *B* refused to pay on the ground that *A* was guilty of fraud. It was held that *B* was bound to pay because he would have bought it even if no deceptive plug was inserted. He was not, therefore, actually deceived by the fraud.

(*ii*) *A*, owner of an unsound horse, forged a veterinary surgeon's certificate stating the horse to be sound and pinned it at the stable door. *B* came to buy the horse. He did not notice the certificate and purchased the horse for a heavy price. Later on *B* sued for setting aside the contract on the ground of fraud. It was held that contract could not be set aside on the ground of fraud because *B* had not seen the certificate and, therefore, he was not deceived by *A*'s fraud.

(5) ***Plaintiff must have suffered :*** 'There is no fraud without damages,' and, therefore, to constitute fraud it is necessary that the plaintiff must have suffered some loss of money or money's worth or some other tangible detriment capable of assessment.

Silence as Fraud

Mere silence without any legal duty to speak will not amount to fraud except where

(*a*) the circumstances of the case are such that regard being had to them, it is the duty of the person keeping silence to speak, or

(*b*) silence, in itself, will be equivalent to speech.

Duty to Speak

In the case of the following types of contracts the law requires that person knowing material facts must speak out the facts, otherwise it will be taken as a fraud on his part.

12. Smith *v*. Chandwick (1884) 9 App. Cas. 187.

1. **Contracts of *uberrimae fidei* :** In the case of contracts *uberrimae fidei* (absolute good faith) law imposes upon parties the duty of making a true and full disclosure of all material facts. Following contracts come within this class.

(*a*) *Contracts of Insurance :* In a contract of insurance the insured is required to make a frank and true disclosure of all material facts known or ought to be known to him and which are likely to influence the insurer in coming to a decision.

(*b*) *Contracts for the sale of immovable properties : Section 55(1)* of The Transfer of Property Act requires the seller to 'to disclose to the buyer any material defects in the property or in the seller's title thereto, of which the seller is, and the buyer is not aware, and which the buyer could not with ordinary care discover.' In case the buyer knows a material fact of which the seller is unaware, he must disclose it to the seller.

Examples : (*i*) *B*, having discovered a mine of ore on the estate of *A*, adopts means to conceal, and does conceal, the existence of the ore from *A*. Through *A*'s ignorance *B* is enabled to buy the estate at an under-value. The contract is voidable at the option of *A*.

(*ii*) *A* is entitled to succeed at the death of *B*. *B* dies. *C*, having received information of *B*'s death, prevents the information reaching *A* and thus, induces *A* to sell him his interest in the estate. The sale is voidable at the option of *A*.

(*c*) *Allotment of shares in companies :* A company inviting the public to subscribe to its shares must disclose all information regarding itself in the prospectus with strict accuracy. This rule is known as the *Rule of Golden Legacy*.

(*d*) *Family settlement :* Full disclosure of all material facts is necessary when family disputes are settled by mutual agreement.

(*e*) *Contracts of marriage :* Each party to a contract of marriage must disclose every material fact known to him and which affects others party's intention to marry.

2. **Contracts of partnership :** Contracts of partnership are not absolutely contracts of *uberrimae fidei* in the sense that they do not need full disclosure of every material fact to an intending partner likely to affect his willingness to become a partner in the firm. But the Partnership Act provides that partners must observe absolute good faith and must be just and faithful to each other. They are also required to render true accounts and full information of all things affecting the firm, to every partner or his legal representative.

3. **Contracts of guarantee :** In case of contracts of guarantee, the creditor must disclose all material facts which are known to him about the debtor. Any guarantee obtained by him by concealment of material facts will not be valid.

4. **Fiduciary relationship :** Parties standing in a fiduciary relation to each other party which are likely to affect his willingness to enter into a contract *e.g.*, contracts between solicitor and client, father and son etc.

Examples : (*i*) *A* sells by auction to *B*, a horse which *A* knows to be unsound. *A* says nothing to *B* about the horse's unsoundness. There is no fraud on the part of *A*.

(*ii*) *B* is *A*'s daughter and has just come of age. Here the relations between the parties would make it *A*'s duty to tell *B* that the horse is unsound.

(*b*) **Silence equivalent to speech :** Silence will amount to fraud in all those cases where it shall be considered equivalent to speech.

Example : *B* says to A, 'If you do not deny it, I shall assume that the horse is sound.' *A* says nothing. Here *A*'s silence is equivalent to speech.

Effects of Fraud *(Sec. 19)*

The party, whose consent to the contract is obtained by fraud can exercise any of the following rights :

(*a*) He may avoid the contract and may (*i*) ask for the damages suffered because of the non-fulfilment of the contract or (*ii*) ask for restitution.

(*b*) He may insist for the performance of the contract and may ask the other party to put him in the position in which he would have been if the representation made have been true, *i.e.*, bring an action for damages for the fraudulent representation.

Examples : (*i*) *A* intending to deceive *B*, falsely represents that five hundred tonnes of indigo are made annually at *A*'s factory, and thereby, induces *B* to buy the factory. The contract is voidable at the option of *B*.

(*ii*) *A* fraudulently informs *B* that *A*'s estate is free from encumbrance. *B*, thereupon, buys the estate. The estate is subject to mortgage. *B* may either avoid the contract, or may insist on its being carried out and mortgage debt redeemed.

However, the party whose consent was caused by fraud shall have no right to avoid the contract in each of the following cases :

(*a*) he has affirmed or ratified the contract in any manner even after becoming aware of the fraud.

(*b*) the parties cannot be restored to their original position.

(*c*) the third parties have acquired right for consideration and in good faith, in the property passing under the contract[13],

(*d*) the aggrieved party had the means of discovering the truth where his consent was caused by fraudulent silence.

MISREPRESENTATION

Misrepresentation is a false representation made innocently without any intention of deceiving the other party. It may include two things :

(*a*) wrong statement of a material fact not known to be false or

(*b*) non-disclosure of facts where there is a legal duty to disclose without any intention to deceive.

In misrepresentation, the knowledge of or belief in particular facts is never based on reasonable grounds. If it is based on reasonable grounds, it will be a case of mutual mistake.

Example : *A*, who is about to sell his horse to *B* says, 'My horse is sound.' *A* does not know that the horse had fallen ill yesterday. *B*, thereupon, buy the horse. There is misrepresentation on the part of *A*.

13. Phillips *v.* Brooks (1919) 2 K.B. 243.

According to *Section 18* misrepresentation may be committed in any of the following ways :

(*i*) *By positive statement* : If a person without any reasonable basis makes an absolute and explicit statement of fact, which is not true though he believes it to be true, it will be said that he is guilty of misrepresentation.

Example : *A* says to *B* without having examined the records that in his factory, 1,000 tonnes of indigo is manufactured every month. *A* believes that his assessment is very correct. *B*, thereupon, buys the factory. The actual production of the factory is found to be only 830 tonnes. *A* is guilty of misrepresentation.

(*ii*) *By breach of duty* : If a person commits a breach of duty on account of which he gains something, while the other party loses, it will be termed as misrepresentation if it has not been done with the intention of deceiving the other party. This sub-section covers all those cases where a party, who has a duty to disclose to the other party all material facts known to him about the subject-matter, innocently does not disclose.

Example : *A* when approached by a life insurance agent for insuring his life, states his age to be 25, believing it to be true. His actual age is 27. The Life Insurance Corporation issues a policy in his favour charging a rate of premium lower than what if should have charged for the actual age of *A*. There is misrepresentation by *A*.

(*iii*) *Causing mistake by innocent misrepresentation* : If on account of misrepresentation of a fact, though not fraudulent, the other party commits a mistake about something which is essential to the contract, it will be said that misrepresentation has been committed.

Example : *A* says to *B*, an intending purchaser of a house, that his house is in perfect condition not knowing that the foundation of the house is very weak and some of the walls have got big cracks. *B*, thereupon, buys the house. *A* is guilty of misrepresentation.

Effects of misrepresentation : Innocent misrepresentation of a material fact will entitle the aggrieved party to the following two rights :

1. **Right of rescission :** The aggrieved party may, it he so likes rescind the contract. However, the right of repudiation will be lost in the following circumstances :

(*i*) Where the party whose consent was caused by misrepresentation had the means to discover truth by ordinary diligence. For example, a person who bought a certain quantity of rice and who was living quite near to the place where the goods were lying, was precluded from alleging misrepresentation about its quality. This was because he could have easily discovered the truth by ordinary diligence.

(*ii*) Where the representation has not instrumental in inducing the other party to enter into a contract. The party enters into the contract in ignorance of the misrepresentation.

(*iii*) Where the party to the contract after having known the misrepresentation expressly affirms the contract or acts in such a manner as to be taken to have impliedly accepted it.

Example : *A*, by misrepresentation, leads *B* to believe erroneously that 5,000 kgs. of flour is made every day in his factory. *B* examines the accounts of the factory which show that only 4,000 kgs. of flour has been made out daily in the past. *B* purchases the factory. *B* cannot avoid the contract for there is no misrepresentation. *B* shall be deemed not to have relied upon the information given to him by *A* but upon his own knowledge. He had verified the true state of affairs and he had full opportunity to disbelieve the statement of *A*.

(*iv*) Where the interest of the third party has intervented before the exercise of the right of rescission of the contract by the party entitled to do so. Repudiation must be done with all haste, since if the rights of third parties for value intervene, the right of repudiation will be lost. Of course the third party must have acquired interest in the subject matter for consideration and in good faith.

2. **Right to claim damages :** Ordinarily, innocent misrepresentation does not entitled the aggrieved party to claim damages. He can simply insist on restitution, *i.e.*, for being restored to the position occupied by him before the entered into the contract. But in the following circumstances the aggrieved party may claim damages :

(*i*) Where innocent misrepresentation was embodied in the contract as a condition or a warranty, damages can be claimed for breach of the condition or warranty.

(*ii*) According to the provisions of the Companies Act, promoters shall be liable for damages to the aggrieved parties if the prospectus is found to have contained any innocent misrepresentation.

(*iii*) An agent, who induces another person to enter into a contract with him as agent, shall be liable for damages to such person if the representation as to his authority as an agent of another turns out to be false in spite of the fact that such misinterpretation might have been innocent.

Distinction between Fraud and Misrepresentation

1. **Intention :** Both fraud and misrepresentation imply a false statement, but in misrepresentation there is no intention to deceive or to gain an advantage as distinguished from fraud. Whereas in fraud the false statement is made deliberately or recklessly with a clear intention of deceiving the other party or inducing him to enter into a contract. Fraud is always intentional, whereas misrepresentation is innocent.

2. **Rights :** Misrepresentation makes the contract only voidable at the option of the party whose consent has been so caused. But in fraud, the injured party, besides avoiding the contract, may also claim damages sustained by him. The remedies of recession and restitution are common in both.

3. **Defence :** In the case of fraud (except fraud by silence), the person who has played it, *i.e.*, the defendant, cannot set up the defence that the injured party, *i.e.*, the plaintiff, had the means of discovering the truth or could have done so with ordinary diligence, but in the case of misrepresentation, it would be a good defence. If the party had the means of discovering the truth with ordinary diligence, but he did not care to do so, the contract shall not be voidable.

MISTAKE

Mistake means erroneous belief concerning something.[14] Mistake may be various types as shown by the chart as on follows :

14. Mistake is something different from miscalculation or error of judgement. According to Anson, "We are not concerned with cases is which a man finds the obligations of a contract more onerous than he intended, or is disappointed in the performance which he receives from the other party."

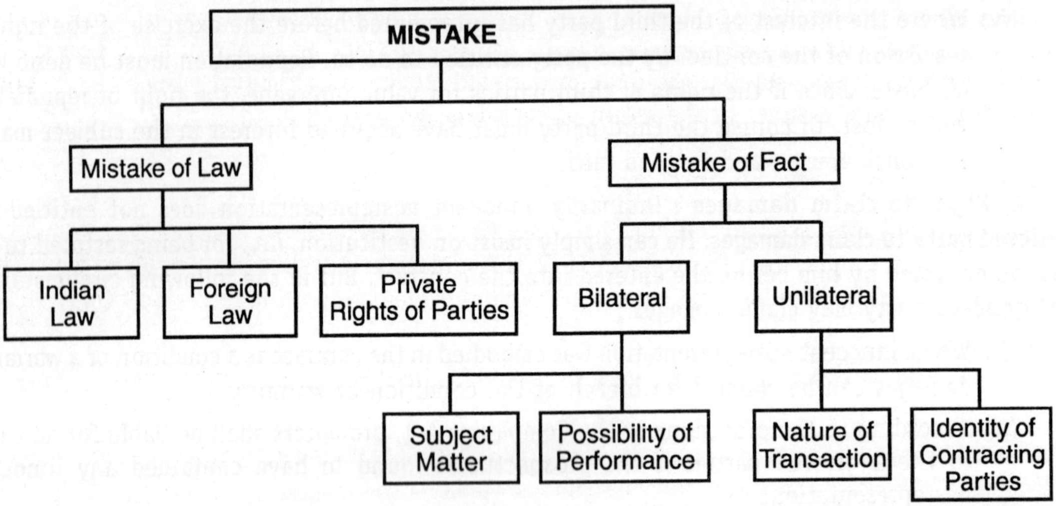

Each of the types of mistakes are being explained below :

Mistake of Law

(*a*) **Mistake as to Indian Law :** A mistake as to Indian law will not make the contract voidable. This is because every person in this country is expected to know the law of this country. Ignorance of law is no excuse (*ignorantia juris nemi nem excusat*).

Examples : (*i*) A and B make a contract on this erroneous belief that a particular debt is barred by the Indian Law of Limitation. The contract cannot be avoided on the ground of mistake because each one of them is expected to know the Law of his own country.

(*ii*) *A*, a widow is entitled to certain occupancy right. *A* remarries and believing that she has lost her occupancy rights by reasons of her remarriage, agrees to hire the same land at enhanced rate from *B*, her zamindar. Both *A* and *B* honestly believe that *A* has lost her occupancy rights. Later, she comes to know that legally her occupancy rights were not withdrawn by her remarriage. She wants to avoid the new agreement. Can she do so?

The widow cannot avoid the new contract. The mistake is as to Indian Law and everybody is expected to know the law of the land. Such a mistake is not a 'mistake' within the meaning of section 20 of the Act. She is, therefore, bound by the new agreement.

However, if a person enters into a contract by making a mistake of law, through the inducement of another, intentional or innocent, the party whose consent is so caused shall have the right to avoid the contract.

(*b*) **Mistake as to foreign law :** Mistake as to a foreign law has the *same effect as a mistake of fact*, and, therefore, the contract can be avoided.

Example : *A* and *B* purchase and sell a plot of land of 192 sq. meters in Dublin believing that a house can be constructed over it. Actually it turns out that in Dublin no house can be constructed on a plot of less than 200 sq. metres. The contract can be avoided.

(*c*) **Mistake as to private rights of the parties :** Existence of private rights is a matter of fact, though depending on the rules of law. A mistake about such rights is considered as a *mistake of fact* and the contract can be avoided on the basis.

Example : *R* after building a house on land purchased from *M*, discovered that the real owner of the land was *X*. This fact was also unknown to *M*. He had sold the land on an honest belief that the land did belong to him. It was held that the contract was void on account of mutual mistakes as to private rights and *R* was only entitled to the return of consideration paid by him.[15]

Mistake of Fact (*Secs. 20 and 22*)

(*A*) **Bilateral mistake :** According to section 20 'where both the parties to an agreement are under a mistake as to a matter of fact, essential to the agreement, the agreement shall be void.' Thus, a mistake shall be termed as bilateral mistake of fact only when both of the following two conditions are satisfied :

1. *It should be committed by both the parties :* The mistake should be common to both the parties to the agreement.

Examples : (*i*) *X* having houses, *A* and *B*, offers to sell house *A*, and *Y* not knowing that *X* has two houses thinks of house *B* and agrees to buy it. Here there is no real consent and, therefore, the contract is void on the ground of bilateral mistake of fact.

(*ii*) *A* agrees to buy from *B* a certain horse. It turns out that the horse was dead at the time of the bargain, though neither party was aware of the fact. The agreement is void.

2. *It should relate to a matter of fact essential to the agreement* : The mistake must relate to a matter of fact and not to a matter of law, expectations or opinion etc. An erroneous opinion as to the value of a thing which forms part of the subject-matter of agreement is not to be deemed to be a mistake as to a matter of fact. Such a matter of fact must be essential to the agreement, *i.e.*, affecting substance of the whole consideration.

Examples : (*i*) *A* and *B* believing themselves to be married, made a separation agreement in which *A* agreed to pay *B* £ 10 a week. It was later discovered that they were not duly married. *B* claimed the promised payments. The agreement was held to be void as there was mistake of fact on their part which was material to the existence of the agreement.[16]

(*ii*) *A* tells certain oats to *B* stating and honestly believing that they are three years old. Oats prove to be only two and half years old. Contract cannot be avoided on the ground of mistake as it is not such which affects the substance of the whole consideration.

It is to be noted that a mutual mistake of fact which goes to the very root of the agreement and frustrates the object of the agreement will make the contract not only voidable but void. There will be no contract even if the mistake is caused by the negligence of a third party.

Bilateral mistakes may be (*i*) common mistakes—when both the parties make a mistake or (*ii*) mutual mistakes—where each party makes a different mistake, *i.e.*, they misunderstand each other. Again, bilateral mistake of fact may be (*i*) as to subject-matter and (*ii*) as to possibility of performance.

(*i*) *Mistake as to subject-matter :* Mistake as to subject-matter may be of the following types :

(*a*) *Regarding existence of the subject-matter*

Example : *A* agrees to sell *B* a specific cargo of goods supposed to be on its way from England to Bombay. It turns out that, before the day of the bargain, the ship conveying the cargo has been cast away and the goods lost. Neither party was aware of the facts. The agreement is void.

15. Rani Kanwar *v.* Mahbub Baksh (1930) 28 All. L.J. 327.

16. Galloway *v.* Galloway (1914) 30 T.L.R. 531.

But in circumstances where the seller is deemed to have warranted the existence of the goods, the seller may be held liable to the buyer for breach of contract, if the goods are non-existent.

Example : *C* invited tenders for the purchase of a wrecked oil tanker and *M* submitted a tender for £ 285, which was accepted. *M* spent considerable sum in searching for the tanker and found that no tanker had been wrecked in the named locality. *M* was allowed to claim £ 285 as damages from *C* on ground of breach of contract by *C*. The defence of *C* that the contract was nullified by mistake was not accepted. "A party cannot rely on mutual mistake where the mistake consists of a belief...entertained by him without any reasonable ground and...deliberately induced by him in the mind of the other party." It was held that no condition could be implied that the contract was not to become binding if the tanker was not in existence.[17]

(b) Regarding identify of the subject-matter

Example : *R* and *W* entered into a contract for the sale of cargo to arrive ex-*'Peerless'* from Bombay. There were two ships of that name sailing about the same time from Bombay and each party had a different ship in his mind. The contract was held to be void for mutual or bilateral mistake.[18]

(c) Regarding title to the subject-matter

Example : At an auction to take a lease of a fishery from *B*. It was unknown to both the parties that fishery actually belonged to *A*. Held, that the agreement was void.

(d) Regarding quality of the subject-matter

Example : At an auction sale table napkins were sold by this description. 'With the crest of Charles I and the authentic property of that monarch.' Actually the napkins were Georgian, but both the parties were ignorant of it. It was held that the agreement was void.[19]

(e) Regarding quantity of the subject-matter

Example : *P* enquired about the price of rifles from-stating that he may buy as many as 50. On receipt of a reply from *H, P* wired 'send three rifles.' The telegraph clerk by mistake transcribed the message as sent the rifles.' *H* sent 50 rifles. *P* accepted only three and returned the rest. *H* filed a case against *P* for damages arising out of non-acceptance of 47 rifles. It was held that there was no *consensus-ad-idem* on account of the mistake of a third party and, therefore, there was no contract. *P* was not held to be liable for damages but was required to pay the price of the three rifles.[20]

(f) Regarding price of the subject-matter

Examples : (*i*) A contract of lease of a house was agreed at a rent of £ 230 p.m. but in the written contract the figure was put as £130 by mistake. Held, that the contract was unenforceable.

(*i*) L & Sons dealers of 'Hindustan 10' motor cars and sold one such car to *A* for a sum of ₹ 9,350 which they believed and represented to be the controlled price of the said car. *A* also paid the price on the belief that the price represented by L & Sons was the controlled price. In fact the controlled price was ₹ 8,195. Held, that the sum of ₹ 1,155 had been paid in excess under a mistake of fact and recoverable by the purchaser.[21]

(*ii*) **Mistake as to the possibility of performance :** If the existence of a certain state of circumstances is essential for the performance of the contract, the contract will be void on the ground of mistake, if both the parties were ignorant about the non-existence of such circumstances at the time of the contract.

---

17. McRae *v.* Commonwealth Disposals Commission (1951) 84 C.L.R. (Australia).
18. Reffles *v.* Wincelhays (1864) 2 H. & C. 906.
19. Nicholson & Venn *v.* Smith Marriott (1947) 177 L.J. 189.
20. Henkel *v.* Pope (1870) L.R. 6 Ex 7.
21. Lakshmana Prasad & Sons *v.* Achutan, A.I.R. (1952) Mad. 799.

Examples : (*i*) *A* hires a room from *B* for watching the coronation procession of King Edward VII. Unknown to both the parties the procession had already been cancelled. The contract is void.

(*ii*) *A* agrees to marry *B*, after taking the consent of *B*'s father *C*. Unknown to both the parties *C* had already died at the time of making of the contract. The contract is void.

(*B*) **Unilateral mistake :** If the mistake is only unilateral, *i.e.*, one party to a contract is under a mistake of fact, the contract is not voidable. Unilateral mistakes do not affect the validity of contract unless they concern some fundamental fact and the other party is aware of the mistake. An error of judgement of one party, a mistake regarding one's ability to perform the promise, a mistake by one party in the expression of his intention or as to the meaning of a trade description, when goods are sold under that trade description, will not enable the party giving consent under such mistakes to avoid the contract.

Examples : (*i*) *A* agreed to buy certain oats from *B* believing that they were old. In fact oats offered were new. It was held that *A* could not avoid the contract on the ground that he had a mistaken impression as to the oldness of oats.[22]

(*ii*) *A* intends to sell his house. B intending to offer ₹ 3,000 for it, by mistake offers ₹ 5,000. *A* accepts the offer. The contract cannot be avoided by *B* on the ground of mistake.

However, a contract can be avoided on the ground of unilateral mistake if it can be shown that mistake was caused by fraud or misrepresentation on the part of the other party. Such a mistake may be committed either about the nature of the contract itself or about the identity of the contracting party. Contract shall also be void where the offerer makes a material mistake in expressing his intention and the other party knows or is deemed to know the error.[23] But if there is a mistake on the part of one party alone and the other does not, or cannot be deemed to know of the mistake, the contract is binding. Mistakes due to the carelessness of the party will not give any right to such a party to avoid the contract.[24]

Unilateral mistake may be of two types :

1. *Mistake as to the nature of the transaction :* A contract shall be void if a party to the contract without any fault of his own, makes a mistake about the very nature of the contract. It may be because of the blindness, illiteracy or servility of the person signing the contract or due to the trick or fraudulent misrepresentation as to the nature of the document.

Examples : (*i*) A document was placed by *A* before an old gentleman *B*. *B* was falsely told that it was a guarantee and he, intending to sign a guarantee, wrote his name on the document in the belief that it was a guarantee. In fact the document was a bill of exchange which was later on endorsed by *A* to *C*, a *bona fide* holder for value. It was held that *A* was not liable for the bill as his signature was fraudulently obtained to a document which he had never intended to sign. There was no consent and consequently there was no contract.[25] A deed executed by a person in such circumstances is a nullity.[26]

(*ii*) A person was induced to sign a deed of exchange and gift on the representation that it was a power of attorney. It was held that there was no contract as his mind did not go with her signature.[27]

An agreement, however, is not a nullity because a party who knew its general character failed to read all its terms or to appreciate them (See chapter 2, special conditions attached to an offer).

---

22. Smith *v*. Jughes (1872) 6 Q.B. 597.
23. Hartog *v*. Colin & Shields (1939).
24. Higgens *v*. Northampton Corporation (1927).
25. Foster *v*. Mckinnon (1869) L.R. 4C.P. 704.
26. Oriental Bank *v*. Fleming, 3 Bom. 242, 267.
27. Surat Chander *v*. Kanai Lal (1921) Cal 786.

But the position stated above is different, because in each of the above cases the document has been signed under a complete misapprehension of its character. In such cases, the plea that the instrument is not my act (*non test factum*) is available.[28]

2. *Mistake as to the identity of the contracting party* : Mistake as to the identity of the person will make the contract void only when the intention was to enter into a contract only with a particular person other than the person with whom the contract has been entered into.[29] Contract shall be valid and binding in spite of the mistake as to the identity of parties in all those cases where the parties were prepared to enter into contract with any person. Mistake as to the identity of a party is to be distinguished from mistake as to the attributes or motives of the person, such as creditworthiness of a man, the latter will not nullify the contract. It may, at the most, make the contract voidable for fraud [*See illustration (iv) given below*].

When a contract is made in which personalities of the contracting parties are or may be of importance, no other person can interpose and adopt the contract.

Mistake as to the identity of the person with whom the contract is made will nullify the contract only if the identity is of material importance to the contract and the mistake is known to the other person.

Examples : (*i*) The managing director of a theatre gave instruction that no tickets were to sold to *S.S* knowing this, asked a friend to buy a ticket for him. With this ticket *S* went to the theatre but was refused admission. His suit for damages for breach of contract was dismissed by the court on the ground that the whole agreement is void for mistake as to identity of the parties. There is no privity of contract between *S* and the managing director of the theatre. The latter had no intention to enter into any contract with *S*, which he had expressed by refusing to issue him a ticket.[30]

(*ii*) *X* falsely representing herself as the wife of a well-known millionaire takes a ring from a jeweller's shop for the approval of her husband. She pledges it with a pawnbroker, who in good faith and without notice of the first transaction pays her ₹ 10,000. Can the jeweller recover the ring from the pawnbroker?

In this case, there was no contract between the jeweller and the woman and the pawnbroker does not get good title and must return the ring to the jeweller. Through the woman got possession physically, there was no mental assent, as the jeweller intended to deal not with her but quite a different person *viz*, the wife of the millionaire.[31]

(*iii*) A person named Blenkarn taking advantage of similarity of his name with Blenkiron & Co., wrote to Lindsay & Co. to supply goods on credit. Lindsay & Co. mistook his order for that of Blenkiron & Co. (as his signature on the order was similar to that of Blenkiron) a respectable firm and delivered the goods to Blenkarn. Blenkarn sold these goods to Cundy but did not pay Lindsay & Co. On a suit being filed by Lindsay & Co. against Cundy for recovery of goods or their price, it was held that owing to mistake caused by Blenkarn, there was no real agreement between him and Lindsay & Co. Cundy did not get any title to the goods and therefore he should return the goods or pay for them.[32]

(*iv*) A man, North, called in person at jeweller's shop and chose some articles of jewellery which the shop-keeper agreed to sell him as a causal customer. He tendered in payment a cheque which he signed in the name of Sir G.B., a person of credit. Thereupon, the jeweller allowed him to take away

28. Keith's Elements of Contracts.
29. Cundy *v*. Lindsay & Co. (1878) 3 A.C. 459.
30. S. Said *v*. Butt (1920) 3 K.B. 497.
31. Lake *v*. Simmons (1927) A.C. 487.
32. Cundy *v*. Lindsay & Co. (infra).

a valuable ring which North pledged with Brooks, who had no notice of fraud. In a suit by the jeweller for the return of the ring, it was held that Brooks, the pawnbroker, had good title to the ring because of contract between North and jeweller was good until the jeweller disaffirmed it. Although the jeweller believed the person to whom he was handing over the ring is Sir G.B., he in fact contracted to sell and deliver to the person who came into his shop. The contract, therefore, was not void on the ground of mistake but voidable on the ground of fraud. It may further be noted that under The Sale of Goods Act the property in the goods passes to the buyer as soon as the contract is made. Goods may be delivered later on. In this case the contract had already been made before the seller took the buyer as Sir G.B., because the cheque was signed later on. But if North had spoken on the telephone that he was Sir G.B., or on entering the shop he had introduced himself as Sir G.B., the contract would have been void on the ground of mistake as to the identify of the contracting parties.[33]

Illustration (*iv*) is to be distinguished from illustration (*i*) to (*iii*) explained above. Though all are cases of fraud, but in case of illustrations (*i*) to (*iii*) there is no contract at all on the ground of want of consent, while in case of illustration (*iv*) there is a contract which is voidable on the ground of fraud. In illustration (*iii*), the deception was effected by a letter, but in illustration (*iv*) the situation is different because the deceived person was treated with fraud face to face. In all the four illustrations, the consequences so far as the person practising the fraud is concerned, are the same, but as explained above they are different and of considerable importance for third parties acting *bona fide*.

KEY TERMS

- **Coercion :** Committing or threatening to commit any Act forbidden by the Indian Penal Code or unlawful detaining or threatening to detain any property to the prejudice of any person whatsoever with the intention of causing any person to enter into an agreement.
- **Consent :** Agreeing upon the same thing in the same sense by the parties concerned.
- **Free Consent :** Consent is said to be free when it is not caused by coercion, undue influence, fraud, misrepresentation and mistake.
- **Undue Influence :** Obtaining unfair advantage over the other by the person enjoying a dominating position.
- **Fraud :** International misrepresentation of facts.
- **Misrepresentation :** A false representation made innocently without any intention to deceive the other party.
- **Mistake :** Erroneous belief concerning something.

TEST QUESTIONS

Objective Type : *Test Your Knowledge*

1. Fill in the blanks
   (*i*) Consensus *ad idem* means...................
   (*ii*) Intentional misrepresentation of facts is known as.......................
   (*iii*) Mistake as to identity of the contracting parties makes the contract..................
   (*iv*) Everyone is expected to know the law of........................
   (*v*) Mistake as to foreign law has the same effect as.......................

33. Phillips *v*. Brooks (1919) 2 K.B. 243.

(*vi*) Mere silence as to facts is not fraud unless the circumstances are such that regard being bad to them, it is the duty of the person........................to speak or his silence is..........................

[***Ans.*** (*i*) identity of minds; (*ii*) fraud; (*iii*) void; (*iv*) one's country; (*v*) mistake of fact;(*vi*) keeping silence, equivalent to speech]

2. Select the most appropriate answer

(*i*) A threat to file or criminal suit—

(*a*) does not amount to coercion. (*b*) amounts to coercion.

(*c*) amounts to undue influence.

(*ii*) Undue influence can be exercised only between the parties who are :

(*a*) related to each other. (*b*) not related to each other.

(*c*) friendly to each other.

(*iii*) A promise made without any intention of performing it amounts to :

(*a*) fraud, (*b*) undue influence, and

(*c*) coercion.

[***Ans.*** (*i*) (*a*); (*ii*) (*a*); (*iii*) (*a*)]

Essay Type : *For Review, Discussion and Practice*

1. 'An agreement requires a meeting of the minds.' Comment.
2. When is consent said to be given under coercion? What is the liability of a person to whom money has been paid or goods have been delivered under coercion? How coercion differs from undue influence?
3. Distinguish between fraud and misrepresentation. What is their effect on the validity of a contract?
4. "Mere silence as to facts likely to affect the willingness of a person to enter into contract is not fraud, unless the circumstances of the case are such that regard being had to them, it is the duty of the person keeping silence to speak or his silence is equivalent to speech." Explain.
5. Explain with illustration, the effect of mistake of fact on an agreement with reference to :
   (*i*) mistake relating to the subject-matter.
   (*ii*) mistake relating to the identity of parties.
6. When is a contract said to be induced by undue influence? Discuss the effect of undue influence on the formation of a contract. Under what circumstances can undue influence by presumed? (*CA Foundation, May 2001*)
7. What is the importance of distinction between Bilateral Mistake and Unilateral Mistake? (*ICWA Foundation, Dec. 1998*)
8. When can we say that consent is not free? (*ICWA Foundation, Dec. 1999*)
9. Explain each of the following statements :
   (*i*) "Amount paid under mistake of law cannot be recovered back." (*ICWA Foundation, June 1998*)
   (*ii*) Mere silence as to facts is not fraud. (*ICWA Foundation, Dec. 1998; B.Com. (Hons.), Delhi 1999, 2000, 2004, CS Foundation, 2012*)
10. Examine the validity of a contract when the acceptance from the offeree is obtained under 'Coercion' or under 'Undue influence'. Point out the distinction between 'Coercion' and 'Undue influence'. (*PEE II, November 2005; GGSIPU, BBA (H), May 2002*)
11. Distinguish between :
    (*a*) Coercion and Undue Influence (*GGSIPU, BBA (H), May 2004; B.Com. (Hons.), Delhi 2005; B.Com. (Pass), Delhi 2004, 2012*)
    (*b*) Fraud and Misrepresentation (*B.Com. (Hons.), Delhi 1988, 1998, 2013; CS Foundation, June 2004, 2012*)
12. "An attempt to deceive which does not deceive is no fraud." Comment. (*B.Com. (Hons.), Delhi 1990*)

13. What is 'undue influence'? How does it differ from 'coercion'?
(*B.Com. (Hons.), Delhi 1991, 1999; B.Com. (Pass), Delhi 2001, 2012*)
14. "The law relating to mistake is a comedy of errors." Comment. (*B.Com. Hons.), Delhi 1996*)
15. What is fraud under Indian Contract Act, 1872? (*ICWA Inter, June 2009*)
16. Write a note on "Effects of Coercion" on a contract. (*ICWA Inter, June 2009*)
17. What do you understand by "coercion" and "undue influence" under the provision of the Indian Contract Act, 1872? What are the differences between them? (*IPCE, ICWA Nov., 2011*)
18. Comment on the following statements:
(*i*) A unilateral mistake cannot become a ground to avoid the contract.
(*B.Com. (Hons.), Delhi 2012*)
(*ii*) Mental acceptance in the eyes of law is no acceptance (*B.Com. (Hons.), Delhi 2010*)
(*iii*) Consideration must be something of value but need not be adequate.
(*B.Com. (Hons.), Delhi 2012*)
19. What is undue influence? State three situations where the presumption of undue influence exists.
(*B.Com. (Hons.), Delhi 2010*)
20. Discuss the impact of mistake on the validity of the contract.(*B.Com. (Hons.), Delhi, Nov. 2013*)

PRACTICAL PROBLEMS

1. *A* sells a horse to *B* knowing well that the horse is vicious. *A* does not disclose the nature of the horse to *B*. Can *A* be made liable to *B* for the transaction.
[***Ans.*** No. *A* has no duty to disclose.]
2. Anil called at a jeweller's shop and chose a costly diamond ring. He tendered in payment a cheque which he signed in the name of Ram Chandra, a man of credit. He took the ring and pledged it to Suresh, who had no notice of the fraud. Can the jeweller recover the ring from Suresh?
[***Ans.*** No. *See* Phillip *v.* Brooks.]
3. *A*, the owner of a ship, by fraudulently representing her to be seaworthy induces *B*, an underwriter to insure the ship. Can *B* obtain cancellation of the policy?
[***Ans.*** Yes, it is a fraud on account of fraudulent misrepresentation under Section 17 of the Contract Act. Moreover, a contract of insurance is contract of *Uberrimae fidei* (*Sec. 19* of the Marine Insurance Act).
4. *A*, a dealer, sold a mare to *B* with the knowledge that the mare has cracked hoof, which *A* had filled up so as to prevent detection even after a diligent examination. Discuss the right of *B* when he subsequently detects it.
[***Ans.*** u/s 17(2) *A* is liable to *B* for playing a fraud.]
5. *A*, a man enfeebled by disease and old age induced by *B*'s influence over him as his medical attendant, to agree to pay *B* an unreasonable sum for his professional services. Discuss.
[***Ans.*** Contract is voidable at the option of *A* on account of undue influence.]
6. M/s. Ganguly & Co. Calcutta, entered into a contract with the General Manager of the Indian Railways at Calcutta for the construction of a bridge and received an advance of ₹ 10 lakhs for the same. He did not complete the work within time and the Railways terminated the contract. This contract was found to be void from its inception for not being in conformity with the Constitution of India. The Indian Railways want to recover the advance given to the contractor. Will it succeed? Discuss. (*CA. Inter, May 1989*)
[***Ans.*** The agreement is void on account of both the parties being under a mistake of law. As per the principle of restitution, the Indian Railways can recover the advance of ₹ 10 lakhs.]
7. The Manager of a Cinema Theatre gave instructions that no tickets were to be sold to *R.R* knowing this, asked his friend to buy a ticket for him. With this ticket *R* went to the theatre but was refused admission. He filed a suit for damages for breach of contract against the theatre. Would he succeed?

Decide giving the provisions of the Indian Contract Act in this regard.

(*CA. Inter, Nov. 1989*)

[**Ans.** *R* would not succeed since the Manager had no intention to enter into contract with him.]

8. A Hindu, well advanced in age, with the object of securing benefits to his soul in the next world, gave away his whole property to his "Guru" or spiritual adviser. Is it a valid contract?

(*ICWA Foundation, June 1998, June 2000*)

[**Ans.** The contract can be void on the ground of undue influence.]

9. *A* applies to a banker for a loan at a time when there is stringency in the money market. The banker reluctantly gives the loan but at an unusual high rate of interest. *A* accepts the loan on the terms at high interest itself. Subsequently, *A* agitates that the transaction was under undue influence. Will he succeed? (*ICWA Foundation, June 1999*)

[**Ans.** *A* will not succeed since there seems to be no undue influence.]

10. A lady *X* induced a jeweller to deliver possession of two pearl necklaces falsely representing that she was the wife of a very prominent M.P. and that she wanted them for showing to her husband for his approval. It is a valid contract? (*ICWA Foundation, June 2000*)

[**Ans.** There is mistake as to identity of person and hence there is no valid contract.]

11. *A* finds a ring of *B* and sells it to a third person who purchases if for value and in good faith. Can the true owner *i.e.,* *B* can compel the innocent purchaser to restore the ring?

(*ICWA Foundation Dec. 2000*)

[**Ans.** *A* does not get any title and hence cannot transfer any title to an innocent purchaser. *B* can recover the ring.]

12. *A* has two houses, one situated in South Delhi and the other in Noida. He offers to sell his Noida House to *B* while *B* is under the impression that he is buying the South Delhi House. Comment.

(*ICWA Foundation, June, 2000*)

[**Ans.** There is no consent. Hence there is no contract.]

13. *A* money lender, advances ₹ 100 to *B*, an agriculturist and by undue influence, induces *B* to execute a bond for ₹ 200 with 6% interest per month. Advise *B*.

(*ICWA Foundation, June 2001*)

[**Ans.** The agreement is voidable on the ground of undue influence.]

14. Arun has two cars – one of white colour and another of red colour. He offers to sell one of the cars to Basu thinking that he is selling the car which has white colour. Basu agrees to buy the car thinking that Arun is selling the car which has red colour. Will this agreement become a valid contract? Give reasons. (*CS Foundation, June 2004*)

[**Ans.** The agreement between Arun and Basu will not become a valid contract because there is no consensus ad idem.]

15. *A* applies to a bank for a loan at a time when there is stringency in the money market. The bank agrees to give loan but at a rate higher than the usual market rate. *A* accepts the loan on these terms. Can *A* prove that the contract was induced by undue influence?

(*B.Com. (Hons.), Delhi 2005*)

[**Ans.** *A* cannot prove that the contract was induced by undue influence. This is a transaction in the ordinary course of business, and the contract is not induced by undue influence.]

16. *A* at a pistol point asked *B* to sell his car for ₹ 10,000 only. *B* sold his car. Can *B* avoid the contract? Give full reasons for your answer. (*B.Com. (Hons.), Delhi 1999*)

[**Ans.** Yes, *B* can avoid the contract as his consent has been obtained by coercion.]

17. *A* intends to sell his horse to *B*. *A*'s horse is not sound. He prepares a forged certificate of fitness seemingly issued by a Veterinary Doctor. He pastes the certificate on the door of the stable. *B*, without looking at the certificate, enters the stable and purchases the horse. Later on *B* comes to know that horse is not sound. Can *B* now cancel the contract on the basis of fraud of *A*? Give reasons. (*B.Com. (Hons.), Delhi 2005*)

[**Ans.** *B* will not succeed because he has not been deceived by the fraud of *A*.]

18. Ajeet, owner of an apple orchard, believes that all the apple trees in his orchard are fruit-bearing trees. However, he has no sufficient ground for his belief. Even then, Ajeet states to Baljeet that his orchard has all fruit-bearing trees. Induced by this statement, Baljeet purchases the orchard. Later on, it is found that only 50% trees are fruit-bearing. Now, Baljeet files a suit for the repudiation of contract. Will Baljeet succeed? Give reasons. *(CS Foundation, Dec. 2006)*

[***Ans.*** Baljeet will succeed.]

19. *G* applies to Colours Bank for a loan of ₹ 80,000 needed for one year. The bank agrees to the loan at a high rate of interest because of the recession in the Indian Capital Market. *G* accepts the loan on these conditions. On due date, *G* refuses to pay back the loan. He (*G*) pleads that the contract has been procured by exercising undue influence. The bank files a suit against *G* for recovery of the said lien. *(PEE-II, ICAI, June 2009)*

[***Ans.*** It is a transaction in the ordinary course of banking business. Hence, the argument of *G* is not tenable and the bank would be given relief by the court for recovery of the said loan.]

20. Aamond has authority from his principal Binod to sell goods on credit. Aamod sells goods on credit to Chandan without making the proper and usual enquires as to Chandan's solvency. At the time of such sale Chandan was insolvent. Should Aamod compensate Binod? *(CS Foundation, Dec. 2008)*

[***Ans.*** Yes, Aamod must compensate Binod.]

21. Mr. *X* buys a ring from Mr. *Y* at a low price employing 'undue influence' and sells the ring to Mr. *Z* who purchased against consideration and without knowing of Mr. *X*'s 'undue influence'. Can Mr. *Y* recover the ring from *Z*? *(ICWA, Inter. Dec., 2010)*

[***Ans.*** Mr. *Y* can not recover the ring from Mr. *Z*]

22. Mr. Sadhu offers to sell his house to Mr. Sarkar at ₹ 221 lakhs but by mistake makes the offer in writing for ₹ 212 lakhs which was accepted by Mr. Sarkar. Can Mr. Sadhu plead the mistake as defence? *(ICWA, Inter. June 2011)*

[***Ans.*** No. Mr. Sadhu can't plead mistake as defence after acceptance of the offer.]

Chapter 5

CONSIDERATION

LEARNING OBJECTIVES

A careful study of this chapter will enable you to :

- understand the concept of consideration;
- describe the essential elements of consideration;
- understand the importance of adequacy of consideration;
- identify the cases where the contract without consideration will be valid; and
- explain the meaning of certain key terms.

MEANING OF CONSIDERATION

Consideration is an essential element of a valid contract. An agreement without consideration is a bare promise and is not binding on the parties (*ex nudo pacto non aritio actio*).

Consideration, broadly speaking, is the price said by the promisee for the obligation of the promisor. The term is used in the sense of *quid pro quo i.e.*, 'something in return'. According to Sir F. Pollock, it is the 'price for which a promise is bought'.

In an English case: *Currie v. Misa*[1] the term consideration was defined as 'some right, interest, profit or benefit, accruing to one party or some forbearance, detriment loss or responsibility given or undertaken by the other'.

Thus, consideration need not be a benefit to the promisor. If the promisee has suffered some loss or detriment, it will be taken as a sufficient consideration for the promisor to fulfil his promise.

According to *Section 2(d)* of the Indian Contract Act 'when at the desire of the promisor, the promisee or any other person has done or abstained from doing or does or abstains from doing or promises to do or to abstain from doing something, such act or abstinence, or promise is called a consideration for the promise.' Consideration, therefore, may be described as something accepted or agreed upon as a return, or equivalent for the promise made. It implies some benefit to the promisor and some injury or inconvenience to the promisee.

Examples : (*i*) *A* agrees to sell his car to *B* for a sum of ₹ 10,000. For *A*'s promise the consideration is a sum of ₹ 10,000 while for *B*'s promise consideration is the car.

(*ii*) The secretary of a Mosque Committee filed a suit to enforce a promise to subscribe ₹ 500 for the rebuilding of the mosque. Court dismissed the suit on the ground that there was no consideration in the sense of benefit. It was held that 'the person who made the promise gained nothing in return for the promise made and the secretary of the committee to whom the promise was made suffered nothing in getting the promise from the subscriber.'[2]

---

1. (1875) L.R. 10 Exch. 153.
2. Abdul Aziz *v.* Masum Ali (1914) 36 All. 268.

(*iii*) In another case of similar nature, where the secretary had acted on the faith of the promise and incurred a liability, the court enforced the claim for the recovery of the amount to the extent of the liability incurred by the promisee.[3]

ESSENTIAL ELEMENTS OF CONSIDERATION

Following are the essential elements of consideration :

1. **Consideration should be furnished at the desire of the promisor :** The first essential element in the definition of 'consideration' is that *the act or forbearance of the promisee or any other person must be done at the desire or request of the promisor.* The desire of the promisor can be implied from the conduct of the parties. Distinction must be made between purely voluntary acts and acts done at the instance of the other party. Acts done on the request of a third person or without the desire of the promisor, *i.e.,* voluntary acts would not constitute good consideration in the eyes of law. It is not necessary that the promisor himself should be benefited by the consideration. It is enough if the act or forbearance constituting consideration was done or given at the promisor's request. On the same principle, plaintiff supplying goods to a third person on credit at the request of the defendant is a good consideration for the guarantee given by the defendant to the plaintiff.

Examples : (*i*) *A*'s son is lost and *B* voluntarily goes in search for him. *B* cannot claim any remuneration or reward for finding out *B*'s son because he had not done it at *A*'s request.

(*ii*) *D* was requested by the collector of the city to spend some money on the improvement of the market. Shopkeepers using the market later on promised to give *D* a commission on articles sold. On a suit by *D* for the recovery of that commission, it was held that he could not demand payment as the consideration did not pass at the desire of the shopkeepers.[4]

2. **Consideration may move from the promisee or any other person :** It is not necessary that consideration should proceed only from the promisee. Consideration furnished by a third party will also be valid if it has been done at the desire of the promisor. This is termed as *'Doctrine of Constructive Consideration'.*

Example : *A*, by a deed of gift, transferred whole of his property in favour of his daughter *C* with instruction that *C* would pay a definite amount as annuity to her uncle *B*. *C* by an agreement on the same date with *B*, promised to carry out *A*'s directions. On *C*'s denial to fulfil the promise on the ground that there was no consideration from *B*, it was held that consideration indirectly moved from *A*'s brother and, therefore, *B* was entitled to recover the amount of annuity.[5]

It is to be noted that though consideration for an agreement may proceed from a third party, it does not follow that the third party can sue on the agreement.

Example : *A*'s father *B* gives an Ambassador car to *C*.*C* in consideration of this promise promises with *A* to give him a Fiat car. On *C*'s refusal to give car to *A*, *B* cannot take any action against him because he not a party to the contract.

Thus, it follows that a stranger to the consideration can only sue another party to a contract to enforce the contract provided he is a party to the contract. A stranger to the contract, however, cannot enforce the promise.

3. **Consideration may be a promise to do something or abstain from doing some-thing:** Consideration may be either negative or positive, *i.e.,* an act to do or not to do something.

---

3. Kedar Nath *v.* Gorie Mohamed (1886) 14 Cal. 64.
4. Durga Prasad *v.* Baldco (1880) 3 All 221.
5. Chinnaya *v.* Ramayya (1881) 4 Mad. 137.

Examples : (*i*) *A* is indebted to *B* to the extent of ₹ 1,000. The debt falls due and *A* fails to pay. *C* promises to stand surety for *A* if *B* does not file a suit against *A*, to which *B* agrees. *B*'s promise regarding forbearance to sue *A* is a good consideration for *C*'s standing as surety.

(*ii*) *B* files a suit against *A* for his failure to pay a sum of ₹ 1,000 on the due date. *C* agrees to pay this amount if *B* withdraws the suit. The suit is withdrawn. *C* is liable to pay the money to *B*.

4. **Consideration may be past, present or future :** Where the promisor had received consideration before the date of the promise, the consideration is termed as *'past consideration'.*

Example : *A* looks after the children of *B* at *B*'s request. A year later *B* agrees to pay *A* a sum of ₹ 1,000 for his services. For the promise of *B*, the services of *A* will be taken as past consideration.

When the promisor receives consideration simultaneously with his promise, the consideration is termed as *'present consideration'.*

Example : *A* agrees to sell his car to *B* for a sum of ₹ 10,000. *B* pays money to *A* at the time of making of the contract. Consideration will be taken as 'present' for *A*

Where the promisor has to receive consideration in future for his promise, the consideration is said to be *'future consideration'.*

Examples : (*i*) *A* looks after the children of *B* and *B* promises to pay *A* all expenses incurred by him in this connection at the end of the year. Consideration is a future one for *A*

(*ii*) On 15th of January, *A* promises to sell his house to *B* for a sum of ₹ 15,000 after fifteen days. Price and property both are to be delivered on a future date and, therefore, consideration in future for both the parties.

5. **There must be an independent consideration to support each independent promise :** A single consideration cannot support two agreements between the same parties unless one of the agreements is a gratuitous promise. There must be as many considerations as the number of contracts. Each agreement in order to be binding must be supported by an independent consideration of its own. It is immaterial that the contract is between the same parties.

6. **Consideration must be real and not illusory, illegal, impossible, uncertain, ambiguous, fraudulent, immoral or opposed to public policy :** Compromising disputed claims, forbearing to sue or to exercise an actually existing and enforceable right are all good considerations for fresh promises. But, when there is a *pre-existing legal obligation* on the part of the promisee by which he is bound to do something and does it, that act cannot be a competent consideration for a promise. Consideration must be something more than the promisee is already bound to do for the promisor. If the promisee did what he was already bound to do, there would be no consideration. A promise to pay an existing debt punctually if the creditor gives a discount is without consideration and the discount cannot be enforced. But where a person promises to do more than what he is legally bound to do, such a promise, if not opposed by public policy, shall be a good and a valid consideration.[6] An agreement by a client to pay his lawyer after the latter had been engaged, a certain sum of money over and above the fee, in the event of success in the case would be void being without consideration.[7] But, where police was requested to arrange for stationary guard for the safety of some property on payment of reasonable remuneration in case where police had thought surveillance by a mobile force to be adequate, the promise to pay the remuneration shall not be without consideration because the

6. Glassbrook Brothers *v.* Glamorgan County Council (1925) A.C. 270.
7. Ramchandra Chintaman *v.* Kalu Raju (1877) 2 Bom. 362.

acceptance by the police to provide more protection than what was deemed to be necessary is a good consideration for the promise of reward.

Consideration is always given in exchange of some benefit accruing or to make good the injury caused to the other party. Consideration should not be fraudulent, forbidden by law or immoral or opposed to public policy. It should not cause injury to any person or property if allowed to be exchanged (*Sec. 23*).

Examples : (*i*) *A* threatens to sue *B*. *B* promises to pay *A* ₹ 1,000 in consideration of *A* agreeing not to sue. *A* had no cause of action against *B*. Is it a valuable consideration in the eyes of law?

Yes. The promise by *B* to pay *A* ₹ 1,000 in consideration of agreeing not to sue, is a good consideration irrespective of the fact that *A* had no cause of action against *B*. If *B* feels himself aggrieved, he has the right to proceed against *A* to test his claim. Refraining of *A* is a valuable consideration to support the promise of *B*.

(*ii*) *A* has contracted to serve throughout a voyage and under any emergency on board a ship. During the voyage some of his fellow seamen deserted. The master of the ship then agreed with the remaining seamen, including *A*, that he would divide the wages of the deserters among them. Can *A* claim the extra wages?

No. The promise of the master of the ship to divide the wages of the deserters among the other employees is not supported by any consideration and, therefore, void. *A* was under an already existing obligation to serve the master throughout the voyage and also under any emergency on board the ship. He cannot claim any extra wages under the second promise of the master as it is not supported by any fresh consideration on the part of *A*.

7. **Consideration must be valuable in the eyes of law :** It must be capable of being valued in terms of money or money's worth. It must result in gain to one and loss to other. Sand near the river bank has no value but the moment it is brought near the building site, it acquires value. Oxygen is a free gift of nature and, therefore, has no value. But the moment it is packed in gas cylinders and is supplied to the hospitals it acquires value.

ADEQUACY OF CONSIDERATION

Consideration need not be adequate. Inadequacy of consideration will not invalidate a contract.

Example : *A* sells his horse worth ₹ 30,000 for a sum of ₹ 10,000 to *B*. The consideration, though inadequate, will not affect the validity of the contract.

However, if the consideration is shockingly inadequate and one party alleges that his consent was not free, the court will take inadequacy of consideration as an evidence in support of such allegation.

Example : *A* agrees to sell a horse worth ₹ 10,000 for ₹ 100. *A* denies that his consent to the agreement was freely given.

The inadequacy of consideration is a fact which the court should take into account in deciding whether or not *A*'s consent was freely given.

Thus, a party cannot set aside a contract on the ground of inadequacy of consideration. Inadequacy of consideration can help him in setting aside the contract only when his consent was not free. It has, therefore, been correctly observed, that, 'in many cases the doctrine of consideration is a mere technicality, irreconciliable either with business expediency or common sense.'

EXCEPTIONS : NO CONSIDERATION, NO CONTRACT

Contracts without consideration are void. According to *Salmond and Winfield* 'A promise without consideration is a gift; one made for a consideration is a bargain.' However, in the following circumstances a contract without consideration will be perfectly valid :

1. **Promise made on account of natural love and affection :** No consideration is required when a contract is made (*i*) on account of natural love and affection between the parties, (*ii*) standing in a near relation to each other, (*iii*) is in writing, and (*iv*) registered under law for the time being in force for the registration of documents [*Sec. 21 (1)*]. It is to be noted that nearness of relationship does not necessarily impart natural love and affection.

Examples : (*i*) *A*, out of his love and affection, promises to give his wife, *B*, ₹ 1,000. This promise is put into writing and is registered. It will be a valid contract without consideration.

(*ii*) *B* after referring to persistent quarrels and disagreement between himself and his wife *R*, promised in writing to pay his wife a sum of money for her maintenance and separate residence. The agreement was also registered. It was held that the promise was not enforceable because it was not entered out of natural love and affection.[8]

2. **Promise to compensate for voluntary services :** When a contract relates to a promise to compensate wholly or in part a person who had already voluntarily done something for the promisor or something which the promisor could be legally compelled to do [*Sec. 25 (2)*]. The act must have been done voluntarily and for the promisor, who must have been in existence at the time when the act was done. The intention of the promisor must have been to compensate the promisee.

Examples : (*i*) *A* finds *B*'s purse and gives it to him. *B* promises to give *A* ₹ 100. This will be a valid contract without any formal consideration.

(*ii*) *A* supports *B*'s infant son. *B* promises to pay *A*'s expenses in so doing. This is a contract.

The difference between a promise given on the basis of past consideration [*Sec. 2(d)*] and a promise given under the above provision [*Sec. 25(2)*] is to be noted. In case the services are rendered at the request of the promisor the matter will fall within the purview of section 2(*d*). While in those cases where the services are rendered voluntarily and a promise is made to compensate for such services the matter will fall within the purview of section 25(2). However, ultimate effect will be same in both the cases, *i.e.*, the promisor will be bound by his promise.

3. **Promise to pay a time-barred debt :** When a debtor makes a written promise under his signature or that of his agent to pay a time-barred debt no fresh consideration is required for this fresh promise [*Sec. 23*(3)]. A mere acknowledgement of a time-barred debt will not be sufficient. There should be a distinct, definite or express promise to pay the debt, which must be a liquidated or an ascertained sum of money.

Example : *A* owes *B* ₹ 1,000 but the debt is barred by The Limitation Act. *A signs a written promise to pay B* ₹ 500 on account of the debt. This will be a valid contract.

In the case of a time-barred debt, the question of reviving the right does not arise for it was never lost. It had always existed, only the remedy had been destroyed by lapse of time which is being now revived by new promise.

4. **Contracts of agency :** According to section 185 of the Indian Contract Act consideration is not required to create an agency.

---

8. Rajlucky Dabee *v.* Bhoothnath (1900) 4 C.W.N. 488.

5. **Completed gifts :** Absence of consideration shall also not affect the validity as between the donor and donee of any gift actually made. [Explanation (2) of section 25]. Thus, gifts once made cannot be recovered on the ground of absence of consideration.

Difference between the Rights of a Stranger to a Contract and a Stranger to the Consideration

According to Indian Contract Act, consideration for an agreement may proceed from a third party, but the third party cannot sue on the agreement. Person, who is a party to the contract, alone can enforce the legal rights arising there from. Since the third party has no *locus standing* in a contract, he is debarred from interfering with the contractual rights or obligations of the parties. *For example*, in a case where a purchaser of mortgaged property agreed with the vendor that he would pay the mortgaged debt, it was held on a suit being filed by the mortgagee that he could not enforce the contract against the purchaser because he was not a party to the contract. A person may be a stranger to the consideration but he should not a stranger to the contract.

A stranger to the consideration can sue to enforce it provided, he is party to the contract, but a person who is not a party to a contract, *i.e.*, a stranger, cannot file a suit to enforce any of the rights arising out of the contract. A contract, therefore, can neither confer any rights nor impose any liability upon a person who is not a party to it. *Lord Haldane* in *Dunlop Co. v. Selfridge.*[9] observed that *'only a person who is a party to a contract can sue on it.'* This rule prevents imposition of contractual obligations upon a person without his consent.

Example : *D* bought tyres from Dunlop Rubber Co. and sold them to *S*, a sub-dealer, who agreed with *D* not to sell below Dunlop's list price and to pay to Dunlop Co. £ 5 as damages on every tyre he undersells. *S* sold two tyres at less that the list price, and thereupon, the Dunlop Co. sued him for the breach. Will the Dunlop Co. succeed?

No. Dunlop Co. cannot claim the benefit of the contract as against *S*, a sub-dealer. There is no privity of contract between the two.[10]

Under the Monopolies and Restrictive Trade Practices Act, 1969, however, now the ruling in the above case may no longer be valid. A retailer who obtains goods from a wholesaler with notice of restrictive conditions imposed on the resale of the goods by the original supplier may be bound by such conditions even though they arose from the contract between the wholesaler and the supplier to which the retailer was not a party.[11]

Exceptions : Following are the important exceptions to the above rule under which third parties, which are strangers to the contract, can bring a suit to enforce their rights arising from a contract.

1. **Beneficiaries in the case of trust :** Beneficiary, in the case of a trust, can enforce his rights given to him under the trust, though he was not a party to the contract between the settler and the trustees.

Example : *A* establishes a trust for the benefit of *B* and appoints *C*, *D* and *E* as trustees. *B* can sue for benefits available to him under trust though he is not a party to the contract.

2. **In case of provision in marriage settlement of minors.**

Example : The father of the bridegroom and the father of the bridge entered into a contract whereby it was agreed that in consideration of marriage the father of the bridgegroom would pay a

9. (1915) A.C. 847.
10. Dunlop Co. *v.* Selfridge (1915) A.C. 847.
11. Goodyear Tyre & Rubber Co. Ltd. *v.* Lakshmi Batteries Ltd. (1958).

definite amount as pin-money or *Kharche-e-Pandan* to his daughter-in-law. The bride and the bridegroom both were minors at that time. On subsequent refusal to pay the pin-money by the father-in-law, the daughter-in-law filed a case against him for recovery of the amount. It was held that, though she was a stranger to the contract, she could sue on the contract. The privy Council observed that it might occasion serious injustice to apply the Common Law doctrine of privity of contract to a country like India where marriages are contracted for minors by parents or guardians.[12]

3. **In case provision is made for the marriage or maintenance of a female member of the family on the partition of a Hindu undivided family :** The female member can enforce the promise though she may be a stranger to the contract.[13]

Example : On partition of a Hindu undivided family, it was agreed between the two brothers that they would jointly (in equal shares) invest money in some fixed property and give the income from such property to their aged mother. The aged mother, though is not a party to the contract, yet she can require the two brothers to invest the money in the fixed property and give its income to her.

4. **Where a charge is created on certain specific immovable property in favour of certain person :** Such charge is enforceable at the instance of the beneficiary entitled. The fact that the beneficiary is a stranger to the document creating charge is immaterial.

Example : In the case of Khwaja Md. *v.* Husaini Begum (as discussed before) a certain specific immovable property was also charged in favour of Husaini Begum for payment of pin-money by a document executed by the father of the bridgegroom and the father of the bridge. It was held that Husaini Begum (the bridge) could recover the amount from her father-in-law (Khwaja Md.).

5. **Assignee of a contract** can enforce the benefits of a contract provided the contract has been assigned to him. Transfer may be voluntary or by operation of law, *e.g.,* transferee of a negotiable instrument or the receiver, who acquires all the rights of the insolvent, case sue on the contract even though originally they were not parties to it.

6. **When a party to the contract has already admitted liability to the third party or has already performed part of the promise,** without any intention to show that the rest is separate to what has already been performed party shall be estopped from denying his liability to the third party arising from a contract.

7. **Contracts, which are entered into through an agent,** can be enforced by the principal.

KEY TERMS

- **Consideration :** Something accepted and agreed upon as a return or equivalent for the promise made.
- **Past consideration :** Consideration received by the promisor before the date of the promise.
- **Present consideration :** The consideration received by the promisor simultaneously with his promise.
- **Future consideration :** Consideration to be received by the promisor in future for his present promise.

12. Khwaja Md. Khan *v.* Husaini Begum (1910) 32 A.H. 410.
13. Dan Kuer *v.* Sarla Devi (1947) 49 Bom. L.R. 23, 73.

TEST QUESTIONS

Objective Type : *Test Your Knowledge*

1. State whether each of the following statements is *True* or *False*
   (*i*) Consideration is essential for the validity of a contract in all cases.
   (*ii*) Adequacy of consideration is essential for validity of a contract.
   (*iii*) A person may be stranger to consideration, but he should not be stranger to a contract.
   (*iv*) Consideration may be past, present or future.
   (*v*) No consideration is required to create agency.
   (*vi*) A stranger to consideration cannot maintain a suit. [*B.Com. (Hons.), Delhi 2010*]
   (*vii*) Consideration need not be adequate. [*B.Com. (Hons.), Delhi 2011*]
   (*viii*) Consideration must move from the promisee. [*CS Foundation, Dec. 2012*]
   [***Ans.*** (*i*) False; (*ii*) False; (*iii*) True; (*iv*) True; (*v*) True; (*vi*) False; (*vii*) True; (*viii*) False]
2. Select the most appropriate answer :
   (*i*) Consideration should be furnished at the desire of :
   (*a*) the promisor, (*b*) the promisee, (*c*) any other person.
   (*ii*) Consideration may be in the form of :
   (*a*) a benefit to the promisor (*b*) a benefit to the promisee
   (*c*) a benefit to the promisor or a detriment to the promisee.
   (*iii*) A promise to pay a time barred debt is enforceable if it is :
   (*a*) an oral promise (*b*) a written promise
   (*c*) a written and registered promise.
   (*iv*) For the enforcement of a promise to pay a time-barred debt without consideration, which of the following condition is not required.
   (*a*) It must be definite and express (*b*) It must be in writing
   (*c*) It must be signed by the promisor of law. (*d*) It must be registered in a court
   (*CS Foundation, June 2008*)
   [***Ans.*** (*i*) (*a*); (*ii*) (*c*); (*iii*) (*b*); (iv) (d)]

Essay Type : *For Review, Discussion and Practice*

1. Explain clearly the meaning of 'Consideration', the presence of which is essential in a contract. Are there any cases in which the Contract Act does not require the presence of consideration? Explain.
2. Can a stranger of a contract enforce it, give exceptions if any.
   (*ICWA Foundation, Dec. 1998; June 1999; CS Foundation, June 1999*)
3. Explain consideration as an element of a valid contract and discuss the effects of (*a*) total absence and (*b*) inadequacy of consideration.
4. 'Offer and acceptance bring the parties together, and constitute the outward semblance of contract, but most systems of law require some further evidence of the intention of the parties and in default of such evidence, refuse to recognise an obligation'—*Anson*. Comment and discuss the nature of the evidence supplied in the Indian Contract Act.
5. What agreements are contracts even though made without consideration? Does an agreement become void merely because consideration is inadequate? Give reasons.
6. 'A promise without consideration is a gift, one made for consideration is a bargain'.—*Salmond and Winfield*. Comment.

7. 'The legal effects of a contract are confined to the contracting parties'. Comment.
8. Discuss the legal rules as to valid consideration. *(ICWA Foundation, June 1999)*
9. Give at least one example when a contract is valid without consideration. *(ICWA Foundation, June 1999)*
10. Define consideration as per the case law in Curie *v.* Misa. What are the exceptions if any to the requirement of consideration in a contract? *(ICWA Foundation, Dec. 1999)*
11. Define consideration. Discuss rules relating to consideration, indicating exception, if any. *(ICWA Foundation, Dec. 2000)*
12. What do you understand by the term consideration under the Indian Contract Act. *(CS Foundation, June 2000)*
13. Explain each of the following statements :
    (*i*) Adequacy of consideration is not a legal requirement. *(ICWA Foundation, June 1998, Dec. 1999, 2000)*
    (*ii*) A stranger to a contract cannot sue. *(ICWA Foundation, Dec. 1998; B.Com. (Hons.), Delhi 1992, 2000)*
    (*iii*) Past consideration is no consideration. *(ICWA Foundation, June 1999; June 2000)*
    (*iv*) A stranger to a consideration may sue on the contract but not a stranger to the contract. *(ICWA Foundation, June 1999)*
    (*v*) A mere verbal or oral promise to pay debt barred by limitation is enforceable. *(ICWA Foundation, June 1999)*
14. State the exceptions to the doctrine that stranger to contract cannot maintain a suit. *(CS Foundation, June 1999)*
15. "Gratuitous promises are not enforceable by law". Explain the statement. *(CS Foundation, June 2005)*
16. "An agreement made without consideration is void." With reference to provisions of the Indian Contract Act, 1872 examine the validity of the statement and explain the cases in which the statement does not apply. *(PEE II, November 2005; GGSIPU, BBA (H), May 2003; B.Com. (Hons.), Delhi 2005)*
17. What do you understand by the term 'consideration'? Is consideration necessary in all cases? *(B.Com. (Hons.), 1990, 1992, 1993, 1996, 1997, 2001, 2003)*
18. Define 'consideration'? What are the legal rules of consideration? *(B.Com. (Hons.), Delhi 1992, 1993; B.Com. (Pass), Delhi 2005)*
19. "Insufficiency of consideration is immaterial but an agreement without consideration is void." Elaborate this statement. *(B.Com. (Hons.), Delhi 1994; B.Com. (Pass), Delhi 2002, 2004)*
20. "Consideration may move from promisee or any other person." Comment. *(B.Com. (Hons.), Delhi 2004)*
21. "Consideration need not be adequate but it must have some value in the eyes of law." Comment. *(B.Com. (Hons.), Delhi 1988)*
22. "A stranger to consideration can sue." Comment. *(B.Com. (Hons.), Delhi, 1990, 1994)*
23. "Consideration in some cases is a mere technically, neither reconcilable with the business expediency nor with the common sense." Comment. *(B.Com. (Hons.), Delhi 1991)*
24. "The law will not enforce a promise given for nothing." Explain. *(B.Com. (Pass), Delhi 2001)*
25. Explain the term 'Consideration' and state the exceptions to the rule 'No consideration, no contract.' *(CS Foundation, June 2002; B.Com. (Pass), Delhi 2005)*

PRACTICAL PROBLEMS

1. *X* agreed to give his house to a school for the library on the condition that the library would be named after him. The management of the school accepted his condition. Later on *X*, changed his mind. Could the management enforce the contract?

   [***Ans.*** Yes, Consideration is present.]

2. *X*, a father died, leaving a house for his two sons. The sons agreed to partition the house. It could not be divided into exactly equal parts and, therefore, one of the sons had agreed not to construct a door at a certain place in his portion of the house. This agreement was later on challenged by the son, on the ground of absence of adequate consideration. Could he succeed?

   [***Ans.*** No. Consideration need not be adequate.]

4. The Highland Bank was indebted to the State Bank under an overdraft. One *M* was the manager of the Highland Bank and his father, *K*, had guaranteed the repayment of the overdraft. *K* gifted his properties to the members of his family. The gift deed provided that the liability, if any, under the guarantee should be met by *M* from the share of the property gifted to him. Can the State Bank sue *M* under the gift deed? Give reasons.

   [***Ans.*** The State Bank is a stranger to a contract and therefore, cannot enforce the terms of the contract.]

5. Mrs. *W* made a gift of certain immovable property to her daughter *D*, by a deed registered with the proper authority, with the stipulation that a sum of ₹ 1,000 in the form of a pension be paid every month to *J*, the sister of Mrs. *W.D* on the same day entered into an agreement in favour of *J*, wherein the former (*D*) promised to give effect to the stipulation, as contained in the deed to gift. *D* later refused to pay the above amount, on the ground that there was no consideration moved from the promisee (*J*). *J* sues *D* for the performance of *D*'s promise.

   [***Ans.*** *D*'s contention is not tenable, hence *J* has a right to get ₹ 1,000 per month.]

6. A rendered some services to *B* at *B*'s request in the month of November, 1997. In December *B* promises to pay *A* a sum of ₹ 100 for his services. Does this promise constitute a valid contract? (*ICWA Foundation, June 1998*)

   [***Ans.*** The past consideration is valid under the Indian Contract Act. Hence *B*'s promise constitute a valid contract.]

7. *A* agrees with *B* to give a motor car to *B*'s son in consideration of his marrying *A*'s daughter. Can *B*'s son sue *A* on this agreement? (*ICWA Foundation, June 1999*)

   [***Ans.*** *B*'s son cannot sue since he is a stranger to the contract.]

8. A renders some services to *B* at *B*'s request in the month of November. In December *B* promises to *A* a sum of ₹ 100 for his services. Can *A* recover the promised amount? (*ICWA Foundation, June 2000*)

   [***Ans.*** Past consideration is valid. Hence, *A* can recover the amount.]

9. A Hindu husband executed and registered a document in favour of his wife, whereby referring to quarrels and disagreement between the parties, he agreed to transfer one of the properties to her. Later, he refused to effect the transfer. Can the wife demand the property? (*ICWA Foundation, June 2000*)

   [***Ans.*** Wife cannot demand the property since promise had been made without natural love and affection.]

10. A person verbally promised the Secretary of the Mosque Committee to subscribe to ₹ 500 for rebuilding a mosque. Later, he declined to pay the same amount. Can the promise be enforced. (*ICWA Foundation, Dec. 2000*)

    [***Ans.*** The agreement is void in the absence of consideration.]

11. *A* finds *B*'s purse and gives it to him. *B* promises to give Rs. 100 to *A*. Is it a valid contract? (*ICWA Foundation, Dec. 2000*)

[***Ans.*** It is a valid contract as per exception u/s 25.]

12. *X* promises his debtor not to file a suit against him on *Y*'s agreeing to pay him ₹ 10,000. Is this agreement supported by consideration? (*ICWA Foundation, June, 2001*)

[***Ans.*** Abstinaence of *X* is good consideration.]

13. *A* saves *B*'s property from fire. Is he entitled for any compensation from *B*? (*ICWA Foundation, June, 2001*)

[***Ans.*** It is a voluntary service and hence *A* is not entitled to any compensation from *B*.]

14. *B* requests *A* to sell and deliver to him certain goods on credit. *A* agrees to do so provided *C* will guarantee the payment of the price of the goods. *C* promises to guarantee the payment in consideration of *A*'s promise to deliver the goods. Is this sufficient consideration for *C*'s promise? (*CS Foundation, June, 1999*)

[***Ans.*** There is sufficient consideration for *C*'s promise.]

15. Anand is a heart patient. He goes to a heart Institute and deposits ₹ 2 lakh, the fixed charges for the operation. But before operation, the concerned doctor informs him that he will operate upon him correctly only if the patient promises to pay him ₹ 50,000 more. Anand agrees to pay. However, after successful operation, Anand refuses to pay this extra amount. Now the doctor files a suit against the patient for breach of contract. Will the doctor succeed? (*CS Foundation, December 2004*)

[***Ans.*** The doctor will not succeed because the promise was without a valid consideration.]

16. *A* gifted the whole of his property to his daughter on the condition that she should pay ₹ 1,000 p.m. to her uncle (father's brother). On the same day, the daughter entered into an agreement with her uncle to pay ₹ 1,000 p.m. Later she refused to pay on the ground that she didn't receive any consideration from her uncle. Advise her. (*B.Com. (Hons.), Delhi 1992*)

[***Ans.*** *A* is entitled to maintain the suit. It is a case of constructive consideration. Consideration need not necessarily move from the promisee.]

17. Ram owed ₹ 5,000 to Mohan. The debt was barred by Limitation Act. Ram signed a written promise to pay ₹ 2,000 to Mohan on account of this time-barred debt. Can Mohan claim ₹ 2,000 from Ram? Explain. (*B.Com. (Hons.), Delhi 2004*)

[***Ans.*** Mohan can claim ₹ 2,000 from Ram, as this promise to pay does not require a fresh consideration.]

18. Anurag promises to pay ₹ 11,000 to the management committee of a school by way of a donation. The management committee, on the basis of Anurag's promise, gets a Water Purifier System (Aquaguard) installed in the school at a cost of ₹ 8,000 on credit. Now, Anurag refuses to pay the donation. What is the remedy available to the management committee of the school? Give reasons. (*CS Foundation, December 2005*)

[***Ans.*** The contract is binding on Anurag because the management committee has undertaken liability on the faith of Anurag's promise. The leading case on the point is Kedar Nath *vs.* Gori Mohammad.]

19. *A* writes to *B* – "At the risk of your life, you saved me from fire. I promise to pay you ₹ 50,000." *A* refuses to pay *B*. Can *B* recover the amount? Give reasons. (*B.Com. (Hons.), Delhi 2005*)

[***Ans.*** *A* promise to pay for a past voluntary service is binding. Thus, *B* can recover the amount.]

20. Sharad, out of natural love and affection for his wife Seema, promised to give ₹ 10,000 to her as a birthday present. On the Birthday, he however, refuses to carry out his promise. Can Seema successfully sue Sharad for the amount? (*CS Executive, Dec. 2012*)

[***Ans.*** Seema cannot sue Sharad for the amount in the absence of writing and registered agreement.]

21. *X*, a Hindu husband executed a registered document in favour of *Y*, his wife, whereby he promised to pay her ₹ 10,000 per month. Later, *X* did not pay. Can *Y* recover from *X* (*a*) if this promise was made without any disgreement and quarrels between them? (*b*) if this promise was made after disagreement and quarrels between them? Discuss. (*B.Com. (Hons.), Delhi, Nov. 2013*)

[***Ans.*** (*a*) Yes, if it is on account of natrual love and affection.
(*b*) No, since there is no natural love and affection]

Chapter 6

LEGALITY OF THE OBJECT AND CONSIDERATION

LEARNING OBJECTIVES

A careful study of this chapter will enable you to :

- differentiate between consideration and object;
- identify the cases where the objects and consideration of an agreement are unlawful; and
- explain the meaning of certain key terms.

CONSIDERATION AND OBJECT

'Consideration' for a contract is different from its 'object'. 'Consideration is the act, abstinence or promise made at the desire of the promisor whereas the 'object' is the purpose for which the agreement is entered into. For example an agreement may be made for purchase of arms for waging a war against the State. In this case, the object of the contract is to wage war while consideration consists of a set of promises, *i.e.*, promise to supply arms and promise to pay for them. In order to make the contract valid both consideration and object of the contract should be lawful. An agreement, the consideration or the object of which is not lawful, cannot be enforced by law. This is because courts will not allow polluted hands to touch the pure foundations of justice.

UNLAWFUL CONSIDERATION AND OBJECT

According to *Sec. 23* the consideration and the object of an agreement shall be unlawful in the following cases :

1. If it is *forbidden by law, i.e.,* it has expressly been declared to be unlawful by any of the laws of the country for the time being in force.

Example : *A* agrees to sell certain goods to *B*. *A* knows that the goods are to be smuggled out of the country. The contract is unlawful.[1]

2. If it is of such a nature that, if permitted, it would *defeat the provisions of law.*

Examples : (*i*) *A*'s estate is sold for arrears of revenue under the provisions of an Act of Legislature, by which the defaulter is prohibited from purchasing the estate. *B*, upon an understanding with *A*, becomes the purchaser, and agrees to convey the estate to *A* upon receiving from him the price which *B* has paid. The agreement is void, as it renders the transaction, in effect, a purchase by the defaulter, and would so defeat the objects of law.

1. Biggs *v.* Lawrence (1789) 3 T.R. 454.

(*ii*) *A* gives a loan of ₹ 10,000 to *B*. *B* agrees not to raise the plea of limitation in case a suit has to be filed against him for recovery of loan even if it becomes timebarred. The agreement is void as it defeats the provisions of the Indian Limitation Act.

(*iii*) *X* agrees to enter *Y*'s service in consideration of a weekly wage of ₹ 100, and a weekly expense allowance of ₹ 20. Both the parties are aware that the expense allowance is a device to conceal the revenues. The agreement is void because it defeats the provisions of law.[2]

(*iv*) *A*, the accused was required under the Indian Penal Code, to furnish a surety in the sum of five thousand rupees for his good behaviour. He deposited this sum with *B* and persuaded him to become his surely. After the expiry of the period of suretyship, *A* sued *B* to recover the sum deposited. It was held that he could not recover since the purpose of the Act that a person should become surety at his own risk was defeated by an agreement of such a sort.[3]

3. If it is *fraudulent, i.e.*, the object is to cheat the other party by concealment of any material fact or otherwise.

Examples : (*i*) *A*, *B* and *C* enter into an agreement for the division among them of gains acquired, or to be acquired by them by fraud. The agreement is void, as its object is unlawful.

(*ii*) *A*, being an agent for the proprietor of land, agrees for money, without the knowledge of his principal, to obtain for *B* a lease of land belonging to his principal. The agreement between *A* and *B* is void, as it implies a fraud on account of the concealment of a material fact by *A* against his principal.

4. If it involves or implies *injury to the person or property of another.*

Examples : (*i*) An agreement by the proprietors of a newspaper to indemnify the printers against claims arising from label printed in the newspaper is void.[4]

(*ii*) An agreement which compels a debtor to do manual labour for the creditor as long as the debt is not repaid in full is void.[5]

5. If the court regards it as *immoral or opposed to public policy.* What is 'immoral' depends upon the standards of morality prevailing at a particular time and as approved by courts. In most cases the meaning is restricted to sexual immorality.

Examples : (*i*) *A*, who is *B*'s mukhtiar, promises to exercise his influence, as such, with *B* in favour of *C* and *C* promises to pay rupees 1,000 to *A*. The agreement is void, because it is immoral.

(*ii*) *A* agrees to let her daughter to *B* for concubinage. The agreement is void, because it is immoral, though the letting may not be punishable under the Indian Penal Code.

(*iii*) *A* person who knowingly lets out his house for prostitution cannot recover the rent thereof because the purpose of the agreement has been immoral.

A promise to pay for past co-habitation has been held to be legal.[6] But where co-habitation is adulterous, *i.e.*, where either party is married, it will be an illegal consideration to support any promise. Similarly, a promise to pay for future co-habitation (whether adulterous or not) is also unenforceable.[7]

2. Napier *v*. N.B. Agency Ltd. (1951) 2 All E.R. 264.
3. Fateh Singh *v*. Sanwal Singh (1878) 1 All. 751.
4. W.H. Smith and Sons *v*. Clinton (1909) 99 .L.T. 840.
5. Ram Sarup *v*. Bansi Mandar (1915) 42 Cal. 742.
6. D. Nagaratanamba *v*. Kunku Ramayya (1968), 1 S.C. R. 43.
7. Alice Mary Hill *v*. William Clark (1907), All. 286.

PUBLIC POLICY

Meaning of Public Policy

Public policy is that principle of law which provides that no person can lawfully do that which has a tendency to be injurious to the public or to the public good. No exhaustive list can be prepared of all the agreements opposed to public policy. Anything which goes against the interest of general public will be deemed to be opposed to public. In *Johnson v. Drietonein Consolidated Mines Ltd.*[8] justice Lord Halsbury observed, 'that categories of public policy are closed, and no court can invent a new head of public policy'. This view seems to be too rigid and it is not applicable in our country because under *Sec. 23* of the Indian Contract Act, courts have been authorised to decide the question of public interest and public policy. However, the doctrine should be invoked only in those clear cases in which harm to the public is materially incontestable. It will be of interest to quote the following observations of Subba Rao J. (afterward C.J.), in *Gherulal v. Mahadeo Das*[9], regarding the doctrine of public policy in India.

'The principles have been crystallised under different heads and though it is permissible for courts to expand and apply them to different situations, it should only be invoked in clear and incontestable cases of harm to the public, though the heads are not closed and though theoretically it may be permissible to evolve a new head under exceptional circumstances of changing world, it is advisable in the interest of stability of society not to make any attempt to discover new heads in these days.'

Meaning of Public Interest

'Public interest' implies common good or general social welfare. The term public interest is, therefore, 'an elusive abstraction', yet it indicates a standard of goodness for judging private acts and conduct in the social context. Public interest is to be distinguished from private interest. According to Dictionary of Sociology, a thing may be said to be in the public interest where it is or can be made to appear to be contributive to the general welfare rather than to the special privilege of a class, group or individual. Anything which is not detrimental to public good shall be in public interest.

Agreements against Public Policy

Following are some cases, in which the courts have held the agreements to be against public policy :

1. **Trading with the enemy :** No Indian national can trade with an alien enemy without prior permission from the Government. Contracts made before the outbreak of hostilities may be performed after the cessation of hostilities unless already cancelled by the parties or the Government.

2. **Agreements for stifling prosecution :** If a person has committed an offence he should be punished and, therefore, 'no court of law can countenance or give effect to an agreement which attempts to take the administration of law out of the hands of the judges and put in the hands of private individuals.'[10] Of course, an agreement to refer a civil dispute to arbitration is perfectly valid.

8. (1902), A.C. 484.
9. (1959), 2 S.C.A. 342 at p. 370.
10. Sudhindra Kumar *v.* Ganesh Chandra (1939), 1 Cal. 241; Eastern Mercantile Bank *v.* Phillip (1960), A. Ker. 194.

Example : *A* promises *B* to drop a prosecution which he has instituted against *B* for robbery, and *B* promises to restore the value of the things taken. The agreements is void, as its object is to stifle prosecution.

3. **Agreements for improper promotion of litigation :** In this connection there are two types of agreements in English law: (1) Maintenance and (2) Champerty.

Maintenance means an agreement in which a person promises to help another by money or otherwise to continue litigation in which he is not himself interested.

Champerty is a bargain whereby one person promises to assist another in recovering property in consideration of the latter giving the former a share in the property so recovered.

In England, all Maintenance and Champerty agreements are illegal and unenforceable, but in India they are perfectly valid if they are made with the *bona fide* object of assisting a claim believed to be just and the amount of compensation is reasonable. The Privy Council, in *Bhagwat Dayal Singh v. Debi Dayal Sahy*[11] held that 'An agreement champertous according to English law was not necessarily void in India, it must be against public policy to render it void here. The principle is taken to be part of the law of justice, equity and good conscience and if any agreement tends to go against these it would not be enforced.'

Example : *A* agrees to defray expenses of prosecuting *B*'s suit to recover a certain property. *B* promises to transfer to *A* in one case 55% share of property, in another 12% share and in a third 50% share. The agreement is *extortionate* and inequitable, and the plaintiff can recover expenses legitimately incurred by him with interest.[12]

4. **Agreements to vary the period of limitation :** Agreements, the object of which is to curtail or extend the period of limitation prescribed by the Law of Limitation, are void. Agreements cannot be allowed to defeat the provisions of law unless otherwise so provided in the law itself.

5. **Marriage brokerage contracts :** An agreement to procure marriage for reward is void. Of course validity of marriage will not be affected but money actually paid cannot be recovered or, if not paid, a suit for the recovery of the promised reward cannot be maintained.[13] If money has been paid but no marriage has taken place, it has been held in a few cases that the money can be recovered since illegal purpose has not been carried out.[13]

Examples : (*i*) *A* promises to a purohit to pay ₹ 3000 in consideration for procuring a second wife for *A*. The promise is illegal.

(*ii*) An agreement to pay money to parents or the guardians in consideration of his giving daughter in marriage is void.

(*iii*) *A* promises to pay a sum of ₹ 1,100 to *B*, the father of the bridegroom, and actually pays ₹ 400. The marriage falls through. ₹ 400 can be recovered by *A*. (In case certain presents were given, they can also be recovered).

6. **Traffic in public offices :** Agreements for the sale of public offices for monetary consideration will corrupt public services and are, therefore, void.

Examples : (*i*) A promise by a person to obtain an employment for the other in any of the government services for some consideration (bribery) shall be void for the reason that traffic in public offices is forbidden by law and considered as an offence.

11. (1907), 35 I.A. 48; 35 Cal. 420.
12. Hiralal *v*. Bhailal (1940), Bom. 143.
13. Baldeodas *v*. Mahamaya (1911), 15 C.W.N. 447.

(*ii*) *A*, secretary of a college, promised *B* that if he made a large donation to the college, he would use his influence to get a knighthood for him. *B* made a large donation but did not get knighthood. He sued *A* for the recovery of money. It was held that he could not recover because the agreement was against public policy.[14]

7. **Agreements creating interest opposed to duty :** If a person enters into an agreement on account of which he will have to follow a course against his public or professional duty, the agreement is void.

Example : An agreement by an agent to enable himself to make secret profits, an agreement for the purchase of property by a public officer where such purchase is prohibited by law or an agreement by an editor for some consideration not to publish reports in his paper about the conduct of a particular person shall be void for being opposed to duty. Besides being opposed to public, they will cause injury to the property of some other.

8. **Agreements interfering with marital status :** Agreements to create interest against marital duties are void.

Example : An agreement to lend money to a woman in consideration of her getting a divorce and marrying the lender shall be void for being against policy in the sense that it encourages people to commit breach of marital duties.

9. **Agreements in restraint of parental rights :** Father is the guardian of the minor child and in the absence of father, mother has this authority. This right cannot be bartered away by any agreement. Therefore, an agreement, in which a father agreed to transfer guardianship of his two minor children in favour of a lady, was held to be void, though the father agreed not to revoke the authority of the lady.[15]

Besides the agreement opposed to public policy discussed above, agreements in restraint of marriage, agreements in restraint of legal proceedings and agreements in restraint of trade are also opposed to public policy. They have been discussed in detail in the next chapter.

Agreements, the consideration or object of which is unlawful in part

Agreements, of which consideration or object is unlawful in part, are subject to the following rules:

1. If the legal part of the agreement cannot be separated from the illegal part then :

(*a*) if there are several objects but a single consideration, the agreement is void if any of the objects is unlawful *(Sec. 24)*.

(*b*) if there is a single object but several considerations, the agreement is void if any one of the considerations is unlawful (*Sec. 24*).

Example : *A* promises to superintend on behalf of *B*, a legal manufacture of indigo, and an illegal traffic in other articles. *B* promises to pay to *A* a salary of 10,000 rupees a month. The agreement is void, the object of *A's* promise and the consideration for *B's* promise being in part unlawful.

2. Where there is a reciprocal promise to do things legal and also other things illegal, and the legal part can be separated from the illegal part, the legal part is a contract and the illegal part is a void agreement (*Sec. 57*).

---

14. Parkinson *v.* College Ambulance Ltd. (1925), 2 K.B. 1.

15. Giddu Narayanish *v.* Mrs. Annie Besant (1907), 38 Mad. 807.

Example : *A* and *B* agree that *A* shall sell to *B* a house for Rs, 10,000 but that if *B* used it as a place for gambling, he shall pay ₹ 50,000 for it to *A*. The first part of the agreement shall be valid and binding but the second part shall be void and unenforceable.

3. In the case of an alternative promise, one branch of which is legal and the other illegal, the legal branch alone can be enforced.

Example : *A* and *B* agree that *A* shall pay *B* ₹ 1,000 for which *B* shall afterwards deliver to *A*, either rice or smuggled opium. There is a valid contract to deliver rice and a void contract as to opium.

Recovery of benefits given under Illegal Agreements[16]

Money paid or property transferred under an illegal agreement is irrecoverable except in the following cases :

(*i*) Where the transferor is not equally guilty with the other party, *i.e.*, transferee.

(*ii*) Where the transferor repents of making the agreement before any part of the illegal purpose is carried out.

(*iii*) Where the transferee was under a fiduciary duty to protect the plaintiff's interests and had abused his duty by making the illegal agreement.

KEY TERMS

- **Object :** The purpose for which an agreement is made.
- **Public Policy :** A principle providing that no person can lawfully do that which has a tendency to be injurious to the public or to the public good.

TEST QUESTIONS

Objective Type : *Test Your Knowledge*

1. State whether each of the following statements is *True* or *False*.

   (*i*) The terms 'consideration' and 'object' have different meanings.

   (*ii*) Agreements relating to traffic in public officers are void.

   (*iii*) Agreements of maintenance and champerty nature may be considered valid in India.

   (*iv*) Money paid or property transferred under an illegal agreement is generally irrecoverable.

   (*v*) Anything which goes against the interest of general public is deemed to be opposed to public policy.

   [*Ans.* All statements are true.]

2. Select the most appropriate answer

   (*i*) In a maintenance agreement :

   (*a*) the promisor gets a share

   (*b*) the promisor does not get share

   (*c*) the third party gets a share; in the property won on account of litigation.

   (*ii*) In case of an alternative promise, one branch which is legal and the other illegal :

   (*a*) the whole agreement is void

   (*b*) the legal branch can alone be enforced.

   (*c*) both legal and illegal branches can be enforced.

16. Please also see 'Restitution' in Chapter 12.

(*iii*) If there are several objects, but a single consideration the agreement is void if :

(*a*) any one of the objects is unlawful.

(*b*) all objects are unlawful.

(*c*) majority of the objects are unlawful.

(*iv*) If there is single object and several considerations, the agreement is void if :

(*a*) all considerations are unlawful.

(*b*) majority of the considerations are unlawful, and

(*c*) any one of the considerations is unlawful.

[***Ans.*** (*i*) (*b*); (*ii*) (*b*); (*iii*) (*a*); (*iv*) (*c*)]

Essay Type : *For Review, Discussion and Practice*

1. What are those cases when the object or the consideration of an agreement is deemed to be unlawful? (*ICWA Foundation, June 1996*)
2. What do you understand by the 'Doctrine of Public Policy'? Are there any limits to it? Give important cases which are ordinarily considered to be opposed to public policy.
3. Differentiate between Champerty & Maintenance. (*CA Foundation, May 2000*)
4. When is consideration illegal? (*ICWA Foundation, June 1998*)
5. What are the contracts of uberrimae fidei? Give any four examples. (*CS Foundation, Dec. 2004*)
6. Explain the doctrine of "Public Policy". Discuss the agreements contrary to Public Policy. [*B.Com. (Hons.), Delhi 2012*]

PRACTICAL PROBLEMS

1. A debtor promises his money-lender that he will not, without the lender's consent, leave his job, or borrow money or dispose of his property, or change his address. Is the agreement valid?
   [***Ans.*** No. It is against public policy since it restricts personal freedom.]
2. *A*, being already married to *B*, agrees with *C*, during *B*'s life-time that he will marry *C* in case *B* dies. Can *C* ask for performance of the promise in the event of *B*'s death?
   [***Ans.*** No. *C*'s contract amounts to interference with the marital status of *A* and *B*.]
3. *X* promises to pay a sum of ₹ 500 to *Y*, who is an intended witness in a suit against *X*, in consideration of *Y*'s absenting himself from the court on one pretext or the other. *Y* absents himself and demands payment from *X* who refuses to pay. Can *Y* recover ₹ 500 from *X*.
   [***Ans.*** No. The agreement is illegal since it is against public policy.]
4. *A* promised to pay ₹ 500 per month to *B*, a married woman in consideration of *B* having adultery with *A* and acting as his house-keeper. *B* lived with *A* as per agreement for three months. On *A*'s refusal to pay any money to her, she filed a suit against him to recover her wages for three months at least for her services as a house-keeper. Would she succeed?
   [***Ans.*** No. Legal and illegal considerations cannot be separated.]
5. *A* promises *B* to drop a prosecution which he has instituted against *B* for robbery and *B* promises to restore the value of the things taken. Is the agreement valid?
   (*ICWA Foundation, June 1998; Dec. 2000*)
   [***Ans.*** The agreement is void since the object is unlawful]
6. *A* promises to pay a sum to *B* in order to induce him to retire so as to provide room for *A*'s appointment to public office held by *B*. Is the agreement valid?
   (*ICWA Foundation, June 1999*)
   [***Ans.*** The agreement is void being against public policy]

7. A police officer agrees with *X* to catch a thief who snatched away his jewellery for a consideration of ₹ 1,000. After the jewellery was recovered from the thief *X* refuses to pay ₹ 1,000. Decide. (*ICWA Foundation, Dec. 1999*)

   [***Ans.*** The consideration is unlawful. Hence police officer will have no remedy against *X*.]

8. *A* applies to city corporation for licence to build additional 15 storeys in a building which has at present 10 storeys. The permission was refused. *A* had to dispose of the building with 10 storeys but later permission was given. A claims damage for loss of excess money he could have bargained if such permission was given earlier. Decide. (*ICWA Foundation, Dec. 1999*)

   [***Ans.*** *MCD* is within its lawful right to refuse license. Hence no claim for damages can be made by *A*.]

9. The city corporation pulls down unauthorised building of *A*. No notice was given. (*ICWA Foundation, Dec. 1999*)

   [***Ans.*** Action of corporation is illegal and hence *A* is entitled for damages.]

10. *A* promised to pay ₹ 10,000 to *B* in consideration of his assaulting *C*. Is this agreement valid. (*ICWA Foundation, June 2000*)

    [***Ans.*** The agreement is void since it opposed to public policy.]

11. Arun promises to pay ₹ 5,000 to Barun who is named as a witness in a suit against Arun, in consideration of Barun's promise to abstain from the trial. Barun abstains, but Arun declines to make the payment. Can Berun recover the money? (*CS Foundation, Dec. 1999*)

    [***Ans.*** Barun cannot recover the money.]

Chapter 7

VOID AGREEMENTS

LEARNING OBJECTIVES

A careful study of this chapter will enable you to :

- enumerate the agreements which have been declared void by the Indian Contract Act;
- describe the agreements in restraints of marriage, trade and legal proceedings;
- differentiate wagering agreements from ordinary commercial transactions and contracts of insurance; and
- explain the meaning of certain key terms.

All agreements may not necessarily be enforceable by law. Agreements, which fulfil all the essentials of a valid contract and have not been expressly declared to be void by law alone can be enforced. Following agreements have been expressly specified to be void by the Indian Contract Act :

1. Agreements made by incompetent parties (*Sec. 11*).
2. Agreements made under a mutual mistake of fact (*Sec. 20*).
3. Agreements, the consideration or object of which is unlawful (*Sec. 23*).
4. Agreements, the consideration or object of which is unlawful in part (*Sec. 24*).
5. Agreements made without consideration (*Sec. 25*).
6. Agreements in restraint of marriage (*Sec. 26*).
7. Agreements in restraint of trade *(Sec. 27)*.
8. Agreements in restraint of legal proceedings (*Sec. 28*).
9. Agreements the meaning of which is uncertain (*Sec. 29*).
10. Agreements by way of wager (*Sec. 30)*.
11. Agreements to do impossible act (*Sec. 56,* Para I).

The first-five cases of void agreements have already been discussed in the earlier chapters.

The remaining classes of void agreements are discussed below :

AGREEMENTS IN RESTRAINT OF MARRIAGE

Every agreement in restraint of marriage of any person, other than a minor, is void (*Sec. 26*). Freedom of choice in marriage has been guaranteed to every person who is major in age. Restrictions on the freedom of people shall be against public policy and, therefore, void.

It is to be noted that under English Law partial restraint, such as an agreement restraining marriage with a particular person or with a person belonging to a particular community etc., is valid. But in India, even partial restraint if not valid.

However, penalty upon remarriage has not been held as a restraint of marriage.

Example : Two widows agreed that if any of them remarried, she would forfeit her right to her share in the deceased husband's property. It was held that it was no restraint on either of the widows to remarry and the agreement was enforceable.[1]

AGREEMENTS IN RESTRAINT OF TRADE

A contract in restraint of trade is one which restricts a person from freely exercising his trade or profession. 'Freedom of contract and freedom of trade are well recognised rules of law. An agreement restraining a person from carrying on a lawful trade or profession shall be opposed to public policy and cannot be enforced by law'. 'Public policy requires that every man shall be at liberty to work for himself and shall not be at liberty to deprive himself of the fruits of his labour, skill or talent, by any contract that he enters into.[2]

Sec. 27 of Indian Contract Act has laid down that every agreement by which anyone is restrained from exercising a lawful profession, trade or business of any kind, is to that extent, void. The words 'to that extent' are significant, so that if a contract is divisible the valid portion will be enforced; but not, if it is not divisible.[3]

Example : *A* and *B* were rival shop-keepers in a locality in Calcutta. *B* agreed to pay *A*, a sum of money if he would close his business in that locality. *A* did so but *B* refused to pay him the money. Held, the agreement was void, and therefore, money could not be recovered.[4]

Certain exceptions have also been provided under the Act where restraint of trade will be valid. Leaving these exceptions, all restraints on the freedom of people to trade, whether they are general or partial, qualified, or unqualified, are void. The test is not whether it is partial or general or limited as to space or unlimited as to time but whether the restraint is reasonable—reasonable in the interest of the parties and reasonable in the interest of the public. Only those restraints on the freedom of the people to trade shall be valid and enforceable which are reasonable both in the interest of the parties to the contract and the general public. Law will not permit anyone to restrain a person from doing what his own interest and the public welfare will require him to do. In order that the restraint imposed may be valid and enforceable, it must be reasonable and necessary for the protection of the party intended to be benefited and must not be injurious to the public interest.

Exceptions

The exceptions to the rule given in Section 27 of the Contract Act can be put into two categories:

(*i*) Statutory exceptions, *i.e.*, those given in the Act itself, and

(*ii*) Judicial exceptions, *i.e.*, those ensuing from judicial interpretation of Section 27.

Statutory Exceptions

1. **Sale of Goodwill :** This is the only exception given under section 27 of the Contract Act. According to it one who sells the goodwill of a business may agree with the buyer to refrain from carrying on a similar business, within specified local limits so long as the buyer, or any person

1. Rao Rani *v*. Gulab Rani, I.L.R. (1942). All. 810.
2. Fraser & Co. *v*. Bombay Ice Mgf. Company (1904), 29 Bombay 107.
3. Parasullah *v*. Chandra Kant (1917), 21 C.W.N. 979.
4. Madub Chander *v*. Raj Coomar (1874), XIV Bengal Law Reports 76.

deriving title to the goodwill from him, carries on a like business therein, provided that such limits appear to be reasonable to the court, regard being had to the nature of the business. The restraint shall be reasonable only when it is no more than necessary for the protection of the interest of the purchaser. The conditions mentioned in the above clause (exception) which will make the agreement by the purchaser of goodwill, though in restraint of trade, a valid one are :

(*a*) that the seller of the business should be restrained only from carrying on a similar business;

(*b*) that the restriction should apply so long as the buyer or person deriving title to the goodwill from him is carrying on a similar business. The seller will be free to resume his business when the buyer ceases to continue it;

(*c*) that the restraint should not amount to a general restraint. It must operate within specified local limits;

(*d*) that the restraint must be reasonable in the eyes of the court in point of time and space.

2. **Under Partnership Act :** (*a*) According to *Sec. 11(2)* of the Indian Partnership Act an agreement amongst the partners that any one of them will not carry on any business other than that of the firm until he is a partner, shall not be void as being in restraint of trade.

(*b*) According to *Sec. 54* of the Indian Partnership Act, partners may enter into an agreement amongst themselves in anticipation of the dissolution of the firm to the effect that no one of them, on ceasing to be a partner, will carry on any business similar to that of the firm within a specified period or within specified local limits. Such an agreement shall not be void if the restrictions imposed are reasonable.

(*c*) *Sec. 36(2)* of the Indian Partnership Act provides that an out-going partner may agree with his other partners not to carry on a business similar to that of the firm within a specified period or within specified local limits.

(*d*) *Sec. 55(3)* of the Indian Partnership Act provides that any partner may, upon the sale of goodwill of a firm, make an agreement with the buyer that such partner will not carry on any business similar to that of the firm within a specified period or within specified local limits.

Judicial Exceptions

1. **Trade combinations etc. :** It is to be noted that agreements, which merely restrain freedom of action in the exercise of business, are not void. Section 27 aims at contracts by which a person is precluded from exercising his profession, trade or business and not at contracts entered into in the ordinary exercise of business, with persons dealing with him, which are really necessary for the carrying on the of the business[5]. On the same principle pooling agreements among the traders to avoid competition and keep up prices are not void under this section. However, if such agreements tend to create monopolies, they will be against public policy, and therefore, void.

***Examples* :** (*i*) A manufacturer of goods sold them to wholesale traders by a contract whereby the latter agreed not to sell goods for less than a certain specified price. The wholesalers had to procure a similar agreement from the retailers who bought goods from them. A wholesaler sold some goods to a retail dealer without procuring from him any such agreement. Held, that the stipulation was valid and the wholesaler was liable for breach of the same.[6]

5. Subba Naidu *v.* Haji Badsha Sahib (1903), 26 Mad. 168.
6. North Western Salt Co. *v.* Electrolytic Co. (1914) A.C. 461.

(*ii*) Certain ice manufacturing companies in Bombay entered into an agreement relating to manufacture and sale of ice by them. It was agreed to sell ice at a minimum price and put profits made by all companies in a common pool and then divide the total profit among different companies in certain proportions. One of the companies committed a breach of the contract and on a suit being instituted, it was held that the defaulting company was liable for damages. The agreement could not be taken as an agreement in restraint of trade.

2. **Sole or exclusive dealing agreement :** In business appointment of sole selling or distributing agents is quite common. The agent agrees to deal only in the goods of a particular manufacturer of whom he is the sole agent and also agrees not to deal in the goods of any other manufacturer. Similarly, the manufacturers may also agree to sell all his output only to one consumer and not to any one else. Such agreements have been held to be perfectly legal.

Examples : (*i*) A manufacturer agreed to supply for a fixed period 1,36,000 pairs of dhotis of a particular make only to *R* and none else. Held the agreement was not in restraint of trade.[7]

(*ii*) An agreement by *A*, a buyer for Calcutta Market with the manufacturer that he would not send goods bought to Madras Market was also to be enforceable.

3. **Service contracts :** Restrictions during the period of service shall not be void. An agreement of service, by which an employee binds himself during the tenure of his service, not to enter into any other service or business of a similar nature or not to compete directly with his employers shall be valid and will not amount to restraint of trade. But an agreement by which a person is restrained from using his skill in competition with his master after leaving his master's employment is always void, even where the skill was acquired in the master's service. However, restrictions can be imposed on a person going out of service so as not to disclose trade secrets and not to wrongfully entice away the customers of the earlier employers.

The reasonableness of restraint will in all cases depend upon :

(*i*) the nature of the employer's business; and

(*ii*) the business position of the employee *e.g.*, a wider restraint will be valid in the case of a manager of the business than in the case of a subordinate.

Examples : (*i*) *A* becomes *B*'s assistant for a period of three years. *B* was a doctor practising at Zanzibar. It was agreed that during the terms of the agreement *A* was not to practise on his own account in Zanzibar. After a year, *A* ceases to act *B*'s assistant and began to practise on his own account. It was held that the agreement was valid and *A* could be restrained by an injunction from doing so.[8]

(*ii*) *A* was engaged by *B* company, who were tea-planters in Assam under an agreement whereby *A* could not at any time during a period of 5 years from the date of termination of his services, engage himself if any other similar business within 40 miles of *B* company's premises in Assam. Held, that the agreement was void.[9]

If a servant is wrongfully dismissed from service by the employer, he can treat the dismissal as repudiation of the contract and is free from the stipulation in the service agreement restraining him from serving anywhere else or running an occupation or profession of his choice.

However, in all such agreements of restraint of trade, the court will see its responsibility and if it finds that the agreement is unreasonable, it may hold it unenforceable.

7. Carlilcs Nephew & Co. *v*. Ricknouth Bucktermull I.L.R. (1882), 8 Cal. 809.
8. Charlesworth *v*. Mcdonald (1898), 23 Bom. 103, 112.
9. Brahmaputra Tea Co. *v*. Scarth (1855), 11 Cal. 545.

Examples : (*i*) A manufacturer agreed to supply his entire production to *A* and to none else, after meeting *A*'s requirements if surplus production was left. Held, the manufacturer could not be restrained from supplying the surplus goods to any other buyer.[10]

(*ii*) All manufacturers of combs of Patna city agreed to supply all combs manufactured by them to *R* during his lifetime and to his heirs after his death and to none else. The court held the agreement to be void. 'It observed, 'It had bound the manufacturers from generation to generation, it was unrestrictive both as to time and place, it was oppressive. It was intended to create monopoly.[11]

Agreements in Restraint of Legal Proceedings (*Sec. 28*)

An agreement which tends to prevent the course of justice is void on account of its being against public policy. Jurisdiction of the courts of law cannot be ousted or restricted by any agreement. Agreements which check a person from enjoying the fundamental right of resorting to a court of law for relief and redress are void.

Section 28 declares the following three types of agreements to be void :

(*i*) **Agreements restricting enforcement of rights by a party :** Every agreement by which any party thereto is restricted *absolutely* from enforcing his rights under or in respect of any contract by the usual legal proceedings in the ordinary tribunals.

(*ii*) **Agreements reducing the limitation period :** Every a agreement which limits the time within which a party may enforce his contractual rights.

(*iii*) **Agreements extinguishing the rights :** Every agreement which extinguishes the rights of any party thereto or discharges any party thereto, from any liability, under or in respect of any contract on the expiry of a specific period so as to restrict any party from enforcing his rights.[12]

It is to be noted that partial restraint will be valid. The Supreme Court in the case of *Hukam Singh* v. *Gammon (India) Ltd.*[13] affirmed the above provision of the Act. The court observed : 'It is not open to the parties by agreement to confer jurisdiction on a court which it does not possess under the Civil Procedure Code. But where two courts or more have under the Code of Civil Procedure jurisdiction to try a suit, an agreement between the parties that the dispute between them shall be tried in one of such courts is not contrary to public policy. Such a provision does not contravene Section 28 of the Contract Act.'

There are two exceptions to the rule given in Section 28.

1. *Agreement to refer a future dispute to arbitration* : An agreement between the parties agreeing to refer a future dispute to arbitration is perfectly valid. The parties may agree that only the amount awarded by the arbitrator will be payable as damages by the defaulting party. Such an agreement does not exclude the jurisdiction of the court. It only stays the plaintiff's hand till some particular amount has been first ascertained by reference.[14]

Example : *A* conductor of a tramway company agreed with the company that in case of breach of rules by him, in any month, he will abide by the decision of the manager as regards his wages for that month. It was held that the stipulation was valid.

10. Har Bilas *v.* Manadco Pd., A.I.R. (1931), All. 539.
11. Shaikh Kalu *v.* Ram Saran Bhagat (1908), 8 C.W.N. 388.
12. Added by the Indian Contract (Amendment) Act, 1997.
13. A.I.R. (1971), S.C. 740.
14. Coringa Oil Co. *v.* Koegler (1876), 1 Cal. 466, 469.

2. *Agreement to refer a present dispute to arbitration* : The parties may agree to refer a present dispute to arbitration. Such an agreement will not be taken as an agreement in restraint of legal proceedings.

However, if the parties agree that they will abide by the arbitrator's award alone, whether just or unjust, the agreement will be void.

In a Madras case, it has been held that an agreement to pay a holy man for the success of a suit is not an interference with the course of justice and is, therefore, not void.[15]

It has also been held that right to appeal also does not come within the purview of this section. A party to a suit may agree not to appeal against the decision.[16]

Agreements the Meaning of which is Uncertain (*Sec. 29*)

Agreements the meaning of which is not certain or capable of being made certain without further agreement between the parties are void. An agreement with uncertain, ambiguous or vague terms is void because in all such cases it is apparent that the parties did not intend to be bound by law. A contract to contract cannot be a contract. But where the parties themselves provide machinery in the contract for resolving uncertainty, it will be a binding contract.[17]

Examples : (*i*) An actor was engaged for a provincial tour. The agreement also provided that if the play is taken to foreign countries, he will be paid on a monthly salary basis to be mutually agreed upon. The agreement was held to be void for being vague in its terms.

(*ii*) *A* agrees to sell to *B* 'hundred tonnes of oil'. There is nothing whatever to show what kind of oil was intended. The agreement is void for uncertainty.

(*iii*) *A* agrees to sell to *B* 'one hundred tonnes of oil of a specified description known as an article of commerce. There is no uncertainty here to make the agreement void.

(*iv*) *A*, who is a dealer in coconut oil only, agreed to sell to *B* 'one hundred tonnes of oil'. The nature of *A*'s trade affords an indication of the meaning of the words, and *A* had entered into a contract for the sale of one hundred tonne of coconut oil.

(*v*) *A* agrees to sell to *B* 'all the grain in my grainary at Ramanagar'. There is no uncertainty here to make the agreement void.

(*vi*) *A* agrees to sell to *B* 'one thousand tonnes of rice at a price to be fixed by *C*'. As the price is capable of being made certain, there is no uncertainty here to make the agreement void.

(*vii*) *A* agrees to sell to *B* 'my white horse for rupees five hundred or rupees one thousand.' There is nothing to show which of the two prices was to be given. The agreement is void.

Now-a-days, however the courts are upholding all those contracts as valid which are freely negotiated and intended to be binding and whenever they can give business efficacy to them. A contract with a clause that disputes will be settled by suitable arbitration[18] or that a party to the contract shall have the first option to purchase an asset at a figure to be agreed[19] may not be void on the ground of uncertainly.

15. Balsundra Muddaliar *v.* Mahomed Osman (1930), Mad. 29.
16. Anant Das *v.* Ashburmer & Co. (1876), All 4267.
17. Foley *v.* Classique Ltd. (1934).
18. Hobbs Padgett & Co. (Reinsurance) Ltd. *v.* J.C. Kirkland (1969), 2 Llyods Rep. 547.
19. Smith *v.* Morgan (1971), 1 W.L.R., 803.

AGREEMENT BY WAY OF WAGER

Meaning : Wager may be defined as an agreement between two parties to the effect that if a given uncertain event is determined in one way, one of them shall pay a certain sum of money to the other and if it is determined the other way, the latter shall pay to the former. Justice Hawkins defines wagering agreement as 'one by which two persons professing to hold opposite views touching the issue of a future uncertain event, mutually agree that, dependent upon the determination of that event one shall win from the other, and that other shall pay or hand over to him a some of money or other stake, neither of the contracting parties having any other interest in that contract than the sum or stake he will so win or lose, there being no real consideration for the making of such contract by either of the parties.'[20]

In cases where one party may win, but cannot lose, or he may lose but cannot win, or he can neither lose nor win, there can be no wagering agreements.

Essential elements : The essentials of a wagering agreement can be summed up as follows :

1. It relates to a promise to pay money or money's worth.
2. The promise must be conditional on an event happening or not happening.
3. Event must be uncertain.
4. Each party must stand equally to win or lose.
5. The gain of one party must be the loss of the other.
6. Neither party should have any interest in the event other than the sum or stake he will win or lose.

Thus 'the essence of gambling and wagering is that one party is to win and the other to lose upon a future event, which at the time of the contract is of an uncertain nature, that is to say, if the event turns out one way *A* will lose, but if it turns out the other way he will win.'[21]

The event on which a wagering agreement is made may be uncertain on account of any of these two reasons : (1) It has not happened so far. (2) It has already happened but the parties are ignorant of the results.

Examples : (*i*) *A* agrees with *B* that if there is rain on a certain day, *A* will pay *B* ₹ 50. If there is no rain *B* will pay *A* ₹ 50. The agreement is of a wagering nature.

(*ii*) *A* bet on a horse race is a wagering transaction, although horse racing is permitted by some local laws and although there may be official agencies through which bets may be placed and the prizes collected.

(*iii*) A test match between India and Pakistan has ended in Calcutta today. Both *A* and *B* are ignorant of the result. *A* agrees with *B* to pay ₹ 50 in case India wins and *B* agrees to pay *A* ₹ 50 in case India does not win. The agreement is of a wagering nature.

Lotteries : A lottery is a game of chance and, therefore, an agreement to buy a lottery ticket is of a wagering nature. The government may authorise a lottery but the only effect of such authorisation is to exempt the persons conducting the lottery from criminal prosecution.[22]

---

20. Carlill *v.* Carbolic Smoke Ball Co. (1893), 1 Q.B. 256.
21. Thacker *v.* Hardy (1878), 4 Q.B. 685.
22. Dorabji *v.* Lance 42 Bombay 676.

A 'chit fund' plan under which all subscribers are repaid their capital by a fixed date, though some of the subscribers, determined by lot, get more and sooner, is not a lottery and, therefore, perfectly valid.

Example **:** An agreement was made between twenty persons whereby it was provided that each should subscribe ₹ 200 by monthly instalments of ₹ 10, and that each in his turn, as determined by lot, should take the whole of the subscriptions for one month. *A* contributed ₹ 10 every month for a period of 10 months, and in the 10th month he got his lot of ₹ 200. Thereupon bond was taken from *A B*, the agent in the business, for remaining ₹ 100 in order to ensure that *A* regularly pays monthly instalments for a further period of 10 months.

On a suit by *B* the recovery of the bond money it was held that the transaction did not amount to a lottery and, therefore, *A* must pay. The court observed, 'Here no such lottery appears to have taken place. It is not the case of a few out of a number of subscribers obtaining prizes by lot. By the arrangement all got a return of the amount of their contribution. It is simply a loan of the common fund to each subscriber in turn, and neither the right of the subscribers to the return of their contributions nor to a loan of the fund is made a matter of risk or speculation.'[23]

Crossword competitions : In an English case, it has been held that a crossward puzzle, in which the prize depends upon the correspondence of competitor's solution with a previously prepared solution kept with the editor of a newspaper, is a lottery, and therefore, a wagering transaction.[24] Prize competitions which are games of skill *e.g.*, picture puzzles, athletic competitions are perfectly valid but the Prize Competition Act, 1955 has declared prize competitions involving prize of more than ₹ 1,000 as gambling and so void.

Example **:** In a wrestling contest it was agreed that the winner was to be rewarded with the whole of the sale proceeds of the tickets. In case of failure of a party to turn up, his deposit of ₹ 500 would be forfeited. It was held that the agreement was of a wagering nature.[25]

Commercial transactions and wager : In order to distinguish a genuine commercial transaction from a wagering transaction, the intention of the parties at the time of entering into agreement must be seen. If the intention of both the parties to the contract was not to give or take delivery of goods, the agreement would be taken as that of a wagering nature. The court will not merely look at the terms of the written contract to decide the real intention of the parties but also will probe among all surrounding circumstances. However, if the real intention of the parties at the time of entering into the contract was to give and take delivery, the contract would be taken as a genuine commercial transaction though it might be settled later on by taking or playing differences.

Option dealings : In case of option dealings, a person by paying some premium to another person, gets an option to purchase certain goods from or sell certain goods to him at a price fixed at the time of entering into the transaction. An option dealing or a 'Teji Mandi' transaction is not a wagering transaction unless it is positively proved that both parties intend not to take and give delivery. Option dealings in securities on a stock exchange are now prohibited by the Securities Contracts (Regulations) Act, 1956.

Agreement between a *Pacca Adatia and his constituents* **:** A *pacca adatia* acts both as an agent as well as a principal for his constituents. He quotes prices to his constituents and takes the liability of performing the contract at that price. The constituents have not to look to the third parties for performance. The *pacca adatia* may or may not enter into a covering contract with the

23. Kamakshi Achari *v.* Appavu Pillai (1863), 1 M.H.C. 448.
24. Coles *v.* Odham's Press (1936), 1 K.B. 416. Also see State of Bombay *v.* R.M.D. Chamarbaughwala (1957), A.S.C. 699.
25. Babasaheb Rahimsaheb *v.* Rajaram (1931), 33 Bom. L.R. 260.

third parties. He may allocate the contract to himself. Thus, a contract between a *pacca adatia* and his constituents may be of a wagering nature, and to decide this the contract between the *pacca adatia* and client must be seen and not the contract between *pacca adatia* and third parties.

Agreement between *Kacha Adatia* and his constituents : A *kacha adatia* acts only as an agent of his constituent, and therefore, no valid contract can arise unless the *kachaadatia* on behalf of his constituent enters into a contract with third parties for the execution of his constituent's order. There cannot be any wagering transaction between a *kacha adatia* and his constituent. The plea of wagering can be established only when it is proved that as between principal and third parties there was a common intention to wager.

Contracts of Insurance and Wagering Agreements

A contract of insurance, though dependent on the happening of an uncertain event, cannot be termed as wagering agreement on account of the following reasons :

1. In a contract of insurance the insured must have *insurable interest* in the life or property insured. Insurable interest means that the insured must suffer in some proprietary or pecuniary sense by the happening of the event insured against. In other words, if the subject matter insured against remains in existence, he shall be benefited and if it is destroyed, he shall be put to some pecuniary loss. A person cannot take insurance policy on that property or life in which he has no insurable interest otherwise, this will amount to a mere gambling, and therefore, void.
2. Besides the presence of insurable interest, insurance other than life insurance is a *contract of indemnity i.e.,* only actual loss is compensated for. Nobody is allowed to make any profit from an insurable claim. In case of life insurance, the assured amount of the policy is taken as the amount of loss (in the event of death of the insured) because it is impossible to estimate the value of one's life. Thus, in a contract of insurance, there is a direct relationship between the amount of compensation and the loss suffered. While in a wagering agreement, no such relationship is found between the amount won and the loss suffered (if any) by the winner.
3. Contracts of insurance are for the general good of the society and therefore, they are encouraged. Wagering agreements, in most cases, bring misery to families and are, therefore, discouraged.

Effects of a Wagering Agreement

Wagering agreements are void but not illegal. However, in the old Bombay State (now States of Gujarat and Maharashtra) on account of the provisions of the Bombay Act, 1865, wagering agreements are considered illegal. Except these two States a wagering agreement is not considered as an offence in the rest of the country. But a wagering agreement is void, and, therefore, the courts do not enforce such agreements. No suit can be brought for recovering anything alleged to be won on any wager or entrusted to any person to abide by the result of any game or other uncertain event on which any wager is made. A winner in wager is, therefore, prevented from recovering by a suit the money from the other party to the contract or the stake-holder. Even a fresh promise to pay a debt arising out of wagering contract would be unenforceable. But the loser of a bet is entitled to recover his deposit provided the plaintiff had demanded its return before the stake-holder had paid it over to the winner. But no suit will lie for recovery of the money from the winner after it had been paid over to him. If the stake-holder pays the money to the winner even after the definite instructions of the loser not to pay, the loser cannot hold the stake-holder liable.

Exception : As an exception to general rule that agreements by way of wager are void, it has been provided by law that subscriptions or contributions made or entered into for or towards any plate, prize or sum of money of the value or amount of five hundred rupees or more to be awarded to the winner or winners of any horse race, shall not be deemed to be rendered unlawful.

Collateral transactions : Though a wagering agreement is void and no suit can lie to recover the fruits of a wager, transactions incidental or collateral to wagering transaction are not void, *e.g.*, a broker in a wagering transaction can recover his brokerage. Similarly, if he has paid losses on behalf of his principal in respect of wagering transactions, his claim for indemnity against the principal will be maintainable. Money lent for the purpose of gambling or for paying a gambling debt, even if advanced with the knowledge of its purpose for which the money is required, can be recovered.

AGREEMENTS TO DO AN IMPOSSIBLE ACT

An agreement to do an act impossible in itself is void. The performance of the contract may be impossible either physically or legally. Economic unprofitableness will not make the performance of the contract impossible. Impossibility of performance will be appearing from the very nature of such contract, *e.g.*, an agreement to discover treasure by magic. Impossibility of performance of the contract may arise subsequent to the formation of the contract and might have not been known to the parties at the time of making the contract. Subsequent impossibility of performance of the contract may arise on account of the change in law or the destruction of the specific thing essential for the performance of the contract.

Examples **:** (*i*) *A* agrees with *B* to draw two parallel lines in such a way that they will cross each other. The agreement is void on the ground of impossibility.

(*ii*) *A* agrees to sell his horse to *B* after three months. The horse dies before the expiry of three months. The agreement becomes void on the ground of subsequent impossibility.

Where one person has promised to do something which he knew or with reasonable diligence might have known and which the promise did not know to be impossible or unlawful, such promisor must make compensation to such promisee for any loss which such promisee sustains through the non-performance of the contract.

Examples **:** *A* contracts to marry *B*, who is already married to *C* and who is forbidden by law to practise polygamy. The contract is void for impossibility of performance since law has forbidden polygamy. But in this case *A* must make compensation to *B* for the loss caused to her by the non-performance to the promise.

KEY TERMS

- **Uncertain Agreement :** An agreement the meaning of which is not certain or capable of being made certain without further agreement between the parties.
- **Wagering Agreement :** An agreement where one party is to win and the other to lose depending upon an event which at the time of the agreement is of an uncertain nature.

TEST QUESTIONS

Objective Type : *Test Your Knowledge*

1. State whether each of the statements is *True* or *False*

   (*i*) Partial restrain such as an agreement restraining marriage with a particular person is valid under the Indian Contract Act.

   (*ii*) An agreement restraining an employee during the period of service is not to be taken as agreements in restraint of trade.

   (*iii*) An agreement to refer a future dispute to arbitration is perfectly valid.

   (*iv*) An agreement by way of wager is illegal.

   (*v*) A contract between *pacca adatia* and his clients may be of a wagering nature.

   (*vi*) Lotteries authorised by the Government are not to be taken as of wagering nature.

   (*vii*) An agreement to divide the gains acquired by fraud is void.

   (*ICWA, Foundation, June 2000*)

   (*viii*) Agreement in restraint of trade is void.

   (*ICWA, Foundation, Dec. 1998*), (*B.Com. (Hons.) 2010*)

   [***Ans.*** (*i*) False; (*ii*) True; (*iii*) True; (*iv*) False (except in old Bombay state); (*v*) True; (*vi*) False; (*vii*) True; (*viii*) True.]

2. State the nature of the agreement in each of the following cases :

   (*a*) *A* agrees with *B* to draw two parallel lines in such a way that they will cross each other.

   (*b*) *A* contracts to pay *B* ₹ 10,000 if it rains tomorrow.

   (*c*) *A* promises to pay *B* ₹ 5,000 if *B* does not marry *C*.

   (*d*) *A* agrees to sell to *B* a 100 tonnes of oil.

   (*e*) *A* buys a lottery ticket of ₹ 500 from *B*.

   [***Ans.*** (*a*) An agreement do an impossible act, (*b*) Wagering agreement, (*c*) Agreement in restraint of marriage, (*d*) Uncertain agreement, (*e*) Wagering agreement.]

Essay Type : *For Review, Discussion and Practice*

1. 'Liberty to trade is not an asset which the law will permit a person to barter except in special circumstances within well recognised limitations.' Comment.
2. What is an agreement by way of wager? What tests would you apply to determine if or not, an agreement is by way of wager? Distinguish a wagering agreement from a good contract.
3. What is meant by agreement in restraint of trade? Describe in brief the various exception thereto.

   (*CA, Foundation, May 1998*)
4. Distinguish between Wagering Contract and Contingent Contract. When can a contract be excused for non performance. (*ICWA, Foundation, June 1998*)
5. Agreement in restraint of trade, profession is void. What are its exceptions.

   (*ICWA, Foundation, Dec. 1998; B.Com. (Hons.), Delhi 1989, 1991, 1995 MBA, GGIPU Dec. 2007*)
6. 'Insurance contracts are basically wagering agreements.' Comment.
7. 'The jurisdiction of courts of law to decide dispute arising from contractual relations cannot be ousted by agreement between parties.' Discuss.
8. 'A person ought not be allowed to restrain himself by contract from exercising any lawful craft or business at his own discretion and in his way.' Discuss.

9. What are the essentials of a wagering agreement? Discuss the effect of wagering agreements. *(B.Com. (Hons.), Delhi 2002, 2013)*
10. Define a wagering agreement. What are the essential elements of a wagering agreement? *(B.Com. (Pass), Delhi 2004)*
11. Discuss briefly whether an agreement by way of wager is a voidable contract. *(CS Foundation, Dec. 2007)*

PRACTICAL PROBLEMS

1. Briefly discuss the legal validity or invalidity of the following :
   (*i*) An agreement to purchase a lottery authorised by Government.
   (*ii*) An agreement to pay fee to a holy man for success of a pending suit.
   (*iii*) An agreement not to plead limitation.
   (*iv*) A champertous agreement in India.
   (*v*) An agreement grounded on erroneous belief that a particular debt is barred by law of limitation.
   (*vi*) An oral agreement to compensate a person who has already voluntarily done something for the promisor.

   [***Ans.*** (*i*) Void, because it is a wagering agreement. (*ii*) Valid, see agreements in restraint of legal proceedings. (*iii*) Void, because it defeats the provisions of the Limitation Act. (*iv*) Valid, unless inequitable and unjust. (*v*) Valid, ignorance of law is no excuse. (*vi*) Valid, exception under section 25(2) regarding consideration.]
2. *A* took a bet of ₹ 1,000 with *B* that a certain horse would win a certain race. Under this agreement *A* had to deposit ₹ 200 with *B*. Since *A* had no money, he approached his friend *C* who advanced him ₹ 200. Subsequently *A* lost the bet and refuses to repay the amount to *C*. Advise *C*.

   [***Ans.*** *C* can recover the sum. Wagering agreements are void but not illegal except in old Bombay State.]
3. *X* instructs *Y* to enter on *X*'s behalf into a wagering transaction. *Y* loses in the transaction and pays from his pocket. Is *Y* entitled to reimbursement from *X*? State reasons.

   [***Ans.*** Yes, Wagering agreements are void not illegal except in old Bombay State. Collateral transactions are valid.]
4. *A* and *B* bet as to whether it would rain on a particular day or not. *A* promises to pay ₹ 100 to *B* if it rained and *B* promises an equal amount to *A* if it did not. Is it a valid contract. *(ICWA, Foundation, Dec. 2000)*

   [***Ans.*** The agreement is of a wagering nature and hence void.]
5. *A* promises to pay one crore of rupees to certain person if he or she can correctly answer few questions on uncertain events or incidents. Is such promise a valid contract. *(ICWA, Foundation, June 2001)*

   [***Ans.*** It is valid agreement since it requires skills.]
6. Mr. Seth, an industrialist has been fighting a long drawn litigation from Mr. Raman, another industrialist. To support his legal campaign, Mr. Seth enlists the services of Mr. *X*, a legal expert stating that an amount of ₹ 5 lakhs would be paid, if Mr. *X* does not take up the brief of Mr. Raman. Mr. *X* agrees, but at the end of the litigation Mr. Seth refuses to pay. Decide whether Mr. *X* can recover the amount promised by Mr. Seth under the provisions of the Indian Contract Act, 1872. *(PEE II, November 2004)*

   [***Ans.*** It is an illegal agreement and hence, Mr. *X* cannot recover the amount.]
7. Amit promises to procure an employment for Bimal in a government department and Bimal promises to pay ₹ 5,000 to Amit for the same. Amit gets the said job for Bimal. However, Bimal refuses to

pay the promised money to Amit who files a suit in the court of law to recover ₹ 5,000 from Bimal. Will Amit succeed? Give reasons. *(CS Foundation, Dec. 2007*

[***Ans.*** Amit will not succeed because the agreement is void.]

8. Point out the reasons whether the following agreements are valid or void:
   (*i*) Kamala promises Ramesh to lend ₹ 50,000 in lieu of consideration that Ramesh gets Kamala's marriage dissolved and himself marries with her.
   (*ii*) Sohan agrees with Mohan to sell his black horse. Unknown to both parties, the horse was dead at the time of agreement.
   (*iii*) Ram sells the goodwill of his shop to Shyam for ₹ 4,00,000 and promises not to carry on such business forever and anywhere in India.
   (*iv*) In an agreement between Prakash and Girish, there is a condition that they will not institute legal proceeding against each other without consent.
   (*v*) Ramamurthy, who is a citizen of India, enters into an agreement with an alien friend. *(PEE-II, ICAI, May 2008)*

   [***Ans.*** (*i*) Void Agreement; (*ii*) Void Agreement; (*iii*) Void Agreement; (*iv*) Void Agreement; (*v*) Valid Agreement]
9. There was an agreement to lend ₹ 5 lakh to Bimla in consideration of her getting a divorce and marrying Govind, the lender. Is the agreement enforceable? Give reasons. *(CS Foundation, Dec. 2008)*

   [***Ans.*** It is an invalid agreement and not enforceable]
10. Sandeep is a jeweller. He deals in artificial jewellery. Sandeep sells his business to Kuldeep and also charges for the goodwill. Sandeep further agrees with Kuldeep that he will not do the business in artificial jewellery as well as in real jewellery within local limits and for a certain period of time. Is this a valid contract? Give reasons. *(CS Foundation, June 2011)*

    [***Ans.*** Contract between Sandeep and Kuldeep is partly valid and partly invalid, not in dealing in artificial jewellery,it is a valid contract. Sandeep will not do the business of real jewellery, it is a void contract. The case on the point is *Goldsoll v.* Goldman, (1915) 1 Ch.D 292.]
11. *X* agreed to become an assistant for 5 years to *Y* who was a doctor practicing at Chennai. It was also agreed that during the term of agreement *X* will not practice on his own account in Chennai. At the end of the year, *X* left the assistantship of *Y* and began to practice on his own account. Referring to the provisions of the Indian Contract Act, 1872, decide whether *X* could be restrained from doing so? *[CA IPC Nov. 2013]*

    [***Ans.*** X can be restrained by an injunction from practicing on his own account in Chennai]

Chapter 8
CONTINGENT CONTRACTS

LEARNING OBJECTIVES

A careful study of this chapter will enable you to :

- understand the meaning of a contingent contract;
- explain the characteristics of a contingent contract;
- differentiate between a contingent contract and a wagering agreement; and
- explain the meaning of certain key terms.

MEANING OF CONTINGENT CONTRACT

A contract may be

(1) absolute, or (2) contingent.

An absolute contract is one where the promisor undertakes to perform the contract in all events.

A contingent contract is a contract to do or not to do something if some event collateral to such contract does or does not happen (*Sec. 31*).

Examples : (*i*) On 1st January, *A* agrees with *B* that he will sell his car to him for ₹ 10,000 on the 15th January. This is an absolute executory contract. In all circumstances both the parties must perform their respective obligations on 15th January.

(*ii*) On 1st January, *A* agrees with *B* that he will sell his car to him for ₹ 10,000 on the 15th January, if he (*A*) gets a new car by 12th January. This is a conditional executory contract. The performance of *A* depends on his getting a new car. If he gets it, he shall perform the contract otherwise not. The contract is, therefore, a contingent contract.

(*iii*) *A* promises, to pay *B* ₹ 10,000 if *B*'s house is burnt. The performance of the contract depends on a future event. It is, therefore, also a contingent contract.

Collateral event : In a contingent contract, the even on which the performance of the contract depends is only collateral to the contract. It is an event regarding which neither of the parties makes any promise. It is important only because it marks the moment at which the rights created by the contract become enforceable.

The Act does not define the term 'collateral event'. But *on the whole* it seems to mean 'an event which is neither a performance directly promised as part of the contract, nor the whole of the consideration for a promise.[1]

Examples : (*i*) *A* agrees to sell his car to *B* for ₹ 10,000. In this contract both *A* and *B* have given promises to each other, regarding selling of the car and making payment of the price, respectively. Though in this contract performance of promise by a party depends on the willingness of another party

1. Pollock and Mulla, 'Indian Contract and Specific Relief Act,' ninth edition. p. 321.

to perform his part, but in case of default by any party, the other party is entitled to have recourse to legal remedies. The contract is, therefore, absolute or unconditional.

(*ii*) *A* agrees to pay *B* a sum of ₹ 1,000 if he (*B*) marries *C*. In this case *B* has not promised to marry *C*. He may or may not marry. The obligation of *A* to pay a sum of ₹ 1,000 will arise only when *B* marries *C* . But *A* cannot compel *B* to marry *C*. Thus 'marriage with *C*' is an event on which the rights and obligations created by the contract will be enforceable. The contract is, therefore, contingent.

(*iii*) *B* agrees to marry *C* and *A* in consideration of this agrees to pay *B* a sum of ₹ 10,000. In this case each party has given a promise to another party and one's promise is consideration for the other. In case a party fails to perform his part, the other can have recourse to legal remedies. The perfomance of the contract does not depend on a collateral event. This is, therefore, not a contingent contract.

ESSENTIAL CHARACTERISTICS

The essential characteristics of a contingent contract are :

1. The performance of the contract depends upon the happening or non-happening of a certain event in future.
2. The event is uncertain. If the event is bound to happen, the contract is due to be performed in every case, and therefore, it will not amount to a contingent contract.
3. The uncertain future event is collateral to the contract.

Contracts of insurance, contracts of indemnity and guarantee etc. are some of important examples of contingent contracts.

Examples **:** (*i*) A contract for the sale by the defendants (Nathmal Hirachand & Co.) of pieces of American fine coloured parachute cloth stated that the goods belonged to H. Bisanesara & Co. and that they were of January and February shipment. The contract then provided that the goods were to be given delivery of when they arrived. The defendants failed to give delivery and the plaintiff (Ranchoddas) sued for damages for breach. The defendants pleaded that the contract was a conditional one and as the goods had not arrived they had no obligation to give delivery. It was held that the provision that the goods were to be given delivery of when they arrived did not constitute a part of the description of the goods. It dealt only with the mode of performance and not with the question of the very obligation to perform the contract, the obligation to perform being absolute and unconditional. The contract was therefore not contingent.[2]

(*ii*) In a contract for sale of certain property, a balance of ₹ 25,000 was left out with the vendee at the time of registration of the sale deed. A clause in the sale deed provided the following in this respect.

'....and the balance of ₹ 25,000 is to be paid by the vendee to the vendor as soon as possible but at a time when the former is in a position to make payment.'

It was held that the above clause did not mean that if the vendee never had the financial reasons or the means to make the payment, he was to be altogether absolved from all liability to make payment of ₹ 25,000. The obligation to pay was absolute and it was only by way of concession in point of time that the vendee was allowed the facility of making payment at a time when he was in a position to make payment. The stipulation 'as soon as possible but at a time when the former is in a position to make the payment' means 'within a reasonable time' and does not make the contract contingent under section 31.[3]

2. Ranchoddas *v*. Nathmal Hirachand & Co. (1949), 51 Bom. L.R. 491.
3. (Mrs.) Sohan Singh *v*. State Bank of India, A.I.R. (1964), Punj. 123 at pp. 126-127.

Contingency Dependent on an Act of a Party

A contract may be contingent on some act of a party to the contract or of a third party. But, if the performance of a promise is contingent upon the discretion of the promisor, the contract will be invalid. In a contract for the manufacture of the goods to order, there may be a condition that the goods shall be to the customer's approval. The decision of the customer if taken *bona fide* shall be binding upon the other party to the contract. But a contract to pay for service whatever the promisor will think right or reasonable will be invalid and not binding on the other party because the performance of the promise is dependent upon the will and pleasure of the promisor. This will not constitute a binding promise. But a promise to pay that amount which shall be fixed up by a third party shall be valid and binding.

RULES REGARDING PERFORMANCE

The rules regarding the performance of the contingent contracts art contained in *Secs. 32* to *36* of the Contract Act. These rules are given below :

1. Contingent contracts to do or not to do anything if an uncertain future event happens cannot be enforced by law unless and until that event has happened. If the event becomes *impossible* such contracts become *void* (*Sec. 32*).

Examples : (*i*) *A* makes a contract with *B* to buy *B*'s horse if *A* survives *C*. This contract cannot be enforced unless and until *C* dies in *A*'s lifetime.

(*ii*) *A* makes a contract with *B* to sell a horse to *B* at a specified price, if *C*, to whom the horse has been offered refuses to buy it. The contract cannot be enforced by law unless and until *C* refuses to buy the horse.

(*iii*) *A* contracts to pay *B* a sum of money when *B* marries *C*. *C* dies without being married to *B*. The contract becomes void.

2. Contingent contracts to do or not to do anything if an uncertain future event does not happen can be enforced when the happening of that event becomes *impossible*, and not before (*Sec. 33*).

Example : *A* agrees to pay *B* a sum of money if a certain ship does not return. The ship is sunk. The contract can be enforced when the ship sinks.

3. If a contract is contingent upon how a person will act at an unspecified time, that event shall be considered to become impossible when such person does anything which renders it impossible that he should so act within any definite time, or otherwise than under further contingencies (*Sec. 34*).

Example : *A* agrees to pay *B* a sum of money if *B* marries *C*. *C* marries *D*. The marriage of *B* to *C* must now be considered impossible, although it is possible than *D* may die and that *C* may afterwards marry *B*.

4. Contingent contracts to do or not to do anything, if a specified uncertain event happens within a fixed time, become *void* if, at the expiration of the time fixed, such event has not happened or if, before the time fixed, such event becomes impossible.

Contingent contracts to do or not to do anything if a specified uncertain event does not happen within a fixed time, may be enforced by law when the time fixed has expired and such event has not happened, or before the time fixed has expired, if it become certain that such event will not happen (*Sec. 35*).

Examples **:** (*i*) *A* promises to pay *B* a sum of money if a certain ship returns within a year. The contract may be enforced if the ship returns within a year, and becomes void if the ship is burnt within a year.

(*ii*) *A* promises to pay *B* a sum of money if a certain ship does not return within a year, or is burnt within the year. The contract may be enforced if the ship does not return within a year, or is burnt within the year.

5. **Contingent agreement to do or not to do anything, if an impossible event happens, are void, whether the impossibility of the event is known or not to the parties to the agreement at the time when it is made (*Sec. 36*).**

Examples **:** (*i*) *A* agrees to pay *B* ₹ 1,000 if two straight lines should enclose a space. The agreement is void.

(*ii*) *A* agrees to pay *B* ₹ 1,000 if *B* will marry *A*'s daughter *C*. *C* was dead at the time of agreement. The agreement is void.

CONTINGENT CONTRACT AND WAGERING AGREEMENT

The following are the points of difference between a contingent contract and a wagering agreement :

1. A wagering agreement consists of reciprocal promises. The performance of promise by each party depends on the happening of an uncertain event. A contingent contract may not consist of reciprocal promises.
2. Every wagering agreement is of a contingent nature while every contingent contract is not a wagering nature.
3. In case of a wagering agreement the parties to the agreement have no other interest in the subject-matter of the agreement except for the winning or losing of the wagering sum. But in a contingent contract parties do have some other interest in the subject-matter. In the absence of such an interest a contingent contract would be of a wagering nature. For example, if *A* who does not have any interest in the house of *B*, gets it insured, it is a wagering agreement. But if *A* has insurable interest in *B*'s house (*e.g.*, he has lent money on the mortgage of the house), and gets it insured, it will be a contingent contract and will be perfectly valid.
4. In a wagering agreement, the future event is the sole determining factor while in a contingent contract, the future event is only collateral. For example, if *A* makes a table for *B* and *B* says to him that it will not be approved by *C* if *C* approves it, he (*B*) will pay a sum of ₹ 200 for it. *A* replies that in case *C* does not approve it, he will give it free of charge to him (*B*). This is a wagering agreement. But in case *A* agrees to sell the table to *B* for ₹ 200 if *C* approves it, the contract will be taken as a contingent contract.
5. A wagering agreement is absolutely void while a contingent contract is perfectly valid.

KEY TERMS

- **Absolute Contract :** A contract where the promisor undertakes to perform a contract in all events.
- **Contingent Contract :** A contract to do or not to do something if some event collateral to the contract does or does not happen.

- **Collateral Event :** An event which is neither a performance directly promised as part of the contract nor the whole of the consideration for a promise.

TEST QUESTIONS

Objective Type : *Test Your Knowledge*

1. Fill in the blanks

(*i*) A contingent contract is dependent on the happening or not-happening of an event which is ......

(*ii*) A contingent contract dependent on not happening of a future event can be enforced when the happening of the event becomes ....

(*iii*) A contingent contract dependent on an event impossible to happen is.....................

(*iv*) A contingent contract dependent on happening of an uncertain event becomes void if the event becomes ....

(*v*) Every wagering agreement is of a .... nature.

(*vi*) A contract of insurance is a .... contract. *(ICE, ICAI, Nov. 2007)*

[***Ans.*** (*i*) collateral to the contract, (*ii*) impossible, (*iii*) void; (*iv*) impossible to happen; (*v*) contingent; (*vi*) contingent.]

Essay Type : *For Review, Discussion and Practice*

1. What do you understand by a 'Contingent Contract'? Discuss how far the contingency may be dependent on the act of the party.
2. To what extent the impossibility of the contingency affects the performance of the contract?
3. Differentiate between wagering agreement and contingent contract. *(CA Inter, Nov. 1989; B.Com. (Hons), Delhi 2010)*
4. Define contingent contract. Discuss also the essential elements of a contingent contract. *(ICWA, Foundation, June 1999)*

PRACTICAL PROBLEMS

1. *X* agrees to pay *Y* ₹ 5,000 if *Y* marries *Z*. *Z* marries *F*. Subsequently *F* dies and *Y* marries *Z*. *Y* sues *X* for the payment of ₹ 5,000. Decide stating reasons.
[***Ans.*** *Y* will fail. Contract became void on the ground of impossibility as soon as *Z* married *F*.]
2. National Construction Corporation agrees to construct a building for Boots Trading Co. for a sum of ₹ 25 lakhs on the condition that no payments shall be made till the completion of the building duly certified by the architect. Is this a contingent contract?
[***Ans.*** The contract is not a contingent one since there is no collateral event on which its performance depends.]
3. *A* agrees to deliver 100 bags of rice and *B* agrees to pay the price only after the bags are delivered to him. State whether it is a contingent contract?
[***Ans.*** It is not a contingent contract since *B*'s liability depends on an event which is a part of the promise itself and not a collateral event.]
4. Are the following contingent contracts.
(*i*) *A* contracts to pay ₹ 1,00,000 to *X*, if his house is burnt. *(ICWA, Foundation, June 2000)*
[***Ans.*** Yes.]

(*ii*) *A* promised to marry none except Miss *B* (aged 19 years) and in default pay her ₹ 50,000.
(ICWA, Foundation, June 2000)
[***Ans.*** No.]

5. *A* participated in the Horse Race at Madras. His horse was successful as No. 1. The Race Club authority refuses to pay the reward on the ground that it is wagering contract. Decide.
(ICWA, Foundation, Dec. 1999)
[***Ans.*** Horse racing has been held as a sport requiring special skills. Hence, *A* is entitled to get the prize money.)

6. *A* and *B* agree that *A* should pay ₹ 1000 to *B* if India wins the World Cup '99' and that *B* should pay *A* if South Africa wins. Is this a valid contract? *(ICWA Foundation, Dec. 1999)*
[***Ans.*** Agreement is by way of wager and hence void.]

Chapter 9

PERFORMANCE OF CONTRACTS

LEARNING OBJECTIVES

A careful study of this chapter will enable you to :

- understand the meaning of performance of contract;
- differentiate between actual performance and attempted performance;
- enumerate the requisites for a valid tender of performance;
- explain the various types of reciprocal promises;
- state the rules regarding appropriation of payments; and
- explain the meaning of certain key terms.

MEANING AND TYPES OF PERFORMANCE

Performance of contract implies fulfilment of the terms of the contract by the respective parties to the contract. *Section 37* of the Contract Act lays down that, 'that parties to a contract must either perform, or offer to perform their respective promises, unless such performance is dispensed with or excused under the provisions of this Act, or of any other law.' 'This means that the performance may be of two types as shown below :

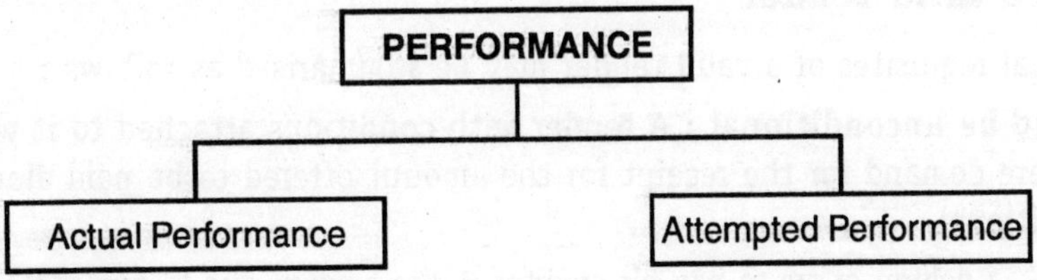

Actual Performance

A party to a contract is said to have actually performed his promise when he has done what he had undertaken to do. In other words, he must have fulfilled all his obligations under the contract.

Attempted Performance or Offer to Perform

An *offer to perform* one's obligations under a contract is called *tender*. It is also called attempted performance because though the promisor has offered to fulfil his obligation under the contract, the performance is not complete unless the offer of performance is accepted by the promisee. The nature of the contract determines whether it requires *actual* or *attempted* performance.

Examples **:** (*i*) *A* contracts to find out the lost child of *B* for a sum of ₹ 100. Here the nature of the contract is such that *A* should actually perform his part.

(*ii*) *A* agrees to sell certain goods to *B* on a fixed date. It is agreed that *B* will send his manager for taking delivery of goods on that date. The nature of the contract requires that *A* should first make an offer of performance to *B* on the fixed date.

It is to be noted that in case the promisee refuses to accept a valid offer of performance of the contract by the promisor, the latter shall be discharged from the responsibility for the non-performance of the contract without in any way prejudicing his own rights against the promisee. A valid tender of performance when rejected by the other party, shall be treated equivalent to the actual performance of the contract and the person, making this valid tender of performance can bring a suit for the breach of contract against the other party.[1] This has been made very clear in *Section 38* of the Act: 'Where a promisor has made an offer of performance to the promisee and the offer has not been accepted, the promisor is not responsible for non-performance, not does he thereby lose his rights under the contract.' However, in case of payment of debt, the rejection of a valid tender of money by the creditor will not discharge the promisor from the liability for the repayment of the debt. He shall continue to be liable for the repayment of the debt without being liable for any interest on the same from the date of valid tender. He shall also be entitled to recover his costs, if any, which he might have incurred in making that valid tender of the payment of the debt.

Kinds of Tender

Tender may be of two kinds : (*i*) Tender of the Goods and (*ii*) Tender of Money. If tender of performance of the promise by delivery of goods is rejected by the other party, the offerer of tender shall not only be discharged from all the consequences of the breach of the contract, but may also maintain a suit for the same. A debtor, however, as stated before, shall not be discharged from the liability for the debt even if his tender of money to repay loan is not accepted by the creditor. Tender of money cannot amount to discharge of the debt. Interest on the debt shall immediately cease to accrue from the date of the rejection of a valid tender of money.

Essentials of a Valid Tender

The essential requisites of a valid tender may be summarised as follows :

1. **It should be unconditional :** A tender with conditions attached to it will not be a valid tender. But a mere demand for the receipt for the amount offered to be paid alone, will not make the tender conditional.

Example : *A*, a debtor, offers to pay his creditor *P*, the amount due to him if *P* sells his car at cost to him. The tender cannot be termed as a valid tender.

2. **It should be an offer to perform in full :** An offer to perform promise in part cannot be taken as a valid tender.

Example : *A* has to deliver 100 bags of wheat to *B* on 1st of December. He offers only 50 bags to *B* on the due date. It is not a valid tender and *B* can refuse to accept delivery of the same.

3. **Tender for the performance of the contract must be made at the fixed time and place or at a proper time and place :** Unless otherwise agreed upon, the place of business of the promisee shall be the proper place to make tender of the performance of the contract.

4. **Tender should be made to the proper promisee :** Tenders made to a stranger would be invalid. Tender made to any one of the joint promisees shall be valid and binding upon all of them.

1. Startup *v*. MacDonald (1943), 6 Man. & G. 593.

5. Tender for the delivery of goods must be for the **quantity and quality agreed upon.**

6. **Reasonable opportunity** must be provided to the promisee to inspect and satisfy himself that the performance is in accordance with the terms of the contract and that the goods offered are the same which the promisor is bound by his promise to deliver.

Example **:** *A* contracts to deliver to *B* at his warehouse, on the 1st March 2000, 100 bales of cotton of a particular quality. In order to make a valid tender of performance, *A* must bring cotton to *B*'s warehouse on the appointed day, under such circumstances that *B* may have a reasonable opportunity of satisfying himself that the thing offered is cotton of the quality contracted for, and that there are 100 bales.

7. **In case of payment of money, tender must be of the precise amount and in terms of legal tender money :** Promisee cannot be compelled to accept cheques in discharge of his debts.

Thus, tender of money by cheque, tender before due date, tender of performance in instalments unless otherwise agreed upon, tender after business hours or at such odd hours which may not permit inspection of goods by the other party, tender of goods in quantity other than agreed, are all examples of invalid tenders of performance.

8. **In case of several promisees a valid tender of performance made to one shall be taken as a valid tender made to all :** This is true only regarding tender of performance and nothing else. A payment by a debtor to one of several joint creditors cannot have the legal effect of discharging the entire contractual obligations as against the other co-creditors. This is because of *Sec. 45* (discussed later) which states that the right to demand performance rests with the joint promisees jointly and not severally.

Effect of the refusal of a party to perform the promise wholly (*Sec. 39*)

When a party to a contract has refused to perform or disabled himself from performing his promise in its entirety, the promisee may put an end to the contract, unless he has signified by his words or conduct, his acquiescence in its continuance.

Examples **:** (*i*) *A*, a singer, enters into a contract with *B*, the manager of a theatre, to sing at his theatre two nights every week during the next two months, and *B* agrees to pay her 100 rupees for each night's performance. On the sixth night *A* wilfully absents herself from the theatre. *B* is at liberty to put an end to the contract.

(*ii*) *A*, a singer, enters into a contract with *B*, the manager of a theatre, to sing at his theatre two nights in every week during the next two months and *B* agrees to pay her at the rate of 100 rupees for each night. On the sixth night *A* wilfully absents herself. With the assent of *B*, *A* sings on the seventh night. *B* has signified his acquiescence to the continuance of the contract, and cannot now put an end to it, but is entitled to compensation for damages sustained by him through *A*'s failure to sing on the sixth night.

RESPONSIBILITY FOR PERFORMANCE

The responsibility of performance of contract lies on the following persons :

1. **The promisor** (Sec. 40) **:** If it appears from the nature of the case that it was the intention of the parties to any contract, that any promise contained in it should be performed by the promisor himself, such promise must be performed by the promisor. Contracts involving personal skill or those depending upon personal trust and confidence must be performed by the promisor himself.

Example **:** *A* promises to paint picture for *B*. *A* must perform this promise personally.

2. **The agent** (*Sec. 40*) **:** Contracts which are not of a personal nature, may be performed by an agent or a deputy appointed by the promisor for this purpose.

Example **:** *A* promises to pay *B* a sum of money. *A* may perform the promise, either by personally paying the money to *B* or by causing it to be paid to *B* by another. If *A* dies before the time appointed for payment, his representative must perform the promise or employ some proper person to do so.

3. **The legal representative** (*Sec. 37*) **:** Promises bind the representatives of the promisors in case of the death of such promisors before performance, unless a contrary intention appears from the contract. On the death of the promisor, the promisee can compel his legal representatives to perform the promise unless it involves the personal skill of the promisor. However, the liability of the legal representative will not be personal, but shall be limited only to the extent of the value of the estate of the deceased promisor inherited by him.

Examples **:** (*i*) *A* promises to deliver goods to *B* on a certain day on payment of ₹ 1,000. *A* dies before that day. *B* can demand performance from the legal representatives of *A*.

(*ii*) *A* promises to paint a picture for *B* by a certain day, at a certain price. *A* dies before that day. The contract cannot be enforced by *A*'s representatives or by *B*.

4. **Performance of a promise by a third person** (*Sec. 41*) **:** When a promisee accepts performance of the promise from a third person, he cannot afterwards enforce it against the promisor.

5. **Performance of joint promises** (*Secs. 42 to 44*) **:** The rules regarding performance of a promise made by joint promisors are as follows :

(*a*) When two or more persons have made a joint promise, then ordinarily all of them, during their life-time must jointly fulfil the promise; and after death of any of them, his legal representatives jointly with the survivor or survivors and after death of the last survivor, the legal representatives of all the original co-promisors must fulfil the promise (*Sec. 42*).

(*b*) In the absence of any contract to the contrary, promisee is free to compel any one or more of the joint promisors to perform the whole of the promise. Thus, a joint promisor cannot claim the right of being sued upon along with his co-promisors (*Sec. 43*).

Example **:** *A*, *B* and *C* jointly promise to pay *D* ₹ 3,000. *D* may compel either *A* or *B* to *C* to pay him ₹ 3,000.

Thus, under Indian law the liability of joint promisors is *joint as well as several.*

(*c*) In all those cases where the debt devoles upon a number of heirs on the death of the individual original debtors, promisee must bring his suit against all the heirs collectively. He cannot compel any one or more of such co-heirs to pay the entire amount because they have only joint liability and not joint and several liability. Severally none of them would be liable for an amount more than his share.

(*d*) A joint promisor, on being compelled to perform the whole contract, can call for equal contribution from others, unless otherwise agreed upon between them (*Sec. 43*).

Example **:** *A*, *B* and *C* jointly promise to pay *D* the sum or ₹ 3,000. *C* is compelled to pay the whole, *C* is entitled to receive ₹ 1,000 each from *A* and *B*.

(*e*) If any of the joint promisors makes default in making his contribution the remaining joint promisors must bear the loss arising from such a default in equal shares. For the purposes of application of this rule of contribution, principal debtor and surety shall not be treated as joint promisors.

Surety shall be entitled to recover from the principal debtor the entire amount paid by him on behalf of the principal debtor (*Sec. 43*).

Examples : (*i*) *A, B* and *C* are under a joint promise to pay *D* ₹ 3,000. *C* is unable to pay anything and *A* is compelled to pay the whole. *A* is entitled to receive ₹ 1,500 from *B*.

(*ii*) *A, B* and *C* are under a joint promise to pay *D* ₹ 3,000. *A*, and *B* being only sureties for *C*. *C* fails to pay *A* and *B* are compelled to pay the whole sum. They are entitled to recover it from *C*.

(*f*) Release of one of the joint promisors by the promisee will not discharge the other joint promisors. They shall continue to be liable to make contribution to the other joint promisors.

DEMAND FOR PERFORMANCE

Performance can be demanded by the following persons :

1. **Promisee :** The performance can be demanded only by the promisee. A third party cannot demand performance of the contract even if it was made for his benefit.

Example : *A* agrees with *B* that as desired by him (*B*), he (*A*) will sell his motor car to *C*. In case *A* refuses to sell his motor car to *C*, only *B* can bring action against him.

2. **Legal representative :** In case the death of the promisee has taken place, the legal representatives of the promisee can demand performance, unless the contract happens to be of a personal nature.

Example : *A* agrees to marry *B*. After some time *B* dies. The legal representatives of *B* cannot demand performance of the promise from *A*.

3. **Joint promisees :** When a person has made a promise to two or more persons jointly, then unless a contrary intention appears from the contract, the right to claim performance rests

(*a*) with all the joint promises jointly;

(*b*) in case of death of any of the joint promisees, with the representatives of such deceased person jointly with the survivor or survivors;

(*c*) in case of death of all joint promises with the representatives of all jointly.

Example : *A*, in consideration of ₹ 500 lent to him by *B* and *C*, promises *B* and *C* jointly to repay them the sum with interest on a day specified. *B* dies. The right to claim performance rests with *B*'s representative jointly with *C* during *C*'s life, and after the death of *C* with the representatives of *B* and *C* jointly.

It has been held by the majority of High Courts in the country that this section does not apply to partnership firm. Surviving partner or partners of a firm can bring suit in their own name to recover a debt to the partnership without joining the representatives of the deceased partner.

RECIPROCAL PROMISES

Meaning

Promises which form consideration or part of the consideration for each other are called reciprocal promises [*Sec. 2(f)*]. Such promises are mutual promises, *i.e.*, a promise for a promise. When one party gives a promise in consideration of the other's promise, both the promises are called reciprocal promises.

Kinds of Reciprocal Promises

Lord Mansfield in *Jones v. Barkley*[2] classified reciprocal promises into three categories:

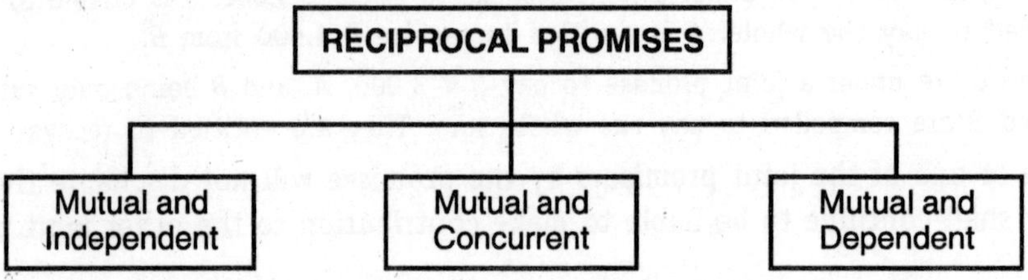

1. **Mutual and independent promises :** In cases where each party has to perform his promise *independently* without waiting for the performance or willingness to perform of the other party, the promises are mutual and independent. Such promises are rare, and, therefore, have not been provided for in the Act.

Example **:** On account of an arbitration award *B* is to pay to *D* the sum of ₹ 2,000 and to deliver 200 ordinary shares held by him and in default of payment within a fortnight, *B* is to pay interest from the expiry of the fortnight. Here the obligation of *D* to deliver shares is quite independent of *B*'s promise to pay.[3]

2. **Mutual and concurrent :** Where the two promises are to be simultaneously performed, promises are mutual and concurrent. This class of cases is covered by section 51 of the Contract Act and section 32 of the Sale of Goods Act.

Example **:** *A* agrees to sell certain goods to *B*. Price is to be paid on delivery. The promises are mutual and concurrent.

3. **Mutual and dependent promises :** Where the performance of promise by one party depends on the *prior performance* of the promise by the other party, the promises are mutual and dependent. This class of cases is covered by Section 54 of the Contract Act.

Example **:** *A* agrees to build a house for *B*. *B* agrees to supply the necessary material required for the construction of the house. The promises are mutual and dependent.

It is to be noted that whether reciprocal promises are dependent, independent or concurrent, depends upon the intention of the parties collected from the agreement as a whole. The Court will not go by technical expressions but by the substance of the contract.[4]

Rules Regarding Performance of Reciprocal Promises

1. **Mutual and independent promises :** In such promises if either party breaks his promise the other party may proceed against him for damages, but he cannot excuse himself from performance by reason of the non-performance of the other.[5]

Example **:** *A* agrees to supply certain goods to *B* on 15th of March. *B* promises to pay the price in advance on 15th February and on default to pay interest @12% p.a. from 15 February till the date of payment. In this case *A*'s promise to deliver goods is quite independent of *B*'s promise to pay price

2. Dough 659, per Lord Mansfield.
3. Brahma Swaroop *v.* Diwan Chand (1963), A Cal. 583.
4. Bradford *v.* Williams (1879), 7 Ex. 259.
5. Mackay *v.* Dick (1881), 6 A.C., 251.

on 15 February. In case *B* does not pay the price, *A* cannot refuse to deliver the goods on 15th March. His only remedy will be to sue *B* for price and damages.

2. **Mutual and concurrent promises :** When a contract consists of reciprocal promises to be simultaneously performed, no promisor need perform his promise unless the promisee is ready and willing to perform his reciprocal promise (*Sec. 51*).

Examples **:** (*i*) *A* and *B* contract that *A* shall deliver goods to *B* to be paid for by *B* on delivery. *A* need not deliver the goods unless *B* is ready and willing to pay for the goods on delivery. *A* need not pay for the goods unless *A* is ready and willing to deliver them on payment.

(*ii*) *A* and *B* contract that *A* shall deliver goods to *B* at a price to be paid by instalments, the first instalment to be paid on delivery. *A* need not pay the first instalment unless *A* is ready and willing to deliver the goods on payment of the first instalment.

3. **Mutual and dependent promises :** Where a contract consists of mutual and dependent reciprocal promises, the promisor who is required to perform his promise first, fails to perform it, such promisor cannot claim the performance of the reciprocal promise and must make compensation to the other party to the contract for any loss which such other party may sustain by the non-performance of the contract (*Sec. 54*).

Examples **:** (*i*) *A* hires *B*'s ship to take in and convey from Calcutta to Mauritius, cargo to be provided by *A*, *B* receiving a certain freight for its conveyance. *A* does not provide any cargo for the ship. *A* cannot claim the performance of *B*'s promise, and must make compensation to *B* for the loss which *B* sustains by the non-performance of the contract.

(*ii*) *A* contracts with *B* to deliver to him, at a specified place, certain merchandise on board a ship which cannot arrive for a month, and *B* engages to pay for the merchandise within a week from the date of the contract. *A* does not pay within the week. *A*'s promise to deliver need not performed, and *B* must make compensation.

(*iii*) *A* contracts with *B* to execute certain builders' work for a fixed price. *B* supplying the scaffolding and timber necessary for the work. *B* refuses to furnish any scaffolding or timber and the work cannot be executed. *A* need not execute the work and *B* is bound to make compensation to *A* for any loss caused to him by the non-performance of the contract.

(*iv*) *A* promises *B* to sell his 100 bales of merchandise, to be delivered next day, and *B* promises *A* to pay for them within a month. *A* does not deliver according to his promise. *B*'s promise to pay need not be performed. *A* must make compensation.

4. **General rules for order of performance :** Where the order in which *reciprocal promises* are to be performed is expressly fixed by the contract, they shall be performed in that order; and where the order is not expressly fixed by the contract, they shall be performed in that order which the nature of the transaction requires (*Sec. 52*).

Examples **:** (*i*) *A* and *B* contract that *A* shall build a house for *B* at a fixed price. *A*'s promise to build the house must be performed before *B*'s promise to pay for it.

(*ii*) *A* and *B* contract that *A* shall make over his stock-in-trade to *B* at a fixed price and *B* promises to give security for the payment of the money. *A*'s promise need not be performed until the security is given, for the nature of the transaction requires that *A* should have security before he delivers his stock.

Consequences where a party prevents performance : When a contract contains of reciprocal promises and one party to the contract prevents the other from performing his promise the contract becomes voidable at the option of the party so prevented, and he is entitled to compensation from the other party for any loss which he may sustain in consequence of the non-performance of the contract (*Sec. 53*).

Example : *A* and *B* contract that *B* shall execute certain work for *A* for a thousand rupees. *B* is ready and willing to execute work accordingly, but *A* prevents him from doing so. The contract is voidable at the option of *B*, and if he elects to rescind it, he is entitled to recover from *A*, compensation for any loss which he has incurred by its non-performance.

Reciprocal promises to do things legal, and also other things illegal : Where persons reciprocally promise, firstly to do certain things which are legal, and secondly, under specified circumstances to do certain other things which are illegal, the first set of promises is a contract, but the second is a void agreement (*Sec. 57*).

Example : *A* and *B* agree that *A* shall sell to *B* a house for 10,000 rupees, but that if *B*uses it as a gambling house, he shall pay *A* 50,000 rupees for it.

The first set of reciprocal promises, namely, to sell the house and pay 10,000 rupees for it is a contract.

The second set is for an unlawful object, that is, *B* may use the house as a gambling house and therefore, will be a void agreement.

Alternative promises, one branch being illegal : In the case of an alternative promise, one branch of which is legal and the other illegal, the legal branch alone can be enforced (*Sec. 58*).

Example : *A* and *B* agrees that *A* shall pay 1,000 rupees, for which *B* shall afterwards deliver to *A* either rice or smuggled opium.

There is a valid contract to deliver rice and void agreement as to the opium.

TIME AND PLACE FOR PERFORMANCE

Time for the performance of a promise where no application is to be made and no time is specified : Where, by the contract, a promisor is to perform his promise without application by the promisee, and no time for performance is specified, the engagement must be performed within a reasonable time.

Explanation : The question 'what is a reasonable time' is, in each particular case, a question of fact (*Sec. 46*).

Time and place for the performance of promise, where time is specified and no application is to be made: Where a promise is to be a performed on a certain day and the promisor has undertaken to perform it without application by the promisee, the promisor may perform it at any time during the usual hours of business on such day and place at which the promise ought to be performed (*Sec. 47*).

Example : *A* promises to deliver goods at *B*'s warehouse on 1st January. On that day *A* brings the goods at *B*'s warehouse, but after the usual hours for closing it, and they are not received. *A* has not performed his promise.

Application for performance on a certain day to be at a proper time and place : Where a promise is to be performed on a certain day and the promisor has not undertaken to perform it without application by the promisee, it is the duty of the promisee to apply for performance at a proper place and within the usual hours of business.

Explanation : The question 'what is a proper time and place' is, in each particular case, is a question of fact (*Sec. 48*).

Place for performance of promise where no application is to be made and no place is fixed for the performance : When a promise is to be performed without application by the promisee, and no place is fixed for the performance of it, it is the duty of the promisor to apply to the promisee to appoint a reasonable place for the performance of the promise, and to perform it at such place (*Sec. 49*).

Example : *A* undertakes to deliver a thousand tonnes of jute to *B* on a fixed day. *A* must apply to *B* to appoint a reasonable place for the purpose of receiving it, and must deliver it to him at such place.

Performance in the manner or at the time prescribed or sanctioned by promisee : The performance of any promise may be made in any manner, or at any time which the promisee prescribes or sanctions (*Sec. 50*).

Examples : (*i*) *B* owes *A* 2,000 rupees. *A* desires *B* to pay the amount to *A*'s account with *C*, a banker. *B*, who also banks with *C*, orders the amount to be transferred from his account to *A*'s credit, and this is done by *C*. Afterwards, and before *A* knows of the transfer, *C* fails. There has been a good payment by *B*.

(*ii*) *A* and *B* are mutually indebted. *A* and *B* settle the account by settling off one item against another, and *A* pays *B* the balance found to be due from him upon such settlement. This amounts to payment by *A* and *B* respectively, of the sums which they owed to each other.

(*iii*) *A* owes *B* rupees 2,000. *B* accepts some of *A*'s goods in reduction of debt. The delivery of the goods operates as a part payment.

Time as the essence of a contract (*Sec. 55*) : In all those cases where parties to the contract have fixed up the time for the performance of the promise as the essence to the contract, if any party fails to perform his promise to the contract within the specified time, the contract shall become voidable at the option of the other party. The applicability of this rule becomes very difficult when the question arises, whether in a particular contract, time was intended to be of the essence of the contract at the time of its formation or not. A mere promise to do something at or before a certain time may not make time the essence of the contract. Whether time was inten-ded to be the essence of the contract or not, can be gathered only from the terms of the contract.

Generally speaking in mercantile transactions the time fixed for delivery of goods is always taken as of essence, but not the time for payment of price, unless otherwise agreed. This is because the prices of goods fluctuate very rapidly and hence, punctuality in the time of delivery of goods must be observed. In contracts relating to those goods, the prices of which remain more or less stable over short periods, *e.g.*, land or immovable property etc., time of the performance of the promise is usually not taken to be an essential condition. Similarly, mortgaged loan can be rapid at any time and mortgaged property can be redeemed even after the due date of the loan. However, even in those contracts where time is usually not taken to be the essence of the contract, it may be expressly agreed upon by the parties that if the contract is not performed by a certain date, the other party shall have the right to rescind the contract.

In those contracts where time is not of essence, failure to perform the contract at the fixed time will not entitle the promisee to set aside the contract but he will be entitled to demand compensation. However, such contracts must also be performed within a reasonable time, otherwise they will become voidable at the option of the promisee.

Promisee is free to waive his right of avoiding the contract when time has been essential for the performance of the contract and the contract has not been performed within the specified time and may accept the performance of the contract at any time other than the agreed time. In such a case of waiver, promisee cannot claim any compensation from the promisor for any loss occasioned by the non-performance of the promise at the agreed time except when, before accepting the performance, he had given notice to the promisor of his intention to claim compensation.

Examples **:** (*i*) *A* promises to sell and deliver on 15th January, 1998 a lorry to *B*. The parties have stipulated that time should be the essence of the contract. But *A* delivers the lorry only on 5th February, 1998. Explain what are the rights of *B* against *A* in this case. Suppose *B* desires to accept the belated delivery and also claim compensation for loss occasioned by the non-performance of the promise at the time agreed. Advise *B* as to whether he can achieve those two objectives.

In the first circumstance, *B* can repudiate the contract since the time is of essence in the contract. He can claim compensation from *A* for loss suffered by him on account of non-performance. In the second case (*i.e.*, when *B* accepts belated delivery) *B* cannot claim damages occasioned by non-performance of the contracts unless, at the time of such acceptance, he gives notice to *A* of his intention to do so.

(*ii*) *B*, the lessee of a petrol pump had to apply for the renewal of the lease within a fixed time as per the terms of the contract. He was late by ten days in submitting his application for renewal. The landlord refused to renew the lease. The Supreme Court held that time was of essence in the contract and the landlord could refuse renewal. Renewal of lease is different from contracts for sale of immovable property. In the latter case time is presumed to be not an essence of the contract.[6]

APPROPRIATION OF PAYMENTS

When a debtor owes several distinct debts to a creditor and makes a payment which is insufficient to discharge his whole indebtedness, there is a problem of appropriating this payment. In England the law on the subject was laid down in *Clayton's Case*.[7] In India, rules regarding appropriation of payments have been laid down in sections 59 to 61 of the Contract Act. In this connection it is important to remember the observations made by the learned judge in *Croft* v. *Lumley's* case.[8]

'There is an established maxim of law that, when money is paid, it is to be applied according to the expressed will of the payer, not the receiver. If the party to whom the money is offered does not agree to apply it according to the expressed will of the party offering it, he must refuse it and stand upon the rights which the law gives him.'

The Indian Contract Act has laid down the following provisions with regard to the appropriation of payments.

1. **Appropriation by the debtor** (*Sec. 59*) : Where money is paid by a debtor to his creditors with the express or implied intimation that money is to be applied to a particular debt, creditor, if accepts the payment, must apply the money received according to the direction of the debtor.[9] If the creditor owns other debts which are also due and payable and the debtor insists upon applying the money to the debt of his choice, the creditors remedy is to refuse to accept the money if he is not prepared to agree with the wishes of the debtor. Appropriation is a right primarily of the debtor and for his benefit. Law on this point is mandatory and the creditor must refuse to accept payment if he does not agree to the specific directions of the debtor as to the appropriation. He may enforce his rights against the debtor in the ordinary course of law. But in no case he can receive the amount under protest or alter the appropriation after he has once accepted it. The debtor's information must synchronise with the payment.

The debtor may give directions as to appropriation either by words or by conduct, *e.g.*, if the debtor owes two debts one of ₹ 50 and another of ₹ 80 and pays ₹ 80, it will be presumed that the latter is the debt intended to be paid.

6. Caltex (India) Ltd. *v.* Bhagwan Devi Marodia (1969), 2 S.C.R. 238.
7. (1816), 1 Mer. 572.
8. (1858), 6 H.L.C. 672.
9. Vasudeo *v.* Namdeo (1951), Nag. 155.

Examples **:** (*i*) *A* ownes *B* among other debts, ₹ 1,000 upon a promissory note which falls due for payment on 1st June. He owes *B* no other debt of that amount. On 1st June, *A* pays to *B* ₹ 1,000. The payment is to be applied to the discharge of the promissory note.

(*ii*) *A* owes to *B* among other debts, the sum of ₹ 567. *B* writes to *A* and demands payment of this sum. *A* sends to *B* ₹ 567. This payment is to be applied to the discharge of the debt of which *B* had demanded payment.

2. **Appropriation by the creditor** (*Sec. 60*) **:** If the debtor fails to intimate to the creditor at the time of payment as to the debt towards the payment of which the money is to be applied and where several debts are due, the right of application may be exercised by the creditor, who may apply it to the payment of any lawful debts at his choice including even the time-barred debts. Creditor may in such cases apply the repayments to the earliest items which are time barred according to law of limitation and sue for such balance as is not so barred. Creditor will exercise such a right of appropriation only after the debtor has had the opportunity to exercise his right but has omitted to do so. Creditor may exercise his right of appropriation until the every last moment. He need not declare his intentions in any express terms.

Creditor's appropriation in such a case, will be revocable till communicated to the debtor, *i.e.*, if he has appropriated the payment to a certain debt, he can afterwards change it to another debt provided he has not disclosed the earlier appropriation to the debtor. But when once an appropriation has been made and communicated to the debtor, the creditor has no right to appropriate it otherwise. Appropriation can be made both to legal and equitable claims, *i.e.*, time-barred debts, though they might not be enforceable by action. But a creditor cannot appropriate a payment to a demand arising out of a contract forbidden by law nor does his right to appropriate remains after a judgement which does not give effect to it.

3. **Where neither party appropriates** (*Sec. 61*) **:** Where neither party makes any appropriation the payment shall be applied in discharge of the debts in order of time, whether they are or not barred by the law in force for the time being as to the limitation of suits. If debts are of equal standing payment shall be applied in discharge of each proportionately. Law here is based on presumption which may be rebutted by evidence showing a contrary intention.

4. **Payment of interest first :** In case of a debt carrying interest and the debtor has not given any specific direction as to the appropriation of money paid, the rule is to apply the money, in ordinary cases, first towards payment of interest and then to apply the surplus in payment of the principal amount.

5. **Hallet's estate case :**[10] The Hallet's estate case lays down the position of trustee who keeps his own money as well as trust's money in one bank account. It was held in this case that in case a series of deposits and withdrawals were made by the trustee from the bank account during the course of which trust funds were misappropriated, the deposits would be first credited to trust funds and then to his own funds; and the withdrawals would be first debited to his money and then to the trust funds. The order of deposits and withdrawals would be immaterial for this purpose.

KEY TERMS

- **Performance of Contract :** It implies fulfilment of the terms of the contract by the respective parties to the contract.
- **Reciprocal Promises :** These are promises which form consideration for each other.
- **Tender of Performance :** It is an offer to perform one's obligation under a contract.

TEST QUESTIONS

Objective Type : *Test Your Knowledge*

1. State whether each of the following statements is *True* or *False*
   (*i*) The liability of joint promisors for performance is joint as well as several under Indian Law.
   (*ii*) A legal representative of a deceased promisee can demand performance of a contract under all circumstances.
   (*iii*) Promises, where each party is to perform his or her promise independently without waiting for the performance of the other party, are termed as mutual and concurrent reciprocal promises.
   (*iv*) In the absence of the debtor's intimation to the creditor regarding appropriation of a payment, the creditor can utilise the payment even towards payment of a time-barred debt.
   (*v*) In the case of an alternative promise one branch of which is legal and the other illegal, only the legal branch can be enforced.
   (*vi*) 'In case of joint promise, the liability to pay the promisee will devolve on any one or more promisors.'

(*PCE, ICAI, May 2007*)

[***Ans.*** (*i*) True; (*ii*) False; (*iii*) False; (*iv*) True; (*v*) True; (*vi*) True.]

2. Fill in the blanks
   (*i*) Contracts involving personal skill must be performed by ....
   (*ii*) Where two promises are to be simultaneously performed, such promises are termed as ....
   (*iii*) Time is taken as of essence generally in ....
   (*iv*) The first right of appropriation for a payment is with........................
   (*v*) Tender is an ....

[***Ans.*** (*i*) the promisor himself; (*ii*) mutual and concurrent; (*iii*) mercantile contracts; (*iv*) the debtor; (*v*) attempted performance.]

Essay Type : *For Review, Discussion and Practice*

1. 'Tender is attempted performance' Comment.
2. State the rules regarding devolution of joint rights and liabilities.
3. State by whom contract should be performed? Is the promisee bound to accept performance from persons other than the promisor?
4. What do you understand by reciprocal promises? State the provisions of the Indian Contract Act which deal with the order of performance of reciprocal promises.
5. What are the rules relating to appropriation of payments made by a debtor who owes a number of distinct debts to his creditor?
6. What is meant by performance of a contract? By whom the contract can be performed? (*CA, Foundation, May 2001*)
7. State the rules of appropriation of payments when
   (*i*) order of discharge is indicated; and (*ii*) the order is not indicated. (*CA, Foundation, May 2001*)
8. What do you mean by reciprocal promises? (*ICWA, Foundation, June 1998*)
9. Explain the law relating to liability of joint promisors in a contract. (*CA, IPC, May, 2014*)

10. Performance of a contract may be made only by the parties to the contract. Comment.

(*ICWA*, Inter. Dec., 2010)

[***Ans.*** Except when specifically required, a contract may be performed by the transferor's representative or by any other person employed by the promisor. When contract requiring personal skill involving personal confidence between the parties can not be performed by others. They are to be performed by the promisors only.]

PRACTICAL PROBLEMS

1. *A* agreed to sell to *B* 25 bags of sugar of July shipment and to declare the name of the vessel and other particulars to *B* within 60 days of the bill of lading. Only 20 bags were delivered within 60 days and the remaining 5 bags delivered subsequently. Can *B* refuse to accept the goods?

   [***Ans.*** Yes. Time is the essence of the contract.]

2. *A, B,* and *C* jointly borrow from *D* ₹ 3,000. *D* proceeds to recover the entire amount from *C* only. Will he succeed?

   [***Ans.*** Yes. Sec. 43 of the Act permits.]

3. *A, B* and *C* jointly lent ₹ 3,000 to *D*. *A* dies. *B* and *C* file a suit against *D* for recovery of the money lent. Will they succeed?

   [***Ans.*** No. The suit should be filed along with the legal representation of *A*.]

4. *A, B* and *C* are partners in a firm. They jointly promise to pay ₹ 1,50,000 to *P.C.* became insolvent and his private assets are sufficient to pay only 1/5 of his share of debts. *A* is compelled to pay the whole amount to *P*. Examining the provisions of the Indian Contract Act, 1872, decide the extent to which *A* can recover and amount from *B*. (*PCE, ICAI, Nov. 2007*)

   [***Ans.*** ₹ 70,000]

5. *'D', 'E'* and *'F'* who are partners in a firm, jointly promised to pay ₹ 1,50,000 to *'A'*. Later on *'F'* became insolvent and his private assets are sufficient to pay only 1/5 of his share of debt. *'A'* recovers the whole amount from *'D'* through a legal action. Decide, under the provisions of the Indian Contract Act, 1872 the extent which *'D'* can recover the amount from *'E'*.

   (*CA, IPC, May, 2014*)

   [***Ans.*** F will contribute ₹ 10,000 (1,50,000 × 1/3 × 1/5) and the remaining ₹ 40,000 (i.e. 50,000-10,000) will be contributed by *D* and *E* in equal ratio. Thus, *D* and *E* have to contribute ₹ 70,000 each (₹ 50,000 for their respective share and 20,000 for deficiency arises due to insolvency of *F*. Thus, *D* has the right to recover ₹ 70,000 from *E* as *E*'s share.]

Chapter 10

DISCHARGE OF CONTRACTS

LEARNING OBJECTIVES

A careful study of this chapter will enable you to :

- understand the meaning of discharge of contracts;
- identify the various modes of discharge of contracts;
- appreciate the significance of Doctrine of Supervening Impossibility;
- differentiate between actual and anticipatory breach; and
- explain the meaning of certain key terms.

MEANING AND MODES OF DISCHARGE

A contract is discharged when the obligation created by it come to an end. A contract may be discharged in any one of the following ways :

1. By Agreement.
2. By Performance of the Contract.
3. By Lapse of Time.
4. By Operation of Law.
5. By Material Alteration.
6. By Subsequent Impossibility of Performance.
7. By Breach.

Each the above modes have been discussed in details in the following pages :

AGREEMENT

The parties may agree to terminate the existence of the contract by any of the following ways (*Sec. 62*) :

(*a*) **By novation :** Substitution of a new contract in place of the old existing one is known as *'novation of contract'.* Novation creates a new contract in exchange of the old contract. It discharges and extinguished the original contract. New contract may be either between the same parties or between different parties, the consideration being mutually the discharge of the old contract. Nature of obligation may also be changed. *'The essence of the novation of a contract lies not in the dissimilarity of the terms between the old contract and the new one, but in the intention of the parties to supersede old by the new.'* Novation, therefore, may take either of the two forms :

(*i*) Substitution of a contract with new terms for an old contract between the same parties.

(*ii*) Substitution of a new party for an old one, the contract remaining the same. Promisee will now look to the third party for the performance of the contract. Original promisor is released of the obligations under the old contract.

Examples : (*i*) *A* owes money to *B* under a contract. It is agreed between *A*, *B* and *C* that *B* shall henceforth accept *C* as his debtor instead of *A*. The old debt of *A* to *B* is at an end, and a new debt from *C* to *B* has been contracted.

(*ii*) *A* owes *B* ₹ 10,000. *A* enters into an arrangement with *B*, and gives *B* a mortgage of his (*A's*) estate for ₹ 5,000 in balance of the debt of ₹ 10,000. This is a new contract and extinguishes the old.

(*iii*) *A* owes *B* ₹ 1,000 under a contract. *A* owes *C* ₹ 1,000, *B* orders *A* to credit *C* with ₹ 1,000 in his books but *C* does not assent to the arrangement. *B* still owes *C* ₹ 1,000, and no new contract has been entered into.

Novation can take place only with the consent of all the parties. It cannot be compulsory. The contract replacing the old one must be capable of legal enforcement. The new contract can be entered into both before and after the breach of the old contract. Novation must relate to the present actual substitution of a new contract for the original one. An agreement to substitute a contract in future will not amount to novation.

As a result of novation, old contract is completely discharged and law will not entertain any action based upon the terms of the old contract.

(*b*) **By rescission :** Rescission means cancellation of the contract. A contract can be rescinded in any of the following ways :

(*i*) *By mutual consent* : Parties may enter into a simple agreement to rescind the contract before its breach.

(*ii*) *By the aggrieved party* : Where a party has committed a breach of contract, the aggrieved party can rescind the contract without in any way affecting his right of getting compensation for the breach of contract.

(*iii*) *By the party whose consent is not free* : In case of a voidable contract, the party whose consent is not free can, if so decides, rescind the contract.

A contract may also be taken to be impliedly rescinded where none of the parties has performed his part till a long time and no party has any complaint against the other.

Though both in novation and rescission the old contract is discharged by mutual agreement yet in the case of novation, a new contract is substituted for the old one, while in the case of rescission only the old contract is cancelled and no new contract is substituted in its place.

(*c*) **By alteration :** Alteration means change in one or more of the conditions of the contract. Alteration made by the mutual consent of the parties will be perfectly valid. But any material alteration, as discussed later, in terms of a written contract by one party without the consent of other party, will discharge such party from its obligation under the contract.

In case of novation, a new contract replaces an old contract. The parties may also change. While in case of alteration only some of the terms of the contract are changed. Parties continue to be the same.

(*d*) **By remission :** Remission means acceptance of a lesser performance than what was actually due under the contract. According to *Sec. 63* a party may dispense with or remit, wholly or in part, the performance of the promise made to him. He can also extend the time of such performance or accept instead of it any satisfaction which he deems fit. A promise to do so will be binding even though there is no consideration for it.

***Examples* :** (*i*) *A* owes *B* ₹ 5,000. *A* pays to *B* and *B* accepts in satisfaction of the whole debt ₹ 2,000 paid at the time and place where ₹ 5,000 were payable. The whole debt is discharged.

(*ii*) *A* owes *B*, under a contract, a sum of money, the amount of which has not been ascertained. *A* without ascertaining the amount gives ₹ 2,000 to *B*, and *B*, in satisfaction, therefore, accepts the sum of the ₹ 2,000. This is a discharge of the whole debt whatever may be its amount.

(*iii*) *A* owes *B* ₹ 2,000 and is also indebted to other creditors. *A* makes an arrangement with his creditors including *B*, to pay them a composition of fifty paise in the rupee upon their respective demands. Payments to *B* of ₹ 1,000 is a discharge of *B's* demand.

(*iv*) *M* was to pay a sum of ₹ 27 lakhs to *K*. Since Hyderabad had been taken over by the Indian Government, a committee was appointed to clear matters. It offered ₹ 20 lakhs to *K* who accepted in full satisfaction of the claim of ₹ 27 lakhs. Later on *K* filed a suit for the recovery of the balance. The Supreme Court held that *K* could not do so as he had accepted 20 lakhs in full satisfaction.[1]

(*e*) **Owing to the occurrence of an event**, on the happening of which it was previously agreed that all rights and liabilities should cease.

(*f*) **By waiver :** A contract may be discharged by agreement between the parties to waive their rights arising from the contract. Thus, in case of waiver, the person who is entitled to any right under the contract, intentionally relinquished them without consideration and without a new agreement.

***Example* :** *A* promises to paint a picture for *B*. *B* afterwards forbids him to do so. *A* is no longer bound to perform the promise.

But extension of time for the performance of the contract by mutual agreement cannot be taken as waiver. The distinction between the two was made clear by the Supreme Court in the case of *M. Sham Singh* v. *State of Mysore.*[2] The facts of the case are being given in the following illustration.

***Example* :** *M* was granted a scholarship by the State of Mysore to study in the United States. Under the terms of the scholarship *M* was to serve the State after completion of his studies provided the State offered him a job within six months of his return, failing which the bond was presumed to have been waived. In case of *M's* failure to do so, he was to refund the scholarship money. The state agreed to extend his period of stay at his request by a year in the United States for practical training. He came to India during this period for a domestic visit but was allowed by the State to rejoin his training. Later on, he joined service in the United States on completion of the training. The State claimed refund of scholarship money. *M* pleaded that by granting extension to him the State had waived its right to recover the scholarship money. Held, the extension was by mutual consent and there was nothing on the part of State which showed that the State had waived its rights.

PERFORMANCE OF CONTRACT

When parties fulfil their obligations and promises under a contract, the contract is said to have been performed and discharged. Performance should be complete and according to the real intentions of the agreement. Offer of performance shall have the same effect as performance. A party to a contract shall become free from all obligations if it has offered to perform his part of the promise but it was not accepted by the other party.

1. Kapur Chand Godha *v.* Mir Nawab Himayat Ali Khan (1963), 2 S.C.R. 168.
2. M. Sham Singh *v.* State of Mysore (1973), 2 S.C.C. 303.

Partial performance will not discharge the contract except in the following circumstance :

(*i*) where the contract is divisible and the other party has had the benefit of the part which has been performed, or

(*ii*) where a promisor has substantially done what he had promised to do, or

(*iii*) where a party is prevented from completing his undertaking because of some act or omission of the other party.

LAPSE OF TIME

Every contract must be performed either within the period fixed or within a reasonable time of the contract. Lapse of time may discharge the contract by barring the right to bring an action to enforce the contract under the Limitation Act.

OPERATION OF LAW

(*a*) **Merger :** Merger implies coinciding and meeting of an inferior and a superior right in one the same person. In such a case, inferior right available to a party under an agreement will automatically vanish.

Example : *A* is holding a property under lease. He subsequently buys that property. *A*'s right as a tenant is inferior to his right as a owner of the property. The right as a tenant and right as an owner have coincided and met in one person, *i.e., A*. Therefore, *A*'s rights as a lessee will terminate.

(*b*) **Death :** In case, a contract is of a personal nature, the death of the promisor will discharge the contract. In other cases, the rights and liabilities of the deceased person shall pass to his legal representatives.

(*c*) **Loss of evidence :** In case there is a destruction of evidence of the existence of the contract.

(*d*) **By insolvency :** An insolvent is released from performing his part of the contract by law. The order of discharge gives a new lease of life to the insolvent and he is discharged from all obligations arising from all his earlier contracts.

MATERIAL ALTERATION

Any material alteration made intentionally in a written contract by the promisee or his agent without the consent of the promisor entitles the latter to regard the contract as rescinded.

An alteration will be taken to be material if it affects directly or indirectly the nature or operation of the contract or the identity, validity or effect of the document.

Example : *C* and *F* entered into a contract of carriage by sea whereby *C* agreed that his ship would sail from Amsterdam on March 15th next to Liverpool and would there load a cargo to be provided by *F*. After the signing of the written contract (charter-party) the broker who acted for *C* wrote in after March next the words 'winds and weather permitting.' This was held to be a material alteration and *C* was precluded from relying on the charter-party in an action against *F* on his refusal to supply the cargo.

SUPERVENING IMPOSSIBILITY OF PERFORMANCE

Impossibility of performance of a contract may be of any of the following three types :

(*i*) **Impossibility known to the parties at the time of making of the contract :** This is called absolute impossibility. In such a case the agreement in void *ab initio*.

Example **:** *A* agrees to pay *B* ₹ 1,000 and *B* promises to bring for *A* stars from heaven. The agreement is void.

(*ii*) **Impossibility unknown to parties at the time of making of the contract :** In such a case the contract becomes void when such an impossibility is discovered, because of mutual mistake of a material fact.

Example **:** *A* agrees to sell his horse to *B*, but unknown to both the parties the horse had already died at the time of making of the contract. The contract is void.

(*iii*) **Impossibility which arises subsequent to the formation of the contract :** This may be due to the happening of certain events which were neither in the contemplation of the parties when they entered into the agreement nor either of the parties are responsible for causing the performance of the contract impossible. In such a case the contract will be void as soon as such events make the performance of the contract impossible. The impossibility must be either legal or physical but not commercial. According to section 56 of the Indian Contract Act :

'An agreement to do an impossible act is void. A contract to do an act, which, after the contract is made, becomes impossible, or by reason of some event which the promisor could not prevent, becomes void when the act becomes impossible or unlawful.' The above principle is called 'Doctrine of Supervening Impossibility'. The supervening or subsequent impossibility may arise due to any of the following reasons :

(*a*) **By the destruction of the subject-matter :** If the subject-matter of the contract is destroyed subsequent to the formation of the contract, without any fault of either of the parties, the contract shall become void.

Examples **:** (*i*) *A* music hall was let for a series of concerts on certain days. The hall was burnt down before the date of the first concert. The contract was held to be void.[3]

(*ii*) A person contracted to deliver a part of specific crop of potatoes. The potatoes were destroyed through no fault of the party. The contract was held to be discharged.[4]

(*iii*) *X* agreed to exhibit a picture at *Y*'s theatre on a certain date. The picture could not be exhibited because before that date, the building was demolished under the orders of authorities on account of its being defective and unsafe. The owner had no knowledge of the defective and unsafe nature of the building. It was held that the contract was discharged because of supervening impossibility.[5]

(*b*) **By the non-existence of a state of things necessary for the performance :** If a contract is made on the basis of continued existence of certain state of circumstances, the contract stands discharged if the state of things changes or ceases to exist.

Examples **:** (*i*) *H* hired a room from *K* for two days to witness the coronation procession of King Edward VII. *K* knew the object of the contract, though the contract contained no reference to the coronation. Owing to king's illness the procession was cancelled.

It was held that *H* was excused from paying rent for the room, as the existence of the procession was the basis of the contract and its abandonment discharged the contract.[6]

(*ii*) *A* and *B* contracted to marry each other. Before the time fixed for marriage, *A* goes mad. The contract becomes void.

---

3. Taylor *v.* Caldwell (1863), 3 B. and S. 826.
4. Howell *v.* Coupland (1876), L.R., Q.B. 462 at pp. 465 and 446.
5. V.L. Narasu *v.* P.S.V. Iyer, I.L.R. (1953), Mad. 831.
6. Krell *v.* Henry (1903), 2 K.B. 740.

(*c*) **Death or personal incapacity of the promisor :** Contracts involving personal skill of the promisor will stand discharged in the case of his death or personal incapacity.

Example : *A* contracts to act at a theatre for six months in consideration of sum paid in advance by *B*. On several occasions *A* is too ill to act. The contract to act on these occasions becomes void.

(*d*) **Change of law :** On account of a subsequent change in law, the performance of the contract may become impossible. The object of the contract may be declared to be unlawful.

Examples : (*i*) *A*, who is governed by Muslim law and who already had a wife, promises to marry *B*. Subsequent to this promise and before it is carried out, Special Marriage Act prohibiting polygamy is passed. The contract to marry becomes void.

(*ii*) *X* sold to *Y* a specific parcel of wheat in a godown. Before the delivery could be made, the godown was sealed by the Government and the entire quantity was requisitioned by the Government under statutory power. The contract was held discharged.[7]

(*iii*) *K* agreed to supply certain raw jute to be imported from Bangladesh to *N*.*N* was to supply the import licence within November, failing which he was to supply in December. The seller was to charge extra price for the delay. If he failed in December, he was to pay the difference between the contract and market prices. *N* applied for licence which was refused because he had sufficient stock of jute in his mills and which could last for two months. He applied again but by this time the rules has changed and to obtain a licence he was required to show that he had used equal quantity of Indian jute. Thus *N* could not get the licence. *N* pleaded frustration of the contract on the ground of change in Government policy.

The Supreme Court held him liable for breach of contract on the ground that there was no complete ban on imports. The Government was permitting imports provided one could satisfy the licensing authority. This was merely an administrative difficulty.[8]

(*e*) **Outbreak of war :** An agreement entered into with an alien enemy during the war is unlawful and, therefore, void *ab initio*. Contracts made before the outbreak of war are either suspended or declared void by the Government. If they are suspended, they may be performed after the termination of the war.

Example : *A* contracts to take in cargo for *B* at a foreign port. *A*'s Government afterwards declares war against the country in which the port was situated. The contract becomes void when war is declared.

It is worthwhile to note that the word 'impossible' under *Sec. 56* has not been used in the physical or literal sense. A contract may not have become literally or physically impossible to perform, but if an untoward event has happened which has totally upset the very foundations of the contract, the contract will be taken to be impossible to perform.

Example : An English company agreed in 1939 to sell certain machinery to a Polish company and deliver the same at Gdynia in Poland. Subsequently war broke out between Germany and Poland and also between Britain and Germany. Poland was occupied by Germany. It was held that the contract was discharged by frustration.[9]

Cases not Covered by Supervening Impossibility

It may be stated that impossibility to perform arising subsequently to the agreement will not, as a rule, relieve the promisor from performing his part in all cases, because 'where there is a positive contract to do a thing, not in itself unlawful, the promisor must perform it or pay damages for not

7. Reshipto, Anderson & Co. *v*. Harrison Bros. and Co's Arbitration (1915), 2 K.B.676.
8. Naihatli Jute Mills Ltd. *v*. Khyaliram Jagannath, A.I.R. (1968), S.C. 522.
9. Fibrosa etc. *v*. Fairbairn etc. (1943), A.C. 32.

doing it, although in consequence of unforeseen accidents, the performance of his promise has become unexpectedly burdensome or even impossible.[10] Therefore, in the following cases the doctrine of supervening impossibility will not apply :

(*a*) **Difficulty in performance :** A contract can be avoided on the ground of supervening impossibility only when the events taking place make the performance of the contract physically or legally impossible as contemplated by the parties at the time of the making of the contract. Difficulty in performance will not discharge a contract on the ground of impossibility of performance.

Examples **:** (*i*) *A* sold to *B* a certain quantity of Finland timber to be delivered between July and September, 1914. No deliveries were made before August when the war broke out and transport was disorganised so that *A* could not bring any timber from Finland. It was held, *B* was not concerned with the way in which *A* was going to get timber and, therefore, impossibility of getting timber from Finland did not excuse performance.[11]

(*ii*) *X* promised to send certain goods from Bombay to Antwerp in September. In August war broke out, and shipping space was not available except at very high rates. It was held that the increase of freight rates did not excuse performance.[12]

(*b*) **Commercial impossibility :** A party cannot be discharged from performing his part of the contract simply on the ground that it will be non-profitable for him to perform the contract.

Example **:** *A* agrees to supply certain goods to *B*. Due to outbreak of war the price of goods suddenly shoots up. *A* is not discharged from his liability to supply goods to *B*.

(*c*) **Impossibility due to behaviour of third person :** A contract, the performance of which depends on the behaviour of a third person, shall not become impossible of performance merely because the third party has not acted in a particular manner agreed upon, this is because that if a person chooses to depend on for the voluntary act of a third person, he must be held to warrant his ability to procure that act.

Example **:** *X* enters into a contract with *Y* for the sale of certain goods to be produced by *Z*, a manufacturer of these goods. *Z* does not manufacture the goods. *X* is liable to *Y* for damages.

(*d*) **Strikes, lock-outs and civil disturbances :** Strikes, lock-outs and civil disturbances will not discharge a party from performing his part of the contract unless a specific provision to this effect has been made in the contract.

Example **:** *X* agreed to supply certain goods to *Y*. The goods were to be procured from Algeria. Due to roits and civil disturbances in that country goods could not be procured. It was held that there was no excuse for the non-performance of the contract.[13]

(*e*) **Partial impossibility :** Where there are several purposes for which a contract is made, failure of one of the objects will not terminate the contracts.

Examples **:** A company agreed to let a boat to *H* to view (*i*) the naval review at the coronation and (*ii*) to cruise round the fleet. Due to the illness of the king the naval review was cancelled, but the fleet was assembled. The boat, therefore, could sail round the fleet. Held, the contract was not discharged.[14]

10. Taylor *v*. Caldwell (1863), 3 B. & S. 826.
11. Blackburn Bobbin Co. *v*. T.W. Allen & Sons (1918) 2, K.B. 467.
12. Karl Etlinger *v*. Chhagandas & Co. (1916), 40 Bom. 301.
13. Jacobs *v*. Credit Lyonnais (1884), 12 Q.B.D. 589.
14. H.B. Steamboat Co. *v*. Hulton (1903), 2 K.B., 683.

Doctrine of Supervening Impossibility and Leases

The Supreme Court has held in the case of *Raja Dhruv Dev Chand* v. *Raja Harmohinder Singh* that doctrine of supervening impossibility is not applicable in case of completed transfer of a leasefold property. The facts of the case are given below in the following example.

Example : *A* gave a lease of an agricultural land to *B* for a year, before partition of India. The rent was paid and *B* got possession of the land. But before the land could be used for agricultural purposes, the country was partitioned and the parties migrated to India leaving the land in Pakistan. *B* sued *A* for recovery of the rent paid on the ground of frustration of the contract. But it was held by the Supreme Court that section 56 does not cover completed transfers regarding leasehold properties.[15]

But where on account of unforeseen circumstances the leasor is not able to transfer the possession of property, the leasee can recover the rent paid.[16]

Effects of Supervening Impossibility

1. The contract becomes void incase its performance becomes subsequently impossible. Parties to the contract will be released from further performance (*Sec. 56*, para 2).

2. The person, who has received any advantage under a contract, which becomes subsequently void, is bound to restore it or to make compensation for it to the person from whom he received it (*Sec. 65*).

3. Where one person has promised to do something which he knew or with reasonable diligence might have known, and which the promisee did not know to be impossible or unlawful, such promisor must make compensation to such promisee for any loss which such promisee sustains through the non-performance of the promise (*Sec. 56*, para 3).

Example : *A* contracts to marry *B* being already married to *C*, and being forbidden by the law to which he is subject to practice polygamy, *A* must make compensation to *B* for the loss caused to her by the non-performance of his promise.

BREACH

Breach means failure of a party to perform his or her obligation under a contract. Breach of contract may be of two types :

Actual Breach

Actual breach means breach committed either

(*i*) at the time when the performance of the contract is due, or

(*ii*) during the performance of the contract.

Examples : (*i*) *A* agrees to supply to *B* on 1st February, 1998, 1,000 bags of sugar. On 1st February, 1998 he fails to supply. This is actual breach of contract. The breach has been committed by *A* at the time when the performance is due.

15. Gurdarshan Singh *v.* Bishen Singh (1962), 2 Punj. 5 F.B.
16. Raja Dhruv Dev Chand *v.* Raja Harmohinder Singh, A.I.R. (1968), S.C.1024.

(ii) If on 1st Feb., 1998 *A* is prepared to supply the required number of bags of sugar and *B* without any valid reason refuses to accept them, *B* is guilty of breach of contract.

(iii) *C* contracted with a railway company to supply it with 3,900 railway chairs. After 1,787 chairs had been delivered, the company told *C* that no more chairs would be required.[17] This is a breach of contract committed during the performance of the contract.

Responsibility of Parties to provide reasonable Facilities for the Performance of the Contract

Section 67 of the Contract Act lays this responsibility on each party to provide reasonable facilities to the other party for the performance of his promise. 'If any promisee neglects or refuses to afford the promisor reasonable facilities for the performance of his promise, the promisor is excused by such neglect or refusal as to any non-performance caused thereby'.

Example : *A* contracts with *C* to repair *A*'s house. *C* neglects or refuses to point out *A* the places in which his house requires repair. *A* is excused from the non-performance of the contract, if it caused by such neglect or refusal.

Anticipatory Breach[18]

Repudiation of an integral part of the contract by the promisor before the actual due date of the performance of the contract is called an *anticipatory* breach of contract (*Sec. 39*). The contract in this case is repudiated before the time fixed for its performances arrives and is so discharged.

Anticipatory or constructive breach of contract may take place because of any of the two causes:

(a) express repudiation of the contract by any party before the date of its performance, or

(b) the act of any party making the performance of the contract impossible.

Examples : (i) *A* agrees to employ *B* from 1st of March. On 1st February, he writes to *B* that he need not join the service. The contract has been expressly repudiated by *A* before the date of its performance.

(ii) *A* agrees to marry *B*. But before the agreed date *A* marries *C*. The contract has been repudiated by *A* by his conduct before the due date of its performance.

Remedies in the Case of Ancipatory Breach

Two remedies are open to a promisee in the case of an anticipatory breach of contract. He may exercise any one of them.

1. To take the anticipatory breach as actual breach and sue for damages and claim other rights as may be available to him under the law. Thus, promisee may treat the contract as over and may bring about an action for the breach of contract without waiting for the arrival of the due date for the performance of the contract.

Example : *K* promised to marry *F* soon after the death of *K*'s father. During the father's lifetime *K* absolutely refused to marry *F*. It was held that though the time for performance of the contract had not arrived, *F* was entitled to sue for breach of promise to marry.[19]

---

17. Cort v. Ambergate Railway Company (1851), 17 Q.B. 127.
18. The term has been used in English Law.
19. Forst v. Knight (1872), L.R. 7 Ex. 111.

2. To wait till the due date of performance of the contract and then avail of legal remedies for breach of contract available against the defaulting party.

If the promisee decides to enjoy the first remedy, *i.e.*, termination of the contract at the time when anticipatory breach of contract is communicated to him, the quantum of damages will be assessed by the difference of prices prevailing on the date of breach of the contract and the contract price. But if the party keeps the contract alive till the due date of performance arrives, damages will be measured by the difference between the contract price and the prices prevailing on the date fixed for the performance of the contract.

In a case when the promisee keeps the contract alive, the contract will remain operative for the benefit of both the parties. If during the interval, *i.e.*, the date of breach and the due date for the performance of the contract, special circumstances intervene which operate for the benefit of the promisor, the promisor would also be legally entitled to take advantage of them. He may still perform the contract irrespective of his earlier repudiation.[20]

Examples : (*i*) *X* agrees to supply 100 tonnes of iron to *Y* on July 1, 2000, at ₹ 50 per tonne. Subsequent to the contract the price of iron rises to ₹ 80 per tonne and on May 1, 2000, *X* intimates to *Y* that he does not intend to perform his promise. *Y* replies that he will hold *X* to his promise. On June 1, 2000, the Government, in order to check the coaring prices of iron, prohibits the sale of more than 10 tonnes of iron and fixes the price at ₹ 60 per toone. Discuss the rights and liabilities of *X* and *Y* on (*a*) May 1, 2000 and (*b*) July 1, 2000.

If *Y* takes on May 1, 2000 anticipatory breach as actual breach of the contract, he will be entitled to get a sum of ₹ 3,000 [100 tonnes × (₹ 80 – ₹ 50] as damages. In case *Y* decides to wait till July 1, 2000, he will be entitled to get only ₹ 100 [10 tonnes × (₹ 60 – ₹ 50] as damages from *X*.

(*ii*) If in the above illustration, *Y* decides to wait till the date of performance and the price of iron goes down to ₹ 45 per toone. *X* may inform *Y* that he is prepared to perform his part. *Y* will have to accept performance or pay damages to *X*.

KEY TERMS

- **Actual Breach :** Breach committed either at the time when the performance of the contract is due or during the performance of the contract.
- **Alteration :** It means change in one or more of the conditions of the contract.
- **Anticipatory Breach :** A breach committed before the actual due date of the performance of the contract.
- **Breach :** Failure of a party to perform his or her obligation under a contract.
- **Discharge of Contracts :** A contract is discharged when the obligation created by it come to an end.
- **Merger :** It implies coinciding and meeting of an inferior and superior right in one and the same person.
- **Novation :** Substitution of a new contract in place of the existing contract.
- **Supervening Impossibility :** It refers to impossibility arising subsequent to the formation of the contract.
- **Recession :** It refers to the cancellation of the contract.

20. Phul Chand *v.* Jugal Kishore (1927), 8 A.L. 501.

TEST QUESTIONS

Objective Type : *Test Your Knowledge*

1. Fill in the blanks
   (*i*) Replacement of an old contract by a new one is termed as..........................
   (*ii*) Acceptance of a less performance than what was actually due under the contract is termed as..........................
   (*iii*) Strikes, lockouts and civil disturbances do not render contract..........................
   (*iv*) A breach committed before the actual due date of the performance of the contract is called..........................

   [*Ans.* (*i*) novation; (*ii*) remission; (*iii*) void; (*iv*) anticipatory breach.]

2. Select the most appropriate answer
   (*i*) Cancellation of a contract by the mutual consent of the parties is called
   (*a*) Novation (*b*) Recession
   (*c*) Satisfaction
   (*ii*) A subsequent change in law will make the contract void because of
   (*a*) Supervening impossibility (*b*) Commercial impossibility
   (*c*) Material alteration.
   (*iii*) A breach committed during the performance of the contract is termed as :
   (*a*) Actual breach (*b*) Anticipatory breach
   (*c*) Waiver.
   (*iv*) A contract may be discharged by:
   (*a*) Lapse of time (*b*) Operation of the law
   (*c*) Mutual agreement (*d*) All the above

   [*Ans.* (*i*) (*b*); (*ii*) (*a*); (*iii*) (*a*); (*iv*) (*d*)]

Essay Type : *For Review, Discussion and Practice*

1. Explain the provisions of the Indian Contract Act relating to the discharge of contract by (*i*) an agreement, and (*ii*) by operation of law.
2. State the various ways in which a contract may be discharged.
   (*CA Foundation, May 1998; GGSIPU, BBA (H), June 2001; CAIPC, Nov., 2013*)
3. What is novation of a contract? How is it effected? What are its legal consequences? How does it differ from alteration?
4. What do you understand by anticipatory breach of contract? State the rights of a promisee in such a case. On what basis should the quantum of the damages by assessed?
   (*B.Com. (Pass), Delhi 2003*)
5. Explain the following :
   (*i*) Promise against a promise is a good consideration. (*ICWA, Foundation, Dec. 2000*)
   (*ii*) Supervening commercial impossibility renders a contract void.
   (*ICWA, Foundation, June 1998*)
   (*iii*) A contract cannot be discharged on account of strikes, lock-outs and civil disobrders.
   (*B.Com., (Hons) Delhi 2012*)
6. State the various methods of termination of contracts. (*CS Foundation, June 2004*)

7. What do you understand by the 'Doctrine of Supervening Impossibility'? Does this excuse the promiser from performing the contract in all cases? *(GGSIPU, BBA (H), May 2003; B.Com. (Hons.) Delhi 1997, 2010)*
8. Distinguish between Actual Breach and Anticipatory Breach. *(GGSIPU, BBA (H), May 2004)*
9. What are the requisites of a valid 'tender of performance'? *(B.Com. (Hons.), Delhi)*
10. "Impossibility of performance is, as a rule, not an excuse for non-performance of a contract." Discuss. *(B.Com. (Hons.), Delhi 2002, 2005)*
11. What is meant by Breach of Contract? Explain the remedies available to an aggrieved party in case of breach of contract. *(B.Com. (Hons.), Delhi 1998, B.Com. (Pass), Delhi 2002)*
12. Explain the circumstances whereunder a party to a contract may be exempted from the performance of contract on the ground of 'supervening impossibility' under the Indian Contract Act, 1872. *(PEE-II, ICAI, May 2006)*
13. When a contract may be discharged under the provisions of Indian Contract Act, 1872? Explain in detail. *(CA IPC Nov. 2013)*
14. Explain the discharge of contract by mutual agreement. *(B.Com. (Hons.), Delhi, Nov., 2013)*
15. Supervening impossibility does not include the difficulty of performance. *(B.Com. (Hons.), Delhi, Nov. 2012)*

PRACTICAL PROBLEMS

1. *A* owes *B* a sum of ₹ 3,000. *C*, who is *A*'s friend, pays to *B* ₹ 1,500. *B* accepts the amount in satisfaction of claim on *A*. Will this payment discharge *A* from the whole debt?

   [***Ans.*** Yes, This is on account of remission.]
2. *A* agreed to deliver his elephant to *B* for Khedda operations on 1st October. *A* later on obtained an extension of time up to 6th October but could not deliver the elephant till 12th October, When *B* refused to accept the elephant. Advise *A*.

   [***Ans.*** *B* was justified in refusing to accept the elephant since the very fact that *A* asked for extension of time, showed that time was intended to be of essence.]
3. *A* enters into a contract with *B* for supplying 600 tonnes of coal to *B* within 6 months. *A* fails to make the delivery in accordance with the terms of the contract, owing to Government's restrictions on the transport of coal from collieries but admitted that coal was available and can be purchased with some difficulty in open market. Can *A* successfully take the plea that the contract is discharged because of impossibility of performance?

   [***Ans.*** The contract does not stand discharged because there is only difficulty and not impossibility of performance.]
4. *A* contracts to pay *B* a sum of money when *B* marries *C*. *C* dies without being married to *B* . Can *B* enforce the contract against *A*. *(ICWA, Foundation, June 1999)*

   [***Ans.*** Contract becomes void on account of *C*'s death.]
5. *A* contracts to sing for *B* at a concert for ₹ 1,000 which is paid in advance. *A* is too ill to sing. Is *A* liable to refund to *B* ₹ 1,000. *(ICWA, Foundation, June 1999)*

   [***Ans.*** The contract becomes void because of supervening impossibility of performance.]
6. *A*, a singer agrees with *B* to give his performance at some particular theatre on a specified date. While on his way to the theatre *A* meets with an accident and is rendered unconscious. Is the agreement enforceable. *(ICWA, Foundation, June 2001)*

   [***Ans.*** Agreement becomes void on the ground of supervening impossibility.]
7. Akhilesh entered into an agreement with Shekhar to deliver him (Shekhar) 5,000 bags to be manufactured in his factory. The bags could not be manufactured because of strike by the workers

and Akhilesh failed to supply the said bags to Shekhar. Decide whether Akhilesh can be exempted from liability under the provisions of the Indian Contract Act, 1872. *(PEE II, May 2004)*

[**Ans.** The difficulty in performance cannot be considered as impossibility of performance and hence Mr. Akhilesh is liable to Mr. Shekhar for non-performance of contract.]

8. Mr. Dubious textile enters into a contract with Retail Garments Show Room for supply of 1,000 pieces of Cotton Shirts at ₹ 300 per shirt to be supplied on or before 31st December, 2004. However, on 1st November, 2004 Dubious Textiles informs the Retail Garments Show Room that he is not willing to supply the goods as the price of cotton shirts in the meantime has gone upto ₹ 350 per shirt. Examine the rights of the Retail Garmets Show Room in this regard. *(PEE II, November 2004)*

   [**Ans.** Retail Garments show room can claim damages from Dubious Textiles immediately after 1st November 2004 without waiting upto 31st December 2004. The damages will be calculated at the rate of ₹ 50 per shirt, *i.e.*, the difference between ₹ 350 (the price prevailing on 1st November) and ₹ 300/-. (the contracted price)]

9. *X* agrees to sell his Maruti Zen to *Y* two months after the date of the contract. But after 25 days of the contract, *X* sells the car to *Z*. Thereupon, *Y* sues *X* for the breach of contract. *X* contends that he could still perform the contract by repurchasing the car from *Z*. Will *X* succeed? Give full reasons for your answer. *(B.Com. (Hons.), Delhi 2001)*

   [**Ans.** *X* will not succeed in this case because it amounts to anticipatory breach of contract.]

10. Baiju, a singer, enters into a contract with Alok, the manager of a theatre, to sing at his theatre three nights in every week during the next three months, and Alok promises to pay him ₹ 5,000 for each night's performance. On the seventh night, Baiju will fully absents himself from the theatre. Can Alok put an end to the contract? *(CS Foundation, June 2008)*

    [**Ans.** Alok is at liberty to put an end to the contract]

11. Mr. Adarsh was due to perform on 20th February but on 17th February 2011 repudiated his obligation. On 25th February the Contract become illegal through a change in Law. Mr. Vasant the other Party requested you to advice action against Mr. Adarsh. *(ICWA, Inter. June 2011)*

    [**Ans.** The repudiation on 17th Feb., 2011 amounts to breach of contract and thereby Mr. Vasant is entitled to claim damages.]

Chapter 11

QUASI-CONTRACTS

(Certain Relations Resembling to those of Contracts)

LEARNING OBJECTIVES

A careful study of this chapter will enable you to :

- understand the concept of quasi-contracts;
- identify the various types of quasi-contracts;
- describe the meaning of quantum meruit;
- appreciate the responsibility of finder of goods, and
- explain the meaning of certain key terms.

CONCEPT OF QUASI-CONTRACTS

It has already been stated in a previous chapter that an agreement forms the very basis of a contract. But in certain categories of cases, the law imposes obligations of contractual nature on one party and confers rights in favour of the other even though there is no offer, no acceptance, no *consensus ad idem* and in fact neither agreement nor promise. These contracts are constituted by law, and are, therefore, termed as *Quasi-Contracts*. They are not contracts in equity because a person cannot be allowed to enrich himself at the expense of another.

The basis for the recognition of quasi-contracts has very nicely been explained by Anson in these words, 'Circumstances must occur under any system of law in which it becomes necessary to hold a person to be accountable to another, without any agreement on the part of the former to be so accountable, on the ground that otherwise he would be retaining money or some other benefit which has come into his hands to which the law regards the other person as better entitled, or on the ground that without such accountability the other would unjustly suffer loss. The law of quasi-contracts exists to provide remedies in circumstances of this kind.'

TYPES OF QUASI-CONTRACTS

The Indian Contract Act has used the term *'Certain relations resembling to those of contracts'* for the term *'quasi-contracts*. These relations are of the following five types :

1. Claim for necessaries supplied to a person incapable of contracting or on his account (*Sec. 68*).
2. Reimbursement of person paying money due by another in payment of which he is interested (*Sec. 69*).
3, Obligation of a person enjoying benefit of a non-gratuitous act (*Sec. 70*).

4. Responsibilities of a finder of goods (*Sec. 71*).
5. Liability of a persons to whom money is paid or things delivered, by mistake or under coercion (*Sec. 72*).

Each of these quasi-contracts will now be discussed in detail :

1. **Claim for necessaries supplied to a person incapable of contracting or on his account** (*Sec. 68*) **:** If a person, incapable of entering into a contract, or any one whom he is legally bound to support, is supplied by another person with necessaries suited to his condition in life, the person who has supplied such necessities is entitled to be reimbursed from the property of such incapable person.

Examples **:** (*i*) *A* supplies, *B*, a lunatic, with necessaries suitable to his condition in life. *A* is entitled to be reimbursed from *B*'s property.

(*ii*) *A* supplies the wife and children of *B*, a lunatic, with articles of necessaries suitable to their condition in life. *A* is entitled to be reimbursed from *B*'s property.

Following conditions are necessary for making claim under this section :

1. Articles supplied should be articles of necessaries. The term 'necessaries' is not limited to such things, as are absolutely necessary to keep the incompetent person alive and decently clothed, but extends to all such things which can reasonably by considered as necessaries in the class of society to which the incompetent person belongs. A watch, a bicycle and engagement ring etc. may also be a necessity.

2. Articles supplied should be necessary both at the time of sale and delivery.[1]

Example **:** *A*, a minor, studying at Cambridge purchased eleven fancy waistcoats from *B*. The waistocoats could have been considered necessaries having regard to his financial position but he was at the time adequately provided with articles of this kind. It was held that waistcoats were not 'necessaries' and *A* was not liable to pay for them.[2]

3. Necessaries should be supplied only to such incompetent person or to persons whom he is legally bound to support, such as his wife and children.

4. Necessaries must not have been supplied gratuitously out of mere kindness, favour or pity etc.

5. Such incompetent person is not personally liable, only his property is liable.

6. Incompetent person's property is liable to pay only a reasonable price and not the agreed price for the goods or services supplied.

Facts of individual cases will help in deciding as to what are necessaries. Following few things have already been decided by some of the legal cases to be necessaries :

Costs incurred in successfully defending a suit on behalf of a minor in which his property is in jeopardy; money advanced to a Hinduminor to meet his marriage expenses or to meet his dependent's marriage expenses; money advanced to save the minor's property from sale in execution; costs incurred for defending the minor in a criminal case; funeral ceremonies of the wife, husband or the children of the minor, shradh, education etc. of the incompetent party will be considered to be for necessaries if bound fit and proper with reference to his position in the society.

2. **Reimbursement of person paying money due by another in payment of which he is interested** (*Sec. 69*)**:** A person who is interested in the payment of money which another is bound by law to pay, and who, therefore, pays it, is entitled to be reimbursed by the other.

---

1. Johnstone *v.* Marks (1887), 19 Q.B.D. 509.
2. Nash *v.* Inman (1908), 2 K.B. 1.

Example : *B* holds land in Bengal on a lease granted by *A*, a Zamindar. The revenue payable by *A* to be the Government being in arrear, his land is advertised for sale. Under the revenue law, the consequence of such sale will be the annulment of *B*'s lease. *B*, to prevent the sale and the consequent annulment of his own lease, pays to the Government the sum due from *A*. *A* would be bound to make good to *B* the amount so paid.[3]

A suit for claim under this section will be valid only when the following conditions are satisfied:

(*i*) *Interest in making payment* : The person paying the money must have interest in the payment being made. The term 'interest' includes 'apprehension of any kind of loss or inconvenience and not merely the actual detriment capable of assessment in money.'[4]

Example : *K* refused improperly to perform the marriage of this deceased brother's daughter. The family was a joint one. The mother of the girl performed the ceremony and made certain payments in connection with the marriage. It was held that *K* was liable for these payments as the widow was interested in the payment.[5]

(*ii*) *Obligation* : There should be obligation to pay the money. Such obligation may be contractual or statutory.

Example : *A* made a gift of some part of his property to *B* and agreed that he (*A*) would pay regularly all taxes in respect of that property. Subsequently he transferred the rest of his property by way of gift to *C*, who agreed to pay all taxes in respect of whole of the property. On *C*'s failure to pay the taxes, *B* paid them and subsequently sued *C* for their recovery. It was held that he was entitled to be reimbursed by *C*.[6]

(*iii*) *Payment to another* : Payment must be made to another person.

Example : *A*, a Zamindar gave his land on lease to the Forest Department of Madras Government. On his failure to pay the land revenue to the Revenue Department of Madras Government, his land was advertised for sale. The Forest Department made payment of the land revenue. Held, the payment was not made to another person and, therefore, it could not be recovered from the landlord.[7]

(*iv*) *Bonafide payment :* The payment must be made *bonafide.*

3. **Obligation of Person enjoying Benefit of Non-gratuitous Act–***Quantum Meruit (Sec. 70)* : Where a person lawfully does anything for another person or delivers anything to him, not intending to do so gratuitously and such other person enjoys the benefit thereof, the latter is bound to make compensation to the former in respect of, or to restore, the things so done or delivered.

Examples : (*i*) *A* manages the estate of his wife and sisters-in-law and is under the impression that he will receive remuneration for his services. He is entitled to get reasonable remuneration.

(*ii*) *A* saves *B*'s property from fire. *A* is not entitled to any compensation if the circumstances show that he had intended to act gratuitously.

A claim under this section can be made only when the following conditions are satisfied :

1. The thing must have been done lawfully and the relationship should be such that it will justify interference of the other party.
2. The person who did it, should have the intention of getting compensation for it at the time when he did the act.
3. The other party must have enjoyed the benefit of it. The action will not be applicable if the services are rendered or benefit is received against the will of the person.[8]

---

3. Hazari Lal *v.* Naurang Lal (1930), 28 All. L.J. 1103.
4. Pankhbati *v.* Nani Lal (1914), 18 Cal. W.N. 778.
5. Vaikuntam *v.* Kallapiram (1900), 23 Mad. 512.
6. Somashastri *v.* Swamairao (1918), 42 Bom. 93, 98.
7. Secretary of State for India *v.* Fernandes (1907), 30 Mad. 375.
8. Jayagopal Patnaik *v.* Chairman, Puri Joint Water Works Committee, A.I.R. (1964), Orissa 69.

4. **Responsibilities of a Finder of Goods (*Sec. 71*) :** A person who finds goods belonging to another and takes them into his custody, is subject to the responsibilities of a baliee. He must take reasonable care of the goods found, *i.e.*, as much care as a man of ordinary prudence would, under similar circumstances, take of his own goods of the same description. The finder of the goods must try to find out the real owner of the goods and deliver the goods to him on demand. Finder of the goods may retain the goods as against the real owner until he receives compensation for trouble and expenses voluntarily incurred by him to preserve the goods and find out the owner. He will enjoy particular lien on the things found, until he is compensated for his trouble and expenses. But he will have no right to sue for such compensation. However, he has the right to sue for the ward if any has been offered by the real owner for finding out the goods and retain possession on the goods until he receives that reward. Finder of the goods is also entitled to the possession of the goods as against every-one except the true owner.

***Example* :** *H* picked up a diamond on the floor of *F*s shop and handed it over to *F* to keep it till the true owner appeared. In spite of the wide advertisement in newspapers, no one appeared to claim it. After the lapse of some weeks, *H* tendered to *F* the cost of advertisement and an indemnity bond and requested him to return the diamond to him. *F* refuses to do so. Held, *F* must return the diamond to *H* as he was entitled to retain goods as against everyone except the true owner.[9]

The finder may sell the goods as per the provisions of section 169 of the Contract Act. These have been explained in Chapter 14.

5. **Liability of person to whom money has been paid or anything delivered by mistake or under coercion** (*Sec. 72*) **:** A person to whom money has been paid, or anything delivered under a mistake of a fact or under coercion must repay or return it.

***Examples* :** (*i*) *A* and *B* jointly owe ₹ 100 to *C*.*A* alone pays the amount to *C*.*B*, not knowing this fact later on also pays ₹ 100 to *C*.*C* is bound to repay the amount to *B*.

(*ii*) *A*, a fruit merchant, sent a parcel of fruits on approval to *B* who was his regular customer, but by mistake the parcel was delivered to *C*.*C* thinking that the parcel was a birthday present from a friend, ate the fruits.

A can recover from *C* the cost of the parcel of fruits. *A* person to whom anything is delivered by mistake must return it or pay for it.

(*iii*) A railway company refuses to deliver up certain goods to the consignee, except upon the payment of illegal charge for carriage. The consignee pays the sum charged in order to obtain the goods. He is entitled to recover to much of the charges as was illegally excessive.

The word 'coercion' in this section has been used in its general or ordinary sense. Mistake may be either of a fact or of law,[10] but it must be of fundamental importance. Money paid to avoid prosecution can be recovered. But voluntary payment cannot be recovered under this section.

***Examples* :** (*i*) *K* had paid sales tax to the Government in respect of forward transactions. The Allahabad High Court subsequently declared levying of sales tax on forward transactions as *ultra-vires*. *K* sued for return of the money paid. Held, he was entitled to get the money Back.[11]

(*ii*) *N* got property of *K* attached in execution of a money decree. Actually the decree was not against *K*, but against another person of a similar name. In order to save his property from being sold away, *K* paid the decretal amount. Subsequently he sued *N* for getting the amount back. Held he would succeed.[12]

---

9. Hollins *v*. Fowler, L.R. 7 H.L. 757.
10. Sales Tax Officer *v*. Kanhiya Lal (1959), 22 Sup. C.J. 53.
11. Seth Kanhiya Lal *v*. National Bank of India (1913), 40 I.A. 56.
12. Manilal *v*. Chandulal (1930), 32 Bom. L.R. 424, 427.

KEY TERMS

- **Quantum Meruit :** A principle which entitles the promisor to get compensation for the work done.
- **Finder of Goods :** A person who finds goods belonging to another and takes them in his custody.
- **Quasi-contracts :** Contracts constituted by law.

TEST QUESTIONS

Objective Type : *Test Your Knowledge*

1. Fill in the blanks
   (*i*) The Indian Contract Act uses the term ....for quasi-contracts.
   (*ii*) The responsibility of a finder of goods is that of a..........................
   (*iii*) A person incompetent to enter into a contract is......................liable for payment towards the articles of necessities.
   (*iv*) A finder of goods is entitled to the possession of the goods as against everyone except the.......................
   (*v*) A person to whom money has been paid under...................must repay.
   [***Ans.*** (*i*) relations resembling to those of contracts; (*ii*) bailee; (*iii*) not personally; (*iv*) true owner; (*v*) coercion.]
2. State whether each of the following statements is *True* or *False*
   (*i*) Quasi contracts are based on principles of equity.
   (*ii*) A finder of goods can sue the true owner for recovery of expenses incurred for the safely of the goods.
   (*iii*) A person doing something for another gratuitously can claim compensation on the principle of quantum meruit.
   (*iv*) Any person taking payment for another can get reimbursement from the person for whom he has paid.
   (*v*) A person supplying articles of the necessities to the wife of a minor is entitled for reimbursement from the property of the minor.
   (*vi*) Explain "A quasi contract is not a contract". (*ICWA Foundation, June 1999; Dec. 2000*)
   [***Ans.*** (*i*) True; (*ii*) False; (*iii*) False; (*iv*) False; (*v*) True; (*vi*) False.]

Essay Type : *For Review, Discussion and Practice*

1. What are implied quasi-contracts? Enumerate the quasi-contracts provided for by the Indian Contract Act. (*CA Foundation, May 2000*)
2. Explain the position of a 'finder of goods' under the Indian Contract Act. What rights may such a person exercise and to what obligations he is subject to? Explain. (*CA Inter, May 1988*)
3. Discuss the responsibility of finder of goods which does not pertain to him.(*ICWA, Foundation, June 1999; B.Com. (Hons), Delhi 2010*)
4. What are Quasi Contracts? Discuss with atleast three examples. (*ICWA, Foundation, June 2000, June 2001; B.Com. (Hons.), Delhi 2005, 2013; B.Com. (Pass), Delhi 2005; CA IPC, May, 2013*)
5. What are Quasi Contracts? Explain the conditions in which Quasi Contractual obligations arise. (*GGSIPU, BBA (H), May 2002*)

6. Explain the concept of Quasi Contracts as provided under the Indian Contract Act, 1872.
(B.Com. (Hons.), Delhi 1996, 1998, 2001, 2003; CS Foundation, Dec. 2008)

7. "A quasi-contract is not a contract at all. It is obligation which the law creates." Explain the statement as recognized under Indian Contract Act. *(B.Com. (Hons), Delhi, Nov. 2012)*

PRACTICAL PROBLEMS

1. A merchant supplied goods for the marriage function of the sister of a Hindu minor who is sole male member of the family. Can he recover?
[**Ans.** The money can be recovered out of the property of the minor in case the goods are supplied according to the class of society to which the minor belongs.]

2. *A* agrees to sell his land to *B*. Before completion of sale, this land is attached by *A*'s creditor. *B* deposits the amount in the Court. Later *A* refuses to complete sale. Can *B* recover the amount paid from *A*?
[**Ans.** No, as at the time of payment he had no interest in the land.]

3. *A* and *B* jointly owe ₹ 1,000 to *C*. *A* alone pays the amount to *C* and *B*, not knowing this fact, pays ₹ 1,000 over again to *C*. Is *C* bound to repay the amount to *B*.
[**Ans.** *C* must pay the money as per Section 72 of the Act.]

4. A Railway company refuses to deliver certain goods to the consignee except upon payment of ₹ 2,000 being excess/illegal charge. The consignee paid the said amount in order to obtain the goods. Is there any remedy? *(ICWAI, Inter, June 2009)*
[**Ans.** Illegal charges can be recovered since paid under coercion.

5. *Y* holds agricultural land in Gujarat on a lease granted by *X*, the owner. The land revenue payable by *X* to the Government being in arrear, his land is advertised for sale by the Government. Under the Revenue Law, the consequence of such sale will be termination of *Y*'s lease. *Y*, in order to prevent the sale and the consequent termination of his own lease, pays the Government, the sum due from *X*. Referring to the provisions of the Indian Contract Act, 1872 decide whether *X* is liable to make good to *Y*, the amount so paid? *(PEE-II, ICAI, May 2007)*
[**Ans.** Yes, *X* is bound to make good to *Y* the amount so paid.]

6. Ravi sent a consignment of goods worth ₹ 60,000 by railway and got railway receipt. He obtained an advance of ₹ 30,000 from the bank and endorsed and delivered the railway receipt in favour of the bank by way of security. The railway failed to deliver the goods at the destination. The bank filed a suit against the railway for ₹ 60,000. Decide in the light of provisions of the Indian Contract Act, 1872, whether the bank would succeed in the said suit? *(PEE-II, ICAI, May 2008)*
[**Ans.** The bank will succeed in the claim of ₹ 60,000 against railway]

7. *Z* rented out his house situated at Mumbai to *W* for ₹ 10,000 per month. A sum of ₹ 5 lakhs, the house tax payable by *Z* to the Municipal Corporation being in arrears, his house is advertised for sale by the Corporation. *W* pays the Corporation, the sum due from *Z* to avoid legal consequences. Referring to the provisions of the Indian Contract Act, 1872 decide whether *W* id entitled to get the reimbursement of the said amount from *Z*. *(IPCE, ICAI, May 2010)*
[**Ans.** *W* has made the payment of lawful dues of *Z* in which *W* had an interest. Therefore, *W* is entitled to get the reimbursement from *Z*.]

8. Mohan and Sohan jointly owe ₹ 1 lakh to Rohan. Mohan pays ₹ 1 lakh to Rohan. Sohan not knowing it, also pays ₹ 1 lakh to Rohan. Is Rohan bound to return ₹ 1 lakh received extra? Give reasons. *(CS Foundation, Dec. 2012)*
[**Ans.** Yes, Rohan is bound to repay the amount as it has been paid to him under mistake as per Section 72 of the Indian Contract Act].

Chapter 12

REMEDIES FOR BREACH OF CONTRACT

LEARNING OBJECTIVES

A careful study of this chapter will enable you to :

- enumerate the remedies available for breach of a contract;
- describe the circumstances under which each of the remedies is available;
- identify the various types of damages;
- appreciate the rules regarding determination of damages;
- appreciate the significance of doctrine of restitution; and
- explain the meaning of certain key terms.

TYPES OF REMEDIES

The remedies available to the aggrieved party in the event of the breach of a contract are shown in the following chart :

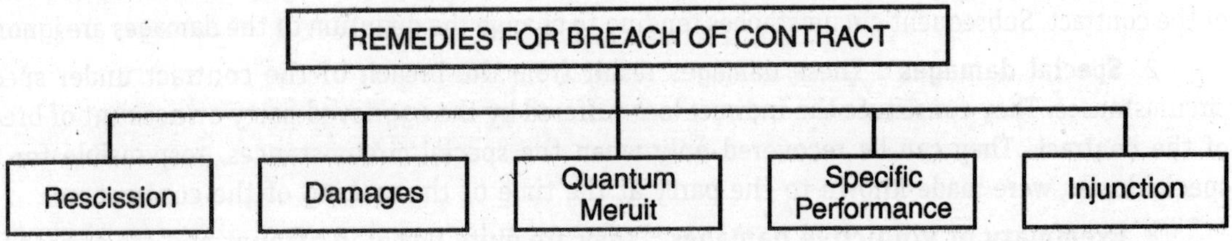

RESCISSION

Rescission means the setting aside of the contract. The aggrieved party may be allowed by the court to treat the contract at an end thereby, terminate all his liabilities under the contract. The court, however, will not allow rescission of the contract in the following cases :

1. Where the party wishing to set aside the contract has expressly or impliedly ratified the contract, *e.g.*, a person loses his right to repudiate the contract to purchase shares to which he had agreed on the basis of a false prospectus after he has exercised his right to vote in general meeting or has accepted dividend. This would amount to implied ratification of the contract after the knowledge of mis-representation.
2. Where only a part of the contract is ought to be set aside and that part cannot be separated from the rest of the contract.

3. Where without fault of either party, there is a change in the circumstances since the making of the contract, on account of which the parties cannot be substantially restored to the position in which they were before the contract was made.
4. Where during the subsistence of the contract, third parties have acquired rights in the subject matter of the contract in good faith and for value.

DAMAGES

Damages means monetary compensation payable by the defaulting party to the aggrieved party in the event of the breach of a contract. The object of providing damages is to put the aggrieved party in the same position, so far as money can do, in which he would have been, had the contract been performed.

Types of Damages

Damages may be of four types as shown in the following chart :

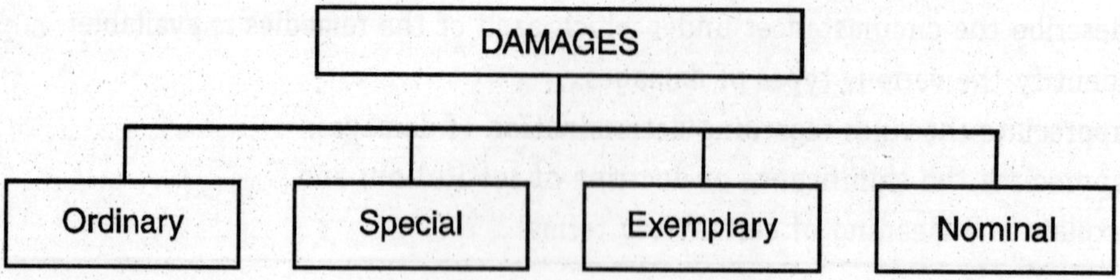

Each of the above types of damages have been explained in the following pages.

1. **Ordinary damages :** Damages which arise in the ordinary course of events from the breach of contract are called ordinary damages. These damages constitute the direct loss suffered by the aggrieved party. They are estimated on the basis of circumstances prevailing on the date of the breach of the contract. Subsequent circumstances tending to change the quantum of the damages are ignored.

2. **Special damages :** These damages result from the breach of the contract under special circumstances. They constitute the indirect loss suffered by the aggrieved party on account of breach of the contract. They can be recovered only when the special circumstances, responsible for the special losses were made known to the party at the time of the making of the contract.

3. **Exemplary or vindictive damages :** They are quite heavy in amount and are awarded by way of punishment only in the following cases :

(*i*) Breach of a contract to marry.

(*ii*) Dishonour of a customer's cheque by the bank without any proper reason.

These damages are awarded with the intention of punishing the defauling party. They are of a deterrent nature and their object is to prevent the parties from committing breach. In the case of a breach of a contract to marry, damages will include compensation for the loss of the feelings and the reputation of the aggrieved party. In the case of a dishonour of cheque damages are awarded taking into consideration the loss to the prestige and goodwill of the customer and the general rule is that the smaller the cheque the greater is the amount of damages.

4. **Nominal damages :** These damages are quite small in amount. They are never granted by way of compensation for the loss. In such cases, usually the actual loss is very negligible. They are awarded simply to recognise the right of the party to claim damages for the breach of the contract.

The Delhi Court in a recent case had held that no damages can be allowed under Section 73 of the Contract Act, unless the aggrieved party has suffered some loss. The facts of the case are being given in the following example :

Example : *T* agreed to supply sleepers to the Railway Administration According to one of the terms of the contract, *T* was required to pay damages to the Railway on his failure to supply whether the Railways suffered any loss or not. *T* failed to supply but the Railways did not suffer any loss. A case was filed against *T.* The High Court disallowed the suit.[1]

In such cases, however, the Court may award nominal damages.

Rules Regarding the Determination of Damages

The rules regarding damages have been very well explained in the English case of *Hadley* v. *Baxendate.*[2] The case is discussed below :

Example : *H*'s mill stopped on account of the breakage of a crankshaft. *B*, a common carrier, was entrusted with the delivery of this machine part for taking it to its makers at Greenwich as a pattern for a new one. *B* did not have this information that delay in carrying the machine would result in loss of profits. The delivery was delayed beyond reasonable time by some neglect on the part of *B.H* claimed from *B* compensation for the wages of workers and depreciation charges which were incurred during the period the factory was idle for the working. The first two items were allowed because they were the natural consequences of breach but the loss of profit was disallowed as it was special or remote loss which could be recovered only when the party had information of it.

Alderson, J. observed in the above case as follows :

"Where two parties have made a contract which one of them has broken, the damages which the other party ought to receive in respect of such breach of contract should be such as may *fairly* and *reasonably* be considered either arising *naturally, i.e.*, according to the usual course of things, from such breach of contract itself or such as may reasonably by supposed to have been in the *contemplation* of the parties, at the time they made the contract, as the *probable* result of the breach of it."

Rules regarding the ascertainment of the amount of damages can be summarised as follows :

1. The principle upon which damages are to be assessed is that where a party sustains a loss by reason of breach of contract, he is, so far as money can do, to be placed in the same situation with respect to damages as if the contract has been performed. Aggrieved party shall be allowed compensation only for the actual loss suffered by him. This also includes costs of getting the decree for damages. Thus, only fair and reasonable damages as arising naturally will be allowed. It is important to note that the fact that damages are difficult to assess will not deprive the plaintiff of his right to recover them.[3]

2. The right to claim damages rests in the party who was sustained loss on account of breach of the contract. The liability to pay damages lies on the party guilty of breach of contract.

3. Compensation can be claimed for damages.

(*a*) which arise naturally in the usual course of things from breach of contract itself, since damages are paid only for the proximate consequences of the breach of a contract[4]. or

---

1. Union of India *v.* Tribhuwan Dasji Patel (1971) A.I.R. Delhi 120.
2. (1854), 9 Ex. 341.
3. Chaplin *v.* Hicks (1911), 2 K.B. 786.
4. Hadley *v.* Baxendale (1854), 9 Ex. 341.

(b) as may reasonably be supposed to have been in the contemplation of both the parties, at the time they made the contract as the probable result of its breach.

Claim for damages must be fair and reasonable.

Examples : *(i) A* contracts to sell and deliver 50 tonnes of saltpetre of *B* at a certain price to be paid on delivery. *A* breaks his promise. *B* is entitled to receive from *A*, by way of compensation, the sum, if any, by which the contract price falls short of the price for which *B* might have obtained 50 tonnes of saltpetre of like quality at the time when the saltpetre ought to have been delivered.

(ii) A contracts to buy of *B*, at a stated price, 50 tonnes of rice, no time being fixed for delivery. *A* afterwards informs *B* that he will not accept the rice if tendered to him. *B* in entitled to receive from *A* by way of compensation, the amount, if any, by which the contract price exceeds that which *B* can obtain for the rice at the time when *A* informs *B* that he will not accept it.

(iii) A contracts to buy *B*'s ship for ₹ 60,000 but breaks his promise. *A* must pay to *B*, by way of compensation, the excess, if any, of the contract price over the price which *B* can obtain for the ship at the time of the breach of promise.

(iv) A, the owner of a boat, contracts with *B* to take a cargo of jute to Mirzapur, for sale at the place, starting on a specified day. The boat, owing to some avoidable cause, does not start at the time appointed. Whereby the arrival of the cargo at Mirzapur is delayed beyond the time when it would have arrived if the boat had sailed according to the contract. After that date, and before the arrival of the cargo, the price of jute falls. The measure of the compensation payable to *B* by *A* is the difference between the price which *B* could have obtained for the cargo at Mirzapur at the time when it would have arrived if forwarded in due course, and the market price at the time when it actually arrived.

(v) A contracts to repair *B*'s house in a certain manner, and receives payment in advance. *A* repairs the house, but not according to the contract. *B* is entitled to recover from *A* the cost of making the repairs conforming to the contract.

(vi) A contract to let his ship to *B* for a year from the first of January, for a certain price. Freights rise, and on the first of January, the hire obtainable for the ship is higher than contract price. *A* breaks his promise. He must pay to *B*, by way of compensation, a sum equal to the difference between the contract price and the price for which *B* could hire a similar ship for a year on and from the first of January.

(vii) A contracts to supply *B* with a certain quantity of iron at a fixed price, being a higher price that for which *A* could procure and deliver the iron. *B* wrongfully refuses to receive the iron. *B* must pay to *A* way of compensation, the difference between the contract price of the iron and the sum for which *A* could have obtained and delivered it.

(viii) A delivers to *B*, a common carrier, a machine to be conveyed without delay, to *A*'s mill, informing *A* that his mill is stopped for want of the machine. *B* unreasonably delays the delivery of the machine, and *A*, in consequence, loses a profitable contract with the Government. *A* is entitled to receive from *B*, by way of compensation, the average amount of profit which would have been made by the working of the mill during the time the delivery of it was delayed, but not the loss sustained through the loss of the Government contract.

(ix) A, having contracted with *B* to supply with 1,000 tonnes of iron at 100 rupees a tonne to be delivered at a stated time, contracts with *C* for the purchase of 1,000 tonnes of iron at 80 rupees a tonne, telling *C* that he does so for the purpose of performing his contract with *B*. *C* fails to perform his contract with *A*, who cannot procure other iron, and *B*, in consequence, rescinds the contract. *C* must pay to *A* 20,000 rupees, being the profit which *A* would have made by the performance of his contract with *B*

(x) A contracts to pay a sum of money to *B* on a day specified. *A* does not pay the money on that day; *B* in consequence of not receiving the money on that day is unable to pay his debts, and is totally

ruined. *A* is not liable to make good to *B* anything except the principal sum he contracted to pay, together with interest upto the day of payment.

(*xi*) *A* contracts to sell and deliver to *B*, on the first of January, certain cloth which *B* intends to manufacture into caps of a particular kind, for which there is no demand, except at that season. The cloth is not delivered till after the appointed time, and too late to be used that year in making caps. *B* is entitled to receive from *A*, by way of compensation, the difference between the contract price of the cloth and its market price at the time of delivery, but not the profit which he expected to obtain by making caps, nor the expenses which he has been put to in making preparations for the manufacturer.

(*xii*) *A*, a shipowner, contracts with *B* to convey him from Calcutta to Sydney in *A*'s ship, sailing on the first of January, and *B* pays to *A*, by way of deposit, one-half of his passage-money. The ship does not sail on the first of January, and *B*, after being, in consequence, detained in Calcutta for some time, and thereby put to some expense, proceeds to Sydney in another vessel and in consequence, arriving too late in Sydney, loses a sum of money. *A* is liable to repay to *B* his deposit, with interest, and expenses to which he is put by his detention in Calcutta, and the excess, if any of the passage-money paid for the second ship over that agreed upon for the first, but not the sum of money which *B* lost by arriving in Sydney too late.

From the above examples following conclusions can be drawn :

(*i*) No compensation will be granted for remote and indirect damages. Damages should be calculated as on the date of breach. Damages will be too remote if they are not the necessary or probable consequences of the breach or they were not in the contemplation of the parties when the contract was made. Loss of profit is never taken into account in estimating damages unless otherwise agreed upon.[5]

(*ii*) A special loss which does not naturally arise from the breach cannot be recovered unless expressly stipulated in the contract. The promisor must make the contract with knowledge, that the promisee is entering into the contract for a special purpose. In other words, special damages will be granted only when it is proved that the other party knew at the time of making the contract that the special loss was likely to result from the breach of the contract.

4. In estimating the amount of loss, the means which existed for remedying the incon-venience occasioned by the non-performance of the contract must be taken into account. All costs of employing such means shall be recoverable from the party at fault. The party suffering from the breach is thus expected to take reasonable steps to minimise the loss. He cannot claim as damages any loss which he has suffered due to his own negligence.

Examples : (*i*) *A* hires *B*'s ship to go to Bombay, and agrees to take on board on the first of January. A cargo which *A* is to provide, and to bring it to Calcutta, the freight to be paid, when earned. *B*'s ship does not go to Bombay, but *A* has opportunities of procuring suitable conveyance for the cargo upon terms as advantageous as those on which he had charted the ship. *A* avails himself of the those opportunities, but is put to trouble and expense in doing so. *A* is entitled to receive compensation from *B* in respect of such trouble and expense.

(*ii*) *A* contracts with *B* to make and deliver to *B*, by a fixed day, for a specified price a piece of machinery. *A* does not deliver the piece of machinery at the time specified, and in consequence of this, *B* is obliged to procure another at a higher price than that which he was to have paid to *A* and is prevented from performing a contract which *B* had made with a third person at the time of this contract with *A* (but which had not been then communicated to *A*), and is compelled to make compensation, for breach of that contract. *A* must pay to *B* by way of compensation, the difference between the contract price of the piece of machinery and the sum paid by *B* for another but not the sum paid by *B* to third person by way of compensation.

5. Damages are given by way of restitution and compensation and not by way of punishment. Aggrieved party can recover only the actual pecuniary loss sustained by him and not exemplary damages, *i.e.*, damages for disappointments or injured feelings etc. Exemplary damages are allowed only in case of breach of promise to marry[6] or where a banker dishonours a cheque of his client while having money to his credit and the client thereby suffers in his business reputation. A businessman, whose credit has been client adversely affected, will get exemplary damages, even if he has sustained no pecuniary loss, but a non-trade cannot get heavy damages unless the damages are alleged and proved as special damages

As stated above, damages are not allowed for injured feelings or mental pain, but they may be allowed in a case where, (*i*) breach was reckless, (*ii*) caused bodily harm and (*iii*) the defaulting party had reason to know that breach would cause mental suffering.

Example : A banking corporation agreed to lend *W* money for a trip of California. It was agreed that *W*'s account would be credited by such sum as he may need on reaching his destination. *W* reached California but the banking corporation refused to give him credit. The court allowed damages to *W* on grounds of mental suffering and humiliation as this could have been thought of by the bank while refusing to give him the credit.[7]

6. Nominal damages may be granted when breach of a contract committed without any real loss.

7. In contracts of sale and purchase of goods, the measure of damages will be the difference between the price agreed upon and the market price. Thus, the measure of damages in such a breach of contract will be the sum by which the contract price falls short of the price at which the purchaser might have obtained goods of like quality at the time and place that they should have been delivered. When no date has been fixed for the performance of the contract and the promisor commits a breach, the measure of damages will be the difference between the contract price and the market price at the date of the refusal to perform. It is to noted that in case of such a contract by the promisee (buyer), he cannot recover from the buyer any further loss of if the market falls, nor will he be liable to have his damages reduced if the market rises.[8]

Example : *A* agreed to sell certain shares to *B* to be delivered on 30th December. On account of heavy fall in the value of the shares on that date, *B* declined to accept the delivery of shares. Subsequently *A* sold the shares at a price higher than that prevailing on 30th December since the share had picked upon the meantime. In a suit brought by *A* it was held that he was entitled to recover from *B* the difference between the contract price of the shares and their market price on 30th December and *B* was not entitled to the benefits of the profits accrued after the breach.

8. As regards damages arising from the breach of contract for the payment of money on a particular date, interest on the principal sum from the date on which the sum was agreed to be paid till the actual date of payment will be a sufficient compensation to the aggrieved party.

9. Damages for breach of service contracts by the employers will be determined with reference to the usual terms of wages for the employment contracted for and the time that would be lost before similar employment can be obtained. In contracts of service for a fixed term, the measure of damages for earlier termination of the service will be salary for the remainder of the term of service.

10. If a sum is named in the contract as the amount to be paid in a case of its breach or if the contract contains any other stipulation by way of penalty for failure to perform his part of the

6. Addis *v.* Gramophone and Co. (1909), A.C. 488.
7. Westesen *v.* Olathe State Bank (1925), 78 Colo 217.
8. Jamal *v.* Molla Dawood and Sons (1916), 43 Cal 493 (I.C.).

obligation under a contract, court will allow reasonable compensation not exceeding the amount so named in the contract.[9]

11. A carrier of goods can be held responsible for damages rising from deterioration caused by delay even without any prior notice. Deterioration in the value of goods includes both physical damage to the goods as well as damages arising from the loss of special opportunity for sale.[10]

LIQUIDATED DAMAGES AND PENALTY

English law : In English law, distinction is made between liquidated damages and penalty. The parties may agree at the time of entering into the contract and predetermine the extent of damages. The amount so agreed upon may be either in the shape of liquidated damages or penalty.

Liquidated damages : When the amount of compensation fixed by an agreement between the parties to be paid in case of breach of contract is in the nature of a fair and honest pre-estimation of probable damages, it is called Liquidated Damages. Liquidated damages are, therefore, a genuine pre-estimate of the probable loss. It is an assessment of the amount, which in the opinion of the parties, will compensate for the breach.

Liquidated damages are to be granted in full, irrespective of the extent of loss, which may be greater or less than the estimates of the parties. Courts have no power to reduce or enhance the amount.

Penalty : When the amount named in the contract at the time of its formation is disproportionate to the damages likely to accrue in the event of breach, it will be termed as penalty. Thus, penalty does not measure actual loss or damage. It is a sort of coercion or pressure on the party used to prevent him from committing breach of the contract. According to *N.H. Jhabvala*, 'The sum will be held to be a penalty, if it is extravagant and unconscionable in comparison with the greatest loss that could possibly flow from the breach.'

Penalty, thus, implies a subsidiary contract besides the main contract. The subsidiary contract aims at providing more drastic consequences in the event of breach of the original and main contract.

In case of penalty, law grant compensation not exceeding the amount fixed. It is not necessary that the whole amount shall be granted. The discretion lies with the court.

Distinction between Liquidated Damages and Penalty

The distinction between liquidated damages and penalty can be summarised in these words. The essence of a penalty is a payment of money stipulated as in *terrorem* of the offending party; the essence of liquidated damages is a genuine covenanted pre-estimate of damage.

In order to decide whether a given sum in a contract is by way of liquidated damages or penalty, the terms and inherent circumstances of each particular contract should be judged at the time of making of the contract and not at the time of its breach. However, the following general rules can be stated.[11]

1. If the sum stipulated is extravagant and unconscionable in amount in comparison with the greatest loss that could conceivably by proved to have followed from the breach, it shall be taken as a penalty.

---

9. Kemble *v.* Farren (1829), 6 Bing 141.
10. Wilson *v.* Lancashire and Yorkshire Rly. Co., 9, C.B.N.S. 632.
11. Desai, T.R. Contract Act (17 Ed.), p. 275.

Example : *A* agreed to repair *B*'s house within a month for a sum of ₹ 500. He also further agrees that if he fails to do so he will pay *B* ₹ 10,000 as damages. The amount is apparently unreasonable, and therefore, is of the nature of penalty.

2. If the breach consists only in not paying a sum of money, and the sum stipulated is greater than the sum ought to have been paid, the amount shall be taken as a penalty.

Example : *A* agrees to pay *B* a sum of ₹ 500 on a particular date. He further agrees to pay ₹ 1,000 in the event of his failure to do so. The sum stipulated shall be taken as penalty.

3. When a single lump sum is made payable by way of compensation, on the occurrence of one or more or all the several events, some of which may cause serious while others only trifling damage, the sum shall be taken as a penalty.

Example : A retail dealer was supplied with certain cars by the Ford Co. He agreed not to sell them below the list price to customers and also to other dealers, etc. It was also agreed that the retailer would pay £ 250 as damages for every breach of this agreement. The amount was held as a penalty since it was payable for various breaches differing in kind some of which might cause only trifling damages.[12]

4. In case the sum stipulated is a genuine pre-estimate of the probable loss, the sum shall be taken as liquidated damages.

Example : *P* sold 200 tyres to *D*, who contracted not to resell them below *P*'s list price and agreed to pay a sum of £ 5 for every tyre he undersold. *D* sold a tyre less than the list price. It was held that *P* could recover £ as damages from *D* as the sum fixed by the parties was a genuine pre-estimate of the probable loss and, therefore, was not a penalty.[13]

Indian Law : The Indian Contract Act does not make any distinction between liquidated damages and penalty. According to *Sec. 74* of the Act.

"When a contract has been broken, if a sum is named in the contract as the amount to be paid in case of such breach, and if the contract contains any other stipulation by way of penalty, the party complaining of the breach is entitled, whether or not actual damage or loss is proved to have been caused thereby, to receive from the party who has broken the contract, reasonable compensation not exceeding the amount so named or, as the case may be, the penalty, stipulated for."

It makes it clear that even in those cases where parties have expressly determined by agreement the amount of damages payable in case of breach of contract, courts are free to reduce it but not to increase it. Courts will award reasonable compensation not exceeding the sum so agreed. It is immaterial if the amount so fixed is in the nature of liquidated damages or penalty. In India law does not require any difference between penalty and liquidated damages to be made nor the courts are required to decide the nature of the amount of compensation agreed upon to be paid on the breach of contract between the parties.

The only exception to the above rule is that when a person enters into any bail bond, recognizance or other instrument of the same nature or under the provisions of nay law or under the orders of central or local governments gives any bond for the performance of any public duty or act in which the public is interested, he shall be liable upon breach of the condition of any such instrument to pay the whole sum mentioned.

Examples : (*i*) *A* contracts with *B* to pay *B* ₹ 1,000 if he fails to pay *B* ₹ 500 on a given day. *A* fails to pay *B* ₹ 500 on that day. *B* is entitled to recover from *A* such compensation, not exceeding ₹ 1,000 (in total) as the court considers reasonable.

12. Ford Motor Co. *v.* Armstrong (1915), 31 T.C.R. 267.
13. Dunlop Pneumatic Tyre Co. Ltd. *v.* New Garage and Motor Co. Ltd., (1915), A.C. 79.

(*ii*) *A* gives *B* a bond for the repayment of ₹ 1,000 with interest at 12 per cent, at the end of six months with a stipulation that in case of default, interest shall be payable at the rate of 75 per cent, from the date of default. This is a stipulation by way of penalty and *B* is only entitled to recover from *A* such compensation as the court considers reasonable.

(*iii*) *A* contracts with *B* that if he practises as a surgeon within Calcutta, he will pay *B* ₹ 5,000 as the court considers reasonable.

(*iv*) *A*, who owes money to *B*, a money-lender, undertakes to repay him by delivering him 10 tonnes of grain on a certain date, and stipulates that in the event of his not delivering the stipulated amount by the stipulated date, he shall be liable to deliver 20 tonnes. This is a stipulation by way of penalty, and *B* is only entitled to reasonable compensation in case of breach.

(*v*) *A* undertakes to repay *B* a loan of ₹ 1,000 by five equal monthly instalments with a stipulation that, in default of payment of any instalment, the whole amount shall become due. This stipulation is not by way of penalty, and the contract may be enforced according to its terms.

(*vi*) *A* borrows ₹ 100 from *B* and gives him a bond for ₹ 200 payable by five yearly instalments of ₹ 40 with a stipulation that, in default of payment of any instalment, the whole amount shall become due. This is a stipulation by way of penalty.

(*vii*) *A* gives a recognizance binding him in a penalty of ₹ 500 to appear in the court on a certain day. *A* fails to appear in the court on the fixed day. He is liable today the whole penalty.

Forfeiture of Earnest Money or Security Deposit

In contracts, sometimes, a party is required to deposit some money with the other party so as to ensure the former's seriousness about the contract. The money so deposited may be as 'earnest money' or as 'security deposit'. Earnest money 'is part of the purchase price when the transaction goes forward; it is forfeited when the transaction falls through by reason of the fault or failure of the promisor.' Security deposit is not appropriated towards the payment of price but it is to kept by promisee as security. Earnest money can be forfeited but security deposit cannot as its forfeiture will amount to penalty.[14]

Examples : (*i*) *A* agreed to sell a plot of land and a bungalow to *B* for a sum of ₹ 1,12,500. As per terms of agreement, the buyer paid ₹ 1,000 as earnest money and later paid ₹ 24,000 on obtaining the possession of the bungalow. It was further provided in the agreement that on failure of the buyer to pay the balance and getting the bungalow registered in his name by a fixed date, the sum of ₹ 25,000 paid so far would stand forfeited; the agreement would be cancelled and the possession of the bungalow would be given back to the seller. The buyer defaulted. The seller forfeited the money and brought an action against the buyer to regain possession and recover compensation for occupation and use of the bungalow.

The Supreme Court in its decision allowed the seller to forfeit ₹ 1,000 being earnest money. It also allowed the seller to retain₹ 24,000 not be way of right but as compensation for occupation and use of the bungalow by the buyer. On a question being raised whether, proof of loss was necessary or recover compensation under section 74, the Court observed that though proof of some loss was required but it was not necessary to prove the extent of it.[15]

(*ii*) *M* contracted to supply to U.P. Military Headquarters potatoes, eggs, fish etc. for one year. He also deposited ₹18,500 for due performance of the contract. *M* made persistent defaults in his supplies. As a consequence of which, as per terms of the contract, the Government forfeited his deposit of

14. Chiranjit Singh *v.* Har Swarup (1926), A.I.R.P.C. 1.
15. Fateh Chand *v.* Bal Kishan Das (1964), I.S.C.R. 515.

₹ 18,500 and rescinded the contracts. It was held by the Supreme Court that this could not be done. At the most the Government could have claimed compensation for the loss suffered by it provided it furnished proof of it. Since in the present case, the Government failed to give any proof of the loss suffered by it, the sum of ₹ 18,500 could not be forfeited as it was not as earnest money but simply as a security deposit.[16]

QUANTUM MERUIT

Literally speaking, the words 'Quantum Meruit' means 'as much as merited' or *'as much as earned.'* This principle of law provides for payment of compensation under certain circumstances, to a person who has rendered goods or services to another person under a contract which could not or has been fully performed. These circumstances can be put as follows :

1. In the case of breach of contract, the aggrieved party can claim reasonable compensation for what he has done under the contract.

Example : In a case where the contractor was prevented by the contractee from completing the work after he had done a part of it, the contractor was held entitled to get reasonable compensation for the work done in addition to the damages for breach of contract as might be allowed by the court.

2. When a contract is discovered to be unenforceable for some technical defect, any person who has done something under the contract, is entitled to a reasonable compensation is spite of the fact the agreement is void.

Example : A person renders some service to a company under a contract of employment which is duly approved by the Board of Directors of that company. Subsequently the constitution of the Board of Directors is found to be illegal and, therefore, the contract of employment becomes void. The employee who has rendered some service to the company shall be entitled to claim remuneration for his service under the doctrine of *quantum meruit.*

3. There is an implied agreement to pay for the services rendered or goods supplied to a person, who had no intentions to do so gratuitously if the benefit of the sum has already been enjoyed by the other party.

Example : *X* forgets certain goods at *Y*'s house. He had no intention to leave them with him gratuitously. *Y* uses those goods for his personal benefit. *X* can compel *Y* to pay for those goods.

Doctrine of *quantum meruit* is, however subject to the following three limitations :

(*a*) In a contract which is not divisible into parts and a lump sum of money is promised to be paid for the complete work, part performance will not entitle the party to claim any payment.

Example : A mate was engaged on the term that he would be paid in a lump sum for a complete voyage. He died before the voyage was complete. It was held that his representatives could not recover the lump sum neither could they sue for payment for the services rendered by the deceased.[17]

(*b*) A person, who himself is guilty of breach of contract, cannot be allowed to claim any payment under the doctrine of *quantum meruit.*

Example : *A*, a builder undertake to build a house on the land of *X* for a lump sum. After *A* has done part of the work he refuses to finish it, and *X* completes the building using some of the materials left on the premises by *A*. Can *A* recover compensation for the work he has done and for the materials used by *X*?

---

16. Maula Bux *v.* Union of India (1969), 2 S.C.C. 554.
17. Cutter *v.* Powell (1785), 6 T.R. 320.

A contract being a complete entity no action lies against *X*, either on the original contract or on a *quantum meruit* in respect of the work done. The fact that *X* completes the work is no evidence of an undertaking to pay for what has been done, following the rule in *Sumpter v. Hedges.*[18]

If, in completing the premises, *X* uses the materials belonging to *A*. *A* will have a good claim in respect of the value of the materials used.

The above rule is subject to following exceptions.

(*i*) If the contract is divisible, part performance will also entitle the defaulting party to claim compensation on the basis of *quantum meruit* if the other party has taken the benefit of what has been done.

Example **:** *A* agreed to supply 200 bales of cotton to *B* @ ₹ 50 per bale. The bales were to be supplied in two instalments of 100 each. *A* supplied the first instalment but failed to supply the second. *B* must pay for 100 bales.

(*ii*) If a lump sum is to be paid for the compensation of an entire work and the work has been completed in full though badly, the defaulting party can recover the lump sum less a deduction for bad workmanship.

Example **:** *H* agreed to decorate *G*'s flat and fit a wardrobe and a book-case for a lump sum of £ 570. The work was done but *G* complained of faulty workmanship. It was estimated that it could be rectified by spending £ 264 more. Held, the *H* could recover £ 306 from *G*.

(*c*) Any claim based upon the doctrine of *quantum meruit* cannot be entertained unless there is an evidence of an express or implied promise to pay for the work which has already been done.

Following two remedies are available to the aggrieved party under equity for breach of a contract:

SPECIFIC PERFORMANCE

Law courts can, at their discertion order for the specific performance of a contract according to the provision of the Specific Relief Act in those cases where monetary compensation will not be an adequate remedy or actual damages cannot accurately be assessed. Specific performance of an agreement will not be granted : (*i*) if the agreement has been made without consideration, or (*ii*) the court cannot supervise its execution, or (*iii*) it will be inequitable, *i.e.*, not fair and just, or (*iv*) if the contract is of a personal nature. In contracts for sale of land and rare articles, courts generally order for specific performance of the contract.

INJUNCTION

Where a contract is of a negative character, *i.e.*, a party has promised not to do something and he does it, and thereby commits a breach of contract, the aggrieved party may, under certain circumstances, seek the protection of the court and obtain an injunction, forbidding the party from committing breach. An injunction is an order of the court instructing a person to refrain from doing some act which has been the subject matter of contract. Courts may, at their discretion, grant a temporary or a perpetual injuction for indefinite period.

Example **:** *A* agreed to sing at *B*'s theatre and to sing no where else for a certain period. Afterwards *A* made a contract with *E* to sing at *E*'s theatre and refused to sing at *B*'s theatre. The court refused to

18. (1898), 1 Q.B. 673.

order specific performance as the contract was of a personal nature but granted an injunction against *A* to restrain him from singing anywhere else.[19]

Equitable rights of specific performance or injunction may be lost by *laches*. Equity is for the benefit of the diligent and not for the sleepy.

RESTITUTION

Restitution means an act of restoration. According to *Anson*, a person who has been unjustly enriched at the expense of another must make compensation to the other. The principle of restitution applies in the following circumstances :

1. *In case of voidable contracts (Sec. 64)* : A party rescinding a voidable contract is required by law to restore back to the other party any benefits that he might have received from him (*Sec. 64*). Contracts become voidable at the option of the party whose consent is obtained by fraud, coercion, misrepresentation or undue influence. In certain cases, contracts become voidable subsequently because of the default of any one party in the performance of the contract, *e.g.*, anticipatory breach of contract or when a party to a contract prevents the other party from performing his part of the contract or when a party to a contract fails to perform his promise in the time fixed when time is of essence in the contract.

Example : *A*, a singer, contracts with *B*, the manager of a theatre to sing at his theatre for two nights in every week, during the next two months, and *B* agrees to pay her a hundred rupees for each night's performance. On the sixth night *A* wilfully absents herself from the theatre, and *B*, in consequence rescinds the contracts *B* must pay *A* for the five nights on which she had sung.

2. *In case of contract becoming void* : When a contract becomes void, all parties who have received benefit under the contract must restore it back to the person from whom it has been received.

Example : *A* contracts to sing for *B* at a concert for ₹ 1,000, which are paid in advance. *A* is too ill to sing. *A* is not bound to make compensation to *B* for the loss of profits which *B* would have made if *A* had been able to sing, but must return to *B* 1,000 rupees paid in advance.

3. *In case an agreement is discovered to be void* : The principle of restitution also applied where an agreement is void *ab initio* but the fact is unknown to both the parties, *e.g.*, mutual mistake regarding existence of the subject matter.

Example : *A* pays ₹ 1,000 in consideration of *B*'s promising to sell his horse to him. Unknown to both the parties the horse is dead at the time of the promise. The agreement is void but *B* must repay *A* ₹ 1,000.

The doctrine of restitution is not applicable in the following circumstances :

(*i*) Where an agreement is known to be void, *e.g.*, where an agreement is impossible to perform or where it is illegal to the knowledge of both the parties from the very beginning. As a matter of fact, a party is deemed to have knowledge of illegality of the agreement at the time when it is entered into. If a party alleges that he came to know of the illegality subsequently, it must be duly proved by him. However, where money has been paid for an executory contract, the purpose of which is illegal, the party who paid money can repudiate the contract before the illegal purpose is carried out and reclaim the money. Similarly, severity of this rule is also miti-gated where both the parties are not equally at fault or when the illegal purpose is not carried out.

---

19. Wather Bros. *v.* Nelson (1937), 1 K.B. 289.

(*ii*) The principle of restitution does not also apply where a party who has to return the benefit is a person incompetent to enter into a contract, *e.g.*, minor. Courts may in these cases also order for the restoration of benefits on equitable ground, *e.g.*, where a minor misrepresents his age and leads other person to believe that he is major.

(*iii*) The principle of restitution is also not applicable where a party is required to give some earnest money which serves as a security that the depositor will perform his part. Such deposit will not be refunded if the depositor fails to perform his promise.

In case where restitution of the same benefit is not possible, reasonable compensation will have to be paid to make good the loss of the other party.

KEY TERMS

- **Damages :** Monetary compensation payable by the defaulting party to the aggrieved party in the event of a breach of contract.
- **Ordinary Damages :** Damages which arise in the ordinary course of events from the breach of contract.
- **Special Damages :** Damages which arise in the ordinary course of event from the breach of contract.
- **Exemplary Damages :** Damages awarded with the intention of punishing the defaulting party rather than compensating the aggrieved party.
- **Nominal Damages :** Damages which are small in amount and are awarded simply to recognise the right of the aggrieved party to claim damages for breach of contract.
- **Specific Performances :** Performance of the contract as promised.
- **Injunction :** An order of the Court restraining a person from doing some act which has been the subject matter of the contract.
- **Restitution :** It means restoring back by a party to the contract to another party any benefit the former might have received from the latter.

TEST QUESTIONS

Objective Type : *Test Your Knowledge*

1. State whether each of the following statements is *True* or *False*

(*a*) Nominal damages are never granted by way of compensation for loss.

(*b*) Penalty can be recovered under the Indian Contract Act.

(*c*) A person who himself is guilty of breach of contract cannot get compensation under the doctrine of quantum of meruit.

(*d*) The order for injunction and specific performance are simultaneously issued by the court.

(*e*) A person incompetent to contract generally cannot be asked to return benefit under the doctrine of restitution.

(*f*) Recoverability of damages for breach of contract depends on foreseability.

(ICWA Foundation, June 2001)

(*g*) The principle of liquidated damages is not relevant to Indian Contract Act.

(ICWA Foundation, June 2001)

(*h*) Earnest money means security for the performance of the contract.
(CS Foundation, Dec. 2008)

(*i*) The object of damages, in case of contract, is to punish the person, who fails to perform his obligation. *(B.Com. (Hons), Delhi 2012)*

[***Ans.*** (*a*) True; (*b*) False; (*c*) True; (*d*) False; (*e*) True; (*f*) True; (*g*) True; (*h*) True; (*i*) False.]

2. Select the most appropriate answer

(*i*) A claim for quantum meruit cannot succeed :
   (*a*) when an indivisible contract for a lump sum is partly performed.
   (*b*) when a divisible contract is partly performed.
   (*c*) when a contract is discovered to be unenforceable due to some technical defect.

(*ii*) Doctrine of restitution is not applicable in case of :
   (*a*) a contract becoming void
   (*b*) a voidable contract
   (*c*) an agreement known to be void.

(*iii*) The order for specific performance will be given by the court in case :
   (*a*) monetary compensation is not an adequate relief.
   (*b*) contract is of a personal nature.
   (*c*) the court cannot supervise execution of the contract.

[***Ans.*** (*i*) (*a*); (*ii*) (*c*); (*iii*) (*a*)]

Essay Type : *For Review, Discussion and Practice*

1. State the different remedies available to the aggrieved party for a breach of contract and explain the principles on which damages are assessed for the breach of a contract.
(CS Foundation, June 2001; B.Com. (Hons.), Delhi 1994)
2. "If the contract is broken, the law will endeavour, so far as money can do to place the injured party, in the same position as if the contract had been performed". Discuss.
3. What is the difference between penalty and liquidated damages? What bearing has this distinction in India upon the question of compensation on breach of contract?
4. State the principles for the assessment of damages in respect of breach of a contract.
5. What do you understand by the Doctrine of Quantum Meruit? When and how does it come in operation? Are there any limitations to this doctrine?
(ICWA Foundation, June 2000; CS Foundation, Dec. 2003)
6. Discuss the circumstances under which restitution could be ordered by the court in respect of benefits received under a contract.
7. Distinguish between ordinary damages and special damages. *(CS Foundation, Dec. 2000)*
8. Explain how special damages differ from ordinary damages with reference to any leading case.
(ICWA Foundation, Dec. 1998)
9. What are the remedies for breach of contract? Discuss with special reference to damages for loss of profits in a contract. *(ICWA Foundation, Dec. 1999)*
10. What do you mean by ordinary damages. When can these damages be claimed.
(CS Foundation, June 1999)
11. Write short notes on the following :
   (*a*) Liquidated Damages and Penalty
   (ICWA Foundation, Dec. 1999; CS Foundation, Dec. 2004; ICWA Inter, Grade I, 2005)
   (*b*) Exemplary Damages *(CS Foundation, Dec. 1998, May 2005)*
   (*c*) Anticipatory Breach of Contract *(CS Foundation, June 2007)*

12. Explain ordinary damages, special damages, exemplary damages and quantum meriut.
(B.Com. (Hons.), Delhi 1986, 1994, 1995)
13. Explain the different types of damages that can be recovered for breach of contract.
(B.Com. (Pass), Delhi 2001)
14. Under what circumstances can an aggrieved party institute a suit for 'injection' and for 'specific performance' of a contract? Explain with examples. *(CS Foundation, Dec. 2006)*
15. Explain the concept of quantum meruit. *(CS Foundation, June 2008)*
16. What is the law relating determination of compensation on breach of contract, contained in Section 73 of the Indian Contract Act, 1872? *(CA, IPCC, May, 2011)*

PRACTICAL PROBLEMS

1. *A* promised to repay a loan of ₹ 5,000 to *B* by five equal instalments. He further agreed that if he defaults to pay any instalment then the whole amount will be due. Is it a valid contract?
(ICWA Foundation, June 2000)
[***Ans.*** It is a void contract since the sum mentioned amounts to be a penalty.]
2. Rohit agreed to erect a plant for Roshan by 31st December, 2001. Rohit further agreed to pay ₹ 1,000 per month as damages in case of delay beyond the agreed date. Roshan sued Rohit for ₹ 6,000 being the actual loss caused to him as a result of delay of four months. What damages will you award and why? *(CS Foundation, June 2001)*
[***Ans.*** Roshan can recover a maximum of ₹ 4,000 as damages.]
3. The plaintiff hired a godown from the defendant for a period of 12 months and paid the whole rent to him in advance. After six months the godown was destroyed by fire and the plaintiff claimed a refund of proportionate amount of the rent. Is the claim valid? State reasons for your answer.
[***Ans.*** Yes. The contract becomes void. Under section 65 restitution is required.]
4. *A* agrees to sell land to *B* for ₹ 30,000. *B* pays to *A* ₹ 1,000 as a deposit at the time of the contract, the amount to be forfeited by *A* if *B* does not complete the sale within a specified period. *B* fails to complete the sale within a reasonable time after the expiry of that period. *A* rescinds the contract and retains the deposits. *B* contends that deposit is a benefit received by *A* under the voidable contract which is rescinded by *A* and so *A* should, under section 64 of the Indian Contract Act, restore the benefit to *B*. Decide.
[***Ans.*** *A* can retain the deposit. It is not a benefit but only a security that the purchaser would fulfil his contract.]
5. In a bond there is a stipulation for payment of compound interest on failure to pay simple interest at the same rate as was payable on the principal. Discuss whether this stipulation is liquidated damage or penalty.
[***Ans.*** Liquidated damages. The sum is not extravagant and unconscionable.]
6. Anil agreed to sell Biswas 10 shares at the rate of ₹ 120 per share to be delivered on November 10, 1998. On that date the prices of shares came down to ₹ 105 per share. Biswas refused to take the shares. On Nov. 12, 1998, Anil sold these shares at the rate of ₹ 140 per share. Is Biswas liable to pay any damages? [***Ans.*** Biswas should pay ₹ 150 as damages.]
7. *A*, a tailor, expected to make good profits at a place on the occasion of a festival there, sent through a railway company a sewing machine and some cloth for carrying to the place of festival. Due to the fault of the servants of the railway company, the machine and the cloth could not be delivered till the termination of the festival. Discuss the rights of the tailor.
[***Ans.*** Since the railway company had no notice of the special purpose, the damages cannot be recovered.]

8. *'A'* contracted with *'B'* to supply him 1,000 tonnes of iron @ ₹ 1,900 per tonne, to be delivered at a stated time. Thereafter, *'A'* contracts with *'C'* for the purchase of 1,000 tonnes of iron @ ₹ 1,800 per tonne and at the same time told *C* that he did so for the purpose of performing his contract entered into with *'B'*, *'C'* failed to perform his contract in due course. Consequently *'A'* could not procure any iron and *'B'* rescinded the contract. What would be the amount of damages which *'A'* could claim from *'C'* in the circumstances? Explain.

[***Ans.*** *'A'* is entitled to claim from *'C'* ₹ 1 lakh, the amount of profit he would have made by the performance of his contract with *'B'*.]

9. *A* lends *B* a sum of ₹ 1,000 @ 12% p.a. repayable after a month, with a stipulation that in case of default, interest @ 24% shall be payable from the date of lending. *B* commits default in the repayment of the loan. State the rights of *A*.

[***Ans.*** *A* can recover the market rate of interest not exceeding 24% from the date of breach of contract and not from the date of lending money.]

10. *X* agrees to sell to *Y* at Delhi certain goods which he has purchased from Madras. The goods were sent from Madras to Delhi through a carrier agency. Unfortunately, the truck carrying the goods caught fire while the truck was on its way to Delhi and the entire goods were destroyed. This fact was known neither to *X* nor to *Y*. The goods, therefore, did not reach Delhi and *X* could not deliver the same to *Y* on the agreed date. *Y*, who had already entered into an agreement for the sale of the same goods to *Z*, also failed to perform his promise, and consequently suffered loss. *Y* now claims the damage from *X*. Decide, giving reasons.

(*i*) Whether *Y* will succeed?

(*ii*) What provisions exist in the Indian Contract Act in this regard?

[***Ans.*** (*i*) If the goods did not exist at the time of the contract, the contract would be voidon the ground of mutual mistake and *Y* will not succeed in claiming damages. (*ii*) If the goods existed at the time of contract but were subsequently destroyed unknown to both the parties, the contract would be void on the ground of supervening impossibility. *Y* will not succeed in claiming damages from *X*.]

11. Arun is a shopkeeper. He enters into a contract with Bhanu, the wholesaler, for the supply of crackers worth ₹ 1 lakh on the condition that the delivery must be made at least 7 days before Diwali. Arun also makes known to Bhanu that if he fails to deliver the crackers in time, Arun is likely to suffer a loss of profit of ₹ 25,000 which he expected to earn from the sale of crackers during Diwali season. But Bhanu supplies crackers 3 days after Diwali. Now Arun sues Bhanu for the loss of profit. Will Arun succeed? Give reasons. *(CS Foundation, Dec. 2004)*

[***Ans.*** Arun will succeed and get special damages.]

12. *M.* Ltd., contracts with Shanti Traders to make and deliver certain machinery to them by 30.06.2004 for ₹ 11.50 lakhs. Due to labour strike, *M.* Ltd., could not manufacture and deliver the machinery to Shanti Traders. Later, Shanti Traders procured the machinery from another manufacturer for ₹ 12.75 lakhs. Shanti Traders was also prevented from performing a contract which it had made with Zenith Traders at the time of their contract with *M.* Ltd. and were compelled to pay compensation for breach of contract. Advise Shanti Traders the amount of compensation which it can claim from *M.* Ltd., referring to the legal provisions of the Indian Contract Act. *(PEE II, May 2005)*

[***Ans.*** (*a*) M. Ltd. is obliged to compensate for the loss of ₹ 1.25 lakhs (*i.e.*, ₹ 12.75 minus ₹ 11.50 lakhs) which had naturally arisen due to default in performing the contract by the specified date. (*b*) M. Ltd. knew about the contract of Shanti Traders and thus will be obliged to reimburse the compensation which Shanti Traders had to pay to Zenith Traders for breach of contract. Otherwise, M. Ltd. will not be liable.]

13. Anil was due to perform a contract on February 20, 2004 but on February 16, repudiated his obligation. On February 23, the contract became illegal through a change in the law. Varun,

the other party on the contract, filed a suit for breach of contract on February 25. Decide the case with reasons. *(B.Com. (Hons.), Delhi 1989)*

[***Ans.*** Varun will not succeed. He did not take immediate action for anticipatory breach. Now there is supervening impossibility.]

14. Miss *X*, a film actress agreed to work exclusively for a period of two years, for a film production company. However, during the said period she enters into a contract to work for another film producer. Discuss the rights of the aggrieved film production company under the Indian Contract Act, 1872. *(ICWA Foundation, June 2000, PEE II, November 2005)*

[***Ans.*** The aggrieved film production company can go to court and get injunction order restraining Miss *X* working for another film production company.]

15. Mr. Ramaswamy of Chennai placed an order with Mr. Shah of Ahmedabad for supply of Urid Dhall on 10.11.2006 at a contracted price of ₹ 40 per kg. The order was for the supply of 10 tonnes within a month's time *viz.*, before 09.12.2006. On 04.12.2006 Mr. Shah wrote a letter to Mr. Ramaswamy stating that the price of Urid Dhall was skyrocketing to ₹ 20 per Kg. and he would not be able to supply as per original contract. The price of Urid Dhall to ₹ 53 on 09.12.06 Advise Mr. Ramaswamy citing the legal position. *(PCE, ICAI, May 2007)*

[***Ans.*** Options available to Ramaswamy: (*i*) can repudiate the contract on 01.04.2006 and claim damages at ₹ 10 per kg. *i.e.*, ₹ 1,00,000. (*ii*) He could wait till 09.12.2006 and claim damages @ ₹ 13 per kg. *i.e.*, ₹ 1,30,000. However if government imposes a ban on movement of dal, the contract becomes void and he would not get any damages.]

16. Anubhav, an author, enters into a contract with Balwant, a publisher, for writing a book for him. But, subsequently Anubhav refuses to write the book for Balwant. Now, Balwant files a suit against Anubhav for specific performance of the contract. Well Balwant succeed? Give reasons. *(CS Foundation, Dec. 2007)*

[***Ans.*** Balwant will not succeed]

17. Mr. *B* (a broker) by the orders of Mr. *A* purchases 10 Drums of oil for *A* from Mr. *C*, Afterwards Mr. *A* refuses to receive oil. Mr. *C* sues Mr. *B* who informs Mr. *A* but Mr. *A* repudiates the contract. Although Mr. *B* defends but failed. Mr. *B* has to pay cost, damages and incurs expense. Can *B* recover any amount from *A*. *(ICWAI Inter, June 2009)*

[***Ans.*** *A* is liable to B for such damages, costs and expenses.]

18. *A* contracted with *B* to supply him (B) 500 tons of iron-steel @ ₹ 5,000 per ton, to be delivered at a specified time. Thereafter, *A* contracts with *C* for the purchase of 500 tons of iron-steel @ ₹ 4,800 per ton, and at the same time told *C* that he did so for the purpose of performing his contract entered into with *B*. *C* failed to perform his contract in due course. Consequently, *A* could not procure any iron-steel and *B* rescinded the contract. What would be the amount of damages which *A* could claim from *C* in the circumstances? Explain with reference to the provisions of the Indian Contract, 1872. *(PEE-II, ICAI, May 2007)*

[***Ans.*** *A* is entitled to claim from *C* ₹ 1,00,000 (difference between the procuring price of iron steel and contracted selling price to *B*) being the amount of profit *A* would have made by the performance of this contract with *B*.]

19. Mohan, a singer agrees to sing at twinkle's theatre for a certain period. He further agrees that during the prescribed period, he will not sing at any other theatre. Afterwards, Mohan makes a contract with Sohan to sing at his theatre during that period and refuses to sing at Twinkle's theatre. What remedies Twinkle has against Mohan? Give reasons. *(CS Foundation, June, 2011)*

[***Ans.*** Twinkle can file suit against Mohan for an injunction, *i.e.*, order of the court restraining Mohan from doing which he promised not to do.]

20. *A.* Das entered into contract to sing for *B.* Roy at a concert for ₹ 10,000 which was received in advance. *A.* Das being too Ill could not sing. *B.* Roy demanded compensation for loss of profit which he would have made it *A.* Das had been able to sing. State *B.* Roy's right.

(*ICWA Inter. Dec., 2010*)

[***Ans.*** *A.* Das is not bound to make compensation to B. Roy. However, *A.* Roy must refund to *B.* Roy ₹ 10,000 which was received in advance. This is being supervening impossibility.]

21. A tailor, ordinarily residing in Agra, wanted to move to Delhi during the marriage season, so as to earn substantial income. He delivered to the Railway company for transmission a package containing his sewing machine and other ancillary tailoring materials. But there was inordinate delay in transmission and the package arrived in Delhi too late for him to take advantage of the marriage season. What damages can the tailor recover from the Railway Company and why?

(*B.Com. (Hons), Delhi, 2011*)

[***Ans.*** The tailor is entitled to recover from the railway company only ordinary damages for the loss as naturally arose due to breach of contract and not any special damages i.e. the ordinary profit that he could normally earn and not additional special earnings he could have made due to marriage ceremonies.]

Chapter 13

CONTRACTS OF INDEMNITY AND GUARANTEE

LEARNING OBJECTIVES

A careful study of this chapter will enable you to :

- understand the meaning of a contract of indemnity and a contract of guarantee;
- identify the rights of indemnity holder;
- differentiate between a contract of indemnity and a contract of guarantee;
- explain different types of guarantee;
- describe the rights of a surety;
- enumerate the circumstances where a surety may be discharged from his liability; and
- explain the meaning of certain key terms.

CONTRACT OF INDEMNITY

Definition : The term 'indemnity' means 'compensation for loss.' Hence, a contract of indemnity implies a promise by one person to another for compensating the latter for the loss suffered by him.

According to section 124 of the Indian Contract Act, a contract of indemnity is 'a contract by which one party promises to save the other from the loss caused to him by the conduct of the promisor himself, or by the conduct of a third party'.

Example : *A* contracts to indemnify *B* against consequences of any proceedings which *C* may take against *B* in respect of a certain sum of ₹ 200. This is a contract of indemnity. *A* will be termed as *'Indemnifier'* and *B* as the *'Indemnity-holder'.*

Definition is not very exhaustive : According to the definition given by Sec. 124 of the Indian Contract Act, a contract of indemnity includes :

(*i*) only express promise to indemnify, and

(*ii*) cases where loss is caused by the conduct of the promisor himself or by the conduct of any other person.

The definition does not cover :

(*i*) implied promise to indemnify and

(*ii*) cases where the loss is caused by accident or by the conduct of the promisee.

The definition of a contract of indemnity as given by the Indian Contract Act is very restrictive. In case it is strictly applied, contracts to compensate for losses caused by happening of events *e.g.*, contracts of insurance will not come within the purview of contracts of indemnity. However, the Indian Courts have taken a very liberal view. They have held in a number of cases that the contracts of indemnity also include contracts to compensate for losses on account of happening of events and implied promises to indemnify.

Examples : (*i*) *A* is the owner of an article. It is lost and is found by *B*. *B* sends it to an auctioneer for selling it. The auctioneer sells the article. *A* recovers damages from the auctioneer for selling away this article. The auctioneer can recover the loss from *B*. There is an implied promise by *B* to save the auctioneer from any loss that may be caused to him on account of any defect in *B*'s authority to let the article sold.

(*ii*) *A*, a broker, forged the signature of *P*, the holder of a Government promissory note and endorsed it to the Bank of India. The bank got the note renewed from the Government. *P* sued Government and recovered damages. It was held that the Government could recover the damages from the Bank of India. The learned judge quoted the following observation of *Lord Halisbury* : "It is general principle of law that when an action is done by one person at the request of another which act is not itself manifestly tortuous to the knowledge of the person doing it, and such act turns out to be injurious to the rights of a third party, the person doing it is entitled to indemnity from him who requested that it should be done."

Commencement of indemnifier's liability : High Court have differed in their judgment regarding commencement of indemnifier's liability. According to High Court of Calcutta, Madras, Allahabad and Patna indemnity-holder when asked to meet a liability, can compel the indemnifier to put him (indemnity-holder) in a position to meet the liability without waiting until he (indemnity-holder) has actually discharged it. High Courts of Bombay, Lahore and Nagpur have, however, held that indemnifier can be made liable only when indemnity-holder has incurred an actual loss, *i.e.*, discharged the liability. The former view seems to be more correct and is also in consonance with the English view : 'to indemnify does not merely mean to reimburse in respect of moneys paid, but to save from loss in respect of liability against which the indemnity has been given....if it be held that payment is a condition precedent to recovery, the contract may be of little value to the person to be indemnified, who may be unable to meet the claim in the first instance.[1]

The above view was also expressed later by Chagla J., in a Bombay case. According to him this would result in an intolerable burden on the indemnity-holder if he was required to first satisfy the liability and then claim the money from the indemnifier. Lord Justice Buckley in a case[2] also observed, 'Indemnity is not necessarily given by repayment after payment. Indemnity requires that the party to be indemnified shall never be called upon to pay.'

Thus, we can conclude that if the indemnity-holder had incurred an absolute liability, he has the right to call upon the indemnifier to save him from that liability and pay it off.

Example : *A* Ltd. was acting as commission agents for *P* for purchase of goods for him. *A* Ltd. bought certain goods for *P*, which *P* failed to take. As a result of this the supplier sued the company and became entitled to recover a certain a amount as damages from the company. Before *A* Ltd. could pay the supplier, it went into liquidation. It is held that the official liquidator of *A* Ltd., could recover the amount of damage payable by it to the supplier from *P*.[3]

Rights of the indemnity-holder when sued : The indemnity-holder is entitled to the following rights, which he is free to enforce provided he has not acted outside the scope of his authority and has not contravened any of the specific direction of the indemnifier.

1. Kennedy L.J. in Liverpool Mortgage Insurance Co's case (1914), 2 Ch. 617.
2. Re Richardson, Exparte the Governor of St. Thomas's Hospital (1911), 2 K.B. 705.
3. Osman Jamal & Sons *v*. Gopal (1928), 56 Cal. 262.

1. *Claim for damages :* Indemnity-holder is entitled to recover all damages which he might have been compelled to pay in any suit in respect of a matter covered by the contract.

2. *Claim for costs :* Indemnity-holder is entitled to recover all costs incidental to the institution or defending of the suit. But the party indemnified cannot recover costs when he has not acted as a prudent man in defending the action against him or has not been authorised by the indemnifier to defend the suit or where the costs incurred are unreasonable in amount.

3. *Claim for sum paid under a compromise :* Indemnity-holder is entitled to recover all sums paid under any compromise of any such suit, provided the compromise was not contrary to the directions of the indemnifier and it has been made on the best available terms. Indemnity-holder-must have acted prudently in making such a promise *(Sec. 125)*.

It is to be noted that a contract of indemnity being a specie of the general contract, and, therefore, must satisfy all essentials of a valid contract such as competent parties, free consent, lawful object etc., otherwise it will not be valid.

Example : *A* agrees to indemnity *B* for all consequences which may arise as a result of his (*B*) giving a good beating to *C*. The object being unlawful the agreement is also void.

CONTRACT OF GUARANTEE

Definition : A 'Contract of Guarantee' is a contract to perform the promise of discharge the liability of a third person in case of his default. The person who gives the guarantee is called the 'surety'; the person in respect of whose default the guarantee is given is called the 'principal debtor' and the person to whom the guarantee is given is called the 'creditor'. The contract of guarantee may be either written or oral *(Sec. 126)*.

Purpose : Contracts of guarantee are usually entered into for the following purpose :

(*a*) to secure the performance of something which may be immediately related to mercantile agreement, or

(*b*) to secure the honesty and fidelity of someone who is to be appointed to some office, or

(*c*) to secure someone from injury arising out of some wrong committed by another.

Essentials of a valid contract must be present : A contract of guarantee, like other ordinary contract, must satisfy all the essentials of a valid contract. However, it has two distinctive features:

(*a*) Something done or any promise made for the benefit of the principal debtor is presumed by law to be a sufficient consideration for the surety to give guarantee. It is not necessary that the surety himself should be benefited.

Examples : (*i*) *A* requests *B* to sell and deliver to him goods on credit and *B* agrees to do so provided *C* will guarantee the payment of the price of the goods. If *C* promises to guarantee the payment in consideration of *A*'s promise to deliver the goods on credit, it is sufficient considerations for *C*'s promise. However, if *A* sells and delivers goods to *B* and if *C* afterwards without any consideration agrees to pay for them in default of *B*, the agreement is void as there is no consideration whatsoever.

(*ii*) *A* sells and delivers goods to *B*. *C* afterwards requests *A* to forbear to sue *B* for the debt for a year and promises that if he does so, *C* will pay for them in default of payment by *B*. *A* agrees to forbear as requested. This is a sufficient consideration for *C*'s promise.

(*b*) In a contract of guarantee, the creditor and surety must be competent to enter into a contract, but debtor may be a minor or a person incapable of entering into a contract, In such a case, the surety will be taken as the principal debtor and will be liable to pay. Section 128 (discussed later) only states the quantum of surety's liability and not its nature.

(*c*) In a contract of guarantee, the liability of the surety is conditional. It arises only when the principal debtor makes a default. A liability which arises independently of a 'default' is not within the definition of guarantee.[4]

Invalid Guarantee

Though a contract of guarantee is not a contract of utmost good faith *(uberimea fidei)*, liable to be avoided by mere non-disclosure of any material contract as would give him the idea about the nature of the transaction for which he is rendering himself answerable.

Following are a few of those cases when the guarantee given by the surety will be invalid and cannot be enforced against him :

(*i*) Guarantee obtained by misrepresentation (*Sec. 142)* : Any guarantee which has been obtained by means of misrepresentation made by the creditor, or with his knowledge and assent, concerning a material part of the transaction, is invalid.

(*ii*) Guarantee obtained by concealment (*Sec. 143)* : Any guarantee which the creditor has obtained by means of keeping silence as to material circumstances is invalid.

(*iii*) In case where co-surety does not join (*Sec. 144)* : Where a person gives a guarantee upon a contract that the creditor shall not act upon it until another person has joined in it as co-surety, the guarantee will be invalid if that other person does not join.

Examples : (*i*) *A* engages *B* as a clerk to collect money for him. *B* fails to account for some of his receipts, and *A*, in consequence, calls upon him to furnish security for his duly accounting. *C* gives his guarantee for *B*'s duly accounting. *A* does not acquaint *C* with *B*'s previous conduct. *B* afterwards makes default. The guarantee is invalid.

(*ii*) *A* guarantee to *C* payment for iron to be supplied by him to *B* to the amount of 2,000 tonnes. *B* and *C* have privately agreed that *B* should pay five rupees per tonne beyond the market price, such excess to be applied in liquidation of an old debt. This agreement is concealed from *A*. *A* is not liable as a surety.

(*iii*) *A* agree with *B* to stand as a surety for *C* for a loan of ₹ 1,000 provided *D* also joins him as surety. *D* refuses to join. *A* is not liable as a surety.

DIFFERENCE BETWEEN A CONTRACT OF INDEMNITY AND A CONTRACT OF GUARANTEE

1. **Nature of liability :** The person giving an indemnity is primarily liable, whereas the surety's liability is secondary, arising only on the default of another person. In a contract of guarantee, there is an undertaking on the part of the surety to be answerable for the debt or default of another, whereas in a contract of indemnity there is no such obligation, promisor merely takes upon himself to indemnify the promisee for loss caused to him by the acts of the promisor or anybody else.

2. **Number of contracts :** A contract of indemnity is a single contract between two parties only, *i.e.*, indemnifier and indemnified. It is an original and direct engagement which may be made independently of the existence of a third party. On the other hand, in a contract of guarantee, there

4. Punjab National Bank *v.* Sri Vikram Cotton Mills, (1970), 1 S.C.C. 60.

are three parties--the creditor, the principal debtor and the surety and three contracts--one between the creditor and the principal debtor, second between the surety and the creditor and the third between the surety and the principal debtor, by means of which the surely is entitled to recover from the principal debtor whatever sums he may have rightfully paid under the contract of guarantee to the creditor.

3. **Purpose of contracts :** A contract of guarantee is to provide necessary security to the creditor against his advance, but a contract of indemnity is made for the reimbursement of loss. Surety gives guarantee only on the request of the debtor but the indemnifier need not necessarily act only on the request of the debtor.

4. **Rights of parties :** In a contract of guarantee surety becomes entitled in law to proceed against the principal debtor in his own right after he has discharged the debt payable by the principal debtor to the creditor. But in the case of a contract of indemnity, indemnifier can bring the suit against third party only in the name of the indemnified and unless he has obtained the assignment of the claim in his favour, he cannot file a suit in his own name.

5. **Existence of risk or liability :** Indemnifier promises to save the idemnity-holder from a contingent risk. But the surety agrees to discharge the liability of the principal debtor which is not contingent but subsisting.

6. **Parities' interest :** The person giving the guarantee should have no other interest in the transaction apart from his guarantee. A person giving an indemnity may have some other interest in the contract, *e.g.*, a *del credere* agent gets commission for his promise to indemnify his principal against bad debts.

KINDS OF GUARANTEE

Contracts of guarantee may be :

(1) Specific, or

(2) Continuing.

1. **Specific guarantee :** Specific guarantee means a guarantee given for one specific transaction. In this case the liability of the surety extends only to a single transaction.

Example : *A* guarantees payment to *B* of the price of five sacks of flour to be delivered by *B* to *C* and to be paid in a month. *B* delivers 5 sacks to *C*. *C* pays for them. Afterwards *B* delivers four sacks to *C*, which *C* does not pay. The guarantee given by *A* was only a specific guarantee and, accordingly, he is not liable for the price of the four sacks.

2. **Continuing guarantee :** A continuing guarantee is that which extends to a series of transactions (*Sec. 129*). It is not confined to a single transaction. Surety can fix up a limit on his liability as to time or amount of guarantee, when the guarantee is a continuing one. The fact that the guarantee is continuing can also be ascertained from the intentions of the parties and the surrounding circumstances.

Examples : (*i*) *A*, in consideration that *B* will employ *C* in collecting the rents of *B*'s zamindari, promises *B* to be responsible, to the amount of 5,000 rupees, for the due collection and payment by *C* of those rents. This is a continuing guarantee.

(*ii*) *A* guarantees payment to *B*, a tea-dealer, to the amount of £ 100, for any tea he may from time to time supply to *C*. *B* supplies *C* with tea to the extent of the agreed value, *i.e.*, £ 100 and *C* pays *B* for it. Afterwards *B* supplies *C* with tea to the value of £ 200. *C* fails to pay. The guarantee given by *A* was a continuing guarantee, and he is accordingly liable to *B* to the extend of £ 100.

Revocation of a continuing guarantee : A continuing guarantee is revoked by any of the following ways :

1. **By notice** *(Sec. 130)* **:** A continuing guarantee may at any time be revoked by the surety as to future transactions, by giving a distinct notice to the creditor.

Examples : (*i*) *A*, in consideration of *B*'s discounting at *A*'s request, bills of exchange for *C* guarantees to *B* for twelve months, the due payment of all such bills to the extent of 5,000 rupees. *B* discounts bill for *C* to the extent of 2,000 rupees. Afterwards, at the end of three months, *A* revokes the guarantee. This revocation discharges *A* from all liability to *B* for any subsequent discount. But *A* is liable to *B* for 2,000 rupees, on the default for *C*.

(*ii*) *A* guarantee to *B*, to the extent of 10,000 rupees, that *C* shall pay all the bills that *B* shall draw upon him. *B* draws upon *C* a bill for ₹ 10,000. *C* accepts the bill. *A* gives notice of revocation. *C* dishonours the bill at maturity. *A* will be liable for his guarantee.

2. **By death** *(Sec. 131)* **:** Death of the surety will operate as a revocation of the continuing guarantee with regard to the future transactions unless the contract provides otherwise. No notice of death need by given to the creditor. Heirs of the surety will not be liable for any fresh transactions entered into by the creditor with the principal debtor after the death of the surety without knowledge of such death.

NATURE OF SURETY'S LIABILITY

Where the parties do not specifically agree as to the extent of the liability or the surety does not put up any limit on his liability at the time of entering into the contract, the liability of the surety will be co-extensive with that of the principal debtor (*Sec. 128*). The quantum or obligation of the surety will be the same as that of a principal debtor. In other words, whatever amount of money a creditor can legally realise from the principal debtor including interest, cost of litigation, damages etc., the same amount he can recover from the surety.

Example : *A* guarantee to *B* the payment of a bill of exchange by *C*, the acceptor. The bill is dishonoured by *C*. A will be liable not only for the amount of the bill but also for any interest and charges which may have become due on it.

The liability of the surety arises immediately on the default of the principal debtor, but the creditor is not bound to give any notice of the default of the principal debtor to the surety or to exhaust all the remedies available to him as against the debtor before proceeding against the surety. Besides that, creditor is free to realise the debt when it becomes due either from the debtor or the surety. It is not necessary for him to proceed against the debtor first. He may sue the surety without suing the principal debtor. It is surety's duty to see that the principal debtor pays or performs his obligation.

Though, generally the liability of surety is co-extensive with that of the principal debtor, yet the surety may by special agreement restrict his liability. In such a case his liability will be limited only to the extent of the amount agreed.

Example : *A* gives a loan of ₹ 2,000 to *B* and *C* agrees to stand as surety for repayment to the extent of ₹ 1,000. *B* fails to pay the whole amount. *C* is liable only to the extent of ₹ 1,000 since he had restricted his liability to that extent by special agreement.

On account of the above reason the surety is sometimes termed as 'a favoured debtor'.

Above provisions of law provide a measure only to the extent of the liability of the surety and do not refer to the nature of the obligation of the principal debtor. Therefore, the liability of the surety is not necessarily simultaneous with that of the principal debtor. The liability of the two is distinct, arising from different contracts. The contract with the surety is not a collateral one, but a principal contract. It cannot be said that the surety will be liable only if the principal debtor is liable or if put the other way, that a surety can never be liable when the principal debtor cannot be held liable. Therefore, when the original contract between the creditor and the principal debtor is void, *e.g.*, when the principal debtor is a minor or that the contract between the two parties was voidable at the option of the principal debtor and who has so exercised his option and has avoided the contract, the surety will not be discharged from liability. He shall be held liable as a principal debtor. A surety continues to be liable even when the claim against the principal debtor becomes barred by limitation. Omission of the creditor to sue the principal debtor within the period of limitation does not discharge the surety.[5] Discharge of the principal debtor by operation of law will not also discharge the surety.[6]

Liability of two persons primarily liable, not affected by arrangement between them that one shall be surety on other's default (*Sec. 132*) **:** Where two persons contract with third person to undertake a certain liability, and also contract with each other that one of them shall be liable only on the default of the other, the third person not being a party to such contract, the liability of each of such two persons to the third person under the first contract is not affected by the existence of the second contract, although such third person may have been aware of its existence.

Example **:** *A* and *B* make a joint and several promissory note to *C*. *A* makes it, in fact as surety for *B*, and *C* knows this at the time when the note is made. The fact that *A*, to the knowledge of *C*, made the note as a surety for *B*, is no answer to a suit by *C* against *A* upon the note.

RIGHTS OF THE SURETY

Rights of the surety can be classified as under :

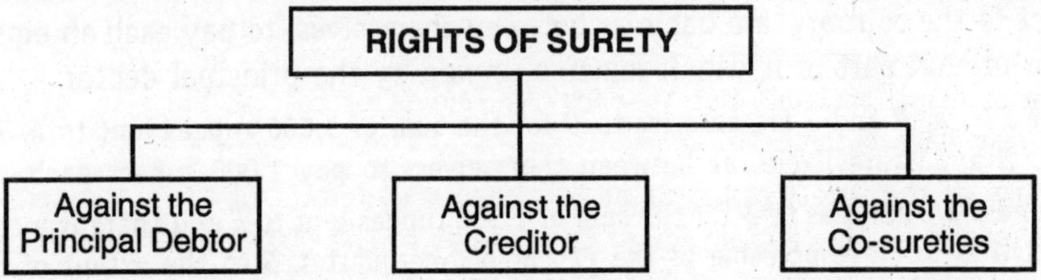

1. Rights of the surety against the principal debtor

(*a*) **Rights to be subrogated :** When the principal debtor has committed the default and the surety pays the debt to the creditor, the surety will stand in the shoes of the creditor and will be invested with all the rights which the creditor had against the debtor (*Sec. 140*).

(*b*) **Right to claim indemnity :** In every contract of guarantee, there is an implied promise by the principal debtor to indemnify the surety, and the surety is to recover from the principal debtor whatever sum he had paid rightfully under the guarantee but no sums which he has paid wrongfully, *e.g.*, cost of fruitless litigation (*Sec. 145*).

Examples **:** (*i*) *B* is indebted to *C*, and *A* is surety for the debt. *C* demands payment from *A*, and on his refusal sues his for the amount. *A* defends the suit, having reasonable grounds for doing so, but

5. Mahant Singh *v.* U. Ba Yi (1939), 66 I.A. 198.
6. Kashiba *v.* Shripat (1894), 19 Bom. 697.

is compelled to pay the amount of the debt with costs. He can recover from *B* the amount paid by him for cost, as well as the principal debt.

(*ii*) *C* lends *B* a sum of money, and *A*, at the request of *B*, accepts bill of exchange drawn by *C* upon *A* to secure the amount. *C*, the holder of the bill, demands payment of it from *A* and, on *A*'s refusal to pay, sues him upon the bill. *A*, not having reasonable grounds for so doing, defends the suit, and has to pay the amount of the bill the costs. He can recover from *B* the amount of the bill, but not the sum paid for costs, as there was no real ground for defending the action.

(*iii*) *A* guarantees to *C* to the extent of 2,000 rupees, payment for rice to be supplied by *C* to *B*. *C* supplies to *B* rice to a less amount that 2,000 rupees, but obtains from *A* payment of the sum of 2,000 rupees is respect of the rice supplied. *A* cannot recover from *B* more than the price of the rice actually supplied.

2. Rights of the surety against the creditor

A surety is entitled to the benefit of every security which the creditor has against the debtor at the time when the contract of suretyship is entered into, whether the surety knows of the existence of such security or not. If the creditor loses or without the consent of the surety parts with such security, the surety is discharged to the extent of the value of the security (*Sec. 141*). But a surety, however, cannot claim the benefit of the securities only on the payment of a part of the debt.

3. Rights against co-sureties

When two or more persons stand as sureties for the same debt or obligation they are termed as co-sureties. The position of co-sureties is as follows :

Co-sureties liable to contribute equally (Sec. 146) : Where two or more person are co-sureties for the same debt or duty, either jointly or severally, and whether under the same or different contracts, and whether with or without the knowledge of each other, the co-sureties in the absence of any contract to the contrary, are liable as between themselves, to pay each an equal share of the whole debt, or of that part of it which remains unpaid by the principal debtor.

Examples : (*i*) *A*, *B* and *C* are sureties to *D* for the sum of 3,000 rupees lent to *E*. *E* makes default in payment. *A*, *B* and *C* are liable, as between themselves, to pay 1,000 rupees each.

(*ii*) *A*, *B* and *C* are sureties to *D* for the sum of 1,000 rupees lent to *E* and there is a contract between *A*, *B* and *C* that *A* is to be responsible to the extent of one-quarter, *B* to the extent of one-quarter and *C* to the extent of one-half. *E* makes default in payment. As between the sureties, *A* is liable to pay 250 rupees, *B* 250 rupees and *C* 500 rupees.

Liability of co-sureties bound in different sums (Sec. 147) : Co-sureties who are bound in different sums are liable to pay equally as far as the limits of their respective obligations permit.

Examples : (*i*) *A*, *B* and *C*, as sureties for *D*, enter into three several bonds, each in a different penalty, namely, *A* in the penalty of 10,000 rupees, *B* in that of 20,000 rupees, *C* in that of 40,000 rupees, conditioned for *D*'s duly accounting of *E*. *D* makes default to the extent of 30,000 rupees. *A*, *B* and *C*, are each liable to pay 10,000 rupees.

(*ii*) *A*, *B* and *C*, as sureties for *D*, enter into three several bonds, each in a different penalty, namely, *A* in the penalty of 10,000 rupees, *B* in that of 20,000 rupees, *C* in that of 40,000 rupees, conditioned for *D*'s duly accounting to *E*. *D* makes default to the extent of 40,000 rupees. *A* is liable to pay 10,000 rupees, and *B* and *C* 15,000 rupees each.

(*iii*) *A*, *B* and *C*, as sureties for *D*, enter into three several bonds each in a different penalty, namely. *A* in the penalty of 10,000 rupees, *B* in that of 20,000 rupees, *C* in that of 40,000 rupees, conditioned for *D*'s duly accounting to *E*. *D* makes default to the extent of 70,000 rupees. *A*, *B* and *C* have to pay each the full penalty of his bond.

A release by the creditor of one or more of the co-sureties will not discharge the others from their obligation, neither will it free the surety so released from his responsibility to the other sureties. A co-surety is also entitled to a share of every collateral security which has been delivered to any of the sureties.

DISCHARGE OF SURETY

A surety will be discharged from his liability in the following cases :

1. **By notice or death** (*Sec. 130 & 131*) **:** A contract of continuing guarantee may be terminated at any time by notice to the creditor. The death of surety brings an end to a continuing guarantee. No notice of death need be given to the creditor. The surety's is estate will not be responsible for acts done after his death.

2. **Variations in the terms of the original contract between the principal debtor and the creditor** (*Sec. 133*)**:** If the contract between the creditor and the principal debtor is materially altered without the consent of the surety, the surety is discharged as to transactions subsequent to the alteration. Even the alteration beneficial to the surety would entitle the surety to claim a discharge.[7] The effect of the alteration is immaterial. But variation in the terms of the contract with the consent of the, express or implied, will not discharge him from the liability. Mere knowledge or silence of the surety, unless otherwise proved, will not necessarily amount to an implied consent. But where a surety is responsible for the performance of several and distinct contracts or duties, a change in one of the those contracts or duties will not effect surety's liability as to rest.[8]

Examples : (*i*) *A* becomes surety to *C* for *B*'s conduct as a manager in *C*'s bank. Afterwards, *B* and *C* contract, without *A*'s consent that *B*'s salary shall be raised, and that he shall become liable for one-fourth of the losses on overdrafts. *B* allows a customer to overdraw, and the bank loses a sum of money. *A* is discharged from his suretyship by the variance made without his consent, and is not liable to make good this loss.

(*ii*) *C* agrees to a appoint *B* as his clerk to sell goods at a yearly salary, upon *A*'s becoming surety to *C* for *B*'s duly accounting for money received by him as such clerk. Afterwards, without *A*'s knowledge or consent, *C* and *B* agree that *B* should be paid by a commission on the goods sold by him and not by a fixed salary. *A* is not liable for subsequent misconduct of *B*.

(*iii*) *C* contracts to lend *B* ₹ 5,000 on 1st March. *A* guarantees repayment. *C* pays the amount to *B* on the 1st January. *A* is discharged from the liability as the contract has been varied in as much as *C* might sue *B* for the money before the 1st March.

(*iv*) *A* guarantees *C* against the misconduct of *B* in the an office to which *B* is appointed by *C*, and of which the duties are defined by an Act, of the legislature. By a consequent Act, the nature of office is materially altered. Afterwards, *B* misconducts himself. *A* is discharged by the change from future liability under his guarantee, though the misconduct of *B* is in respect of a duty not affected by the latter Act.

---

7. Blest *v*. Brown (1862), 4 De G.G. & J. 367 : Lord Westbury in this case observed, "You bind him (surety) to the letter of his engagement. If that engagement be altered without the surety's consent in a single line, no matter whether it is altered for his benefit, no matter whether the alteration be innocently made he has a right to say : The contract is no longer that for which I engaged to be surety, you have put an end to the contract that I guaranteed and my obligation therefore is at an end."
8. Skillet *v*. Fletcher (1866-67), L.R., 2 C.P. 469.

(*v*) *A* gives to *C* a continuing guarantee to the extent of 3,000 rupees for any oil supplied by *C* to *B* on credit. Afterwards *B* becomes embarrassed, and without the knowledge of *A, B* and *C* contracts that *C* shall continue to supply *B* with oil for ready money, and, that the payments shall be applied to the then existing debts between *B* and *C. A* is not liable on his guarantee for any goods supplied after this new arrangement.

3. **By release or discharge of the principal debtor** (*Sec. 134*) **:** The surety is discharged by any contract between the creditor and the principal debtor, by which the principal debtor is released or by any act or omission of the creditor, the legal consequence of which is the discharge of the principal debtor. But the discharge of a surety on one agreement will not release the other surety bound for the same debt by a separate agreement for his engagement, unless the effect of such release is to adversely affect the other's right to contribution.

Examples **:** (*i*) *A* gives guarantee to *C* for goods to be supplied by *C* to *B. C* supplies goods to *B*, and afterwards *B* becomes embarrassed and contracts with his creditors (including *C*) to assign to them his property in consideration of their releasing him from their demands. Here *B* is released from his debt by the contract with *C*, and *A* is discharged from his suretyship.

(*ii*) *A* contracts with *B* for a fixed price to build a house for *B* within a stipulated time. *B* supplying the necessary timber. *C* guarantees *A's* performance of the contract. *B* omits to supply the timber. *C* is discharged from suretyship.

(*iii*) *A* contracts with *B* to grow a crop of indigo on his (*A's*) land and to deliver it to *B* at a fixed rate. *C* guarantees *A's* performance of this contact. *B* diverts a stream of water which is necessary for the irrigation of *A's* land and thereby prevents him from raising the indigo. *C* is no longer liable on his guarantee.

4. **Compounding by creditor with the principal debtor** (*Sec. 135*) **:** A contract between the creditor and the principal debtor, by which creditor makes a composition with, or promises to give time to, or not to sue the principal debtor discharges the surety unless the surety assents to such contract.

But where a contract to give time to the principal debtor is made by the creditor with a third person and not with the principal debtor, the surety is not discharged (*Sec. 136*).

Example **:** *C*, the holder of an overdue bill of exchange drawn by *A* as surety for *B*, and accepted by *B*, contracts with *M* to give time to *B. A* is not discharged.

Similarly, mere forbearance on the part of the creditor to sue the principal debtor or to enforce any other remedy against him does not in the absence of any provision in the guarantee to the contrary discharge the surety (*Sec. 137*).

The Privy Council has held that even if the creditor fails to sue the principal debtor within the limitation period, the surety will not be discharged from his liability.[9]

Example **:** *B* owes to *C* a debt guaranteed by *A*. The debt becomes payable. *C* does not sue *B* for a year after the debt has become payable. *A* is not discharged from the suretyship.

Where there are co-sureties, a release by the creditor of one of them does not discharge the other; neither does it free the surety so released from his responsibility to other sureties (*Sec. 138*).

9. Mahant Singh *v.* U. Ba Yi (1939), 181 I.C. 1 (P.C.).

Claim barred against the Debtor but not against Surety.

The surety will not be discharged from liability to pay a debt which has become time-barred against the principal debtor but not against surety. Though creditor cannot realise the amount from the principal debtor as it has become time-barred, yet he can realise the same from the surety against whom it has not become time-barred. This is because the obligation of the surety arises on the date the principal debtor commits a default.[10] This has been decided by various Indian High Courts on the basis of *Sec. 137* of the Indian Contract Act, stated above.

5. **Creditor's act or omission impairing surety's eventual remedy** (*Sec. 139*) **:** If the creditor does any act which is inconsistent with the rights of the surety, or omits to do any act which his duty to the surety requires him to do, and the eventual remedy of the surety himself against the principal debtor is thereby impaired, the surety is discharged.

Examples **:** (*i*) *B* contracts to build a ship for *C* for a given sum to the paid by instalments as the work reaches certain stages. *A* become surety to *C* for *B*'s due performance of the contract. *C*, without the knowledge of *A*, prepays to *B* the last two instalments. *A* is discharged by this prepayment.

(*ii*) *A* puts *M* as apprentice to *B*, and gives a guarantee to *B*, for *M*'s fidelity. *B* promises on his part that he will, at least once a months, see *M* to make up the cash. *B* omits to see *M* as promised, and *M* embezzles. *A* is not liable to *B* on his guarantee.

(*iii*) *C* lends money to *B* on the security of a joint and several promissory note made in *C*'s favour by *B*, and *A* is surety for *B*, together with a bill of sale of *B*'s furniture, which gives power to *C* to sell the furniture, and apply the proceeds in discharge of the note. Subsequently *C* sells the furniture, but owing to his misconduct and wilful negligence, only a small price is realised. *A* is discharged from liability on the note.

6. **Loss of security** (*Sec. 141*) **:** If the creditor loses, or without the consent of the surety, parts with any security given to him at the time of the contract of guarantee, the surety is discharged from liability to the extent of the value of security. The term security is not used here in a technical sense. It includes all rights which the creditor had against the property at the date of the contract.[11]

Examples **:** (*i*) *C* advances to *B*, his tenant, ₹ 2,000 on the guarantee of *A*. *C* has also a further security for ₹ 2,000 by a mortgage of *B*'s furniture. *C* cancels the mortgage, *B* becomes insolvent, and *C* sues *A* on his guarantee. *A* is discharged from liability to the amount of the value of the furniture.

(*ii*) *A*, as surety for *B*, makes a bond jointly with *B* to *C* , to secure a loan from *C* to *B*. Afterwards, *C* obtains from *B* a further security for the same debt. Subsequently, *C* gives up the further security. *A* is not discharged.

(*iii*) *C*, a creditor, whose advance to *B* is secured by a decree, receives also a guarantee for the advance from *A*. *C* afterwards takes *B*'s goods in execution under the decree, and then, without the knowledge of *A*, withdraws the execution. *A* is the discharged.

7. **By invalidation of the contract of guarantee** (*Secs. 142, 143* and *144*) **:** A contract of guarantee becomes invalid if guarantee was obtained by fraud or concealment etc. about material facts as discussed before. Surety, in such a case will be discharged from his liability.

Guarantee without consent or knowledge of the principal debtor or co-surety: Though a contract of guarantee is a direct contract between the creditor and the surety yet it is necessary that it must be entered into with the knowledge and consent of the principal debtor. Surety must undertake

10. Montosh Kumar Chatterji *v.* Central Calcutta Bank Ltd., 57 C.W.N. 852.
11. State of M.P. *v.* Kaluram (1967), A.I.R., S.C. 1105.

the obligation at the request of the principal debtor. Such a request can be made both expressly or impliedly. Even contract of guarantee, therefore, must be supported by the concurrence of all the three parties, *i.e.*, principal debtor, creditor and surety. If a person becomes a surety, without the consent and knowledge of the principal debtor, the surety cannot enjoy any right of action in his own name against principal debtor in the event of his default.

Example : *A* agreed to supply certain goods to *B* and *C* guaranteed the due performance of the contract by *A*. *C* was neither a party to the contract between *A* and *B* nor was *A* a party to the contract between *A* and *C*. *A* broke his promise and *C* had to compensate *B*. In a suit by *C* against *A* it was held that a surety could undertake an obligation only at the express or implied request of the principal debtor. The contract between *B* and *C* was not a contract of guarantee but only a contract of indemnity. Thus, *C* was not entitled to recover anything from *A*.

Two persons can become co-sureties for the same debt both jointly and severally even without the consent and knowledge of each other. If a person becomes a surety without the consent and knowledge of the co-surety, he will be entitled to recover from the latter, the excess of what he has paid above his share.

KEY TERMS

- **Contract of Indemnity :** A contract by which one party promises to save the other from the loss caused to him by the conduct of the promisor/third party or on account of happening of an event.
- **Indemnifier :** The person promising to indemnify is termed as indemnifier.
- **Indemnity Holder :** The person agreed to be identified is termed as indemnity holder.
- **Contract of Guarantee :** A contract to perform the promise or discharge the liability of a third person in case of his default.
- **Specific Guarantee :** A guarantee given for a specific transaction.
- **Continuing Guarantee :** A guarantee which extends to a series of transactions.

TEST QUESTIONS

Objective Type : ***Test Your Knowledge***

1. State whether each of the following statements is *True* or *False* :

(*i*) A contract of insurance is also a contract of indemnity.

(*ii*) The liability of the indemnifier is a primary liability.

(*iii*) The discharge of the principal debtor will discharge the surety also.

(*iv*) Guarantee given for a person incompetent to enter into a contract is not enforceable.

(*v*) A guarantee given for minor's debt is void. *(CS Foundation, Dec. 2003)*

(*vi*) Where there are co-surities a release by the creditor of one of them does not discharge the others. *(PCE, ICAI, Nov. 2007)*

(*vii*) A specific guarantee once given is 'irrevocable'. *(CS Foundation, Dec. 2007)*

(*viii*) A continuing guarantee can be revoked as to the past transaction by giving notice to the creditor. *(CS Foundation, June 2007)*

(*ix*) Any promise made for the benefit of the principal debtor may be a sufficient consideration to the surety for giving the guarantee. *(CS Foundation, June 2008)*

(*x*) In contract of guarantee there are three contracts. *(CAIPC, Nov. 2013)*

[***Ans.*** (*i*) True; (*ii*) True; (*iii*) False; (*iv*) True; (*v*) False; (*vi*) True; (*vii*) True; (*viii*) False; (*ix*) True; (*x*) True]

2. Select the most appropriate answer
   (*i*) The number of contracts in a contract of guarantee are : (*a*) One (*b*) Two (*c*) Three.
   (*ii*) Co-sureties bound in different sums are liable to pay :
      (*a*) equally as far as the limits of their respective obligations permit;
      (*b*) proportionately according to their respective obligations;
      (*c*) none of the above.
   (*iii*) Liability of the surety is :
      (*a*) coextensive with the principal debtor,
      (*b*) primary with the principal debtor, or
      (*c*) secondary to the principal debtor. (*c*) none of the above.
   (*iv*) The liability of a surety
      (*a*) May be less than that of debtor. (*b*) May be more than that of debtor.
      (*c*) Always remains the same as that of debtor.
      (*d*) Depends upon the judgement of court.

   (CS Foundation, June 2007, Dec. 2008)
   (*v*) In a contract of guarantee a person, who promises to discharge another's liability is called
      (*a*) Principal Debtor (*b*) Creditor
      (*c*) Indemnifier (*d*) Surety

   (PCE, ICAI, May 2007)

   [***Ans.*** (*i*) (*c*); (*ii*) (*a*); (*iii*) (*a*); (*iv*) (*a*); (*v*) (*d*).]

Essay Type : *For Review, Discussion and Practice*

1. What is a Contract of Indemnity? Give instances of liability to indemnify arising by operation of law. Discuss the right of indemnity-holder when sued.
2. Define a 'Contract of Guarantee'. How and in what respects is it different from a 'Contract of Indemnity'? *(B.Com., (Hons.), Delhi 2013)*
3. Briefly explain the rights of a surety against co-sureties.
4. What is a 'Continuing Guarantee'? When can it be revoked?
5. What do you understand by contracts of 'Indemnity' and 'Guarantee'? Point out the distinction between the two. *(ICWA Foundation, June 1998, Dec. 2000; CA Foundation May 2000; B.Com. (Pass), Delhi 2005, PEE II, Nov. 2004)*
6. What is a 'Contract of Indemnity'? Explain the rights of the 'Indemnified' and the 'Indemnifier' under the Indian Contract Act.
7. "Liability of a surety is co-extensive with that of the principal debtor." Explain with an illustration. *(CA Foundation, November 2000; CS Foundation, Dec. 2003; B.Com. (Hons.), Delhi, 1989, 1992, 1995, 1996, 1998, 1999, B.Com. (Pass), Delhi 2002)*
8. When a surety is discharged from liability. *(ICWA Foundation, Dec. 1998; B.Com. (Hons.), Delhi, 1993)*
9. What is the nature of the liability of a surety? State his rights against the creditor, principal debtor and co-sureties. *(ICWA Foundation, Dec. 1998; B.Com. (Hons.) Delhi, 1998, 1994, 2001)*
10. What are the essentials of a contract of guarantee? *(ICWA Foundation, June 2001)*
11. Is a specific guarantee once given revocable? *(ICWA Foundation, June 2001)*
12. Is a minor competent to be a surety of a contract of guarantee? *(ICWA Foundation, June 2001)*
13. Explain :
    (*i*) Guarantee once given is irrevocable. *(ICWA Foundation, Dec. 1999)*
    (*ii*) "The ambit of definition of contract of indemnity is narrow one"—Do you agree with this view. *(ICWA Foundation, Dec. 2000)*
14. What is the difference between 'Indemnity' and 'Guarantee'. *(CS Foundation, June 2004, Dec. 2008)*
15. Describe the rights of a surety against various parties. *(B.Com. (Hons.), Delhi, 1993, 2002)*
16. What is continuing guarantee? How can it be revoked? Comment. *(B.Com. (Hons.), Delhi 1987)*

17. "Between co-sureties there is equity of burden and benefit." Comment. *(B.Com. (Hons.), Delhi 1988)*
18. "The surety is a favoured debtor." Comment. *(B.Com. (Hons.), Delhi 1996, 1997)*
19. Write short note on nature and extent of surety's liability. *(B.Com. (Hons.), Delhi 2005)*
20. Discuss the nature of surety's liability. *(B.Com. (Pass), Delhi 2002; B.Com. (Hons), Delhi 2012)*
21. What are the rights of a surety against a creditor? *(B.Com. (Pass), Delhi 2005)*
22. What is a Contract of Guarantee? What are its important characteristics? State the rights of the surety against the creditor, the Principal Debtor and the co-sureties. Give suitable examples. *(B.Com. (Hons.), Delhi 2005)*
23. Write note on 'Continuing Guarantee". *(CS Foundation, June 2008)*
24. How the surety is discharged from liability? *(ICWA Inter. Dec., 2010)*
25. Discuss the rights of surety against various parties. *(B.Com. (Hons.), Delhi 2010)*
26. 'Surety' is a favoured debtor. Discuss. *(B.Com. (Hons.), Delhi 2011)*
27. Distinguish between contract of indemnity and contract of guarantee. *(B.Com. (Hons.), Delhi 2012)*

PRACTICAL PROBLEMS

1. *A* and *B* are co-sureties for *C*. *A* agrees to be liable to the extent of ₹ 1,000 and *B* to the extent of ₹ 1,500. *C* makes a default of ₹ 1,500. How much should *A* and *B* pay?

   [***Ans.*** ₹ 750 each]
2. *A* advances ₹ 500 to a minor on the guarantee of *G*. On demand for repayment the borrower pleads minority. Can *A* recover the amount from *G*?

   [***Ans.*** Yes. The surety in such a case will be taken as principal debtor. The contract with the surety is not a collateral but a principal contract.]
3. *B* is the principal debtor of *A*. *C* is the surety for the debt. *A*, the creditor makes a promise to a neighbour of *B* to give time to *B*. Discuss the effect, if any, of this promise on the contract of guarantee.

   [***Ans.*** Surety is not discharged because the contract is with a third party and not with the debtor.]
4. *C* had advanced *P* a loan of ₹ 5,000 against some securities. *S* has guaranteed ₹ 2,500 out of the above loan. *S* pays ₹ 2,500 to *C* against the loan. He then claims his right to the securities. Decide.

   [***Ans.*** *S* will not succeed. Surety is not entitled to the benefit of a portion of securities.]
5. *C* guaranteed the payment of a sum of ₹ 500 advanced by *A* to *B*. On *A*'s pressing *B* for payment, *B* passed a demand promissory note and *A* did not sue *B* for some time. Later on *A* filed a suit against *C*. Would he succeed?

   [***Ans.*** No. *B*'s passing a demand promissory note was a variance of the contract.]
6. *A* contracted to indemnify *B & Co.*, *a* publishing firm against the consequence of any libel which might appear in any of their publications. *B & Co.* were forced to pay damages for a statement published by them which they knew to be libellous. The firm sues *A* on the basis of the agreement. Is this agreement enforceable?

   [***Ans.*** The agreement is illegal and hence cannot be enforced.]
7. *DJA* guarantees payment to *V* of the price of 10 cycles to be delivered to *S*. The price as per the agreement is to be paid within three months. *V* delivers the above cycles to *S*, and gets the payment, as agreed upon. Afterwards, *V* delivers three more cycles for which *S* did not pay. *V* sues *DJA* for the recovery of the price of the three cycles. Would *V* succeed? What provisions exist in the Indian Contract Act in this regard?

   [***Ans.*** The guarantee given was not a continuing guarantee. Therefore, '*V*' will not succeed.]
8. *X* of Calcutta agrees to indemnify Mr. *A* of Delhi, a newspaper proprietor, against any claims arising out of the libels printed in the newspaper concerning Mr. *Z*, a reputed businessman of Bombay. Is this contract of indemnity enforceable and can *A* recover any amount paid by him in a suit for damages filed by Mr. *Z*?

   [***Ans.*** The contract shall not be enforceable and *A* shall not be entitled to recover any amount paid by him as damages to *Z*.]

9. Ashok appointed Bose as his agent to collect his rents and required him to execute a fidelity bond, in which Chandra was surety. Sometime after the execution of the bond Chandra died and Bose committed various acts of dishonesty. Is Chandra's estate liable for the loss caused to Ashok? Decide, giving the provisions of the Indian Contract Act in this regard.

[***Ans.*** Chandra's estate is not liable for act of dishonesty committed by Bose after Chandra's death.]

10. *P* contracts to indemnify *R* against the consequences of the proceedings which *S* might take against *R* in respect of a debt due by *R*. *S* obtains judgement against *R* for the amount. Without paying any portion of the decreed amount, *R* sues *P* for its recovery. Decide with reference, to the provisions of the Indian Contract Act in this regard.

[***Ans.*** *R* can sue *P* for the recovery of the amount for which *S* has obtained judgment against him.]

11. *A* took a loan from *B*. *C* was surety. *B* agreed to reduce the interest rate afterwards without informing *C*. *A* defaults repayment of principal and interest. Decide legal rights of *B* and *C*.

(ICWA Foundation, Dec. 1999)

[***Ans.*** *B* cannot proceed against *C*. He can file a civil suit against *A* only.]

12. Sunil delivered his car to Mahesh for repairs. Mahesh completed the work, Mahesh completed the work, but did not return the car to Sunil within reasonable time, though Sunil repeatedly reminded Mahesh for the return of car. In the meantime a big fire occurred in the neighbourhood and the car was destroyed. Decide whether Mahesh can be held liable under the provisions of the Indian Contract Act, 1872. *(PEE II, November 2003)*

[***Ans.*** Mahesh is liable for the loss since he failed to deliver the car within reasonable time.]

13. Explaining the provisions of the Indian Contract Act, 1872, answer the following :
    (*i*) *A* contracts with *B* for a fixed price to construct a house for *B* within a stipulated time. *B* would supply the necessary material to be used in the construction. *C* guarantees *A*'s performance of the Contract. *B* does not supply the material as per the agreement. Is *C* discharged from his liability?
    (*ii*) *C*, the holder of an over due bill of exchange drawn by *A* as surety for *B*, and accepted by *B*, contracts with *X* to give time to *B*. Is *A* discharged from his liability?

(PEE, ICAI, Nov. 2006)

[***Ans.*** (*i*) *C* is discharged from his liability (*ii*) *A* is not discharged.]

14. Ravi becomes guarantor for Ashok for the amount which may be given to him by Nalin within six months. The maximum limit of the said amount is ₹ 1 lakh. After two months Ravi withdraws his guarantee. Upto the time of reconviction of guarantee, Nalin had given to Ashok ₹ 20,000.
    (*i*) Whether Ravi is discharged from his liabilities to Nalin or any subsequent loan.
    (*ii*) Whether Ravi is liable if Ashok fails to pay the amount of ₹ 20,000 to Nalin?

(PEE-II, ICAI, May 2006)

[***Ans.*** (*i*) Yes, Ravi is discharged from all the subsequent loan because it's a case of continuing guarantee. (*ii*) Ravi is liable for payment of ₹ 20,000 Nalin because the transaction has already completed.]

15. "*A*" executed a guarantee in favour of State Bank of India as Security for a loan to '*B*' Later '*A*' contended that the guarantee was not enforceable as it was not supported by consideration as he was not paid guarantee commission. Is '*A*'s stand correct in law? *(ICWAI Inter, June 2009)*

[***Ans.*** No.]

16. Anil gives a guarantee to Kamal in January for supply of goods worth of ₹ 10,000 to Vimal on credit basis. The payment was to be made in April. However, Vimal made the payment in March itself and again took goods on credit basis from Kamal for the same amount but failed to pay. Now, Kamal files a suit against Anil for the payment. Will Kamal Succeed? Give reasons.

(CS Foundation, Dec., 2010)

[***Ans.*** Kamal will not succeed. It was a case of specific guarantee.]

17. *X* sent a consignment of mobile phones worth ₹ 60,000 to *Y* and obtained a railway receipt therefore. Later, he borrowed a loan of ₹ 40,000 from Star bank and endorsed the railway receipt in favour

of the Bank as security. In transit the consignment of mobile phones was lost. The Bank files a suit against the railway for a claim of ₹ 60,000, the value of the consignment. The railway contended that the Bank is entitled to recover the amount of loan, *i.e.* ₹ 40,000 only. Examining the provisions of the Indian Contract Act, 1872, decide, whether the contention of the railway is valid. (*IPCE, ICAI, Nov., 2010*)

[***Ans.*** As a Pledgee, a bankers' rights are not limited to his interest in the goods pledged. In the case of injury to the goods or their deprivation by a third party, the Pledgee would have all such remedies that the owner of the goods would have against them. In this case the Supreme Court also held that the Bank (Pledgee) was entitled to recover not only the amount of the advance due to it, but also the full value of the consignment. However, the amount over and above his interest is to be held by him in trust for the pledger. Thus, the Star Bank will succeed in recovering the claim of ₹ 60,000 against the railway.]

18. Mr. Bose in indebted to Mr. Das and Mr. Ghosh is the surity. When Mr. Bose and Mr. Ghosh refused to pay, Mr. Das sued the surety (Mr. Ghosh) who paid the amount and cost as per orders of the court. Can the surety recover the amount from Mr. Bose? (*ICWA Inter, Dec., 2010*)

[***Ans.*** Yes. The surety is entitled to recover the legitimate and rightful amount from the Principle Debtor.]

Chapter 14

CONTRACTS OF BAILMENT

LEARNING OBJECTIVES

A careful study of this chapter will enable you to :

- understand the concept of bailment;
- describe the various types of bailment;
- enumerate the rights of a bailor and a bailee;
- explain the concept of lien and pledge;
- discuss the rights and duties of a pawner and a pawnee;
- identify the circumstances whether the pledge by non-owners is valid; and
- explain the meaning of certain key terms.

MEANING OF CONTRACT OF BAILMENT

In our daily life possession of goods passes from one person to another. For example, a person may deliver his pen or book to another. This constitutes bailment. According to Section 148 of the Indian Contract Act, bailment is the delivery of goods by one person to another for some purpose, upon a contract that they shall, when the purpose is accomplished, be returned or otherwise disposed of according to the direction of the person delivering them. The person delivering the goods is called the 'bailor'. The person to whom they are delivered is called the 'bailee'.

Examples : (*i*) *A* lends his motor cycle to *B* for his use.

(*ii*) *A* gives a piece of cloth to a tailor to make it into a coat.

(*iii*) *A* gives his radio set to a mechanic for repairs.

All the above are contracts of bailment.

ESSENTIAL CHARACTERISTICS

The essential characteristics of bailment can be summed up as under :

(*a*) Bailment is always based upon a contract. In exceptional cases it may arise without a contract also. *i.e.*, it may be implied by law, *e.g.*, in case of finder of goods.

Example : *A* firm had failed to pay the income-tax dues. On account of instructions of income-tax authorities, the officials of collectorate locked the godown of the firm in which its tobacco packages were lying pledged to a bank. The key was handed over to the police. On account of heavy rains, the roof of the godown leaked and the tobacco was damaged. The court held that there was bailment without being a contract. It was the duty of the Government officers as bailee to take such care as every prudent manager would take his own goods. Since this was not done, the Government was liable for the loss.[1]

---

1. Merchants Co-operative Bank Ltd., *v.* Prabhudas Hathibhai (1966), A.I.R. Bombay 134.

The above view was also accepted by the Supreme Court in the case of State of *Gujarat* v. *Memon Mohomed.*[2] In this case the State seized certain motor vehicles etc. under a Sea Customs Act. The goods remained uncared for while in the custody of the State. The Supreme Court observed that "bailment may arise without an enforceable contract" and, therefore, the State is liable for the loss.

(*b*) There can be a bailment of movable properties only but *money* is not included in the category of movable goods.

(*c*) In bailment the possession of goods must change. Bailment requires temporary delivery of goods. Mere custody of goods without possession will not be sufficient to constitute bailment. A servant or a guest using his master's or host's goods will not be a bailee.

In bailment the delivery of goods may be actual or constructive. An actual delivery implies actual physical transfer of goods from one person to another. Constructive delivery may be made by doing anything which has the effect of putting the goods in the possession of the intended bailee or any person authorised to hold them on his behalf. For example, if a person is already in possession of the goods of another and contracts to hold them as a bailee, it will be taken to be a good delivery by way of bailment even though there is no actual transfer of goods.

Examples : (*i*) *A* delivers his radio-set to *B* for repairs. This is a case of actual delivery of goods by *A* to *B*. *A* is the bailor and *B* is the bailee.

(*ii*) *A* purchases a radio-set from *B*'s shop and leaves it with *B* to send it to his (*A*'s) residence. In this case *B* has not taken actual delivery of the radio-set from *A* but there is a contract of bailment between *A* and *B*, the delivery being constructive.

(*iii*) *A* employed a goldsmith to melt old jewellery and prepare new jewels. Every evening she used to receive half-made jewels from the goldsmith and put them in a box and leave the box in the goldsmith's room. She kept the key of the room with her. On one night jewels were stolen. It was held that there was a re-delivery of jewels to the lady and the goldsmith could not be regarded as a bailee. The lady herself must bear the loss.[3]

(*d*) In bailment, ownership is not transferred. The bailor continues to be the owner of the goods.

(*e*) Goods are delivered upon a condition that they are to be returned in *specie.* On the accomplishment of the purpose of the contract of bailment, the very goods in their original form are to be returned by the bailee or are otherwise to be disposed of according to the directions of the bailor.

All transactions of safe custody, deposit of goods, (where one man keeps goods of another), *commodatum* (goods lent to a friend), hire, pawn, carriage and repair etc. are in the nature of contracts of bailment. The legal relation between the guest and the hotel keeper in respect of the furniture used by the former is that of the bailee and bailor, since, the guest hires not only the room but also the furniture therein. Similarly, the position of the railways with regard to the goods accepted by them for carriage is that of a bailee. Purchaser of a car, under hire-purchase agreement, is a bailee till such time he pays up all the instalments.

There is no contract of bailment when there is a delivery of property on a contract for an equivalent money or some other valuable commodity and not for the return of the identical article

2. A.I.R. (1967), S.C. 1885.
3. Kailiaperumal *v.* Visalakshami, A.I.R. (1938), Mad. 32.

in its original form. This is a transfer of property for value amounting to a sale or exchange and not bailment.

Does the Deposit of Money in a Bank constitute Bailment?

Deposit of money in a bank is not a case of bailment since the return of money will not be of the identical coins deposited. Moreover, the money handed over to the bank is not for safe custody but to be credited to some kind of account. The relation between the bank and the depositor of money is that of a borrower and the lender and not that of a bailor and bailee. On the same basis, an agent who has collected money on his principal's behalf is not a bailee of the money.[4]

CLASSIFICATION OF BAILMENT

Bailments may be classified on the basis of (*a*) benefit and (*b*) reward.

On the basis of benefit

(*i*) Those for the exclusive benefit of bailor.

(*ii*) Those for the exclusive benefit of the bailee,

(*iii*) Those for the mutual benefit of both.

Examples : (*i*) *A* wants to send his horse to his uncle *B*. He requests *C* to do this job. *C* agrees. Here bailment is for the exclusive benefit of the bailor *A*.

(*ii*) *C* wants to go to *A*'s uncle *B*. He requests *A* to lend him his horse. *A* does so, Here bailment is for the exclusive benefit of the bailee *C*.

(*iii*) *A* wants to send his horse to his uncle *B*. *C* has also a work with *B*. *A* lends *C* his horse. The bailment is for the mutual benefit of both bailor *A* and bailee *C*.

On the basis of reward

(*i*) **Gratuitous bailment :** Where neither the bailor nor the bailee gets any remuneration, bailment is termed as gratuitous.

Example : *A* lends his book to his friend *B*. The bailment is gratuitous.

(*ii*) **Non-gratuitous bailment :** Where either the bailor or the bailee gets remunerations, the bailment is termed as non gratuitous.

Example : *A* gives his watch to a watch maker for repairs. The bailment is non-gratuitous.

RIGHTS OF BAILOR

1. **Right of termination :** Bailor has the right to terminate the bailment and claim damages, if any, if the conditions of bailment are disobeyed by the bailee, *e.g.*, bailee uses the goods bailed in a manner in consistent with the conditions of bailment (*Sec. 153*).

Example : *A* lets *B*, for hire, a horse for his own riding. *B* drives the horse in his carriage. *A* can terminate the contract of bailment.

2. **Right to demand return of goods any time in case of gratuitous bailment :** In the case of a gratuitous bailment, the bailor can demand back the goods bailed at any time he chooses in spite

4. Shanker Lal *v.* Bhura Lal, A.I.R. (1951), Ajm. 24.

of the fact that he had lent them for a fixed period or for a specified purpose. But if the bailee had, in this case, acted in such a manner that the return of the goods before the stipulated time would cause loss greater than the benefit which he had derived, the bailor shall be asked to indemnify him for the loss if he compels immediate return of the specified object.

3. **Enforcement of rights :** The duties of the bailee are the rights of the bailor and he can sue bailee for their enforcement.

DUTIES OF BAILOR

1. **To disclose faults in the goods bailed** (*Sec. 150*) **:** The bailor is bound to disclose to the bailee faults in the goods bailed, of which the bailor is aware, and which materially interfere with the use of them or expose the bailee to extraordinary risks. In case the bailee does not make such disclosure, he is responsible for damage arising to the bailee directly from such faults.

If the goods are bailed for hire, the bailor is responsible for such damage, whether he was or was not aware of the existence of such faults in the goods bailed.

Examples : (*i*) *A* lends a horse to *B*, which he knows to be vicious. *A* does not disclose the fact of viciousness of the horse to *B*. The horse runs aways. *B* is thrown and injured. *B* can claim damages from *A* for the injury caused.

(*ii*) *A* hires a carriage from *B*. The carriage is unsafe, though *B* is not aware of it and *A* is injured. *B* is responsible to *A* for the injury.

(*iii*) *R* hired a motor launch from *D* for a holiday on river Thames. The launch caught fire and *R* could not extinguish the fire as the fire fighting equipment was out of order. *R* was injured. Held, *D* was liable to pay him damages.[5]

2. **Responsibility for title to the goods** (*Sec. 164*) **:** The bailor is responsible to the bailee for any loss which the bailee may sustain by reason that the bailor was not entitled to make the bailment or to receive back the goods or to give directions respecting them.

3. **To bear necessary expenses of bailment** (*Sec. 158*) **:** Where by the condition of the bailment the goods are to be kept or to be carried or to have work done upon them by the bailee for the bailor and the bailee is to receive no remuneration (bailment is gratuitous), the bailor shall repay the bailee the necessary expenses incurred by him for the purpose of the bailment.

4. **To bear risk for loss etc. :** Bailor is to bear the risk of loss, destruction or deterioration of the thing bailed if the bailee has taken as much care as a man of ordinary prudence would, under similar circumstances, take of his own goods of the same bulk, quality and value as the goods bailed.

RIGHTS OF BAILEE

1. **Right to interplead** (*Sec. 165*) **:** If a person other than the bailor, claims the goods bailed, bailee may apply to the court to stop the delivery of the goods to the bailor and to decide the title to the goods.

2. **Right against third person :** If a third person wrongfully deprives the bailee of the use or possession of the goods bailed, or causes them any injury, the bailee is entitled to use such remedies as the owner might have used in a like case if no bailment has been made. Bailee can thus bring a suit against a third person for such deprivation or injury (*Sec. 180*).

---

5. Reed *v.* Dean (1949), 1 K.B. 188.

3. **Right of particular lien for payment for service** (*Sec. 170*) : Where the bailee has (*a*) in accordance with the purpose of bailment, (*b*) rendered any service involving the exercise of labour or skill, (*c*) in respect of the goods, he shall have, in the absence of a contract to the contrary, right to retain such goods until he receives due remuneration for the services he has rendered in respect to them. Bailee has, however, only a right to retain the article and not to sell it. The services must have entirely been performed within the time agreed or a reasonable time and the remuneration must have become due. This right of particular lien shall be available only against the property in respect of which skill and labour have been used.

Examples : (*i*) *A* delivers a rough diamond to *B*, a jeweller, to be cut and polished, which is accordingly done. *B* is entitled to retain the stone till he is paid for the services he has rendered.

(*ii*) *A* gives cloth to *B*, a tailor, to make it into a coat. *B* promises *A* to deliver the coat as soon as it is finished and to give three months' credit for the price. *B* is not entitled to retain the coat until he is paid.

4. **Right of general lien** (*Sec. 171*) : Bankers, factors, wharfingers, attorneys of a High Court and policy brokers will be entitled to retain, as a security for a general balance of account, any goods bailed to them in the absence of a contract to the contrary. By agreement other types of a bailees may also be given this right of general lien.

5. **Right to indemnity** (*Sec. 166*) : Bailee is entitled to be indemnified by the bailor for any loss arising to him by reason that the bailor was not entitled to make the bailment or to receive back the goods or to give directions respecting them. If the bailor has no title to the goods, and the bailee in good faith, delivers them back to, or according to the directions of the bailor, the bailee shall not be responsible to the owner in respect of such delivery. Bailee can also claim all the necessary expenses incurred by him for the purpose of gratuitous bailment.

6. **Right to claim compensations in case of faulty goods** (*Sec. 150*) : *A* bailee is entitled to receive compensation from the bailor for any loss caused to him due to the failure of the bailor to disclose any faults in the goods known to him. If the bailment is for hire, the bailor will be liable to compensate even though he was not aware of the existence of such faults.

7. **Right to claim necessary expenses** (*Sec. 158*) : Where the bailee is not to receive any remuneration for the work to be done by him as per terms of the bailment, he is entitled to recover from the bailor all necessary expenses incurred by him for the purposes of bailment.

8. **Right of delivery of goods to any one of the several joint bailors of goods** (*Sec. 165*) : Delivery of goods to any one of the several joint bailors of goods will amount to delivery of goods to all of them in the absence of any contract to the contrary.

DUTIES OF THE BAILEE

1. **To take reasonable care** (*Secs. 151* and *152*) : Bailee is bound to take as much care of the goods bailed to him as a man of ordinary prudence would, under similar circumstances, take of his own goods of the same bulk, quality and value as the goods bailed. It will not make any difference whether the bailment is gratuitous or for reward. If any loss is caused to the goods, inspite of such reasonable care by the bailee, he shall not be liable for the loss. Bailee shall be held liable for all losses arising due to his negligence. Bailee shall be held liable for having not taken reasonable care of the goods bailed as a prudent man would have taken in all those cases where goods bailed are used for any other purpose which is inconsistent with the terms of the agreement. However, a bailee will not be liable

for any loss resulting from action of the third parties over which the bailee has no control or for destruction or deterioration of the things bailed if he has taken the amount of care required of him.

Examples : (*i*) *A* delivered to *B* certain gold ornaments for safe custody. *B* kept the ornaments in a locked safe and kept the key in a cash box in the same room. The room was on the ground and was locked from outside, and therefore, was easily accessible to burglars. The ornaments were stolen. It was held that the bailee did not take reasonable care, and therefore, was liable for the loss.[6]

(*ii*) *A* deposited his goods in *B*'s godown. On account of unprecedented floods, a part of the goods were damaged. Held *B* is not liable for the loss.[7]

The fact that bailee's goods were also lost or damaged with those of the bailee cannot be taken as a reasonable proof of this fact that the bailor has taken reasonable care of the goods. In case the goods are lost from bailee's custody, it is his duty to take reasonable steps for recovering them.

Liability for the acts of servants : A bailee is liable to compensate the bailor for any damage done to the thing bailed by the negligence of his servants acting in the course of their employment. He may, however, protect himself from such loss by a special agreement with the bailor.

Example : *A*, an owner of a car, deposited it for sale with a broker. The receipt contained a clause, 'customers' cars are driven by our men at customers' sole risk.' The car was sent out by the broker in charge of one of his drivers to be shown to a prospective purchaser and was damaged on account of negligence of the driver. In a suit by *A* against the broker, it was held that the broker was not responsible for the damages on account of the above clause.[8]

2. **To use goods according to the conditions of bailment** (*Sec. 154*) **:** Bailee must use the goods according to the conditions of the contract of bailment or the directions of the bailor. He shall be held liable for compensation to the bailor if any damage is caused to the goods because of his unauthorised use. Liability on this account will arise even if the bailee is not found to be guilty of any negligence and the damages may result from an accident. Bailee must not do any act with regard to the goods bailed which is inconsistent with the terms of the bailment, otherwise the contract shall become voidable at the option of the bailor and bailee shall be held liable to compensate for any damages caused to the goods.

Examples : (*i*) *A* lends his horse to *B* for his own riding only. *B* allows *C*, a member of his family, to ride the horse. *C* rides with care but the horse accidentally falls and is injured. What remedy has *A* against *B*?

A can claim damages from *B* for the injury caused to the horse from an unauthorised use. *B* in this case has failed to use the horse according to the conditions of bailment, and, therefore, he shall be liable to pay compensation to the bailor for the damages caused to the horse because of his unauthorised use.

(*ii*) *A* hires a motor car from *B* expressly to go to Agra. *A* goes to Meerut and in the course of his journey meets with an accident, wherein the car is completely smashed. Can *B* claim compensation from *A* for the loss of car?

B can certainly claim compensation from *A* for the destruction of his car. Loss in this case has been caused due to the breach of an express condition by *A*. *A* made an unauthorised use of the car. Instead of going to Agra, he went to Meerut and, therefore, he shall be held liable to compensate. *A* for the loss of his car.

3. **Must not mix up the goods with his own goods :** Baliee is not entitled to mix up the goods bailed with his own goods except with the consent of the bailor. If he, with the consent of the bailor,

6. Rampal *v.* Gauri Shankar (1952), A.I.R. Nag. 8.
7. Shanit Lal *v.* Tara Chand, A.I.R. (1933), All. 158.
8. Rutter *v.* Palmer (1922), 2 K.B. 87.

mixes the goods bailed with his own goods, both the parties shall have an interest in proportion to their respective shares in the mixture thus produced (*Sec. 155*).

If the bailee, without the consent of the bailor, mixes the goods bailed with his own goods and the goods can be separated or divided, the property in the goods remains in the parties respectively. Bailee is bound to bear the expenses of separation and division and any damage arising from the mixture (*Sec. 156*).

If the bailee, without the consent of the bailor, mixes the goods of the bailor with his own goods in such a manner that it is impossible to separate the goods, bailed from the other goods and deliver them back, the bailor is entitled to compensation from the bailee for the loss of the goods (*Sec. 157*).

Examples : (*i*) *A* bails 100 bales of cotton marked with a particular mark to *B*. *B*, without *A*'s consent, mixes the 100 bales with other bales of his own, bearing a different mark. *A* is entitled to have his 100 bales returned, and *B* is bound to bear all the expenses in the separation of the bales and any other incidental damages.

(*ii*) *A* bails a barrel of cape flour worth ₹ 45 to *B*. *B*, without *A*'s consent, mixed the flour with country flour of his own, worth only ₹ 25 a barrel. *B* must compensate *A* for his flour.

4. **To return the goods :** Bailee must return or deliver the goods bailed according to the directions of the bailor, on the expiry of the time of bailment or on the accomplishment of the purpose of bailment (*Sec. 160*). Bailee shall be responsible to the bailor for any loss, destruction or deterioration of the goods from the date of the expiry of the contract of bailment, if he fails to return, deliver, or tender the goods at the proper time (*Sec. 161*). As a Railway Contracts the liability is governed by the Railways Act, 1989.

Example : *S* delivered certain books to *C*, a binder, who promised to bind and return them to *S* within a reasonable time. The binder could not complete his job within a reasonable time. The books were subsequently burnt by an accidental fire in *C*'s premises. Held, *C* was liable for the loss and the plea that the fire was accidental or 'an act of God' was of no avail.

5. **To return any increase or profit from the goods** (*Sec. 163*) **:** Bailee is bound to deliver to the bailor any increase or profit which might have accrued from the goods bailed provided the contract does not provide otherwise.

Example : *A* leaves a cow in the custody of *B*. The cow gives birth to a calf. *B* is bound to deliver the calf as well as the cow to *A*.

6. **Must not set up an adverse title :** Bailee must not set up a title adverse to that of the bailor. He must hold the goods on behalf of and for the bailor. He cannot deny the title of the bailor.

RIGHTS OF BAILOR AND BAILEE AGAINST THIRD PARTIES

1. **Suit by bailor or bailee against a wrong-doer** (*Sec. 180*) **:** If a third person wrongfully deprives the bailee of the use or possession of the goods bailed, or does them any injury, the bailee is entitled to use such remedies as the owner might have used in a like case if no bailment had been made. The bailor or the bailee may bring a suit against the third person for such deprivation or injury.

Example : *A* railway company was induced to deliver goods to a cheat on the basis of a food railway receipt. The cheat pledged the goods. Held, the railway company could sue for recovery of goods from the pledgee.[9]

9. Purshottamdas *v.* Union of India (1967), A.I.R. All. 549.

2. **Apportionment of relief or compensation obtained by such suits** *(Sec. 181)* **:** Whatever is obtained by way of relief or compensation in any such suit shall, as between the bailor and the bailee, be dealt with according to their respective interests.

Liability of Hotel-keepers and Common Carriers

The liability of a hotel-keeper towards his guests is governed by *Section 151* of the Indian Contract Act. His liability is that of an ordinary bailee. He is bound to take reasonable care of the property of his guests lying in the botel.

Example **:** *A* stayed in a room in a hotel. The hotel-keeper knew that room occupied by *A* was in an insecure condition. While *A* was dining in another part of the hotel, building, some articles were stolen from his room. It was held that the hotel-keeper was liable as he should have taken reasonable steps to rectify the insecure condition of the room.[10]

The liability of common carriers in India is governed by the Carriers Act, 1865, and the Railways Act, 1989. A common carrier under English Law is taken as an insurer of goods. In India, the Common Carriers Act permits a common carrier to restrict his liability as insurer by special contract in the case of the certain goods. The Railways Act makes the liability of railways higher than that of an ordinary bailee with powers to limit it by special contract subject to the provisions of *Sections 93* to *98* of the Act.

RIGHTS AND LIABILITY OF FINDER OF GOODS

One who finds goods belonging to another and takes them in his possession is called the finder of goods. His rights and liabilities have been discussed in *sec. 168* and *169* of the Contract Act as follows:

(*i*) A finder of the goods is free to take or not to take the goods found out under his custody. A person who finds goods belonging to another and takes them into his custody is subject to the same responsibility as a bailee. He must restore the goods on demand to the real owner. He must take reasonable care of the goods, *i.e.*, as much care of the goods as a man of ordinary prudence would take of similar goods of his own, so long as the goods remain in his custody. He must try to find out the real owner of the goods. No one except the real owner can claim possession of goods from him.

(*ii*) Finder of goods is not entitled to bring a suit for the realisation of compensation for the trouble and expenses voluntarily incurred by him in preserving the goods and in finding out the real owner. However, he can exercise his right of particular lien on the goods found out and may refuse to deliver them to the real owner until he receives compensation for his trouble and expenses.

(*iii*) In case where the real owner of the goods has offered a specific reward for the return of goods lost, the finder of the goods may sue for the realisation of such reward and may also retain his possession over the goods until he receives the reward with all other necessary costs.

(*iv*) Finder of the goods has no right to sell the goods found out except when all the following conditions are satisfied :

(*a*) when the thing found out is commonly the subject of sale;

(*b*) when the owner cannot be found out with reasonable diligence or when the owner refuses to pay the lawful charges of the finder;

10. Jan. & Son *v.* Cameron (1992), 44 All. 735.

(c) when the thing is in the danger of perishing or losing the greater part of its value or when the lawful charges of the finder in respect of thing found out exceed two-third of the value of the goods.

LIEN

Lien is a right of a person to retain that which is in his possession and which belongs to another, until the demands of the person in possession are satisfied. Lien may arise by statutes, contract or by general course of dealing in a particular trade where it is claimed. Lien gives to a person only a right to retain the possession of the goods and not the power to sell unless such a right is expressly conferred by statute (*e.g.,* unpaid seller or pawnee) or by custom or usage.

Kinds of Lien

There are two kinds of lien :

(*a*) Particular Lien

(*b*) General Lien.

(*a*) **Particular lien :** It is attached to some specific goods. It is a right to retain possession over those particular goods in connection with which the debt arose. It is restricted to those goods which are the subject matter of the contract and are liable for certain demands of the person in possession of those goods.

Section 170 lays down that where the bailee has, in accordance with the purpose of the contract of bailment, rendered any service involving the exercise of labour or skill in respect of the goods bailed, he has, in the absence of a contract to the contrary, a right to retain such goods in his possession until he receives due remuneration for the services, he has rendered in respect of them. A bailee, therefore, has a particular lien which he can exercise on the goods bailed till he is paid for his services, provided;

(*a*) there is no contract to the contrary,

(*b*) bailee has rendered some service involving labour or skill, to the goods bailed, and

(*c*) the service is not contrary to the purpose of bailment.

Particular lien can be exercised when the services when the services have been performed entirely and the remuneration has become due. Bailee's particular lien in contracts of service may be lost if he does not complete the work within the agreed time or reasonable time.

Example : *S* delivered to *J* an organ to repair. *J* promised to repair it for ₹ 100. Subsequently *J* refused to repair it for ₹ 100, and claimed to be entitled to retain the organ until he received certain remuneration for the work done. It was held that as there was an express contract, it must be done in its entirety or nothing could be claimed under it and that *J* was not entitled to retain the organ.[11]

Besides the bailee, other persons who are entitled to exercise particular lien are—unpaid seller of goods, finder of goods, pawnee, agents etc.

General lien : A general lien entitles a person to retain possession of goods belonging to another for a general balance of account. It will entitle a person in possession of the goods to retain them until all claims or accounts of the person in possession against the owner of the goods are satisfied. It is not necessary that the demands should arise only out of the articles detained under

11. Skinmer *v.* Jager (1833), All. 1394.

possession. General lien is a kind of a special privilege which the law has granted only to a few persons: (*i*) bankers, (*ii*) factors (agents entrusted with possession of goods for the purpose of sale), and (*iii*) wharfingers (persons who own a wharf, *i.e.*, landing site along the shore), (*iv*) attorneys of the High Courts, (*v*) policy brokers, (insurance agents employed to effect a marine insurance policy), and (*vi*) others by express agreements (*Sec. 171*). The general balance of account must include only lawful claims, which must have arisen to them while acting in any of the above-mentioned capacities. These parties therefore, can exercise general lien against any goods under their possession and for any sum legally due on a general balance of account. But, where goods are deposited for a some special purpose, *e.g.*, safe custody, they will not come under the spell of general lien. This is because acceptance of goods for special purpose impliedly excludes general line. As to lien of Railway Administration, the provisions of the Railway Act 1989 will be applicable.

Examples : (*i*) *K* deposited certain jewels with the Madras Bank to secure certain debt. After payment of this debt he demanded the return of these jewels from the bank. He was still indebted to the bank for certain debts. On bank's refusal to return, it was held that he was not entitled to recovery unless he proved that the bank has agreed to give up its general lien.[12]

(*ii*) *A* solicitor has a general lien on all the papers of the client in his possession in his professional capacity as solicitor. He can claim a lien for all costs due to him from the client but not for money loans.[13]

(*iii*) *R* gave his bankers a sum of money to transfer it telegraphically to his own firm at another place. The bank wanted to hold the money for their balance of account against the firm. Held that the bank could not do so because the money was given to the bank for a special purpose which therefore, excluded the bank's right of lien.[14]

PLEDGE

Pledge is the bailment of goods as security for the payment of a debt or performance of a promise. Bailor, in this case, is called the 'pawner' and the bailee is called the 'pawnee' (*Sec. 172*). In a contract of pledge, pawner must deliver the goods pledged to the pawnee either actually or constructively. Transfer of possession, in the judicial sense, is essential in a valid pledge. Mere contract to give possession cannot constitute a pledge[15] but it has been held that delivery of documents of title which would enable the pledgee to obtain possession, is equally effective to create a pledge.[16]

Pledge is not necessarily terminated by return of goods to the owner. The goods pledged may be redelivered to the pawner for a limited purpose. But in case the pawner fraudulently sells away the goods pledged to a *bona fide* purchaser for value, he will get a good title to the goods.

Pledge can be made only of movable properties. Properties which can not be the subject-matter of sale, *e.g.*, sky, rivers etc., cannot be pledged.

It is not necessary that delivery of the goods and making of the advance should be simultaneous, to create a valid pledge. Delivery of the goods may be made before or in contemplation of an advance. The transaction will ripen into a pledge as soon as the advance is made. Similarly, delivery of goods

12. Kunhan *v.* Bank of Madras (1895), 19 Mad. 234.
13. Re. Taylor (1891), 1 Ch. 590.
14. Mercantile Bank of India *v.* Rochaldas Gidumal & Co. (1926), A.I.R. Sind 225.
15. Parson's 16 Q.B.D. 532.
16. Morvi Mercantile Bank *v.* Union of India (1965), A.I.R. S.C. 1954.

may be made after getting the advance. In such a case, the pledge will be effective as soon as the delivery is given.[17]

Difference between Pledge and Bailment

Pledge is a kind of bailment made for a specific purpose, *i.e.*, as a security for payment of a debt or performance of a promise. Both the contracts are created by agreement between the parties and both necessitate transfer of possession of movable goods from one person to another. In both the cases the same goods are to be returned on the accomplishment of the purpose of the contract. In spite of these similarities, the difference between bailment and pledge can be put as follows :

1. The objectives of the two are different. A pledge is made for a specific purpose, *i.e.*, as security for payment of a debt or performance of a promise, while a bailment may be made for any purpose.
2. A pawnee does not have a right to use the goods. But a bailment may be made entitling the bailee to use the goods.

Difference between Pledge and Lien

Following are the points of difference between a contract of pledge and a right of lien :

1. Though in both the cases possession of property is transferred to the creditor, yet in lien the party in possession of the goods cannot have in general any right to sell the goods. Goods remain in the full ownership of the borrowers. In pledge, the creditor or the pawnee gets a right to sell the goods in his possession on the default of the debtor.
2. Pledge is always created by contract as against lien, which in most of the cases, is created by law.
3. Right of lien is lost with the loss of the possession of the goods. Pledge may not be extinguished by the return of goods to the owner.
4. Lien is purely a passive right. Lien-holder cannot enforce his claim except through the law courts. Pawnee, on the other hand, enjoys the right to sue as also of sale in addition to the right of lien.

Difference between Pledge and Hypothecation

Both in pledge and hypothecation, movable property is given by way of security for the payment of loan or performance of a promise. But in case of hypothecation, the debtor continues to enjoy the possession of goods. He has also a right to deal in them subject to the terms of the contract. Frequently, he has to send details of property hypothecated to the creditor, who has also a right to inspect the property at his convenience. While in case of pledge the debtor loses the possession of the property as well as his right to deal in the property pledged.

Rights and Duties of the Pawner

1. **Duty of repay loan :** The pawner should repay the loan and take back the delivery of his property from the pawnee within the stipulated time.

17. Blundell Leigh *v.* Attenborough (1921), 3 K.B. 233.

2. **Right to receive goods till sold** (*Sec. 177*) **:** If a time is stipulated for the payment of the debt or performance of the promise for which the pledge is made, and the pawner makes default in the payment of the debt or the performance of the promise at the stipulated time, he may still redeem the goods pledged at any subsequent time before the actual sale of them, but he must in that case pay, in addition, any expenses which might have arisen from his default.

In case there is any increase in the goods, the pawner is entitled to such increase. For example, in case bonus shares are issued against the shares pledged, the pledger will be entitled to these shares after he has paid off the amount due.[18]

Rights and Duties of the Pawnee

1. **Right to receive payment from the debtor or obtain the performance of promise with interest and expenses** (*Sec. 173*) **:** Pawnee has a right to retain possession on the goods pledged till he obtains payment of his debt, interest on that debt and all other necessary expenses which he might have incurred for the preservation of the goods pledged or in respect of his possession.

2. **Right of particular lien** (*Sec. 174*) **:** Pawnee has no right to retain his possession over the goods pledged for any debt or promise other than the debt or promise for which they were pledged, unless otherwise provided for, by the contract. Law will presume such a contract with regard to the subsequent advances made by the pawnee, in the absence of anything to the contrary.

3. **Right to receive extraordinary expenses** (*Sec. 175*) **:** Pawnee is also entitled to receive from the pawner any extraordinary expenses which he might have incurred for the preservation of the goods pledged. But he has no right of lien for such expenses.

4. **Pawnee's right in case of default of the pawner** (*Sec. 176*) **:** In the case of default by the pawner in the payment of debt or the performance of promise at the stipulated time, the pawnee can exercise the following two rights :

(*a*) He has a right to bring a suit on the debt or promise and can retain the goods pledged as a collateral security.

(*b*) He has also a right to sell the goods pledged after giving reasonable notice of sale to the pawner. The requirement of 'reasonable notice' is a statutory requirement and, therefore, cannot be excluded by a contract to the contrary.[19] The pledgee may sell the goods to himself but in case he has given a value less than the market price of the goods, the pledger may make him liable for the balance.[20]

The pledgee has a right to claim any deficit arising from the sale of the goods pledged from the pawner. He will have to return to the pawner any excess obtained by the sale of goods pledged beyond the amount necessary to pay the debt and other expenses due.

5. **Pawnee must not use the goods pledged :** He must not use the goods pledged unless they are such as will not deteriorate by wear.

Besides the above rights and duties, all other rights and duties of the bailer and bailee apply to the pawner and the pawnee.

18. M.R. Dhawan *v.* Madan Mohan (1969), A.I.R. Delhi 313.
19. Prabhat Bank *v.* Babu Ram, A.I.R. (1966), All. 134.
20. Dhani Ram & Sons *v.* Frontier Bank, A.I.R. (1962), Punj. 321.

Pledge by Non-owners

Ordinarily only a person who is the real owner of the goods can make a valid pledge, but in the following cases pledge made by non-owners will also be valid :

1. **Pledge by a mercantile agent** (*Sec. 178*) **:** Where a mercantile agent is, with the consent of the owner, in possession of goods or the documents of title to goods, makes a pledge acting in the ordinary course of his business, the pledge shall be as *valid* as if he were expressly authorised by the owner of the goods to make the same, provided that the pawnee acts in *good faith* and has not at the time of the pledge notice that the pawner has no authority to pledge.

The term 'mercantile agent' is defined in *Sec. 2(9)* of the Sale of Goods Act, thus :

'Mercantile agent means a mercantile agent having in the customary course of business as such agent, authority either to sell goods or to consign goods for the purposes of sale or to buy goods or to raise money on the security of goods.'

Example **:** *A*, a mercantile agent was entrusted with certain diamonds for sale. He pledged them through a friend with *B*. Held, the pledge was not valid since it was not in the ordinary course of business of a mercantile agent to ask a friend to pledge goods entrusted to him. He should have pledged the goods himself.[21]

2. **Pledge by person in possession under voidable contract** (*Sec. 178A*) **:** When the pawner has obtained possession of the goods pledged by him under a contract voidable under *Section 19* or *Section 19A*, but the contract has not been rescinded at the time of the pledge, the pawnee acquires a good title to the goods, provided he acts in good faith and without notice of the pawner's defect of title.

Example **:** *A* purchases a car worth ₹ 10,000 from his student *B* for ₹ 5,000 by exercising undue influence over him. Before *B* takes any action for rescinding the contract, *A* pledges the car with *C* for a sum of ₹ 5,000 who accepts this in good faith. The pledge made by *A* is valid.

3. **Pledge where pawner has only a limited interest** (*Sec. 179*) **:** Where a person pledges goods in which he has only a limited interest, the pledge is valid to the extent of that interest.

Example **:** *A* finds a watch on the road and spends ₹ 25 on its repair. He pledges it with *B* for ₹ 50. The real owner can get the watch by paying ₹ 25 to the pawnee.

A pledgee himself may repledge the goods. But in such a case the pledge is valid only to the extent of his interest, *i.e.*, the amount due to him (including interest).[22] In case the original pledge is found to be valid, the repledge will also be equally invalid.[23]

4. **Pledge by a co-owner in possession :** If there are several joint owners of goods and goods are in the sole possession of one of the co-owners with the consent of other co-owners, such a co-owner can make a valid pledge of goods.

5. **Pledge by seller or buyer in possession after sale :** A seller who has got possession of goods even after sale, can make a valid pledge, provided the pawnee acts in good faith.

Example **:** *A* buys goods from *Y*, pays for them, but leaves them in the possession of *Y*, and *Y* then pledges the goods with *Z* who does not know of sale to *X*, the pledge is valid.

---

21. De Gorsgter *v.* Attenborough & Son (1908), 1. K.B. 221.
22. Thakurdas *v.* Mathura Pd. (1958), A.I.R. All 66.
23. Jaswantrai Manilal Akhaney *v.* State of Bombay (1956), S.C.R. 483.

Similarly, if the buyer obtains possession of goods with the consent of the seller before payment of price and pledges them, the pawnee will get a good title provided he does not have the notice of seller's right of lien or any other right (*Section 30* of the Sale of Goods Act).

TERMINATION OF BAILMENT

A contract of bailment shall terminate in the following circumstances :

1. **On expiry of stipulated period :** If the goods were given for a stipulated period, the contract of bailment shall terminate after the expiry of such period.

2. **On fulfilment of the purpose :** If the goods were delivered for a specific purpose, bailment shall terminate on the fulfilment of that purpose.

3. **By notice :** (*a*) Where the bailee acts in a manner which is inconsistent with the terms of the bailment, the bailor can always terminate the contract of bailment by giving a notice to the bailee.

(*b*) A gratuitous bailment can be terminated by the bailor at any time by giving a notice to the bailee.

4. **By death :** A gratuitous bailment terminates upon the death of either the bailor or the bailee.

KEY TERMS

- ❑ **Bailment :** The delivery of goods by one person to another for a purpose.
- ❑ **Bailor :** The person delivering the goods is called as 'Bailor'.
- ❑ **Bailee :** The person to whom the goods are delivered is called as 'Bailee'.
- ❑ **Lien :** The right of a person to retain that which is in his possession and which belongs to other until the demand of the person in possession are satisfied.
- ❑ **Pledge :** The bailment of goods as security for the payment of a debt or performance of promise.

TEST QUESTIONS

Objective Type : ***Test Your Knowledge***

1. State whether each of the following statements is *True* or *False* :

(*i*) Bailment may arise without a contract also.

(*ii*) Bailment must be for the mutual benefit of both the parties.

(*iii*) Bailee has a right of specific lien.

(*iv*) Pledge is a type of bailment.

(*v*) Deposit of money in a bank constitutes bailment.

(*vi*) A contract of Bailment does not result when a person leaves some goods with his friend for being looked after. (*CS Foundation, Dec. 1998*)

(*vii*) Hiring of bank locker is a contract of Bailment. (*CS Foundation, Dec. 1999*)

(*viii*) Bailee has a right of general lien. (*CS Foundation, June 2000; (B.Com. (Hons.), Delhi 2002*)

(*ix*) Placing of ornaments in a bank locker is a contract of bailment. (*CS Foundation, June 2001*) (*x*) "Pledgee may further pledge the goods". (*ICWA Foundation, June 1999*)

(*xi*) Money deposited in fixed deposit with a bank is a contract of bailment. (*CS Foundation, June 2004; PCE, ICAI, May 2007*)

(*xii*) The bailor may determine the bailment where the bailee wrongfully uses or disposes of the goods bailed. (*CS Foundation, June 2005*)

(*xiii*) In Gratuitous bailment, no remuneration passes between the bailor and the bailee. (*CS Foundation, Dec. 2012*)

[***Ans.*** (*i*) True; (*ii*) False; (*iii*) True; (*iv*) True; (*v*) False; (*vi*) False; (*vii*) True; (*viii*) False; (*ix*) True; (*x*) True; (*x*) True; (*xi*) False; (*xii*) True; (*xiii*) True]

2. Select the most appropriate answer

(*i*) When a person deposits with another, goods by way of security for the payment of a loan, it is a contract of :

(*a*) bailment (*b*) pledge
(*c*) hypothecation.

(*ii*) The bailor is responsible for loss caused to the bailee on account of defects in goods bailed but unknown to him in case of :

(*a*) gratuitous bailment (*b*) non-gratuitous bailment
(*c*) bailment for mutual benefit.

(*iii*) Any increase of profit from the goods bailed belongs to :

(*a*) the bailor (*b*) the bailee
(*c*) both.

(*iv*) The delivery of goods by one person to another as security for payment of a debt is called.

(*a*) Bailment (*b*) Pledge
(*c*) Mortgage (*d*) Hypothecation

(*PCE, ICAI, May 2007*)

[***Ans.*** (*i*) (*b*); (*ii*) (*b*); (*iii*) (*a*); (*iv*) (*b*)]

Essay Type : *For Review, Discussion and Practice*

1. Define 'Bailment'. What are requisites of a contract of bailment? Explain.
2. Explain the meaning of 'Gratuitous' and 'Non-Gratuitous' bailments.
3. Define 'Pledge'. In what way does 'Pledge' differ from 'Bailment'? Explain.
4. Explain clearly the meaning of 'Bailment' as provided in the Indian Contract Act. When does a contract of bailment terminate? Explain.
(*B.Com. (Pass), Delhi 2003*)
5. Distinguish between 'general lien' and 'particular lien.' In what category would you place the bailee's lien? Who are entitled to a general lien?
(*CA Foundation, May 1998; May 2001*)
6. When will a pledge made by a non-owner of the goods be valid?
7. Does deposit of money in a bank amount to bailment? (*ICWA Foundation, June 1999*)
8. What are the duties and rights of a bailee in a contract of bailment?
(*ICWA Foundation, June 1999; B.Com. (Hons.), Delhi 1992*)
9. Explain 'Delivery of goods is essential for effecting bailment'. (*ICWA Foundation, June 2000*)
10. Discuss at least three rights of a Bailor and three rights of a Bailee.
(*ICWA Foundation, June 2001; B.Com. (Hons.), Delhi 2002*)
11. What do you mean by "Particular Lien"? (*ICWA Foundation, June 2001*)

12. Distinguish between
    (a) Gratuitous and Non-gratuitous Bailment (*B.Com. (Hons.), Delhi 2005*)
    (b) Bailment and Pledge (*B.Com. (Hons.), Delhi 1990, 1998; B.Com. (Pass), Delhi 2004*)
    (c) Particular Lien and General Lien (*CS Foundation, Dec. 1999; B.Com. (Pass), Delhi 2002*)
13. Explain what relief is available to the bailor in case of bailor's goods being mixed with that of the bailee. (*B.Com. (Hons.), Delhi 1986*)
14. Discuss the position of finder of goods. (*B.Com. (Hons.), Delhi 1989*)
15. "The status of a finder of lost goods is just like a bailee." Comment. (*B.Com. (Hons.), Delhi 2005*)
16. "Goods can be pledged by the owner only" Discuss. State the circumstances in which the goods can be pledged by non-owners. (*PCE, ICAI, May 2007*)
17. Write a note on 'Bailee's particular lien'. (*ICWAI Inter, June 2009*)
18. State the different kinds or types of Bailment(*ICWAI Inter, June 2011; B.Com. (Hons.) Delhi 2013*)
19. State the essential elements of a contract of bailment. Distinguish between the 'contract of bailment' and 'contract of pledge'. (*CA IPC, Nov 2012; B.Com. (Hons.), 2012*)
20. Define the term Lien. Differentiate between Particular and General Lien. (*B.Com. (Hons), Delhi 2011*)

PRACTICAL PROBLEMS

1. *A* finds a costly ring and after making reasonable efforts to trace the owner, sells it to *B*, who buys in good faith and without having the knowledge that *A* was merely a finder. Can the true owner recover the ring from *B*?

   [***Ans.*** No, if other conditions regarding 'sale by finder' are satisfied.]
2. *H* entered into a hire-purchase agreement with *B* in relation to a piano on the condition that on paying 12 instalments of ₹ 100 each the piano should be his property. After payment of 6 instalments *B* pawned the piano with *M* who took it in good faith. Can *H* take back the piano from *M*.

   [***Ans.*** Yes, Ownership was not transferred.]
3. *A* delivered gold to a jeweller for making certain ornaments. *B* refused to deliver the ornaments when ready. He claims that until *A* pays him the charges for making the ornaments and also the sum of ₹ 1,000 which was due to him from '*A*' on certain earlier transactions, he is entitled to retain ornaments. Advice *A*.

   [***Ans.*** *A* can have the ornaments by only paying charges for making ornaments. The jeweller has only particular lien and not general lien.]
4. *A* lends a sum of ₹ 500 to *B*, on the security of twenty shares of a limited company on 1st January, 1998. On 15th January, 1998, the company issued five bonus shares. *B* repays the amount of ₹ 500 with interest. *A* returns twenty shares but refuses to return the five bonus shares. Advice *B*.

   [***Ans.*** *B* must succeed. *B* is entitled to any increase in shares as per Section 163.]
5. *X* enters in a restaurant for dining. His bag containing some important documents was taken by a waiter at the gate, who placed it on a shelf behind *X*. After having his dinner when *X* rose to leave, the bag was gone. *X* wants to hold the proprietor of the restaurant liable for the loss. Decide.

   [***Ans.*** U/s. 151, *X* can hold the proprietor liable for the loss on account of his failure to take a reasonable care.]
6. *X*, a warehouseman, was entrusted with certain goods for safe custody. *X* had taken reasonable precautions for the safety of the goods by providing a safe building, safe locks and a competent watchman. But the goods were lost due to the negligence of the watchman who did not lock or watch properly. *X* denies his liability urging that there was no negligence on his part. Decide the question of *X*'s liability.

[*Ans.* *X* is responsible for the loss.]

7. *X* lends his car to *Y* for going to attend the Annual General Meeting of *ABC* Limited, being held at Juhu, a place in Bombay. The brakes of the car are not in working order. This fact is already known to *X*, but he did not tell *Y* about the defect. *Y* holds a valid driving licence. *Y*, instead of going to attend the Annual General Meeting at Juhu, drives the car to the Gateway of India on a pleasure trip. The car meets with an accident and *Y* get injured. *Y* wants to hold *X* liable for the injury. Giving the provisions of the Indian Contract Act, decide whether *Y* would succeed.
   [*Ans.* Bailee *Y* has himself committed a breach of duty and hence he cannot hold *X* liable for the injury.]
8. *X* lends his car to *Y* for his own driving. *Y* ask *Z*, his son to drive the car while *Y* and his family were going on picnic. *Z* drives the car with care but unfortunately meets with an accident with a truck. The car is damaged and *X* has to pay a sum of ₹ 5,000 for the repairs. *X* wants to claim this amount from *Y*, who refused to pay on the ground that the car was not driven by him. Decide giving reasons : (*i*) Whether *Y*'s contention is tenable? (*ii*) What provisions exist in the Indian Contract Act in the regard?
   [*Ans.* *Y* will have to compensate *X* for breach of duty.]
9. *A* lets to *B* for hire, a horse for his own riding. *B* drives the horse in his carriage. Can *A* exercise to terminate the bailment? Will *A* succeed? *(ICWA Foundation, June 1999)*
   [*Ans.* *A* can terminate the contract of bailment since *B* has violated the terms of contract.]
10. *A* lends his car to *B* for his own driving only. *B* allows *C*, an expert driver to drive the car. *C* drives the car with care but hits it with an electric pole. The car is damaged. *A* files a suit against *B* for claiming damages. Will *A* succeed. Give reasons. *(CS Foundation, June 1999)*
   [*Ans.* *A* will succeed.]
11. *A* hire a carriage of *B* and agrees to pay ₹ 500 as hire charges. The carriage is unsafe, though *B* is unaware of it. *A* is injured and claims compensation for injuries suffered by him. *B* refuses to pay. Discuss the liability of *B*. *(CS Foundation, Dec. 2000, PEE II, May 2005)*
   [*Ans.* *B* is liable for damages since it is a bailment for hire.]
12. A lady went to a jeweller, falsely representing herself to be the wife of a particular zamindar. She took a ring on the pretext of getting the approval of her husband. She pledged the ring with someone else. Can the jeweller recover the ring from the pawnee? Elaborate your answer with the relevant provisions and decided case law. *(B.Com., (Hons.), Delhi 1991)*
   [*Ans.* There was no valid contract between the jeweller and the lady. The pawnee did not get good title and therefore, must return the ring to the jeweler.]
13. *A* delivers some stock of sugar to *B* for the purpose of storage. On *A*'s refusal to *B*'s lawful charges, *B* declines to return the sugar on the ground of his right of lien. Will *B* succeed? Give reasons. *(B.Com. (Hons.), Delhi 2005)*
   [*Ans.* This type of custody does not involve the exercise of labour or skill; therefore, the bailee was not entitled to lien.]
14. Ajay found a defective video camera lying in a park. He pledged it with Vijay for ₹ 3,000. Mohan, the real owner, came to know about it. Mohan sued Vijay to recover his camera. Vijay had incurred ₹ 500 on repaid to make the camera operational. Can Mohan recover his camera? *(CS Foundation, June 2007)*
   [*Ans.* Mohan can recover his camera only by paying ₹ 500 to Vijay.)
15. Ajoy finds a mobile phone lying on a table in a Coffee House. He hands over the mobile phone to Bijoy, the manager of the Coffee House, so that the true owner can claim it back. However, no one claims the mobile phone. After sometime, Ajoy goes to Bijoy, the manager and requests him to return the mobile phone to him. On Bijoy's refusal, Ajoy files a suit against him for recovery of the mobile phone. Will Ajoy succeed? Give reasons. *(CS Foundation, June 2008)*
   [*Ans.* Yes, Ajoy will succeed]
16. State the legal consequences, if any in the following case: 'Pawnee received a property from Pawner who pledged the property as security for payment of debts of ₹ 10,000. Pawner failed to repay. Pawanee sold the property at ₹ 15,000. *(ICWAI Inter, June 2009)*

[***Ans.*** The Pawnee must pay ₹ 5,000 being excess amount to the Pawner immediately.]

17. Examine whether the following constitute a contract of 'Bailment' under the provisions of the Indian Contract Act, 1872:
    (*i*) V parks his car at a parking lot, locks it and keeps the keys with himself. (*ii*) Seizure of goods by customs authorities. *(PEE-II, ICAI, May 2007)*
    [***Ans.*** (*i*) No, mere custody of goods does not mean possession.
    (*ii*) Yes, the possession of the goods is transferred to the custom authorities.]

18. Mr. Saxena a Pledgee incurred extra-ordinary expense for preservation of goods pledged. Pledgee refused to return such goods till the payment is settled, can he retain
    (ICWAI Inter, June 2011)
    [***Ans.*** To Pledgee is entitled to receive extra ordinary expense from pledger but he has not right to retain the goods for recovery of such expense. He can sue the pledger to pay such amount in case of pledger's refusal.]

19. *X*, a lady handed over her old jewellery to *Y*, a goldsmith, for the purpose of remaking after melting it. Every evening as soon as *Y*'s work for the day is over, the lady used to take the semifinished jewellery and put it in a box and keep the box in the goldsmith's shop, but carry the key of the box with her. One night the jewellery was lost from the box. Explain the liability of the goldsmith in this regard. *(B.Com. (Hons), Delhi 2012)*
    [***Ans.*** The goldsmith is not liable for the loss of jewellery, because the lady *X* has not bailed the jewellery to the goldsmith *Y*. Every evening the lady used to take it back and keep it in the box, but carry the keys of the box with her.]

20. Amrit hires a van from Bhim and agrees to pay ₹ 2,000 as hire charges. The van was unsafe, though Bhim was aware of it. Amrit was injured and he claims compensation for injuries suffered by him, from Bhim. Bhim refuses to pay. Discuss the liability of Bhim in this regard.
    (B.Com. (Hons.), Delhi, Nov. 2012)
    [***Ans.*** Bhim is liable to reimburse Amrit for injuries suffered by him. In case of a non-gratutious bailment, the bailor is responsible for all defects in the goods bailed whether he is aware of the defects or not.]

Chapter 15

CONTRACTS OF AGENCY

LEARNING OBJECTIVES

A careful study of this chapter will enable you to :

- understand the concept of agency;
- classify agents into different categories;
- describe the modes of creating agency;
- differentiate between sub-agent and substituted agent;
- identify the circumstances where the agent may be personally liable;
- enumerate the rights and duties of an agent;
- state the circumstances whether the agency may get terminated; and
- explain the meaning of certain key terms.

MEANING AND NATURE OF AGENCY

According to Section 182 of the Indian Contract Act an *agent* is a person employed to do any act for another or to represent another in dealings with third persons. The person for whom such act is done, or who is so represented is called the *principal.*' The 'relationship' between the agent and the principal is called *'agency'*.

The definition given by the Act is quite wide so as to include even a servant, a casual employee or a shoe-shine boy engaged for polishing the shoes within the definition of an agent. But it is not the intention of law. The term 'agent' is to be used only for a person who represents another and who has the power to effect contractual relationship between the person he represents, *i.e.*, his principal and the third parties.

Thus, the duty of the agent is to enter into contractual relations on behalf of the principal with third parties. He derives his authority to do so from the consent of the principal. But, by doing so, he himself does not become a party to the contract nor does he incur any liability under that contract. The principal shall be responsible for all the acts of his agent provided they are not outside the scope of his authority. Except for unauthorised acts, an agent does not incur any personal liability in respect of contracts made by him for his principal. An agent, therefore, simply brings his employer, the principal into legal relationship with third parties. A person, whose business is to give advice to his principal in matters of business, does not become an agent by doing so.

Contracts of agency are based upon two important principles of law :

(*a*) *Qui facit per alium facit per se, i.e.,* he who does through another does by himself. The acts of the agent shall, for all legal purposes, be considered to be the acts of the principal.

(*b*) Whatever a person is competent to do by himself, shall also be allowed to do through an agent except in the case of contracts involving personal services such as painting, marriage etc.

Competence of the parties to enter into a contract of agency

The person employing the agent must himself have the legal capacity or be competent to do the act for which he employs the agent. A minor or a person with unsound mind cannot appoint an agent so as to be legally represented by him (*Sec. 183*). But an agent so appointed need not necessarily be competent to contract (*Sec. 184*). As between the principal and the third parties, the act of an agent will be looked upon as an act of the principal who authorised it and hence, a person, who is incompetent to contract (*e.g.*, a minor) on his own behalf, will be competent to contract on behalf of the principal so as to bind him but such an incompetent agent cannot personally be held liable to the principal. Principal cannot realise any compensation for the losses caused to him by the faults of the incompetent agent. Incompetent parties, therefore, can be appointed agents only at the risk of the principal himself.

Consideration not required

A contract of agency requires no consideration. It comes under the category of those contracts which law has declared to be valid without consideration (*Sec. 185*).

AGENT AND SERVANT

An agent differs from a servant in the following respects :

(*i*) An agent is employed for the purpose of establishing contractual relationship between the principal and the third parties, while a servant is employed to work under direct and immediate control, guidance and supervision of his employer, *i.e.*, master. He does not necessarily create relationship between his employer and the third persons.

(*ii*) In case of an agent, the principal has the right to direct him what work he has to do. However, the agent will not be subject to the control or supervision of the principal while exercising his authority. But in case of a servant, the master has the further right to direct him how the work has to be done.[1] He must obey all the reasonable orders of his employer.

(*iii*) A person generally acts an agent for several principals while a servant generally works for only one master.

AGENT AND BAILEE

An agent differs from a bailee also. A person is a bailee so long he has the possession of the goods of the bailor, but a person may act as an agent of another person without having the possession of his goods. Moreover, an agent represents the principal in his dealings with the third parties, which is not the case with a bailee.

KINDS OF AGENTS

The word 'agent' is used in different contexts. As a matter of fact 'no word is more commonly and constantly abused than the word agent.'[2] It may refer to General Agent, Special Agent, Universal

1. Lakshminarayan Ram Gopal & Sons *v.* Hyderabad Government (1954), A.I.R. S.C. 364.
2. Kennedy *v.* De Trafford (1897), A.C. 180 at p. 188.

Agent, Mercantile Agent, Cleaning Agent, Secret Agent, etc. In this chapter, the word 'agent' has been used only as Mercantile Agent.

Mercantile Agent : He is an agent who has in the customary course of his business, authority to sell goods, to consign goods for purposes of sale or to buy goods or to raise money on the security of goods on behalf of his principal. When a mercantile agent in possession of the goods, with the consent of the real owner, sells goods in the ordinary course of his business to a *bona fide* buyer for value, the buyer will get better title to the goods even though the mercantile agent had no authority to sell.

Factor : A factor is an agent employed to sell goods or merchandise consigned or delivered to him by or for his principal. He has wide powers regarding selling of the goods in his possession. He can sell them in his own name, receive payment and give valid receipts of discharge. He has interest in the goods and also a lien in respect of any claim he may have arising out of the agency. A *bona fide* buyer of goods from a factor will acquire better title to the goods.

Broker : A broker is an agent who has been engaged by his principal to sell or buy goods on his behalf. A broker differs from a factor in many respects. A broker does not deal in his own name, while a factor does. A broker does not have possession of goods, while a factor has. A factor receives payment and gives valid receipts of discharge while a broker cannot do so. A broker has a particular lien while a factor has a general lien.

Auctioneer : He is an agent to sell goods at a public auction to the highest bidder. He has the possession of goods and has the authority to receive the purchase price and can sue for it in his own name. But he has only a particular lien and not a general lien.

Del credere agent : He is an agent employed to sell goods and who undertakes that purchasers he procures will pay for any goods they take. In case they do not pay, he indemnifies the principal for the loss. He gets an extra commission for bearing this extra risk. Such commission is called del credere commission.

A del credere agent is not liable to the buyer for any default on the part of his principal.[3] He is also not liable for any disputes between the principal and the buyer regarding the contract or the amount due.[4] He will not be liable for the non-performance of the contract if the buyer refuses to take delivery.

CREATION OF AGENCY

Agency may be created by any of the following ways :

1. **Expressly (*Sec. 187*) :** When an agent is appointed by words spoken or written, his authority is said to be express. It is usual in many cases to appoint agents by executing formal power of attorney on a written and stamped document. The power of attorney may be either general or special. Agents to execute deeds or to grant or surrender leases, to sign prospectus of a company, to act as proxy for a shareholder must be appointed by a written deed.

2. **Impliedly (*Sec. 187*) :** When agency arises from the conduct of the parties or inferred from the circumstances of the case it is called an implied agency. Partners, servants and wives are usually regarded as agents by implications because of their relationship. In an implied agency, principal will

3. Shaw *v.* Woodcock (1872), 7 B & C. 73.
4. Churchill & Sim *v.* Goddard (1937), K.B. 92.

not be entitled to limit the implied authority of the agent without notice to the third party, so as to adversely affect his rights, *e.g.*, where a husband allows his wife to pledge his credit and without repudiating future contracts meets the liability, his conduct will debar him from repudiating future contracts unless he gives express notice to the third parties.[5]

Example : *A* of Calcutta has a shop in Delhi. *B*, the manager of the shop, has been ordering and purchasing goods from *C* for the purpose of the shop. The goods purchased were being regularly paid for out of the funds provided by *A*. *B* shall be considered to be an agent of *A* by his conduct.

Agreement of agency must disclose intention of one person to act on behalf of the other. Intention to act on behalf of another may create implied agreement of agency. A person shall cease to be an agent the moment he intends acting of his own behalf.

Wife as an implied agent to her husband

(*a*) Where the *husband and wife are living together in a domestic establishment of their own,* the wife shall have an implied authority to pledge the credit of her husband for necessities. In case a person is a manager of a domestic establishment, the agency will be presumed even if the person is not the wife. But in the absence of a domestic establishment, the agency will not be presumed even if the person happens to be the wife.

Example : *M* was manager of a hotel where his wife also worked as manageress. They lived together in the same hotel but did not have any domestic establishment of their own. The wife purchased certain clothes etc. for which the payment was demanded from *M*, the husband. Held, he was not liable since there was no domestic establishment.[6]

This implied authority can be challenged by the husband if he is able to prove any of the following:

1. He had expressly forbidden the wife from borrowing money or buying goods on credit. However, in case of traders who had dealt with the wife and whom the husband in the past had paid, it is necessary that the husband must inform them that he has forbidden his wife to pledge his credit.[7]

2. The articles purchased did not constitute necessities (*i.e.*, articles suited to the style in which the husband chooses to live).

3. He had given sufficient funds to the wife for purchasing the articles she needed to the knowledge of the seller,[8] or

Example : A wife was supplied with clothes to the value of £ 215 and the husband refused to pay for them. On his being sued by the supplier, the husband proved that he had been paying £ 960 a year as an allowance. The husband was not held liable by the court.

4. The creditor had been expressly told not to give credit to the wife.[9]

(*b*) Where the *wife lives apart from husband without any of her own fault,* she shall have an implied authority to bind the husband for necessaries, if he does not provide for her maintenance. The husband cannot escape liability by telling the wife not to pledge his credit; nor even by telling the tradesmen not to supply her necessaries on credit. However, if the wife lives apart of her own

5. Jolly *v.* Rees (1864), 15 C.B. (N.S.), 628.
6. Debenham *v.* Mellon (1880), 6 A.C. 24.
7. *Ibid.*
8. Jolly *v.* Rees (1864), 15 C.M. (N.S.) 628.
9. Miss Gray Ltd. *v.* Cathcart (1922), 38 T.L.R. 562.

will and without any justification, she cannot be treated as an agent to her husband even for necessities, as the husband is under no obligation to maintain her.

3. **Agency by necessity :** Under certain circumstances, a person may be compelled to act as an agent to the other, *e.g.*, master of the ship can borrow money at a port where the owner of the ship has no agent, to carry out necessary repairs to the ship in order to complete the voyage. In such a case of necessity, person acting as an agent need not necessarily have the authority of the principal. However, the agent must act under pressing conditions and for the benefit of the principal. Law confers authority upon a person to act in a reasonable manner in order to save the property of any person in times of emergency without having any prior instructions from the owner thereof. Law assumes the consent of the owner to the creation of the relationship of the principal and agent. But to constitute a valid agency by necessity, each of the following conditions must be satisfied :

(*a*) The agent should not be in position or have any opportunity to communicate with his principal within the time available.

(*b*) There should have been actual and definite commercial necessity for the agent to act promptly.

(*c*) The agent should have acted *bona fide* and for the benefit of the principal.

(*d*) The agent should have adopted the most reasonable and practicable course under the circumstances.

(*e*) The agent must have been in possession of the goods belonging to his principal and which are the subject of contract.

Examples : (*i*) The master of the ship on finding that the cargo is rapidly perishing is entitled to dispose it of at the best price available so as to bind the consignor as an agent by necessity.

(*ii*) *M* allowed *S* to store certain furniture in his house without any charge. Then they lost contact with each other. Three years after *M* needed space for himself and therefore wrote two letters to *S* at the address supplied by this bank. No reply was received. His efforts to contract *S* on phone also failed. *M* sold the furniture. *S* returned back after six years and claimed the furniture. Held, that there was no such emergency which could entitled *M* to work as an agent for *S* and sell the furniture. However, *S* would be entitled to recover only the actual sale proceeds and no damages if he had received the letters. But he would be entitled to recover any notional appreciation also in the value of furniture between the date of sale and his discovery of it, if he had not received the letters.[10]

4. **Agency be estoppel** (*Sec. 237*) **:** When an agent has, without authority done acts or incurred obligations to third person on behalf of his principal, the principal is bound by such acts and obligations if he has by his words or conduct induced such third person to believe that such acts and obligations were within the scope of the agent's authority. Anson puts this principle of estoppel in these words: *"Where a person permits or represents another to act on his behalf, so that a reasonable man would infer that the relationship of principal and agent had been created, he will not be permitted to relieve himself of his obligations to a third party by proving that no such relationship in fact existed, provided that the third party acted in reliance on his assumption and to his detriment, the principal will be estopped from denying his agent's authority."*

Examples : (*i*) *A* says to *B* in the presence of and within the hearing of *C* that he is *C*'s agent. *C* remains mum. *B* supplied goods of ₹ 10,000 to *A* taking him as *C*'s agent. *C* is responsible for the payment of the price of those goods.

10. Sachs *v.* Milkos (1948), 2 K.B. 23.

(*ii*) *A* consigns goods to *B* for sale and gives him instructions not to sell under a fixed price. *C*, being ignorant of *A*'s instructions, enters into a contract with *B* to buy the goods at a price lower than the reserved price. *A* is bound by the contract.

(*iii*) *A* entrusts *B* with negotiable instruments endorsed in blank. *B* sells them to *C* in violation of private orders from *A*. The sale is good.

5. **Agency by ratification** (*Sec. 196 to 200*) **:** Ratification means subsequent acceptance and adoption of an act by an principal originally done by the agent without authority. This is *agency ex-post facto* or agency arising after the event. According to Section 196, "Where acts are done by one person on behalf of another but without his knowledge or authority, he may elect to ratify or to disown such acts. If he ratifies them, the same effects will follow as if they had been performed by his previous authority." In such circumstances the contract of agency shall come into effect from a retrospective date. The date will be the date on which agent has first acted. Thus, ratification tantamounts to prior authority.

Example : The manager of a company purporting to act as an agent on the company's behalf but without its authority, accepted an offer by *L*, the defendant. *L* subsequently withdrew the offer, but the company ratified the manager's acceptance. *L* was held to be bound by the acceptance. His revocation of the offer was held to be invalid. Ratification relates back to the date when the agent had first acted, and, therefore, subsequent revocation shall have no effect.[11] An offer once accepted cannot be withdrawn.

Ratification may be express or implied in the conduct of the person on whose behalf the acts are done.

Examples : (*i*) *A*, without authority, buys goods for *B*. Afterwards *B* sells them to *C* on his own account. *B*'s conduct implies a ratification of the loan.

Ratification will bind the principal by the effects of the act. It will be immaterial if the contract results to his profit or loss or it is founded on a tort or an agreement. Where an agent makes a contract in the name of his principal, but with the intention of fraudulently taking the benefit of the contract for himself, the principal may ratify and enforce the contract as against the other parties to it.

In order that ratification may be legal and valid, it must satisfy the following essentials :

1. The act must be done for or on account of the principal and not on account of the agent himself. It must be done in the name of the principal. Principal cannot subsequently ratify an act done not in his name but in the name of the agent.

Example : *R* authorised by *K* to buy wheat at a certain price, exceeded his authority and bought at a higher price from *D*. *R* bought in his own name, but intended to buy for *K*. *K* agreed with *R* to take the wheat at the price, but failed to take delivery. Held, *K* was not liable to *D* as he could not ratify *R*'s contracts.[12]

2. Principal must have been in existence and competent to contract at the time when agent acted on his behalf as well as on the date of ratification. An act done on behalf of a minor, without his authority, cannot be ratified by him on attaining majority. A newly promoted company cannot ratify an act done by its directors and promoters in its name before its incorporation. Since ratification authorises a contract from a back date, the party must be competent to contract on the date when the agent entered into the contract.

---

11. Bolton Partners *v*. Lambert (1889), 41 Ch. D. 295.
12. Keighley, Maxsted & Co. *v*. Durant (1901), A.C. 240.

Example : A promoter makes a contract on behalf of the company he is promoting .Can the company, when formed, ratify the contract?

A company has no existence in the eyes of law until it has been registered. It cannot incur any liability on a contract, even through an agent, till it is duly registered and property established. An important essential of valid ratification is that the principal must be in actual existence at the time when the agent entered into contract on its behalf, company cannot ratify such contract after it has come into existence.[13]

3. The act must be legal which the principal must be competent to do. Transactions void *ab initio* cannot be ratified. Therefore, there can be no valid ratification of a void or an illegal agreement. Similarly a company cannot ratify those unauthorised acts of the directors which are beyond its Memorandum of Association.

4. Ratification must be made with full knowledge of all the material facts.[14] Ratification by a person whose knowledge of the facts of the case is materially defective shall be bad in the eyes of law and will not bind the parties to the contract (*Sec. 198*).

5. Ratification must relate to the whole act and not to a part of it. Ratification of a part of the act will not be valid. Thus, either whole contract should be ratified or avoided (*Sec. 199*).

6. An act done by one person on behalf of another, without such person's authority, which if done with authority would have the effect of subjecting a third person to damages or of terminating any right or interest of a third person, cannot, by ratification, be made to have such effect (*Sec. 200*). Thus, there can be no valid ratification of an act which is to the prejudice of a third person.

Examples : (*i*) *A*, not being authorised thereto by *B*, demands on behalf of *B*, the delivery of a chattel, the property of *B* from *C*, who is in possession of it. The delivery cannot be ratified by *B*, so as to make *C* liable for damages for his refusal to deliver.

(*ii*) *A* holds a lease from *B*, terminable on three months notice. *C*, an unauthorised person, gives notice of termination to *A*. The notice cannot be ratified by *B*, so as to be binding on *A*.

7. Ratification of an act must be made either within the time fixed for this purpose or within a reasonable time after the contract was entered into by the agent. Ratification made after the expiry of time fixed for ratification will not be valid.

EXTENT OF AGENT'S AUTHORITY

Principal is responsible for the acts of the agent done by him within the scope of his authority. The authority of an agent may be express or implied. An authority is said to be express when it is given by words spoken or written. An authority is said to be implied when it is to be inferred from the circumstances of the case (*Secs. 186 and 187*).

Example : *A* owns a shop in Serampur, living himself in Calcutta, and visiting the shop occasionally. The shop is managed by *B*, and he is in the habit of ordering goods from *C* in the name of *A* for the purpose of the shop, and of paying for them out of *A's* funds with *A's* knowledge. *B* has an implied authority from *A* to order goods from *C* in the name of the *A* for the purposes of the shop.

Ostensible Authority of an Agent

The authority of an agent extends to the performance of every lawful thing necessary to do an act for which he is appointed. When he is appointed to carry on business, he can do every lawful

13. Kelner *v.* Baxter (1866), L.R. 2 C.P. 174.

14. Marsh *v.* Joseph (1897), 1 Ch. 213.

thing necessary for the purpose or as is usually done in the course of conducting such business (*Sec. 188*).

Examples : (*i*) *A* is employed by *B* residing in London, to recover at Bombay a debt due to *B*. *A* may adopt any legal process necessary for the purpose of recovering the debt and may give a valid discharge for the same.

(*ii*) *A* appoints *B* his agent to carry on his business of a ship-builder. *B* may purchase timber and other materials and hire workmen, for the purpose of carrying on the business.

Ordinarily, an agent has not power to borrow money on behalf of his principal unless such an authority is expressly given to him. Authority to borrow can be implied where the nature of business is such or the duties of the agent are of such a nature that he is bound to borrow in order to carry out the instructions of the principal and the duties of his office.

An agent has authority in an emergency to do all such acts for the purpose of protecting the principal from loss as would be done by a person of ordinary prudence, in his own case, under similar circumstances (*Sec. 189*). The emergency must be real not permitting the agent to communicate with the principal.

Examples : (*i*) An agent for sale may have goods repaired if it be necessary.

(*ii*) *A* consigns provisions to *B* at Calcutta, with directions to send them immediately to *C* at Cuttack. *B* may sell the provisions at Calcutta, if they will not bear journey to Cuttack without spoiling.

DELEGATION OF AGENT'S AUTHORITY

The principle is "A delegate cannot further delegate" (*Delegatus non-potest delegare*). An agent himself being the delegate of his principal, cannot further delegate his powers. However, under certain circumstances the agent may delegate some or all of his powers to another person. Such person may be either a sub-agent or a substituted agent.

Sub-agent

A "sub-agent" is a person employed by an acting under the control of the original agent in the business of agency (*Sec. 191*). In the following cases an agent can appoint a sub-agent unless he is expressly forbidden to do so :

(*i*) When the ordinary custom of trade permits the appointment of a sub-agent.

(*ii*) When the nature of the agency business requires the appointment of a sub-agent.

(*iii*) When the act to be done is purely ministerial and involves no exercise of discretion or confidence.

(*iv*) When the principal agrees to the appointment of such a sub-agent expressly or impliedly.

(*v*) When some unforeseen emergency has arisen.

The relations of the sub-agent to the principal depend on the question whether the agent had an authority to appoint the sub-agent and whether the sub-agent is properly appointed.

Where the sub-agent is properly employed, the principal is, so far as regards third persons, represented by the sub-agent and is bound by and is responsible for his acts as if he was an agent originally appointed by the principal. Principal, therefore, will be responsible for the acts of a properly appointed sub-agent. But the sub-agent will not be responsible for his acts to the principal, except in case of fraud or wilful wrong. Principal can hold the agent responsible for the acts of the sub-agent (*Sec. 192*).

Where an agent, without having authority to do so, has appointed a person to act as a sub-agent, *i.e.*, a sub-agent is improperly appointed, the principal is not represented by or responsible for the acts of the sub-agent as between himself and the third parties. The sub-agent is also not responsible to the principal for anything. The agent is responsible for the acts of the sub-agent both to the principal and to the third persons (*Sec. 193*).

Substituted Agent

Where an agent holding an express or implied authority to name another person to act in the business of the agency, has accordingly, named another person, such a person is not a sub-agent but a substituted agent. The substituted agent shall be taken as the agent of the principal for such part of the work as is entrusted to him (*Sec. 194*).

Examples : (*i*) *A* directs *B*, his solicitor, to sell his estate by auction, and to employ and auctioneer for the purpose. *B* names *C*, an auctioneer to conduct the sale. *C* is not a sub-agent, but is an agent for *A* for the conduct of the sale.

(*ii*) *A* authorises *B*, a merchant in Calcutta, to recover the money due to *A* from *C* & Co. *B* instructs *D*, the solicitor to take legal proceedings against *C* & Co. for the recovery of the money. *D* is not a sub-agent, but is a solicitor for *A*.

In selecting substituted agent for his principal an agent is bound to exercise the same amount of discretion as a man of ordinary prudence would exercise in his own case, and if he does this, he is not responsible to the principal for acts of negligence of the substituted agent.

Examples : (*i*) *A* instructs *B*, a merchant, to buy a ship for him. *B* employed a ship surveyor of good reputation to choose a ship for *A*. The surveyor makes the choice negligently and the ship turns out to be unseaworthy and is lost. *B* is not, but the surveyor is responsible to *A*.

(*ii*) *A* consigns goods to *B*, a merchant, for sale. *B* in due course employs an auctioneer in good credit to sell the goods of *A*, and allows the auctioneer to receive the proceeds of the sale. The auctioneer afterwards becomes insolvent without having accounted for the proceeds. *B* is not responsible to *A* for the proceeds.

Difference between a Sub-agent and a Substituted Agent

1. A substituted agent is only named by the agent but acts under the direct control of the principal. He is the agent of the principal though named by the agent on the request of the principal, while a sub-agent works under the control of the agent.
2. There is no privity of contract between the sub-agent and the principal. Neither the principal can sue the sub-agent nor the sub-agent can sue the principal. Of course, both can sue the agent, while an case of a substituted agent there is privity of contract between the principal and the substituted agent and both can sue each other.
3. The agent is responsible to the principal for the acts of sub-agent, while he is not responsible for the acts of the substituted agent.

AGENCY AND CONTRACTS WITH THIRD PERSONS

The consequences of agent's acts, done in the course of his employment, in relation to third parties can be studied under the following three heads :

1. When the agent expressly contracts as an agent for a *named* principal.
2. When the agent expressly contracts as an agent for an *unnamed* principal.
3. When the agent acts for an undisclosed principal.

1. When the agent contracts for a named principal

(*a*) *Acts within authority of agent* : The principal is bound by the acts done by the agent within his actual authority. He will also be liable to the third parties for the acts of the agent which may be beyond his actual authority but which come with in his ostensible or apparent authority unless the third party knows of the limitations on the agent's apparent authority.

Example : *A* leaves a watch with *B*, an auctioneer, with the instruction that it is not to be sold below ₹ 100. *B* sells the watch to *C* for ₹ 80, who does not know about the special instruction. *A* cannot set aside the contract.

(*b*) *Acts beyond agent's authority* : When an agent does more than what he is authorised to do and when the part of what he does, which is within his authority, can be separated from the part which is beyond his authority, so much only of what he does as is within his authority, is binding as between him and his principal (*Sec. 227*).

Example : *A*, being an owner of a ship and cargo, authorises *B* to procure an insurance for ₹ 4,000 on the ship. *B* procures a policy of ₹ 4,000 on the ship and another for the like sum on the cargo. *A* is bound to pay the premium for the policy on the ship, but not the premium for the policy on the cargo.

Where an agent does more then he is authorised to do, and what he does beyond the scope of his authority cannot be separated from what is within it, the principal is not bound to recognise the transaction (*Sec. 228*).

Example : *A* authorises *B* to buy 500 sheep for him. *B* buys 500 sheep and 200 lambs for one sum of ₹ 6,000. *A* may repudiate the whole transaction.

(*c*) *Liability of principal inducing belief that agent's unauthorised acts were authorised* : When an agent has, without authority, done acts or incurred obligations to a third person on behalf of his principal, the principal is bound by such acts or obligation if he has by his words or conduct induced such third persons to believe that such acts and obligations were within the scope of the agent's authority (*Sec. 237*).

Example : *A* consigns goods to *B* for sale, and gives him instructions, not to sell under a fixed price. *C*, being ignorant of *B*'s instructions, enters into a contract with *B* to buy the goods at a price lower than the reserved price. *A* is bound by the contract.

(*d*) *Notice to the agent* : Any notice given to or information obtained by the agent, provided it has been given or obtained in the course of business transacted by him for the principal, shall as between the principal and the third parties, have the same legal consequences as if it had been given to or obtained by the principal (*Sec. 229*).

Examples : (*i*) *A* is employed by *B* to buy from *C* certain goods of which *C* is the apparent owner and buys them accordingly. In the course of the treaty for the sale, *A* learns that goods really belonged to *D*, but *B* is ignorant of that fact. *B* is not entitled to set off a debt owing to him from *C* against the price of the goods.

(*ii*) *A* is employed by *B* to buy from *C*, goods of which *C* is apparent owner. *A* was, before he was so employed, a servant of *C*, and than learnt that the goods really belonged to *D*, but *B* is ignorant of that fact. In spite of the knowledge of his agent, *B* may set off against the price of goods a debt owing to him by *C*.

(e) *Misrepresentation or fraud by an agent* : The principal is liable for misrepresentation or fraud of the agent committed in the course of the employment or within the scope of agent's apparent authority (*Sec. 238*). It is immaterial for whose benefit such fraud or misrepresentation has been done. The liability of the principal will not however exclude the personal liability of the agent. He may also be sued.

Of course, the principal is not liable for misrepresentation made or fraud committed by his agent in matters which do not fall in agent's authority.

Principal will be liable for the torts of the agent if the agent was employed or appeared to have been employed to do honestly or carefully those things which he has done fraudulently or negligently.

Examples : (*i*) *A* being *B*'s agent for the sale of goods, induces *C* to buy them by misrepresentation, which he was not authorised by *B* to make. The contract is voidable, as between *B* and *C* at the option of *C*.

(*ii*) *A*, the captain of *B*'s ship, signs bills of lading without having received on board the goods mentioned therein. The bills of lading are void as between *B* and the pretended consignor.

(*iii*) *L* consulted *G*, in her capacity as solicitor, over some property. *L* was referred to the managing clerk of the firm of *G*, who fraudulently induced her to execute the conveyance of the property to himself. He then mortgaged the property and absconded with the proceeds. Held that the firm was liable to reimburse *L*, as the fraud was committed by its agents. The clerk had authority to do the very thing he did do. That he did it fraudulently was besides the point. The firm was liable for his fraud.[15]

(*f*) *Admission made by an agent* : The law considers the principal and agent as one person, and therefore, any admission made by the agent in the course of agency business will be taken to have been made by the principal and the principal will be bound by that admission. In a case where the station master reported to the police that one of the porters had run away with the parcel, it was held that admission made by the station master was admission made by the railway company itself, and therefore, it was responsible to compensate for the loss.

2. When the agent contracts for an unnamed principal

An agent is not personally liable to third parties when he has disclosed the fact that he is an agent but has not disclosed the name of his principal to them. The third parties can proceed only against the principal and not against the agent. However, if the agent declines to disclose the identity of his principal when asked by the third parties, they can sue him personally also.

3. When the agent contracts for an undisclosed principal

When an agent makes a contract with a person who neither knows nor has reason to suspect that he is an agent, his principal is termed as an undisclosed principal. The position of the third party, the principal and the agent in such a case is as follows :

(*i*) If the third party comes to know of the existence of the principal before obtaining judgement against the agent, he may sue either the principal or the agent or both. If he decides to sue the

15. Lloyd *v*. Grace Smith & Co. (1912), A.C. 716.

principal, he must allow the principal the benefit of all payments received by him (third party) from the agent (*Sec. 231*).

Example : *A* enters into a contract with *B* to sell him bales of cotton and receives ₹ 500 in advance from *B*. Afterwards he (*A*) discovers that *B* was acting as agent for *C*. *A* may sue *C* but he must give credit to *C* for ₹ 500 paid by his agent, *B*, to him.

(*ii*) The principal, if he likes, may intervene and sue the third party. In such a case he can obtain such performance subject to the rights and obligations subsisting between the agent and the other party to the contract (*Sec. 232*).

Example : *A*, who owes 500 rupees to *B*, sells 1,000 rupees' worth of rice to *B*. *A* is acting as agent for *C* in the transaction, but *B* has to knowledge nor reasonable ground of suspicion that such is the case. *C* cannot compel *B* to take the rice without allowing him to set off *A*'s debt.

(*iii*) Para 2 of *Sec. 231* states that 'if the principal discloses himself before the contract is completed, the other contracting party may refuse to fulfil the contract if he can show that, if he had known who was the principal in the contract, or if he had known that agent was not a principal, he would not have entered into the contract.'

It is to be noted that right of the third party to repudiate the contract arises only when the principal himself makes the disclosure. It does not arise where the disclosure is made by some other person or information reaches him from some other source.[16]

Choice of remedy : When a person who has made a contract with an agent, induces the agent to act upon the belief that the principal only will be held liable, or induces the principal to act upon the belief that the agent only will be held liable, he cannot afterwards hold liable the agent or the principal respectively (*Sec. 234*).

Example : *G* authorised *L* & Co. to buy goods for him from *A*. Later on *G* himself approached *A* for purchasing them. *A* knew that *L* & Co. were buying goods for *B* but preferred to treat *L* & Co. as principal and debited their account. *L* & Co. failed to pay the money and *A* sued *G* for payment. It was held that *A* was not entitled to recover payment from *G* because he (*A*) had shown a clear intention from the beginning that he had given credit to the agent alone and he also knew of the principal.[17]

Liability of pretended agent : A person untruly representing himself to be the authorised agent of another, and thereby inducing a third person to deal with him as such agent, is liable, if his alleged employer does not ratify his acts, to make compensation to the other in respect of any loss or damage which he has incurred by so dealing (*Sec. 235*).

Example : *A* and *B*, directors of a company, borrowed money from *D* on its behalf. The company had no power to borrow money under its memorandum of association. *D* was unable to recover the amount of the loan from the company, and he, therefore, sued the directors. They were held liable.[18]

However, the pretended agent will not be liable if the plaintiff knew that no authority was given or the agent could not possess that authority, *e.g.*, the person giving the authority happens to be a minor.

PERSONAL LIABILITY OF AGENT

As a general rule, neither an agent can personally enforce contracts entered into by him on behalf of the principal nor can be personally held liable for them unless the contract provides otherwise.

16. Laksmandas *v*. Anna R. Lane (1904), 32 Bom., 356.
17. Addison *v*. Gandasequi (1812), 4 Taunt 574.
18. Collen *v*. Wright (1857), 7 E. & B 301.

Principal is the right person to enforce such contracts and to be held liable. In the following cases, law presumes a contract to the contrary to be in existence and the agent can be held personally liable for the contracts entered into by him on behalf of the principal. Most of these cases are based on the principle that if by his conduct one person causes another to believe that a principal is being dealt with, he cannot put that other in a worse position by any subsequent disclosure of his character as agent.

1. **Foreign principal :** When the contract is made for the sale or purchase of goods for a merchant resident abroad, in case of breach of contract the third party can make the agent personally liable. The presumption of law in case of such contracts is that credit has exclusively been given to the agent and not to the foreigner.

2. **Undisclosed or concealed principal :** When the agent does not disclose the name of the principal, the third party can make the agent personally liable if he has solely relied upon the responsibility of the agent.[19] He must not have any knowledge of the fact that the person contracting is not a principal but an agent, at the time of contracting. If he comes to know or have the means to know that the party contracting is an agent, the name of the principal may not have been disclosed, the third party cannot hold the agent personally liable for the contract.

Where subsequently the contracting party comes to know of the existence of the principal, he gets an option either to proceed against the principal or the agent. Once having made his election, he may not be allowed afterwards to proceed against the other, *i.e.*, if he sues the agent and obtains no satisfaction, he may not be able then to sue the principal.[20] The third party may also be estopped from suing the principal at all if he allows the principal to think that he has settled matters satisfactorily with the agent. If credit was given exclusively to the agent and the principal pays the agent before the third party discovers his existence, the third party cannot sue the principal.

3. **Principal cannot be sued :** Where the principal though disclosed cannot be sued, *e.g.*, foreign sovereign ambassador etc. or the principal is disqualified from contracting though otherwise competent to contract and this inability of the principal was not communicated to the third party at the time of contracting, he can hold the agent personally liable.

4. **Personal liability by agreement :** When the agent expressly by agreement or impliedly by conduct undertakes personal liability for the contract.

5. **Agent's liability for breach of warranty :** When the agent acts without or beyond his authority and in this way commits a breach of warranty of authority, he can be held personally liable.[21] If the agent knows that he is exceeding his authority, the breach of warranty will amount to deceit.[22]

6. **Agent signs the contract in his own name :** An agent who signs a Negotiable Instrument *e.g.*, Bills of Exchange, Promissory Notes etc., in his own name without making it clear that he is signing as an agent, shall be held personally liable.

7. **Agency coupled with interest :** Where the contract of agency relates to a subject matter in which the agent has a special interest, agent shall be personally liable to the extent of his interest since he shall be a principal for that interest.

19. Thomson *v.* Davenport (1829), 2 Sm. L.C. (12th Ed.) 355.
20. Militz *v.* Bomering Wood (1954).
21. Collen *v.* Wright (1857), 7 E. & B. 301.
22. Polhill *v.* Walter (1832), B. & Ad. 114.

8. **Misrepresentation or fraud :** When the misrepresentation made or fraud committed by an agent in matters which do not fall within his authority or in the ordinary course of his business for his principal, agent can be personally held liable.

9. **Non-existent principal :** If an agent acts for a non-existent principal, he shall be held personally liable as if he had contracted on his own account, *e.g.*, liability of promoters entering into contracts on behalf of a company yet to come into existence. But mere singing of a non-existent company's name does not make the signor a party.[23]

Right of person dealing with agent personally liable : In cases where the agent is personally liable, a person dealing with him hold either him or his principal, or both of them liable (*Sec. 233*).

Example : *A* enters into a contract with *B* to sell him 100 bales of cotton and afterwards discovers that *B* was acting as an agent for *C*. *A* may sue either *B* or *C*, or both, for the price of the cotton.

RIGHTS OF AN AGENT

1. **Right to claim reimbursement for expenses :** Agent has the right to retain, out of the money received on behalf of the principal, money advanced or expenses properly incurred in conducting the agency business (*Sec. 217*). The agent may have paid the money at the request of the principal, or on account of the understanding implied by the terms of the agency or through mercantile usage.

2. **Right to receive remuneration :** Agent has also a right to claim remuneration as may be payable to him for acting as an agent. The amount of remuneration may be retained by him out of the money received on account of principal in the business of agency. But an agent cannot retain sums received by him in one business for his commission in other business, though it may be on behalf of the same principal.[24]

In the absence of any contract to the contrary, the right to claim remuneration will arise only when the agent has carried out the object of the agency in full without being guilty of misconduct (*Sec. 219*). It is to be noted that once a binding contract for sale has been entered into and commission has been earned, the fact that the contract is never brought to completion is immaterial. Thus, an agent cannot be deprived of his commission if he has brought the parties to the contract together but the contract did not materialise on account of the principal taking advantage of legal technicality which made the contract unenforceable.[25]

Examples : (*i*) *A* promises to pay *B* a commission of 5% if he sells a house for him. *B* finds a purchaser, whom he brings to *A*, but in the meantime *A* has sold the house to a purchaser found by himself. Has *B* any right against *A*?

The question is purely one of the contract. There is a contract of agency between *A* and *B*, which has never been revoked. *B* still remains the agent entitled to 5% commission, but his commission is not due until a contract of sale has been made binding between *A* and the proposed purchaser. If, however, it becomes difficult to bring about such a contract through the fault of *A*, *A* must be content to bear the loss. Therefore, in the above case, *B* will be entitled to commission on the sale which his principal has himself negotiated provided the sale arranged by *A* was not due to *B*'s neglect to find a purchaser.

(*ii*) A broker, who was engaged to negotiate a lease deed succeeded in getting a lessee to agree to the terms of the lease but the lease could not be put through as the defendant (the employer of the

23. Newborne *v*. Sensolid (1954).
24. Sardar Mohammad *v*. Surajmal Govindram (1907), 33 Bom. 364.
25. Prickett *v*. Badger (1856), 1 C.B. (N.S.) 296, Sheikh Farid Baksh *v*. Hargular Singh, A.I.R. (1937), All 46.

broker) had failed to make out a title to the premises. It was held that the broker was entitled to recover his brokerage.[26]

An agent who is guilty of misconduct in the business of the agency is not entitled to any remuneration in respect of that part of the business which has been misconducted (*Sec. 220*).

Examples : (*i*) *A* employs *B* to recover 1,00,000 rupees from *C,* and lay it out on good security. *B* recovers the 1,00,000 rupees and lays out 90,000 rupees on goods security, but lays out 10,000 rupees on security which he ought to have known to be bad, whereby *A* loses 2,000 rupees. *B* is entitled to remuneration for recovering the 1,00,000 rupees and for investing the 90,000 rupees. He is not entitled to any remuneration for investing the 10,000 rupees, and he must make good the loss of 2,000 rupees to *A*.

(*ii*) *A* employs *B* to recover 1,000 rupees from *C*. Through *B's* misconduct the money is not recovered *B* is entitled to no remuneration for his services, and must make goods the loss.

3. **Right of indemnification against consequences of all lawful acts :** An agent has a right to be indemnified by the principal against the consequences of all lawful acts done in exercise of his authority (*Sec. 222*). The losses and damages must be direct and natural consequences of his acts under the contract of agency. The exercise of authority must be according to the rules and customs of the particular trade or market in which the agent has to deal, provided the same is a reasonable one.[27] Right of indemnification will be lost if the agent acts beyond his authority or performs his duties negligently.

Examples : (*i*) *B,* at Singapore, under instructions from *A* of Calcutta, contracts with *C* to deliver certain goods to him. *A* does not send the goods to *B,* and *C* sues *B* for breach of contract. *B* informs *A* of the suit, and *A* authorises him to defend the suit. *B* defends the suit, and is compelled to pay damages and costs, and incurs expenses. *A* is liable to *B* for such damages, costs and expenses.

(*ii*) *B,* a broker at Calcutta, by the orders of *A,* a merchant there, contracts with *C* for the purchase of 10 casks of oil for *A.* Afterwards *A* refuses to receive the oil and *C* sues *B. B* informs *A,* who repudiates the contract altogether. *B* defends, but unsuccessfully, and has to pay damages and incurs expenses. *A* is liable to *B* for such damages, costs and expenses.

4. **Right of indemnification against consequences of acts done in good faith :** An agent has a right to be indemnified by the principal for any compensation which he may be required to pay to the third parties for injuries caused to them by his wrongful acts within the scope of his actual authority done in his good faith, *i.e.*, without any wrong or dishonest (*Sec. 223*).

Examples : (*i*) *A,* a decree-holder in execution of his decree against *B,* requires the officer of the Court to seize certain goods, representing them to be the goods of *B.* The officer seizes the goods, and is sued by *C,* the true owner of the goods. *A* is liable to indemnify the officer for the sum which he is compelled to pay to *C,* in consequence of obeying *A's* directions.

(*ii*) *B,* at the request of *A,* sells goods in the possession of *A,* but which *A* had no right to dispose of. *B* does not know this, and hands over the proceeds of the sale to *A.* Afterwards *C,* the true owner of the goods. sues *B* and recovers the value of the goods and cost, *A* is liable to indemnify *B* for what he has been compelled to pay to *C* and for *B's* own expenses.

But where one person employs another to do an act which is criminal. The employer is not liable to the agent either upon an express or an implied promise, to indemnify him against the consequences of that act (*Sec. 224*).

26. Raghu Nandan *v.* Madan Mohan, 38 C.L.J. 139.

27. Davis *v.* Howard (1890), 24 Q.B.D. 691.

Examples : (*i*) *A* employs *B* to beat *C*, and agree to indemnify him against all consequences of the act. *B* thereupon beats *C*, and has to pay damages to *C* for doing so. *A* not liable to indemnify *B* for those damages.

(*ii*) *B*, the proprietor of a newspaper, publishes, at *A*'s request, a libel (defamation in writing) upon *C* in the paper, *A* agrees to indemnify *B* against the consequences of the publication and all costs and damages of any action in respect thereof. *B* is sued by *C* and has to pay damages and also incurse expenses. *A* is not liable to *B* upon the indemnity.

5. **Right of indemnification for injuries caused by principal's neglect :** An agent has a right to claim compensation from the principal for injuries caused to him by the negligence or want of skill on the part of the principal (*Sec. 225*). But he cannot claim compensation if the injury results from his own negligence or acquiescence after knowledge of the risk of agency. This is because the agent is presumed to undertake ordinary consequences of the risk incidental to the nature of agency.

Example : *A* employs *B* as a bricklayer in building a house, and puts up the scaffolding himself. The scaffolding is unskilfully put up, and *B* is in consequence hurt. *A* must make compensation to *B*.

6. **Right of particular lien :** An agent it entitled to retain under his possession both movable and immovable property of the principal received by him until the amount due to him for commission, disbursements and services has been paid or accounted to him, provided the contract does not provide otherwise (*Sec. 221*). The property on which the agent claims his lien must have not been received by him by a wrongful act. No sooner the agent parts with the possession of the goods, his right of lien is lost. The right of lien can equally be claimed by a properly appointed sub-agent.

DUTIES OF AN AGENT

1. **To follow the instructions of his principal :** The agent must conduct the business of the principal according to the directions of the latter. In the absence of any such directions, he must follow the custom of the business prevailing in the locality where the agent is conducting such business. If the agent acts otherwise and the principal sustains a loss, the former must compensate the latter for it. He will also lose his remuneration (*Sec. 211*).

Examples : (*i*) *A*, as agent engaged in carrying on for *B* a business in which it is the custom to invest from time to time, at interest, the moneys which may be in hand, omits to make such investment. *A* must make good to *B* the interest usually obtained by such investment.

(*ii*) *B*, a broker, in whose business it is not the custom to sell on credit, sells goods of *A* on credit to *C*'s, whose credit at the time was very high. *C*, before payment, becomes insolvent. *B* must make good the loss to *A*.

2. **Duty to act with skill and diligence :** The agent must conduct the business of agency with as much skill as is generally possessed by persons engaged in a similar business unless the principal has notice of his want of skill.[28] An agent must act with reasonable diligence and to the best of his skill. An agent must compensate the principal for any loss directly attributable to the agent's neglect, want of skill or misconduct. But he is not responsible for indirect or remote losses caused by such neglect, want of skill or misconduct (*Sec. 212*).

Examples : (*i*) *A*, a merchant in Calcutta, has an agent *B* in London to whom a sum of money is paid on *A*'s account, with orders to remit. *B* retains the money for a considerable time. *A* in consequence of not receiving the money, becomes insolvent. *B* is liable for the money and interest from the day on

28. Keppel *v*. Wheeler (1927), 1 K.B. 577.

which it ought to have been paid, according to the usual rate, and for any further direct loss such as losses by variation of rate of exchange but nothing else.

(*ii*) *A*, an agent for the sale of goods, having authority to sell on credit, sells to *B* on credit, without making the proper and usual enquiries as to the solvency of *B*. *B* at the time of such sale is insolvent. *A* must make compensation to his principal in respect of any loss thereby sustained.

(*iii*) *A*, an insurance broker, employed by *B* to effect an insurance on a ship, omits to see that the usual clauses are inserted in the policy. The ship is afterwards lost. In consequence of omission of the clauses nothing can be recovered from the underwriters. *A* is bound to make good the loss to *B*.

(*iv*) *A*, a merchant in England, directs *B*, his agent at Bombay, who accepts the agency, to send him 100 bales of cotton by a certain ship. *B*, having it in his power to send the cotton, omits to do so. The ship arrived safely in England. Soon after her arrival the price of cotton rises. *B* is bound to make good to *A* the profit which he might have made by the 100 bales of cotton at the time the ship arrived but not any profit he might have made by the subsequent rise.

3. **Duty to render account :** An agent is bound to render proper accounts to his principal on demand. He must explain those accounts to the principal and produce the vouchers in support of the entries (*Sec. 213*).

4. **Duty to communicate with the principal :** In cases of difficulty, it is duty of the agent to use all reasonable diligence in communicating with the principal and in seeking to obtain his instructions (*Sec. 214*). It is only in an emergency where there is no time to communicate that he may act *bona fide* without consulting the principal. Principal can repudiate the act of the agent in cases where communication with him was possible and the agent did not ask for his instructions.

5. **Duty not to deal on his own account :** The relationship of principal and agent is of a fiduciary character. An agent, therefore, should not deal on his own account and should not do anything which may indicate a clash between his interest and duties. An agent can deal on his own account only with the consent of the principal which should be obtained after a full disclosure of all the material circumstances which have come to his knowledge on the subject. Principal has the right to repudiate those transactions where the agent has dishonestly concealed any material facts or the dealing of the agent have been disadvantageous to him (*Sec. 215*). An agent shall have to pay all the benefits to the principal, which may have resulted to him from his dealings on his own account in the business of the agency without the knowledge of the principal (*Sec. 216*).

Examples **:** (*i*) *A* directs *B* to sell *A*'s estate. *B* buys the estate for himself, in the name of *C*. *A*, on discovering that *B* has bought the estate for himself, may repudiate the sale, if he can show that *B* has dishonestly concealed any material fact, or that the sale has been disadvantageous to him.

(*ii*) *A* directs *B* to sell *A*'s estate. *B*, on looking over the estate before selling it, finds a mine on the estate which is unknown to *A*. *B* informs *A* that he wishes to buy the estate for himself, but conceals the discovery of the mine. *A* allows *B* to buy in ignorance of the existence of the mine. *A* on discovering that *B* knew of the mine at the time he bought the estate, may either repudiate or adopt the sale at his option.

(*iii*) *A* directs *B*, his agent, to buy a certain house for him. *B* tells *A* it cannot be bought, and buys the house for himself. *A* may, on discovering that *B* has bought the house, compel him to sell it to *A* at the price he gave for it.

6. **Duty not to delegate his authority :** An agent cannot delegate his authority to another person unless authorised or warranted by the usage of trade or nature of the agency. A work entrusted to the agent must be done by him.

7. **Duty to protect the interest of principal or his legal representative in the event of principal's unsoundness of mind or his death :** When an agency is terminated by the principal dying or becoming of unsound mind, the agent is bound to take on behalf of the representatives of his late principal, all reasonable steps for the protection and preservation of the interests entrusted to him (*Sec. 209*).

8. **Duty to pay sums received for principal :** The agent is bound to pay to his principal all sums received on his account after deducting for his own claim (*Sec. 218*).

Rights and Duties of Principal

The agent's duties are principal's rights and agent's rights are principal's duties.

TERMINATION OF AGENCY

Agency may be terminated by any of the following ways:

(*a*) **By act of the parties :** A contract of agency may come to an end either on account of the act of the principal or agent or both. Thus, agency may be terminated :

1. By agreement between principal and agent.
2. By revocation of agency by the principal.
3. By renunciation of business by the agent.

(*b*) **By operation of law :** In the following cases agency will terminate on account of operation of law :

1. By completion of the business of agency.
2. By efflux of time.
3. By death or insanity of principal or agent.
4. By the insolvency of the principal.
5. By the destruction of the subject matter of agency.
6. By the principal becoming an alien enemy.

By Acts of Parties

1. **By agreement between the principal and agent :** In some cases contract of agency itself may contain provisions as regards the termination of agency. They may be express or implied, which may be inferred from the circumstances of the case and the terms of the contract. Parties to a contract of agency may enter into a fresh agreement terminating or replacing the earlier contract.

2. **By revocation of agency by the principal :** Principal may either expressly or impliedly, after giving reasonable notice, revoke the authority of the agent before it has been exercised by the latter so as to bind the former (*Sec. 207*).

Example : *A* empowers *B* to let *A*'s house. Afterwards lets it himself. This is an implied revocation of *B*'s authority.

Principal shall have to pay compensation to the agent for any earlier revocation of his authority without sufficient cause than the period for which it was given to him.

Irrevocable agency : However, the principal will not be entitled to revoke the authority of the agent in the following circumstances :

(*i*) *Where the agency is coupled with interest :* An agency where the agent himself has an interest in the property which forms the subject matter of agency is said to be agency coupled with interest.

Sec. 202 of the Indian Contract Act provides :

"Where the agent has himself an interest in the property which forms the subject matter of agency, the agency cannot, in the absence of an express contract, be terminated to the prejudice of such interest." Thus, the law has made it very clear than an authority coupled with interest is irrevocable if the effect of such a revocation; would be to prejudice the interest of the agent in the subject matter of the agency or will cause any loss to the agent. Even the death or insanity of the principal will not terminate the authority of the agent in this case. However, an express agreement between the principal and an agent may provide for an exception to this general rule.

The following are the requisites to constitute agency coupled with interest :

(*i*) the interest of the agent in the subject matter of the contract of agency must be substantial, mere prospects of remuneration alone cannot be an interest within the meaning of this section, the interest of the agent must be over and above his remuneration as an agent;

(*ii*) the interest of agent must exist at the time of creation of agency; and

(*iii*) the primary object or giving power to the agent should be to secure an interest of the agent.

An interest of the agent in the subject matter may arise when the principal has entered into an agreement to give something to a person and has appointed the latter as agent to collect and secure it for himself. Another example may be where an agent has been authorised to recover a sum of money due from a third person to the principal and to pay himself out of the sum so recovered, the debts due to him from the principal.

Examples : (*i*) *A* gives authority to *C* to sell *A*'s land and to pay himself out of the proceeds the debt due to him from *A*. *A* cannot revoke this authority, nor can it be terminated by his insanity or death.

(*ii*) *A* consigned certain goods to *B* for sale. Subsequently *B* advanced some money to *A*. It was held that the subsequent advance could not convert the agency into one coupled with interest.[29]

(*ii*) *Where authority has been partly exercised by the agent :* If the authority has partly been exercised by the agent, the principal cannot revoke the authority of the agent so far as regards such acts and obligations as arise from acts already done in the agency (*Sec. 204*). The principal cannot revoke agent's authority in such a way as to damage the interests of innocent third parties *viz.* by breaking contracts the agent has already made with them.

Example : *A* asks *B*, his agent, to pay out of *A*'s funds a sum of ₹ 1,000 to *C* in two equal instalments. By a subsequent letter *A* revokes *B*'s authority. Before this revocation *B* had already paid a sum of ₹ 500 to *C*. *A* is bound by this payment.

(*iii*) *Where agent has incurred personal liability :* Where the agent has entered into contracts in his personal name for the principal and has thereby made himself personally liable, the principal cannot revoke agent's authority without his consent.

---

29. Smart *v.* Sanders (1848), 75 R.R. 849.

Examples : (*i*) *A* authorised *B* to buy 1,000 bales of cotton on account of *A* and to pay for it out of *A's* money remaining in *B's* hands. *B* buys 1,000 bales of cotton in his own name, so as to make himself personally liable for the price. *A* cannot revoke *B's* authority so far as regards payment for the cotton.

(*ii*) *A* authorises *B* to buy 1,000 bales of cotton on account of *A* and to pay for it out of *A's* money remaining in *B's* hands. *B* buys, 1,000 bales of cotton in *A's* name and so as not to render himself personally liable for the price. *A* can revoke *B's* authority to pay for the cotton.

3. **By renunciation of business by the agent :** Agent after giving reasonable notice to the principal may renounce the business of agency. In case the contract of agency is entered into for a fixed period, agent shall have to pay compensation to the principal for his earlier renunciation of the business of agency.

Reasonable notice : Reasonable notice must be given of revocation of agency by the principal or renunciation of agency by the agent, to each other as the case may be. In the absence of such a notice the principal or the agent, as the case may be, can be held liable for loss suffered by the other.

By Operation of Law

1. **By completion of the agency business :** When a person is employed as an agent for a particular work and that work is completed, the agency will come to an end.

2. **By efflux of time :** When a person is appointed agent for a fixed term, the contract of agency will terminate on the expiry of the fixed period. The quantity of work done is immaterial. Agent will have no right to represent his principal after the fixed period is over.

3. **By death or insanity of the agent or principal :**[30] The death or insanity of any of the two parties to the contract of agency will cause its termination. The death or insanity of the principal cannot operate to bring about an end to the contract of agency until it comes to the knowledge of the agent.

4. **By insolvency of the principal :** The contract of agency will come to an end when the principal becomes insolvent and the fact of his insolvency comes to the knowledge of the agent. As against third persons, the agency will terminate when the fact of the insolvency of the principal comes to their knowledge. Insolvency of an agent will not lead to the termination of the contract of agency.

5. **Destruction of the subject matter of the contract of agency :** The contract of agency will come to an end when the subject matter of the agency ceases to exist or when the principal is deprived of his powers on the subject matter of the contract of agency.

6. **Principal becoming an alien enemy :** Breaking out of war between two countries, in one of which resides the principal and in the other resides the agent, shall cause the termination of the authority of an agent.

When termination of agent's authority takes effect as to agent, and as to third persons : The termination of the authority of an agent does not, so far as regards the agent, takes effect before it becomes known to him, or so far as regards third parties, before it becomes known to them (*Sec. 208*). Where notice of revocation has not been given to third parties, they may still regard the former agent as having actual authority to enter into contracts on behalf of the former principal.

30. In case the principal or agent is a corporation or a firm, the agency will stand terminated on its dissolution.

Examples : *(i)* *A* directs *B* to sell goods for him, and agrees to give *B* five per cent commission on the price fetched by the goods. *A* afterwards by letter, revokes *B*'s authority. *B*, after the letter is sent, but before he receives it, sells the goods for 100 rupees. The sale is binding on *A*, and *B* is entitled to five rupees as his commission.

(ii) *A*, at Madras, by letter directs *B* to sell for him some cotton lying in a warehouse in Bombay, and afterwards by letter, revokes his authority to sell, and directs *B* to send the cotton to Madras. *B* after receiving the second letter, enters into a contract with *C*, who knows of the first letter but not of the second, for the sale to him of cotton. *C* pays *B* the money, with which *B* absconds. *C*'s payment is good as against *A*.

(iii) *A* directs *B*, his agent, to pay certain money to *C*. *A* dies, and *D* takes out probate to his will. *B*, after *A*'s death, but before hearing of it, pays the money to *C*. The payment is good as against *D*, the executor.

Agent's duty on termination of agency by principal's death or insanity : When an agency is terminated by the principal dying or becoming of unsound mind, the agent is bound to take, on behalf of the representatives of his late principal, all reasonable steps for the protection and preservation of the interests entrusted to him (*Sec. 209*).

Termination of sub-agent's authority : The termination of the authority of an agent causes the termination (subject to the rules herein contained regarding the termination of an agent's authority) of the authority of all sub-agents appointed by him (*Sec. 210*).

KEY TERMS

- ❑ **Agent :** A person employed to do an act for another or to represent another in dealing with third person.
- ❑ **Agency :** The relationship between the principal and the agent.
- ❑ **Sub-agent :** A person employed by and acting under the control of the original agent in the business of agency.
- ❑ **Substituted Agent :** An agent named by another agent to act on behalf of the principal.

TEST QUESTIONS

Objective Type : *Test Your Knowledge*

1. State whether each of the following statements is *True* or *False*

   (i) An agent need not necessarily by competent to contract.

   (ii) A contract of agency is not valid without consideration.

   (iii) Ratification tantamounts to prior authority.

   (iv) The authority of the substituted agent terminates with the expiry of the authority of the agent who appoint him.

   (v) In case the sub-agent is improperly appointed, the principal continues to be responsible to the third party for the acts of the sub-agent.

   (vi) Agency coupled with interest can be terminated any time by the principal.

   (ICWA Foundation, June, 2001)

   (vii) A person who is appointed by the agent is known as Sub-agent.

   (CS Foundation, Dec. 2012)

(*viii*) Agency cannot be created without consideration. (*CAIPC, Nov. 2013*)

[***Ans.*** (*i*) True; (*ii*) False; (*iii*) True; (*iv*) False; (*v*) False; (*vi*) False; (*vii*) True; (*viii*) False.]

2. Select the most appropriate answer

(*i*) A person employed by and acting under the control of the original agent in the business of agency is termed as :

(*a*) substituted agent (*b*) sub-agent,

(*c*) factor.

(*ii*) After appointment of a substituted agent, the agent appointing him :

(*a*) continues to be responsible to the principal (*b*) walks out of the transaction

(*c*) none of the above.

(*iii*) The principal can legally ratify only those unauthorised acts of his agent which were done by the agent on his behalf and on the date when the principal was :

(*a*) competent to contract (*b*) in existence

(*c*) in existence and competent to contract.

[***Ans.*** (*i*) (*b*), (*ii*) (*b*), (*iii*) (*c*)]

Essay Type : *For Review, Discussion and Practice*

1. (*a*) Describe the various ways by which an agency may be terminated.
(*CA Foundation, May 2000*)

(*b*) What is agency coupled with interest? Is such an agency revocable? If so, when?
(*ICWA Foundation, June 1998*)

2. (*a*) Discuss the extent to which an agent can delegate his authority. State the consequences where the agent properly employs a sub-agent and when he appoints him without authority.

(*b*) An agent having an authority to do an act has authority to do every lawful thing which is necessary in order to do such act.

3. Explain clearly the meaning of creation of agency by 'ratification'. What conditions must be fulfilled for a valid ratification? Explain the effects of a valid ratification.
(*ICWA Foundation, Dec. 1998*)

4. Discuss the rights of an agent against his principal.

5. What is meant by 'Agency by Estoppel' and 'Agency by Necessity'? Explain the provisions of the Indian Contract Act relevant to the above under the Contract of Agency.

6. Briefly state the circumstances under which an agent is held personally liable in a contract of agency. (*CA Foundation, Nov. 2000*)

7. State the rights and obligations of an agent.

8. When and how far an agent can delegate his duties. (*ICWA Foundation, June 2001*)

9. Can an agent delegate his authority? State how a sub-agent differs from a substituted agent.
(*ICWA Foundation, Dec. 1998*)

10. Distinguish between agent and co-agent (*ICWA Foundation, Dec. 1999*)

11. Discuss the different modes in which the authority of an agent may terminate.
(*B.Com. (Hons.); ICWA Foundation, Dec. 1999*)

12. Write a short note on Irrevocable Agency. (*CS Foundation, Dec. 1998; June 1999*)

13. Write a short note on Agency by Holding out. (*June 2007*)

14. Differentiate between Sub-agent and Substituted agent. (*CS Foundation, Dec. 1999*)

15. Write a short note on responsibilities of principal to third parties in a contract of agency.
(*CS Foundation, Dec. 2000*)

16. What do you understand by "Agency by Ratification"? What is the effect of ratification? Point out any four elements of a valid ratification. *(PEE II, November 2003)*
17. "A delegate cannot further delegate." Explain the statement and give the exceptions to the rule. *(CS Foundation, Dec. 2004; B.Com. (Hons.), Delhi 1991, 2003)*
18. State the circumstances when an agent is personally liable for the contracts entered into by him on behalf of his principal.
(ICAI, PEE II, May 2005; B.Com. (Hons.), Delhi, 1987, 1992, 1996, 1998, B.Com. (Pass), Delhi 2005)
19. Write a note on 'agency by ratification'.
(B.Com. (Hons.), Delhi, 1987, 1989, 1990, 1992, 1995, 1997, 2000, 2001, 2012; B.Com. (Pass), Delhi 2000)
20. When can an agency be not revoked?
21. Who is a sub-agent? When can an agent appoint a sub-agent?
(B.Com. (Hons.), Delhi, 1999, 2001, B.Com. (Pass), Delhi 2003)
22. "An agency can be terminated by operation of law." Comment. *(B.Com. (Hons.), Delhi, 2005)*
23. What is a Contract of Agency? What are its important characteristics? State the circumstances when an agent is personally liable to the third parties for the acts done during the course of agency. Give suitable examples. *(B.Com. (Hons.), Delhi 2005)*
24. "The relationship of principal and agent (*i.e.*, Agency) may be constituted by subsequent ratification by the principal". Examine the validity of the statement and state the requisites of a valid ratification in the light of the provisions of the Indian Contract Act, 1872. *(PEE, ICAI, Nov. 2006)*
25. Write short note on 'Irrevocable agency'. *(CS Foundation, June 2007)*
26. What is 'agency by ratification'? State the conditions of valid ratification.
(CS Foundation, Dec., 2011)
27. Sub-agent and substitued agent are interchangeable terms. Comment.
(B.Com. (Hons), Delhi 2011; 2013)

PRACTICAL PROBLEMS

1. *X* holds a lease from *Y* terminable on six months notice. *Z* an unauthorised person gives a notice of termination to *X*. Can this notice be ratified by *Y* so as to be binding on *X*? State reasons for your answer.

[***Ans.*** No. Refer agency by ratification.]

2. *X* owes *Y* ₹ 5,000. *Z* contracts to sell to *Y* goods belonging to *X* for ₹ 10,000 without disclosing that he was acting as an agent to *X*. *Y* comes to know later that *Z* has contracted as an agent. Can *Y* claim that his dues of ₹ 5,000 should be set off against the price? State giving reasons.

[***Ans.*** Yes. Refer contracts for an undisclosed principal.]

3. *X* is employed by *Y* to buy from *Z* certain goods of which *Z* is the apparent owner and *X* buys them accordingly. In the course of treaty for the sale *X* learns that goods really belonged to *F* but *Y* is ignorant of that fact. Is *Y* entitled to set off a debt owing to him from *Z* against the price of the goods? Give reasons for your answer.

[***Ans.*** No. Information obtained by agent in course of business is as good as obtained by the principal.]

4. *X* owes ₹ 1,000 to *Y*. *X* sells sugar worth ₹ 5,000 to *Y*. *X* is acting as an agent for *Z* in this transaction. But *Y* has no knowledge at all that such is the case. Just after the sale, *Z* gives a notice to *Y* that *X* was merely acting as an agent of *Z* and demands the entire sum of ₹ 5,000 from *Y* without allowing to set off the debt due to *Y*. Discuss the legal rights of *X*, *Y* and *Z*.

[*Ans.* Z can recover only ₹ 4,000. *Y* can set off ₹ 1,000. *X* will have to compensate *Z* to the extent of ₹ 1,000.]

5. *X* employs *Y* as an agent to assault *Z* and agrees to indemnify him (*Y*) against all consequences of the act. *Y* thereupon assaults *Z* and has to pay damages to *Z* for doing so. *Y* seeks indemnity from *X*. Decide whether *Y* is entitled to it.

[*Ans.* No. It is a criminal act. Refer Section 224.]

6. *X* holds a lease from two joint owners *Y* and *Z*. *Y* without *Z*'s authority gives notice to *X*. Can this notice be ratified by *Z* so as to bind *X*?

[*Ans.* No. Refer agency by ratification.]

7. An agent was appointed to introduce a customer to purchase the principal's property. The agent did introduce a customer, the sale was settled and the earnest money was paid to the principal. But the sale fell through because of the customer's failure to find money. Is the agent entitled to his agreed commission? State reasons.

[*Ans.* Yes. The agent had performed his part.]

8. *X* being *Y*'s agent for the sale of goods induces *Z* to buy them by a misrepresentation, which *X* was not authorised by *Y* to make. Can this contract be set aside at the option of *Z*. State reasons for your answer.

[*Ans.* Principal is bound by the misrepresentation made by the agent acting in the course of agency business. *Z* can, therefore, set aside the contract.]

9. *A* authorises *B* to buy 500 sheep from him. *B* buys 600 sheep for ₹ 12,000. Can *A* repudiate the whole transaction? What will be the right of *A* in case *B* buys 500 sheep and 100 goats for a lump sum of ₹ 12,000?

[*Ans.* U/s 228, in the first case *A* must accept the transaction to the extent of the purchase of 500 sheep. In the second case he can repudiate the whole.]

10. *A* consigns 300 cases of tea to *B*, who has advanced amount to him and desired *B* to sell tea and to repay himself out of the price, the amount of his own advance. *A* wants to revoke this authority. Decide.

[*Ans.* *A* cannot revoke the authority since the "agency is coupled with interest".]

11. *A* authorizes *B* to sell a camera for him, and agrees to give *B*, a commission of 10 per cent on the sale price. *A* afterwards, by a telegram, revokes *B*'s authority. *B* after the telegram is sent, but before he receives it, sells the camera to *C* for ₹ 10,000. *C* is also not aware of the revocation of authority by *A*. *A* later refuses to deliver the camera to *C* and pays commission to *B* for the sale, on the ground that the sale was not binding upon him. Decide.
   (*i*) Whether *A*'s contention is valid?
   (*ii*) Whether *B* is entitled to commission on the sale price?
   (*iii*) What are the provisions of the Indian Contract Act in this regard?

[*Ans.* *A*'s contention is not valid. *B* is entitled to his commission.]

12. *B* of Bombay sends his agent *D* to buy certain goods for him, on credit. Later, he pays for the goods, On another occasion *B* again sends *D* to buy goods but pays sufficient amount for the purpose. *D*, however, buys goods on credit. After sometime *D* runs away. Is *B* bound to pay for the goods? Decide giving the provisions of the Indian Contract Act in this regard.

[*Ans.* *B* is liable to pay the price of the goods.]

13. *S* entered into a contract with *T* for sale of horses to him subject to the conditions that *R*, *T*'s agent should certify that horses were sound. *S* secretly offered *R* to a certain sum (if the sale would be completed) by way of bribe. *R* having accepted the offer of *S* certified that the horses were sound. On coming to know of *R*'s duplicity *T* refused to affirm the contract. Is *S* entitled to enforce the contract against *R*. Decide giving reasons.

[*Ans.* *S* cannot enforce the contract against *T*.]

14. *A* purporting to act as an agent of *B* but without his authority accepted an offer by *C*, the defendant. *C* subsequently withdrew the offer, but *B* ratified the authority of *A*. Can *C* be held bound by the acceptance?

[***Ans.*** *C* is bound by the acceptance.]

15. *A* appoints *B*, a minor to sell his bicycle to anybody but not below the price of ₹ 200. *B* sold it to *C* for ₹ 150. Can *A* cancel the contract. *(ICWA Foundation, June 2000)*

[***Ans.*** *A* cannot cancel the contract since a minor can be appointed as an agent.]

16. Mr. Ahuja of Delhi engaged Mr. Singh as his agent to buy a house in West Extension area. Mr. Singh bought a house for ₹ 20 lakhs in the name of a nominee and then purchased it himself for ₹ 24 lakhs. He then sold the same house to Mr. Ahuja for ₹ 26 lakhs. Mr. Ahuja later comes to know the mischief of Mr. Singh and tries to recover the excess amount paid to Mr. Singh. Is he entitled to recover any amount from Mr. Singh? If so, how much? Explain. *(PEE II, November 2005)*

[**Ans.** According to Sections 215 & 216 of the Indian Contract Act, the agent without the knowledge of the principal cannot deal on his own account in the business of agency. Hence, in the instant case, Mr. Ahuja is entitled to recover ₹ 6 lakhs from Mr. Singh, the amount of profit earned by Mr. Singh out of the transaction.]

17. *A* instructed *B*, a mechanic, to buy a ship for him. *B* employed a ship-surveyor of good repute to choose a ship for *A*. The surveyor made the choice negligently and the ship turned out to be unseaworthy and is lost. Who is liable for the loss? Give full reasons for your answer.

(B.Com. (Hons.), Delhi 1999)

[***Ans.*** The surveyor himself is liable to *A*, the principal.]

18. Ashish consigns to Bashish 100 radio sets for sale and authorizes him to deduct ₹ 5,000 out of the proceeds which Bashish had sent as advance to Ashish. Ashish wishes to revoke Bashish's authority. Can he do so? Give reasons. *(B.Com. (Hons.), Delhi 2002)*

[***Ans.*** No, Ashish cannot revoke his authority nor can it be terminated by his insanity or death.]

19. *R* of New Delhi sends his agent M to purchase certain goods from Global Enterprise, Mumbai on credit for him. Later on *R* pays the amount for the goods purchased. On another occasion, he again sends *M* to purchase goods but this time pays sufficient cash to *M* for the purpose. *M*, however again purchases the goods from Global Enterprises but on credit and soon thereafter he dies. Global Enterprise files a suit against *R* for recovery of the said amount. Decide whether Global Enterprise would be given any relief by the Court under the provisions of the Indian Contract Act, 1872.

(PEE-II, ICAI, June 2009)

[***Ans.*** *R* has through an affrimative act, held out M as his agent to purchase goods for him on credit. Thus, based on principle of estoppel, Global Enterprises will succeed against R for recovery of the value of goods.]

20. Mr. *B* (a broker) by the orders of Mr. *A* purchases 10 Drums of oil for *A* from Mr. C, Afterwards Mr. *A* refuses to receive oil. Mr. *C* sues Mr. *B* who informs Mr. *A* but Mr. *A* repudiates the contract. Although Mr. B defends but failed. Mr. *B* has to pay cost, damages and incurs expense. Can B recover any amount from *A*. *(ICWAI Inter, June 2009)*

[***Ans.*** *A* is liable to *B* for such damages, costs and expenses.]

21. Suresh, an agent, has authority from his principal Bhupesh to sell goods on credit. Suresh sells goods on credit to Chandan without making proper enquiries about Chandan's financial status. At the time of sale, Chandan was insolvent. Is Suresh under liability to compensate his principle Bhupesh? Why? *(CS Foundation, June 2010)*

[***Ans.*** Subhash must compensate Bhupesh in respect of any loss thereby sustained. Since, he has not observed reasonable diligence.]

22. Mr. Roy consigns come fruits to his agent Mr. Paul at Mumbai with direction to send those fruits to Mr. Kar at Chembur. Mr. Paul sold fruits, which were spoiling at Mumbai below cost price without prior consent of Mr. Roy. Whether Mr. Paul's action was valid? *(ICWA Inter, Dec., 2010)*

[***Ans.*** Mr. Paul's action was justified.]

23. Mr. Bose directs Mr. Roy to sell wheat for which Mr. Bose agreed to pay 10% commission on the price fetched by the goods. Mr. Bose afterwords by a letter revoked Mr. Roy's Authority. But before receiving that revocation letter Mr. Roy sold wheat for ₹ 10,000 Mr. Bose refused to pay commission to Mr. Roy. Offer your views. *(ICWA Inter, June, 2011)*

[***Ans.*** Mr. Roy sold wheat before receiving the revocation letter, sale is binding to Mr. Bose and Mr. Roy is entitled to commission of ₹ 1,000.]

24. *K* is the wife of *A*. She purhased a saree on credit from *B*. *B* demanded the amount from *A*. *A* refused to make the payment, *B* filed a suit against *A* for the same amount. Decide in light of provisions of the Indian Contract Act, 1872 whether *B* would succeed. *(CA IPC, May, 2013)*

[***Ans.*** *'B'* will succeed. He can recover the said amount from *'A'* if saree purchased by *'K'* is a necessity for her.]

25. Sunil borrowed a sum of ₹ 3 lakh from Rajendra. Sunil appointed Rajendra as his agent to sell and authorized him to appropriate the amount of loan out of the sale proceeds. Afterwards, Sunil revoked the agency. Decide under the provisions of the Indian Contract Act, 1872 whether the revocation of the said agency by Sunil is lawful? *(CA IPC, May, 2014)*

[***Ans.*** Sunil cannot revoke the contract of agency with Rajendra as contract of agency is coupled with interest and it is irrevocable.]

SECTION 2

THE SALE OF GOODS ACT, 1930

Chapter 1

GENERAL PRINCIPLES

LEARNING OBJECTIVES

A careful study of this chapter will enable you to :

- understand the meaning of a contract of sale;
- differentiate between sale and agreement to sell;
- describe the term goods and its types; and
- explain the meaning of certain key terms.

The Sale of Goods Act came into force July 1,1930. It extends to the whole of India except the State of Jammu and Kashmir.

MEANING OF CONTRACT OF SALE

According to Section 4 of the Act, a contract of sale means "a contract where the seller transfers or agrees to transfer the property in goods to the buyer for price." Thus, a contract of sale may be of two types :

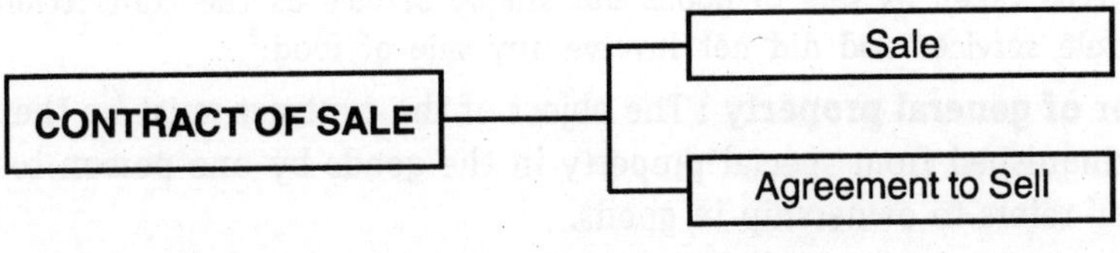

Sale : Where under a contract of sale the property in the goods is immediately transferred from the seller to the buyer, the contract is called a *'sale'*.

Example : On 15th March, *A* sells 10 bags of rice to *B* for a sum of ₹ 100. It is a sale since the ownership of 10 bags of rice has been transferred from *A* to *B*.

Agreement to sell : Where under a contract of sale, the transfer of property in goods is to take place at a future time or subject to the fulfilment of certain conditions, the contract is called an *agreement to sell.*

Example : On 15th March, *A* agrees with *B* that he will sell to *B*, his horse on 21st of March for a sum of ₹ 1,000. It is an agreement to sell, since *A* agrees to transfer the ownership of the horse to *B* in future.

An agreement to sell becomes a sale when the time elapses or the conditions are fulfilled subject to which the property in the goods will be transferred.

ESSENTIALS OF CONTRACT OF SALE

The essential characteristics of a contract of sale can be summarised as follows :

1. **Two Parties :** There must be two parties—a buyer and a seller—to constitute a contract of sale. The same person cannot be both a purchaser and a seller.

Example : *A* is the owner of certain goods but he does not know. *B* pretends to be the owner of those goods and sells them to *A*. There is no sale since there is nothing for *A* to buy.

However, the same person may work in both capacities, *i.e.*, buyer as well as the seller. For example in case of pledge, a pawnee may sell the goods pledged with him on non-payment of his money. In such a case the pawner himself may buy such goods. Actually speaking, here are also two different persons, the pawnee and the buyer. One the same basis, a partner can also buy the goods belonging to his principal. A part-owner can also sell his share to the other part-owner.

Example : *A* and *B* own 10 bags of cement jointly. *A* can sell to *B* his share in the bags so as to make *B* the owner of goods.

But when a club supplies meals, drinks etc., to its members against payment there is no sale. Members of a club are not part-owners but are undivided joint owners. Every member, as a matter of fact, is consuming his own property on the basis of understanding that he must restore to the club what he consumed. The club is not to make any profit out of him. The mode of payment is only a matter of internal arrangement regulated by the rules of club which were agreed to by each member on his admission.[1]

2. **Goods :** Contract of sale relates to goods, *i.e.*, movable property. Transactions involving purchase and sale of immovable property are out of the purview of the Sale of Goods Act. They are regulated by the Transfer of Property Act. Similarly, contracts for providing a certain service cannot be taken as a contract for the sale of goods.

Example : According to a contract between the hotelier and resident customers, the hotelier made a consolidated charge for residence, services and supply of food. No rebate was allowed if food was not taken. On a question being raised whether supply of food amounted to "sale", it was held that the supply of food could not be taken as sale of goods but simply service as the transaction was an indivisible contract of multiple services and did not involve any sale of food.[2]

3. **Transfer of general property :** The object of the contract must be the transfer of general property as distinguished from special property in the goods by one person to another. The term 'general property' refers to ownership in goods.

4. **Price :** Transfer of property must take place for some money consideration called 'price'. Where goods are exchanged for goods, it is not a contract of sale but simply a barter transaction. But in case the consideration consists partly of goods and partly of money, it will be taken as a contract of sale.[3]

DISTINCTION BETWEEN SALE AND AGREEMENT TO SELL

1. **Nature of contract :** Sale is an executed contract, whereas an agreement to sell is an executory contract.

1. Metford *v.* Edwards (1915), 1 K.B. 119.
2. Associated Hotels of India *v.* Excise and Taxation Officer, A.I.R. (1966), Punjab 249.
3. Aldridge *v.* Johnson (1857), 7 E. & B. 885.

2. **Transfer of ownership :** In a sale, property in the goods passes to the buyer immediately, while in an agreement to sell the property in the goods is agreed to be passed at some future time or on the fulfilment of some condition.

3. **General and particular property :** Sale implies contract plus conveyance of ownership in the goods. It gives to the buyer *jus in rem* (right against the whole world). He becomes the absolute owner of the goods and can use them in the way he likes. But an agreement to sell is a mere contract which secures to the buyer only *jus in personam* (right a against a particular individual). In case, a breach of contract is committed, the aggrieved party can sue the defaulting party only for damages.

4. **Seller's right of resale :** In a sale, since there is immediate transfer of the property in the goods to the buyer, the seller has no right to resell or deal in those goods even though the goods may be in his possession. When the seller is in possession of the goods after the sale and sells it to another, he will be 'guilty of conversion' and for this default the buyer may ask the seller to compensate him. In certain cases, *e.g.*, where the new buyer has not purchased the goods in good faith, the original buyer can recover the goods from the new buyer. In an agreement to sell, the property in the goods remains with the seller, who may deal with those goods in any way he may like though he will be running the risk of committing a breach of the agreement. Since the property in the goods does not pass to the buyer in an agreement to sell, goods can be disposed of by the seller. They can also be attached in execution of a decree against the seller.

5. **Right to recover price and damages :** (*i*) In a sale, buyer can be sued for the contracted price of the goods in case he refuses to pay the price though the goods may still be in the possession of the seller. But in an agreement to sell, buyer can be sued only for the loss caused to seller by his default.

(*ii*) In a sale, if the seller commits a breach of contract, the buyer may compel the seller to deliver him the goods or pay him damages on the basis of difference between the contract price and price prevailing in the market on the date of breach of contract. But in the case of breach of an agreement to sell, since the ownership in goods has not been transferred to the buyer, the buyer can only sue the seller for damages.

6. **Incidence of risk of loss :** In a sale, buyer is to bear, as a rule, the risk of subsequent loss of or damages to the goods not caused by the fault of the seller, even though the goods may be in possession of the seller. In an agreement to sell, the seller is to bear this risk.

7. **Insolvency of the buyer :** On the insolvency of the buyer in a sale, the Official Assignee of Receiver can claim delivery of goods from the seller, who will be entitled to a rateable dividend for the price of the goods out of the property of the buyer. In an agreement to sell, the seller can refuse to deliver the goods to the Receiver of the insolvent buyer unless he is paid for in full.

8. **Insolvency of the seller :** On the insolvency of the seller in a sale, buyer can compel the Receiver to deliver the goods to him. In an agreement to sell, the buyer cannot compel the Receiver to sell and deliver the goods to him. Moreover, if the buyer had made some advance to the seller in an agreement to sell he can only claim a reteable dividend on that account.

SALE DISTINGUISHED FROM OTHER CONTRACTS

Because of the essential characteristics discussed earlier, a contract of sale of goods differs in one or the other way from other types of contracts such as a contract of bailment, gift, barter, mortgage, hypothecation, contract of work and labour, hire purchase etc.

Sale and Bailment

In the case of a contract of bailment the ownership does not pass to the bailee. The goods are delivered for a specific purpose with the condition that the same goods shall be returned back to the bailor or otherwise disposed of according to his directions on the accomplishment of the purpose. Thus, in the case of bailment, only possession passes to the buyer, while in the case of sale it is the ownership which passes to the buyer, who can use the goods in any way he likes.

Sale and Gift

In the of sale, the ownership of goods is transferred to another person for a consideration termed as 'price', while in the case of gift, ownership passes without any consideration.

Sale, Barter and Exchange

In the case of sale, goods are exchanged for money; in a barter dealings, goods are exchanged for goods; and in the case of exchange transactions, money is exchanged for money. Thus, barter and exchange transactions are not contracts of sale. But, as stated before, where consideration for goods is received partly in the form of goods and partly in money, it will be taken as a contract of sale.

Sale, Mortgage and Hypothecation

In the case of sale, general property in goods is transferred to the buyer, while in the case of mortgage only special property in the goods is transferred by the mortgager to the mortgagee. Mortgager continues to be the owner of the property. Same is the case of pledge or hypothecation. Mortgage is done in respect of immovable property, while sale relates to movable property. Both pledge and hypothecation relate to movable properties, but in the case of pledge, possession of the property pledged is given to the creditor, while in the case of hypothecation the property hypothecated continues to be in the possession of the debtor.

Sale and Contract for Work and Labour

The difference between a contract of sale and a contract for work and labour is difficult to make. This is particularly so when the contract is a composite one involving both a contract of work and labour and a contract of sale. Nevertheless, the distinction between the two rests on a clear principle. A contract of sale is one whose main object is the transfer of property in, and the delivery of the possession of, a chattel (a movable item) as a chattel to the buyer. Where the principal object of the work undertaken by the payee of the price is not the transfer of chattel as a chattel, the contract is one for work and labour. The court would have to find out in each case the principal object of the transaction and the intention of the parties for determining whether a contract is a contract of sale or a contract for work and labour.[4] For example, contract for the supply of a mink coat has been held to be a sale[5] but making and affixing a cocktail cabinet has been held to be a contract for work and materials.[6]

4. State of Punjab *v.* Associated Hotels of India Ltd. (1972), S.C.C. 476-478.
5. Marcell Ltd. *v.* Tapper (1953).
6. Brooks Robinson Ltd. *v.* Rockfield (1951).

Example : (*i*) *A* promises to print and deliver to *B* 500 copies of manuscript, which *B* entrusted to *A*. For that job, paper and ink is supplied by *A*. Is this a contract of sale?

The present contract is not a contract for sale because though *A* uses his own paper and ink for printing books and delivers them to *B*, the substance of the contract is skill and experience of the printer and supply of materials is only subsidiary to work and labour of *A*.

(*ii*) *A* promise by a dentist to make a set of artificial teeth to fit in the mouth of a customer is a contract of sale of goods.[7] But an agreement by a painter to paint a portrait for the promisee on the condition that paint and canvas will be supplied by the latter is a contract of work and labour and not a contract of sale of goods.[8]

In a recent case *State of Gujarat v. Variety Body Buklders,*[9] the Supreme Court has very well differentiated between a contract of sale and a contract for work and labour. In this case M/s Variety Body Builders entered into three contracts with the Western Railway Administration for construction of railway coaches on under-frames supplied by the said Railway Administration. The Sale Tax Officer held the transactions as of sales of these coaches by the Variety Body Builders and levied sales tax on them accordingly. The case came before the Supreme Court which held that the contract was a contract for work and labour. It observed, "To constitute transaction of sale, there should be an agreement express or implied relating to the goods to be completed by passing of title in those goods. It is of the essence of this concept that both the agreement and sale should relate to the same subject matter. On the true interpretation of the expression 'sale of goods' there must be an agreement between the parties for the sale of very goods in which eventually property passes. In the instant case, It cannot be said that there is an agreement to supply a completed railway coach which when produced will be the property of the contractor. Along with those of contractors, materials and labour of them are also required to be put in for production of the completed railway coach."

Sale and Hire Purchase Agreement

A hire purchase agreement differs from a contract of sale. An ordinary hire purchase agreement is a contract of bailment. It differs from a contract of an outright sale since in hire purchase the ownership or property in the goods will pass on to the buyer when he pays off all the stipulated instalments. An a matter of fact, in the case of hire purchase contract, the seller gives an *option* to the purchaser to buy the goods. The goods are delivered to the buyer for his use at the time of making the contract. It is not a contract for sale since the hirer enjoys a right to terminate the agreement at his pleasure by stopping to pay further instalment of rent. Hirer may return the property hired at any time of his choice. Though the seller delivers the goods to the possession of the buyer, yet he retains with him ownership in them until he receives all the stipulated instalments of hire. Seller continues to enjoy two rights (*i*) to take back the goods on the failure of the purchaser to pay any of the instalment and (*ii*) to keep all the instalments paid by the buyer with him as hire charge for the use of the goods by the buyer.

A hire purchase agreement, therefore, is an *irrevocable offer* for sale, which will become a contract of sale on the fulfilment of the condition by the intending buyer, *i.e.*, payment of all the hire instalment. Unlike a seller, a hirer cannot exercise any ownership rights on the goods, *i.e.*, right to resell or pledge the goods till he has paid all the instalments of hire. However, he will continue to use the goods for his benefit till they are in his possession.

---

7. Robinson *v.* Greaves (1955), 1 K.B. 579.
8. Lee *v.* Griffin (1861), L.J.B. 252.
9. (1976) S.C. 2108.

The difference between a contract of sale and a hire-purchase contract can be put as follows :

1. **Transfer of ownership :** In a contract of sale the ownership of the goods is transferred to the buyer either immediately or on fulfilment of certain conditions.

In a hire-purchase contract the buyer becomes the owner of the goods only when he pays all the instalment.

2. **Buyer's status :** In a contract of sale the position of the buyer is that of the owner of the goods.

In a hire-purchase contract the buyer is only in the capacity of the bailee.

3. **Buyer's option :** The buyer has no option to put and end to the contract. He is, therefore, bound to pay the price.

The buyer has the option to set aside the contract. In case he decides to do so, he cannot be held liable to pay the price.

4. **Use of instalments payment :** In case the buyer has to pay the price in instalment, each instalment's payment will be taken as a part payment towards the price of the goods.

The instalments paid by the buyers will be taken as a part payment towards the price only when the buyer exercises his option to buy the article. In case, he decides otherwise, it be taken as hire for use of the article.

FORMATION OF CONTRACT OF SALE

A contract of sale is just like any other contract and, therefore, it must satisfy all the essentials of a valid contract as laid down in Section 10 of the Indian Contract Act. It may be verbal or in writing or partly in writing and partly oral. It is not necessary that price should be immediately paid or delivery of goods should be immediately made. In case the seller transfers of agrees to transfer the ownership in goods for a price it is a contract of sale, even though the payment of price and the delivery of goods might have been fixed for a later date.

GOODS

Definition : The subject matter of a contract of sale must be goods. According to *Section* 2(7) the term 'goods' means "every kind of movable property other than actionable claims and money and includes stock and shares, growing crops, and things attached to or forming part of the land which are agreed to be severed before sale or under the contract of sale."

Thus, every type of movable property comes within the definition of the term 'goods'. Goodwill, patents, trade marks, water, gas, electricity[10] etc. are also considered movable properties and are, therefore, treated as goods. Actionable claims and money have been excluded from the definition of the term goods. The actionable claim means a claim which can be recovered only by means of a suit or an action in the court of law, *e.g.*, debt. A debt is not goods. It cannot be sold though it can be assigned. Money currently in circulation is not included in the definition of goods but old and rare coins easily be treated as goods and can be the subject matter of a contract of sale.

10. The supply of the water electricity and gas is governed by special Acts, but they are goods within the meaning of the description given in the Sale of Goods Act.

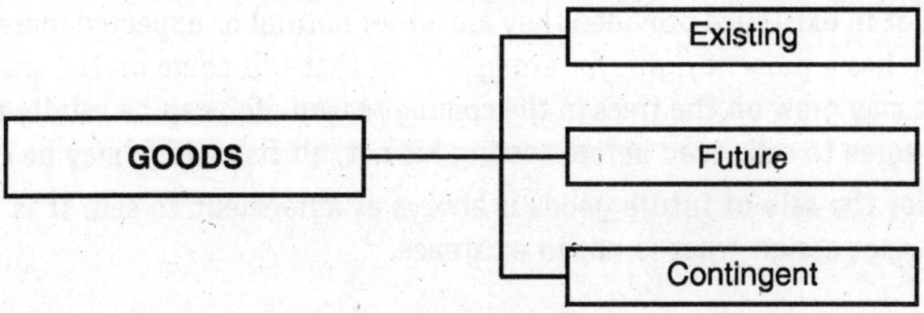

Types of goods : Goods may be of the following types :

1. **Existing goods :** Goods owned or possessed by the seller at the time of making of the contract of sale are called existing goods. In case of sale by an agent or pawnee, the goods are possessed but not owned by the seller (agent or pawnee). Existing goods may be classified as follows :

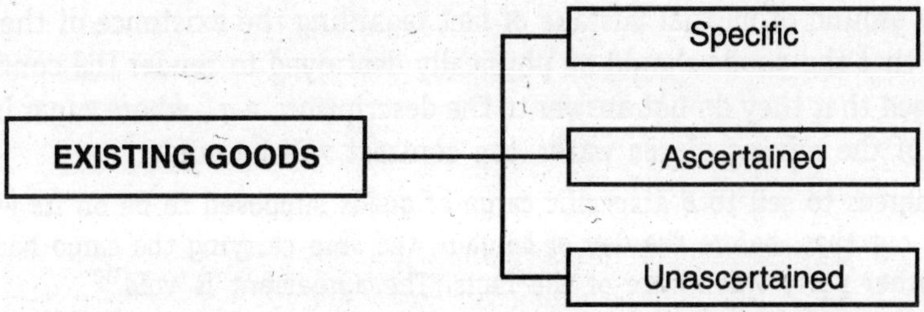

(*a*) *Specific goods* : Goods identified and agreed upon at the time of making of the contract of sale of goods.

(*b*) *Ascertained goods :* Goods identified subsequent to the formation of the contract of sale. The terms, ascertained and specific, are commonly used for the same kind of goods.

(*c*) *Unascertained or Generic goods* : Goods not identified or agreed upon at the time of making of the contract of sale. They are goods defined by description only.

Example : *X* has ten cows. He promises to sell one of them to *Y*, pointing it out to *Y* at the time of sale. Goods have been identified at the time of sale and, therefore, it is a contract of sale of 'specific goods'.

If in the above example, *X* only agrees to sell one of the cows, but does not specify which cow he will sell, it is a contract of sale of unascertained goods. The cow will become 'ascertained' when *X* makes up his mind as to which cow he will sell and *Y* gives his assent thereto.

2. **Future goods :** Goods to be manufactured, produced or acquired after the making of the contract are called future goods.

Example : *A* contract, on 1st January, to sell *B* 50 shares in Reliance Ltd., to be delivered and paid for on the 1st March of the same year. At the time of making of the contract, *A* is not in possession of any shares. The contract is a contract for the sale of future goods.

3. **Contingent goods :** Goods, the acquisition of which by the seller, depends upon an uncertain contingency are called 'contingent goods'. They are also a type of future goods.

Example : *A* agrees to sell 100 units of an article provided the ship which is bringing them, reaches the port safely. This is an agreement for the sale of *contingent goods*.

It is to be remembered that only those things which are owned by some one can be the subject matter of a contract of sale. Birds flying in the air, wild animals in a jungle, fish in a river are no one's property, and therefore, cannot be purchased and sold. *A* person may also agree to sell those goods which are not in existence provided they are either natural or expected increase of something to which the seller has a present right, *for example* wool that will come on the sheep in the coming winter, fruits that may grow on the trees in the coming season etc., can be validly agreed to be sold. *A* fisherman may agree to sell, even before casting his net, all fish which may be caught in his net.

A contract for the sale of future goods is always as agreement to sell. It is never actual sale because a man cannot assign what is not in existence.[11]

PERISHING OF GOODS

1. Perishing of goods before making of the contract *(Sec. 7)*

(*a*) Where specific goods are the subject matter of sale, the goods must be in existence at the time of making of the contract. If the goods perish at or before the time of the contract, the contract will be void on the ground of mutual mistake of fact regarding the existence of the subject matter. It is not necessary that the goods should be physically destroyed to render the contract void. If the goods are so damaged that they do not answer to the description, *e.g.*, where sugar is converted into syrup on account of the mixing of sea water, the contract will be void.

Example : *A* agrees to sell to *B* a specific cargo of goods supposed to be on its way from England to Bombay. It turns out that, before the day of bargain, the ship carrying the cargo had been cast ways and goods lost. Neither party was aware of the facts. The agreement is void.[12]

(*b*) In case only a part of the goods are destroyed or damaged the performance of the contract will depend upon the nature of the contract, whether it can be avoided or not. If the contract is divisible, the buyer will have to accept the goods which are in good conditions. If the contract is indivisible, destruction or damage of goods in part will render the whole contract void.

Example : *A* agreed to supply one wagon containing 700 bags of groundnuts to *B*. Only. 591 bags could be delivered because the rest 109 bags had been stolen. It was held that *B* was not bound to accept 591 bags.[13]

It is to be noted that *Section* 7 applies only to specific goods and not to unascertained goods, and therefore, in the case of destruction of unascertained goods, the contract will not be void.

Examples : (*i*) *A* agreed to sell 100 bales of Egyptian cotton, bearing a particular mark, to *B* and lying in his godown. Unknown to both the parties, the bales had already been destroyed on account of a fire in the godown. Held, the contract was for the sale of specific goods, and therefore, void.

(*ii*) *A* agreed to sell 20 bales of Egyptian cotton of *B*. On account of fire the cotton bales in the godown were completely destroyed. Held that the contract was not void because the sale was not of specific goods, but of a certain quantity of unascertained goods.

2. Goods perishing before sale but after agreement to sell *(Sec. 8)*

"Where there is an agreement to sell specific goods, and subsequently the good without any fault on the part of the seller or buyer perish or become so damaged as no longer to answer to their description in the agreement before the risk passes to the buyer, the agreement is thereby avoided."

Thus, according to *Section* 8, contract can be avoided on the ground of supervening impossibility of the performance of the contract, if it satisfies following conditions :

11. Moti Ram *v.* Khyali Ram, A.I.R. (1967), 484 (B).
12. Hastley *v.* Conturire (1853), 5 H.L. Cas. 673.
13. Barrow, Lane and Ballard Ltd. *v.* Philip Philips & Co. Ltd. (1927), K.B. 574, 582.

(1) the contract is an agreement to sell and not an actual sale,
(2) the loss is specific,
(3) the loss is not caused by the wrongful act or default of any party.
(4) the goods have perished before the risk passed to the buyer.

Example **:** (*i*) *A* delivered a horse to *B* upon trial for 8 days. It was agreed that if found suitable for intending buyer's purpose, the bargain then would become absolute. The horse died within 8 days without any fault of either party. Held, the contract was void and the seller must bear the loss.[14]

(*ii*) *X* had contracted to erect machinery on *Y*'s premises. The price was to be paid on completion. During the course of the work there was a fire, which completely destroyed the premises and machinery. It was held that both parties were excused from further performance. *X* was not entitled to any remuneration as the specific sum was payable on the completion of the entire work.

Section 8 also applies to the sale of ascertained goods. In the case of a contract of sale of unascertained goods, the destruction of even the whole quantity of such goods in the possession of the seller will not discharge him from his obligation.

The provisions of these sections can, however, be negatived or varied by an express agreement.

PRICE

Sec. 2(10) defines price "as money consideration for a sale of goods." Money means "legal tender money in circulation." Old and rare coins are not included in the definition of the term money.

Ascertainment of Price

1. The price in a contract of sale may be fixed by the contract or may be left to be fixed in a manner thereby agreed or may be determined by the course of dealings between the parties [*Sec. 9(1)*].

2. Where the price is not determined in accordance with the foregoing provisions, the buyer shall pay the seller a reasonable price. What is a reasonable price is a question of fact depending on the circumstances of each particular case [*Sec. 9(2)*].

3. Where there is an agreement to sell goods on the terms that the price is to be fixed by the valuation of a third party and such third party cannot or does not make such valuation, the agreement is thereby avoided [*Sec. 10(1)*].

Provided that, if the goods or any part thereof have been delivered to and appropriated by the buyer, he shall pay a reasonable price thereof.

4. Where such third party is prevented from making the valuation by the fault of the seller or buyer, the party not in fault may maintain a suit for damages against the party in fault [*Sec. 10(2)*].

Example **:** *A* agreed to sell ten casks of oil to *B* at a price to be fixed by *C*. In case *C* refuses to fix the price, the contract between *A* or *B* will be void. If however *C* is willing to fix up the price but is prevented either by *A* or *B* from doing so, the aggrieved party will be entitled to sue the defaulting party for damages.

14. Elphick *v.* Barense (1880), 5 C.P.D. 321.

SOME IMPORTANT LEGAL TERMS

Document of Title to Goods [*Sec. 2(4)*]

Documents, which in the ordinary course of trade, are regarded as proof of the ownership of the goods are called documents of title. They authorise the holder thereof to transfer or receive goods which are mentioned therein. These documents contain an undertaking on the part of the issuing authority to deliver the goods to the possessor of the documents unconditionally. Bill of lading, dock warrants, railway receipts warehouse keeper's certificate, wharfinger's certificate, multimodal transport document order for the delivery of goods etc., can easily be cited as a few examples of the documents of title. It is presumed that the holder of document of title shall have the right to claim possession of the goods from every other person. Since they are regarded as equivalent to possession of goods, they can be transferred just like goods. However, it is not necessary that these documents of title should be negotiable instruments.

Insolvent [*Sec. 2(8)*]

The meaning of the term 'insolvent' under The Sale of Goods Act is different from what has been given under the Insolvency Law. According of the Insolvency Law, a person is deemed to be insolvent if he has committed an act of insolvency and has been declared as an insolvent by a competent court. But according to The Sale of Goods Act a person is said to be insolvent if he has ceased to pay his debts in the ordinary course of business, or cannot pay his debts as they become due, whether he has committed an act of insolvency or not.

Mercantile Agent [*Sec. 2(9)*]

Mercantile agent means an agent who has, in the customary course of his business, authority to sell goods, to consign goods for purposes of sale or to buy goods or to raise money on the security of goods on behalf of his principal, *e.g.*, a broker of jewellery, who is given the jewellery by the owners for sale, is a mercantile agent.[15]

KEY TERMS

- **Contract of Sale :** A contract whether the seller transfers or agrees to transfer the property in goods to the buyer for a price.
- **Goods :** The term includes every type of moveable property other than actionable claim and money.
- **Actionable Claim :** A claim which can be recovered only by means of a suit or an action in a court of law.
- **Documents of Title :** Documents which in the ordinary course of trade are regarded as a proof of ownership of the goods.
- **Insolvent :** A person who has ceased to pay his debts in the ordinary course of business or who cannot pay his debts as they become due.
- **Mercantile Agent :** An agent who in the ordinary course of his business has authority to sell or otherwise dispose of the goods on behalf of his principal.

15. V. Sulaiman *v.* Ma Ywet A.I.R. (1934) Rang. 198.

TEST QUESTIONS

Objective Type : *Test Your Knowledge*

1. State whether each of the following statements is *True* or *False*

(*i*) In case of "sale" the property in goods is transferred to the buyer immediately.

(*ii*) The term goods include actionable claims.

(*iii*) A person would be deemed to be insolvent under the Sale of Goods Act if he commits an act of insolvency.

(*iv*) Contract of sale requires immediate fixation of price.

(*v*) In case of an agreement to sell, the ownership of goods passes to the buyer at a future date.

(*vi*) The Hire Purchase transaction is regulated by Sales of Goods Act.

(*ICWA Foundation, Dec. 2000*)

(*vii*) Property in the goods can pass from seller to the buyer even if the buyer has not paid the price. (*CS Foundation, Dec. 1998*)

(*viii*) A contract for the sale of future goods is always knows as an agreement to sell.

(*CS Foundation, June 1999, Dec. 2006*)

(*ix*) Old coins may be treated as goods. (*B.Com. (Hons), Delhi 2011; 2012*)

(*x*) Future goods can be the subject matter of a "sale". (*CS Foundation, Dec. 2007, Dec. 2008*)

(*xi*) In the case of an 'agreement to sell', ownership in the goods passes from seller to the buyer immediately.' (*CS Foundation, June 2008*)

(*xii*) A contract of sale of goods is a bilateral contract. (*CS Foundation, Dec. 2012*)

[***Ans.*** (*i*) True; (*ii*) False; (*iii*) False; (*iv*) False; (*v*) True; (*vi*) False; (*vii*) True; (*viii*) True; (*ix*) True; (*x*) False (It will be an "agreement to sell") (*xi*) False; (*xii*) True]

2. Select the most appropriate answer

(*i*) A transaction involving exchange of goods for goods is termed as :

(*a*) bailment (*b*) exchange (*c*) barter.

(*ii*) Goods identified and agreed upon at the time of the making of the sale are termed as :

(*a*) specific goods (*b*) ascertained goods (*c*) generic goods.

(*iii*) A contract of sale includes :

(*a*) sale only (*b*) an agreement to sell only

(*c*) both sale and agreement to sell.

(*iv*) There is a contract for sale of goods when :

(*a*) *A* agrees to give his horse to *B* on his giving a cow to *A*.

(*b*) *A* supplies artificial teeth to fit into the mouth of *B* for ₹ 500.

(*c*) *A* agrees to paint a picture on a canvas with the materials supplied by *B*.

(*d*) *A* agrees to construct a building with the materials to be supplied by *B*.

(*v*) The term 'goods' under the Sale of Goods Act, 1930 does not include :

(*a*) Harvested crops (*b*) Actionable claims

(*c*) Grass (*d*) Stocks and shares

(*Foundation, ICSI, June 2007*)

(*vi*) Which of the following is not a contract of sale under the Sale of Goods Act, 1930.

(*CS Foundation, Dec. 2008*)

(*a*) *A* partner agreed to buy goods from the firm.

(*b*) *X* agreed to sell his building for ₹ 10 lakh to *Y*

(c) M agreed to sell 20 kgs rice worth ₹ 1,000 on a future date.

(d) P agreed to sell 100 shares for ₹ 20,000 to R.

[**Ans.** (i) (c); (ii) (a); (iii) (c); (iv) (b); (v) (b); (vi) (b)]

Essay Type : *For Review, Discussion and Practice*

1. Distinguish 'sale' from an 'agreement to sell' under the Sale of Goods Act, 1930. *(CS Foundation, December 2005, Dec. 2007; B.Com. (Hons), Delhi 2010, 2012, 2013)*
2. Briefly discuss the essential characteristics of a contract of sale of goods. *(GGSIPU, BBA (H), June 2001)*
3. Distinguish between Sale and Hire Purchase Agreement with specific reference to ownership transfer. *(GGSIPU, BBA (H), May 2002)*
4. Distinguish between "Sale" and "Hire-purchase" Agreement. *(ICAI PII, Nov. 2003, May 2006; CS Foundation, Dec. 2008)*
5. Define a contract of sale of goods. Distinguish between a 'contract of sale' and an 'agreement to sell'. *(B.Com. (Pass), Delhi, 2002)*
6. Explain the term 'goods' as defined in the Sale of Goods Act, 1930. *(B.Com. (Hons.), Delhi, 2003)*
7. "Appropriation is a right primarily of the buyer and for his benefit." Comment. *(B.Com. (Hons.), Delhi, 2002)*
8. State briefly the essential element of a contract of sale under the Sale of Goods Act, 1930. Examine whether there should be an agreement between the parties in order to constitute a sale under the said Act. *(PEE II, November 2004)*
9. What is meant by 'specific goods'? State the rules regarding passing of property from a seller to a buyer in a contract for the sale of specific goods. *(CS Foundation, June 2005)*
10. Explain clearly the essential elements which must co-exist for constituting a valid sale of goods. In what respects does a 'sale' differ from an 'agreement to sell'?
11. Define 'Goods'. Distinguish between Specific, Ascertained, and Unascertained goods. *(B.Com. (Hons.) Delhi, 2011)*
12. State the rules regarding ascertainment of price in a contract of sale.
13. Distinguish between Sale Agreement and Hire Purchase Agreement. *(CS Foundation, June 2000)*
14. Write a note on 'Contingent goods'. *(CS Foundation, June 2008)*
15. What are the essentials of a contract of Sale? *(ICWA Inter, June 2011)*
16. Explain the term Contract of Sale of Goods. Will an exchange of cow with horse and ₹ 500 be covered under the Contract of Sale of Goods? *(B.Com. (Hons.), Delhi, 2011)*
17. How is the price fixed in a contract of sale? If price is not decided between the parties, what price the buyer has to pay? *(B.Com. (Hons.), Nov. 2012)*
18. Define the term 'Goods' and 'Price under the Sale of Goods Act.' *(B.Com. (Hons.), Nov. 2013)*

PRACTICAL PROBLEMS

1. State giving reasons, the nature of the transaction in each of the following cases :

   (a) *A* promises to make a set of false teeth for *B* with materials wholly found by *A* and *B* promises to pay for them when made.

   (b) A member of an ordinary club pays for provisions in the club's store and carries them away for his use at home.

   (c) *A* sells his motor car to *B* for ₹ 5,000 on the conditions that *B* will reconvey the car to *A* if within six months he repays the amount to *B* with interest @ 6%.

   [*Ans.* All are contract of sale since ownership in the goods has been transferred. In the last case the sale is conditional but it does not alter the nature of the contract.]

2. *X* agrees to sell two of his cars to *Y* at a price to be fixed by *Z*. He immediately gives delivery of the first car. *Z* refuses to fix the price. *X* asks for return of the car already delivered while *Y* claims the delivery of the second car too. Decide.

   [***Ans.*** *X* can not get the first back, he will get a reasonable price for it. However, he need not deliver the second car since the contract regarding it sale is now void.]

3. *X* agrees to sell *Y* fine sugar, out of 2,000 bags stock in his godown, for ₹ 12,000 @ ₹ 3,000 per bag. Before the delivery of sugar there is fire in the godown which completely destroys the stock. Can *Y* compel *X* to supply the sugar as per agreement?

   [***Ans.*** *X* cannot be compelled to supply the sugar since it was a contract for sale of specific goods which perished before transfer of title to the buyer without fault of either party.]

4. *G* commissioned *R*, an artist, to paint a portrait for *A* for ₹ 250. *R* supplied the canvas and other materials. State with reasons whether this is a contract for sale of goods.

   [***Ans.*** It is contract for service and not for sale of goods.]

5. *A* agreed to exchange with *B* 100 tins of baby food at ₹ 10 per tin, for 10 cows at ₹ 500 per cow and pay the difference in cash. State with reasons whether this is a contract for sale of goods?

   [***Ans.*** It is a contract for sale of goods since money values have been taken into consideration.]

6. *A* agrees to sell a flower-pot to *B* at a price to be fixed by *B*. Is it a valid contract? Give reasons.

   (CS Foundation, June, 1998)

   [***Ans.*** It is a valid contract.]

Chapter 2

CONDITIONS AND WARRANTIES

LEARNING OBJECTIVES

A careful study of this chapter will enable you to :

- understand the meaning of the terms conditions and warranties;
- differentiate between conditions and warranties;
- describe different implied conditions and warranties in a contract of sale;
- appreciate the importance of conditions and warranties in a contract of sale;
- explain the doctrine of Caveat Emptor; and
- explain the meaning of certain key terms.

MEANING OF CONDITIONS AND WARRANTIES

It is usual for the seller to make certain statements about the goods he is selling before a contract of sale is concluded. These statements or representations may or may not form part of the contract depending on this fact whether they amount to stipulations or mere expression of opinion. A representation made by the seller will be taken as a stipulation if he assumes to assert a fact of which the buyer is ignorant. However, if he merely states a judgment upon a matter of which he has no special knowledge and on which the buyer may also be expected to have an opinion, representation made by him will simply amount to an expression of an opinion. A stipulation is considered to be a part of the contract of sale and its breach provides remedy to the buyer against the seller. The nature of remedy depends on whether the stipulation is a condition or a warranty. While an expression of an opinion is not considered to be a part of the contract, and therefore, it creates no obligation on the seller.

Examples : (*i*) *A* wants to sell his horse. He says to *B*, an intending buyer, "The horse is a beauty and is worth ₹ 1,000". In this case *A* is simply commending his goods and his representation is a mere expression of an opinion. The buyer in such a case will not have any remedy against the seller if later on the representation proves to be incorrect.

(*ii*) If in the above case *A* says *B*, "the horse is a beauty and only yesterday he bought it for ₹ 1,000". Here in the later part of his statement the seller is making an assertion about which the buyer is ignorant. This amounts to a stipulation. The remedy of the buyer in case of the stipulation proving to be untrue will depend upon this fact whether it is a condition or a warranty.

The terms 'condition' and 'warranty' have been defined by the Sale of Goods Act as under :

Condition : 'A condition is a stipulation essential to the main purpose of the contract, the breach of which gives rise to a right to reject goods and treat the contract as repudiated' [*Sec. 12(2)*].

Warranty : "A warranty is stipulation collateral to the main purpose of the contract, the breach of which gives rise to claim for damages but not a right to reject goods and treat the contract as repudiated" [*Sec. 12(3)*].

"Whether a stipulation in a contract of sale is a condition or a warranty depends in each case on the construction of the contract. A stipulation may be a condition, though called a warranty in the contract" [*Sec. 12(4)*].

Examples : (*i*) *A* goes to *B*, a horse dealer, and says, "I want a horse which can run at a speed of 40 m.p.h." The horse dealer points out at a particular horse and says, "This will suit you." *A* buys the horse. Later on, *A* finds that horse can run only at the speed of 30 m.p.h.

There is a breach of condition because the stipulation made by the seller forms the, very basis of the contract.

(*ii*) *A* goes to *B* a horse dealer, and says, "I want a good horse." The horse dealer shows him a horse and says, "it can run at a speed of 60 m.p.h." *A* buys the horse. Later on, *A* finds that the horse can run at a speed of 30 m.p.h.

There is a breach of warranty because the stipulation made by the seller was only a collateral one.

Stipulations as to time : Unless a different intention appears from the terms of the contract, stipulations as to time of payment are not deemed to be of essence in a contract of sale. Whether any other stipulation as to time is of the essence of the contract or not depends on the terms of the contract (*Sec. 11*). But in mercantile contracts, time for delivery of goods is always taken as of essence unless otherwise agreed.

Examples : (*i*) There was a sale of goods C.I.F. Antwerp to be shipped in October. The buyer was to reject delivery even if there was any difference in the type or value or grade specified. The goods could not be shipped till November on account of strike at the port. It was held that the buyer could refuse to take delivery of the goods.[1]

(*ii*) There was a sale of some oak trees on the term that the trees might remain on the seller's land for four months and the buyer should pay for them within twelve weeks from the date, the contract was made. The buyer failed to pay the price on due date. Further time for payment was asked for, but it was not granted by the seller who treated the contract as at an end. The buyer then tendered the price which the seller refused to accept. The seller then sold away the oak trees to some other buyer. It was held that the first buyer was entitled to damages as there was a wrongful avoidance of the contract.[2]

DIFFERENCE BETWEEN CONDITION AND WARRANTY

The difference between a condition and a warranty can be summarised as follows :

1. **Nature :** Condition is essential to the main purpose of the contract. It is of a fundamental nature. The main purpose of the contract cannot be fulfilled without the prior fulfilment of this stipulation.

Warranty is only collateral to the main purpose of the contract. It is of a subsidiary of inferior character. Fulfilment of the main purpose of the contract does not depend upon the fulfilment of the warranty.

2. **Remedies for Breach :** Breach of condition gives right to the party not at fault either to repudiate the contract or to claim damages or to do both.

Breach of warranty entitles party not at fault only to claim damages. Right to rescind the contract is not available to such a party.

---

1. Aron and Co. *v.* Comptoir Wegmont (1921), 3 K.B. 435.
2. Martindale *v.* Smith (1841), 1 Q.B. 389.

3. **Condition as warranty and *vice versa* :** A breach of condition may be treated as a breach of warranty.

A breach of warranty cannot be treated as a breach of condition.

When a breach of condition is taken as a breach of warranty

In the following two cases a breach of condition will be taken as a breach of warranty :

1. **Voluntary waiver :** The buyer may, if he so desires, treat the breach of a condition by the seller as a breach of warranty and make him liable only for paying damages [*Sec. 13(1)*]. However, if the buyer prevents the possibility of the seller fulfilling the conditions he will be deemed to have waived it.[3]

It is to be noted that once the buyer decides to waive the condition, he cannot afterwards insist on its fulfilment.

2. **Compulsory treatment of a condition as a warranty :** Where a contract is not severable and the buyer has accepted the goods or part thereof, the breach of any condition to be fulfilled by the seller can only be treated as a breach of warranty, unless there is a contrary term in the contract, express or implied to that effect [*Sec. 13(2)*].

Examples : (*i*) *B* agrees to buy from *A* twenty five sacks of flour by sample, the flour is delivered to *B* who pays the price. *B*, upon examination, finds it not equal to sample but uses two sacks and sells one. He cannot now rescind the contract and recover the price. But he is entitled to get compensation from *A* for any loss caused by the breach of warranty.

(*ii*) *A* bought a bale of dhoties from *B* and resold it to *C*. *C* found the bale infested with white ants, and therefore, returned it to *A*. It was held that *A* must be deemed to have accepted goods, and therefore, he could not repudiate the contract but could claim only damages.[4]

EXPRESS AND IMPLIED CONDITIONS AND WARRANTIES

Conditions and warranties may be express or implied. Express conditions and warranties are those which have been expressly agreed upon by the parties at the time of the contract of sale.

Implied conditions and warranties are those which the law incorporates into the contract unless the parties stipulate to the contrary. They may be cancelled or varied by an express agreement or by the course of dealings or by usage and custom (*Sec. 62*).

But such exclusion by an express agreement or otherwise does not entitle a party to give up his fundamental obligation under the contract. For example, if a person agrees to deliver a car, he cannot escape his liability by delivering a pig even though parties might have agreed to exclude all conditions and warranties express or implied.

Implied conditions (*Secs. 14 to 17*)

The following are the implied conditions :

Each of the above conditions are discussed below in the following pages :

1. **Condition as to title :** Unless a different intention appears from the contract, there is an implied condition that the seller has a right to sell the goods in the case of a sale, and he will have a right to sell the goods in the case of an agreement to sell at the time when the property is to pass.

---

3. Mackey *v.* Dick (1881), 6 A.C. 251.
4. Mithan Lal Narain *v.* Suraj Prasad, M.I.R. (1932) Lah. 52.

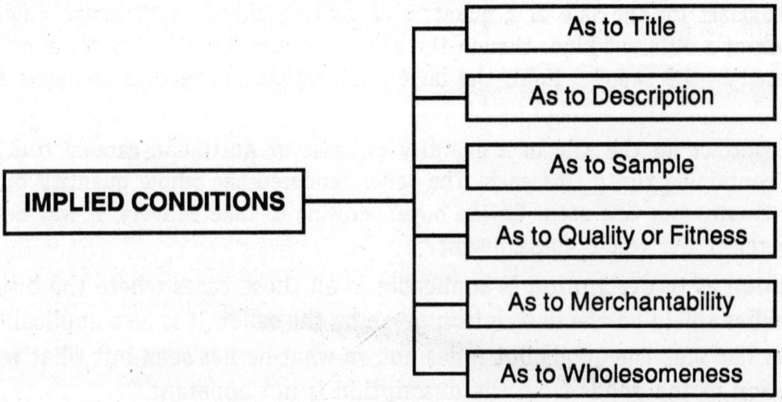

Buyer is entitled to repudiate the contract if he finds the title of the seller to the goods defective [*Sec. 14(a)*]. If the goods delivered can only be sold by infringing a trade mark, the seller shall be deemed to have broken the condition that he has a right to sell the goods.

Examples : (*i*) *R* bought a motor car from *D* and used it for four months. *D* had no title to the car. *R* was forced to return the car to the true owner. *R* can claim back the price paid to *D* notwithstanding the fact that he had used the car for four months because of the breach of implied condition as to title.[5]

(*ii*) *A* bought 3,000 tonnes of preserved milk from U.S.A. The tins were labelled in such a way as to infringe Neselle's trade mark. As a result they were detained by custom authorities. To get the clearance from the custom authorities, *A* had to remove the labels and had to sell the tins at a loss. Held, the seller had broken the condition that he had a right to sell because goods could be sold only by infringing the trade mark.[6]

It is to be noted that if a seller who had no title to the goods at the time of sale, subsequently acquires title to the goods, he will purify both the title of the original buyer and the sub-buyer.[7] Similarly, if the true owner leads the buyer to believe that the seller is either the owner of the goods or has the authority to sell the goods, the buyer purchasing the goods in good faith shall acquire a good title.[8]

2. **Condition as to description :** Where there is a contract of sale of goods by description there is an implied condition that the goods shall correspond with the description (*Sec. 15)*. The term 'correspond to description' means that the buyer must get the 'article' that was described in the contract. Thus, where a seller described a car as of 10 h.p. when it was of 8 h.p., it was held that there was a breach of condition.[9]

In *Bowes v. Shand,*[10] the learned judge observed : "if you contract to sell peas you cannot oblige a party to take beans. If the description of the article tendered is different in any respect, it is not the article bargained for and the other party is not bound to take it."

Example : (*i*) *A* wants to sell his typewriter. He says to *B*, intending buyer who has not seen the machine, that it is a brand new machine. *B* agrees to purchase it. On delivery *B* finds that the machine is old and repaired. *B* can repudiate the contract.[11]

5. Rowland *v.* Divall (1932), 2 K.B. 500.
6. Niblett *v.* Confectioners Materials Co. Ltd. (1921), 2 K.B. 387.
7. Butter Worth *v.* Kingsway Motors (1954), 1 W.L.R. 1286.
8. Eastern Distributors Ltd. *v.* Goldring (1957), 2 Q.B. 600.
9. M'loor *v.* Mickie (1953), S.L.J. 53.
10. (1877), 2 App. Cas. 455.
11. Varley *v.*Whipp (1900), 1 Q.B. 513.

(*ii*) In a contract for the sale of a quantity of seed described as "Common English Sainfoin" the seed supplied was of a different kind, though the difference was not discoverable except by sowing. The defect also existed in the sample. Held, the buyer was entitled to recover damages for the breach of condition.[12]

(*iii*) In a contract for the sale of a quantity of cases of Australian canned fruit, the goods were stated in cases containing thirty tins each. The seller tendered the whole quantity but nearly half the cases contained twenty-four tins each. On the buyer refusing to take delivery, it was held that the buyer was entitled to reject the whole consignment.[13]

The condition as to description is applicable in all those cases where the buyer has not seen the goods but relies solely on the description given by the seller. It is also applicable in those cases where the buyer has seen the goods but relies not on what he has seen but what was stated to him and the "deviation of the goods from the description is not apparent."

Example : *A* set of line napkins and table cloths, described as of seventeenth century, was sold at an auction sale to an antique dealer who had seen the set. Later on, it was found by the dealer that the set was of eighteenth century and, therefore, he wanted to reject the set. Held, he could do so since he relied on the description given by the auctioneer and the discrepancy between the actual quality and the description could not have been discovered by a casual examination.[14]

3. **Condition as to sample :** A contract of sale is a contract of sale by sample *when there is a term in the contract express or implied to that effect.* In the case of a contract for the sale of goods by sample, there is an implied condition:

(*a*) that the bulk of the goods shall correspond with the sample quality;

(*b*) that the buyer shall have reasonable opportunity of comparing the bulk with sample;

(*c*) that the goods shall be free from any defect, rendering them unmerchantable, which would not be apparent on reasonable examination of the sample (*Sec. 17*).

Example **:** Some mixed worsted coatings were sold by sample. It was found that owing to a latent defect, coats made out of it were not fit to stand ordinary wear. The same defect appeared in the sample but could not be detected on reasonable examination. Held, the buyer could reject the goods.[15]

In case goods have been sold by description as well as by sample, they must correspond to both.

Example : *A* seller undertakes to supply 100 tonnes of Java sugar warranted to be equal to the sample. The sugar when supplied, corresponds to the sample but is not Java sugar. The buyer can repudiate the contract.

It is to be noted that it does not follow merely because a sample is exhibited that the seller intends to sell by sample because he may by express warranty exclude its operation or may exhibit the specimen merely to enable the purchaser to form his own reasonable opinion.[16] Lord *Macanaughten* also observed, "The office of a sample is to present to the eye the real meaning and intention of the parties with regard to the subject matter of the contract which owing to the imperfection of language, it may be difficult or impossible to express in words." It is open for the seller to show the sample but decline to sell by it, and require the buyer to purchase at his own risk. Similarly, the buyer may not trust the sample and ask the seller to give a specific warranty to that effect.

12. Wallis etc. *v.* Pratt & Haynes (1911) A.C. 394.
13. Johnson *v.* Raylton, 7 Q.B.D. 438.
14. Nicholson and Venn *v.* Smith Marriott (1947), 177 L.T. 189.
15. James Drimmond and Sons *v.* E.H. Van Ingen and Co. (1887), 12 A.C. 284.
16. Gardiner *v.* Grav. 4 Camp. 143.

4. **Condition as to quality or fitness** *(Sec. 16)* **:** Normally in a contract of sale there is no implied condition as to quality or fitness of the article for any particular purpose. It is the duty of the buyer to see and satisfy himself whether the article will be suitable for the purpose for which he requires.

Following points in this connection are important to note :

1.(*a*) Where the goods are required for a particular purpose which the buyer makes known to the seller either expressly or impliedly, (*b*) the buyer relies on the seller's skill and judgment and (*c*) it is the seller's business to supply goods of that description (whether he is the manu-facturer or producer or not), there will be an implied condition that the goods must be reasonably fit for the purpose intended. The buyer cannot be said to rely on the seller's skill and judgment when he selects the article himself after inspection.

Example : An order was placed for six lorries to be used for ' heavy traffic in a hilly country.' Five lorries were supplied by the seller which were unfit for this purpose and broke down. It was held that there was a breach of condition as to fitness.

2. Where the article can be used for only one particular purpose, the buyer need not to tell the seller the purpose for which he requires the goods.

A 'particular purpose' is not some purpose necessarily distinct from a 'general purpose.' In the case of food items, eating is both a general as well as a particular purpose. Thus, even if the purpose is not expressly made known to the seller, it will be deemed to be known to him if it can be readily gathered from a description of the goods.

Example : *A* purchased a hot water bottle from *B*, a chemist. *A* was draper, who could not be expected to have special knowledge with regard to hot water bottles. While being used by *A*'s wife, the bottle burst and injured her. Held, the seller was responsible for damages.[17]

3. In case the article can be used for a number of purposes, the buyer should tell the seller the purpose for which he requires the goods if he wants to make the seller responsible.

Example : There was a sale by sample of indigo cloth to a tailor who required the cloth for the purpose of making it into liveries. The purpose was not made known to the seller. The cloth was unfit for that purpose owing to a latent defect but could be used for other purposes. Held, the buyer could not reject the contract.[18]

4. In case the goods are purchased under a patent or other trade name, there is no implied condition as to their fitness for any particular purpose.

Example : *A*, the owner of a brewery, placed an order with *B*, a manufacturer, to supply him his patent smoke consuming furnace for fitting up in his (*A*'s) brewery. The furnace was supplied but it was not fit for the buyer's purpose. Held, the purchase was of a defined and well known type of furnace and *B*, the seller, was not liable for its unsuitability for the buyer's purpose.

It is to be noted that the mere fact that an article sold is described in the contract by its trade does not necessarily make the sale, a sale under a trade name. For this it is necessary that the buyer should specify the article under its trade name in such a way as to indicate that he is satisfied, rightly or wrongly that it will answer his purpose, and that he is not relying on the skill or judgment of seller, however great skill or judgment may be.[19] If the buyer takes the goods because they are

17. Priest *v.* Last (1903), 2 K.B. 148.
18. Jones *v.* Padgett (1890), 24 Q.B.D. 650.
19. Badry *v.* Marshall (1925), 1 K.B. 260.

recommended by the seller as being suitable for the purpose intended, there is an implied condition of fitness for the purpose.

Examples **:** (*i*) A went to a car dealer and said that he wanted a car for touring purposes. The seller recommended 'Bugatti' car for the purpose. The buyer ordered for one. The car was found unfit for the purpose. Held, that the buyer can claim damages because condition as to fitness had been broken though the sale was under as trade mark.

(*ii*) In the above example if the buyer had told the seller that he had been recommended by some one Buggatti car for touring purposes and he would like to have one such car. The seller should not be liable if the car is found unfit for the purpose.

5. In case the seller supplies an article of the description in which he usually deals, under its patent or trade name, there is an implied condition that goods will be fit for the purpose for which it is generally used.

Example **:** *A*, a dealer in refrigerators, sells a 'Godrej' refrigerator to *B*. The name of the article itself implies that the seller warrants the machine to be fit for a particular purpose.[20]

6. An implied condition as to quality or fitness for a particular purpose may also be fixed or annexed by the usage of trade [*Sec. 16(6)*].

5. **Condition as to merchantability :** Where goods are brought by description from a seller who deals in goods of that description (whether he is the manufacturer or producer or not), there is an implied condition that the goods shall be of merchantable quality [*Sec. 16(2)*]. Even goods sold under a patent or trade mark must be of a merchantable quality.[21]

Merchantable quality implies that the goods should be of such quality and in such a condition that a reasonable man acting reasonably would accept the goods after a full examination under the same circumstances whether he buy for his own use or reselling.[22] In other words, goods should be such as are reasonably saleable under the description by which they are known in the market. However, this does not mean that there will be buyers ready to by the goods or that the goods will comply with the law of a foreign country in order to be saleable there. Goods will be unmerchantable if they have defect which will make them unfit for ordinary use or are such that a reasonable person knowing of their conditions would not buy them.[23]

Examples **:** (*i*) *A* agreed to sell *B* some motor horns. Goods were to be delivered by instalments. The first instalment was accepted but the second contained a substantial quantity of horns which were damaged owing to bad packing. Held, the buyer was entitled to reject the whole instalment, as the goods were not of a merchantable quality.[24]

(*ii*) A manufacturer of mineral waters sold F.O.B. in England a large quantity of 'Webb's Indian Tonic', among the ingredients of which was a certain percentage of salicylic acid, a fact of which the buyer was ignorant. The seller was aware that the purchase was for the purpose of shipment to Argentina, where, however, by a law of the country, the sale of any article of food containing salicylic acid was prohibited, a circumstance unknown to him. On the arrival of the goods in Argentine the authorities, finding that they contained salicylic acid, condemned them as unfit for human consumption. Held, there was no breach of implied condition as to merchantability.[25]

20. E.W. Ewans *v.* Stella Benjamin, 1951, Cal. 470.
21. Bristol Tramway etc. Co. Ltd. *v.* Fiat Motors, (1910), 2 K.B. 831.
22. Bristol Tramway etc. Co. Ltd. *v.* Fiat Motors Ltd., *ibid.*
23. Taylor *v.* Combined Buyers Ltd. (1924).
24. Jackson *v.* Rotex Motor and Cycle Co. (1910), 2 K.B. 937.
25. Summer Permain and Co. *v.* Webb and Co. (1922), 1 K.B. 55 C.A.

(*iii*) *M* asked for bottle of Stone's Ginger Wine at *F*'s shop, which was licensed for the sale of wine. While *M* was drawing the cork with due care the bottle broke and *M* was injured. Held, the bottle was unmerchantable, and *M* was entitled to recover damages.[26]

It is to be noted that there is no implied condition as regards those defects which could have been revealed if the buyer had examined the goods. But if the examination of the buyer does not reveal the defects and he approves and accepts the goods but when put to work the goods are found to be defective, there is breach of condition of merchantability.

Examples **:** (*i*) *X* wanted to purchase some glue. The glue was stored in the seller's warehouse in barrels. Every facility was given to *X* for its inspection. *X* did not have the barrels opened, but only looked at the outside of the barrels. The glue was found to have defects which would have been found out if *X* has inspected the contents of the cases. Held, there was no breach of any implied condition as to merchantability.[27]

(*ii*) *A*, a dealer in watches of a particular make, sells one watch to *B*, a layman with the usual guarantee of keeping the watch in running condition for a period of one year. The watch was found to be very unsatisfactory within one year. *B* wanted a new watch or its price. State on what basis such a claim can be made. Can *B* succeed?

The claim should be made on the basis of breach of an implied condition as to merchantability. Merchantability does not merely mean that a thing is saleable in the market because it apparently looks all right. An article may be considered to be unmerchantable if it has latent defects rendering it unfit for its only proper use. In the instant case *B* had an opportunity to examine that watch, but the defect was latent which could not have been found out by a buyer like *B*. Therefore, *B* must succeed.

The implied condition as to fitness for a particular purpose and merchantability must be construed reasonably, and a seller will not be liable when the unsuitability of the article arises from state of affairs relating to the buying of which the seller was not made aware, *e.g.*, when an article is sold to a customer who is allergic to it, there is a duty on the customer to disclose known peculiarity.[28]

Example **:** *G* a woman with abnormally sensitive skin bought a Haris tweed coat and got rashes through wearing it. She was not allowed to claim any compensation. There was no breach of condition as she had not disclosed the fact of her skin being abnormally sensitive.[29]

6. **Condition as to wholesomeness :** This condition applies in the case of provisions and foodstuffs. The provisions supplied must not only answer to description and be merchantable but also wholesome, pure unadulterated and suitable for consumption at the time of sale.

Examples **:** (*i*) *A* purchased tinned salmon from *B*, a grocer and provisions merchant. The salmon was poisonous and *A* and his wife, who ate, fell ill. While *A* recovered from his illness, his wife died from the effects of the poison. *A* claimed damages against *B* both for his illness and for the death of his wife, which deprived him of the services rendered by her. Held, *A* was entitled to get damages because the condition of wholesomeness was violated by the seller.[30]

(*ii*) *X* purchased milk from *Y*, a milk dealer. The milk contained typhoid germs. *X*'s wife, on taking the milk, got infection and died. Held, *X* was entitled to get damages.[31]

---

26. Morelli *v.* Fitch and Gibbons (1928), 2 K.B. 636.
27. Thornett and Fehr. *v.* Beers and Sons (1919), 1 K.B. 486.
28. Ingham *v.* Emem (1955), 2 Q.B. 306.
29. Graffiths *v.* Peter Conway Ltd. (1939), 1 All E.R. 685.
30. Jackson *v.* Watson and Sons (1909), 2 K.B. 193.
31. Forst *v.* Aylesbury Dairy Co. Ltd., (1905), 1 K.B. 608.

Implied Warranties : The implied warranties can be put as follows :

1. **Warranty of quiet enjoyment :** This warranty implies the buyer shall have and enjoy quiet possession of the goods [*Sec. 14(c)*].

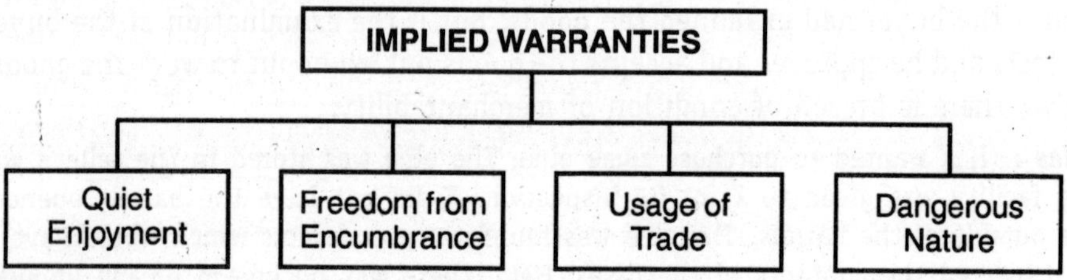

Example **:** *A* had given his bicycle on hire for a period of ten days to *B*. Soon after *A* sold it to *C* without disclosing to him that *B* was entitled to use bicycle on account of the hire agreement. *B* claims the bicycle from *C*. *C*'s possession is disturbed. He is entitled to get damages from *A*.

The breach of implied condition as to title may also result in breach of warranty as to quiet possession. The buyer, therefore, will be entitled to recover compensation for breach of both a condition as well as a warranty.

Example **:** *M* purchased a second-hand typewriter from *B*. *M* spent some money on its repairs but was dispossessed of it after six months by the true owner. It was held that *M* was entitled to recover from *B* not only price paid but also cost of repair.[32]

2. **Warranty of freedom from encumbrance :** This warranty implies that the goods shall be free from any charge or encumbrance in favour of a third party not declared or known to the buyer before or at the time when the contract was made [*Sec. 16(3)*]. Buyer shall have no right of action if the seller had disclosed the charge or encumbrance at the time of contract.

Example **:** *A* pledges his bicycle with *C* for a loan of ₹ 100 and promises him to give its possession the next day. Soon after he sells the bicycle to *B*, an innocent buyer, who does not know about the fact of bicycle being pledged. *B* may either ask *A* to clear the loan or may himself pay the money and then file a suit against *A* to recover this money with interest.

3. **By usage of trade :** An implied warranty or condition as to quality or fitness for a particular purpose may be annexed by the usage of trade [*Sec. 16(3)*].

Where drugs are sold by auction and where it is a usage of trade to disclose beforehand any sea-damage such disclosure must be made. In case no such disclosure has been made the goods are found to be defective, it will be taken as a breach of warranty.[33]

4. **Dangerous goods :** Where the goods are dangerous and the seller knows that the buyer is ignorant about the dangerous nature of the goods, the seller should warn the buyer about the probable danger otherwise, he will be liable for damages to the buyer for the injury caused to the buyer because of the dangerous quality of the goods.

Example **:** *A* sold a tin of disinfectant powder to *C*. *A* knew that the tin was to be opened with special care otherwise it might prove dangerous. He also knew that *C* was ignorant about it. He did not warm *C*.*C* opened the tin and his eyes were injured by the powder. Held, *A* was liable as he should have warned *C* of the probable danger.[34]

---

32. Mason *v.* Burnigham (1949), 2 K.B. 545.
33. Jones *v.* Bowden (1813), 4 Taunt 847.
34. Clarke *v.* Army and Navy Co-operative Society Ltd. (1903), 1 K.B. 155.

DOCTRINE OF "CAVEAT EMPTOR"

The maxim *Caveat Emptor* (let the buyer beware) means that the buyer must take care of his own interest while purchasing the goods. Buyer in a contract of sale of specific goods will purchase them at his own risk as regards the quality or fitness of the goods except in case of fraud or where a condition to that effect is laid down in the contract itself. Buyer cannot hold the seller liable if the goods turn out to be defective or do not suit his purpose or if the buyer makes a mistake in assessing the quality of the goods. If is for the buyer to ensure at the time of purchase that the goods conform to his requirements.

Section 16 of the Indian Sale of Goods Act has enunciated this principle in the following words : "Subject to the provisions of this Act and of any other law for the time being in force, there is no implied warranty or condition as to the quality or fitness for any particular purpose of goods supplied under contract of sale.........." When a person sells goods, he only warrants that they shall be fit for some purpose but he does not warrant that they will be fit for any particular purpose. The buyer, unless otherwise agreed upon, cannot reject the goods on the basis of latent defect unless they render the goods unmerchantable or the seller had deliberately concealed such defects.

Following are important *exceptions* to this general rule :

1. **Implied condition as to quality or fitness :** Where the buyer has made known to the seller the purpose for which he requires the goods and depends on the skill and judgment of the seller, there is an implied condition that the goods will be fit for the purpose for which the buyer requires them. This condition is not applicable in those cases where the goods have been sold under a patent mark or trade name.

2. **Sale of goods by description :** Where the goods are purchased by description from a seller, who deals in such class of goods, there will be an implied condition that the goods shall be of a merchantable quality.

3. **Usage of trade :** Proof of reasonable usage or custom of trade may also establish an implied condition as to quality or fitness of goods for a particular purpose.

4. **Consent by fraud :** The doctrine of *Caveat Emptor* shall not apply to all those purchases which have been made by a buyer under a contract where his consent was obtained by the seller by fraud *i.e.*, where the buyer relies on false representation of the seller and suffers damage. A seller, who is guilty of fraud, shall have no protection of the doctrine of *caveat emptor.*

KEY TERMS

- ❑ **Condition :** A stipulation essential to the main purpose of the contract.
- ❑ **Warranty :** A stipulation collateral to the main purpose of the contract.
- ❑ **Caveat Emptor :** It implies "let the buyer be aware."

TEST QUESTIONS

Objective Type : *Test Your Knowledge*

1. Fill in the blanks

(*i*) Condition may be expressed or..........in a contract of sale.

(*ii*) In case of breach of ....the buyer has a right to rescind the contract.

(*iii*) The condition as to wholesomeness is applicable in case of provisions and.............

(*iv*) The quality of goods of their being of the description by the which they are known in the market is termed as...........

(*v*) A breach of..............may be treated as a breach of ....

(*vi*) A condition will sink to the level of warranty where the buyer treats the breach of condition as a breach of.................

(CS Foundation, Dec. 2000)

(*vii*) A warranty is a stipulation which is .... to the main purpose of the contract.

(CS Foundation, Dec. 2012)

[***Ans.*** (*i*) implied; (*ii*) condition; (*iii*) food stuffs; (*iv*) merchantability; (*v*) condition, warranty; (*vi*) warranty; (*vii*) collateral.]

2. Select the most appropriate answer

(*i*) A stipulation essential to the main purpose of the contract is known as

(*a*) condition (*b*) warranty

(*c*) mere expression of opinion.

(*ii*) In a contract of sale of goods there is implied warranty and not implied condition that

(*a*) the bulk shall correspond with the sample in quality.

(*b*) the buyer shall have and enjoy quiet position of the goods.

(*c*) the goods shall correspond with the description as given in the contract.

(*d*) the seller has a right to sell the goods.

(*iii*) There is an implied condition in a contract of sale that

(*a*) goods would be fit for the purpose the buyer requires.

(*b*) the goods shall correspond the description given by the seller.

(*c*) the goods will be free from all encumbrances.

(*iv*) Caveat emptor means *(CS Foundation, Dec. 2008)*

(*a*) Let the seller beware (*b*) Let the buyer beware

(*c*) Let the govt. beware (d) None of the above

[***Ans.*** *(i) (a); (ii) (b); (iii) (b); and (iv) (b)*]

Essay Type : *For Review, Discussion and Practice*

1. Distinguish between a 'condition' and a 'warranty'. What conditions and warranties are implied in a contract of sale?

(C.A. Foundation, May 1998; May 2001; CS Foundation, Dec. 2012)

2. What is meant by 'sale by sample'? What are the condition implied is such a sale?
3. "In a contract for the sale of goods, there is no implied condition or warranty as to the quality of the goods or their fitness for any purpose." Comment.
4. Explain the doctrine of 'Caveat Emptor' with its exceptions.

(C.A Inter, Nov. 86, Nov. 98 and May 1991)

5. "If a person sells an article he thereby warrants that it is fit for some purpose, but he does not warrant that it is fit for any particular purpose." State the various qualifications subject to which this preposition should be received.
6. Distinguish between condition and warranty?

(ICWA Foundation, Dec. 1998; June 1999; CS Foundation, June 2007)

7. What are the rules regarding sale by sample. *(ICWA Foundation, Dec. 1998)*
8. Discuss the Rule of *Caveat Emptor* and state its exceptions.

(ICWA Foundation, Dec. 1999; CS Foundation, June 2000)

9. What do you understand by the terms condition and warranty. *(ICWA Foundation, Dec. 2000)*
10. Write short note on implied condition as to sample and description. *(CS Foundation, Dec. 1998)*
11. Distinguish between condition and warranty? *(CS Foundation, June 1999)*
12. Explain the implied condition in a contract for sale of goods by sample. Give one example. *(CS Foundation, June 1998)*
13. What are the implied conditions in a contract of 'Sale by Sample' under the Sale of Goods Act, 1930? State also the implied warranties operative under the said Act. *(PEE II, November 2003)*
14. When does a 'condition' become a 'warranty' and *vice versa*? *(CS Foundation, Dec. 2003)*
15. Point out the differences between conditions and warranties under the Sale of Goods Act, 1930. *(PEE II, May 2004)*
16. State the implied conditions 'as to title' and 'as to sample' in a contract of sale of goods. *(CS Foundation, June 2004)*
17. "........ there is no implied warranty or condition as to quality or fitness for any particular purpose of goods supplied under a contract of sale.........." Discuss the significance and state exceptions, if any. *(PEE II, May 2005)*
18. Differentiate between "Warranty" and "Guarantee". Explain and illustrate the "Warranties" in a contract of sale. *(GGSIPU, BBA (H), June 2001)*
19. Distinguish between 'Condition' and 'Warranty' in a contract of sale. *(GGSIPU, BBA (H), May 2002, B.Com. (Pass), 2nd Year, Delhi 2005 (Correspondence & External))*
20. When can a condition be treated as a warranty? What are the various implied conditions in a contract of sale? *(GGSIPU, BBA (H), May 2003)*
21. Distinguish between 'condition' and 'warranty'. State the circumstances under which a condition can be treated as a warranty. *(B.Com. (Pass), 2000, 2001, 2003; CA PEE, Nov. 2006)*
22. "The seller of goods is not bound to disclose defects in the goods that he intends to sell." Comment. *(B.Com. (Hons.), Delhi 1988, 1991)*
23. Distinguish between condition and warranty. Discuss the implied conditions and warranties in a contract of sale of goods. *(B.Com. (Hons.), Delhi 1995, 1998, 1999)*
24. When can 'condition' be treated as 'warranty'? Comment. *(B.Com. (Hons.), Delhi 1989, 1996, 2011, 2012)*
25. What is a 'sale by sample'? Explain the implied conditions inherent in a sale by sample. *(B.Com. (Hons.), Delhi 1991)*
26. "In a contract of sale of goods the buyer has always to bear the risk." Comment. *(B.Com. (Hons.), Delhi 1998)*
27. Distinguish between Sale by Sample and Sale by Description. *(B.Com. (Hons.), Delhi 2004)*
28. Explain the rule of *'Caveat emptor'*. Discuss the circumstances under which it is not applicable. *(B.Com. (Hons.), 1st Year, Delhi 2003, B.Com. (Pass), Delhi 2005)*
29. "A breach of condition cannot be treated as a breach of warranty." Comment. *(B.Com. (Hons.), Delhi 2005)*
30. Describe the various implied conditions and warranties in a contract of sale. *(B.Com. (Hons.), Delhi 2005)*
31. Write a short note on "Doctrine of Caveat Emptor". *(MBA, Dec. 2007, IPU; B.Com. (Hons), Delhi 2012)*

32. There is no implied condition as to fitness or quality of the goods sold? Critically examine this statement. *(B.Com. (Hons.), Delhi 2011)*
33. Distinguish between a condition and a warranty. When can a breach of condition be treated as a breach of warranty? *(B.Com. (Hons.), Delhi 2010)*

PRACTICAL PROBLEMS

1. Worsted cloth of quality equal to sample was sold to tailors who could not stitch in into coats owing to some defect in its texture. The buyers had examined the cloth before effecting the purchase. Are they entitled to damages?

   [***Ans.*** Yet, if the defect is a latent one.]
2. *F* bought milk form *A*. The milk contained typhoid germs. *F*'s wife took the milk and got infection as a result of which she died. What damages can *F* recover from *A*?

   [***Ans.*** Reasonable damages. See rules regarding damages.]
3. *A* bought a car from *B* who had no title to it. *A* used the car for several months. After that the true owner came forward and demanded the car. State the rights of *A* and the true owner of the car.

   [***Ans.*** *A* is bound to hand over the car to the true owner. He can sue *B* for breach of 'condition as to title'.]
4. A boiler was sold for manufacturing carbon paper and the seller knew that it was so required. But the boiler was not fit as required under the Indian Boilers' Act. State the rights and the liabilities of the buyer and the seller.

   [***Ans.*** The seller must know the requirements under the Indian Boilers' Act. The principle of Caveat Emptor is not applicable. Buyer can cancel the contract and recover compensation from the seller.]
5. *A* sold a new singer car to *B*. On delivery, *B* found that it was not a new car. What is the remedy of *B*?

   [***Ans.*** There is a breach of condition as to description. *B* may repudiate the contract.]
6. *H* sold to *G* certain quantity of 'foreign refined palm oil' warranted only equal to sample. The sample consisted of palm oil mixed with vegetable oil. The oil tendered corresponded with the sample but it was not such as is known in the market as 'foreign refined palm oil.' *G* wants to reject the goods on the ground that the oil supplied was not in accordance with the sample. Advise him giving reasons.

   [***Ans.*** *G* can reject the goods as they do not correspond to the description.]
7. *D* purchases a video-cassette-recorder (VCR) from a dealer of repute. *D* being a non-technical person does not know about the technical details of the *VCR*. On being put to use, the *VCR* was found to be defective from the very beginning and it did not work inspite of the repairs undertaken by the dealer. *D* wants to return the set and claim refund. Dealer refuses to take the set back and also refuses to accept the claim for refund. State the provisions of the Sale of Goods Act regarding the liability of the seller in this case. Is the action of the dealer justified? *(C.A. Inter, Nov. 1987)*

   [***Ans.*** The seller cannot refuse to take back the set. He will have to accept the claim for refund.]
8. Mrs. *K*, a housewife, purchased a tin of standard quality kerosene form *G*, a kerosene dealer of repute. When part of the kerosene was put to use in a stove for cooking by Mrs. *K*, an explosion occurred causing damages. Mrs. *K* claims damages form the dealer. The dealer refuses to pay for the damages. Decide giving the provisions of the Indian Sale of Goods Act in this regard.

   [***Ans.*** Mrs. *K* is entitled to claim damages from the dealer since the goods were not of merchantable quality.]

9. *A* sold a refrigerator to *B*. The refrigerator performs all other function but fails to make ice. Is it a valid sale. *(ICWA Foundation, June 1998; Dec. 2000)*

[***Ans.*** It is a breach of an implied condition as to fitness. Hence the buyer can repudiate the contract.]

10. *A* goes to *B*'s shop and purchases a silk saree thinking that it is made of banarasi-silk. The shopkeeper knows that *A*'s thinking is wrong. He, however, does not correct *A*'s impression. Later on, when *A* discovers that the saree is not made of banarasi-silk, He wants to avoid the contract. Would *A* succeed? Give reasons. *(CS Foundation, June 1999)*

[***Ans.*** *A* will not succeed. Let the buyer be aware.]

11. Aman borrows ₹ 200 from Bhuvan against the security of his wrist-watch. After a week's time, Aman obtains the watch from Bhuvan on some pretext and then sells the same watch to Chandan, an innocent buyer, who has no knowledge about Bhuvan's charge on the watch. Subsequently, Bhuvan disturbs Chandan's possession and gets payment of ₹ 200 from him. Now Chandan files a suit against Aman for recovery of ₹ 200 from him. Will Chandan succeed? Give reasons. *(CS Foundation, December 2004)*

[***Ans.*** Chandan can recover ₹ 200 from Aman since Aman had not disclosed any charge in favour of Bhuvan to him.]

12. For the purpose of making uniform for the employees, Bansi Bhaiya bought dark blue coloured cloth from Vivek, but did not disclose to the seller the purpose of said purchase. When uniforms were prepared and used by the employees, the cloth was found unfit. However, there was evidence that the cloth was fit for caps, boots and carriage lining. Advise Bansi Bhaiya whether he is entitled to have any remedy under the Sale of Goods Act, 1930. *(PEE II, May 2004)*

[***Ans.*** Bansi will not succeed since there is no implied condition of the article being fit for a particular purpose.]

13. Ram sells by auction a horse to Rahim without disclosing that the horse was unsound. Can Rahim cancel the contract? Answer with reasons. *(CS Foundation, June 2004)*

[***Ans.*** No. The principle of *Caveat Emptor* is applicable.]

14. *A* agreed to sell to *B* 20 kg of rice described as 'Dehradun Basmati' as per the sample shown. Although the rice supplied was in accordance with the sample but the sample itself was of 'Punjab Sela'. The buyer refuses to make payment. What remedies are available to the seller? *(B.Com. (Hons.), Delhi 1991)*

[***Ans.*** There is breach of an implied condition of 'Sale by sample as well as description' and the buyer has got right to set aside the contract.]

15. *B* purchased some glue. The glue was stored in barrels. Every facility was given to the buyer to examine the glue. However, the purchaser did not get the barrel open to examine them. He having looked the barrels from outside purchased the glue. *B* wants to avoid the contract on the ground of breach of implied condition. Advise giving full reasons for your answer. *(B.Com. (Hons.), Delhi 1999)*

[***Ans.*** There was no breach of any implied condition as to the merchantability and, therefore, *B* was not entitled to avoid the contract and also not entitled to any relief against the seller.]

16. *M* agreed to supply to *N* a certain quantity of timber of half-inch thickness. The timber actually supplied varied in thickness from one-third inch to five-eighth inch. The timber was merchantable and commercially fit for the purpose for which it was ordered. *N* rejected the timber. Is this action justified? *(B.Com. (Hons.), Delhi 2001)*

[***Ans.*** Yes, *N* can reject the goods.]

17. Mr. *A* purchased some glue. The glue was stored in barrels. Every facility was given to him to examine the glue. However, he did not get the barrels opened to examine them. He, having looked the barrel from outside, purchased the glue. He wants to avoid the contract on the ground of breach of implied condition. Advise him giving full reasons for your answer.

(*GGSIPU, BBA (H), May 2003*)

[***Ans.*** No, the principle of *Caveat Emptor* is applicable.]

18. *A* purchases a television from *B* on *B*'s plea that though it is old, it is in excellent condition. *A* finds later on that the television does not work at all. Can he reject the set and recover his money.

(*B.Com. (Hons.), Delhi 1987*)

[***Ans.*** Condition as to description has been broken. Hence, *A* can reject the set and recover his money.]

19. *A* asked a car dealer to suggest him a suitable car for touring purposes. The dealer suggested him to buy 'Buggati Car'. Accordingly, *A* purchased the car but found it unsuitable for touring purposes. Can *A* return the car the get back the price. (*B.Com. (Hons.), Delhi 1992*)

[***Ans.*** Condition as to fitness broken. Hence, *A* can return the car and get back the price.]

20. *A* contracts to sell *B*, by showing sample, certain quantity of rape-seed oil described as 'foreign refined rape-seed-oil'. The oil when delivered matches with the sample, but is not foreign refined rape-seed oil. Referring to the provisions of Sale of Goods Act, 1930 advise the remedy, if any, available to *B*. (*PEE, ICAI, Nov. 2006*)

[***Ans.*** *B* has a remedy to repudiate the contract.]

21. Roshan purchases a desktop computer from Harish on Harish's plea that though the said computer is used, it is an excellent condition. Later on, Roshan finds that the computer does not work at all. Can he reject the purchase of the said computer and recovery his money? Give reasons.

(*CS Foundation, Dec. 2006*)

[***Ans.*** Roshan can reject the computer and recover his money from Harish.]

22. Mr. Amit was shopping in a self-service Super Market. He picked up a bottle of cold drink from a shelf. While he was examining the bottle, it exploded in his hand and injured him. He files a suit for damages against the owner of the market on the ground of breach of condition. Decide, under the Sale of Goods Acts, 1930, whether Mr. Amit would succeed in his claim?

(*PEE-II, ICAI, May 2008*)

[***Ans.*** Mr. Amit would succeed in claim for damage from the owner of the shop.]

23. Raman purchases a pastry from Standar Pastry Shop. It contained a piece of stone which broke one of Raman's teeth. What remedy has Raman against the shop-keeper? Give reasons.

(*CS Foundation, Dec., 2010*)

[***Ans.*** Raman can file a suit against Standard Pastry Shop for damages. There is breach of implied condition as to wholesomeness on the part of the seller.]

24. *L* sold to *S* wheat by sample. The wheat was contained in 2 parcels and *S* was given the opportunity of comparing the bulk of only one parcel with the sample. *S* refuses to accept the delivery of the goods. Can he be held liable for breach of contract?

(*B.Com. (Hons), Delhi 2011*)

[***Ans.*** No, *S* cannot be held liable for breach of contract. In this case, S was given opportunity of comparing only one parcel of wheat with the sample and not the other. This amounted to breach of an implied condition.]

25. Ashok sold wheat to Babu by showing a sample, the wheat was contained in two parcels. Babu was given opportunity to inspect the bulk of one parcel only with the sample, Babu refused to accept the delivery of the goods. Can Babu be held liable for breach of contract? Explain.

(*B.Com. (Hons), Delhi, Nov. 2012*)

[*Ans.* No, Babu cannot be held liable for breach of contract. Babu was given the opportunity to inspect the bulk of one parcel only, so he can refuse to accept the goods and rescind the contract.)

26. *X* purchased a hot water bottle from a chemist. The bottle burst, when the hot water was poured into it and injured his wife. What are the rights of *X* against the chemist? Explain briefly.

(*B.Com. (Hons), Delhi, Nov. 2013*)

[*Ans.* *X* can claim damages for the injury. There is a breach of condition as to fitness. The buyer's purpose was clear from the nature of the bottle and thus the chemist must reimburse *X*.]

Chapter 3
TRANSFER OF OWNERSHIP

LEARNING OBJECTIVES

A careful study of this chapter will enable you to :

- appreciate the importance of transfer of ownership;
- enumerate the rules regarding transfer of ownership;
- identify the circumstances of valid transfer of title by non-owners; and
- explain the meaning of certain key terms.

IMPORTANCE OF TRANSFER OF OWNERSHIP

A contract of sale of goods involves transfer of ownership from seller to the buyer. Transfer of ownership or property in goods is in fact the main object of making a contract of sale. It is important to know the precise moment of time at which property in goods passes from the seller to the buyer because of the following reasons :

1. **Risk *prima facie* passes with ownership :** In case of destruction of or damage to the goods, it is the owner who has to bear the loss because the general rule is *'res perit domino' risk follows ownership* or whosoever is the owner must bear the loss. The payment of price or possession of goods is immaterial.

***Examples* :** (*i*) *A* buys goods from *B*. The goods remain in *B*'s warehouse. Before delivery of goods to *A*, there is a fire in *B*'s warehouse and all the goods are destroyed. *A* must pay the price of goods, to *B*, if he has not paid it so far.

(*ii*) *A* agrees to purchase *B*'s car for ₹ 10,000. The ownership from *A* to *B* is to pass on 15th January, 2002, while the price is paid in advance on 10th January, 2002. On 11th January, 2002 the car is damaged in an accident. *B* will have to bear the loss.

The above rule is applicable in the absence of any contract or custom of trade to the contrary, *e.g.*, in case of fur trade even if the goods are purchased on approval, they are at the risk of the intending purchaser.

2. **Action against third parties :** In case the goods have been damaged by a third party, it is only the owner who can take action against him.

3. **Insolvency of the seller or the buyer :** In the event of the insolvency of the seller or the buyer, in order to decide whether official receiver or assignee can take over the goods or not, it is important to determine whether the ownership in goods is with the buyer or the seller. This has been already explained in details while discussing the difference between an actual sale and an agreement to sell.

RULES REGARDING TRANSFER OF OWNERSHIP

In a contract of sale of goods, property or ownership in the goods will pass from seller to the buyer when the parties intend to pass it. Parties are free to make any arrangement as to the passing of the property. It is only when the intentions of the parties are not known that the provisions laid down in *Sections* 18 to 25 of the Sale of Goods Act shall be a applicable. These rules can be classified as under :

Passing of property or ownership in case of specific or ascertained goods

In the case of ascertained goods, the property in them is transferred at such time as the parties intend it to be transferred. The intentions of the parties can be ascertained from the terms of the contract, the conduct of the parties and the circumstances of the case (*Sec. 19*). In order to decide the intention of the parties, the following rules are applicable :

1. **When goods are in a deliverable state :** In an unconditional contract of sale of specific goods, which are in deliverable state, property in the goods will pass from the seller to the buyer as soon as the contract is made and the sale is effected, unless a contrary intention appears from the dealings of the two parties. Time for the payment of the price or delivery of the goods shall be immaterial (*Sec. 20*).

Goods are said to be in a deliverable state when they are in such a state that the buyer would, under the contract, be bound to take delivery of them [*Sec. 2(3)*].

Examples : *(i) B* offers *A* for his horse a sum of ₹ 1,000. The horse is to be delivered to *B* on a fixed day and the price is to be paid on another fixed day. *A* accepts the offer. The horse becomes *B's* property as soon as the offer is accepted.

(ii) A sold haystack lying on his land to *B* on 4th January. According to the terms of the agreement the price was to be paid after a month and the haystack was to remain on *A's* land till May and that no hay was to be cut till the price was paid. On the burning of the hystack by fire before the payment of the price was made, the purchaser, *B*, was held liable for the loss because the property in the haystack had already passed to him on the day he had entered into the contract.[1]

(iii) A offered *B* to sell his machinery to him for a fixed price. *B* agreed to buy subject to the condition that *A* should get it repaired in order to put it into running condition. *A* replied that *B* might himself get the machinery repaired and pay him the agreed price less the actual cost of repairs. While being repaired the machine was destroyed without any fault of the mechanic. It was held that A must bear the since the contract of sale was conditional and the ownership of the machine has not passed to *B*.[2]

2. **When the seller has to do something :** Where there is a contract for the sale of specific goods and the seller is bound to do something for putting the goods in a deliverable state, the property will pass when such thing is done and the buyer has notice thereof (*Sec. 21*).

Examples : (*i*) X contracted to purchase timber from oak trees which belonged to *Y*. *X* marked out the selected part of the trees. *Y* had to remove the rejected portions from the trees according to the custom of the trade. But before this could be done, *Y* became bankrupt. Held, *X* could not take away the selected portions because the property in the goods could pass to him only when the goods were put in a deliverable state.[3]

---

1. Clarke *v.* Army and Navy Co-operative Society Ltd. (1903), 1 K.B. 155.
2. Appleby *v.* Myers (1867), L.R. 2 C.P. 651
3. Acraman *v.* Morrice (1849), 137 E.R. 584.

(*ii*) The entire quantity of oil in a cistern was sold. Under the contract the seller was required to full the oil in barrels and then the buyer was to take them away. Some of the barrels were filled in the presence of the buyer but before the remainder could be filled, a fire broke out and the entire quantity of oil was destroyed. Held the buyer must bear the loss of the remainder.[4]

3. **When goods are to be measured etc. :** When there is a contract for the sale of specific goods in a deliverable state, but something has to be done by the seller to ascertain the price, *e.g.*, weighing, measuring or testing the goods, the property in the goods will pass from the seller to the buyer when that thing is done and the buyer has notice of it (*Sec. 22*).

If nothing remains to be done to the goods by the seller for the purpose of ascertaining the price, the title shall pass on to the buyer though they have not been weighed by the buyer.[5]

Examples : (*i*) A contract of sale was made to sell a heap of bark at an agreed price per tonne. The bark was to be weighed by the agents of the seller and also of the buyer. A part of the bark was weighed and taken away by the buyer's agents and servants, but before the remaining could be weighed and carried away, a flood swept away the remaining bark. It was held that the loss of remainder should fall on the seller, because the property in the remainder has not passed as the required weighing for ascertainment of price was not done.[6]

(*ii*) A heap of clay was sold as a whole, at an agreed price per tonne. The buyer was to load the clay on his own carts and take it away. Each load was to be weighed at a machine which the carts had to pass while going on the seller's grounds. It was held that since the sale was of a heap of clay as a whole, it was an unconditional contract for sale of specific goods. The ownership passed on to the buyer as soon as the contract was made. The clay was to be weighed only for the satisfaction of the buyer and not a necessary condition for the transfer of property or ascertainment of price.[7]

4. **When goods are sold on approval :** When the goods are delivered to the buyer on 'approval' or on 'sale or return' basis, the property in the goods will pass from seller to the buyer, when any of the following conditions are satisfied :

(*a*) the buyer accepts the goods, or

(*b*) the buyer does something which is similar to his act of accepting the goods, *e.g.*, pledges the goods or sells away the goods, or

(*c*) the buyer retains the goods without giving notice of rejection beyond the period fixed or reasonable period if no time is fixed (*Sec. 24*).

Examples : (*i*) *A* sends *B* a gas meter on approval or return in March, 2000. *B* returns the gas meter after a trial in December, 2000. The meter has not been returned within a reasonable time, and therefore, *A* is not bound to accept it and he can sue *B* for the price.

(*ii*) Jewellery was sent by *A* to *B* 'on sale or return.' *B* pledged the jewellery with *C*. *A* can recover the price of jewellery from *B*.[8]

(*iii*) *G* sold certain diamonds to *W* on 'sale or return basis.' *W* sold them to *X* and *X* sold them to *Y* on the same terms, *i.e.*, 'sale or return basis'. The diamonds were lost while in possession of *Y*. Held, W was responsible to *G* for payment of price as by reselling them he has deprived himself of the right to return goods.[9]

---

4. Rugg *v.* Minett (1809), 11 East 210.
5. Turiey *v.* Bates (1863), 2 H. and C.200.
6. Zagury *v.* Furnell (1809), Camp. 240.
7. Turley *v.* Bates *op. cit.*
8. Kirkham *v.* Attenborough (1807), 1 Q.B. 201.
9. Genn *v.* Winkel (1911), 28 T.L.R. 438

A contract of sale on the basis of *'sale or, return'* differs from a contract of *'sale for cash only or return'.* In the latter case, the ownership of the goods will pass to the buyer only when the price is paid.

Example : *A* delivered to *B* a necklace on sale or return basis. It was agreed that the ownership was to pass only on payment of cash by *B* on a particular date. *B* pledged the necklace with *C* before that date. In an action by *A* to recover the necklace from *C* it was held that the property in the necklace has not passed to *B* when he had pledged with *C*, and therefore, *A* could succeed.[10]

Passing of property on case of unascertained goods

No property can pass from the seller to the buyer in the case of unascertained goods until the goods are ascertained. In the case of a contract for the sale of unascertained or future goods by description, property will pass from the seller to the buyer when goods of the same description, in a deliverable state, are unconditionally appropriated to the contract by one party with the consent of the other.[11]

Appropriation of goods

Appropriation means separating the goods sold from other goods so as to determine and identify the actual goods to be delivered.

Appropriation should be unconditional. It can be done either

(*i*) by the seller with the buyer's consent, or

(*ii*) by the buyer with the seller's consent.

Normally goods are in the seller's possession, and therefore, he appropriates the goods. But in those cases where the buyer is acting as the warehouseman or godownkeeper of the seller's goods, he may appropriate the goods with the consent of the seller.

Appropriation of goods can be done in any of the following ways :

(1) *By separating the quantity contracted from the other goods.*

Example : *A* has 100 tins of oil in his godown. He agrees to sell 10 tins out of them to *B*. The goods will be said to be appropriated when 10 tins of oil are set apart as those meant for buyer and the buyer has been informent about it.

(2) *By putting the quantity contracted for in suitable receptacles.*

Example : A agrees to sell 10 tonnes of sugar to B. The goods will be said to be appropriated when the seller puts the required quantity in proper bags, and informs the buyer.

(3) *By delivery to the common carrier or other sort of bailee for the purpose of transmission to the buyer without reserving the right of disposal.* The seller is said to have reserved the right of disposal where his actions show that he has an intention not to part with the control over the goods till the fulfilment of certain conditions.

The following are two cases given under the Act where it can be presumed that the seller has reserved the right of disposal :

(*i*) Where goods are shipped or delivered to a railway administration for carriage by railway and by the bill of lading or railway receipt, as the case may be, the goods are deliverable to the order of the seller or his agent, the seller is, *prima facie,* deemed to have reserved the right of disposal.

10. Edward *v.* Vaghan (1910) 26 T.L.R. 438.
11. Loonkaran *v.* John and Co. A.I.R. (1967), All 308.

(*ii*) Where the seller of goods draws on the buyer for the price and transmits to the buyer the bill of exchange together with the bill of lading or, as the case may be, the railway receipt, to secure acceptance or payment of the bill of exchange, the buyer is bound to return the bill of lading or the railway receipt if he does not honour the bill of exchange; and, if he wrongful retains the bill of lading or the railway receipt, the property in the goods does not pass to him.

Example **:** *A* sold some tins of oil to *B*. *B* had paid the price but the goods were not yet in the possession of *B*. Subsequently, *A* received the railway receipt of the goods and he endorsed and delivered it to *B*. After endorsement of railway receipt by *A* to *B*, the goods got burnt while in transit. It was held that *B* must bear the loss since the property in the tins of oil has passed to *B* before the goods got burnt down.[12]

Effect of Customs and Conventions

Customs and conventions override the law (*Modus et conventio vincunt legem*), *e.g.*, in the case of fur trade, there is a custom that the person who orders for the goods bears the risk in the course of transit, thought the goods might have been purchased on approval.[13]

TRANSFER OF TITLE BY NON-OWNERS

The rules regarding transfer of ownership, discussed in the preceding pages, are based on the presumption that the seller is either the absolute owner of the goods or is authorised to sell the goods, and therefore, the sale made by him also makes the buyer an absolute owner of the goods. But, where the seller is neither the absolute owner nor has any authority to sell, the title of the buyer will also not be absolute. His title will be equally wanting and defective as that of the seller.

Section 27 of The Sale of Goods Act lays down, "Subject to the provisions of the Act and of any other law at the time in force, where goods are sold by a person, who is not the owner thereof and who does not sell under the authority or with the consent of the owner, the buyer acquires no better title to the goods than the seller has, unless the owner is precluded by his conduct from denying the seller's authority to sell."

As a general rule, a seller cannot convey a better title to the buyer than he himself has (*Nemo dat quod non habet*) 'No one can give that which he has not.' In other words, a buyer cannot acquire a better title that the seller possesses.

A purchaser of goods from a thief will not acquire any title to the goods as against the real owner even though he may have honestly purchased the goods for value. Real owner of the goods will be entitled to recover possession of the goods from such purchaser without returning to him the price that he might have paid to the seller.[14]

Therefore, a buyer cannot get good title to the goods unless he has purchased the goods from a person who was the owner of the goods or a person who is properly authorised by the seller to sell the goods. The title of the buyer will remain defective if the title of the seller was defective in spite of the fact that the buyer may have purchased the goods *bona fide* and for value.

Following are the exceptions to the above general rule. It is in these cases that the non-owners can convey a better title to the *bona fide* purchaser of goods for value.

12. Shankar Dass *v.* Bhanoo Dial (1926), 7 Lah. 406.
13. Brevington *v.* Dale (1902), Com. Cas. 112.
14. Cundy *v.* Lindasy (1878), 47 L.J.Q.B. 481.

1. **Title by estoppel :** Where the true owner by his words or conduct causes the buyer to believe that the seller was the owner of the goods or had the owner's authority to sell them and induced him to by goods in that belief, he will be estopped afterwards from setting up seller's want of title or authority to sell (*Sec. 27*).

Examples : (*i*) *A* says to *B* in the presence of *C*, the real owner of the goods, that the (*A*) is the owner of goods. *C* remains mum. Subsequently *A* sells the same goods to *B*. *C* cannot recover the goods from *B* since by his conduct he has accepted that *A* is the owner of the goods.

(*ii*) *A*, the owner of certain machinery, had left them in the possession of *B*. *C* who had obtained a decree against *B*, seized the goods in the execution of the decree. *A* did not take any steps for several months to claim the goods. Rather, he had also conversed with *C*'s solicitor regarding the execution of decree by *C*, without mentioning the fact of his title to the machinery. *C* got the machinery sold in execution of the decree. *A* will be estopped from pleading his title to the machinery and the *bona fide* purchaser for value will acquire better title to the machinery.[15]

2. **Sale by a mercantile agent :** Where goods are sold by a mercantile agent, who is in the possession of the goods or any document of title to the goods, with the consent of the real owner, in the ordinary course of the business, the buyer will get good title if he acts in good faith (*Sec. 27*). The essential elements of this exception are :

(*i*) The goods must have been sold by a mercantile agent and not by an ordinary agent.

(*ii*) The mercantile agent must be in the possession of the goods or any document of title to the goods with the consent of the real owner.

(*iii*) The mercantile agent while selling the goods must act in the ordinary course of his business.

(*iv*) The buyer must act in good faith. He should not have any knowledge of the defect in the title of the seller of the goods at the time, he enters into the contract.

Examples : (*i*) *A* entrusts his car to his agent *B* for sale. He instructs *B* not to sell the car below a sum of ₹ 10,000. *A* sell it to *C* for a sum of ₹ 8,000 and absconds with the money. *A* cannot recover the car from *C* since sale was made by a mercantile agent who transferred valid title to *C*.

(*ii*) *A*, a cotton broker, is appointed by *B* to sell 1,000 bales of cotton belonging to *B*. Subsequently *B* entrusts him 100 tolas of gold to get it converted into ornaments. *A* sells away the gold to *C*, a *bona fide* purchaser for value. *C* will not get good title over the gold since *A* is a mercantile agent for sale of bales of cotton and not gold. Moreover, the gold has not been received by him (*A*) in the ordinary course of his business.

3. **Sale by a co-owner :** A buyer who purchases goods from a co-owner will get valid title if all of the following conditions are satisfied :

(*i*) The co-owner must be in the sole possession of goods with the consent of the other co-owners.

(*ii*) The buyer should purchase the goods for value and in good faith.

(*iii*) The buyer should not have notice or suspicion at the time of sale of the seller's authority to sell (*Sec. 28*).

Example : *A* and *B* are co-owners of a lantern projector with several slides. They use the projector by turns. While the projector is with *A*, with the consent of *B*, he wrongfully sells it away to *C*, a *bona fide* purchaser for value. *C* gets a good title.

15. Picard *v. Sears (1937), 6 A. & E. 474.*

4. **Sale by a person in possession of goods under voidable contract :** Where a person who is in the possession of the goods under a contract voidable under *Sections 19* and 19A of the Contract Act (*i.e.*, where consent is obtained by coercion, undue influence, fraud, misrepresentation), sells such goods to another before the contract is avoided by the party having the option to do so and the buyer purchases them for value, in good faith and without notice of the seller's defect of title, he (the buyer), will under such conditions acquire a good title (*Sec. 29*).

Examples **:** (*i*) *A*, by misrepresentation, induces *B* to sell and deliver him a car. *A* sells the car to *C* before *B* has rescinded the contract. *C* does not know about the defective title of *A*. *C* gets a good title to the car and *B* cannot recover it from him.

(*ii*) *A* was induced to sell a car to *B* on 12th January on the basis of a forged cheque. He came to know of the forgery the very next day and he immediately informed the police and the Automobile Association to trace the car. *B* sold the car on 15th January to *C* who acted in good faith. Held, *C* did not get good title to the car since *A* had effectively shown his intention to rescind the contract.[16]

It is to be noted that the above rule presupposes a contract and will not apply unless there is a contract. It will not apply to contracts which are originally void or to those cases where goods have been obtained by theft. Further, it does not cover the cases of the mutual mistake or cases where there is no contract at all.

Example **:** *A* obtains goods from *B* by falsely representing that he is *X*'s agent. He subsequently sells them to *C*, a *bona fide* purchaser for value. *C* does not get any title to the goods since the person who sold the goods to him, himself did not have any title.

5. **Sale by seller in possession after sale :** Where a person, having sold goods, is in possession of the goods or the documents of title to the goods, resells the goods, the new buyer will get a good title over the goods provided he (*i*) acts in good faith, (*ii*) does not have notice of the prior sale, and (*iii*) obtains possession of goods or documents of title to the goods [*Sec. 30(1)*].

Example **:** *A* buys from *B*, a furniture maker, an almirah for ₹ 300 and pays the amount. He informs *B* that he will take the almirah away after a fortnight. Subsequently *B* sells the almirah to *C* who received the same in good faith, for value, and without having any knowledge of the previous sale to *A*. *C* gets a good title to the almirah. *A*'s only remedy is against *B* for loss suffered by *A* on account of *B*'s conduct.

It is to be noted that to enable the seller to pass a good title, he must continue in possession of the goods or of the documents of title to the goods. It has been held that possession as a hirer or bailee of the goods from the buyer after delivery of the goods to him will not give a valid right even to a *bona fide* purchaser for value.[17]

Example **:** *A* bought a motor lorry from *B*, a dealer in motor lorries and took its delivery. Subsequently, *A* let out the vehicle to *B* on a hire purchase agreement. *B* then sold it away to *C* who bought it in good faith. It was held that sale to *C* was not valid because he took it not from a seller in possession but a bailee of goods.

6. **Sale by a buyer in possession of goods :** Where a person having bought or agreed to buy goods, obtains, with consent of the seller, possession of goods or of the documents of title to the goods, the delivery or transfer by such person or by a mercantile agent acting for such person of the goods or documents, by way of sale, pledge or other disposition thereof will be valid and effective if the person receiving the same acted *bona fide* and without notice of the seller's lien [*Sec. 30(2)*].

Example **:** *A* sold 100 bales of cotton to *B* for a sum of ₹ 10,000. *A* had not received the payment

16. Car and Universal Finance Co. Ltd. *v. Calwell (1964), All E.R. 290.*
17. Staffe Motor Guarantee Ltd. *v.* British Wagon Co. (1934), 2 K.B. 305.

of the price but he sent the railway receipt to *B* without reserving his right of disposal. *B* immediately endorsed the railway receipt to *C*, a *bona fide* purchaser for value. *B* became insolvent before the goods could reach their destination. *A* exercised his right of stoppage of the goods in transit. It was held that goods could not be stopped in the way since *C* had a good title over them.

A difference must be made between having bought or agreed to buy goods and having an option to buy goods. In case of a hire purchase agreement, the hirer has the option to terminate the agreement at anytime he pleases. He will, therefore, be not in a position to give a good title to even a *bona fide* purchaser for value. Similarly, wheher a buyer obtains goods on sale for cash or return, he is not a buyer in possession of goods and cannot give a better title.[18]

Example : *A* took a car from *B* on this condition that *A* would pay a monthly hire of ₹ 400 and could also, if he so desired, purchase it by paying a sum of ₹ 9,000 in 24 equal monthly instalments. After some time *A* sold the car to *C*. It was held that *B* could recover the car from *C* since *A* had neither bought the car nor had agreed to buy the car but only had the option to buy the car.[19]

7. **Unpaid seller's right of re-sale :** A purchaser of goods for value from an unpaid seller, who has the goods in his possession in the exercise of his right of lien or stoppage of goods in transit, shall get an absolute title to the goods even though re-sale may not be justified under the circumstances (*Sec. 54*).

8. **Sale under the provisions of other Acts :** (*a*) A purchaser of goods for value from a pawnee who is selling goods under default of the pawnor shall acquire a valid title to goods (*Sec. 176 of The Indian Contract Act*).

(*b*) Purchaser of goods from a finder of goods shall acquire a valid title provided the sale made by the finder is valid (*Sec. 169 of The Indian Contract Act*).

(*c*) Sale by a person acting in execution of law or under a power of sale will confer a good title to the buyer. For example, sale by an Official Receiver or Assignee or Liquidator of a company, executor of a will, administrator of the estate of an intestate (*i.e.*, a person who dies without making a will) will give to the purchaser a valid title.

KEY TERMS

- ❑ **Appropriation of Goods :** It refers to separating the goods sold from other goods so as to determine and identity the actual goods to be delivered.
- ❑ **Deliverable State :** It is such a state of goods that the buyer under the contract would be bound to take their delivery.

TEST QUESTIONS

Objective Type : ***Test Your Knowledge***

1. Fill in the blanks
   (*i*) Risk follows....................
   (*ii*) In case of unascertained goods the ownership will pass to buyer only when the goods are......................
   (*iii*) In case of specific goods in a..........the property in goods passes from a seller to the buyer

---

18. Edwards *v.* Vanghu (1910).
19. Belsizw Motor Supply Co. *v.* Cox (1924), 1 K.B. 244.

as soon as the contract of sale is effected.

(*iv*) The right of resale is available to an..................

(*v*) No one can convey a better title than what............

[***Ans.*** (*i*) ownership; (*ii*) ascertained; (*iii*) deliverable sate; (*iv*) unpaid seller; (*v*) he has.]

2. Select the most appropriate answer

(*i*) A buyer acquires a better title than the seller when :

(*a*) the seller obtained the possession of goods under a voidable contract which has been rescinded and buyer buys goods in good faith.

(*b*) one of several joint owners has obtained possession of goods by murdering other co-owners and the buyer buys the goods from such co-owners in good faith.

(*c*) a seller who has already sold the goods continues to be in their possession and sells them again to a buyer who receives them in good faith and without notice of the previous sale.

(*ii*) In case of 'sale or return' the buyer is deemed to have accepted the goods when :

(*a*) he does not intimate to the seller that he has accepted them

(*b*) he pledges the goods

(*c*) he retains without intimating the seller that he has rejected them

(*d*) he rejects the goods but does not intimate the seller.

(*iii*) In case of an agreement to sell action against a third party for damaging the goods can be taken by :

(*a*) the seller (*b*) buyer (*c*) both

[***Ans.*** (*i*) (*c*); (*ii*) (*b*); (*iii*) (*a*)]

Essay Type : *For Review, Discussion and Practice*

1. In a contract of sale of goods 'no one cane transfer a better title than what he himself has'—Explain.
2. State the circumstances in which ownership of unascertained goods passes from the seller to the buyer under the Sale of Goods Act.
3. When does property in the goods pass in case of unascertained goods?
4. When does the property in goods sold pass from seller to the buyer.
5. When the property in specific or ascertained goods passes to the buyer? (*CS Foundation, May 2000*)
6. State the rules as to passing of property when goods are delivered on approval in a contract for sale? (*CA Foundation, May 2001*)
7. "No seller of goods can give the buyer of goods a better title to the goods than he himself has"-Discuss this rule with their exceptions. (*ICWA Foundation, June 1999;CS Foundation, Dec. 2007*)
8. State the rules relating to passing of property in the goods under the Sale of Goods Act, 1930. (*ICWA Foundation, Dec. 1999*)
9. When does the property in goods pass from seller to buyer in a contract for sale of ascertained and unascertained goods? (*CS Foundation, June 1999*)
10. "Risk prima facie passes with ownership." Comment. (*CS Foundation, Dec. 2005, Dec. 2007*)
11. The rule in the sales of goods is "no one can transfer better title than he himself possess". Are there any exceptions to this rule? Discuss. (*GGSIPU, BBA (H), May 2004*)
12. Why is it important to know the exact time when the property in goods passes from a seller to

the buyer? Explain with examples the rules regarding the transfer of ownership of goods from seller to the buyer. *(B.Com. (Hons.), Delhi 1987, 1994, 1997)*

13. Discuss briefly the cases in which a seller can give a better title to the goods than he himself has. *(B.Com. (Hons.), 1st Year, Delhi 1988, 1993, 1997, 2002, 2004)*
14. "Nemo Dat Quod Non Haber"–None can give or transfer goods what he himself does not himself own. Explain. *(ICAI, PEE II, Nov. 2005)*
15. Explain the rules regarding transfer of ownership from seller to the buyer. *(B.Com. (Pass), Delhi 2005)*
16. "No seller of goods can give the buyer of goods a better title to those goods than what he himself possesses." Examine this statement and mention whether there are any exception to this rule. *(B.Com. (Hons.), Delhi 1988, 1993, 2002, B.Com. (Pass), Delhi 2005)*
17. "An hirer, who obtains possession of a car from its owner under a hire purchase agreement sells the car to a buyer who buys in good faith and without notice of the right of the owner." Comment. *(ICWAI Inter, June 2009)*
18. When a property passes to the buyer under 'goods on approval' or 'on sale or return'? *(ICWAI Inter, June 2009)*
19. "A seller cannot transfer to the buyer of goods a title better than what he himself has." Comment, giving exceptions to the rule. *(B.Com. (Hons), Delhi 2010)*
20. "Custody or control of goods" implies "Property in Goods". Comment. *(B.Com. (Hons), Delhi 2012)*

PRACTICAL PROBLEMS

1. The plaintiff handed over a motor car to a mercantile agent for sale on condition that the car should not be sold below a specified price. The agent agreed to do so, but sold it below such price to *A* and misappropriated the proceeds. *A* bought the car in good faith and resold it to the defendant. Can the plaintiff recover the car from the defendant? State reasons for your answer.
   [***Ans.*** No. See sale by mercantile agent under 'Transfer of title by non-owners'.]
2. *A* sold and delivered a motor car to *B*. Subsequently *A* gets possession of the same car on hire from *B*. *A*, the former seller, who is now in possession of the car as the hirer sells and delivers it to *C* who, in good faith and without notice of the previous sale, purchases it for consideration. Has *B* any right to get the car from *C*? Decide stating reasons.
   [***Ans.*** Yes. See, 'Sale by a seller in possession after sale'.]
3. *X*, the owner of a motor car, leaves its certificate of registration in the car. The certificate of registration is equivalent to a document of registration in the car. The driver of the car by forgery, procures its registration to his own name and sells it to Z, a *bona fide* purchaser for value. Is *X* estopped from denying Y's authority to sell? Give reasons for your answer.
   [***Ans.*** No. Mere negligence is not enough. He could not have anticipated the forgery. No disregard to buyer's interests.]
4. *A* delivered his horse to *B* on trial for a week with a condition that if found suitable he will buy the horse for ₹ 1,000. The horse died on the third day. Is *B* liable to pay the price?
   [***Ans.*** No. Ownership was not transferred.]
5. A hirer, who obtains possession of a refrigerator from its owner under hire purchase agreement sells the refrigerator to a buyer who buys in good faith and without notice of the right of the owner. Does this buyer get a good title to the refrigerator? State reasons for your answer.
   [***Ans.*** No. The hirer has no title and therefore cannot transfer any title to the buyer.]

6. *A* delivered to *B* certain goods on 'sale or return.' It was agreed that the property would not pass except on payment of cash by *B* by a particular date. Before the date *B* pledged the goods with *C*. Can *A* recover the goods from *C* by filling a suit?
[***Ans.*** *B*'s pledging of goods with *C* was not valid and hence *A* could recover the goods from *C*.]
7. *B* selects certain furniture in a shop. The price is settled. He arranges to takes delivery of the furniture the next day through his servant and agrees to pay for the furniture on the first of the next month. The furniture was destroyed by fire the same evening. Is *B* liable to pay the price? Give reasons.
[***Ans.*** *B* is liable to pay the price. This is an unconditional contract for sale of specific goods in a deliverable state.]
8. *A* sells 80 kilograms of grain out of a large quantity lying in his granary. *B* sells 60 kilograms out of these, the goods not yet being ascertained, to *C*. Then *C* having a delivery order from *B*, forwards it to *A* who informs *C* that he will send the grain in due course. *B* then becomes insolvent. Can *A* refuse to deliver the 60 kilograms of grain to *C*. Give reasons.
[***Ans.*** *A* cannot refuse to deliver grains to *C*.]
9. *J*, the owner of a fiat car wants to sell his car. For his purpose he hands over the car to *P*, a mercantile agent for sale at a price not less than ₹ 50,000. The agent sells the car for ₹ 40,000 to *A*, who buys the car in good faith and without notice of any fraud. *P* misappropriated the money also. *J* sues *A* to recover the car. Decide giving reasons whether *J* would succeed.
[***Ans.*** *J* would not succeed.]
10. Mr. Shah agreed to purchase 50 bales of cotton from Mr. Bose from his large stock and sent his men to take delivery of the goods. They could pack only 30 bales. Then there was accidental fire and the entire stock was destroyed including the 30 bales that were packed. Who will bear the loss and to what extent? Explain. *(CA Inter, May 1989)*
[***Ans.*** In case the bales have been selected with the buyer's consent the loss will be borne to the extent of 30 bales by Mr. Shah.]
11. While travelling in a bus Ashish finds a *VCR*. After making reasonable efforts to discover the owner, he sells the VCR to Deepika, who buys the VCR with the knowledge that Ashish was merely a finder. On coming to know about the deal, *M*, the owner of the VCR files a suit against Deepika for the recovery of VCR from her. Decide giving reasons, whether *M* will succeed in getting the VCR back from Deepika?
[***Ans.*** *M* would succeed in getting the VCR back.]
12. *A* delivers his watch to *B* on 'sale or return' basis *B* delivers the same watch to *C* on 'sale or return' basis. *C* delivers it to *D* on 'sale or return' basis and *D* delivers the same watch to *E* on 'sale or return' basis. While in the possession of *E*, the watch is damaged. Who will bear the loss? Give reasons. *(CS Foundation, Dec. 1998)*
[***Ans.*** *D* will bear the loss.]
13. *A* delivered a horse to *B* for trial for three days. It was agreed that if found suitable to the buyer for his purposes, the sale would then be absolute. The horse died on the 2nd day without the fault of either party, who will bear the loss. *(GGSIPU, BBA (H), May 2004)*
[***Ans.*** The seller will bear the loss since the ownership had not been transferred.]
14. *A* delivered a diamond ring to *B* on "Sale or Return" basis. *B* delivers that ring to *C* and then *C* delivers it to *D* on similar terms. *D* lost the ring. Is *B* liable to *A* for the loss? Give reasons. *(B.Com. (Hons.), Delhi 2005)*
15. *A* agrees to purchase bales of cotton from *B* at Chennai. The goods are sent by rail, delivery to be given against payment by *A* through bank. *A* pays the amount and obtains a delivery note. But the goods had been destroyed by fire before he pays the amount. Has the property in goods passed to *A*? Give reasons. *(B.Com. (Hons.), Delhi 2002)*
[***Ans.*** No, *A* will not bear the loss as property in goods has not passed to *A*.]

16. *B* buys furniture and makes full payment. He promises to take delivery of furniture in the next week to which the seller agreed. Next day, the shopkeeper sold that furniture to *C* on cash basis. Examine *C*'s title to the furniture.

(*B.Com. (Hons.), Delhi 2004*)

[***Ans.*** In the present case, *B* has bought furniture but the possession of the furniture is still with the shopkeeper. *C* is the subsequent purchaser who is not aware of the previous sale to *B*. *C* gets a valid title.]

17. *J*, the owner of a Fiat car wants to sell his car. For this purpose, he handed over the car to *P*, a mercantile agent for sale at a price not less than ₹ 50,000. The agent sells the car for ₹ 40,000 to *A*, who buys the car in good faith and without notice of any fraud. *P* misappropriated the money also. *J* sues *A* to recover the car. Decide giving reasons whether *J* would succeed.

(*PEE II, November 2005*)

[***Ans.*** *P*, the agent, was in the possession of the car with *J*'s consent for the purpose of sale. *A*, the buyer, therefore obtained a good title to the car. Hence, *J* in this case, cannot recover the car from *A*. A similar decision, in analogous circumstances, was taken in *Folkes vs. King*.]

18. *A* sells his horse to *B*. The delivery of the horse is to be made in the next week. *B* agrees to pay the price of the horse on delivery. *A* requires his servant to keep the horse separate from the other horses. The horse is kept separately with the knowledge and consent of *B*. The horse, however, dies before it is delivered and paid for. Now *A* files a suit against *'B'* for recovery of the price. Will *A* succeed? Give reasons. (*B.Com. (Hons.), Delhi 2005*)

[***Ans.*** *A* will succeed. It is a contract of sale of specific goods in a deliverable state and therefore, the property in the horse passes to *B* at once at the time of contract.]

19. Goods are delivered by *A to B* on 'sale or return' basis. They are further delivered by *B* to *C* and then by *C* to *D* on similar terms. The goods are stolen while in the custody of *D*. Who is to bear the loss of goods and why? (*B.Com. (Hons.), Delhi 1989*)

[***Ans.*** *C* can recover the loss from *D*. *C* is bound to pay the price to *B* and *B* is bound to pay the price to *A*.]

20. A horse was delivered to *B* on the condition of sale or return within 8 days. The horse died within 8 days. Who shall bear the loss of the horse? Give full reasons. (*B.Com. (Hons.), Delhi 2000*)

[***Ans.*** The loss would fall on the seller as the property in the goods had not yet been transferred from the seller to the buyer since the sale was on sale or return basis.]

21. With a view to boost the sales Hanuman Automobiles sells a motorcar to Mr. *A* on trial basis for a period of three days with a condition that if Mr. *A* is not satisfied with the performance of the car, he can return back the car. However, the car was destroyed in a fire accident at the place of Mr. *A* before the expiry of three days. Decide whether Mr. *A* is liable for the loss suffered.

(*PEE II, November 2004*)

[***Ans.*** There was no transfer of owndership to *A*. Hence *A* is not liable for the loss due to the fire accident. M/s Hanuman Automobiles will have to bear the loss.]

22. Gautam delivers some jewellery to Priya on approval without specifying any time for its return in case of non-acceptance. Priya keeps the jewellery with her without signifying her approval or refusal. After one month, a burglary takes place in Priya's house and the jewellery is stolen. Can Gautam sue Priya for the price of jewellery? Give reasons. (*B.Com. (Hons.), Delhi 2001*)

[***Ans.*** Ownership transferred to Priya on expiry of reasonable period if there is no specified period. Hence, Gautam can sue Priya.]

23. Sanjay delivers some goods to Tarun on 'Sale or return' basis for 7 days. State the legal position in each of the following different situations:

(*CS foundation, Dec. 2008*)

(*i*) Such goods are destroyed by fire on the second day itself with no fault of Tarun.

(*ii*) Tarun informs acceptance of goods over phone to Sanjay and immediately thereafter goods are destroyed by fire.

(*iii*) These goods are further delivered by Tarun to Umesh on fourth day, and then by Umesh to Vivek on same terms. The goods are stolen while in the custody of Vivek.

(*iv*) Tarun neither returns goods nor gives any notice of rejection even after the expiry of ninth day. Goods are destroyed by fire on the tenth day.

(*v*) Tarun retains goods but gives the notice of rejection on the seventh day. Goods are destroyed by fire on the eighth day.

[***Ans.*** (*i*) Sanjay shall bear the loss; (*ii*) Tarun shall bear the loss; (*iii*) Tarun is liable to pay the price to Sanjay. Umesh is also liable to pay the price to Tarun; (*iv*) Tarun shall bear the loss; (*v*) Sanjay shall bear the loss.]

24. L delivered sarees valuing ₹ 50,000 to *R* on 'Sale or Return Basis'. *R* further delivered these sarees to V and *V* to *M* on the same terms and conditions. Subsequently, these sarees were burnt by fire while in the custody of *M, L* filed a suit against *M* for the recovery of the price. With reference to provisions of the Sale of Goods Act, 1930, examine whether *L's* suit for the price shall be maintainable. (*PEE-II, ICAI, June 2009*)

[***Ans.*** Loss shall fall on *R*, the owner (risk being associated with ownership unless otherwise is agreed between the parties).]

25. *A, B* and *C* were joint owners of a truck and possession of the said truck was with *B*. *X* purchases the truck from *B* without knowing that *A* and *C* were also owners of the truck. Decide in light of provisions of the Sale of Goods Act, 1930, whether the sale betwen *B* and *X* is valid or not? (*PEE-II, ICAI, May 2008*)

[***Ans.*** *X* acquires good title and becomes full owner.]

26. Asha delivers some furniture to Bipasha on 'sale or return' basis. Bipasha then delivers the same furniture to Chitra, and Chitra further delivers it to Divya on similar basis. Before Divya could give her acceptance furniture is suddenly destroyed by fire. Who is to bear the loss of furniture? Give reasons. (*CS Foundation, June 2008*)

[***Ans.*** As between Asha and Bipasha there is a complete sa le. But as between Chitra and Divya, the property in the goods has not passed to Divya. As such Chitra cannot recover the loss from Divya.]

27. Mr. *S* agreed to purchase 100 bales of cotton from *T*, out of his large stock and sent his men to take delivery of the goods. They could pack only 60 bales. Later on, there was an accidental fire and the entire stock was destroyed including 60 bales that were already packed. Referring to the provisions of the Sale of Goods Act, 1930 explain as to who will bear the loss and to what extent? (*PEE-II ICAI, May 2007, ICWAI Inter, June 2009*)

[***Ans.*** The property in the goods shall not been transferred at all and hence the loss of 100 bales would be borne by Mr. *V* completely.]

28. Aman, Raman and Chaman were joint-owners of a truck and possession of the said truck was with Raman. Sudhir purchased the truck from Raman without knowing that Aman and Chaman were also co-owners of the truck. Decide in the light of the provisions of the Sale of Goods Act, 1930 whether the sale between Raman and Sudhir is valid. (*CS Foundation, June 2010*)

[***Ans.*** The sale between Raman and Sudhir is valid. A buyer who buys in good faith from one of the several joint owners who is in sole possession of the goods with the permission of his co-owners will get good title to the goods.]

29. Mr. Bose settled the price after selecting two chairs. He arranges to take delivery of chairs next day and agrees to pay next month. Said chairs were destroyed by fire before delivery. Seller demanded the price. Mr. Bose refused. State legal position. (*ICWA Inter. Dec., 2010*)

[***Ans.*** Mr. Bose is liable because the contract was unconditional for the sale of specific goods in a deliverable state.]

30. Mr. Saxena received cheque dated 02.05.2010 for ₹ 10,000 from Mr. Malhotra towards cost of furniture. On 13.11.10 Mr. Malhotra closed the Bank Account. What action Mr. Saxena can take to receive the amount against the cheque which is still with him. *(ICWA Inter. Dec., 2010)*

[**Ans.** If the period of validity of the cheque is not specified in the cheque, the cheque must have been presented to the Bank within a period of six months from the date of cheque. Mr. Saxena failed to present the cheque within the validity of the cheque. Hence, Mr. Malhotra is not responsible. He may however request Mr. Malhotra for fresh cheque stating the circumstances of delay in presenting by 2.11.2010.]

31. Ramen sold 50 kg. of rice to Khagen who paid by cheque and Ramen gave the delivery order to Khagen. Khagen resold such rice to Bhaben who purchased on good faith and for consideration. Khagen's cheque was dishonoured. Ramen refused to deliver rice to Bhaben on the plea of non-payment. Advise Bhaben. *(ICWA Inter, Dec., 2010)*

[**Ans.** Bhaben can not claim delivery of goods because Khagen cannot give what he does not have. Khagen's title having become defective by dishonor of cheque, cannot confer good title to Bhaben.

32. Jewellery was sent by *A* to *B* on Sale or Return basis. *B* pledged the jewelry with *C*. Discuss the rights and liabilities of the parties. *(B.Com. (Hons), Delhi 2011)*

[**Ans.** *A* has the right to recover the price of the jewellery from *B* but has no right to claim the jewellery from *C*. Where goods are sent on 'sale or return' basis, the property in the goods passes to the buyer when he does an act adopting the transaction. Pledging of goods by the buyer is an act amounting to an adoption of transaction.

33. *X* delivered his old laptop to *Y*, for sale, he also instructed *Y* not to sell below ₹ 10,000. However, *Y* sold the laptop to *Z* for ₹ 8,000 and Y misappropriated the sale amount. When *X* comes to know about the deal, *X* decided to cancel the deal and demanded his laptop back from *Z*. Discuss the legal position of all the parties. *(B.Com. (Hons), Delhi 2012)*

[**Ans.** *X* cannot demand his laptop back from *Z*, because *Z* has bought it from *Y* in good faith and for lawful consideration. However, *X* can claim the decided amount, i.e., ₹ 10,000 from *Y*, because he has delivered it for sale not below ₹ 10,000].

34. Binod finds a diamond ring of Anand and sells the same for ₹ 50,000 to Chirage who purchases the ring for value and in good faith. Can Anand, the real owner recover the ring from Chirag? Explain. *(CS Foundation, Dec. 2012)*

[**Ans.** The real owner Anand can recover the ring from Chirag, for Binod having no title to the ring could not pass a better title.]

35. *B*, a lady, purchased from *A*, a second-hand typewriter, used it for some time and also spent some money on its repairs. Subsequently, she discovered it to be stolen and had to return it to the true owner. She sued the sellers. Whether *B* would be entitled to the refund and compensation for the cost of the overhaul? Explain. *(B.Com. (Hons), Nov. 2013)*

[**Ans.** There is a breach of Condition as to Title. *B* would be entitled to the refund and compensation for the cost of the overhaul.]

Chapter 4
PERFORMANCE OF A CONTRACT OF SALE

LEARNING OBJECTIVES

A careful study of this chapter will enable you to :

- appreciate the duties of the seller and the buyer under a contract of sale;
- explain the term delivery and its types;
- enumerate the rules regarding delivery;
- appreciate the importance of a *CIF* contract; and
- explain the meaning of certain key terms.

DUTIES OF SELLER AND BUYER

It is the duty of the seller to deliver the goods and of the buyer to accept and pay for them, in accordance with the terms of the contract of sale (*Sec. 31*).

Payment and delivery are concurrent conditions : Unless otherwise agreed, delivery of the goods and payment of the price are concurrent conditions, that is to say, the seller shall be ready and willing to give possession of the goods to the buyer in exchange for price, and the buyer shall be ready and willing to pay the price in exchange for the possession of the goods (*Sec. 32*).

Thus, it is the duty of the seller to deliver the goods and the buyer's duty is to accept delivery and pay the price.

DELIVERY

Delivery of goods implies voluntary transfer of possession of goods from seller to buyer. Delivery should have the effect of putting the buyer in possession of the goods. Buyer should acquire the position of exercising some degree of control over the goods, directly or through any of his representatives.

Modes of Delivery

Delivery of goods may be of the following types :

1. **Actual delivery :** Where the goods are physically handed over by the seller or his authorised agent to the buyer.

2. **Symbolic delivery :** Where the goods are bulky and incapable of actual delivery, the 'means of obtaining possession' of goods are delivered by the seller to the buyer. Delivery of the key of the warehouse where the goods are stored or the bill of lading etc. are all examples of symbolic delivery.

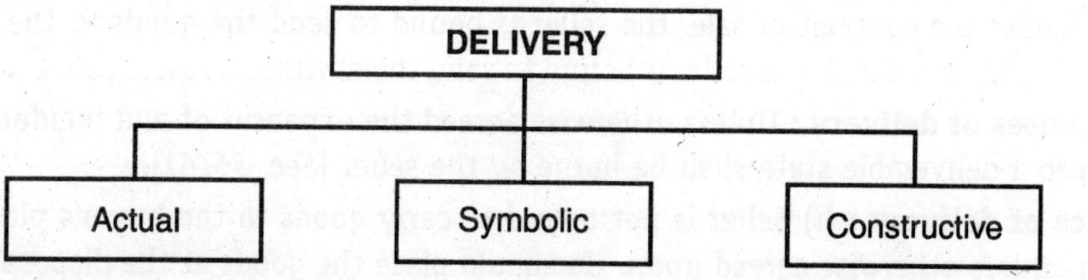

3. **Constructive delivery :** Where a third person in possession of goods acknowledges to hold goods on behalf of and at the disposal of the buyer, the delivery is constructive.

Example : *A* is the warehouseman of *B*. *B* gives a delivery order to *C*, the buyer, asking *A* to deliver a certain quantity of goods to *C*. *C* goes to *A* with this delivery order. *A* agrees to deliver goods the next day. It is a symbolic delivery of goods because now *A* is holding goods on behalf of and the disposal of *C*. *B* cannot now stop *A* from delivering the goods to *C*.

Rules regarding delivery

1. **Buyer should be in a position to exercise control over the goods :** Delivery of goods sold may be made by doing anything which the parties agree shall be treated as delivery or which has the effect of putting the goods in the possession of buyer or of any person authorised to hold them on his behalf (*Sec. 33*).

Example : *A* sold the wood of some fallen trees to *B*. *B* after cutting up the trees was about to remove them, when he was prevented from doing so by *C*. *B* sued *A* for refund of purchase money. It was held that he would succeed since there was no delivery of goods to *B*. This was because the mere fact that the buyer has cut the tree did not mean that the could exercise his control over the goods until he carted them away.

2. **Effect of part delivery :** A delivery of the part of the goods, in progress of the delivery of the whole has the same effect, for the purpose of passing the property in such goods, as a delivery of the whole, but a delivery of the part of the goods, with an intention of severing it from the whole, does not operate as a delivery of the remainder (*Sec. 34*).

Examples : (*i*) *A* ship arrives in a harbour laden with cargo consigned to *A*, the buyer. The captain begins to unload it and delivers a part of the goods to *A* in progress of the delivery of the whole. The part delivery of the cargo is equivalent to the delivery of the cargo as a whole and the ownership in whole of the goods shall pass on the buyer.

(*ii*) *A* agreed to buy from *B* ten bales of cotton or any part thereof that might be in merchantable condition. Each bale was to weigh eight quintals to be paid for on or before delivery in Bombay. *A* took delivery of and paid of only two bales. He rejected the rest eight. *B* sued *A* for recovery of the price of bales rejected. It was held that *B* could not recover the price since the delivery and acceptance of two bales did not pass the property in all bales so as to make *A* liable to pay the price them. The fact that each bale was to be paid separately was a strong indication of the intention of the parties that the delivery of one bale was not intended to pass the property in all. The only remedy available to the seller was to recover from the buyer damages for breach of contract.[1]

3. **Buyer to apply for delivery :** Apart from any express contract, the seller of goods is not bound to deliver them until the buyer applies for delivery [*Sec. 35*].

The demand for delivery should be made at a reasonable hour. Where according to the terms of the contract, it is the duty of the seller to deliver the goods, the tender of delivery should similarly be also made at a reasonable hour. What is reasonable hour is a question of fact [*Sec. 36(4)*].

1. Mitchell Reid & Co. *v.* Baldeo Das (1888), 15 Cal.1.

Where under the contract of sale, the seller is bound to send the goods to the buyer, but no time for sending them is fixed, the seller is bound to send them within a reasonable time [*Sec. 36(2)*].

4. **Expenses of delivery :** Unless otherwise agreed the expenses of and incidental to putting the goods into a deliverable state shall be borne by the seller [*Sec. 36(6)*].

5. **Place of delivery :** (*i*) Seller is not bound to carry goods to the buyer's place of business or residence, unless otherwise agreed upon. He should place the goods at the disposal of the buyer.

(*ii*) Delivery of the goods is to be made at the place where the goods are lying at the time of sale unless otherwise agreed upon. If the goods were not then in existence, they are to be delivered at the place where they are produced [*Sec. 36(2)*].

(*iii*) Where the seller has agreed to deliver goods to the buyer at a place other than that where they were when sold, the buyer must in the absence of agreement to the contrary take the risk of deterioration necessarily incidental to the course of transit (*Sec. 40*).

6. **Where goods are with a third person :** Where the goods are in the hands of a third person, there can be no delivery to the buyer unless the third person acknowledges that he holds them on behalf of the buyer [*Sec. 36(3)*].

7. **Delivery of wrong quantity :** (*i*) Where the seller delivers to the buyer a quantity of goods less he had contracted to sell, the buyer may reject them, but if the buyer accepts the goods so delivered he shall pay for them at the contract rate.

(*ii*) Where the seller delivers to the buyer a quantity of goods larger than he had contracted to sell, the buyer may accept the goods included in the contract and reject the rest, or he may reject the whole. If the buyer accepts the whole of the goods so delivered, he shall pay for them at the contract rate.

(*iii*) Where the seller delivers to the buyer the goods he had contracted to sell mixed with goods of a different description not included in the contract, the buyer may accept the goods which are in accordance with the contract and reject the rest, or may reject the whole.

(*iv*) The provisions of this section are subject to any usage of trade, special agreement or course of dealing between the parties (*Sec. 37*).

Examples : (*i*) *A* sells 2,000 gross of '200-meter reels' of sewing cotton to *B*. After taking delivery *B* comes to know that the length per reel is on an average 6% short. *B* may reject the goods but in case he accepts them, he will have to pay for the actual quantity of thread in the reels at the contract rate.

(*ii*) *A* contracted to sell 50 bottles of syrup to *B*. *A* offers to deliver only 30 bottles to *B* on the date of performance of the contract. *B* can reject delivery but in case he accepts, he will have to pay for 30 bottles at the contract rate.

(*iii*) If in the above example *A* sends for delivery sixty bottles, *B* may (*a*) accept the whole consignment, or (*b*) accept 50 bottles and reject the rest, or (*c*) reject the whole consignment.

It is to be noted that if the delivery of goods is slightly less or slightly more than the contracted quantity, the buyer would not be entitled to reject such delivery unless the goods are very precious like platinum, gold, diamonds etc. This is based on the maxim that the law does not take account of trifles (*de minimis non curat lex*).[2]

8. **Instalment deliveries :** (*i*) Unless otherwise agreed, the buyer of goods in not bound to accept delivery thereof by instalments.

2. Jackson *v.* Rotax Motor and Cycle Co. (1910), 2 K.B. 937 (C.A.).

(*ii*) Where there is a contract for the sale of goods to be delivered by the stated instalments which are to be separately paid for, and the seller makes no delivery or defective delivery in respect of one or more instalments, or the buyer neglects or refuses to take delivery of or pay for one or more instalments, it is a question in each case, depending on the terms of the contract and the circumstances of the case, whether the breach of contract is repudiation of the whole contract, or whether it is a severable breach giving rise to a claim for compensation, but not to a right to treat the whole contracts as repudiated (*Sec. 38*).

Examples : (*i*) *A* purchased from *B* 25 tonnes of pepper March-April shipment. *B* shipped 20 tonnes in April and 5 tonnes in November. It was held that the contract did not provide for delivery of goods in instalments, and therefore, *A* could reject the entire consignment.[3]

(*ii*) It was agreed in a contract of sale of steel tinplate bars that (*a*) goods would be delivered over a period of three months, (*b*) payment would be made in cash in fourteen day after delivery and (*c*) all payment were to be made on due dates as a condition precedent to future deliveries. This purchaser failed to pay the money on the due date. It was held that the seller was entitled to refuse any further deliveries of goods.[4]

If in the above example, the payment on due date had not been made a condition precedent for future deliveries, the seller could not have repudiated the contract.[5]

Example : *A* agrees to sell 300 tonnes of sugar. The shipment to be made during November and December next in lots of about 75 tonnes in a shipment, payment to be made in cash for delivery. *A* informs *B* of the arrival of the first shipment and demands payment, but *B* fails to pay. Discuss whether the failure of *B* to pay discharges *A* from making further deliveries.

B's failure to pay will not discharge *A* from liability to make further deliveries of sugar. It is a severable breach which gives rise only to compensation and not to a right of repudiation of the whole contract.

9. **Delivery to carrier or wharfinger :** (*i*) Where, in pursuance of a contract of sale, the seller is authorised or required to send the goods to the buyer, delivery of the goods to a carrier, whether named by the buyer or not, for the purpose of transmission to the buyer, or delivery of the goods to a wharfinger for safe custody, is *prima facia* deemed to be delivery of the goods to the buyer.

(*ii*) Unless otherwise authorised by the buyer, the seller shall make such contract with the carrier or wharfinger on behalf of the buyer as may be reasonable having regard to the nature of the goods and the other circumstances of the case. If the seller omits so to do, and the goods are lost or damaged in course of transit or whilst in the custody of the wharfinger, the buyer may decline to treat the delivery to the carrier or wharfinger as a delivery to himself, or may held the seller responsible for damages.

Example : *A* of Agra places an order with *B* of Bombay to supply him three casks of oil to be sent to him by railway. *A* delivers casks to the railway company without conforming to the rules which must be complied with in order to render the railway company liable for their safety. The goods do not reach *B*. *B* is not liable to pay the price since there has not been a sufficient delivery to make *B* liable.

(*iii*) Unless otherwise agreed, where goods are sent by the seller to the buyer by a route involving sea transit, in circumstances in which it is usual to insure, the seller shall give such notice to the buyer as may enable him to insure them during their sea transit, and if the seller fails to do so, the goods shall be deemed to be at his risk during such sea transit (*Sec. 39*).

3. Renter *v.* Sala (1889) 48 L.J. 492.
4. Ebb Vale Steel, etc. Co. *v.* Blaina Iron etc. Co. (1901), 6 Com. Cas. 33 (C.A.).
5. Ct. Mersey Steel and Iron Co. *v.* Naylor Benzon Co. (1884), 9 App. Cas. 434.

Example : *A* sold certain goods to *B* F.O.B. Antwerp. The goods were to be shipped according to *B*'s directions. Subsequently. *A* received instructions from *B* asking him to ship the goods to Odessa and pay freight on *B*'s account. The choice of the ship was left to *A*. *B* knew that the insurance of goods should be effected and he had all information for getting the goods insured but he preferred not to get the goods insured. The goods were shipped but were lost in the transit. *B* refused to make the payment on the ground that *A* had not given him notice regarding custom of insurance. It was held that though technically notice was to be given by the seller to the buyer, yet the buyer must suffer since he elected not to insure the goods knowing it well that insurance of goods should be effected.[6]

10. **Buyer's right of examining the goods :** (*i*) Where goods are delivered to the buyer which he has not previously examined, he is not deemed to have accepted them unless and until he has had a reasonable opportunity of examining them for the purpose of ascertaining whether they are in conformity with the contract.

(*ii*) Unless otherwise agreed, when the seller tenders delivery of goods to the buyer, he is bound, on request, to afford the buyer a reasonable opportunity of examining the goods for the purpose of ascertaining whether they are in conformity with the contract (*Sec. 41*).

Acceptance by Buyer

The buyer is deemed to have accepted the goods in each of the following cases (*Sec. 42*) :

(*i*) He intimates to the seller that he has accepted them or

(*ii*) He deals with the goods[7] in a manner inconsistent with the ownership of the seller *i.e.*, resells or pledges the goods or makes some alteration in the goods or

(*iii*) After the lapse of a reasonable time, he retains the goods without intimating to the seller that he has rejected the goods.

Buyer is not bound to return those goods to the seller which he has rightfully rejected. Seller after getting intimation of their rejection shall have to bring back the goods at his own cost (*Sec. 43*).

Liability of buyer for neglecting or refusing delivery of goods : When the seller is ready and willing to deliver the goods and requests the buyer to take delivery and the buyer does not within a reasonable time after such request take delivery of the goods, he is liable to the seller for any loss occasioned by his neglect or refusal to take delivery, and also for a reasonable charge for the care and custody of the goods.

Provided that nothing in this section shall affect the right of the seller where the neglect or refusal of the buyer to take delivery amounts to a repudiation of the contract (*Sec. 44*).

C.I.F. CONTRACT

The abbreviation *CIF* is used for the terms Cost, Insurance and Freight. CIF contract is one in which the seller agrees to sell the goods to be carried by sea at a price which will cover the cost of the goods, insurance and freight charges.

A *CIF* contract is performed by delivery of the shipping documents relating to the goods and not be actual delivery of goods by the seller to the buyer. Documents of title to the goods are

6. Wimble *v.* Resenberg (1913), 3 K.B. 743.
7. It has been held that dealing with documents of title does not amount to acceptance Choa *v.* British Traders & Shippres Ltd. (1954), 1 All E.R. 779.

delivered so as to symbolise the delivery of goods. Buyer is not allowed to inspect the goods. He is asked to pay price against the delivery of complete and regular documents of title to the goods. Payment of price is not dependent on the safe arrival of the goods. Buyer will have to pay the price even if the goods are damaged or destroyed. He can realise the loss from the shipping or the insurance company. But by paying the price on the presentation of shipping document, buyer will not be precluded from subsequently rejecting the goods or recovering damages for breach of contract of sale if on receipt of the delivery of goods, they are found to be not in accordance with the contract.

Is a CIF contract, a contract for the sale of documents only? A CIF contract is not a contract for the sale of documents but a contract of sale of goods to be performed through the delivery of documents. This was clearly stated by *Chakravarti, C.J. In Joseph Pyke and Son* v. *Kedaranath.*[8]

"The delivery of goods is not necessary under *CIF* contract but obligation as to delivery is discharged by the delivery of goods on board a ship instead of directly and at once to the buyer. It cannot be said that a *CIF* contract is not a contract for the delivery of any article. I have already pointed that even after the shipping documents have been presented to the buyer and even after he has paid out the invoice price, he still retains the right to examine the goods shipped to him and to reject them, if he finds any deficiency in regard to either quantity or quality. It is, thus, impossible to see how it can be said that under a *CIF* contract delivery of goods to the buyer is not material or not contemplated."

A buyer under A CIF contract has two rights. He has the right to reject the documents if they are not complete and in order. He can also reject the goods if they are not in perfect condition.[9]

Duties of the Seller

Seller, under a *CIF* contract, is required to fulfill the following obligations :

1. To make out an invoice of the goods sold in the usual form showing the price of the goods.
2. To ship at the port of shipment goods of the description contained in the contract within the time fixed or within a reasonable time if no time is fixed.
3. To procure a proper contract of affreightment (Bill of Lading) under which the goods will be delivered at the destination contemplated by the contract.
4. To arrange for an insurance upon the terms current in the trade which will be available for the benefit of the buyer.
5. To tender at the earliest to the buyer, either at the place named in the contract or at the place of business of the buyer, all the necessary shipping documents, *viz.*, Invoice, Bill of Lading, Insurance Policy etc., so that the buyer may know what freight he has to pay, to obtain delivery of the goods, if they arrive, or recover for their loss if they are lost on the voyage.

Duties of the Buyer

1. Buyer is bound to accept all the complete and regular shipping documents when they are tendered to him.
2. He must pay the price irrespective of the arrival of the goods. He is bound to pay the price even before the arrival of the goods or even if the goods are destroyed because he can claim compensation for the loss in the value of goods from the insurance company.

---

8. A.I.R. (1959), Cal. 328.
9. Kwei Lek Chao *v.* British Traders and Shippers Ltd. (1954), 2 Q.B. 459.

Ex-ship Contract

In case of an ex-ship contract, the seller agrees to sell and deliver goods from a ship which has come overseas. The ownership in the goods passes on to the buyer only when they are actually delivered to the buyer at the port of destination. It is the duty of the seller to meet all expenses of the voyage and hand over to the buyer a proper delivery order which will enable him to have delivery of goods. Since the goods are at the seller's risk during the course of voyage, it is in his interest to get the goods insured.

KEY TERMS

- **Actual Delivery :** Physical handing over of the possession of the goods by the seller to the buyer.
- **Constructive Delivery :** Acknowledgement by a third person in possession of goods to hold them on behalf of and at the disposal of the buyer.
- **Delivery :** Voluntary transfer of possession of goods from seller to buyer.
- **Symbolic Delivery :** Delivery of means of obtaining possession of goods by the seller to the buyer.

TEST QUESTIONS

Objective Type : ***Test Your Knowledge***

1. State whether each of the following statements is *True* or *False*
   (*i*) In case of a *CIF* contract, the seller agrees to sell and deliver the goods from a ship which has come overseas.
   (*ii*) Unless otherwise agreed the expenses incidental to putting the goods in a deliverable state are to be borne by the seller.
   (*iii*) In the absence of any contract to the contrary, the buyer must apply for delivery.
   (*iv*) Unless otherwise agreed the buyer is not bound to accept delivery of goods in instalments.
   (*v*) In an ex-ship contract property passes when goods are unloaded from the ship.
   [***Ans.*** (*i*) False; (*ii*) True; (*iii*) True; (*iv*) True; (*v*) False.]
2. Select the most appropriate answer
   (*i*) Delivery of the key of the warehouse by the seller to the buyer will amount to :
   (*a*) symbolic delivery (*b*) constructive delivery
   (*c*) actual delivery.
   (*ii*) Unless otherwise agreed :
   (*a*) delivery of goods and payment of price have to be done concurrently,
   (*b*) payment of price should precede delivery,
   (*c*) delivery of goods should precede payment of price.
   (*iii*) A *CIF* contract is performed by delivery of :
   (*a*) shipping documents relating to the goods, (*b*) actual delivery of goods, and
   (*c*) constructive delivery of goods.
   [***Ans.*** (*i*) (*a*); (*ii*) (*a*); (*iii*) (*a*)]

Essay Type : *For Review, Discussion and Practice*

1. Explain the term 'delivery' as used in a contract of sale and state the rules regarding valid delivery of goods. *(CA Inter, May 1992)*
2. "The CIF contract is not a contract for sale of goods but a contract for the sale of documents relating to the goods." Comment and explain the duties of a seller and a buyer in such a contract.
3. Write short notes on :
   (*a*) Instalment Deliveries. (*b*) Ex-ship Contract.
4. Define the term "Delivery of Goods". State the different modes of effective delivery of goods. [*B.Com. (Hons), Delhi 2012*]

PRACTICAL PROBLEMS

1. A contract is made for the supply of 100 tonnes of flock by instalments. The first 15 deliveries are satisfactory but the sixteenth instalment contains much more chlorine than what is permitted. However, the next deliveries are to the complete satisfaction of the buyer. The buyer wants to repudiate the whole contract. Advise.
   [***Ans.*** The buyer cannot do so. The chances of supplying goods not according to terms seem to be negligible.]
2. *A* buys certain bags of wheat from *B*. Without making proper inspection of the quality of wheat he sells these bags to different buyers. After a few days, *A* comes to know that the wheat is not of the quality as agreed. Can he repudiate the contract?
   [***Ans.*** No. Sale of wheat amounts to his acceptance of goods.]
3. *B* agrees to sell and deliver to *A* 300 quintals of rice. Only 200 quintals are delivered. *A* gets the rice weighed and accepts the quintals sent. *A* afterward, objects that the whole of the 300 quintals was not delivered and refuses to pay for 200 quintals. Can *A* be compelled to pay the price for 200 quintals? What are the provisions of the Indian Sale of Goods Act in this regard?
   [***Ans.*** *A* can be compelled to compensate *B* for the price of 200 quintals.]

Chapter 5

REMEDIAL MEASURES

LEARNING OBJECTIVES

A careful study of this chapter will enable you to :

- understand the meaning of an unpaid seller;
- describe the rights of an unpaid seller;
- enumerate the rights of an aggrieved party under the Sales of Goods Act; and
- explain the meaning of certain key terms.

MEANING OF UNPAID SELLER

Unpaid seller means a seller :

(*i*) who has not been paid or tendered the whole of the price of the goods sold, or

(*ii*) who had received a bill of exchange or any other negotiable instrument as a conditional payment but which is subsequently dishonoured.

The term seller in this case will include every person in the position of a seller, *e.g.*, an agent of the seller to whom the bill of lading has been endorsed, or consignor or agent who has himself paid, or is directly responsible for the price (*Sec. 45*).

Example : *A* purchased some goods in his personal name on behalf of his principal *B*. *B* refuses to pay the price of the goods. Since *A* has incurred personal liability, the relationship between him and his principal will be taken as that of a seller and a buyer. *A* will be taken as unpaid seller under the provisions of section 45.[1]

The term *unpaid seller* however does not include a buyer, who after having paid the price, rejects the goods. He will, therefore, be not entitled to the right of lien on rejected goods as available to an unpaid seller.[2]

RIGHTS OF UNPAID SELLER

The unpaid seller has the following two types of rights under the Sale of Goods Act :

1. Rights of an unpaid seller against the goods

(*a*) *When the property in the goods has been transferred*

(*i*) Right of lien.

(*ii*) Right of stoppage of goods in transit.

(*iii*) Right of resale.

---

1. Hiralal Chimanlal *v.* Pehladrai & Co. (1929), 31 Bom. L.R. 508.
2. Shah Trilok Chand Poosaji *v.* Crystal Co., A.I.R. (1955), Mad. 481.

(*b*) *When the property in the goods has not been transferred.*

Right of withholding delivery.

2. Rights of an unpaid seller against the buyer personally

(*a*) Right to sue for price.

(*b*) Right to sue for damages.

(*c*) Right to sue for interest.

Each of the above rights are being discussed in the following pages :

1. Rights against goods

(*I*) *When property in goods has been transferred.*

(*i*) Right of Lien (*Secs. 47 to 49*)

Lien is a right of an unpaid seller to retain possession on the goods which are under his actual possession until he is paid or tendered the price of those goods. If the goods are in the actual possession of the seller, transfer of property, title or ownership in those goods to the buyer will be immaterial for the exercise of the lien on the goods by the unpaid seller. Right of lien will not also be affected by the seller parting with a document capable of transferring title, *e.g.*, bill of Lading or any other type of delivery order, provided the goods remain in the actual possession of the seller. The unpaid seller may exercise his right of lien notwithstanding that he may be holding the goods with the consent of the buyer as his agent or bailee.

Unpaid seller's right of lien will extend to the whole of the goods in his possession. He may refuse to deliver a part of the goods on payment of a proportionate part of the price by the buyer.

Unpaid seller's right of lien extends only to the price, and not for any other type of maintenance or custody charges etc. Wharehousing charges for keeping the goods in a godown in exercise of lien for the price will not be allowed.

Unpaid seller is entitled to exercise his right of lien on the remainder of the goods if part of them have already been delivered to the buyer, except when such part delivery has been made under such circumstances as to show an agreement to waive the lien (*Sec. 48*).

When can lien be exercised? Following are the cases where an unpaid seller may exercise his right of lien on the goods sold until price is paid or tendered for them :

1. Where goods have been sold on credit, but the period of credit has expired without payment of price.

2. Where the buyer becomes insolvent. It may be noted that an unpaid seller can exercise his right of lien even within the period of credit if the buyer becomes insolvent within that period (*Sec. 47*).

When lien is lost? Unpaid seller will lose his right of lien on the goods in the following three cases :

1. When the seller delivers the goods to a carrier or other bailee for the purpose of transmission to the buyer without reserving the right of disposal of the goods.

2. When the buyer or his agent lawfully obtains possession of the goods. In case the goods are redelivered to the seller for some specific purpose *e.g.*, repair etc. it does not revive the unpaid seller's lien.[3]

3. When the seller expressly or implied waives his right of lien, *e.g.*, grants fresh term of credit or accepts a negotiable instrument from the buyer for the payment of price of the goods (*Sec. 49*).

Seller is entitled to exercise right of lien until the payment or tender of price. A decree for the price being passed by the court alone will not destroy lien until it is satisfied by payment of the amount due. A tender of the price will put an end to the lien even though the seller may have declined to receive the money. Right of lien, if once lost, will not revive if the buyer redelivers the goods to him for any particular purpose.

(*ii*) Right of Stopping the Goods in Transit (*Sec. 50 to 50*)

Right of stopping the goods in transit is just an extension of the unpaid seller's right of lien. It arises when the seller has lost the opportunity of exercising the right of lien, *i.e.*, the goods are no more under his physical possession. This right places the unpaid seller in a position similar to that which he had lost by parting with the goods. It does not amount to rescinding of the contract of sale. An unpaid seller can exercise right of stoppage of goods in transit when each of the following conditions are satisfied :

1. Seller had parted with the possession of the goods.

2. Goods are in the course of transmission to the buyer, *i.e.*, they have not reached in the possession of the buyer thought they have gone out of the seller's actual possession.

3. The buyer of the goods has become insolvent.

4. The seller must not have been prevented by any other provision of the Act from exercising this right, *e.g.*, seller will lose this right where the buyer who has obtained document of title assigns or pledges or sells the goods for value to a *bona fide* transferee.

Unpaid seller may resume possession of the goods so long as they are in the course of transit and may retain those goods under his possession until he is paid or tendered the price thereof.

Duration of Transit (*Sec. 51*)

Goods are deemed to be in the course of transit from the time when they are delivered to a carrier or other bailee for the purpose of transmission to the buyer, till the buyer or his agent on his behalf takes delivery of them from such carrier or bailee. Following are the cases where transit is presumed to be at an end and the seller's right of stopping the goods in transit terminates :

1. When the buyer or his agent obtains delivery of the goods before their arrival at the fixed destination. Such an unauthorised delivery by the carrier to the buyer may make him liable to the seller for damages but so far as seller's right of stoppage in transit is concerned, it will terminate.

2. When after the arrival of the goods at the appointed destination, the carrier or other bailee acknowledges to the buyer or his agent that he holds the goods on his behalf.

3. When goods are delivered to the carrier hired by the buyer and who acts as an agent of the buyer.

---

3. Eduljee *v.* John Bros. (1944), I.L.R. Nag. 37.

4. Where the carrier or other bailee wrongfully refuses to deliver the goods to the buyer or his agent.

5. Where part delivery of the goods has been made to the buyer or his agent under such circumstances as to show an agreement to give up possession of the whole of the goods, the transit will be at an end for the remainder of the goods which are yet in the course of transit.

Transit does not come to an end where the goods have been rejected by the buyer and the carrier or the bailee continues in their possession. The fact that the seller refuses to take them back will be immaterial for ascertaining the duration of the transit.

How Stoppage in Transit can be Effected? (*Sec. 52*)

There are two modes of effecting stoppages of the delivery of the goods to the buyer which are in the course of transmission :

(*a*) by the seller taking actual possession of the goods, or

(*b*) by the seller giving notice of his claim to the carrier or other bailee who has the actual possession over the goods.

Where the goods are in the actual possession of a person (servant or agent) other than the principal carrier, notice to be effective must be given at such time and under such circumstances that the principal or the employer, by the exercise of reasonable diligence may communicate it to his servant or agent in time to prevent the delivery of the goods to the buyer.

Distinction between Right of Lien and Right of Stoppage in Transit

(*a*) Though both the rights arise only when the property in the goods has passed to the buyer yet the right of lien can be exercised only when the goods are in the actual possession of seller, while right of stoppage in transit can be enforced so long as the goods have not reached the possession of the buyer though the seller has parted with their possession. Both of these rights will terminate if the buyer obtains possession of the goods.

(*b*) Right of stopping the goods in transit arises only when the buyer has become insolvent, while a seller can exercise lien so long as the price of the goods has not been paid or tendered to him. Buyer's solvency or otherwise is immaterial in this respect.

(*c*) The right of lien is exercised to retain possession of goods while the right of stoppage of goods in transit is exercised to retain possession of goods from the carrier of the goods.

Effect of Sub-sale or Pledge by Buyer (*Sec. 53*)

The unpaid seller's right of lien or stoppage of goods in transit is not at all affected even if the buyer has sold or made any other disposition of the goods unless the seller has given his assent thereto.

Example : *X* sold 80 quintals of barley out of a granary to *Y*, who sold 60 quintals to *K* before the goods had been ascertained by *X*. *K* paid *Y* and obtained a delivery order and presented it to *X* who consented to forward barley on being requested to do so. Held *X* the unpaid seller had recognised the title of *K*, the sub-buyer, and therefore, was estopped from exercising the lien which he had waived.

But, where a document of title to goods has been issued or lawfully transferred to any person as buyer or owner of the goods, and that person transfers the document to a person who takes the document in good faith and for consideration, then, if such last mentioned transfer was by way of sale, the unpaid seller's right of lien or stoppage in transit is defeated, and, if such last mentioned transfer was by way of pledge other than disposition for value, the unpaid seller's right of lien or stoppage in transit can only be exercised subject to the right of the transferee.

Examples **:** (*i*) *A* sends and consigns certain goods to *B* and sends him the bill of lading. *A* is still an unpaid seller. While the goods are in transit, *B* becomes insolvent, *B* assigns the bill of lading for cash to *C* who is not aware of his insolvency. *A* cannot stop the goods in transit.

(*ii*) If in the above example, the goods are worth ₹ 10,000 and *B* pledges them with *C* for a sum of ₹ 6,000. *A* can exercise his right of stoppage of goods in transit provided he pays *C* ₹ 6,000 with interest thereon.

Where the transfer is by way of pledge, the unpaid seller may require the pledgee to have the amount secured by the pledge satisfied in the first instance, as far as possible, out of any other goods or securities of the buyer in the hands of the pledgee and available against the buyer.

Example **:** *A* sells some goods to *B* and sends him the bill of lading. *B* pledges the bill of lading together with some government securities with *C* for a loan of ₹ 5,000. As a matter of fact *B* has become insolvent by that time. *C* accepts the documents in absolute good faith. *A* can exercise his right of stoppage of goods in transit only when he pays the loan of *C* to *B*. However, he may ask *C* to satisfy his claim first out of government securities and make him liable only for the balance.

(iii) Right of Resale (*Sec. 54*)

An unpaid seller who has the possession of goods can resell them under the following circumstances :

(*a*) **When the goods are of a perishable nature :** The term perishable has not been defined in the Act, but it means perishable not only physically buy also commercially, *e.g.*, deterioration in the market value by delay. No notice or resale to the buyer is necessary in case of these goods.

(*b*) **When he gives notice of his intention to resell :** An unpaid seller after having exercised his right of lien or stoppage in transit may give notice to the buyer asking him to pay the price within a reasonable time failing which he will be reselling the goods. In case the buyer fails so to pay price after such notice the unpaid seller should sell away the goods within a reasonable time. He will be entitled to recover from the original buyer any loss occasioned by his breach of contract, but the buyer shall not be entitled to any profit which may occur on resale. If such notice is not given, the unpaid seller shall not be entitled to recover such damages and the buyer shall be entitled to the profit, if any, on the resale.

The notice to the buyer has been made obligatory on account of two reasons :

(*i*) The buyer gets one more opportunity of fulfilling the contract by paying the price at the last moment, and

(*ii*) The buyer may, if he is enable to pay the price, see that the goods are sold at a proper price.

It is to be noted that default in giving notice to the original buyer by the unpaid seller will not affect the rights and title of the second purchaser of the same goods which have been resold to him.

(*c*) **When he expressly reserves a right of resale :** Where the seller expressly reserves right of resale in case the buyer should make default, the seller may resell the goods in the event of such a default. No notice to the buyer will be necessary in such a case. The original contract of sale shall thereby be rescinded, but the seller will be entitled to get damages from the buyer for the loss suffered by him.

(II) *When the property in goods has not been transferred.*

Right of withholding Delivery

If the property in the goods has not passed to the buyer, the unpaid seller cannot exercise right of lien, but gets a right of withholding the delivery of goods, similar to and co-extensive with lien.

2. Rights against the Buyer personally

The following rights are available to the unpaid seller against the buyer personally :

(*i*) Right to sue for price (*Sec. 55*).

(*ii*) Right to sue for damages (*Sec. 56*).

(*iii*) Right to sue for interest (*Sec. 61*).

These rights have been discussed below under the heading 'Suits for Breach of Contract.'

Suits for the Breach of Contract

Following rights have been given to the *aggrieved party* by the Sale of Goods Act, in addition to the rights to an unpaid seller as discussed above :

1. **Suit for price** (*Sec. 55*) **:** (1) Where under a contract of sale, the property in the goods has passed to the buyer and the buyer wrongful neglects or refuses to pay for the goods according to the terms of the contract, the seller may sue him for the price of the goods.

(2) Where under a contract of sale, the price is payable on a certain day irrespective of delivery and the buyer wrongfully neglects or refuses to pay such price, the seller may sue him for the price although the property in the goods has not passed and the goods have not been appropriated to the contract.

2. **Damages for non-acceptance** (*Sec. 56*) **:** Where the buyer wrongfully neglects or refuses to accept and pay for the goods, the seller may sue him for damages for non-acceptance.

The damages for non-acceptance will be such as directly and naturally arise in the ordinary course of events from the breach and where there is an available market for the goods in question. *The measure of damage is a fair price to be ascertained by the difference between the contract price and the market or current price at the time when the goods ought to have been accepted.*

3. **Damages for non-delivery** (*Sec. 57*) **:** Where the seller wrongfully neglects or refuses to deliver the goods to the buyer, the buyer may sue the seller for damages for non-delivery.

4. **Specific performance** (*Sec. 58*) **:** In any for breach of contract to deliver specific or ascertained goods, the court may, if it thinks fit, on the application of the plaintiff, by its decree, direct that the contract shall be performed specifically, without giving the defendant the option of retaining the goods on payment of damages. The decree may be unconditional, or upon such terms and conditions as to damages, payment of the price or otherwise, as the court may deem just. The power of the court to order specific performance in such a case is to be used subject to rules contained in the Specific Relief Act regarding specific performance of the contract.

5. **Remedy for breach or warranty** (*Sec. 59*) **:** Where there is a breach of warranty by the seller, or where the buyer elects or is compelled to treat any breach of a condition on the part of the seller

as a breach of warranty, the buyer is not by reason only of such breach of warranty entitled to reject the goods; but may :

(*a*) set up against the seller the breach of warranty, in diminution or extinction of the price; or

(*b*) sue the seller for damages for breach of warranty.

Example : *A* sold cingfoin seeds to *B* with a warranty that they were good new growing seeds. Soon after, *B* found out that the seeds did not correspond with the warranty. He afterwards sowed a part of the seeds and sold the remainder. In an action by *A* to recover the price of the seeds, it was held that *B* was competent to sow the seeds to show that the seeds did not correspond with the warranty. *B* was also not bound to return the seeds without using it. He had not precluded himself from bringing an action for breach of the warranty, or from insisting on such breach in an action by *A* in order to show that the seed was of less value than the seller represented it to be.[4]

6. **Repudiation of contract before due date** (*Sec. 60*) **:** Where either party to a contract of sale repudiates the contract before the date of delivery, the other may either treat the contract as subsisting and wait till the date of delivery, or he may treat the contract as rescinded and sue for damages of the breach.

7. **Interest by way of damages and special damages** (*Sec. 61*) **:** The seller or the buyer is entitled to recover interest or special damages in any case, where under the law, interest or special damages may be recoverable, or to recover the money paid where the consideration for the payment of it has failed.

In the absence of a contract to the contrary, the court may award interest at such rate as it thinks fit on the amount of the price--

(*a*) to the seller in a suit by him for the amount of the price--from the date of the tender of the goods or from the date on which the price was payable;

(*b*) to the buyer in a suit by him for the refund or the price in a case of a breach of the contract on the part of the seller--from the date on which the payment was made.

Effect of increase or decrease in taxes [*Sec. 64*(*a*)] : Unless a different intention appears from the terms of the contract in the event of any taxes of the nature of customs or excise duty on goods or taxes on sale or purchase of goods being imposed is increased or decreased in respect of any goods after the making of any contract for the sale of purchase of such goods without stipulation as to the payment of tax where tax was not chargeable at the time of making of the contract, or for the sale or purchase of such goods tax-paid where tax was chargeable at that time,-

(*a*) If such imposition or increase so takes effect that the tax or increased tax, as the case may be, or any part of such tax is paid or is payable, the seller may add so much to the contract price as will be equivalent to the amount paid or payable in respect of such taxes or increase of tax, and he shall be entitled to be paid and to sue for and recover such addition and

(*b*) if such decrease or remission so taken effect that the decreased tax only or no tax, as the case may be, is paid or is payable, the buyer may deduct so much from the contract price as will be equivalent to the decrease of tax or remitted tax, and he shall not be liable to pay, or be sued for, or in respect of, such deduction.

4. Poulton *v.* Lattimole (1829), 9 B & C. 259.

KEY TERMS

- **Lien :** A right to retain goods belonging to another person till satisfaction of certain outstanding claims.
- **Sub-sale :** A subsequent sale made by the original buyer of the goods to a third party.
- **Unpaid Seller :** A seller who has not been paid the whole price of the goods sold.

TEST QUESTIONS

Objective Type : ***Test Your Knowledge***

1. State whether each of the following statements is *True* or *False*

(*i*) A buyer, who after having paid the price, rejects the goods is also an unpaid seller.

(*ii*) Right of stopping the goods in transit is just an extension of the unpaid seller's right of lien.

(*iii*) The unpaid seller lost his right of lien in the event of the buyer making a sub-sale.

(*iv*) The transit is deemed to be at an end when the buyer or his agent obtains delivery of goods before their arrival at the fixed destination.

(*v*) The right of stopping the goods in transit arises only when buyer has become insolvent.

(*vi*) A seller may deliver goods to a carrier with right of disposal.
(ICWA Foundation, June 1998)

(*vii*) The right of an unpaid seller for stoppage in transit can be exercised along with the right of lien. *(ICWA Foundation, June 2001)*

(*viii*) An unpai seller can also stop in transit even in those cases where the buyer is solvent.
(CS Foundation, Dec. 2004)

[***Ans.*** (*i*) False; (*ii*) True; (*iii*) False; (*iv*) True; (*v*) True; (*vi*) True; (*vii*) False; (*viii*) False.]

2. Select the most appropriate answer

(*i*) Unpaid seller of goods has no right of lien where :

(*a*) the goods have been sold without any stipulation as to credit.

(*b*) he has parted with the possession of the goods,

(*c*) buyer become insolvent,

(*d*) the goods have been sold on credit but the term of credit has expired.

(*ii*) The unpaid seller can exercise the right of resale of the goods when :

(*a*) goods are of a perishable nature

(*b*) property in goods has not been transferred to the buyer

(*c*) the buyer has become insolvent.

(*iii*) The right of lien is exercised :

(*a*) to retain possession of goods

(*b*) to regain possession of goods

(*c*) to resell the goods.

[***Ans.*** (*i*) (*b*), (*ii*) (*a*), (*iii*) (*a*)]

Essay Type : ***For Review, Discussion and Practice***

1. When can seller of goods be deemed to be an unpaid seller? What conditions must be satisfied before the right of lien over the goods sold may be exercised by the seller?
2. Explain the rights of a buyer against the seller for breach of contract under the Sale of Goods Act.
3. When is a seller of goods deemed to be an 'Unpaid Seller' under the Sale of Goods Act? When can an unpaid seller re-sell goods? Explain.

4. Distinguish between right of lien and right of stoppage in transit of an unpaid seller. (*B.Com. (Hons), Delhi 2012*)
5. Discuss the remedies available to seller against the buyer in case of breach of contract of sales. (*C.A. Foundation, May 1998*)
6. Who is an unpaid seller? State his rights. (*ICWA Foundation, Dec. 2000; CS Foundation, June 2007; Dec. 2007*)
7. Write short note on Unpaid Seller's right for stoppage of goods in transit. (*CS Foundation, Dec. 2000*)
8. Who is an unpaid seller? Can unpaid seller resell the goods? If so when? (*CS Foundation, June 1998; B.Com. (Hons), Delhi 2011*)
9. When can an unpaid seller of goods exercise his right of lien over the goods under the Sale of Goods Act? Can he exercise his right of lien even if the property in goods has passed to the buyer? When such a right is terminated? Can he exercise his right even after he has obtained a decree for the price of goods from the court? (*ICAI, PEE II, May 2005*)
10. What do you understand by the term "unpaid seller" under the Sale of Goods Act, 1930? When can an unpaid seller exercise the right of stoppage of goods in transit? (*ICAI, PEE II, May 2004*)
11. Briefly discuss the rights of an unpaid seller under the Sale of Goods Act? (*GGSIPU, BBA (H), June 2001*)
12. Explain the rights of unpaid seller against – (*a*) The goods, and (*b*) The buyer personally. (*GGSIPU, BBA (H), May 2002*)
13. Explain the term 'Unpaid Seller' with suitable examples. Discuss his rights against the buyer personally. (*GGSIPU, BBA (H), May 2003*)
14. Who is unpaid seller and what are his rights against the goods? (*B.Com. (Hons.), Delhi 1990, 1992, 1993, 1997, 1998, 2001, B.Com. (Pass), Delhi 2003*)
15. Under what circumstances can an unpaid seller exercise the right of resale? (*B.Com. (Pass), Delhi 2000*)
16. Compare the right of lien and stoppage in transit in case of an unpaid seller. (*B.Com. (Hons.), Delhi 1990*)
17. Discuss three remedies available to a buyer against the seller for a breach of a contract of sale. (*B.Com. (Hons.), Delhi 2001*)
18. What are the rules as to delivery of goods by instalments under Sale of Goods Act? (*B.Com. (Hons.), Delhi 2002*)
19. Explain the effect of sub-sale or pledge bv the buyer on the rights of an unpaid seller. (*B.Com. (Hons.), Delhi 2003*)
20. Distinguish between particular lien and general lien. (*B.Com. (Hons.), Delhi 2004*)
21. "The right of stoppage in transit is an extension of the unpaid seller's right of lien." Comment. (*B.Com. (Hons.), Delhi 2011, 2012*)
22. Define the term 'Unpaid Seller' as per Sale of Goods Act, 1930. Discuss the rights of unpaid seller against the goods. (*B.Com. (Hons.), Delhi 2005, 2013*)
23. What are the rights of an unpaid seller against the goods? (*CS Foundation, Dec., 2011*)

PRACTICAL PROBLEMS

1. *X* sold a quantity of wheat to *Y*, who paid by cheque which was dishonoured upon presentation. *X* gave a delivery order to *Y* for the wheat and *Y* resold it to *Z*, a purchaser in good faith for consideration endorsing the delivery order to him. *X* refuses to deliver the goods to *Z* on the plea of non-receipt of price. Advise *Z*.

   [***Ans.*** *Z* is entitled to the goods. See 'Effect of sub-sale or pledge by the buyer'.]

2. *X* sells and consigns goods to *Y* of the value of ₹ 10,000. *Y* assigns the bill of lading for these goods to *Z* to secure the sum of ₹ 4,000 due from his to *Z*. *Y* becomes insolvent. Can *X* stop the goods in transit.

[***Ans.*** *X* can stop goods only on payment of ₹ 4,000 to *Z*. See 'Effect of sub-sale or pledge by the buyer'.]

3. *X* sells and consigns goods to *Y*, *X* being still unpaid, *Y* becomes insolvent and while the goods are still in transit *Y* assigns the bill of lading for cash to *Z* who knows that *Y* is insolvent. Can *X* stop the goods in transit?

[***Ans.*** *X* can still stop the goods in transit since the assignee has not acted in good faith.]

4. Goods were sold and sent by the sellers at the request of the buyer to shipping agents of the buyer and were put on board a ship by those agents. Subsequently they were re-loaded and sent back to sellers for the purpose of re-packing. While they were still in possession of the sellers for that purpose the buyer became insolvent. The sellers refused to deliver them to the buyer's trustee in bankruptcy except upon payment of price. Are the sellers entitled to refuse to deliver the goods to the trustee? State reasons for your answer.

[***Ans.*** The sellers had lost their lien by delivering goods to the shipping agents. Their refusal to deliver goods to the trustee in bankruptcy was wrong.]

5. Goods were delivered by the vendor to the railway company for conveyance and the endorsee of the railway receipt paid the freight and obtained delivery. Before the goods were taken out of the station compound the unpaid vendor gave a telegram which was received. State with reasons whether the right of stopping in transit is available.

[***Ans.*** The transit having come to an end, the right of stopping in transit cannot therefore, be exercised.]

6. *X* of Delhi orders *Y* of Madras, to deliver certain goods to him at Delhi. While the goods are lying at the Delhi Railway station, the station master informs *X* that the goods are held at *X*'s risk. But *X* has become insolvent. Has *Y* any right over the goods as an unpaid seller?

[***Ans.*** The transit is at an end and hence *Y* cannot exercise the right of stoppage of goods in transit.]

7. *R* sells and consigns certain goods to *P* for cash and sends the Railway Receipt to him. *R*, being still the unpaid seller, *P* becomes insolvent and while the goods are in transit, *P* assigns the Railway Receipt to *N*, who does not know that *P* is insolvent. *R*, being an unpaid seller wants to exercise his right of stoppage of goods in transit. Advise :

(*i*) Whether *R* can do so?

(*ii*) Would your answer be different if *N* was aware of *P*'s insolvency, before the assignment of the Railway Receipt in favour of *N*?

(*iii*) What are the provisions of the Indian Sale of Goods Act in this regard?

[***Ans.*** (*i*) *R* can not stop the goods in transit. (*ii*) *R* can stop the goods in transit.]

8. *A* sells goods to *B*. *B* pays to *A* through a cheque. Before *B* could obtain the delivery of goods, his cheque was dishonoured by the bank. *A*, therefore, refuses to deliver the goods until paid. Is *A*'s action justified? (*B.Com. (Hons.), Delhi 1988, 2010*)

[***Ans.*** *A* can retain possession of the goods exercising his right of lien under Section 47]

9. Certain goods were sold by sample by *A* to *B*, who in turn sold them by sample to *C*. The goods were not according to the sample. Therefore, *C* rejected the goods and gave notice to *B*. *B* sued *A*. Advise *B*. (*B.Com. (Hons.), Delhi 1990*)

[***Ans.*** There is breach of an implied condition as to 'sale by sample'. Thus, *B* can repudiate the contract, refuse the goods and if he has already paid for them, he can even recover the price.]

10. Suraj sold his car to Sohan for ₹ 75,000. After inspection and satisfaction, Sohan paid ₹ 25,000 and took possession of the car and promised to pay the remaining amount within a month. Later

on Sohan refuses to give the remaining amount on the ground that the car was not in a good condition. Advise Suraj as to what remedy is available to him against Sohan.

(*PEE-II, ICAI, May 2006*)

[***Ans.*** Suraj will succeed against Sohan for recovery of the remaining amount. Apart from this Suraj is also entitled to interest on the remaining amount, interest during the pendency of the suit and costs of the proceedings.]

11. *A*, an agent of a buyer, had obtained goods from the Railway organization and loaded the goods on his truck. In the meantime, the Railway organization received a notice from *B*, the seller, for stopping goods in transit as the buyer had become insolvent. Referring to the provisions of the Sale of Goods Act, 1930 decide whether the Railway organization can stop the goods in transit, as instructed by the seller? (*PEE-II, ICAI, May 2007*)

[***Ans.*** Railway Organization cannot act as instructed by the seller, who has lost the light of stoppage of the goods in transit.]

Chapter 6

AUCTION SALE

LEARNING OBJECTIVES

A careful study of this chapter will enable you to :

- understand the meaning of auction sale;
- enumerate the rules regarding auction sale; and
- explain the meaning of certain key terms.

MEANING AND RULES

Sale by auction is a public sale where the goods are generally sold to the highest bidder.[1] Following are the rules regarding auction sales :

(1) When goods are sold by auction in separate lots, each lot will *prima facie* be deemed to be the subject of a separate contract of sale.

(2) The sale is complete when the auctioneer announces its completion by the fall of the hammer or in other customary manner and until such announcement is made, any bidder may retract his bid.

Examples : (*i*) *A* made a bid of ₹ 1,000 for an old and rare stamp at an auction sale but withdrew it before the fall of the hammer. One of the conditions of the sale was 'bid once made shall not be withdrawn' and this was known to *A*. Discuss the rights of the auctioneer and *A*.

The condition in the auction sale, 'a bid once made shall not be withdrawn', is against the provisions of law, and therefore, is not enforceable, Thus, *A* has every right to withdraw his bid before it is accepted by the auctioneer.

(*ii*) *A* sold his car by auction. It was knocked down to *B*, who allowed to take it away on the condition that he would give a cheque for the price and the ownership would not pass to him till the cheque was cleared. The cheque was not cleared but *B* sold away the car to *C* in the meanwhile. It was held that the ownership of the car had passed on to *B* when it was knocked down to him. *C* therefore, has a good title to the car.[2]

In case goods are damaged before completion of sale, the seller will have to bear the loss.

Example : *A* bids ₹ 5,000 for a costly flower was at an auction sale. The auctioneer purports to accept the bid by striking his hammer, but accidentally strikes the vase, which is broken to pieces. The sale is not complete, and therefore, the seller shall bear the loss.

(3) A right to bid may be reserved expressly by or on behalf of the seller and where such right is expressly so reserved, but not otherwise, the seller or any one person on his behalf may, subject to the provisions hereinafter contained, bid at the auction.

---

1. An auctioneer has the right to make the auction subject to such conditions as he likes. He may reserve for himself the right to accept a lower hid in preference to a higher bid. (The Coffee Board *v.* Famous Coffee and Tea Works (1965), A.I.R. Mad. 14).
2. Dennant *v.* Skinner (1948), 2 K.B. 164.

(4) Where the sale is not notified to be subject to a right to bid on behalf of the seller, it will not be lawful for the seller to bid himself or to employ any person to bid at such sale, of for the auctioneer knowingly to take any bid from the seller or any such person; and any sale contravening this rule may be treated as fraudulent by the buyer.

(5) If the seller makes use of pretended bidding to raise the price, the sale is voidable at the option of the buyer.

The person employed by the seller to make pretended bids are known by different technical names such as *puffers, by-bidders, white bonnets or decoy ducks.*

(6) The sale may be notified to be subject to a reserve or upset price in order to protect auctioneer from too low a bid. In such a case the auction is called *with reserves.* The auctioneer in this case reserves with himself the right not to sell the article in case the highest bid does not come upto the level of the minimum price fixed. An auction is said to be *without reserves*, when no minimum price has been fixed and the auctioneer shall sell the article to the highest bidder irrespective of the amount of the bid.

In case of an auction sale *with reserves,* the auctioneer can refuse to sell the goods to highest bidder if he, by mistake, knocks down the lot for less than the minimum or reserve price. The buyer will have no remedy against the auctioneer.[3]

Example : *F* conducted an auction sale of certain properties. The offer of each lot of properties was subject to a reserve price. *M* made a bid which was lower than the reserve price. *F* knocked down the lot to *M*. It was held that the sale was not valid. The court observed, *"A* sale by auction subject to a reserve price on the article sold, where the fact that there is a reserve price is known, the invitation by the auctioneer calling for bids, the bidding and the knocking down of article to the highest bidder are all subject to the condition that the reserve price must be reached. The auctioneer could not effectively accept such a bid, because he could not make a contract so as to bid his principal, to accept less than the reserve price."[4]

Original bidder, whose bid was accepted but who has failed to pay the price, shall continue to be liable for the price even after resale of goods to some other party. He shall be liable for the difference of price which he had agreed to pay the price which the goods are able to fetch on their resale.

Implied Warranties in an Auction Sale

All auction sales are subject to the following implied warranties for which the auctioneer is held responsible :

(*a*) he warrants his authority to sell;
(*b*) he knows of no defects in his principal's title;
(*c*) he guarantees to give quiet and undisturbed possession against payment of price.

Knock out Agreement

A *bona fide* agreement between persons not to bid against each other at an auction sale is called a 'knock out agreement.' Such an agreement is perfectly valid.[5] An agreement between two or more

3. Rainbow *v.* Howkins (1904), 2 K.B. 322.
4. Manus *v.* Fortesque (1907), 2 K.B. 1.
5. Jyoti *v.* Jhownull, 36 Cal. 134.

persons not to bid against each other at an auction sale and to divide the property purchased by one of the bidders amongst themselves is perfectly valid provided, it does not amount to defrauding a third person. Seller may protect his interest against any such combination by placing a reserve price on the goods.

Example : In an auction sale of a fishery by a public authority, the villagers colluded that only one of them shall bid for all of them. The fishery was sold for a very low price. On a suit being filed by the public authority for setting aside the contract on the ground of its being misguided by the villagers, it was held that the suit was not maintainable and agreement among the villagers was perfectly legal.[6]

Damping

Damping is an overt act to dissuade the would be purchasers from bidding or from raising the price by pointing out defects in the goods. Damping is illegal and the auctioneer can withdraw the property from auction.

KEY TERMS

- **Auction Sale :** A public sale where the goods are generally sold to the highest bidder.
- **Damping :** An overt act to dissuade the would be purchaser from bidding or raising the price by pointing out defects in the goods.
- **Knockout Agreement :** A *bona fide* agreement between persons not to bid against cash other at an auction sale.
- **Puffers :** Persons employed to make pretended bids. They are also known as by bidders, white bonnets or decoy ducks.

TEST QUESTIONS

Objective Type : *Test Your knowledge*

1. State whether each of the following statements is *True* or *False*
   (*i*) An auctioneer may reserve for himself expressly the right to bid.
   (*ii*) Damping is illegal.
   (*iii*) The ownership of the goods in a sale by auction is transferred to the bidder as soon as he makes a bid.
   (*iv*) The auctioneer can always notify that the auction sale is subject to a reserve price.
   (*v*) The liability of the original bidder whose bid was accepted but who failed to pay the price terminates soon after the sale of goods to some other party.
   (*vi*) The bidder cannot revoke his bid. (*CS Foundation, June 1998*)
   (*vii*) An auctioneer can refuse to accept the highest bid. (*CS Foundation, June 2007*)
   (*viii*) The sale is complete when the auctioneer announces its completion by the fall of hammer or .... manner. (*CS Foundation, June 2008*)

[***Ans.*** (*i*) True; (*ii*) False; (*iii*) False; (*iv*) False; (*v*) False; (*vi*) False; (*vii*) True; (*viii*) In the other customary manner]

6. Pattipati Ramalingaiah *v.* Nafulanganta A.I.R. 1951, Mad, 390. In United States of America such agreements have been held to be illegal.

2. Fill in the blanks
   (*i*) White bonnets are person employed to make.........
   (*ii*) A seller may protect his interest against a..............by placing a reserve price on the goods.
   (*iii*) In case the goods are sold in separate lots, each lot will be deemed to be subject of....................
   (*iv*) In case the seller makes use of pretended bids, the sale is................at the option of the buyer.
   (*v*) The sale by auction is complete when the auctioneer announce its completion by the fall of.................. *(CS Foundation, June 2007)*
   (*vi*) The sale is complete when the auctioneer announces its completion by the fall of hammer or .... manner. *(CS Foundation, June 2008)*

   [***Ans.*** (*i*) pretended bids, (*ii*) knockout agreement, (*iii*) a separate contract of sale, (*iv*) voidable, (*v*) the hammer, (*vi*) in the other customary manner.]

Essay Type : *For Review, Discussion and Practice*

1. State the rules regarding 'Auction Sales.' Under what circumstances, the auctioneer can refuse to sell goods after having advertised to sell goods by auction or after having accepted the highest bid? *(CA Foundation, May 2000)*
2. Write a note on "knock out agreements".
3. Write a short note on "Auction Sales". *(CS Foundation, Dec. 2006)*
4. In an aution sale, a bid once made can be withdrawn by the Bidder. Comment citing rules. *(ICWAI Inter, June 2009)*

PRACTICAL PROBLEMS

1. *A* sold a car by an auction to *B*. The buyer was in fact a swindler. He gave a fake cheque and obtained delivery. *A* in order to protect himself, inserted a clause in the agreement that the property in the car would not pass to *B* until the cheque was cleared. *B* sold the car to *C* before the fraud could be detected. *A* claims the car from *C*. Will he succeed?

   [***Ans.*** No. Ownership passed when the hammer fell. *C* gets goods title.]

2. In an auction sale on of the conditions was, "The seller does not bind himself to accept the highest bid or any bid, he is not bound to assign any reason for his decision and his decision shall be final conclusive," Is such a condition valid?

   [***Ans.*** Yes. Auctioneer may impose such conditions as he likes.]

3. An auctioneer advertised in the newspaper that a sale of office furniture will be held at Bangalore. Ajay, a broker of Mumbai, reached Bangalore on the appointed date and time. But the auctioneer withdrew all the office furniture from the auction sale. The broker sued for his loss of time and expenses. Will he succeed? *(CS Foundation, December 2003)*

   [***Ans.*** The broker will not succeed.]

SECTION 3

MISCELLANEOUS

Chapter 1

THE LIMITED LIABILITY PARTNERSHIP ACT

LEARNING OBJECTIVES

A careful study of this chapter will enable you to :

- Understand the meaning and nature of Limited Partnership;
- Identify the steps to be taken for formation of Limited Partnership;
- Understand the concept of designated partners;
- Differentiate Limited Liability Partnership from Ordinary Partnership and from Company;
- Explain the mutual relationship of partners of a limited liability firm;
- Determine the extent and limitation of liability of limited liability partnership and partners;
- Explain the requirements as to financial disclosures, winding up and dissolution of a limited liability partnership; and
- Explain the meaning of certain key terms.

INTRODUCTION

The formation of Limited Liability Partnership in India is a sequel to the recommendations of the Naresh Chandra Committee (2003) and Irani Committee (2005) as a new form of business entity. A limited liability partnership is a hybrid between a company and a partnership firm. The limited liability partnership (LLP) is a separate legal entity with unlimited capacity but limited liability of the partners.

The Limited Liability Partnership Act, 2008 has come into effect from 1st April 2009. The Act makes provisions for the formation and regulation of limited liability partnership and for matters connected therewith or incidental thereto. It extends to whole of India. The Act is administered by the Ministry of Corporate Affairs. It comprises of 81 Sections in 14 Chapters and 4 Schedules.

MEANING AND NATURE OF LIMITED LIABILITY PARTNERSHIP

A Limited Liability Partnership means a partnership formed and registered under the Limited Liability Partnership Act. The provisions of the Partnership Act, 1932 are not applicable to Limited Partnership. The following are the essentials of a limited liability partnership as per Sections 3 and 4 of the LLP Act:

(*i*) It is a body corporate formed and incorporated under the *LLP* Act and is a legal entity separate from that of its partners. It has perpetual succession.

(*ii*) Any change in the partners of a LLP shall not affect the existence, rights and liabilities of the limited liability partnership.

(*iii*) The minimum number of partners is 2 but there is not ceiling on maximum number of partners.

(*iv*) It is created by registration of an incorporation document with the Registrar of Joint Stock Companies.

(*v*) Any individual or body corporate can be a partner of a limited liability partnership.

FORMATION OF LIMITED LIABILITY PARTNERSHIP

The following steps are to be taken according to Secs. 11 to 15 of LLP Act for getting a limited liability formed or incorporated:

(*i*) ***Filing of Documents:*** For a limited liability partnership to be incorporated–

(*a*) two or more persons associated for carrying on a lawful business with a view to profit shall subscribe their names to an incorporation document;

(*b*) the incorporation document shall be filed in such manner and with such fees, as may be prescribed with the Registrar of Companies of the State in which the registered office of the limited liability partnership is to be situated; and

(*c*) there shall be filed along with the incorporation document, a statement in the prescribed form, made by either an Advocate, or a Company Secretary or a Chartered Accountant or a Cost Accountant, who is engaged in the formation of the limited liability partnership and by any one who subscribed his name to the incorporation document, that all the requirements of this Act and the rules made thereunder have been complied with, in respect of incorporation and matters precedent and incidental thereto.

(*ii*) ***Contents of the Incorporation Document:*** The incorporation document shall be in the prescribed form with the following details:

(*a*) Name of the limited liability partnership. The words 'limited liability partnership' or *LLP* should be added as the last word of the partnership name. Moreover, the name should not resemble the name of any other limited partnership nor be considered as undesirable by the Central Government;

(*b*) Proposed business of the limited liability partnership;

(*c*) Address of the registered office of the limited liability partnership;

(*d*) Name and address of each of the persons who are to be partners of the limited liability partnership on incorporation;

(*e*) Name and address of the persons who are to be designated partners of the limited liability partnership on incorporation;

(*f*) Other information concerning the proposed limited liability partnership as may be prescribed.

(*iii*) ***Incorporation by Registration:*** The Registrar shall retain the incorporation document on complying with the above requirements and shall within a period of fourteen days-

(*a*) register the incorporation document;

(*b*) give a certificate that the limited liability partnership is incorporated by the name specified therein;

(*c*) shall be signed by the Registrar and authenticated by his official seal;

(*d*) the certificate shall be conclusive evidence that the limited liability partnership is incorporated by the name specified therein.

(*iv*) ***Effect of Registration:*** On registration, a limited liability partnership shall, by its name, be capable of –

(*a*) suing and being sued;
(*b*) acquiring, owning, holding and developing or disposing of property, whether movable or immovable, tangible or intangible;
(*c*) having a common seal, if it decides to have one; and
(*d*) doing and suffering such other acts and things as bodies corporate may lawfully do and suffer.

DESIGNATED PARTNERS

According to Section 7 of LLP Act, the designated partners occupy a unique position in the scheme envisaged in the LLP Act. The following are the summarized provisions in this regard:

1. Every limited liability partnership shall have at least two designated partners who are individuals and at least one of them shall be a resident in India provided that in case of a limited liability partnership in which all the partners are bodies corporate or in which one or more partners are individuals and bodies corporate, at least two individuals who are partners of such limited liability partnership or nominees of such bodies corporate shall act as designated partners.
2. An individual shall not become a designated partner in any limited liability partnership unless he has given his prior consent to act as such to the limited liability partnership in such form and manner as may be prescribed.
3. Every limited liability partnership shall file with the Registrar the particulars of every individual who has given his consent to act as designated partner in such form and manner as may be prescribed within thirty days of his appointment.
4. Every designated partner of a limited liability partnership shall obtain a Designated Partner Identification Number (DPIN) from the Central Government.

Penalty for improper use of words "limited liability partnership" of "LLP" [Section 20]: If any person or persons carry on business under any name or title of which the words "Limited Liability Partnership" or "LLP" or any contraction or imitation thereof is or are the last words, that person or each of those persons shall, unless duly incorporated as limited liability partnership, be punishable with fine which shall not be less than fifty thousand rupees but which may extend to five lakh rupees.

LIMITED LIABILITY PARTNERSHIP V/S PARTNERSHIP FIRM

A comparative study of a Limited Liability Partnership and a Partnership firm established under Indian Partnership Act can be done as under:

Basis	*Partnership under Indian Partnership Act*	*Limited Liability Partnership*
Liability	There is unlimited personal liability of each partner for dues of the partnership firm.	Liability limited to the properties of LLP except in case of unauthorized acts, fraud and negligence of partner(s) when the delinquent partner will be personally liable.
Registration	Registration of partnership is not mandatory.	Incorporation of partnership as LLP is mandatory.
Separate Legal Entity	It is not a legal entity separate from its partners. Firm cannot hold property in its own name; cannot sue or be sued in its own name. The firm is a convenient name of all the partners taken together.	It is a legal entity separate from its partners. The firm may hold property in its own name and sue or be sued in its own name.

Partnership Deed	Partnership deed is executed.	'Incorporation Document' is executed. LLP Agreement/First Schedule governs the mutual rights and duties of partners *inter se* and between the partners and the LLP.
Number of Partners	Minimum 2 partners; maximum 10 partners for banking business and 20 in other cases.	Minimum 2 partners; no maximum limit.
Filing of Documents	Documents are required to be filed with Registrar of firms (of respective states).	MCA/ROC is the administrative ministry/ authority.
Liability of Partners	Partners are liable for statutory compliances.	Only Designated Partners are liable for statutory compliances except when LLP has only one Designated Partner (when all the partners are liable).
Business	A Partner cannot enter into business with firm since the latter is not a separate legal entity.	Partners may enter into contracts with their LLP including lending of money. They have rights and obligations therefore as in the case of third parties/ outsiders.
Agency	Every partner of a firm is an agent of the firm and also of other partners.	Every partner of LLP is an agent only of the firm and not of the other partner(s).
Filing of Accounts	There is no requirement as to filing of Annual Accounts or Solvency Statement or Annual Return with Registrar of Firms.	Statement of Accounts, Solvency Statement and Annual Return are to be filed with RoC each year.
Resolution	A Partnership firm can be dissolved as per Act/ Partnership Deed.	LLP is to be wound up and dissolved as per LLP Act.

LIMITED LIABILITY PARTNERSHIP V/S LIMITED LIABILITY COMPANY

The following is the comparative position of a limited liability firm with that of a limited liability company:

Basis	*Limited Liability Company*	*Limited Liability Partnership*
Filing of Documents	Memorandum and Articles of Association are to be filed with RoC. Table A applies in the absence of Articles.	Incorporation document and LLP Agreement are to be filed. First Schedule applies in the absence of LLP Agreement.
Name	Name to end with 'Limited or Private Limited' (Government Companies exempted from latter).	Name to end with 'Limited Liability Partnership' or 'LLP'.
Managerial Power	Managing Director/Manager vested with powers of day-to-day administration subject to the supervision, control and direction of the Board of Directors.	Management rests with those Partners (including designated partners) who are authorized by LLP agreement. (As Designated Partners, they are responsible only for legal compliances).
Remuneration	There are certain restrictions on remuneration payable to the Directors, their relatives etc.	There is no legal restriction on remuneration to partner. Partners will be eligible for remuneration as per LLP Agreement.
Registration of Charges	Charges/mortgages to be valid should be registered with RoC.	No such provision exists for LLPs.
Annual General Meeting	The AGM of shareholders is mandatory.	There is no AGM of partners.

Restrictions on Inter-corporate Loans	There are restrictions on inter-corporate investments and loans.	There are no such restrictions.
Fee	The incorporation fee and Document Registration fees are high. Moreover, many forms are to be filed in.	There is moderate fee for incorporation and filing of documents. Documents are also filed.

PARTNERS AND THEIR RELATIONS

The mutual relations between the partnership and LLP are governed by Sections 22 to 26 of the LLP Act as summarized below:

(*i*) ***Eligibility to be Partners:*** On the incorporation of a limited liability partnership, the persons who subscribed their names to the incorporation document shall be its partners and any other person may become a partner of the limited liability partnership by and in accordance with the limited liability partnership agreement.

( ) ***Relationship of Partners:*** Save as otherwise provided by this Act, the mutual rights and duties of the partners of a limited liability partnership, and the mutual rights and duties of a limited liability partnership and its partners, shall be governed by the limited liability partnership agreement between the partners, or between the limited liability partnership and its partners. In the absence of any agreement between the partners, the mutual rights and duties of the partners of LLP will be governed by the provisions given by in the 1st schedule of the Act as detailed below:

The First Schedule

1. All the partners of a limited liability partnership are entitled to share equally in the capital, profits and losses of the limited liability partnership.
2. The limited liability partnership shall indemnify each partner in respect of payments made and personal liabilities incurred by him–
   (*a*) in the ordinary and proper conduct of the business of the limited liability partnership; or
   (*b*) in or about anything necessarily done for the preservation of the business or property of the limited liability partnership.
3. Every partner shall indemnify the limited liability partnership for any loss caused to it by his fraud in the conduct of the business of the limited liability partnership.
4. Every partner may take part in the management of the limited liability partnership.
5. No partner shall be entitled to remuneration for acting in the business or management of the limited liability partnership.
6. No person may be introduced as a partner without the consent of all the existing partners.
7. Any matter or issue relating to the limited liability partnership shall be decided by a resolution passed by a majority in number of the partners, and for this purpose, each partner shall have one vote. However, no change may be made in the nature of business of the limited liability partnership without the consent of all the partners.
8. Every limited liability partnership shall ensure that decisions taken by it are recorded in the minutes within thirty days of taking such decisions and are kept and maintained at the registered office of the limited liability partnership.

9. Each partner shall render true accounts and full information of all things affecting the limited liability partnership to any partner or his legal representatives.
10. If a partner, without the consent of the limited liability partnership, carries on any business of the same nature as and competing with the limited liability partnership, he must account for and pay over to the limited liability partnership all profits made by him in that business.
11. Every partner shall account to the limited liability partnership for any benefit derived by him without the consent of the limited liability partnership from any transaction concerning the limited liability partnership, or from any use by him of the property, name or any business connection of the limited liability partnership.
12. No majority of the partners can expel any partner unless a power to do so has been conferred by express agreement between the partners.
13. All disputes between the partners arising out of the limited liability partnership agreement which cannot be resolved in terms of such agreement shall be referred for arbitration as per the provisions of the Arbitration and Conciliation Act, 1996.

CESSATION OF PARTNERSHIP

Section 24 of the LLP Act gives the following provisions regarding cessation of a limited liability partnership :

1. A person may cease to be a partner of a limited liability partnership in accordance with an agreement with the other partners or, in the absence of agreement with the other partners as to cessation of being a partner, by giving a notice in writing of not less than thirty days to the other partners of his intention to resign as partner.
2. A person shall cease to be a partner of a limited liability partnership—
   (*a*) on his death or dissolution of the limited liability partnership; or
   (*b*) if he is declared to be of unsound mind by a competent court; or
   (*c*) if he has applied to be adjudged as an insolvent or declared as an insolvent.
3. Where a person has ceased to be a partner of a limited liability partnership (hereinafter referred to as 'former partner'), the former partner is to be regarded (in relation to any person dealing with the limited liability partnership) as still being a partner of the limited liability partnership unless–
   (*a*) the person has notice that the former partner has ceased to be a partner of the limited liability partnership; or
   (*b*) notice that the former partner has ceased to be a partner of the limited liability partnership has been delivered to the Registrar.
4. The cessation of a partner from the limited liability partnership does not by itself discharge the partner from any obligation to the limited liability partnership or to the other partners or to any other person which he incurred while being a partner.
5. Where a partner of a limited liability partnership ceases to be a partner, unless otherwise provided in the limited liability partnership agreement, the former partner or a person entitled to his share in consequence of the death or insolvency of the former partner, shall be entitled to receive from the limited liability partnership–

(a) an amount equal to the capital contribution of the former partner actually made to the limited liability partnership; and

(b) his right to share in the accumulated profits of the limited liability partnership,

After the deduction of accumulated losses of the limited liability partnership, determined as at the date the former partner ceased to be a partner.

EXTENT AND LIMITATION OF LIABILITY OF LIMITED LIABILITY PARTNERSHIP AND PARTNERS

Sections 26 to 31 provide about the liability of partners of an LLP as detailed below:

1. ***Partner as Agent:*** Every partner of a limited liability partnership is, for the purpose of the business of the limited liability partnership, the agent of the limited liability partnership, but not of other partners.

2. ***Extent of liability of Limited Liability Partnership:***

   (i) A limited liability partnership is not bound by anything done by a partner in dealing with a person if–

   (a) the partner in fact has no authority to act for the limited liability partnership in doing a particular act; and

   (b) the person knows that he has no authority or does not know or believe him to be a partner of the limited liability partnership.

   (ii) The limited liability partnership is liable if a partner of a limited liability partnership is liable to any person as a result of a wrongful act or omission on his part in the course of the business of the limited liability partnership or with its authority.

   (iii) An obligation of the limited liability partnership whether arising in contract or otherwise, shall be solely the obligation of the limited liability partnership.

   (iv) The liability of the limited liability partnership shall be met out of the property of the limited liability partnership.

3. ***Holding Out:*** Any person, who by words spoken or written or by conduct, represents himself, or knowingly permits himself to be represented to be a partner in a limited liability partnership is liable to any person who has on the faith of any such representation given credit to the limited liability partnership, whether the person representing himself or represented to be a partner does or does not know that the representation has reached the person so giving credit.

   Provided that where any credit is received by the limited liability partnership as a result of such representation, the limited liability partnership shall, without prejudice to the liability of the person so representing himself or represented to be a partner, be liable to the extent of credit received by it or any financial benefit derived thereon.

4. ***Unlimited liability in case of fraud:*** In the event of an act carried out by a limited liability partnership, or any of its partners, with intent to defraud creditors of the limited liability partnership or any other person, or for any fraudulent purpose, the liability of the limited liability partnership and partners who acted with intent to defraud creditors or for any fraudulent purpose shall be unlimited for all or any of the debts or other liabilities of the limited liability partnership.

WHISTLE-BLOWING POLICY

1. Concept

In an organisation, Whistle-blowing Policy aims at providing a vigil mechanism to ensure that the officers and the employees of the company act in a fair and transparent manner by adopting highest standard of professionalism, honesty, integrity and ethical behaviour. Towards this purpose, the organisation adopts a code of conduct for its officers and employees which lays down the principles and standards that should govern the actions of the organisation, its associates and its employees. Any actual and potential violation of code, howsoever insignificant, is a matter of serious concern for the organisation and should be brought to the attention of the concerned authority. The Whistle Mechanism also provides for adequate safeguards against the victimization of persons reporting such violations.

The person reporting or exposing any kind of information or activity that is deemed illegal, dishonest or incorrect within organisation is known as a whistleblower. The following are a few examples of wrongful activities:

(i) Abuse of authority

(ii) Breach of contract

(iii) Negligence causing substantial and specific danger to public health and safety

(iv) Manipulation of company data/records

(v) Financial irregularities, including fraud, or suspected fraud

(vi) Criminal offence

(vii) Pilferation of confidential/propriety information

(viii) Deliberate violation of law/regulation

(ix) Wastage/misappropriation of company funds/assets

(x) Breach of employee Code of Conduct or Rules.

A whistleblower may be an employee, a former employee or member of an organisation, a government agency, who have willingness to take corrective action on the misconduct.

2. Whistle-Blowing under the LLP Act

The Limited Liability Partnership Act makes the following provisions regarding whistle-blowing as per Section 31 of the said Act:

(i) The Court or Tribunal may reduce or waive any penalty leviable against any partner or employee of a limited liability partnership, if it is satisfied that –

(a) Such partner or employee of a limited liability partnership has provided useful information during investigation of such limited liability partnership; or

(b) When any information given by any partner or employee (whether or not during investigation) leads to limited liability partnership or any partner or employee of such limited liability partnership being convicted under this Act or any other Act.

(ii) No partner or employee of any limited liability partnership may be discharged, demoted, suspended, threatened, harassed or in any other manner discriminated against the terms and conditions of his limited liability partnership or employment merely because of his providing information or causing information to be provided pursuant to para (i) above.

FINANCIAL DISCLOSURES

Sections 34 to 40 of the LLP Act give the following provisions regarding financial disclosures:

1. ***Maintenance of books of accounts, other records and audit etc:***

   (*i*) The limited liability partnership shall maintain such proper books of accounts as may be prescribed relating to its affairs for each year of its existence on cash basis or accrual basis and according to double entry system of accounting and shall maintain the same at its registered office for such period as may be prescribed. [*Sec. 34(1)*]

   (*ii*) Every limited liability partnership shall, within a period of six months from the end of each financial year, prepare a Statement of Account and Solvency for the said financial year as at the last day of the said financial year in such form as may be prescribed, and such statement shall be signed by the designated partners of the limited liability partnership. [*Sec. 34(2)*]

   (*iii*) Every limited liability partnership shall file within the prescribed time, the Statement of Account and Solvency prepared pursuant to sub-section (2) with the Registrar every year in such form and manner and accompanied by such fees as may be prescribed. [*Sec. 34(3)*]

   (*iv*) The accounts of limited liability partnerships shall be audited in accordance with such rules as may be prescribed provided that the Central Government may, by notification in the Official Gazette, exempt any class or classes of limited liability partnerships from the requirements of this sub-section.

   Provided that the Central Government may by notification in the Official Gazettee any class or classes of limited liability partnership from the above requirement [*Sec. 34(4)*].

   (*v*) Any limited liability partnership which fails to comply with the provisions of this section shall be punishable with fine which shall not be less than twenty-five thousand rupees but which may extend to five lakh rupees and every designated partner of such limited liability partnership shall be punishable with fine which shall not be less than ten thousand rupees but which may extend to one lakh rupees. [*Sec. 34(5)*]

2. ***Annual Return:*** Every limited liability partnership shall file an annual return duly authenticated with the Registrar within sixty days of closure of its financial year in such form and manner and accompanied by such fee as may be prescribed. [*Sec. 35(1)*]

   Any limited liability partnership which fails to comply with the provisions of this section shall be punishable with fine which shall not be less than twenty-five thousand rupees but which may extend to five lakh rupees [*Sec. 35 (2)*]. Any limited liability partnership which fails to comply with the provisions of this section shall be punishable with fine which shall not be less than twenty-five thousand rupees but which may extend to five lakh rupees.

Inspection of documents kept by Registrar [Section 36]

The incorporation document, names of partners and changes, if any, made therein, Statement of Account and Solvency and annual return filed by each limited liability partnership with the

Registrar shall be available for inspection by any person in such manner and on payment of such fee as may be prescribed.

Penalty for false statement [Section 37]

If in any return, statement or other document required by or for the purposes of any of the provisions of this Act, any person makes a statement –

(a) which is false in any material particular, knowing it to be false; or

(b) which omits any material fact knowing it to be material,

he shall, save as otherwise expressly provided in this Act, be punishable with imprisonment for a term which may extend to two years, and shall also be liable to fine which may extend to five lakh rupees but which shall not be less than one lakh rupees.

CONTRIBUTIONS

Sections 32 and 33 provide as under for contributions by partners of an LLP.

1. ***Form of contribution*** **(*Sec. 32*)**

   (*i*) A contribution of a partner may consist of tangible, movable or immovable or intangible property or other benefit to the limited liability partnership, including money, promissory notes, and other agreements to contribute cash or property and contracts for services performed or to be performed.

   (*ii*) The monetary value of contribution of each partner shall be accounted for and disclosed in the accounts of the limited liability partnership in the manner as may be prescribed.

2. ***Obligation to contribute*** **(*Sec. 33*)**

   (*i*) The obligation of a partner to contribute money or other property or other benefit or to perform services for a limited liability partnership shall be as per the limited liability partnership agreement.

   (*ii*) A creditor of a limited liability partnership, which extends credit or otherwise acts in reliance on an obligation described in that agreement, without notice of any compromise between partners, may enforce the original obligation against such partner.

Power of Registrar to obtain information [Section 38]

In order to obtain such information as the Registrar may consider necessary for the purposes of carrying out the provisions of this Act, the Registrar may require any person including any present or former partner or designated partner or employee of a limited liability partnership to answer any question or make any declaration or supply any details or particulars in writing to him within a reasonable period.

Destruction of old records [Section 40]

The Registrar may destroy any document filed or registered with him in physical form or in electronic form in accordance with such rules as may be prescribed.

ASSIGNMENT AND TRANSFER OF PARTNERSHIP RIGHTS

Section 42 of LLP Act provides for assignment and transfer of partnership rights as under:

(1) The rights of a partner to a share of the profits and losses of the limited liability partnership and to receive distributions in accordance with the limited liability partnership agreement are transferable either wholly or in part.

(2) The transfer of any right by any partner pursuant to para (1) does not by itself cause the disassociation of the partner or a dissolution and winding up of the limited liability partnership.

(3) The transfer of right pursuant to this section does not, by itself, entitle the transferee or assignee to participate in the management or conduct of the activities of the limited liability partnership, or access information concerning the transactions of the limited liability partnership.

INVESTIGATION

Section 43 provides for Investigation of the Affairs of a Limited Liability Partnership as under:

(1) The Central Government shall appoint one or more competent persons as inspectors to investigate the affairs of a limited liability partnership and to report thereon in such manner in the following circumstances:

(*a*) The National Company Law Tribunal, either on its own motion, or any application received from not less than one fifth of the total number of partners of limited liability partnership, by order, declares that the affairs of the limited liability partnership ought to be investigated; or

(*b*) Any Court, by order, declares that the affairs of a limited liability partnership ought to be investigated.

(2) The Central Government may appoint one or more competent persons as inspectors to investigate the affairs of a limited liability partnership and to report on them in such manner as it may direct.

(3) The appointment of inspectors pursuant to para (2) may be made in the following circumstances:

(*a*) If not less than one-fifth of the total number of partners of the limited liability partnership make an application along with supporting evidence and security amount as may be prescribed; or

(*b*) If the limited liability partnership makes an application that the affairs of the limited liability partnership ought to be investigated; or

(*c*) If, in the opinion of the Central Government, there are circumstances suggesting:

(*i*) that the business of the limited liability partnership is being or has been conducted with an intent to defraud its creditors, partners or any other person, or otherwise of a fraudulent or unlawful purpose, or in a manner oppressive or unfairly prejudicial to some or any of its partners, or that the limited liability partnership was formed for any fraudulent or unlawful purpose; or (*ii*) that the affairs of the limited partnership are not being conducted in accordance with the provisions of this Act; or

(*iii*) that, on receipt of a report of the Registrar or any other investigating or regulatory agency, there are sufficient reasons that the affairs of the limited liability partnership ought to be investigated.

Person ineligible for appointment as Inspector [Section 45]

No firm, body corporate or other association shall be appointed as an inspector.

Production of documents and evidence [Section 47]

The following are the duties of partnership in case of investigation–

(*a*) To preserve and to produce before an inspector or any person authorized by him in their behalf with the previous approval of the Central Government, all books and papers of, or relating to, the limited liability partnership or, as the case may be, the other entity, which are in their custody or power; and

(*b*) To give to the inspector all assistance in connection with the investigation which they are reasonably able to give.

Inspector's Report [Section 49]

(1) The inspector may, and if so directed by the Central Government, shall make interim reports to that Government, and on the conclusion of the investigation, shall make a final report to the Central Government and any such report shall be written or printed, as the Central Government may direct.

(2) The Central Government

(*a*) shall forward a copy of any report (other than an interim report) made by the inspector to the limited liability partnership at its registered office, and also to any other entity or person dealt with or related to the report; and

(*b*) may, if it thinks fit, furnish a copy thereof, on request and on payment of the prescribed fee, to any person or entity related to or affected by the report.

CONVERSION FROM FIRM INTO LIMITED LIABILITY PARTNERSHIP

According to Section 55 a firm may be converted into a limited liability partnership in accordance with the rules and procedure given in second schedule to the Limited Liability Partnership Act as given below:

A partnership firm may convert into a limited liability partnership by complying with the requirements as to the conversion set out in Second Schedule to the Act. Upon such conversion, the partners of the firm shall be bound by the provisions of this Schedule that are applicable to them.

(1) A firm may apply to convert into a limited liability partnership in accordance with this Schedule if and only if the partners of the limited liability partnership into which the firm is to be converted, comprise, all the partners of the firm and no one else.

(2) A firm may apply to convert into a limited liability partnership by filing with the Registrar –

(*a*) A statement by all its partners in such form and manner and accompanied by such fee as the Central Government may prescribe, containing the following particulars, namely:

The name and registration number, if applicable, of the firm; and

The date on which the firm was registered under the Indian Partnership Act, 1932 or under any other law, if applicable, and

(*b*) Incorporation document and statement referred to in Section 11 of the LLP Act.

(3) On receiving the documents referred to in paragraph 2, the Registrar shall subject to the provisions of this Act, register the documents and issue a certificate of registration in such form as the Registrar may determine stating that the limited liability partnership is, on and from the date specified in the certificate, registered under this Act:

Provided that the limited liability partnership shall, within fifteen days of the date of registration, inform, the concerned Registrar of Firms with which it was registered under the provisions of the Indian Partnership Act, 1932 about the conversion and of the particulars of the limited liability partnership in such form and manner as the Central Government may prescribe.

Nothing in this Schedule shall be constructed as to require the Registrar to register any limited liability partnership if he is not satisfied with the particulars or other information furnished under the provisions of this Act:

Provided that an appeal may be made before the Tribunal in case of refusal of registration by the Registrar.

The Registrar may, in any particular case, require the documents referred to in para (2) to be verified in such manner, as he considers fit.

On and from the date of registration specified in the certificate of registration issued under para (3):

(a) There shall be a limited liability partnership by the name specified in the certificate of registration registered under this Act;

(b) All tangible (movable and immovable) property as well as intangible property vested in the firm, all assets, interests, rights, privileges, liabilities, obligations relating to the firm and the whole of the undertaking of the firm shall be transferred to and shall vest in the limited liability partnership without further assurance, act or deed; and

(c) The firm shall be deemed to be dissolved and if earlier registered under the Indian Partnership Act, 1932 removed from the records maintained under that Act.

CONVERSION FROM PRIVATE COMPANY INTO LIMITED LIABILITY PARTNERSHIP

According to Section 56 of the Limited Liability Partnership Act, a private company may convert itself into a limited liability partnership by complying with the requirements as to the conversion set out in the Third Schedule to the Act. The provisions for conversion are as under:

(1) A company may apply to convert into a limited liability partnership in accordance with this Schedule if and only if:

(a) There is no security interest in its assets subsisting or in force at the time of application; and

(b) The partners of the limited liability partnership to which it converts comprise all the shareholders of the company and no one else.

(2) Upon such conversion, the company, its shareholders, the limited liability partnership into which the company has converted and the partners of that limited liability partnership shall be bound by the provisions of this Schedule that are applicable to them.

(3) A company may apply to convert into a limited liability partnership by filing with the Registrar

(*a*) a statement by all its shareholders in such form and manner to be accompanied by such fees as the Central Government may prescribe, containing the following particulars, namely:

(*i*) the name and registration number of the company;

(*ii*) the date on which the company was incorporated; and

(*b*) incorporation document and statement referred to in Section 11.

(4) On receiving the documents referred to in para (3), the Registrar shall, subject to the provisions of this Act and the rules made thereunder, register the documents and issue a certificate of registration in such form as the Registrar may determine stating that the limited liability partnership is, on and from the date specified in the certificate, registered under this Act:

Provided that the limited liability partnership shall, within fifteen days of the date of registration, inform the concerned Registrar of Companies with which it was registered under the provisions of the Companies Act, 2013 about the conversion and of the particulars of the limited liability partnership in such form and manner as the Central Government may prescribe.

(5) Nothing in this Schedule shall be construed as to require the Registrar to register any limited liability partnership if he is not satisfied with the particulars or other information furnished under the provisions of this Act:

Provided that an appeal may be made before the Tribunal in case of refusal of registration by the Registrar.

The Registrar may, in any particular case, require the documents referred to in para (3) to be verified in such manner, as he considers fit.

(6) On and from the date of registration specified in the certificate of registration issued under para (4) –

(*a*) There shall be a limited liability partnership by the name specified in the certificate of registration registered under this Act;

(*b*) All tangible (movable or immovable) and intangible property vested in the company, all assets, interests, rights, privileges, liabilities, obligations relating to the company and the whole of the undertaking of the company shall be transferred to and shall vest in the limited liability partnership without further assurance, act or deed; and

(c) The company shall be deemed to be dissolved and removed from the records of the Registrar of Companies.

CONVERSION FROM UNLISTED PUBLIC COMPANY INTO LIMITED LIABILITY PARTNERSHIP

According to Section 57, an Unlisted Public Company may convert into a limited liability partnership by complying with the requirements as to the conversion set out in Fourth Schedule to the Act.

Upon such conversion, the company, its shareholders, the limited liability partnership into which the company has converted and the partners of that limited liability partnership shall be bound by the provisions of this Schedule that are applicable to them.

The following provisions are relevant in this regards:

(1) A company may apply to convert into a limited liability partnership in accordance with the provisions of this Schedule if and only if:

(a) There is no security interest in its assets subsisting or in force at the time of application; and

(b) The partners of the limited liability partnership to which it converts comprise all the shareholders of the company and no one else.

(2) A company may apply to convert into a limited liability partnership by filing with the Registrar –

(a) A statement by all its shareholders in such form and manner to be accompanied by such fee as the Central Government may prescribe containing the following particulars, namely:

(i) The name and registration number of the company;

(ii) The date on which the company was incorporated; and

(b) Incorporation document and statement referred to in Section 11.

(3) On receiving the documents referred to in paragraph (2), the Registrar shall, subject to the provisions of this Act, and the rules made thereunder, register the documents and issue a certificate of registration in such form as the Registrar may determine stating that the limited liability partnership is, on and from the date specified in the certificate, registered under this Act:

Provided that the limited liability partnership shall, within fifteen days of the date of registration, inform the concerned Registrar of Companies with which it was registered under the provisions of the Companies Act, 2013 about the conversion and of the particulars of the limited liability partnership in such form and manner as the Central Government may prescribe.

(4) On and from the date of registration specified in the certificate of registration issued under paragraph (3):

(a) There shall be a limited liability partnership by the name specified in the certificate of registration registered under this Act;

(*b*) All tangible (movable or immovable) and intangible property vested in the company, all assets, interests, rights, privileges, liabilities, obligations relating to the company and the whole of the undertaking of the company shall be transferred to and shall vest in the limited liability partnership without further assurance, act or deed; and

(*c*) The company shall be deemed to be dissolved and removed from the records of the Registrar of Companies.

TAXATION OF LIMITED PARTNERSHIP

The Income Tax Act, 1961 treats Limited Liability Partnership (LLP) and general partnership as equivalent. The definition of a partnership firm and a partner has been suitably amended for taxation purpose after the enactment of The Limited Liability Partnership Act. These definitions are as under:

(a) Firm shall have the meaning assigned to it in the Indian Partnership Act 1932 and shall include a limited liability partnership as defined in the Limited Liability Partnership Act 2008.

(b) Partner shall have the meaning assigned to it in the Indian Partnership Act 1932 and shall include:

- Any person, being a minor, has been admitted to the benefits of partnership; and
- A partner of a limited liability partnership as defined in the Limited Liability Partnership Act 2008.

(c) Partnership shall have the meaning assigned to it in the Indian Partnership Act 1932 and shall include a limited liability partnership as defined in the Limited Liability Partnership Act 2008.

The key highlights concerning taxation of an LLP are being summarized below:

(i) LLP's will be treated as Partnership Firms for the purpose of Income Tax.

(ii) No surcharge will be levied on income tax.

(iii) Profit will be taxed in the hands of the LLP and not in the hands of the partners.

(iv) Minimum Alternate Tax and Dividend Distribution Tax will not be applicable for LLP.

(v) Remuneration to partners will be taxed as "Income from Business and Profession."

(vi) No capital gain on conversion of partnership firm into LLP.

(vii) Designated Partners will be liable to sign and file the Income Tax return.

(viii) LLP shall not be eligible for presumptive taxation.

(ix) Capital Gain on conversion of company into LLP will be exempt from tax, if prescribed conditions are complied with.

(x) On conversion, the successor LLP, will be allowed to carry forward and set off of accumulated loss and unabsorbed depreciation allowance.

(xi) On conversion, the successor LLP will be allowed to amortize the expenditure incurred under voluntary retirement scheme. On conversion, the successor LLP will not be allowed to take the credit of MAT paid by the predecessor company.

WINDING UP AND DISSOLUTION

Sections 63 and 64 provide as under for winding up and dissolution of a LLP.

1. **Modes of Winding Up (*Sec. 63*):** The winding up of a limited liability partnership may be by one of the following:

   (*i*) Voluntary;

   (*ii*) By the National Company Law Tribunal constituted under the Companies Act; and Limited Liability Partnership, so wound up may be dissolved.

2. **Winding Up by Tribunal (*Sec. 64*):** The following are the circumstances under which limited liability partnership may be wound up by National Company Law Tribunal:

   (*i*) if the limited liability partnership decides that limited liability partnership be wound up by the Tribunal;

   (*ii*) if, for a period of more than six months, the number of partners of the limited liability partnership is reduced below two;

   (*iii*) if the limited liability partnership is unable to pay its debts;

   (*iv*) if the limited liability partnership has acted against the interests of the sovereignty and integrity of India, the security of the State or public order;

   (*v*) if the limited liability partnership has made a default in filing with the Registrar the Statement of Account and Solvency or annual return for any five consecutive financial years; or

   (*vi*) if the Tribunal is of the opinion that it is just and equitable that the limited liability partnership be wound up.

KEY TERMS

- ❑ **Designated Partners:** A partner designated as such under the provisions of Limited Liability Partnership Act. He is responsible for doing all acts, matters and things which are required to be done by the limited liability partnership in respect of compliance of the provisions of the Act.
- ❑ **Limited Liability Partnership:** A Partnership firm registered under Limited Liability Partnership Act.

TEST QUESTIONS

Objective Type: ***Test Your Knowledge***

1. State whether each of the following statements is *True* or *False*:

   (*a*) A Limited Liability Partnership is governed by the provisions of Indian Partnership Act, 1932.

   (*b*) Only an individual can become a partner in Limited Liability Partnership.

   (*c*) There is no maximum limit as to number of Partners in a Limited Liability Partnership.

   (*d*) There have to be atleast two designated partners in a limited liability partnership who are individuals.

   (*e*) The liabilities of a limited partnership firm can be met out of personal assets of the partners.

(*f*) A partner of a Limited Liability Partnership is not the agent of other partners.

(*g*) An obligation of a Limited Liability Partnership shall be solely the obligation of Limited Liability Partnership.

[**Ans.** (*a*) False; (*b*) False; (*c*) True; (*d*) True; (*e*) False; (*f*) True; (*g*) True]

2. Select the most appropriate answer:

(*a*) A Limited Liability Partnership has to be registered with–

(*i*) Registrar of Companies (*ii*) Registrar of Partnership firms

(*iii*) Registrars of Societies

(*b*) The minimum number of designated partners in Limited Partnership should be–

(*i*) 2 (*ii*) 5

(*iii*) 7

(*c*) The maximum number of partners in a Limited Partnership is–

(*i*) 20 (*ii*) 10

(*iii*) No Limit

(*d*) The agreement creating Limited Partnership is known as–

(*i*) Partnership Deed (*ii*) Incorporation Document

(*iii*) Memorandum of Association

(*e*) Every Limited Liability Partnership has to file with the Registrar the following documents under financial disclosure–

(*i*) Profit & Loss Account and Balance Sheet (*ii*) Income & Expenditure Account and Balance Sheet

(*iii*) Statement of Accounts and Solvency

[**Ans.** (*a*) (*i*); (*b*) (*i*); (*c*) (*iii*); (*d*) (*ii*); (*e*) (*iii*)]

Essay Type: *For Review, Discussion and Practice*

1. Explain the meaning and essential features of a Limited Liability Partnership. Enumerate the steps to be taken for formation of a Limited Partnership.
2. Differentiate a Limited Liability Partnership from an Ordinary Partnership and a Company.
3. State the mutual rights of partners of a Limited Liability Partnership Firm in the absence of any agreement between the partners.
4. Write short notes on :
   (*i*) Designated Partners
   (*ii*) Financial Disclosures by Limited Liability Partnership
   (*iii*) Winding up of a Limited Liability Partnership
5. (*i*) Define and explain the essential features of a Limited Liability Partnership (LLP).
   (*ii*) Who can be appointed as designated partner in an LLP? Also discuss, the procedure of his appointment.
   (*iii*) Discuss briefly the powers and duties of auditors of an LLP. [*B.Com. (Hons.), Delhi, 2012*]
6. (*i*) Explain the procedure and effects of conversion of a partnership into LLP.
   (*ii*) How can LLP be incorporated and registered under LLP Act, 2008?
   (*iii*) How can a person become a partner of an LLP? What are the disqualifications for becoming a partner in an LLP?
   (*iv*) Explain the duties if a liquidator under LLP Act, 2008? [*B.Com. (Hons.), Delhi, 2012*]

7. (*i*) Explain the winding up of an LLP Discuss the various grounds under which LLP, can be wound up by the Court. *[B.Com. (Hons.), Delhi, 2012]*

   (*ii*) Discuss the provision of filing return of an LLP. *[B.Com. (Hons.), Delhi, 2012]*

8. (*i*) Discuss the extend of liability of an LLP. *[B.Com. (Hons.), Delhi, 2012]*

   (*ii*) Discuss the contents of incorporation documents of an LLP. *[B.Com. (Hons.), Delhi, 2012]*

   (*iii*) Explain the legal effect of incorporation of an LLP. *[B.Com. (Hons.), Delhi, 2012]*

9. How is an LLP formed under the LLP Act, 2008? Enumerate the various documents to be filed with the Registrar in this connection. *[B.Com. (Hons.), Delhi, Nov. 2012]*

10. What is meant by Statement of Account and Solvency in an LLP? *[B.Com. (Hons.), Delhi, Nov. 2012]*

11. State the procedure of conversion from partnership firm into LLP. *[B.Com. (Hons.), Delhi, Nov.2012, 2013]*

12. Discuss the features of separate legal entity and perpetual existence in relation to an LLP. *[B.Com (Hons.), Delhi, Nov. 2012]*

13. State the liability of the LLP for the wrongful act of partner. *[B.Com. (Hons.), Delhi, Nov. 2012]*

14. Discuss in brief the provisions of the LLP Act, 2008 relating to the voluntary winding up of an LLP. *[B.Com. (Hons.), Delhi, Nov. 2012]*

15. "An LLP is a definite improvement over the partnership in the matter of promoting entrepreneurship."Discuss. *[B.Com. (Hons.), Delhi, Nov. 2012].*

16. Discuss the provisions regarding appointment and eligibility condition for a Designated Partner under the LLP Act, 2008. *[B.Com. (Hons.), Delhi, Nov. 2012]*

17. Who may file petition for winding up an LLP? Discuss powers of court on hearing such petition. *[B.Com. (Hons.), Delhi, Nov. 2012]*

18. Explain the procedure for change of registered office of LLP from one state to another. *[B.Com. (Hons.), Delhi, Nov. 2013]*

19. "The validity of a certificate of incorporation of LLP cannot be disputed on any ground whatsoever". Critically examine the statement. *[B.Com. (Hons.), Delhi, Nov. 2013]*

20. Discuss the various grounds under which a LLP can be wound up by the court. *[B.Com. (Hons.), Delhi, Nov. 2013]*

21. State the provisions relating to whistle-blowing in case of a LLP. *[B.Com. (Hons.), Delhi, Nov. 2013]*

22. State the provisions for conversion of a private company into a LLP. *[B.Com. (Hons.), Delhi, Nov. 2013]*

23. Briefly describe any five important features of Limited Liability Partnership Act, 2008 *[B.Com. (Hons.), Delhi, 2013]*

24. Write a short note on Taxation of Limited Liability Partnership.

Chapter 2

THE INFORMATION TECHNOLOGY ACT, 2000

LEARNING OBJECTIVES

A careful study of this chapter will enable you to :

- understand the objectives and application of the Act;
- define certain key terms;
- state the meaning and procedure applicable to 'Digital Signature';
- enumerate the rules applicable to electronic governance and electronic records;
- explain the procedure for securing electronic records and digital signatures;
- state the functions of the certifying authorities;
- explain the rules applicable to digital signature certificates;
- identify the duties of the subscribers;
- state the provisions applicable to Appellate Tribunal; and
- state the activities which will be considered as offences under the Act and the relevant provisions for penalties and adjudication.

OBJECTIVES OF THE ACT

The technological revolution in the field of communication has brought out revolutionary changes in the mode of carrying out business and commerce. The exchange of physical documents is no longer necessary for carrying out business transactions. The electronic commerce is the new buzzword in both national and international trade. Electronic commerce involves carrying out of business transactions by means of electronic data interchange and other means of electronic communication involving the use of alternatives to paper based methods of communication and storage of information. The international trade is growing at a vast pace and the whole world has become almost a global village. The World Trade Organization (WTO) has further contributed towards the blast growth in trade, commerce and other fields amongst different countries of the world.

The General Assembly of the United Nations, recognizing this fact also resolved on 30.01.1997, to adopt a model law on electronic commerce framed by United Nations Commission of International Trade Law. The resolution recommends that all states give favourable consideration to the said model law when they communicate or revise their laws in view of the need of uniformity in the law applicable to alternatives to paper based methods of communication and storage of information.

The Government of India, keeping in view the above facts, got enacted by Parliament the Information Technology Act, 2000.

The Act has been amended by the Information Technology (Amendment) Act, 2008 effective from 5th February, 2009. The amendments have been incorporated at proper places in the book.

The Act has been framed keeping in view the following objectives:

(*i*) To bring uniformity in the law applicable to paperless methods of communication and storage of information prevalent in India on the pattering international law.

(*ii*) To promote efficient delivery of government services by means of reliable electronic records.

SCOPE AND APPLICATION

The Information Technology Act, 2000 has come into effect from 17th October, 2000. It extends to whole of India. It also applies to any offence or contravention committed under the Act by any person outside India except as otherwise provided in the Act.

The Act does not apply to the following:

(*a*) a negotiable instrument as defined in Section 13 of the Negotiable Instruments Act, 1881.

(*b*) a power-of-attorney as defined in Section 1A of the Powers-of-Attorney Act, 1882.

(*c*) a trust as defined in Section 3 of the Indian Trusts Act, 1882.

(*d*) a will as defined in clause and Section (2)(h) of the Indian Succession Act, 1925 including any other testamentary disposition by whatever name called;

(*e*) any contract for the sale or conveyance of immovable property or any interest in such property;

(*f*) any such class of documents or transactions as may be notified by the Central Government in the Official Gazette.

DEFINITIONS

Definitions of certain importants terms as given in Section 2 of the Act are as under:

1. **Access**, with its grammatical variations and cognate expressions, means gaining entry into, instructing or communicating with the logical, arithmetical or memory function resources of a computer, computer system or computer network.

2. **Addressee** means, 'a person who is intended by the originator to receive the electronic record but does not include any intermediary'.

3. **Affixing electronic signature** with its grammatical variations and cognate expressions means adoption of any methodology or procedure by a person for the purpose of authenticating an electronic record by means of digital signature.

4. **Appropriate Government** means, as respects any matter,—

(*i*) enumerated in List *II* of the Seventh Schedule to the Constitution;

(*ii*) relating to any State law enacted under List *III* of the Seventh Schedule to the Constitution,

the State Government and in any other case, the Central Government.

5. **Asymmetric Crypto System** means, a system of a secure key pair consisting of a private key for creating a digital signature and a public key to verify the digital signature.

6. **Certifying Authority** means, a person who has been granted a licence to issue a Electronic Signature Certificate under Section 24.

7. **Certification Practice Statement** means, a statement issued by a Certifying Authority to specify the practices that the Certifying Authority employs in issuing Electronic Signature Certificates.

8. **Computer** means, any electronic, magnetic, optical or other high-speed data processing device or system which performs logical, arithmetic and memory functions by manipulations of

electronic, magnetic or optical impulses, and includes all input, output, processing, storage, computer software or communication facilities which are connected or related to the computer in a computer system or computer network.

9. **"communication device"** means cell phones, personal digital assistance or combination of both or any other device used to communicate, send or transmit any text, video, audio or image;

10. **"computer network"** means the interconnection of one or more computers or computer systems or communication device through:

(*i*) the use of satellite, microwave, terrestrial line, wire, wireless or other communication media; and

(*ii*) terminals or a complex consisting of two or more inter-connected computers or communication device whether or not the interconnection is continuously maintained.

11. **"cyber cafe"** means any facility from where access to the interest is offered by any person in the ordinary course of business to the members of the public.

12. **"cyber security"** means protecting information, equipment, devices, computer, computer resources, communication device and information stored therein from unauthorised access, use disclosure, disruption, modification or destruction."

13. **Computer Resource** means computer, computer system, computer network, data, computer database or software.

14. **Computer System** means, a device or collection of devices, including input and output support devices and excluding calculators which are not programmable and capable of being used in conjunction with external files which contain computer programmes, electronic instructions, input data and output data that perform logic, arithmetic, data storage and retrieval, communication control and other functions.

15. **Data** means a representation of information, knowledge, facts, concepts or instructions which are being prepared or have been prepared in a formalised manner, and is intended to be processed, is being processed or has been processed in a computer system or computer network, and may be in any form (including computer printouts, magnetic or optical storage media, punched cards, punched tapes) or stored internally in the memory of the computer.

16. **Digital Signature** means authentication of any electronic record by a subscriber by means of an electronic method or procedure in accordance with the provisions of Section 3.

17. **Electronic Form**, with reference to information, means any information generated, sent, received or stored in media, magnetic, optical, computer memory, micro film, computer generated micro fiche or similar device.

18. **Electronic Gazette** means, the Official Gazette published in the electronic form.

19. **Electronic Record** means data, record or data generated, image or sound stored, received or sent in an electronic form or micro film or computer generated micro fiche.

20. **"Electronic signature"** means authentication of any electronic record by a subscriber by means of the electronic technique specified in the Second Schedule and includes digitial signature.

21. **"Electronic Signature Certificate"** means an Electronic Signature Certificate issued under Section 35 and includes Digital Signature Certificate.

22. "Indian Computer Emergency Response Team" means an agency established under Sub-section (i) of Section 70B.

23. **"intermediary"**, with respect to any particular electronic records, means any person who on behalf of another person receives, stores or transmits that record or provides any service with

respect to that record and includes telecom service providers, network service providers, Interest service providers, web-hosting service providers, search engines, online payment sites, online auction sites, online marketplaces and cyber cafes'.

24. **Function**, in relation to a computer, includes logic, control, arithmetical process, deletion, storage and retrieval and communication or telecommunication from or within a computer.

25. **Information** includes data, menage text images, sound, voice, codes, computer programmes, software and databases or micro film or computer generated micro fiche.

26. **Key Pair**, in an asymmetric crypto system, means a private key and its mathematically related public key, which are so related that the public key can verify a digital signature created by the private key.

27. **Licence** means a licence granted to a Certifying Authority under Section 24.

28. **Originator** means a person who sends, generates, stores or transmits any electronic message; or causes any electronic message to be sent, generated, stored or transmitted to any other person but does not include an intermediary.

29. **Private Key** means the key of a key pair used to create a digital signature.

30. **Public Key** means they key of a key pair used to verify a digital signature and listed in the Digital Signature Certificate.

31. **Secure System** means computer hardware, software, and procedure that—

(*a*) are reasonably secure from unauthorised access and misuse;

(*b*) provide a reasonable level of reliability and correct operation;

(*c*) are reasonably suited to performing the intended functions; and

(*d*) adhere to generally accepted security procedures;

32. **Subscriber** means a person in whose name the Electronic Signature Certificate is issued;

33. **Verify**, in relation to a digital signature, electronic record or public key, with its grammatical variations and cognate expressions, means to determine whether—

(*a*) the initial electronic record was affixed with the digital signature by the use of private key corresponding to the public key of the subscriber;

(*b*) the initial electronic record is retained intact or has been altered since such electronic record was so affixed with the digital signature.

DIGITAL SIGNATURE AND ELECTRONIC SIGNATURE

Section 3 deals with the mode of verifying the electronic records through digital signature. The relevant provisions are summarised below :

(1) Any subscriber may authenticate an electronic record by affixing his digital signature.

(2) The authentication of the electronic record shall be effected by the use of asymmetric crypto system and hash function which envelop and transform the initial electronic record into another electronic record.

Hash function is an algorithm mapping that translates a sequence of bits into smaller sequence of bits called 'Hash Result'. Algorithm mapping whenever executed with the same electronic record produces the same hash result. Whenever the above algorithm is executed with the same electronic record as its input, it becomes infeasible:

(*i*) that two electronic records can produce the same hash result.

(*ii*) to get back the original electronic record from the hash result obtained from algorithm.

(3) Any person by the use of a public key of the subscriber can verify the electronic record.

(4) The private key and the public key are unique to the subscriber and constitute a functioning key pair.

Section 3A deals with the authentication of electronic signature as under:

(1) Notwithstanding anything contained in Section 3, but subject to the provisions of sub-section (2), a subscriber may authenticate any electronic record by such electronic signature or electronic authentication technique which:

(*a*) is considered reliable; and

(*b*) may be specified in the Second Schedule.

(2) For the purposes of this section any electronic signature or electronic authentication technique shall be considered reliable if:

(*a*) the signature creation data or the authentication data are, within the context in which they are used, linked to the signatory or, as case may be, the authenticator and to no other person;

(*b*) the signature creation data or the authentication data were, at the time of signing, under the control of the signatory or, as the case may be, the authenticator and of no other person;

(*c*) any alteration to the electronic signature made after affixing such signature is detectable,

(*d*) any alternation to the information made after its authentication by electronic signature is detectable; and

(*e*) it fulfils such other conditions which may be prescribed.

ELECTRONIC GOVERNANCE

Sections 4 to 10 deal with provisions relating to electronic governance as summarised below :

1. **Legal recognition of electronic records** (*Sec. 4*) : Where any law provides that information or any other matter shall be in writing or in the typewritten or printed form, then, notwithstanding anything contained in such law, such requirement shall be deemed to have been satisfied if such information or matter is—

(*a*) rendered or made available in an electronic form; and

(*b*) accessible so as to be usable for a subsequent reference.

2. **Legal recognition of electronic signatures** (*Sec. 5*) : Where any law provides that information or any other matter shall be authenticated by affixing the signature or any document shall be signed or bear the signature of any person, then, notwithstanding anything contained in such law, such requirement shall be deemed to have been satisfied, if such information or matter is authenticated by means of electronic signature affixed in such manner as may be prescribed by the Central Government.

Explanation : For the purposes of this section, 'signed', with its grammatical variations and cognate expressions, shall, with reference to a person, mean affixing of his handwritten signature or any mark on any document and the expression 'signature' shall be construed accordingly.

3. **Use of electronic records and electronic signatures in Government etc.** (*Sec. 6*) :

(1) Where any law provides for—

(*a*) the filing of any form, application or any other document with any office, authority, body or agency owned or controlled by the appropriate Government in a particular manner;

(*b*) the issue or grant of any licence, permit, sanction or approval by whatever name called in a particular manner;

(*c*) the receipt or payment of money in a particular manner then, notwithstanding anything contained in any other law for the time being in force, such requirement shall be deemed to have been satisfied if such filing, issue, grant, receipt or payment, as the case may be, is effected by means of such electronic form as may be prescribed by the appropriate Government.

(2) The appropriate Government may, for the purposes of sub-section (1), by rules, prescribe—

(*a*) the manner and format in which such electronic records shall be filed, created or issued;

(*b*) the manner or method of payment of any fee or charges for filing, creation or issue any electronic record under clause (a).

The appropriate Government may, for the purposes of this Chapter and for efficient delivery of services to the public through electronic means authorise, by order, any service provider to set up, maintain and upgrade the computerised facilities and perform such other services as it may specify by notification in the Official Gazette. (*Sec. 6A*)

4. **Retention of electronic records** (*Sec. 7*) : Where any law provides that documents, records or information shall be retained for any specific period, then, that requirement shall be deemed to have been satisfied if such documents, records or information are retained in the electronic form, if—

(*a*) the information contained therein remains accessible so as to be usable for a subsequent reference;

(*b*) the electronic record is retained in the format in which it was originally generated, sent or received or in a format which can be demonstrated to represent accurately the information originally generated, sent or received;

(*c*) the details which will facilitate the identification of the origin, destination, date and time of despatch or receipt of such electronic record are available in the electronic record :

Provided that this clause does not apply to any information which is automatically generated solely for the purpose of enabling an electronic record to be despatched or received.

5. **Audit of Documents** (*Sec. 7A*) : Where in any law for the time being in force, there is a provision for audit of documents, records or information, that provision shall also be applicable for audit of documents, records or information processed and maintained in the electronic form.

6. **Publication of rule, regulation, *etc.*, in Electronic Gazette** (*Sec. 8*) : Where any law provides that any rule, regulation, order, bye-law, notification or any other matter shall be published in the Official Gazette, then, such requirement shall be deemed to have been satisfied if such rule, regulation, order, bye-law, notification or any other matter is published in the Official Gazette or Electronic Gazette :

Provided that where any rule, regulation, order, bye-law, notification or any other matter is published in the Official Gazette or Electronic Gazette, the date of publication shall be deemed to be the date of the Gazette which was first published in any form.

7. **Acceptance of electronic documents cannot be insisted** (*Sec. 9*) : Nothing contained in sections 6, 7 and 8 shall confer a right upon any person to insist that any Ministry or Department of the Central Government or the State Government or any authority or body established by or under any law or controlled or funded by the Central or State Government should accept, issue, create, retain and preserve any document in the form of electronic records or effect any monetary transaction in the electronic form.

8. **Power of Central Government to make rules** (*Sec. 10*) : The Central Government may, for the purposes of this Act, by rules, prescribe—

(*a*) the type of electronic signature;

(*b*) the manner and format in which the electronic signature shall be affixed;

(*c*) the manner or procedure which facilitates identification of the person affixing the electronic signature;

(*d*) control processes and procedures to ensure adequate integrity, security and confidentiality of electronic records or payment; and

(*e*) any other matter which is necessary to give legal effect to electronic signatures.

9. **Validity and Contracts** (*Sec. 10A*) : Where in a contract formation, the communication of proposals, the acceptance of proposals, the revocation of proposals and acceptances, as the case may be, are expressed in electronic form or by means of an electronic record, such contract shall not be deemed to be unenforceable solely on the ground that such electronic form or means was used for that purpose.

ATTRIBUTION, ACKNOWLEDGMENT AND DESPATCH OF ELECTRONIC RECORDS

Sections 11 to 13 provide for attribution, acknowledgment and despatch of electronic records. These provisions are enumerated below :

1. **Attribution of electronic records** (*Sec. 11*) : An electronic record shall be attributed to the originator—

(*a*) if it was sent by the originator himself;

(*b*) by a person who had the authority to act on behalf of the originator in respect of that electronic record; or

(*c*) by an information system programmed by or on behalf of the originator to operate automatically.

2. **Acknowledgment of receipt** (*Sec. 12*) : (1) Where the originator has not stipulated that the acknowledgment of receipt of electronic record be given in a particular form or by a particular method, an acknowledgment may be given by—

(*a*) any communication by the addressee, automated or otherwise; or

(*b*) any conduct of the addressee, sufficient to indicate to the originator that the electronic record has been received.

(2) Where the originator has stipulated that the electronic record shall be binding only on receipt of an acknowledgment of such electronic record by him, then, unless acknowledgment has been so received, the electronic record shall be deemed to have been never sent by the originator.

(3) Where the originator has not stipulated that the electronic record shall be binding only on receipt of such acknowledgment, and the acknowledgment has not been received by the originator within the time specified or agreed or, if no time has been specified or agreed to within a reasonable time, then, the originator may give notice to the addressee stating that no acknowledgment has been received by him and specifying a reasonable time by which the acknowledgment must be received by him and if no acknowledgement is received within the aforesaid time limit he may after giving notice to the addressee, treat the electronic record as though it has never been sent.

3. **Time and place of despatch and receipt of electronic record** (*Sec. 13*) : (1) Save as otherwise agreed to between the originator and the addressee, the despatch of an electronic record occurs when it enters a computer resource outside the control of the originator.

(2) Save as otherwise agreed between the originator and the addressee, the time of receipt of an electronic record shall be determined as follows, namely:

(*a*) if the addressee has designated a computer resource for the purpose of receiving electronic records :

(*i*) receipt occurs at the time when the electronic record enters the designated computer resource; or

(*ii*) if the electronic record is sent to a computer resource of the addressee that is not the designated computer resource, receipt occurs at the time when the electronic record is retrieved by the addressee;

(*b*) if the addressee has not designated a computer resource along with specified timings, if any, receipt occurs when the electronic record enters the computer resource of the addressee.

(3) Save as otherwise agreed to between the originator and the addressee, an electronic record is deemed to be despatched at the place where the originator has his place of business, and is deemed to be received at the place where the addressee has his place of business.

(4) The provisions of sub-section (2) shall apply notwithstanding that the place where the computer resource is located may be different from the place where the electronic record is deemed to have been received under sub-section (3).

(5) For the purposes of this section—

(*a*) if the originator or the addressee has more than one place business, the principal place of business, shall be the place of business;

(*b*) if the originator or the addressee does not have a place of business, his usual place of residence shall be deemed to be the place of business;

(*c*) 'usual place of residence', in relation to a body corporate, means the place where it is registered.

SECURE ELECTRONIC RECORDS AND SECURE ELECTRONIC SIGNATURES

Sections 14 to 16 of the Act provide the circumstances under which electronic records and electronic signatures can be considered as secure. These provisions are as under:

1. **Secure electronic record** (*Sec. 14*): Where any security procedure has been applied to an electronic record at specific point of time, then such record shall be deemed to be a secure electronic record from such point of time to the time of verification.

2. **Specific electronic signature** (*Sec. 15*): The electronic signature shall be deemed to be a secure electronic signature if:

(*i*) the signature creation data, at the time of affixing signature, was under the exclusive control of signatory and no other person; and

(*ii*) the signature creation data was stored and affixed in such exclusive manner as may be prescribed.

Explanation—In case of digital signature, the "signature creation data" means the private key of the subscriber.

3. **Security procedures and practices** (*Sec. 16*) **:** The Central Government may, for the purposes of sections 14 and 15, prescribe the security procedures and practices:

Provided that in prescribing such security procedures and practices, the Central Government shall have regard to the commercial circumstances, nature of transactions and such other related factors as it may consider appropriate.

REGULATION OF CERTIFYING AUTHORITIES

Following are the various authorities created under the Act for enforcement of different requirements under the Act.

1. **Appointment of Controller and Other Officers** (*Sec. 17*): (1) The Central government may, by notification in the Official Gazette, appoint a Controller of Certifying Authorities for the purposes of this Act and may also by the same or subsequent notification, appoint such number of Deputy Controllers and Assistant Controllers, other officers and employees as it deems fit.

(2) The Controller shall discharge his functions under this Act subject to the general control and directions of the Central Government.

(3) The Deputy Controllers and Assistant Controllers shall perform the functions assigned to them by the Controller under the general superintendence and Control of the Controller.

2. **Functions of Controller** (*Sec. 18*) : The Controller may perform all or any of the following functions:

(*a*) exercising supervision over the activities of the Certifying Authorities;
(*b*) certifying public keys of the Certifying Authorities;
(*c*) laying down the standards to be maintained by the Certifying Authorities;
(*d*) specifying the qualifications and experience which employees of the Certifying Authority should possess;
(*e*) specifying the conditions subject to which the Certifying Authorities shall conduct their business;
(*f*) specifying the contents of written, printed or visual materials and advertisements that may be distributed or used in respect of a Digital Signature Certificate and the public key;
(*g*) specifying the form and content of a Digital Signature Certificate and the key;
(*h*) specifying the form and manner in which accounts shall be maintained by the Certifying Authorities;
(*i*) specifying the terms and conditions subject to which auditors may be appointed and the remuneration to be paid to them;
(*j*) facilitating the establishment of any electronic system by a Certifying Authority either solely or jointly with other Certifying Authorities and regulation of such systems;
(*k*) specifying the manner in which the Certifying Authorities shall conduct their dealings with the subscribers;
(*l*) resolving any conflict of interests between the Certifying Authorities and the subscribers;
(*m*) laying down the duties of the Certifying Authorities;
(*n*) maintaining a database containing the disclosure record of every Certifying Authority containing such particulars as may be specified by regulations, which shall be accessible to public.

3. **Recognition of Foreign Certifying Authorities** (*Sec. 19*) : (1) Subject to such conditions and restrictions as may be specified, by regulations, the Controller may, with the previous approval of the Central Government, and by notification in the Official Gazette, recognise any foreign Certifying Authority as a Certifying Authority for the purposes of this Act.

(2) The Controller may, if he is satisfied that any Certifying Authority has contravened any of the conditions and restrictions subject to which it was granted recognition under sub-section (1) he may, for reasons to be recorded in writing, by notification in the Official Gazette, revoke such recognition.

4. **Power to Delegate** (*Sec. 27*) : The Controller may, in writing, authorise the Deputy Controller, Assistant Controller or any officer to exercise any powers of the Controller under this Chapter.

5. **Power to Investigate Contraventions** (*Sec. 28*) : (1) The Controller or any officer authorised by him in this behalf shall take up for investigation any contravention of the provisions of this Act, rules or regulations made thereunder.

(2) The Controller or any officer authorised by him in this behalf shall exercise the like powers which are conferred on Income-tax authorities under Chapter XIII of the Income Tax Act, 1961, and shall exercise such powers, subject to such limitations laid down under that Act.

GRANTING OF LICENCE

Sections 21 to 26 empower the Controller to issue licence to persons authorising them to issue Digital Signature Certificates. The various provisions are explained below:

1. **Licence to issue Digital Signature Certificates** (*Sec. 21*): (1) Subject to the provisions of sub-section (2), any person may make an application to the Controller for a licence to issue Digital Signature Certificates.

(2) No licence shall be issued under sub-section (1), unless the applicant fulfils such requirements with respect to qualification, expertise, manpower, financial resources and other infrastructure facilities, which are necessary to issue Digital Signature Certificates as may be prescribed by the Central Government.

(3) A licence granted under this section shall—

(*a*) be valid for such period as may be prescribed by the Central Government;

(*b*) not be transferable or heritable;

(*c*) be subject to such terms and conditions as may be specified by the regulations.

2. **Application for licence** (*Sec. 22*) : (1) Every application for issue of a licence shall be in such form as may be prescribed by the Central Government.

(2) Every application for issue of a licence shall be accompanied by—

(*a*) a certification practice statement;

(*b*) a statement including the procedures with respect to identification of the applicant;

(*c*) payment of such fees, not exceeding twenty-five thousand rupees as may be prescribed by the Central Government;

(*d*) such other documents, as may be prescribed by the Central Government.

3. **Renewal of licence** (*Sec. 23*) : An application for renewal of a licence shall be—

(*a*) in such form;

(*b*) accompanied by such fees, not exceeding five thousand rupees, as may be prescribed by the Central Government and

(*c*) shall be made not less than forty-five days before the date of expiry of the period of validity of the licence.

4. **Procedure for grant or rejection of licence** (*Sec. 24*) : The Controller may, on receipt of an application under sub-section (1) of Section 21, after considering the documents accompanying the application and such other factors, as he deems fit, grant the licence or reject the application:

Provided that no application shall be rejected under this section unless the applicant has been given a reasonable opportunity of presenting his case.

5. **Suspension of licence** (*Sec. 25*) : (1) The Controller may revoke the licence if he is satisfied after making such inquiry, as he may think fit, that a Certifying Authority has—

(*a*) made a statement in, or in relation to, the application for the issue or renewal of the licence, which is incorrect or false in material particulars;

(*b*) failed to comply with the terms and conditions subject to which the licence was granted;

(*c*) failed to maintain the standards specified under clause (*b*) of sub-section (2) of Section 20;

(*d*) contravened any provisions of this Act, rule, regulation or order made thereunder;

Provided that no licence shall be revoked unless the Certifying Authority has been given a reasonable opportunity of showing cause against the proposed revocation.

(2) The Controller may, if he has reasonable cause to believe that there is any ground for revoking a licence under sub-section (1), by order, suspend such licence pending the completion of the enquiry ordered by him.

Provided that no licence shall be suspended for a period exceeding ten days unless the Certifying Authority has been given a reasonable opportunity of showing cause against the proposed suspension.

(3) No Certifying Authority whose licence has been suspended shall issue any Digital Signature Certificate during such suspension.

6. **Notice of suspension or revocation of licence** (*Sec. 26*) : (1) Where the licence of the Certifying Authority is suspended or revoked, the Controller shall publish notice of such suspension or revocation, as the case may be, in the database maintained by him.

(2) Where one or more repositories are specified, the Controller shall publish notices of such suspension or revocation, as the case may be, in all such repositories:

Provided that the database containing the notice of such suspension or revocation, as the case may be, shall be made available through a website which shall be accessible round the clock.

Provided further that the Controller may, if he considers necessary, publicise the contents of database in such electronic or other media, as he may consider appropriate.

7. **Certifying Authority to follow certain procedures** (*Sec. 30*) : Every Certifying Authority shall—

(*a*) make use of hardware, software, and procedures that are secure from intrusion and misuse;

(*b*) provide a reasonable level of reliability in its services which are reasonably suited to the performance of intended functions;

(*c*) adhere to security procedures to ensure that the secrecy and privacy of the digital signatures are assured;

"(*ca*) be the repository of all Electronic Signature Certificates issued under this Act;

(*cb*) publish information regarding its practices, Electronic Signature Certificates and current status of such certificates; and"

(*d*) observe such other standards as may be specified by regulation.

8. **Certifying Authority to ensure compliance of the Act, *etc.*** (*Sec. 31*) : Every Certifying Authority shall ensure that every person employed or otherwise engaged by it complies, in the course

of his employment or engagement, with the provisions of this Act, rules, regulations or orders made thereunder.

9. **Display of licence** (*Sec. 32*) : Every Certifying Authority shall display its licence at a conspicuous place of the premises in which it carries on its business.

10. **Surrender of licence** (*Sec. 33*) : (1) Every Certifying Authority whose licence is suspended or revoked shall immediately after such suspension or revocation, surrender the licence to the Controller.

(2) Where any Certifying Authority fails to surrender a licence under sub-section (1), the person in whose favour a licence is issued, shall be guilty of an offence and shall be punished with imprisonment which may extend up to six months or a fine which may extend up to ten thousand rupees or with both.

11. **Disclosure** (*Sec. 34*) : Every Certifying Authority shall disclose in the manner specified by regulations—

(*a*) its Electronic Signature Certificate;

(*b*) any certification practice statement relevant thereto;

(*c*) notice of the revocation or suspension of its Certifying Authority certificate, if any; and

(*d*) any other fact that materially and adversely affects either the reliability of Electronic Signature Certificate, which that Authority has issued, or the Authority's ability to perform its services.

ELECTRONIC SIGNATURE CERTIFICATES

Sections 35 to 38 provide for the issue and suspension of electronic certificate. The provisions are explained below :

1. **Certifying authority to issue Electronic Signature Certificate** (*Sec. 35*) : (1) Any person may make an application to the Certifying Authority for the issue of a Electronic Signature Certificate in such form as may be prescribed by the Central Government.

(2) Every such application shall be accompanied by such fee not exceeding twenty-five thousand rupees as may be prescribed by the Central Government, to be paid to the Certifying Authority :

Provided that while prescribing fees under sub-section (2), different fees may be prescribed for different classes of applicants.

(3) Every such application shall be accompanied by a certification practice statement or where there is no such statement, a statement containing such particulars, as may be specified by regulations.

(4) On receipt of an application under sub-section (1), the Certifying Authority may, after consideration of the certification practice statement or the other statement under sub-section (3) and after making such enquiries as it may deem fit, grant the Digital Signature Certificate or for reasons to be recorded in writing, reject the application :

Provided that no application shall be rejected unless the applicant has been given a reasonable opportunity of showing cause against the proposed rejection.

2. **Representations upon issuance of Digital Signature Certificate** (*Sec. 36*) : A Certifying Authority while issuing a Digital Signature Certificate shall certify that—

(*a*) it has complied with the provisions of this Act and the rules and regulations made thereunder;

(*b*) it has published the Digital Signature Certificate or otherwise made it available to such person relying on it and the subscriber has accepted it;

(*c*) the subscriber holds the private key corresponding to the public key listed in the Electronic Signature Certificate;

(*ca*) the subscriber holds a private key which is capable of creating a digital signature;

(*cb*) the public key to be listed in the certificate can be used to verify a digital signature affixed by the private key held by the subscriber,".

(*d*) the subscriber public key and private key constitute a functioning key pair;

(*e*) the information contained in the Digital Signature Certificate is accurate; and

(*f*) it has no knowledge of any material fact, which if it had been included in the Digital Signature Certificate would adversely affect the reliability of the representations in clauses (a) to (d).

3. **Suspension of Digital Signature Certificate** *(Sec. 37)* : (1) Subject to the provisions of sub-section (2), the Certify Authority which has issued a Digital Signature Certificate may suspend such Digital Signature Certificate—

(*a*) on receipt of a request to that effect from—

(*i*) the subscriber listed in the Digital Signature Certificate; or

(*ii*) any person duly authorised to act on behalf of that subscriber;

(*b*) if it is of opinion that the Digital Signature Certificate should be suspended in public interest.

(2) A Digital Signature Certificate shall not be suspended for a period exceeding fifteen days unless the subscriber has been given an opportunity of being heard in the matter.

(3) On suspension of a Digital Signature Certificate under this section, the Certifying Authority shall communicate the same to the subscriber.

4. **Revocation of Electronic Signature Certificate** (*Sec. 38*) : (1) A Certifying Authority may revoke a Digital Signature Certificate issued by it—

(*a*) where the subscriber or any other person authorised by him makes a request to that effect; or

(*b*) upon the death of the subscriber, or

(*c*) upon the dissolution of the firm or winding up of the company where the subscriber is a firm or a company.

(2) A Digital Signature Certificate shall not be revoked unless the subscriber has been given an opportunity of being heard in the matter.

(3) On revocation of a Digital Signature Certificate under this section, the Certifying Authority shall communicate the same to the subscriber.

5. **Notice of suspension or revocation** (*Sec. 39*) : Where a Digital Signature Certificate is suspended or revoked under Section 37 or Section 38, the Certifying Authority shall publish a notice of such suspension or revocation, as the case may be, in the repository specified in the Digital Signature Certificate for publication of such notice.

DUTIES OF SUBSCRIBERS

Sections 40 to 42 of the Act have given the following duties of the subscribers—

1. **Generating Key pair** (*Sec. 40*) : Where any Digital Signature Certificate the public key of which corresponds to the private key of that subscriber which is to be listed in the Digital Signature Certificate has been accepted by a subscriber, then, the subscriber shall generate the key pair by applying the security procedure.

In respect of Electronic Signature Certificate, the subscriber shall perform such duties as may be prescribed (*Sec 40A*).

2. **Acceptance of Digital Signature Certificate** (*Sec. 41*) : (1) A subscriber shall be deemed to have accepted a Digital Signature Certificate if he publishes or authorises the publication of a Digital Signature Certificate—

(*a*) to one or more persons;

(*b*) in a repository; or

(*c*) otherwise demonstrates his approval of the Digital Signature Certificate in any manner.

By accepting a Digital Signature Certificate, the subscriber certifies to all who reasonably rely on the information contained in the Digital Signature Certificate that—

(*a*) the subscriber holds the private key corresponding to the public key listed in the Digital Signature Certificate and is entitled to hold the same;

(*b*) all representations made by the subscriber to the Certifying Authority and all material relevant to the information contained in the Digital Signature Certificate are true;

(*c*) all information in the Digital Signature Certificate that is within the knowledge of the subscriber is true.

3. **Control of private key** (*Sec. 42*) : (1) Every subscriber shall exercise reasonable care to retain control of the private key corresponding to the public key listed in his Digital Signature Certificate and take all steps to prevent its disclosure to a person not authorised to affix the digital signature of the subscriber.

(2) If the private key corresponding to the public key listed in the Digital Signature Certificate has been compromised, then, the subscriber shall communicate the same without any delay to the Certifying Authority in such manner as may be specified by the regulations.

PENALTIES COMPENSATION AND ADJUDICATION

Sections 43 to 47 provide for Penalties Compensation and Adjudication incase of contravention of various offences committed under the Act. The provisions are explained below :

1. **Penalty and compensation for damage to computer, computer system, etc.** (*Sec. 43*) : If any person without permission of the owner or any other person who is incharge of a computer, computer system or computer network, commits any of the following, acts he shall be liable to pay damages by way of compensation not exceeding one crore rupees to the person so affected.

(*a*) Accesses or secures access to such computer, computer system or computer resource;

(*b*) Downloads, copies or extracts any data, computer database or information from such computer, computer system or computer network including information or data held or stored in any removable storage medium;

(*c*) Introduces or causes to be introduced any computer contaminant or computer virus into any computer, computer system or computer network;

(*d*) Damages or causes to be damaged any computer, computer system or computer network, data, computer database or any other programmes residing in such computer, computer system or computer network;

(*e*) Disrupts or causes disruption of any computer, computer system or computer network;

(*f*) Denies or causes the denial of access to any person authorised to access any computer, computer system or computer network by any means;

(*g*) Provides any assistance to any person to facilitate access to a computer, computer system or computer network in contravention of the provisions of this Act, rules or regulations made thereunder;

(*h*) Charges the services availed of by a person to the account of another person by tempering with or manipulating any computer, computer system, or computer network.

(*i*) destroys, deletes or alters any information residing in a computer resource or diminishes its value or utility or affects it injuriously by any means,

(*j*) steal, conceals, destroys or alters or causes any person to steal, conceal, destroy or alter any computer source code used for a computer resource with an intention to cause damage."

Hacking : Broadly, hacking means intentionally accessing a computer system without authorisation or exceeding authorised access. All the above activities therefore, come within the meaning of hacking.

2. **Penalty for failure to furnish information, return, etc.** (*Sec. 44*) : If any person who is required under this Act or any rules or regulations made thereunder to—

(*a*) furnish any document, return or report to the Controller or the Certifying Authority, fails to furnish the same, he shall be liable to a penalty not exceeding one lakh and fifty thousand rupees for each such failure;

(*b*) file any return or furnish any information, books or other documents within the time specified therefor in the regulations, fails to file return or furnish the same within the time exceeding therefor in the regulations, he shall be liable to a penalty not exceeding five thousand rupees for every day during which such failure continues;

(*c*) maintain books of account or records, fails to maintain the same, he shall be liable to a penalty not exceeding ten thousand rupees for every day during which the failure continues.

3. **Residuary penalty** (*Sec. 45*) : Whoever contravenes any rules or regulations made under this Act, for the contravention of which no penalty has been separately provided, shall be liable to pay a compensation not exceeding twenty-five thousand rupees to the person affected by such contravention or a penalty not exceeding twenty-five thousand rupees.

4. **Power to adjudicate** (*Sec. 46*) : (1) For the purpose of adjudging under the Act, whether any person has committed a contravention of any of the provisions of this Act or of any rule, regulation, direction or order made thereunder which renders him liable to pay penalty or compensation, the Central Government shall, subject to the provisions of sub-section(3), appoint any officer not below the rank of a Director to the Government of India or an equivalent officer of a State Government to be an adjudicating officer for holding an inquiry in the manner prescribed by the Central Government.

The adjudicating officer appointed as above shall exercise jurisdiction to adjudicate matters in which the claim for injury or damage does not exceed rupees five crore:

Provided that the jurisdiction in respect of the claim for injury or damage exceeding rupees five crore shall vest with the competent court."

(2) The adjudicating officer shall, after giving the person referred to in sub-section(1), a reasonable opportunity for making representation in the matter and if, on such inquiry, he is satisfied that the person has committed the contravention, he may impose such penalty or award such compensation as he thinks fit in accordance with the provisions of that section.

(3) No person shall be appointed as an adjudicating officer unless he possesses such experience in the field of Information Technology and legal or judicial experience as may be prescribed by the Central Government.

(4) Where more than one adjudicating officers are appointed, the Central Government shall specify by order the matters and places with respect to which such officers shall exercise their jurisdiction.

5. **Factors to be taken into account by the adjudicating officer**—While adjudging the quantum of compensation under the Act, the adjudicating officer shall have due regard to the following factors, namely:

(*a*) the amount of gain of unfair advantage, wherever quantifiable made as a result of the default;

(*b*) the amount of loss caused to any person as a result of the default;

(*c*) the repetitive nature of the default.

THE CYBER APPELLATE TRIBUNAL

Sections 48 to 64 of the Act provides for establishment and functioning of Cyber Appellate Tribunal, to whom appeal can be made by any person aggrieved by the decision of the Controller. The relevant provision are summarised below:

1. Establishment of Cyber Appellate Tribunal (*Sec. 48*)

The Central Government shall, by notification, establish one or more appellate tribunals to be known as the Cyber Regulations Appellate Tribunal.

2. Composition of Cyber Appellate Tribunal (*Sec. 49*)

The Cyber Appellate Tribunal shall consist of a Chairperson and such number of other members, as the Central Government may, by notification in the Official Gazette, appoint.

3. Qualifications for appointment as Presiding Officer of the Cyber Appellate Tribunal (*Sec. 50*)

(*i*) **A person shall not be** qualified for appointment as Chairperson of the Cyber Appellate Tribunal unless he is, or has been, or is qualified to be, a Judge of a High Court.

(*ii*) The Members of the Cyber Appellate Tribunal, except the Judicial Member to be appointed under sub-section (3), shall be appointed by the Central Government from amongst persons, having special knowledge of, and professional experience in, information technology, telecommunication, industry and management of consumer affairs.

(*iii*) The Judicial Members of the Cyber Appellate Tribunal shall be appointed by the Central Government from amongst persons who is or has been a member of the Indian Legal Service and has held the post of Additional Secretary for a period of not less than one year or Grade I post of that Service for a period of not less than five years.

4. Term of office (*Sec. 51*)

The Chairperson or Member of a Cyber Appellate Tribunal shall hold office for a term of five years from the date on which he enters upon his office or until he attains the age of sixty five years, whichever is earlier.

5. Filling up of vacancies (*Sec. 53*)

If, for reason other than temporary absence, any vacancy occurs in Tribunal, the Central Government shall appoint another person in accordance with the provisions of this Act to fill the vacancy and the proceedings may be continued before the Cyber Appellate Tribunal from the stage at which the vacancy is filled.

6. Resignation and Removal (*Sec. 54*)

1. The Chairperson or the Member of a Cyber Appellate Tribunal may, by notice in writing under his hand addressed to the Central Government, resign from his office.
2. The Chairperson or the Member of a Cyber Appellate Tribunal shall not be removed from his office except by an order by the Central Government on the ground of proved misbehaviour or in capacity after an inquiry made by a Judge of the Supreme Court in which the Presiding Officer concerned has been informed of the charges against him and given a reasonable opportunity of being heard in respect of these charges.

7. Orders constituting Appellate Tribunal to be final and not to invalidate its proceedings (*Sec. 55*)

No order of the Central Government appointing any person as the Chairperson or Member of a Cyber Appellate Tribunal shall be called in question in any manner and no act or proceeding before a Cyber Appellate Tribunal shall be called in question in any manner on the ground merely of any defect in the constitution of a Cyber Appellate Tribunal.

8. Appeal to Cyber Regulations Appellate Tribunal (*Sec. 57*)

1. Save as provided in sub-section (2), any person aggrieved by an order made by Controller or an adjudicating officer under this Act may prefer an appeal to a Cyber Appellate Tribunal having jurisdiction in the matter.
2. No appeal shall lie to the Cyber Appellate Tribunal from an order made by an adjudicating officer with the consent of the parties.
3. Every appeal under sub-section (1) shall be filed within a period of forty-five days from the date on which a copy of the order made by the Controller or the Adjudicating Officer is received by the person aggrieved and it shall be in such form and be accompanied by such fee as may be prescribed :

   Provided that the Cyber Appellate Tribunal may entertain an appeal after the expiry of the said period of forty-five days if it is satisfied that there was sufficient cause for not filing it within that period.
4. On receipt of an appeal under sub-section (1), the Cyber Appellate Tribunal may, after giving the parties to the appeal, an opportunity of being heard, pass such orders thereon as it thinks fit, confirming, modifying or setting aside the order appealed against.
5. The Cyber Appellate Tribunal shall send a copy of every order made by it to the parties to the appeal and to the concerned Controller or Adjudicating Officer.
6. The appeal filed before the Cyber Appellate Tribunal under sub-section (1) shall be dealt with by it as expeditiously as possible and endeavour shall be made by it to dispose off the appeal finally within six months from the date of receipt of the appeal.

9. Procedure and Powers of the Cyber Appellate Tribunal (*Sec. 58*)

1. The Cyber Appellate Tribunal shall not be bound by the procedure laid down by the Code of Civil Procedure, 1908 (5 of 1908) but shall be guided by the principles of natural justice and, subject to the other provisions of this Act and of any rules, the Cyber Appellate Tribunal shall have powers to regulate its own procedure including the place at which it shall have its sittings.

2. The Cyber Appellate Tribunal shall have, for the purposes of discharging its functions under this Act, the same powers as are vested in a civil court under the Code of Civil Procedure, 1908 while trying a suit, in respect of the following matters, namely :

(*a*) summoning and enforcing the attendance of any person and examining him on oath;
(*b*) requiring the discovery and production of documents or other electronic records;
(*c*) receiving evidence on affidavits;
(*d*) issuing commissions for the examination of witnesses or documents;
(*e*) reviewing its decisions;
(*f*) dismissing an application for default or deciding it *ex parte*;
(*g*) any other matter which may be prescribed.

10. Civil court not to have jurisdiction (*Sec. 61*)

No court shall have jurisdiction to entertain any suit or proceeding in respect of any matter which an adjudicating officer appointed under this Act or the Cyber Appellate Tribunal constituted under this Act is empowered by or under this Act to determine and no injunction shall be granted by any court or other authority in respect of any action taken or to be taken in pursuance of any power conferred by or under this Act.

11. Appeal to High Court (*Sec. 62*)

Any person aggrieved by any decision or order of the Cyber Appellate Tribunal may file an appeal to the High Court within sixty days from the date of communication of the decision or order of the Cyber Appellate Tribunal to him on any question of fact or law arising out of such order.

OFFENCES

Sections 65 to 78 provide the following penalties for various offences committed under the Act:

1. Tampering with computer source documents (*Sec. 65*)

Whoever knowingly or intentionally conceals, destroys or alters or intentionally or knowingly causes another to conceal, destroy or alter any computer source code used for a computer, computer programme, computer system or computer network, when the computer source code is required to be kept or maintained by law for the time being in force, shall be punishable with imprisonment up to three years, or with fine which may extend up to two lakh rupees, or with both.

2. Computer related offences (*Sec. 66*)

If any person, dishonestly or fraudulently, does any act referred to in Section 43, he shall be punishable with imprisonment for a term which may extend to three years or with fine which may extend to five lakh rupees or with both.

Explanation—For the purposes of this section:

(*a*) the word"dishonestly" shall have the meaning assigned to it in Section 24 of the Indian Penal Code;

(*b*) the word "fraudulently" shall have the meaning assigned to it in Section 25 of the Indian Penal Code.

3. Punishment for sending offensive messages through communication service, etc. (*Sec. 66A*)

Any person who sends, by means of a computer resource or a communication device:

(*a*) any information that is grossly offensive or has menacing character, or

(*b*) any information which he knows to be false, but for the purpose of causing annoyance, inconvenience, danger, obstruction, insult, injury, criminal intimidation, enmity, hatred or ill-will, persistently by making use of such computer resource or a communication device; or

(*c*) any electronic mail or electronic mail message for the purpose of causing annoyance or inconvenience or to deceive or to mislead the addressee or recipient about the origin of such messages,

4. Publishing of information which is absence in electronic form (*Sec. 67*)

Whoever publishes or transmits or causes to be published in the electronic form, any material which is lascivious or appeals to the prurient interest or if its effect is such as to tend to deprave and corrupt persons who are likely, having regard to all relevant circumstances, to read, see or hear the matter contained or embodied in it, shall be punished on first conviction with imprisonment of either description for a term which may extend to three years and with fine which may extend to five lakh rupees and in the event of a second or subsequent conviction with imprisonment of either description for a term which may extend to five years and also with fine which may extend to ten lakh rupees.

5. Protected system (*Sec. 70*)

1. The appropriate Government may, by notification in the Official Gazette, declare that any computer resource which directly or indirectly affects the facility of critical information infrastructure to be a protected system.
2. The appropriate Government may, by order in writing, authorise the persons who are authorised to access protected systems notified under sub-section (1).
3. Any person who secures access or attempts to secure access to a protected system in contravention of the provisions of this section shall be punished with imprisonment of either description for a term which may extend to ten years and shall also be liable to fine.
4. "The Central Government shall prescribe the information security practices and procedures for such protected system."

6. Indian Computer Emergency Response Team to (*Sec. 70B*)

(*i*) The Central Government shall, by notification in the Official Gazette, appoint an agency of the **Government to be called the Indian Computer Emergency Response Team.**

(*ii*) The Central Government shall provide the agency referred to in sub-section (*I*) with a Director-General and such other officers and employees as may be prescribed.

(*iii*) The salary and allowances and terms and conditions of the Director-General and other officers and employees shall be such as may be prescribed.

(*iv*) The Indian Computer Emergency Response Term shall serve as the national agency for performing the following functions in the area of cyber security:

(*a*) collection, analysis and dissemination of information on cyber incidents;

(*b*) forecast and alerts of cyber security incidents;

(*c*) emergency measures for handling cyber security incidents:

(*d*) coordination of cyber incidents response activities;

(*e*) issue guidelines, advisories, vulnerability notes and whitepapers relating to information security practices, procedures, preventation, response and reporting of cyber incidents;

(*f*) such other functions relating to cyber security as may be prescribed.

(*v*) The manner of performing functions and duties of the agency referred to in sub-section (*1*) shall be such as may be prescribed.

7. Penalty for misrepresentation (*Sec. 71*)

Whoever makes any misrepresentation to, or suppresses any material fact from, the Controller or the Certifying Authority for obtaining any licence or Digital Signature Certificate, as the case may be, shall be punished with imprisonment for a term which may extend to two years, or with fine which may extend to one lakh rupees, or with both.

8. Breach of confidentiality and privacy (*Sec. 72*)

Save as otherwise provided in this Act or any other law for the time being in force, any person who, in pursuance of any of the powers conferred under this Act, rules or regulations made thereunder, has secured access to any electronic record, book, register, correspondence, information, document or other material without the consent of the person concerned discloses such electronic record, book, register, correspondence, information, document or other material to any other person shall be punished with imprisonment for a term which may extend to two years, or with fine which may extend to one lakh rupees, or with both.

9. Penalty for publishing Digital Signature Certificate false in certain particulars (*Sec. 73*)

1. No person shall publish a Digital Signature Certificate or otherwise make it available to any other person with the knowledge that :

(*a*) the Certifying Authority listed in the certificate has not issued it; or

(*b*) the subscriber listed in the certificate has not accepted it; or

(*c*) the certificate has been revoked or suspended,

unless such publication is for the purpose of verifying in digital signature created prior to such suspension or revocation.

2. Any person who contravenes the provisions of sub-section (1) shall be punished with imprisonment for a term which may extend to two years, or with fine which may extend to one lakh rupees, or with both.

10. Publication for fraudulent purpose (*Sec. 74*)

Whoever knowingly creates, publishes or otherwise makes available a Digital Signature Certificate for any fraudulent or unlawful purpose shall be punished with imprisonment for a term which may extend to two years, or with fine which may extend to one lakh rupees, or with both.

11. Confiscation (*Sec. 76*)

Any computer, computer system, floppies, compact disks, tape drives or any other accessories related thereto, in respect of which any provision of this Act, rules, orders or regulations made thereunder has been or is being contravened, shall be liable to confiscation.

12. Compensation, penalties or confiscation not to interfere with other punishment (*Sec. 77*)

No compensation awarded, penalty imposed or confiscation made under this Act shall prevent the award of compensation or imposition of any other penalty or punishment under any other law for the time being in force.

13. Compounding of offences (*Sec. 77A*)

A court of competent jurisdiction may compound offences other than offerences for which the punishment for life or imprisonment for a term exceeding three years has been provided, under this Act;

KEY TERMS

- ❑ **Access :** With its grammatical variations and cognate expressions means gaining entry into, instructing or communicating with the logical, arithmetical, or memory function resources of a computer, computer system or computer network [*Sec. 2(a)*].
- ❑ **Addressee :** Means a person who is intended by the originator to receive the electronic record but does not include any intermediary [*Sec. 2(b)*].
- ❑ **Affixing Electronic Signature :** With its grammatical variations and cognate expressions means adoption of any methodology or procedure by a person for the purpose of authenticating an electronic record by means of digital signature [*Sec. 2(d)*].
- ❑ **Asymmetric Crypto System** means a system of a secure, key pair consisting of a private key for creating a digital signature and a public key to verify the digital signature. (*Sec. 2(f)*)
- ❑ **Certifying Authority** means a person who has been granted a licence to issue a Electronic Signature Certificate under section 24 [*Sec. 2(g)*].
- ❑ **Certification practice statement** means a statement issued by a Certifying Authority to specify the practices that the Certifying Authority employs in issuing Electronic Signature Certificates (*Sec. 2(h)*).
- ❑ **Computer resource** means computer, computer system, computer network, data, computer database or software. (*Sec. 2(k)*)
- ❑ **Computer system** means a device or collection of devices, including input and output support devices and excluding calculator which are not programmable and capable of being used in conjunction with external files, which contain computer programmes, electronic instructions, input data, and output data, that performs logic, arithmetic, data storage and retrieval, communication control and other functions (*Sec. 2(l)*).

- **Data** means a representation of information, knowledge, facts, concepts or instructions which are being prepared or have been prepared in a formalised manner, and is intended to be processed, is being processed or has been processed in a computer system or computer network, and may be in any form (including computer printouts, magnetic or optical storage media, punched cards, punched tapes) or stored internally in the memory of the computer [*Sec. 2(o)*].
- **Electronic Form** with reference to information means any information generated, sent, received or stored in media, magnetic, optical, computer memory, microfilm, computer generated micro fiche or similar device [*Sec.2(n)*].
- **Electronic Gazette** means Official Gazette published in the electronic form (*Sec. 2 (s)*).
- **Electronic record** means data, record or data generated, image or sound stored, received or sent in an electronic form or microfilm or computer generated micro fiche [*Sec. 2 (t)*].
- **Intermediary** with respect to any particular electronic message means any person who on behalf of another person receives, stores or transmits that message or provides any service with respect to that message [*Sec.2(w)*].
- **Key Pair** in an asymmetric crypto system, means a private key and its mathematically related public key, which are so related that the public key can verify a digital signature created by the private key [*Sec. 2(x)*].
- **Originator** means a person who sends, generates, stores or transmits any electronic message or causes any electronic message to be sent, generated, stored or transmitted to any other person but does not include an intermediary [*Sec. 2(za)*].
- **Prescribed** means prescribed by rules made under this Act;
- **Private Key** means the key of a key pair used to create a digital signature (*Sec. 2(zc)*).
- **Public Key** means the key of a key pair used to verify a digital signature and listed in the Digital Signature Certificate [*Sec. 2(zd)*].
- **Secure System** means computer hardware, software, and procedure that :
  (*a*) are reasonably secure from unauthorised access and misuse;
  (*b*) provide a reasonable level of reliability and correct operation;
  (*c*) are reasonably suited to performing the intended functions; and
  (*d*) adhere to generally accepted security procedures [*Sec. 2(ze)*].
- **Subscriber** means a person in whose name the Digital Signature Certificate is issued [*Sec. 2(zg)*].
- **Verify** in relation to a digital signature, electronic record or public key, with its grammatical variations and cognate expressions means to determine whether :
  (*a*) the initial electronic record was affixed with the digital signature by the use of private key corresponding to the public key of the subscriber;
  (*b*) the initial electronic record is retained intact or has been altered since such electronic record was so affixed with the digital signature [*Sec. (zh)*].

TEST QUESTIONS

Objective Type : *Test Your Knowledge*

1. State whether each of the following statements is *True* or *False*
   (*a*) The provisions of the Information Technology Act do not apply to a cheque.
   (*b*) The term 'Adressee' does not include a person who is an intermediary between the originator and receiver of the electronic record.

(c) The term 'Digital Signature' means signatures downloaded from the Internet.
(d) The term 'Public Key' means the key of key-pair used to verify a digital signature.
(e) An electronic record shall be attributed to the originator if it was send by the information system programmed by or on behalf of the originator to operate automatically.
(f) The application for a licence to issue digital signature certificate should be made to the Central Government.
(g) The Cyber Appellate Tribunal consists of at least three persons appointed by the Central Government.

[*Ans.* (a) True; (b) True; (c) False; (d) True; (e) True; (f) False; (g) False]

2. Select the most appropriate answer :
   (i) Private key means :
      (a) A key of a lock of a private limited company.
      (b) Key of a key-pair used to verify a digital signature.
      (c) A key of a key-pair used to create a digital signature.
   (ii) Electronic Gazette means :
      (a) Official gazette published in the electronic form.
      (b) Data record or data generated or sent in electronic form.
      (c) Data, text images or film software notified in the official gazette.
   (iii) Application for licence to issue digital signature certificates is to be made in such form as may be prescribed by the :
      (a) The Central Government.
      (b) The Controller appointed under the Information Technology Act.
      (c) Certifying authority recognized under the Act.

[*Ans.* (i) c; (ii) a; (iii) a]

Essay Type : *For Review, Discussion and Practice*

1. Define the term 'Digital Signature'. State the mode of authentication of an electronic record through digital signature.
2. State the provisions of the Information Technology Act regarding :
   (a) Electronic Governance; and
   (b) Attribution, Acknowledgment and Despatch of Electronic Records.
3. State the considerations which are kept in mind by the Central Government while prescribing the security procedure for securing electronic records or digital signatures.
4. Enumerate the procedure for appointment of the Controller of Certifying Authorities. State his functions and duties.
5. State the provisions of the Information Technology Act regarding issue, suspension and revocation of Digital Signature Certificates.
6. State the duties of the subscribers listed in the Digital Signature Certificate.
7. Explain the consequences in case of :
   (a) Tempering with computer source documents.
   (b) Hacking with computer system.
   (c) Publishing of information which is passing in electronic form.
8. Explain the duties of 'Certifying Authority' under the Information Technology Act, 2000.
(B.Com. (Hons.), Delhi 2005)

9. Define the following terms as per Information Technology Act, 2000 :
   (*a*) Addresses (*b*) Computer
   (*c*) Data (*d*) Information
   (*B.Com. (Hons.), Delhi 2005*)
10. Give the definitions of the following terms as per Information Technology Act, 2000 :
    (*a*) Certifying Authorities (*b*) Computer Network
    (*c*) Originator (*d*) Information
    (*B.Com. (Hons.), Delhi 2005*)
11. Explain the concept of Digital Signature and Digital Certificate as per Information Technology Act, 2000. (*B.Com. (Hons.), Delhi 2005*)
12. Briefly discuss the following (*B.Com. (Hons.), Delhi 2010*)
    (*i*) Digital signature certificate (*ii*) Private key and public key
    (*iii*) Duties of a subscriber
13. Comment on the following statements: [*B.Com. (Hons.), Delhi 2010*]
    (i) Hacking is an offence punishable under IT Act, 2000
    (ii) Electronic records are as authentic as the hard copies.
    (iii) The Cyber Appellate Tribunal has the same powers as a Civil Court but an aggrieved party may appeal to the High Court.
14. How is the Controller of Certifying Authorities appointed? What are his functions?
    [*B.Com. (Hons.), Delhi 2010*]
15. State the objectives of Information Technology Act, 2000. [*B.Com. (Hons.), Delhi 2011*]
16. Define the following terms:
    (*i*) Hacking (*ii*) Digital signature
    (*iii*) Key pair [*B.Com. (Hons.), Delhi 2011*]
17. Do any *Five* [*B.Com. (Hons.), Delhi 2012*]
    (*i*) Describe the term "Subscriber". Explain the duties of a subscriber under I.T. Act as amended in 2008.
    (*ii*) Explain the powers of controller of certifying authority under I.T. Act.
    (*iii*) What do you mean by "Cyber Terrorism" as under I.T. Act.
    (*iv*) Explain the duties of certifying authority under I.T. Act.
    (*v*) Explain "Digital Signature" under I.T. Act.
    (*vi*) Role of Certifying authorities. [*B.Com. (Hons.), Delhi, 2012*]
18. Do any *Five*
    (*i*) Comment on "Digital Signature Certificate" (*ii*) Write a short note on "Electronic Governance"
    (*iii*) Explain – The legal recognition of electronic records.
    (*iv*) Discuss the objects of I.T. Act
    (*v*) Explain the meaning and punishment for publishing or transmitting obscene material in electronic form.
    (*vi*) Computer network, Computer Resource. [*B.Com. (Hons.), Delhi, 2013*]
19. What are the areas involving paper based documents in which I.T. Act does not apply?
    [*B.Com. (Hons.), Delhi, Nov. 2012*]
20. What are the functions performed by public and private keys?
    [*B.Com. (Hons.), Delhi, Nov. 2012*]

21. What are the provisions regarding the issue and revocation of a Digital Signature Certificate? [*B.Com. (Hons.), Delhi, Nov. 2012*]
22. What is meant by E-Governance with reference to I.T. Act? [*B.Com. (Hons.), Delhi, Nov. 2012*]
23. The Cyber Appellate Tribunal has the same powers as a Civil Court but an aggrieved party may appeal to the High Court. Explain. [*B.Com. (Hons.), Nov. 2012*]
24. How is the Controller of Certifying Authority appointed? What are his functions under Information Technology Act, 2000? [*B.Com. (Hons.), Nov. 2012*]
25. Explaint the terms: Electronic Governance and Cyber Terrorism under the IT Act, 2000. [*B.Com. (Hons.), Nov. 2013*]
26. Explain the duties of Certifying Authority under IT Act, 2000. [*B.Com. (Hons.), Nov. 2013*]
27. What are the areas involving paper based documents in which IT Act does not apply? [*B.Com. (Hons.), Nov. 2013*]
28. What is meant by Digital Signature Certificate as under the IT Act, 2000? [*B.Com. (Hons.), Nov. 2013*]
29. Discuss the functions of Controller appointed under the IT Act, 2000. [*B.Com. (Hons.), Nov. 2013*]
30. Discuss the objects of IT Act, 2000. [*B.Com. (Hons.), Nov. 2013*]
31. Briefly discuss the following:
    (*i*) Digital Signature Certificate
    (*ii*) Private Key and Public Key
    (*iii*) Duties of a Subscriber [*B.Com. (Hons.), Delhi, 2010*]

PRACTICAL PROBLEM

1. A person knowingly or intentionally conceals, destroys or alters any computer source, computer program, computer system or network. In such an act an offence? If so, what is the punishment? [*B.Com.(Hons.), Delhi 2011*]

   [***Ans.*** Yes. Imprisonment for 3 years or fine of ₹ 5 lakh or both]

APPENDIX

QUESTION PAPER

Business Laws

Delhi University B.Com. (Hons.) CBCS - 2015

Semester I

Duration : **3 Hours** Maximum Marks: **75**

Attempt **all** questions.

All questions carry equal marks.

1. (a) State, with reasons in brief, whether the following statements are true or false:
   (i) In commercial and business agreements, the presumption is that the parties intend to create legal obligation.
   (ii) Communication of offer is complete when the letter of offer is posted.
   (iii) Lotteries authorised by government are not wagering agreements. (9)

   (b) Discuss the position of a minor in a contract. (6)

   OR

   (a) State, with reasons in brief, whether the following statements are true or false:
   (i) A contract cannot be discharged on account of strikes, lock-outs and civil disorders.
   (ii) The object of damages, in case of breach of contract, is to punish the person who fails to perform his obligation.
   (iii) Inadequacy of consideration will make an agreement void. (9)

   (b) Define undue influence. How does it differ from coercion? (6)

2. (a) (i) Distinguish between 'Sale' and 'Agreement to sell'.
   (ii) X shows a sample to Y describing it as 'Chinese silk'. Y approves of the sample and places an order for the supply of 'Chinese silk'. The goods delivered are according to sample but it turns out that the sample as well as bulk is 'Japanese silk'. Discuss the rights of buyer Y against seller X.
   (iii) A funds a costly ring and after making reasonable efforts to discover the owner, sells it to B who buys without knowledge that A was merely a finder of the ring. Can the true owner recover the ring from B? State reasons. (9)

   (b) Explain the rights of an unpaid seller against the goods. (6)

   OR

   (a) (i) When can a breach of condition be treated as a breach of warranty?
   (ii) Agreed to purchase 200 tonnes of wheat from B out of a larger stock. A sent his men with sacks and 150 tonnes of wheat were put into the sacks. Then there was a sudden fire and entire stock was gutted. Who will bear the loss and why?

(iii) A agreed to sell his new LCD TV to Y for ₹ 25,000 payable partly in cash of ₹ 15,000 and partly in exchange of old TV set. Is it a valid contract of Sale of Goods? Give reason. (9)

(b) Discuss the rules as to passing of property in case of specific goods. (6)

3. (a) (i) State the contents of Incorporation Document of an LLP.

(ii) "An LLP is a definite improvement over the partnership firm in the matter of promoting entrepreneurship." Discuss.

(iii) Write a note on Whistle Blowing. (9)

(b) State the provisions regarding taxation of LLP. (6)

OR

(a) (i) "A partner shall never be liable to an unlimited extent for the debts of the LLP." Critically examine the statement.

(ii) "The court can wind up an LLP on just and equitable grounds." Comment.

(iii) Explain the rules regarding change of name of an LLP. (9)

(b) Discuss the provisions regarding appointment and eligibility conditions for a Designated Partner under Limited Liability Partnership Act, 2008. (6)

4. (a) Distinguish between:

(i) Digital signature and Electronic signature

(ii) Cyber contraventions and cyber offences

(iii) Public key and Private key (9)

(b) "E-governance is SMART governance". Discuss the provisions of Information Technology Act, 2000 to facilitate and strengthen e-governance. (6)

OR

(a) (i) "The IT Act is not applicable to some specified documents." Comment.

(ii) The Cyber Appellate Tribunal has same powers as a civil court, but an aggrieved party may appeal to the high court." Explain.

(iii) Write a note on Tempering with computer source documents. (9)

(b) What is meant by digital signature? State the procedure of creation and verification of digital signature. (6)

5. Distinguish between:

(a) (i) Sub-agent and Substituted agent

(ii) Indemnity and Guarantee

(iii) Novation and Alteration as modes of discharge of a contract. (9)

(b) Explain Declaration of solvency under voluntary winding up. Is it necessary to obtain the approval of creditors in voluntary winding up of an LLP? (6)

OR

(a) "An agreement in restraint of trade is void". Examine the statement giving exceptions, if any. (9)

(b) Describe the procedure of conversion of a partnership firm into LLP. (6)